FUNDAMENTALS OF LITERATURE

SECOND EDITION

DONNALYNN HESS
JUNE CATES

bju press®

Greenville, South Carolina

NOTE: The fact that materials produced by other publishers may be referred to in this volume does not constitute an endorsement of the content or theological position of materials produced by such publishers. Any references and ancillary materials are listed as an aid to the student or the teacher and in an attempt to maintain the accepted academic standards of the publishing industry.

FUNDAMENTALS OF LITERATURE
Second Edition

Donnalynn Hess, MA
June Cates

Coordinating Writers
Bethany Harris, MA, MEd
Judith W. Lanier, MA
Elizabeth Rose, MEd, MA
Stephen Rowley, MA
Kimberly Y. Stegall, MEd

Consultant
Steven N. Skaggs, MEd
Manager of Product Development, BJU Press

Page Design
Drew Fields
Jennifer Lowry

Page Layout
Carol Ingalls

Editor
Rebecca Moore

Photo Acquisition
Joyce Landis
Rita Mitchell
Carla Thomas

Project Managers
Lesley Morris
Benjamin Sinnamon

Bible Integration
Bryan Smith, PhD

Acknowledgments begin on page iv, which is an extension of this copyright page.
Illustrators and Photograph Credits appear on pages 517–19.

ACKNOWLEDGMENTS

UNIT 1

Harold Matson Co., Inc.: *"Top Man"* © 1939, 1941, 1944, 1945, 1948, 1951, 1952, 1953 by James Ramsey Ullman. © renewed in 1967, 1969, 1972, 1973, 1976, 1979, 1980, 1981 by James Ramsey Ullman and the Estate of James Ramsey Ullman. Permission to reprint granted by Harold Matson Co., Inc.

HarperCollins Publishers: All pages from "Through the Tunnel" from THE HABIT OF LOVING by Doris Lessing. Copyright © 1955 by Doris Lessing. Originally appeared in *The New Yorker*. Reprinted by permission of HarperCollins Publishers (world excluding the UK).

Jonathan Clowes Ltd: THROUGH THE TUNNEL Copyright © 1954 by Doris Lessing. Reprinted by kind permission of Jonathan Clowes Ltd., London, on behalf of the Estate of Doris Lessing (UK).

Penguin Random House: "Robert Louis Stevenson Banks aka Chimley" from A GATHERING OF OLD MEN by Ernest J. Gaines. Copyright © 1983 by Ernest J. Gaines. Used by permission of Alfred A. Knopf, an imprint of the Knopf Doubleday Publishing Group, a division of Penguin Random House LLC (worldwide excluding the UK) and reprinted by permission of G Agency LLC (UK). All rights reserved.

UNIT 2

Hachette Book Group USA: "Phaëthon" from *Mythology* by Edith Hamilton, copyright © 1942. Reprinted by permission of Little, Brown and Company, an imprint of Hachette Book Group, Inc.

Copyright Clearance Center: "Old Man" by Ricardo Sánchez from *Selected Poems*, 2001. Reproduced with permission of Yvonne Sánchez via Copyright Clearance Center.

Penguin Random House: "Neighbour Rosicky" from OBSCURE DESTINIES by Willa Cather, copyright © 1930, 1932 by Willa Sibert Cather, copyright renewed 1958, 1960 by Edith Lewis and The City Bank Farmers Trust Co. Used by permission of Alfred A. Knopf, an imprint of the Knopf Doubleday Publishing Group, a division of Penguin Random House LLC. All rights reserved.

UNIT 3

Penguin Random House: "Go Down Death - A Funeral Sermon" from GOD'S TROMBONES by James Weldon Johnson, copyright © 1927 by Penguin Random House LLC, renewed © 1955 by Grace Nail Johnson. Used by permission of Viking Books, an imprint of Penguin Publishing Group, a division of Penguin Random House LLC. All rights reserved.

New Directions Publishing Corporation: "Do Not Go Gentle Into That Good Night" by Dylan Thomas, from THE POEMS OF DYLAN THOMAS, copyright ©1952 by Dylan Thomas. Reprinted by permission of New Directions Publishing Corp. for U.S., its territories, and Canada. **David Higham Associates** granted world print rights excluding the USA.

A P Watt Ltd: "When You Are Old" by W. B. Yeats. Reprinted by permission of A P Watt Ltd. on behalf of Gráinne Yeats.

Harold Ober Associates Incorporated: "A Black Man Talks of Reaping" by Arna Bontemps. Reprinted by permission of Harold Ober Associates Incorporated. Copyright © 1963 by Arna Bontemps.

UNIT 4

HarperCollins Publishers: "By Any Other Name" from *Gifts of Passage* by Santha Rama Rau. Copyright 1951 by Santha Rama Rau. Copyright renewed © 1979 by Santha Rama Rau. Reprinted by permission of HarperCollins Publishers for United States and Canada and William Morris Agency for all other territories.

Unit 5

Penguin Random House: "The Possibility of Evil," copyright © 1965 by Stanley Edgar Hyman; from JUST AN ORDINARY DAY: STORIES by Shirley Jackson (Penguin Books, 2017). Copyright © Laurence Jackson Hyman, J.S. Holly, Sarah Hyman DeWitt and Barry Hyman, 1996. Used by permission of Bantam Books, an imprint of Random House, a division of Penguin Random House LLC (worldwide excluding the UK & Commonwealth) and reproduced by permission of **Penguin Books Ltd** (UK & Commonwealth). All rights reserved.

"The Lightning Flashes" and "A Lightning Gleam" from AN INTRODUCTION TO HAIKU by Harold Gould Henderson, copyright © 1958 by Harold G. Henderson. Used by permission of Doubleday, an imprint of the Knopf Doubleday Publishing Group, a division of Penguin Random House LLC. All rights reserved.

Harold Ober Associates Incorporated: "In the Ring with Jack Dempsey" by Paul Gallico. Reprinted by permission of Harold Ober Associates Incorporated. Copyright 1938 by Paul Gallico. Copyright renewed 1966 by Paul Gallico.

Jonathan Clowes Ltd.: "The Adventure of the Beryl Coronet" from *The Adventures of Sherlock Holmes*, Authorised Edition by Sir Arthur Conan Doyle. Copyright 1996 Sir Arthur Conan Doyle Copyrights Holders. Printed with kind permission of Jonathan Clowes Ltd., London, on behalf of Andrea Plunket, the Administrator of the Sir Arthur Conan Doyle Copyrights.

Houghton Mifflin Harcourt Publishing Company: "Splinter" from *Good Morning, America,* copyright 1928 and renewed 1956 by Carl Sandburg, reprinted by permission of Houghton Mifflin Harcourt Publishing Company.

Maxine W. Kumin Literary Trust: "400-Meter Freestyle" by Maxine Kumin. Copyright © 1959 and renewed 1987 by Maxine Kumin, from SELECTED POEMS 1960-1990 by Maxine Kumin. Used by permission from the Maxine W. Kumin Literary Trust.

Farrar, Straus and Giroux: "Freedom to Breathe" from STORIES AND PROSE POEMS by Aleksandr Solzhenitsyn, translated by Michael Glenny. Translation copyright © 1971 by Michael Glenny. Reprinted by permission of Farrar, Straus and Giroux (worldwide excluding the UK & Canada) and **Librairie Arthème Fayard** (UK & Canada). « ETUDES ET MINIATURES » de Alexandre Soljénitsyne. © Alexandre Soljénitsyne pour la langue russe. © Librairie Arthème Fayard, 2004 pour la traduction française.

Unit 6

Berlin Associates: "The Crime" by Sir Max Beerbohm. Reprinted by permission of Berlin Associates.

Brooks Permissions: "We Real Cool" by Gwendolyn Brooks. Reprinted By Consent of Brooks Permissions.

CONTENTS

Unit II: Character

UNIT III: Theme

UNIT IV: Point of View

Unit V: Structure

POETRY

Unit VI: Tone

TO THE STUDENT

By now you have become familiar with reading literature for relaxation and for education, for entertainment and for instruction. You may even have learned to recognize various techniques that authors or poets use to construct their works. If so, you have begun to experiment with literary criticism. *Fundamentals of Literature* intends to take you further toward a basic understanding of literary criticism and even help you become a literary critic.

WHAT IS LITERARY CRITICISM?

In this context, the word *criticism* does not mean *condemnation*. Rather, **literary criticism** refers to the act of analyzing and evaluating literary works. Literary criticism demands that the reader interpret an author's message and determine how—and how skillfully—he communicates that message in his work. This textbook will introduce you to a variety of works by authors from different times and different places. You will examine their approaches to six fundamental components of literature: conflict, character, theme, point of view, structure, and tone.

THE AUTHOR, THE CRITIC, AND WORLDVIEW

While examining how an author communicates with his audience, a critic also responds to the author's message. Just as an author incorporates a specific worldview into his work, a critic likewise evaluates and responds to the work from the perspective of his own worldview. A **worldview** is a person's set of beliefs about the universe, the lens through which a person looks at all of life, both the physical and spiritual world. It answers the most important questions of humanity's existence: Where did the world come from? Where is it headed? What is a

human being? What is the difference between good and evil, right and wrong? In other words, a person's worldview tells him what reality is. However, the critic also employs his view of truth when deciding how skillfully and accurately an author's work reflects truth.

THE CHRISTIAN AND LITERARY CRITICISM

Christian literary critics also must evaluate a work from a biblical worldview. In other words, a Christian critic must accurately analyze, evaluate, and respond to the work of literature through the lens of Scripture. It isn't enough for a Christian to ask, "Do I like it?" Rather, the Christian critic judges a work of literature according to the criteria of beauty, goodness, and truth. A beautiful work of literature delights the reader with its excellence. The main criterion of goodness in literature is whether something reflects God's view of morality. And since truth is defined as an accurate representation of reality, literary criticism asks, "Does the work represent reality accurately?" To do this, one must first carefully read a work to discern what the author believes to be true about the world. Then the Christian critic evaluates that viewpoint based on the Word of God. In doing so, a

Christian critic may find a work of literature technically well-written while judging its author's worldview to be inaccurate. Unfortunately, the reverse may also be true.

WHY IS ALL OF THIS SO IMPORTANT?

You may wonder why it is important for a Christian to become a critic of literature. Three key reasons present themselves.

First, when God made humans in His own image, He instructed Adam and Eve to subdue the earth and gave them the abilities needed to do so (Gen. 1:26–28). Language is one of these God-given gifts, and literature may be said to be the ultimate use of it in its capacity both to communicate and to do so beautifully.

Second, we live in a world corrupted by sin (Gen. 3:16–19). Everything in our world has been likewise corrupted, including our use of language and literature. When Adam and Eve succumbed to Satan's lies (Gen. 3:1–6), they began to use language deceptively themselves (Gen 3:12). But all of us still reflect the image, though flawed, of God. Throughout history, human writers have used language both to glorify God and to blaspheme Him, to instruct others and to confuse them. All works of human literature mix truth and error, depicting to some degree the sinful human heart in all its twists and turns (Jer. 17:9). Studying literature can help us to distinguish truth from error. Studying literature can also help us recognize the problems in our own hearts, though only Scripture and the Holy Spirit can adequately address those problems.

Finally, God has provided a solution to the problem of sin (Gen. 3:15). Even now He is working to redeem the world to Himself. God has called Christians to live redemptively in their jobs, hobbies, and in every part of their lives. Literature can often play a role in carrying out one's role in life. For instance, Christians are called to reach out to others with the gospel of Christ. A knowledge of literature enhances both one's ability to communicate with other people—either saved or unsaved—and the ability to understand and address their view of the world. Indeed, God's Word is a perfectly executed collection of literary works. Of course, the technical perfection of Scripture is merely the frame for its more important function as the vehicle of God's truth. Only the Bible can lay claim to this combination of ideal form and infallible content.

Fundamentals of Literature will help you to understand and appreciate literature. But the final goal is to equip you go beyond this stage to respond to literature in a Christian way. God has called you to live redemptively in a fallen world. As the apostle Paul knew (Acts 17:28–29, Titus 2:11–14), you will find that understanding literature will play an important role in fulfilling that calling.

The Adventure of the Beryl Coronet

SIR ARTHUR CONAN DOYLE

As a hero, Doyle's master detective Sherlock Holmes has ample physical courage, strength, and agility. But he relies mainly on his brainpower: his ability to see significance in details that everyone else overlooks and to reason accurately from them. He is also a student of human nature and can construct hypotheses on the basis of people's actions. Notice that his interpretations of certain characters' actions often oppose the interpretations of others. What moral lessons are hinted at in these differences?

Keep in mind that detective stories often rely heavily on dialogue and exposition as characters relate their version of an incident or as the narrator relates the details of a setting or a character's reactions. As a result, the events of the plot can appear out of sequence or even overlap.

"Holmes," said I, as I stood one morning in our bow-window* looking down the street, "here is a madman coming along. It seems rather sad that his relatives should allow him to come out alone."

bow-window: curved bay window

My friend rose lazily from his arm-chair and stood with his hands in the pockets of his dressing-gown, looking over my shoulder. It was a bright, crisp February morning, and the snow of the day before still lay deep upon the ground, shimmering brightly in the wintry sun. Down the center of Baker Street it had been plowed in a brown crumbly band by the traffic, but at either side and on the heaped-up edges of the foot-paths it still lay as white as when it fell. The gray pavement

✺ CONFLICT ✺

To be human is to be enmeshed in conflict. When God introduced the first human to this world, He introduced him to conflict: "Of the tree of the knowledge of good and evil, thou shalt not eat of it" (Gen. 2:17). This conflict became both painful and tragic when man disobeyed that command. But God Himself entered the battle, and He is still working to deliver His world. Shortly after the first sin, God told the serpent that He would give His people victory: "I will put enmity between thee and the woman, and between thy seed and her seed; it shall bruise thy head, and thou shalt bruise his heel" (Gen. 3:15). The end of the Bible's story records the final arrival of this triumph: "The kingdoms of this world are become the kingdoms of our Lord, and of his Christ; and he shall reign for ever and ever" (Rev. 11:15). This conflict of good versus evil—God versus the powers of darkness—is all around us, between us, and even in us. Since literature imitates reality, we should not be surprised to discover that conflict is basic to any story.

Conflict is broadly defined as the opposition of two or more characters or forces. The forms each conflict takes may differ widely: the setting may be a small town or a stormy sea; the adversary may be an evil ruler or a guilty conscience; and the prize may be a parcel of land or a human soul. But regardless of its time, place, characters, or situation, a story without conflict is a story with no significance to the reader, for our lives are framed by physical and spiritual conflict.

TYPES OF CONFLICT

In literature, we recognize three main types of conflict. One story that aptly illustrates all three types of conflict is the Bible's account of the Fall. Genesis 3 tells us that at the beginning of the world, Adam and Eve rebelled against the Creator in the Garden of Eden. As a direct result of this first conflict, God cursed the ground, and

man found himself at odds with both God and nature. These incidents form our first record of **man against a greater force.**

Out of this initial struggle a second type of conflict emerged: **man against himself.** After the fall, Adam and Eve hid themselves upon "[hearing] the voice of the Lord God." When the Lord asked them why they had fled, Adam replied, "I heard thy voice in the garden, and *I was afraid*" (Gen. 3:8, 10). Man's sin not only severed his fellowship with God but also destroyed his inner peace.

This second conflict produced yet another—**man against man.** Once he was confronted with his disobedience, Adam's loving attitude toward his wife vanished. Driven by fear for himself, Adam blamed Eve for his sin: "The woman whom thou gavest to be with me, she gave me of the tree and I did eat" (3:12). Eve, quick to follow her husband's

November Night

ADELAIDE CRAPSEY

Listen.
With faint dry sound,
Like steps of passing ghosts,
The leaves, frost-crisp'd, break from the trees
And fall.

Full-color illustrations and photographs throughout not only add visual interest but also reinforce theme and tone.

The book includes interesting selections from a variety of cultures, eras, and genres.

About the Author

The contribution of Adelaide Crapsey (1878–1914) to poetry, though small in volume, is significant because of her invention of the cinquain, a compact yet highly expressive verse form. Instead of explicitly presenting her emotions on themes such as life, death, and change, Crapsey chose to organize sensory images into a compressed verse form that expresses her worldview.

Born in Rochester, New York, Adelaide Crapsey led a life as brief and concise as her poetry. She died when only thirty-six years old, after having taught English literature and history at a girls' school and also at Smith College. She followed her interests in archeology and English poetry until tuberculosis made these hobbies impossible. She devoted her later years to writing her own highly personalized cinquains. Most of these have been included in the first collection of her poems entitled *Verse*, which was published after her death. She also left an unfinished scholarly work, *Analysis of English Metrics*.

---

number five shells, blowed the dust off them, and went out to the road to wait for Clatoo.

About the Story

1. How does the setting of the story influence its conflicts?

2. What is the primary conflict of the story? Is it external or internal?

3. How do the past conflicts mentioned in the story affect the primary conflict?

4. Mat and Chimley face a difficult choice. What are the possible consequences of either option?

5. Why do Mat and Chimley make the choice they do? What do they hope to accomplish?

Discussion questions following each story guide students toward higher-order thinking skills.

About the Author

Ernest J. Gaines (b. 1933) was born on River Lake Plantation in Pointe Coupée Parish, Louisiana, into a fifth generation of sharecroppers. The first of twelve children, Gaines was working in the fields by age nine. At fifteen, however, Gaines moved to California to live with his mother and stepfather and to attend high school. After graduation, he served two years in the army and then enrolled in San Francisco State University. Upon graduating in 1957, he attended Stanford University on a scholarship for creative writing. Though he received favorable reviews for his early novels, his first major work was *The Autobiography of Miss Jane Pittman* (1971). Later novels receiving similar acclaim include *A Gathering of Old Men* (1983) and *A Lesson Before Dying* (1993).

Gaines's writing focuses primarily on the rural African-American culture of Louisiana. His style echoes the oral traditions of that culture as he frequently uses a first-person narrator, employs the dialects of his youth, and creates characters who give personal perspectives on the African-American past. Gaines has never been afraid to confront the continuing tensions of race relations in America in a nuanced manner. Throughout his long career as a writer and professor of writing, Gaines has earned a multitude of honors and awards, both national and international. Among the most notable are the 1994 Pulitzer Prize (for *A Lesson Before Dying*) and a 2004 nomination for the Nobel Prize in Literature. He is currently a writer-in-residence at the University of Southwestern Louisiana.

When information is available, a brief biographical sketch of the author accompanies the selection, alerting students to author purpose and philosophy.

Both contemporary and classic authors are featured.

ROBERT LOUIS STEVENSON BANKS, AKA CHIMLEY   51

❧ THINKING ZONE ❧

Within a work of fiction, the descriptions, actions, and dialogue of well-drawn characters will always coax a response from the reader. The extent to which an author encourages a reader to respond favorably or unfavorably toward a character will lend support to the message that the author wishes to communicate. Characters that a reader favors or identifies with are known as **sympathetic characters**, while characters for whom the reader feels disdain are known as **unsympathetic characters**. Some authors encourage readers to find wicked characters sympathetic or virtuous characters unsympathetic; therefore, the Christian reader should thoughtfully examine each author's attitude toward the actions and attitudes of his characters.

While one may assume that flawed characters will always appear unsympathetic to the reader, this is not necessarily true. Within literary works known as **tragedies**, the protagonist's flaws cause him tremendous suffering that eventually results in

a catastrophe, or disastrous conclusion. Consequently, though the protagonist in such works may not be a likable character, we nevertheless are led to sympathize with him because of the universality of his flaws and the severity of his woes. In these literary works, the protagonist is also the **tragic hero**, and his **tragic flaw**, or most significant flaw—often pride (known as hubris)—triggers his downfall. According to critics, tragedies not only cause us to feel pity for the protagonist but also instill the reader or viewer with a sense of fear. We take pity on the tragic hero because he suffers terribly, yet we also fear that the same unchecked weaknesses in our own lives may lead us to a similar fate. The true story of Samson from Judges 13–16 illustrates characteristics of the basic tragic plot, with the protagonist facing a ruinous end because of his flaw (lust) yet finally realizing his fallibility. Though Samson's initial hubris and rashness detract significantly from our sympathy, we eventually pity him because he suffers greatly because of his flaw.

1. Identify each of the following characters from *Treasure Island* as either sympathetic or unsympathetic: Jim Hawkins, Pew, Jim's mother, and Black Dog. Explain your answer for each character, identifying the traits that make each either **sympathetic** or **unsympathetic**.

2. Do you find Phaëthon sympathetic or unsympathetic? Explain.

3. How does Freeman encourage the reader to sympathize with Mrs. Penn in "The Revolt of Mother"?

4. Is the reader ever encouraged by Freeman to sympathize with Adoniram Penn?

5. Would it ever be morally permissible for an author to render a flawed character sympathetic to the reader? Can you think of any examples from the Bible?

6. Which of the four selections that you have read thus far in this unit best fits the definition of a **tragedy**? What is the catastrophe in that selection?

7. For the story you identified in the previous question, who is the **tragic hero**? What is his **tragic flaw**?

⚜ ——————————————

> At the end of each selection or group of selections, the Thinking Zone highlights or reviews literary terms and concepts being studied.

[THINK]ING ZONE ❧

[...]ques [...]rds, [...]s to [...]ech-[...]on. [...]h of [...]ings [...]tice emphasizes the repeated words and can allow a writer to extend a statement without losing audience comprehension. Dickens's famous beginning to *A Tale of Two Cities*—"*It was the* best of times, *it was the* worst of times, *it was the* age of wisdom, *it was the* age of foolishness, *it was the* epoch of belief, *it was the* epoch of incredulity"—is an excellent example of a long sentence using anaphora for clarity as well as for emphasis. Also, in both poetry and prose, anaphora can be used to enhance rhythm. For instance, Tennyson's "The Charge of the Light Brigade" employs anaphora in every stanza. In this context, the technique creates not only emphasis but also a rhythmic effect, combining with the short lines to create a driving beat of sound evoking an actual charge.

Another technique for arranging word groups is **parallelism**, or similarity in the structure of two or more phrases, clauses, or sentences. The main appeal of parallelism

is its symmetry, which both satisfies readers' aesthetic senses and attracts attention to the content. Writers can exhibit parallelism in both grammar and thought. In fact, the Dickens quotation provides a fine example of grammatical parallelism as well as anaphora: each clause follows the same sentence pattern of subject ("it"), verb ("was"), article ("the"), predicate noun ("best"), prepositional phrase ("of times"). Parallelism of thought is less common in English language poetry. However, Hebrew poetry makes good use of this form, as the Bible clearly illustrates. Verses such as Proverbs 10:1—"A wise son maketh a glad father: but a foolish son is the heaviness of his mother"—display parallelism of two precisely contrasted ideas, whereas many like Proverbs 22:1—"A good name is rather to be chosen than great riches, and loving favour rather than silver and gold"—rephrase an idea for emphasis. An alternate form of parallelism is chiasmus. **Chiasmus** inverts the parallel structure, keeping the elements of the original phrase, clause, or sentence but reversing them in the following unit. For example, in Shakespeare's line from "Sonnet 29"—"With what I most enjoy contented least"—the final four words display chiasmus on a small scale (adverb, verb, verb, adverb).

1. According to the description in your text, what common feature of ballads exhibits repetition?

2. In this unit, two poems besides Tennyson's employ **anaphora**. Name one and explain what effect the anaphora might contribute to the poem.

3. Aside from the refrain, what parallel structures exist in "Bonnie George Campbell"? Cite an example and tell what effect **parallelism** might create in the poem.

4. The haiku form requires parallelism. What must be parallel?

5. You have already seen an example of **chiasmus** from "Sonnet 29." Line 6 contains another. Explain how this line shows chiasmus.

⚜ ——————————————

THINKING ZONE   325

> Questions specifically target literary terms and concepts from the Thinking Zone.

UNIT II REVIEW

REMEMBER THE TERMS

Review the following terms from the opening essay, "Character," and the Thinking Zone pages. Be prepared to discuss their meanings and uses.

character trait	round character	unsympathetic character
description	flat character	tragedy
direct characterization	foil	tragic hero
indirect characterization	static character	tragic flaw
action	dynamic character	normative character
dialogue	sympathetic character	character motivation

APPLY THE CONCEPTS

Answer the following questions about how the literary concepts you have studied are used in this unit.

1. In Chapter 1 of *Treasure Island*, what is Billy Bones's motivation for choosing to stay at the Admiral Benbow?
2. What is the source of the conflict between Dr. Livesey and Billy Bones in Chapter 1?
3. What method or methods of characterization does Stevenson use at the beginning of Chapter 3 to reveal Billy Bones's state of mind?
4. In Chapter 3 how do Pew's actions contradict his initial dialogue with Jim?
5. Identify each of the following characters as round or flat: Jim Hawkins, Jim's mother, Billy Bones, Black Dog. Explain your answers.
6. In "Phaëthon" what is Phaëthon's motivation for visiting the sun-god?
7. Is Phaëthon a round character or a flat character? Explain.
8. In "Old Man" what do the old man's words reveal about his view of his heritage?
9. Is Sarah Penn from "Th[e]...
10. Which story in the first [...] tragic flaw?
11. In "Neighbour Rosicky" [...] appearance suggest his [...]
12. Is Mary Rosicky a symp[...]
13. Is Polly a dynamic chara[...]
14. How does Sancho Panza [...]
15. What does the title "My [...] point toward his late wi[...]

156   CHARACTER

EVALUATE THE IDEAS

Identify each of the following statements as true or false. If false, rewrite the underlined portion of the sentence to make it true.

16. The description of a character's appearance <u>sometimes</u> qualifies as indirect characterization.
17. Job's friends are examples of <u>round</u> characters.
18. Billy Bones from *Treasure Island* is a <u>dynamic</u> character.
19. In *Treasure Island*, because Dr. Livesey reprimands Billy Bones, the reader finds the doctor <u>unsympathetic</u>.
20. <u>Pride</u> is a common flaw found in tragic heroes.
21. <u>Dynamic</u> characters undergo changes within themselves in a story.
22. The <u>norm</u> is the character whose traits emphasize opposing traits in the main character.
23. <u>Nanny</u> Penn from "The Revolt of Mother" is a flat character.
24. One difference between round and flat characters is that <u>flat</u> characters are more likely to be dynamic characters.
25. Rudolph from "Neighbour Rosicky" is a <u>static</u> character.
26. Most tragedies end in a <u>catastrophe</u>.
27. We sympathize with the <u>duchess</u> in "My Last Duchess."
28. Cervantes uses <u>description</u> in Chapter 1 of *Don Quixote* to tell the reader about the main character.
29. Tragic heroes are generally <u>unsympathetic</u>.

WRITE A RESPONSE

Completely answer each of the following questions.

30. Throughout *Treasure Island* how does Robert Louis Stevenson use description, action, and dialogue to reveal the character of Billy Bones to the reader?
31. How does the character of Anton Rosicky from "Neighbour Rosicky" contrast with Adoniram Penn in "The Revolt of Mother"?
32. What is the Duke's main character flaw in "My Last Duchess"? How do his words reveal this flaw?

UNIT II REVIEW   157

A LITERARY JOUST

Jonathan Wolstenholme

I

❧ CONFLICT ❧

Artist Jonathan Wolstenholme (b. 1950) is an illustrator whose works have appeared in a number of magazines and newspapers. Because of his love for old books and writing instruments, many of his watercolors feature writing and the written word. His style is often referred to as "idiosyncratic painting," which could be described as contemporary painting that combines touches of realism, surrealism, and humorous whimsy.

✤ How does *A Literary Joust* fit the definition of idiosyncratic painting as described above?

✤ Is *A Literary Joust* a good fit for a unit entitled "Conflict"? Why or why not?

✤ If you were to select two stories to joust with each other, what would they be?

✤ What dialogue could be written for Wolstenholme's painting?

❧ CONFLICT ❧

To be human is to be enmeshed in conflict. When God introduced the first human to this world, He introduced him to conflict: "Of the tree of the knowledge of good and evil, thou shalt not eat of it" (Gen. 2:17). This conflict became both painful and tragic when man disobeyed that command. But God Himself entered the battle, and He is still working to deliver His world. Shortly after the first sin, God told the serpent that He would give His people victory: "I will put enmity between thee and the woman, and between thy seed and her seed; it shall bruise thy head, and thou shalt bruise his heel" (Gen. 3:15). The end of the Bible's story records the final arrival of this triumph: "The kingdoms of this world are become the kingdoms of our Lord, and of his Christ; and he shall reign for ever and ever" (Rev. 11:15). This conflict of good versus evil—God versus the powers of darkness—is all around us, between us, and even in us. Since literature imitates reality, we should not be surprised to discover that conflict is basic to any story.

Conflict is broadly defined as the opposition of two or more characters or forces. The forms each conflict takes may differ widely: the setting may be a small town or a stormy sea; the adversary may be an evil ruler or a guilty conscience; and the prize may be a parcel of land or a human soul. But regardless of its time, place, characters, or situation, a story without conflict is a story with no significance to the reader, for our lives are framed by physical and spiritual conflict.

TYPES OF CONFLICT

In literature, we recognize three main types of conflict. One story that aptly illustrates all three types of conflict is the Bible's account of the Fall. Genesis 3 tells us that at the beginning of the world, Adam and Eve rebelled against the Creator in the Garden of Eden. As a direct result of this first conflict, God cursed the ground, and man found himself at odds with both God and nature. These incidents form our first record of **man against a greater force**.

Out of this initial struggle a second type of conflict emerged: **man against himself**. After the fall, Adam and Eve hid themselves upon "[hearing] the voice of the Lord God." When the Lord asked them why they had fled, Adam replied, "I heard thy voice in the garden, and *I was afraid*" (Gen. 3:8, 10). Man's sin not only severed his fellowship with God but also destroyed his inner peace.

This second conflict produced yet another— **man against man**. Once he was confronted with his disobedience, Adam's loving attitude toward his wife vanished. Driven by fear for himself, Adam blamed Eve for his sin: "The woman whom thou gavest to be with me, she gave me of the tree and I did eat" (3:12). Eve, quick to follow her husband's example, sought to protect herself by blaming the serpent for her sin.

In addition to these three types of conflict, another useful method labels each conflict in reference to a character. In this system, **external conflicts** occur between a character and an outside force (such as society, nature, or another character) whereas **internal conflicts** occur between a character and his thoughts, emotions, and beliefs. Generally, conflicts of man against a greater force or of man against man are external, while the struggles of man against himself are internal.

PARTICIPANTS IN CONFLICT

Though stories often contain numerous conflicts, usually one primary conflict drives the plot. When considering the primary participants in the major conflict, certain labels are helpful. The central character of the story is known as the **protagonist**. If a particular force or character strongly opposes the protagonist, that force or character is called the **antagonist**.

Sometimes a protagonist behaves virtuously in a story. If so, that character may be labeled a **hero**. Similarly, if the antagonist in a story is particularly evil or cruel, he is known as a **villain**. At the same time, readers should remember that a protagonist may not always be admirable nor an antagonist evil. For example, in 2 Samuel 12, when the prophet Nathan confronts King David over unconfessed sin, David is the protagonist of the story and Nathan is the antagonist. Yet Nathan clearly has behaved more uprightly than David in the story.

RESOLUTION OF CONFLICT

Conflict resolution refers to how the opposing forces in a particular conflict come to grips with the issues at hand. The resolution may involve victory and defeat or simple compromise. But how a conflict is resolved (or not resolved) is important since the resolution often emphasizes what the author wishes to say. Conflict resolutions may teach the value of seeing life from another's point of view, illustrate the principle of "be sure your sin will find you out," or reinforce qualities such as kindness, integrity, or perseverance, among many others.

Sometimes, an author may leave a conflict unresolved so that the reader will consider a particular problem. For example, the book of Jonah ends with the Lord's rebuking the prophet for his selfish vindictiveness towards the Ninevites. Though Jonah's response is not recorded, leaving his internal conflict unresolved, we are left to ponder God's thoughts on the matter and—hopefully—apply them to ourselves.

In your first reading selection, "Miss Hinch," the author uses two techniques that further emphasize conflict resolution. First, he induces audience **suspense** (anxiety resulting from an author's withholding of plot details). This technique plays on the reader's curiosity and gives the resolution greater emotional weight when it finally comes. At the same time, the author employs **foreshadowing** (hinting at events that will occur later in the story). Both methods are common occurrences in literature.

Here are some questions to keep in mind as you read the stories in this unit: What is the central conflict of the story and what type of conflict is it? Is it internal or external? Who is the protagonist of the story? Who is the antagonist? Are there any secondary conflicts? How are the main conflict and any other conflicts resolved?

Miss Hinch

Henry Sydnor Harrison

It seems unlikely that an aging clergyman and a decent-looking old woman would be pitted against each other in a life-and-death struggle. As the story of "Miss Hinch" unfolds, you will discover that things are not always as they seem nor is it always easy to discern who is the hero and who is the villain. If you follow the details of the action carefully, however, you can unravel the mystery before reaching the story's end.

In going from a given point on 126th Street to a subway station at 125th, it is not usual to begin by circling the block to 127th Street, especially in sleet, darkness, and deadly cold. When two people pursue such a course at the same time, moving unobtrusively on opposite sides of the street, in the nature of things the coincidence is likely to attract the attention of one or the other of them.

In the bright light of the entrance of the tube* they came almost face to face, and the clergyman took a good look at her. Certainly she was a decent-looking old body, if any woman was: white-haired, wrinkled, spec-tacled, and stooped. A poor but thoroughly respectable domestic servant of the better class she looked, in her old black hat, neat veil, and grey shawl; and her brief glance at the reverend gentleman was precisely what it should have been from her to him—def-erence* itself. Nevertheless, he, going more slowly down the draughty* steps, continued to study her from behind with a singular intentness.

tube (British): subway
deference: a humble yielding to the wishes or judgment of another
draughty (DRAF tee; British): drafty

An express was just thundering in, which the clergyman, handicapped as he was by his clubfoot and stout cane, was barely in time to catch. He entered the same car with the woman and chanced to take a seat directly across from her. It must have been then after twelve o'clock, and the wildness of the weather was discouraging to travel. The car was almost deserted. Even in this underground retreat the bitter breath of the night blew and bit, and the old woman shivered under her shawl. At last, her teeth chattering, she got up in an apologetic sort of way, and moved toward the better protected rear of the car, feeling the empty seats as she went, plainly in search of hot pipes. The clergyman's eyes followed her candidly, and watched her sink down, presently, into a seat on his own side of the car. A young couple sat between them now; he could no longer see the woman, beyond occasional glimpses of her black knees and her faded bonnet, fastened on with a long steel hatpin.

Nothing could have seemed more natural or more trivial than this change of seats on the part of a thin-blooded and half-frozen passenger. But it happened to be at a time of mutual doubt and misgivings, of alert suspicions and hair-trigger watchfulness, when men looked askance into every strange face and the smallest incidents were likely to take on a hysterical importance. Through days of fruitless searching for a fugitive outlaw of extraordinary gifts, the nerve of the city had been slowly strained to the breaking-point. All jumped, now, when anybody cried "Boo!" and the hue and cry went up falsely twenty times a day.

The clergyman pondered; mechanically he turned up his coat collar and fell to stamping his icy feet. He was an Episcopal clergyman, by his garb—rather short, very full-bodied, not to say fat, bearded and somewhat puffy-faced, with heavy cheeks cut by deep creases. Well-lined against the cold though he was, however, he, too, began to suffer visibly, and presently was forced to retreat in his turn, seeking out a new place where the heating apparatus gave a better account of itself. He found one, two seats beyond the old serving-woman, limped into it, and soon relapsed into his own thoughts.

The young couple, now half a dozen seats away, were thoroughly absorbed in each other's society. The fifth traveler, a withered old gentleman sitting next the middle door across the aisle, napped fitfully upon his cane. The woman in the hat and shawl sat in a sad kind of silence; and the train hurled itself roaringly through the tube. After a time, she glanced timidly at the meditating clergyman, and her look fell swiftly from his face to the discarded "ten o'clock extra" lying by his side. She removed her dim gaze and let it travel casually about the car; but before long it returned, pointedly, to the newspaper. Then, with some hesitation, she bent forward and said, above the noises of the train:

"Excuse me, Father, but would you let me look at your paper a minute, sir?"

The clergyman came out of his reverie instantly, and looked up with a quick smile.

"Certainly. Keep it if you like: I am quite through with it. But," he added, in a pleasant deep voice, "I am an Episcopal minister, not a priest."

"Oh, sir—I beg your pardon! I thought—"

He dismissed the apology with a nod and a good-natured hand.

The woman opened the paper with decent cotton-gloved fingers. The garish headlines told the story at a glance: "Earth Opened and Swallowed Miss Hinch—Headquarters Virtually Abandons Case—Even Jessie Dark," so the bold capitals ran on—"Seems Stumped." Below the spread was a luridly written but flimsy narrative "By Jessie Dark," which at once confirmed the odd implication of the caption. "Jessie Dark," it appeared, was one of those most extraordinary of the products of yellow journalism,* a woman "crime expert," now in action. More than this, she was a "crime expert" to be taken seriously it seemed—no mere office-desk sleuth, but an actual performer with, unexpectedly enough, a somewhat formidable list of notches on her gun. So much, at least, was to be gathered from her paper's display of "Jessie Dark's Triumphs:"

March 2, 1901. Caught Julia Victorian, alias Gregory, the brains of the "Heally Ring" kidnappers.

October 7–29, 1903. Found Mrs. Trotwood and secured the letter that convicted her of the murder of her lover, Ellis E. Swan.

December 17, 1903. Ran down Charles Bartsch in a Newark laundry and trapped a confession from him.

July 4, 1904. Caught Mary Calloran and recovered the Stratford jewels.

And so on—nine "triumphs" in all; and nearly every one of them, as the least observant reader could hardly fail to notice, involved the capture of a woman.

Nevertheless, it could not be pretended that the "snappy" paragraphs in this evening's extra seemed to foreshadow a new or tenth triumph for Jessie Dark at an early date; and the old serving-woman in the car presently laid down the sheet with a look of marked depression.

The clergyman looked at her again. Her expression was so speaking that it seemed to be almost an invitation; besides, public interest in the great case made conversation between total strangers the rule wherever two or three were gathered together.

"You were reading about this strange mystery, perhaps."

The woman with a sharp intake of breath, answered. "Yes, sir. Oh, sir, it seems as if I couldn't think of anything else."

"Ah?" he said, without surprise. "It certainly appears to be a remarkable affair."

Remarkable, indeed, the affair seemed. In a tiny little room within ten steps of Broadway at half-past nine o'clock on a fine evening, Miss Hinch had killed John Catherwood with the light sword she used in her famous representation of the Father of his Country. Catherwood, it was known, had come to tell her of his coming marriage, and ten thousand amateur detectives, fired by unusual rewards, had required no further motive of a creature already notorious for fierce jealousy. So far the tragedy was commonplace enough, and even vulgar.* What had redeemed it to romance from this point on was the extraordinary faculty of the woman, which had made her celebrated while she was still in her teens. Coarse, violent, utterly unmoral she might be, but she happened also to be the most astonishing impersonator of her time. Her brilliant "act" consisted of a series of character changes, many of them done in full view of the audience with the assistance only of a small table of properties half concealed under a net. Some of these transformations were so amazing as to be beyond belief, even after one had sat and watched them. Not her appearance only, but voice, speech, manner, carriage, all shifted incredibly to fit the new part; so that the woman appeared to have no permanent form or fashion of her own, but to be only so much plastic human material out of which her cunning could mold at will man, woman, or child, great lady of the Louisan Court* or Tammany statesman* with the modernest of East Side modernisms upon his lip.

vulgar: common, lacking good breeding

Louisan Court: the court of any of a line of extravagant French monarchs

Tammany statesman: a member of a Democratic party organization in New York City that was very powerful in the nineteenth and early twentieth centuries

With this strange skill, hitherto used only to enthrall large audiences and wring extortionate contracts from managers, the woman known as Miss Hinch—she appeared to be without a first name—was now fighting for her life somewhere against the police of the world. Without artifice, she was a tall, thin-chested young woman with strongly marked features and considerable beauty of a bold sort. What she would look like at the present moment nobody could venture a guess. Having stabbed John Catherwood in her dressing-room at the Amphitheater, she had put on her hat and coat, dropped two wigs and her make-up kit into a handbag, and walked out into Broadway. Within ten minutes the dead body of Catherwood was found and the chase had begun. At the stage door, as she passed out, Miss Hinch had met an acquaintance, a young comedian named Dargis, and exchanged a word of greeting with him. That had been ten days ago. After Dargis, no one had seen her. The earth, indeed, seemed to have opened and swallowed her. Yet her natural features were almost as well known as the President's, and the newspapers of a continent were daily reprinting them in a thousand variations.

"A very remarkable case," repeated the clergyman, rather absently; and his neighbor, the old woman, respectfully agreed that it was. Then, as the train slowed up for the stop at 86th Street, she added with sudden bitterness:

"Oh, they'll never catch her, sir—never! She's too smart for 'em all, Miss Hinch is."

Attracted by her tone, the stout divine inquired if she were particularly interested in the case.

"Yes, sir—I got reason to be. Jack Catherwood's mother and me was at school together, and great friends all our life long. Oh, sir," she went on, as if in answer to his look of faint surprise, "Jack was a fine gentleman, with manners and looks and all beyond his people. But he never grew away from his old mother—no, sir, never! And I don't believe ever a Sunday passed that he didn't go up and set the afternoon away with her, talking and laughing just like he was a little boy again. Maybe he done things he hadn't ought, as high-spirited lads will, but oh, sir, he was a good boy in his heart— a good boy. And it does seem too hard for him to die like that—and that hussy free to go her way, ruinin' and killin'—"

"My good woman," said the clergyman presently, "compose yourself. No matter how diabolical this woman's skill is, her sin will assuredly find her out."

The woman dutifully lowered her handkerchief and tried to compose herself, as bidden.

"But, oh, she's that clever—diabolical, just as ye say, sir. Through poor Jack we of course heard much gossip about her, and they do say that her best tricks was not done on the stage at all. They say, sir, that, sittin' around a table with her friends, she could begin and twist her face so strange and terrible that they would beg her stop, and jump up and run from the table—frightened out of their lives, sir, grown-up people, by the terrible faces she could make. And let her only step behind her screen for a minute—for she kept her secrets well, Miss Hinch did—and she'd come walking out to you, and you could go right up to her in the full light and take her hand, and still you couldn't make yourself believe it was her."

"Yes," said the clergyman, "I have heard that she is remarkably clever—though, as a stranger in this part of the world, I never saw her act. I must say, it is all very interesting and strange."

He turned his head and stared through the rear of the car at the dark flying walls. At the same moment the woman turned her head and stared full at the clergyman. When the train halted again, at Grand Central Station, he turned back to her.

"I'm a visitor in the city, from Denver, Colorado," he said pleasantly, "and knew little or nothing about the case until an evening or two ago, when I attended a meeting of gentlemen here. The men's club of St. Matthias' Church—perhaps you know the place? Upon my word, they talked of nothing else. I confess they got me quite interested in their gossip. So tonight I bought this paper to see what this extraordinary woman detective it employs had to say about it. We don't have such things in the West, you know. But I must say I was disappointed after all the talk about her."

"Yes, sir, indeed, and no wonder, for she's told Mrs. Catherwood herself that she never made such a failure as this so far. It seemed like she could always catch women, up to this. It seemed like she knew in her own mind just what a woman would do, where she'd try to hide and all, and so she could find them time and time when the men detectives didn't know where to look. But, oh, sir, she's never had to hunt for such a woman as Miss Hinch before!"

"No! I suppose not," said the clergyman. "Her story here in the paper certainly seems to me very poor."

"Story, sir! Bless my soul!" suddenly exploded the old gentleman across the aisle, to the surprise of both. "You don't suppose the clever little woman is going to show her hand in those stories, with Miss Hinch in the city and reading every line of them! In the city, sir—such is my positive belief!"

The approach to his station, it seemed, had roused him from his nap just in time to overhear the episcopate criticism. Now he answered the looks of the old woman and the clergyman with an elderly cackle.

"Excuse my intrusion, I'm sure! But I can't sit silent and hear anybody run down

Jessie Dark—Miss Mathewson in private life, as perhaps you don't know. No, sir! Why, there's a man at my boarding-place—astonishing young fellow named Hardy, Tom Hardy—who's known her for years! As to those stories, sir, I can assure you that she puts in there exactly the opposite of what she really thinks!"

"You don't tell me!" said the clergyman encouragingly.

"Yes, sir! Oh, she plays the game—yes, yes! She has her private ideas, her clues, her schemes. The woman doesn't live who is clever enough to hoodwink Jessie Dark. I look for developments any day—any day, sir!"

A new voice joined in. The young couple down the car, their attention caught by the old man's pervasive tones, had been frankly listening; and it was illustrative of the public mind at the moment that, as they now rose for the station and drew nearer, the young man felt perfectly free to offer his contribution.

"Dramatic situation, isn't it, when you stop to think. Those two clever women pitted against each other in a life-and-death struggle, fighting it out silently in the underground somewhere—keen professional pride on one side and the fear of the electric chair on the other. Good heavens, there's—"

"Oh, yes! Oh, yes!" exclaimed the old gentleman rather testily. "But my dear sir, it's not professional pride that makes Jessie Dark so resolute to win. It's sex jealousy, if you follow me—no offense, madam! Yes, sir! Women never have the slightest respect for each other, either! I tell you, Jessie Dark'd be ashamed to be beaten by another woman. Read her stories between the lines, sir—as I do. Invincible determination—no weakening—no mercy! You catch my point, sir?"

"It sounds reasonable," answered the Colorado clergyman, with his courteous smile. "All women, we are told, are natural rivals at heart—"

"Oh, I'm for Jessie Dark every time!" the young fellow broke in eagerly—"especially since the police have practically laid down. But—"

"Why, she's told my young friend Hardy," the old gentleman rode him down, "that she'll find Hinch if it takes her lifetime! Knows a thing or two about actresses, she says. Says the world isn't big enough for the creature to hide from her. Well! What do you think of that?"

"Tell what we were just talking about, George," said the young wife, looking at her husband with admiring eyes.

"But oh, sir," began the old woman timidly, "Jack Catherwood's been dead ten days now, and—and—"

"Ten days, madam! And what is that, pray?" exploded the old gentleman, rising triumphantly. "A lifetime, if necessary! Oh, never fear! Mrs. Victorian was considered pretty clever, eh? Wasn't she? Remember what Jessie Dark did for her? Nan Parmalee, too—though the police did their best to steal her credit. She'll do just as much for Miss Hinch—you may take it from me!"

"But how's she going to make the capture, gentlemen?" cried the young fellow, getting his chance at last. "That's the point my wife and I've been discussing. Assuming that she succeeds in spotting this woman-devil, what will she do? Now—"

"Do! Yell for the police!" burst from the old gentleman at the door.

"And have Miss Hinch shoot her—and then herself, too? Wouldn't she have to—"

"Grand Central!" cried the guard for the second time; and the young fellow broke off reluctantly to find his bride towing him strongly toward the door.

"Hope she nabs her soon, anyway," he called back to the clergyman over his shoulder.

"The thing's getting on my nerves. One of these kindergarten reward-chasers followed my wife for five blocks the other day, just because she's got a pointed chin, and I don't know what might have happened if I hadn't came along and—"

Doors rolled shut behind him, and the train flung itself on its way. Within the car a lengthy silence ensued. The clergyman stared thoughtfully at the floor, and the old woman fell back upon her borrowed paper. She appeared to be re-reading the observations of Jessie Dark with considerable care. Presently she lowered the paper and began a quiet search for something under the folds of her shawl; and at length, her hands emerging empty, she broke the silence in a lifted voice.

"Oh, sir—have you a pencil you could lend me, please? I'd like to mark something in the piece to send to Mrs. Catherwood. It's what she says here about the disguises, sir."

The kindly divine felt in his pockets, and after some hunting produced a pencil—a white one with blue lead. She thanked him gratefully.

"How is Mrs. Catherwood bearing all this strain and anxiety?" he asked suddenly. "Have you seen her today?"

"Oh, yes, sir! I've been spending the evening with her since nine o'clock, and am just back from there now. Oh, she's very much broke up, sir."

She looked at him uncertainly. He stared straight in front of him, saying nothing, though conceivably he knew, in common with the rest of the reading world, that Jack Catherwood's mother lived, not on 126th Street, but on East Houston Street. Possibly he might have wondered if his silence had not been an error of judgment. Perhaps that misstatement had not been a slip, but something cleverer?

The woman went on with a certain eagerness: "Oh, sir, I only hope and pray those gen-tlemen may be right, but it does look to Mrs. Catherwood, and me too, that if Jessie Dark was going to catch her at all, she'd have done it before now. Look at those big blue eyes she had, sir, with the lashes an inch long, they say, and that terrible long chin of hers. They do say she can change the color of her eyes, not forever of course, but put a few of her drops into them and make them look entirely different for a time. But that chin, ye'd say—"

She broke off; for the clergyman, without preliminaries of any sort, had picked up his heavy stick and suddenly risen.

"Here we are at Fourteenth Street," he said nodding pleasantly. "I must change here. Good night. Success to Jessie Dark, I say!"

He was watching the woman's faded face and he saw just that look of respectful surprise break into it that he had expected.

"Fourteenth Street! I'd no notion at all we'd come so far. It's where I get out, too, sir, the express not stopping at my station."

"Ah?" said the clergyman, smiling a little.

He led the way, limping and leaning on his stick. They emerged upon the chill and cheerless platform, not exactly together, yet still with some reference to their acquaintanceship on the car. But the clergyman, after stumping along a few steps, all at once realized that he was walking alone, and turned. The woman had halted. Over the intervening space their eyes met.

"Come," said the man gently. "Come, let us walk about a little to keep warm."

"Oh, sir—it's too kind of you, sir," said the woman, coming forward.

From other cars two or three blue-nosed people had got off to make the change; one or two more came straggling in from the street; but scattered over the bleak concrete expanse, they detracted little from the isolation that seemed to surround the woman and the clergyman. Step for step, the odd pair made their way to the extreme northern end of the platform.

"By the way," said the clergyman, halting abruptly, "May I see that paper again for a moment?"

"Oh, yes, sir—of course," said the woman, producing it from beneath her shawl. "I thought you had finished with it, and I—"

He said that he wanted only to glance at it for a moment; but he fell to looking through it page by page, with considerable care. The woman glanced at him several times. At last she said hesitatingly:

"I thought, sir, I'd ask the ticket-chopper could he say how long before the next train. I'm very late as it is, sir, and I still must stop to get something to eat before I go to bed."

"An excellent idea," said the clergyman.

He explained that he, too, was already behind time, and was spending the night with cousins in Jersey, to boot. Side by side, they retraced their steps down the platform, questioned the chopper with scant results,

and then, as by tacit* consent, started back again. However, before they had gone far, the woman stopped short and, with a white face, leaned against a pillar.

tacit: unspoken

"Oh, sir, I'm afraid I'll have to stop and get a bite somewhere before I go on. You'll think me foolish, sir, but I missed my supper entirely tonight, and there is quite a faint feeling coming over me."

The clergyman looked at her with apparent concern. "Do you know, my friend, you seem to anticipate all my own wants. Your mentioning something to eat just now reminded me that I myself was all but famishing." He glanced at his watch, appearing to deliberate. "Yes—it will not take long. Come, we'll find a modest eating-house together."

"Oh, sir," she stammered, "but—you wouldn't want to eat with a poor old woman like me, sir."

"And why not? Are we not all equal in the sight of God?"

They ascended the stairs together, like any prosperous parson and his poor parishioner, and coming out into Fourteenth Street, started west. On the first block they came to a restaurant, a brilliantly lighted, tiled and polished place of a quick-lunch variety. But the woman timidly preferred not to stop here, saying that the glare of such places was very bad for her old eyes. The divine accepted the objection as valid, without an argument. Two blocks farther on they found on a corner a quieter resort, an unpretentious little haven which yet boasted a "Ladies' Entrance" down the side street.

They entered by the front door, and sat down at a table, facing each other. The woman read the menu through, and finally, after some embarrassed uncertainty, ordered poached eggs on toast. The clergyman ordered the same. The simple meal was soon dispatched.

Just as they were finishing it, the woman said apologetically:

"If you'll excuse me, sir—could I see the bill of fare a minute? I think I'd best take a little pot of tea to warm me up, if they do not charge too high."

"I haven't the bill of fare," said the clergyman.

They looked diligently for the cardboard strip, but it was nowhere to be seen. The waiter drew near.

"Yes, sir! I left it there on the table when I took the order."

"I'm sure I can't imagine what's become of it," repeated the clergyman, rather insistently.

He looked hard at the woman, and found that she was looking hard at him. Both pairs of eyes fell instantly.

The waiter brought another bill of fare; the woman ordered tea; the waiter came back with it. The clergyman paid for both orders with a bill that looked hard-earned.

The tea proved to be very hot; it could not be drunk down at a gulp. The clergyman, watching the woman sidewise as she sipped, seemed to grow more restless. His fingers drummed the tablecloth: he could hardly sit still. All at once he said: "What is that calling in the street? It sounds like newsboys."

The woman put her old head on one side and listened. "Yes, sir. There seems to be an extra out."

"Upon my word," he said after a pause. "I believe I'll go get one. Good gracious! Crime is a very interesting thing, to be sure!"

He rose slowly, took down his shovel-hat from the hanger near him, grasped his heavy stick, limped to the door. Leaving it open behind him, much to the annoyance of the proprietor in the cashier's cage, he stood a moment in the little vestibule, looking up and down the street. Then he took a few slow steps eastward, beckoning with his hand as he went, and so passed out of sight of the woman at the table.

The eating-place was on the corner, and outside the clergyman paused for half a breath. North, east, south and west he looked and nowhere he found what his flying glance sought. He turned the corner into the darker cross-street, and began to walk, at first slowly, continually looking about him. Presently his pace quickened, quickened, so that he no longer even stayed to use his stout cane. In another moment he was all but running, his clubfoot pounding the icy sidewalk heavily as he went. A newsboy thrust an extra under his very nose, but he did not even see it.

Far down the street, nearly two blocks away, a tall figure in a blue coat stood and stamped in the freezing sleet; and the hurrying divine sped straight toward him. But he did not get very near. For, as he passed the side entrance at the extreme rear of the restaurant, a departing guest dashed out so recklessly as to run full into him, stopping him dead.

Without looking at her, he knew who it was. In fact, he did not look at her at all, but turned his head hurriedly north and south, sweeping the dark street with a swift eye. But the old woman, having drawn back with a sharp exclamation as they collided, rushed breathlessly into apologies:

"Oh, sir—excuse me! A newsboy popped his head into the side door just after you went out, and I ran to get you the paper. But he got away too quick for me, sir, and so I—"

"Exactly," said the clergyman in his quiet deep voice. "That must have been the very boy I myself was after."

On the other side, two men had just turned into the street, well muffled against the night, talking cheerfully as they trudged along. Now the clergyman looked full at the

woman, and she saw that there was a smile on his face.

"As he seems to have eluded us both, suppose we return to the subway?"

"Yes, sir; it's full time I—"

"The sidewalk is so slippery," he went on gently, "perhaps you had better take my arm."

Behind the pair in the dingy restaurant, the waiter came forward to shut the door, and lingered to discuss with the proprietor the sudden departure of his two patrons. However, the score had been paid with a liberal tip for service, so there was no especial complaint to make. After listening to some unfavorable comments on the ways of the clergy, the waiter returned to his table to set it in order.

On the floor in the carpeted aisle between tables lay a white piece of cardboard, which his familiar eye recognized as part of one of his own bills of fare, face downward. He stooped and picked it up. On the back of it was some scribbling, made with a blue lead pencil.

The handwriting was very loose and irregular, as if the writer had had his eyes elsewhere while he wrote, and it was with some difficulty that the waiter deciphered this message:

"Miss Hinch 14th St. subway Get police quick."

The waiter carried this curious document to the proprietor, who read it over a number of times. He was a dull man, and had a dull man's suspiciousness of a practical joke. However, after a good deal of irresolute discussion, he put on his overcoat and went out for a policeman. He turned west, and halfway up the block met an elderly bluecoat trudging east. The policeman looked at the scribbling, and dismissed it profanely as a wag's foolishness of the sort that was bothering the life out of him a dozen times a day. He walked along with the proprietor, and as they drew near to the latter's place of business both become aware of footsteps thudding nearer up the cross-street from the south. As they looked up, two young policemen, accompanied by a man in uniform like a street-car conductor's, swept around the corner and dashed straight into the restaurant.

The first policeman and the proprietor ran in after them, and found them staring about rather vacantly. One of the arms of the law demanded if any suspicious characters had been seen about the place, and the dull proprietor said no. The officers, looking rather flat, explained their errand. It seemed that a few moments before, the third man, who was a ticket-chopper at the subway station, had found a mysterious message lying on the floor by his box. Whence it had come, how long it had lain there, he had not the slightest idea. However, there it was. The policeman exhibited a crumpled scrap torn from a newspaper, on which was scrawled in blue pencil:

"Miss Hinch Miller's Restaurant Get police quick."

The first policeman, who was both the oldest and the fattest of the three, produced the message on the bill of fare, so utterly at odds with this. The dull proprietor, now bethinking himself, mentioned the clergyman and the old woman who had taken poached eggs and tea together, called for a second bill of fare, and departed so unexpectedly by different doors. The ticket-chopper recalled that he had seen the same pair at his station; they had come up, he remembered, and questioned him about trains. The three policemen were momentarily puzzled by this testimony. But it was soon plain to them if either the woman or the clergyman really had any information about Miss Hinch—a highly improbable supposition in itself—they would never have stopped with peppering the neighborhood with silly little contradictory messages.

"They're a pair of old fools tryin' to have sport with the police, and I'd like to run them in for it," growled the fattest of the officers; and it was the general verdict.

The little conference broke up. The dull proprietor returned to his cage, the waiter to his table; the subway man departed for his chopping box; the three policemen passed out into the bitter night. They walked together, grumbling, and their feet, perhaps by some subconscious impulse, turned toward the subway. And in the next block a man came running up to them.

"Officer, look what I found on the sidewalk a minute ago. Read that scribble!"

"Police! Miss Hinch 14th St subw"

The hand trailed off on the *w* as though the writer had been suddenly interrupted. The fat policeman blasphemed and threatened arrests. But the second policeman, who was dark and wiry, raised his head from the bill of fare and said suddenly: "Tim, I believe there's something in this."

"There'd ought to be ten days on the Island in it for them," growled fat Tim.

"Suppose, now," said the other policeman, staring intently at nothing, "the old woman was Miss Hinch, herself, f'r instance, and the parson was shadowing her, and Miss Hinch not darin' to cut and run for it till she was sure she had a clean getaway. Well, now, Tim, what better could he do—"

"That's right!" exclaimed the third policeman. "'Specially when ye think that Hinch carries a gun, an'll use it, too! Why not have a look in at the subway station?"

The proposal carried the day. The three officers started for the subway, the citizen following. They walked at a good pace and without more talk; and both their speed and their silence had a psychological reaction. As the minds of the policemen turned inward upon the odd behavior of the pair in Miller's Restaurant, the conviction that, after all,

something important might be afoot grew and strengthened within each one of them. Unconsciously their pace quickened. It was the wiry policeman who first broke into a run, but the two others had been for twenty paces on the verge of it.

However, these consultations had taken time. The stout clergyman and the poor old woman had five minutes' start on the officers of the law, and that, as it happened, was all that the occasion required. On Fourteenth Street, as they made their way arm in arm to the station, they were seen and remembered by a number of belated pedestrians. It was observed by more than one that the woman lagged as if she were tired, while the club-footed divine, supporting her on his arm, steadily kept her up to his own brisk gait.

So walking, the pair descended the subway steps, came out upon the bare platform again, and presently stood once more at the extreme uptown end of it, just where they had waited half an hour before. Nearby a careless porter had overturned a bucket of water, and a splotch of thin ice ran out and over the edge of the concrete. Two young men who were taking lively turns up and down distinctly heard the clergyman warn the woman to look out for this ice. Far away to the north was to be heard the faint roar of the approaching train.

The woman stood nearer the track, and the clergyman stood in front of her. In the vague light their looks met, and each was struck by the pallor of the other's face. In addition, the woman was breathing hard, and her hands and feet betrayed some nervousness. It was difficult now to ignore the fact that for an hour they had been clinging desperately to each other, at all costs; but the clergyman made a creditable effort to do so. He talked ramblingly, in a voice sounding only a little unnatural, for the most part of the deplorable weather and his train to Jersey, for which he was now so late. And all the time both of them were incessantly turning their heads toward the station entrances, as if expecting some arrival.

As he talked, the clergyman kept his hands unobtrusively busy. From the bottom edge of his black sack-cloth he drew a pin, and stuck it deep into the ball of the middle finger. He took out a handkerchief to dust the hard sleet from his hat; and under his overcoat he pressed the handkerchief against his bleeding finger. While making these small arrangements, he held the woman's eyes with his own, talking on; and, still holding them, he suddenly broke off his random talk and peered at her cheek with concern.

"My good woman, you've scratched your cheek somehow! Why, bless me, it's bleeding quite badly."

"Never mind—never mind," said the woman and swept her eyes hurriedly toward the entrance.

"But good gracious, I must mind! The blood will fall on your shawl. If you will permit me —ah!"

Too quick for her, he leaned forward, and, through the thin veil, swept her cheek hard with the handkerchief; removing it, he held it up so that she might see the blood for herself. But she did not glance at the handkerchief; and neither did he. His gaze was riveted upon her cheek, which looked smooth and clear where he had smudged the clever wrinkles away.

Down the steps and upon the platform pounded the feet of three flying policemen. But it was evident now that the train would thunder in just ahead of them. The clergyman, standing close in front of the woman, took a firmer grip on his heavy stick, and a look of stern triumph came into his face.

"You're not so terribly clever, after all!"

The woman had sprung back from him with an irrepressible exclamation, and in that instant she was aware of the police.

However, her foot slipped upon the treacherous ice—or it may have tripped on the stout cane, when the clergyman suddenly shifted its position. And in the next breath the train came roaring past.

By one of those curious chances which sometimes refute all experience, the body of the woman was not mangled or mutilated in the least. There was a deep blue bruise on the left temple, and apparently that was all; even the ancient hat remained on her head, skewered fast by the long pin. It was the clergyman who found the body huddled at the side of the dark track where the train had flung it—he who covered the still face and superintended the removal to the platform. Two eyewitnesses of the tragedy pointed out the ice on which the unfortunate woman had slipped, and described their horror as they saw her companion spring forward just too late to save her.

Not wishing to bring on a delirium of excitement among the bystanders, two policemen drew the clergyman quietly aside and showed him the mysterious messages. Much affected by the shocking end of his sleuthery* as he was, he readily admitted having written them. He briefly recounted how the woman's strange movements on 126th Street had arrested his attention and how, watching her closely on the car, he had finally detected that she wore a wig. Unfortunately, however, her suspicions had been aroused by his interest in her, and thereafter a long battle of wits had ensued between them—he trying to summon the police without her knowledge, she dogging him close to prevent that, and at the same time watching her chance to give him the slip. He rehearsed how, in the restaurant, when he had invented an excuse to leave her for an instant, she had made a bolt and narrowly missed getting away; and finally how, having brought her back to the sub-

way and seeing the police at last near, he had decided to risk exposing her make-up with this unexpectedly shocking result.

---

sleuthery: acting as a detective

"And now," he concluded in a shaken voice, "I am naturally most anxious to know whether I am right—or have made some terrible mistake. Will you look at her, officer, and tell me if it is indeed—she?"

But the fat policeman shook his head over the well-known ability of Miss Hinch to look like everybody but herself.

"It'll take God Almighty to tell ye that, sir, saving your presence. I'll leave it f'r headquarters," he continued, as if that were the same thing. "But, if it is her, she's gone to her reward, sir."

"God pity her!" said the clergyman.

"Amen! Give me your name, sir. They'll likely want you in the morning."

The clergyman gave it: Rev. Theodore Shaler, of Denver; city address, a number of East 11th Street. Having thus discharged his duty in the affair, he started sadly to go away; but, passing by the silent figure stretched on a bench under the ticket-seller's overcoat, he bared his head and stopped for one last look at it.

The parson's gentleness and efficiency had already won favorable comments from the bystanders, and of the first quality he now gave a final proof. The dead woman's balled-up handkerchief, which somebody had recovered from the track and laid upon her breast, had slipped to the floor; and the clergyman, observing it, stooped silently to restore it again. This last small service chanced to bring his head close to the head of the dead woman; and, as he straightened up again, her projecting hatpin struck his cheek and ripped a straight line down it. This in itself would have been a trifle, since scratches soon heal. But it happened that the point of the hatpin caught the lining of the clergyman's perfect beard and ripped it clean from him; so that, as he rose with a suddenly shrilled cry, he turned upon the astonished onlookers the bare, smooth chin of a woman, curiously long and pointed.

There were not many such chins in the world, and the urchins in the street would have recognized this one. Amid a sudden uproar which ill became the presence of the dead, the police closed in on Miss Hinch and handcuffed her with violence, fearing suicide, if not some new witchery; and at the station-house an unemotional matron divested the famous impersonator of the last and best of her disguises.

This much the police did. But it was everywhere understood that it was Jessie Dark who had really made the capture, and the papers next morning printed pictures of the unconquerable little woman and of the hatpin with which she had reached back from another world to bring her greatest adversary to justice.

About the Story

1. What type of conflict does the story reveal?

2. Who is the protagonist? the antagonist?

3. What is the first clue to the true identity of the old woman?

4. How is the conflict resolved?

5. How does Harrison create suspense throughout the story? How does that suspense affect the conflict resolution?

About the Author

Henry Sydnor Harrison (1880–1930) was born in Sewanee, Tennessee, the son of a professor of classical languages at the University of the South. Harrison attended Columbia University in New York City and then went into newspaper work as a staffer at the Richmond *Times-Dispatch* from 1902 to 1910, the year he published his first novel. His experiences in journalism helped him in creating the main character of his second novel, *Queed*. Instantly popular, this novel was later made into a play. Five more novels and a nonfiction piece followed in addition to short stories such as "Miss Hinch," an excellent example of using a story's structure to create conflict and sustain a high level of suspense.

Like Charles Dickens, Harrison used his pen to promote social reform, though he never enjoyed Dickens's critical acclaim. Yet even when dealing with problems such as factory working conditions and child-labor disputes, Harrison maintained a lively, entertaining, and optimistic style. It is this light-hearted quality in his writing that still makes Henry Sydnor Harrison a pleasure to read.

Top Man

JAMES RAMSEY ULLMAN

After reading only the first few paragraphs of "Top Man," you will see that one conflict in the story is man against nature. But as you continue reading about the men and their ascent, you will notice that Ullman brings two other conflicts to our attention: man struggling with himself and man struggling with man. Which of these conflicts becomes the dominant conflict?

The gorge bent. The walls fell suddenly away, and we came out on the edge of a bleak, boulder-strewn valley. . . . *And there it was.*

Osborn saw it first. He had been leading the column, threading his way slowly among the huge rock masses of the gorge's mouth. Then he came to the first flat bare place and stopped. He neither pointed nor cried out, but every man behind him knew instantly what it was. The long file sprang taut, like a jerked rope. As swiftly as we could, but in complete silence, we came out one by one into the open space where Osborn stood, and we raised our eyes with his.

In the records of the Indian Topographical Survey it says: "Kalpurtha: altitude 27,930 feet. The highest peak in the Garhwal Himalayas and probably fourth highest in the world. Also known as K3. A tertiary formation of sedimentary limestone. . . ."

There were men among us who had spent months of their lives—in some cases years—reading, thinking, planning about what now lay before us; but at that moment statistics and geology, knowledge, thought, and plans, were as remote and forgotten as the faraway western cities from which we had come. We were men bereft of everything but eyes, everything but the single electric perception: *there it was!*

Before us the valley stretched into miles of rocky desolation. To right and left it was bounded by low ridges; which, as the eye followed them, slowly mounted and drew closer together, until the valley was no longer a valley at all, but a narrowing, rising corridor between the cliffs. What happened then I can describe only as a stupendous crash of music. At the end of the corridor and above it—so far above it that it shut out half the sky—hung the blinding white mass of K3.

It was like the many pictures I had seen, and at the same time utterly unlike them. The shape was there, and the familiar distinguishing features: the sweeping skirt of glaciers; the monstrous vertical precipices of the face and the jagged ice-line of the east ridge; finally, the symmetrical summit pyramid that transfixed the sky. But whereas in the pictures the mountain had always seemed unreal—a dream-image of cloud, snow, and crystal—it was now no longer an image at all. It was a mass: solid, immanent, appalling. We were still too far away to see the windy whipping of its snow plumes or to hear the cannonading of its avalanches, but in that sudden silent moment every man of us was for the first time aware of it not as a picture in his mind, but as a thing, an antagonist. For all its twenty-eight thousand feet of lofty grandeur it seemed, somehow, less to tower than to crouch—a white-hooded giant, secret and remote, but living. Living and on guard.

I turned my eyes from the dazzling glare and looked at my companions. Osborn still stood a little in front of the others. He was absolutely motionless, his young face tense and shining. One could feel in the very set of his body the overwhelming desire that swelled in him to act, to come to grips, to conquer. A little behind him were ranged the other white men of the expedition: Randolph, our leader, Wittmer and Johns, Dr. Schlapp and Bixler. All were still, their eyes cast upward. Off to one side a little stood Nace, the Englishman, the only one among us who was not staring at K3 for the first time. He had been the last to come up out of the gorge and stood now with arms folded on his chest, squinting at the great peak he had known so long and fought so tirelessly and fiercely. His lean British face, under its mask of stubble and windburn, was expressionless. His lips were a thin line, and his eyes seemed almost shut. Behind the sahibs* ranged the porters, bent forward over their brown seamed faces straining upward from beneath their loads.

sahibs: Europeans

For a long while no one spoke or moved. The only sounds between earth and sky were the soft hiss of our breathing and the pounding of our hearts.

Through the long afternoon we wound slowly between the great boulders of the valley and at sundown pitched camp in the bed of a dried-up stream. The porters ate their rations in silence, wrapped themselves in their blankets, and fell asleep under the stars. The rest of us, as was our custom, sat close about the fire that blazed in the circle of tents, discussing the events of the day and the plans for the next. It was a flawlessly clear Himalayan night, and K3 tiered up* into the blackness like a monstrous beacon lighted from within. There was no wind, but a great tide of cold air crept down the valley from the ice fields above, penetrating our clothing, pressing gently against the canvas of the tents.

tiered up: ascended in layers

"Another night or two and we'll be needing the sleeping bags," commented Randolph.

Osborn nodded. "We could use them tonight would be my guess."

Randolph turned to Nace. "What do you say, Martin?"

The Englishman puffed at his pipe a moment. "Rather think it might be better to wait," he said at last.

"Wait? Why?" Osborn jerked his head up.

"Well, it gets pretty nippy high up, you know. I've seen it thirty below at twenty-five thousand on the east ridge. Longer we wait for the bags, better acclimated we'll get."

Osborn snorted. "A lot of good being acclimated will do, if we have frozen feet."

"Easy, Paul, easy," cautioned Randolph. "It seems to me Martin's right."

Osborn bit his lip, but said nothing. The other men entered the conversation, and soon it had veered to other matters: the weather, the porters and pack animals, routes, camps, and strategy, the inevitable, inexhaustible topics of the climber's world.

There were all kinds of men among the eight of us, men with a great diversity of background and interest. Sayre Randolph, whom the Alpine Club had named leader of our expedition, had for years been a well-known explorer and lecturer. Now in his middle fifties, he was no longer equal to the grueling physical demands of high climbing, but served as planner and organizer of the enterprise. Wittmer was a Seattle lawyer who had recently made a name for himself by a series of difficult ascents in the Coast Range of British Columbia. Johns was an Alaskan, a fantastically strong, able sourdough,* who had been a ranger in the U.S. Forestry Service and had accompanied many famous Alaskan expeditions. Schlapp was a practicing physician from Milwaukee, Bixler a government meteorologist with a talent for photography. I, at the time, was an assistant professor of geology at an eastern university.

sourdough: northern prospector, pioneer

Finally, and preeminently, there were Osborn and Nace. I say "preeminently" because, even at this time, when we had been together as a party for little more than a month, I believe all of us realized that these were the two key men of our venture. None, to my knowledge, ever expressed it in words, but the conviction was nonetheless there that if any of us were eventually to stand on the summit of K3, it would be one of them, or both. They were utterly dissimilar men. Osborn was twenty-three and a year out of college, a compact, buoyant mass of energy and high spirits. He seemed to be wholly unaffected by either the physical or mental hazards of mountaineering and had already, by virtue of many spectacular ascents in the Alps and Rockies, won a reputation as the most skilled and audacious of younger American climbers. Nace was in his forties—lean, taciturn,* introspective. An official in the Indian Civil Service, he had explored and climbed in the Himalayas for twenty years. He had been a member of all five of the unsuccessful British expeditions to K3, and in his last attempt had attained to within five hundred feet of the summit, the highest point which any man had reached on the unconquered giant. This had been the famous, tragic attempt in which his fellow climber and lifelong friend, Captain Furness, had slipped and fallen ten thousand feet to his death. Nace rarely mentioned his name, but on the steel head of his ice ax were engraved the words: TO MARTIN FROM JOHN. If fate were to grant that the ax of any one of us should be planted upon the summit of K3, I hoped it would be this one.

taciturn: untalkative

Such were the men who huddled about the fire in the deep, still cold of a Himalayan night. There were many differences among us, in temperament as well as in background. In one or two cases, notably that of Osborn and Nace, there had already been a certain amount of friction, and as the venture continued and the struggles and hardships of the actual ascent began, it would, I knew, increase. But differences were unimportant. What mattered—all that mattered—was that our purpose was one: to conquer the monster of rock and ice that now loomed above us in the night; to stand for a moment where no man, no living thing, had ever stood before. To that end we had come from half a world away, across oceans and continents to the fastnesses* of inner Asia. To that end we were prepared to endure cold, exhaustion, and danger, even to the very last extremity of human endurance. . . . Why? There is no answer, and at the same time every man among us knew the answer; every man who has ever looked upon a great mountain and felt the fever in his blood to climb and conquer knows the answer. George Leigh Mallory, greatest of mountaineers, expressed it once and for all when he was asked why he wanted to climb unconquered Everest.

---

fastnesses: fortifications, mountain heights

"I want to climb it," said Mallory, "because it is there."

Day after day we crept on and upward. Sometimes the mountain was brilliant above us, as it had been when we first saw it; sometimes it was partially or wholly obscured by tiers of clouds. The naked desolation of the valley was unrelieved by any motion, color, or sound; and as we progressed, the great rock walls that enclosed it grew so high and steep that its floor received the sun for less than two hours each day. The rest of the time it lay in ashen half-light, its gloom intensified by the dazzling brilliance of the ice slopes above. As long as we remained there we had the sensation of imprisonment; it was like being trapped at the bottom of a deep well or in a sealed court between great skyscrapers.

Soon we were thinking of the ascent of the shining mountain not only as an end in itself, but as an escape.

In our nightly discussions around the fire our conversation narrowed more and more to the immediate problems confronting us, and during them I began to realize that the tension between Osborn and Nace went deeper than I had at first surmised. There was rarely any outright argument between them—they were both far too able mountain men to disagree on fundamentals—but I saw that at almost every turn they were rubbing each other the wrong way. It was a matter of personalities, chiefly. Osborn was talkative, enthusiastic, optimistic, always chafing* to be up and at it, always wanting to take the short straight line to the given point. Nace, on the other hand, was matter-of-fact, cautious, slow. He was the apostle of trial-and-error and watchful waiting. Because of his far greater experience and intimate knowledge of K3, Randolph almost invariably followed his advice, rather than Osborn's, when a difference of opinion arose. The younger man usually capitulated with good grace, but I could tell that he was irked.

---

chafing: straining against a prohibition, delay, or limitation

During the days in the valley I had few occasions to talk privately with either of them, and only once did either mention the other in any but the most casual manner. Even then, the remarks they made seemed unimportant and I remember them only in view of what happened later.

My conversation with Osborn occurred first. It was while we were on the march, and Osborn, who was directly behind me, came up suddenly to my side. "You're a geologist, Frank," he began without preamble. "What do you think of Nace's theory about the ridge?"

"What theory?" I asked.

"He believes we should traverse* under it from the glacier up. Says the ridge itself is too exposed."

traverse: pass across

"It looks pretty mean through the telescope."

"But it's been done before. He's done it himself. All right, it's tough—I'll admit that. But a decent climber could make it in half the time the traverse will take."

"Nace knows the traverse is longer," I said. "But he seems certain it will be much easier for us."

"Easier for *him* is what he means." Osborn paused, looking moodily at the ground. "He was a great climber in his day. It's a shame a man can't be honest enough with himself to know when he's through." He fell silent and a moment later dropped back into his place in line.

It was that same night, I think, that I awoke to find Nace sitting up in his blanket and staring at the mountain.

"How clear it is!" I whispered.

The Englishman pointed. "See the ridge?"

I nodded, my eyes fixed on the great, twisting spine of ice that climbed into the sky. I could see now, more clearly than in the blinding sunlight, its huge indentations and jagged, wind-swept pitches. "It looks impossible," I said.

"No, it can be done. Trouble is, when you've made it you're too done in for the summit."

"Osborn seems to think its shortness would make up for its difficulty."

Nace was silent a long moment before answering. Then for the first and only time I heard him speak the name of his dead companion. "That's what Furness thought," he said quietly. Then he lay down and wrapped himself in his blanket.

For the next two weeks the uppermost point of the valley was our home and work-shop. We established our base camp as close to the mountain as we could, less than half a mile from the tongue of its lowest glacier, and plunged into the arduous tasks of preparation for the ascent. Our food and equipment were unpacked, inspected and sorted, and finally repacked in lighter loads for transportation to more advanced camps. Hours were spent poring over maps and charts and studying the monstrous heights above us through telescope and binoculars. Under Nace's supervision, a thorough reconnaissance of the glacier was made and the route across it laid out; then began the backbreaking labor of moving up supplies and establishing the chain of camps.

Camps I and II were set up on the glacier itself, in the most sheltered sites we could find. Camp III we built at its upper end, as near as possible to the point where the great rock spine of K3 thrust itself free of ice and began its precipitous ascent. According to our plans, this would be the advance base of operations during the climb. The camps to be established higher up, on the mountain proper, would be too small and too exposed to serve as anything more than one or two nights' shelter. The total distance between the base camp and Camp III was only fifteen miles, but the utmost daily progress of our porters was five miles, and it was essential that we should never be more than twelve hours' march from food and shelter. Hour after hour, day after day, the long file of men wound up and down among the hummocks* and crevasses of the glacier, and finally the time arrived when we were ready to advance.

hummocks: mounds or ridges

Leaving Dr. Schlapp in charge of eight porters at the base camp, we proceeded easily and on schedule, reaching Camp I the first night, Camp II the second, and the advance base the third. No men were left at Camps I and

II, inasmuch as they were designed simply as caches for food and equipment; and furthermore we knew we would need all the manpower available for the establishment of the higher camps on the mountain proper.

For more than three weeks now the weather had held perfectly, but on our first night at the advance base, as if by malignant prearrangement of nature, we had our first taste of the fury of a high Himalayan storm. It began with great streamers of lightning that flashed about the mountain like a halo; then heavily through the weird glare, snow began to fall. The wind rose. At first it was only sound—a remote, desolate moaning in the night high above us—but soon it descended, sucked down the deep valley as if into a gigantic funnel. Hour after hour it howled about the tents with hurricane frenzy, and the wild flapping of the canvas dinned in our ears like machine-gun fire.

There was no sleep for us that night or the next. For thirty-six hours the storm raged without lull, while we huddled in the icy gloom of the tents, exerting our last ounce of strength to keep from being buried alive or blown into eternity. At last, on the third morning, it was over, and we came out into a world transformed by a twelve-foot cloak of snow. No single landmark remained as it had been before, and our supplies and equipment were in the wildest confusion. Fortunately there had not been a single serious injury, but it was another three days before we had regained our strength and put the camp in order.

Then we waited. The storm did not return, and the sky beyond the ridges gleamed flawlessly clear; but night and day we could hear the roaring thunder of avalanches on the mountain above us. To have ventured so much as one step into that savage vertical wilderness before the new-fallen snow froze tight would have been suicidal. We chafed or

waited patiently, according to our individual temperaments, while the days dragged by.

It was late one afternoon that Osborn returned from a short reconnaissance up the ridge. His eyes were shining and his voice jubilant.

"It's tight!" he cried. "Tight as a drum. We can go!" All of us stopped whatever we were doing. His excitement leaped like an electric spark from one to another. "I went about a thousand feet, and it's sound all the way. What do you say, Sayre? Tomorrow?"

Randolph hesitated, then looked at Nace.

"Better give it another day or two," said the Englishman.

Osborn glared at him. "Why?" he challenged.

"It's usually safer to wait till—"

"Wait! Wait!" Osborn exploded. "Don't you ever think of anything but waiting? The snow's firm, I tell you!"

"It's firm down here," Nace replied quietly, "because the sun hits it only two hours a day. Up above it gets the sun twelve hours. It may not have frozen yet."

"The avalanches have stopped."

"That doesn't necessarily mean it will hold a man's weight."

"It seems to me Martin's point—" Randolph began.

Osborn wheeled on him. "Sure," he snapped. "I know. Martin's right. The cautious English are always right. Let him have his way, and we'll be sitting here chewing our nails until the mountain falls down on us." His eyes flashed to Nace. "Maybe with a little less of that cautiousness you English wouldn't have made such a mess of Everest. Maybe your pals Mallory and Furness wouldn't be dead."

"Osborn!" commanded Randolph sharply.

The youngster stared at Nace for another moment, breathing heavily. Then abruptly he turned away.

The next two days were clear and windless, but we still waited, following Nace's advice. There were no further brushes between him and Osborn, but an unpleasant air of restlessness and tension hung over the camp. I found myself chafing almost as impatiently as Osborn himself for the moment when we would break out of that maddening inactivity and begin the assault.

At last the day came. With the first paling of the sky a roped file of men, bent almost double beneath heavy loads, began slowly to climb the ice slope, just beneath the jagged line of the great east ridge. In accordance with the prearranged plan, we proceeded in relays, the first group consisting of Nace, Johns, myself, and eight porters. It was our job to ascend approximately two thousand feet in a day's climbing and establish Camp IV at the most level and sheltered site we could find. We would spend the night there and return to the advance base next day, while the second relay, consisting of Osborn, Wittmer, and eight more porters, went up with their loads. This process was to continue until all necessary supplies were at Camp IV, and then the whole thing would be repeated between Camps IV and V and V and VI. From VI, at an altitude of about twenty-six thousand feet, the ablest and fittest men—presumably Nace and Osborn—would make the direct assault on the summit. Randolph and Bixler were to remain at the advance base throughout the operations, acting as directors and co-ordinators. We were under the strictest orders that any man—sahib or porter—who suffered illness or injury should be brought down immediately.

How shall I describe those next two weeks beneath the great ice ridge of K3? In a sense there was no occurrence of importance, and at the same time everything happened that could possibly happen, short of actual disaster. We established Camp IV, came down

again, went up again, came down again. Then we crept laboriously higher. With our axes we hacked uncountable thousands of steps in the gleaming walls of ice. Among the rocky outcroppings of the cliffs we clung to holds and strained at ropes until we thought our arms would spring from their sockets. Storms swooped down on us, battered us, and passed. The wind increased, and the air grew steadily colder and more difficult to breathe. One morning two of the porters awoke with their feet frozen black; they had to be sent down. A short while later Johns developed an uncontrollable nosebleed and was forced to descend to a lower camp. Wittmer was suffering from racking headaches and I from a continually dry throat. But providentially, the one enemy we feared the most in that icy gale-lashed hell did not again attack us. No snow fell. And day by day, foot by foot, we ascended.

It is during ordeals like this that the surface trappings of a man are shed and his secret mettle* laid bare. There were no shirkers or quitters among us—I had known that from the beginning—but now, with each passing day, it became more manifest which were the strongest and ablest among us. Beyond all argument, these were Osborn and Nace.

mettle: courage

Osborn was magnificent. All the boyish impatience and moodiness which he had exhibited earlier were gone, and, now that he was at last at work in his natural element, he emerged as the peerless mountaineer he was. His energy was inexhaustible, his speed, both on rock and ice, almost twice that of any other man in the party. He was always discovering new routes and short cuts. Often he ascended by the ridge itself, instead of using the traverse beneath it, as had been officially prescribed; but his craftsmanship was so sure and his performance so brilliant that no one

from them had he tried. Osborn attacked the mountain head-on. Nace studied it, sparred with it, wore it down. His spirit did not flap from his sleeve like a pennon;* it was deep inside him—patient, indomitable.

pennon: flag

The day soon came when I learned from him what it is to be a great mountaineer. We were making the ascent from Camp IV to V, and an almost perpendicular ice wall had made it necessary for us to come out for a few yards on the exposed crest of the ridge. There were six of us in the party, roped together, with Nace leading, myself second, and four porters bringing up the rear. The ridge at this particular point was free of snow, but razor-thin, and the rocks were covered with a smooth glaze of ice. On either side the mountain dropped away in sheer precipices of five thousand feet.

Suddenly the last porter slipped. I heard the ominous scraping of boot nails behind me and, turning, saw a gesticulating figure plunge sideways into the abyss. There was a scream as the next porter was jerked off too. I remember trying frantically to dig into the ridge with my ax, realizing at the same time it would no more hold against the weight of the falling men than a pin stuck in a wall. Then I heard Nace shout, "Jump!" As he said it, the rope went tight about my waist, and I went hurtling after him into space on the opposite side of the ridge. After me came the nearest porter . . . .

What happened then must have happened in five yards and a fifth of a second. I heard myself cry out, and the glacier a mile below, rushed up at me spinning. Then both were blotted out in a violent spasm, as the rope jerked taut. I hung for a moment, an inert mass, feeling that my body had been cut in two; then I swung in slowly to the side of the mountain. Above me the rope lay tight and

ever thought of taking him to task. Indeed, there was such vigor, buoyancy, and youth in everything he did that it gave heart to all the rest of us.

In contrast, Nace was slow, methodical, unspectacular. Since he and I worked in the same relay, I was with him almost constantly, and to this day I carry in my mind the clear image of the man: his tall body bent almost double against endless shimmering slopes of ice; his lean brown face bent in utter concentration on the problem in hand, then raised searchingly to the next; the bright prong of his ax rising, falling, rising, falling, with tireless rhythm, until the steps in the glassy incline were so wide and deep that the most clumsy of the porters could not have slipped

motionless across the crest of the ridge, our weight exactly counterbalancing that of the men who had fallen on the far slope.

Nace's voice came up from below. "You chaps on the other side!" he shouted. "Start climbing slowly. We're climbing too."

In five minutes we had all regained the ridge. The porters and I crouched panting on the jagged rocks, our eyes closed, the sweat beading our faces in frozen drops. Nace carefully examined the rope that again hung loosely between us.

"All right, men," he said presently. "Let's get on to camp for a cup of tea."

Above Camp V the whole aspect of the ascent changed. The angle of the ridge eased off, and the ice, which lower down had covered the mountain like a sheath, lay only in scattered patches between the rocks. Fresh enemies, however, instantly appeared to take the place of the old. We were now laboring at an altitude of more than twenty-five thousand feet—well above the summits of the highest surrounding peaks—and day and night, without protection or respite, we were buffeted by the fury of the wind. Worse than this was that the atmosphere had become so rarefied it could scarcely support life. Breathing itself was a major physical effort, and our progress upward consisted of two or three painful steps followed by a long period of rest in which our hearts pounded wildly and our burning lungs gasped for air. Each of us carried a small cylinder of oxygen in his pack, but we used it only in emergencies and found that, while its immediate effect was salutary,* it left us later even worse off than before. My throat dried and contracted until it felt as if it were lined with brass. The faces of all of us, under our beards and windburn, grew haggard* and strained.

salutary: beneficial to health

haggard: appearing worn and tired

But the great struggle was now mental as much as physical. The lack of air induced a lethargy of mind and spirit; confidence and the powers of thought and decision waned, and dark foreboding crept out from the secret recesses of the subconscious. The wind seemed to carry strange sounds, and we kept imagining we saw things which we knew were not there. The mountain, to all of us, was no longer a mere giant of rock and ice; it had become a living thing, an enemy, watching us, waiting for us, hostile, relentless, and aware. Inch by inch we crept upward through that empty forgotten world above the world, and only one last thing remained to us of human consciousness and human will: to go on. To go on.

On the fifteenth day after we had first left the advance base we pitched Camp VI at an altitude of almost twenty-six thousand feet. It was located near the uppermost extremity of the great east ridge, directly beneath the so-called shoulder of the mountain. On the far side of the shoulder the monstrous north face of K3 fell sheer to the glaciers, two miles below. And above it and to the left rose the symmetrical bulk of the summit pyramid. The topmost rocks of its highest pinnacle were clearly visible from the shoulder, and the intervening two thousand feet seemed to offer no insuperable* obstacles.

insuperable: not able to be overcome

Camp VI, which was in reality no camp at all, but a single tent, was large enough to accommodate only three men. Osborn established it with the aid of Wittmer and one porter; then, the following morning, Wittmer and the porter descended to Camp V, and Nace and I went up. It was our plan that Osborn and Nace should launch the final assault—the next day, if the weather held—with myself in support, following their progress through binoculars and going to their aid or summoning help from below if anything went wrong. As the three of us lay in the tent that night, the summit seemed already within arm's reach, victory securely in our grasp.

And then the blow fell. With malignant timing, which no power on earth could have made us believe was a simple accident of nature, the mountain hurled at us its last line of defense. It snowed.

For a day and a night the great flakes drove down on us, swirling and swooping in the wind, blotting out the summit, the shoulder, everything beyond the tiny white-walled radius of our tents. Hour after hour we lay in our sleeping bags, stirring only to eat or to secure the straining rope and canvas. Our feet froze under their thick layers of wool and rawhide. Our heads and bodies throbbed with a dull nameless aching, and time crept over our numbed minds like a glacier. At last, during the morning of the following day, it cleared. The sun came out in a thin blue sky, and the summit pyramid again appeared above us, now whitely robed in fresh snow. But still we waited. Until the snow either froze or was blown away by the wind it would have been the rashest courting of destruction for us to have ascended a foot beyond the camp. Another day passed. And another.

By the third nightfall our nerves were at the breaking point. For hours on end we had scarcely moved or spoken, and the only sounds in all the world were the endless moaning of the wind outside and the harsh sucking noise of our breathing. I knew that, one way or another, the end had come. Our meager food supply was running out; even with careful rationing there was enough left for only two more days.

Presently Nace stirred in his sleeping bag and sat up. "We'll have to go down tomorrow," he said quietly.

For a moment there was silence in the tent. Then Osborn struggled to a sitting position and faced him.

"No," he said.

"There's still too much loose snow above. We can't make it."

"But it's clear. As long as we can see—"

Nace shook his head. "Too dangerous. We'll go down tomorrow and lay in a fresh supply. Then we'll try again."

"Once we go down we're licked. You know it."

Nace shrugged. "Better to be licked than . . ." The strain of speech was suddenly too much for him and he fell into a violent paroxysm of coughing. When it had passed there was a long silence.

Then suddenly Osborn spoke again. "Look, Nace," he said, "I'm going up tomorrow."

The Englishman shook his head.

"I'm going—understand?"

For the first time since I had known him I saw Nace's eyes flash in anger. "I'm the senior member of this group," he said. "I forbid you to go!"

Osborn jerked himself to his knees, almost upsetting the tiny tent. "You forbid me? This may be your sixth time on this mountain, and all that, but you don't *own* it! I know what you're up to. You haven't got it in you to make the top yourself, so you

don't want anyone else to make it. That's it, isn't it? Isn't it?" He sat down again suddenly, gasping for breath.

Nace looked at him with level eyes. "This mountain has beaten me five times," he said softly. "It killed my best friend. It means more to me to climb it than anything else in the world. Maybe I'll make it and maybe I won't. But if I do, it will be as a rational intelligent human being—not as a fool throwing my life away. . . ."

He collapsed into another fit of coughing and fell back in his sleeping bag. Osborn, too, was still. They lay there inert, panting, too exhausted for speech.

It was hours later that I awoke from dull, uneasy sleep. In the faint light I saw Nace fumbling with the flap of the tent.

"What is it?" I asked.

"Osborn. He's gone."

The words cut like a blade through my lethargy. I struggled to my feet and followed Nace from the tent.

Outside, the dawn was seeping up the eastern sky. It was very cold, but the wind had fallen and the mountain seemed to hang suspended in a vast stillness. Above us the summit pyramid climbed bleakly into space, like the last outpost of a spent and lifeless planet. Raising my binoculars, I swept them over the gray waste. At first I saw nothing but rock and ice; then, suddenly, something moved.

"I've got him," I whispered.

As I spoke, the figure of Osborn sprang into clear focus against a patch of ice. He took three or four slow upward steps, stopped, went on again. I handed the glasses to Nace.

The Englishman squinted through them, returned them to me, and reentered the tent. When I followed, he had already laced his boots and was pulling on his outer gloves.

"He's not far," he said. "Can't have been gone more than half an hour." He seized his ice ax and started out again.

"Wait," I said. "I'm going with you."

Nace shook his head. "Better stay here."

"I'm going with you," I said.

He said nothing further, but waited while I made ready. In a few moments we left the tent, roped up, and started off.

Almost immediately we were on the shoulder and confronted with the paralyzing two-mile drop of the north face; but we negotiated the short exposed stretch without mishap, and in ten minutes were working up the base of the summit pyramid. The going here was easier, in a purely climbing sense: the angle of ascent was not steep, and there was firm rock for hand- and foot-holds between the patches of snow and ice. Our progress, however, was creepingly slow. There seemed to be literally no air at all to breathe, and after almost every step we were forced to rest, panting and gasping as we leaned forward against our axes. My heart swelled and throbbed with every movement until I thought it would explode.

The minutes crawled into hours and still we climbed. Presently the sun came up. Its level rays streamed across the clouds, far below, and glinted from the summits of distant peaks. But, although the pinnacle of K3 soared a full three thousand feet above anything in the surrounding world, we had scarcely any sense of height. The wilderness of mountain valley and glacier that spread beneath us to the horizon was flattened and remote, an unreal, insubstantial landscape seen in a dream. We had no connection with it, or it with us. All living, all awareness, purpose, and will, was concentrated in the last step and the next: to put one foot before the other; to breathe; to ascend. We struggled on in silence.

I do not know how long it was since we had left the camp—it might have been two hours, it might have been six—when we suddenly sighted Osborn. We had not been able to find him again since our first glimpse through the binoculars; but now, unexpectedly and abruptly, as we came up over a jagged outcropping rock, there he was. He was at a point, only a few yards above us, where the mountain steepened into an almost vertical wall. The smooth surface directly in front of him was obviously unclimbable, but two alternate routes were presented. To the left, a chimney* cut obliquely across the wall, forbiddingly steep, but seeming to offer adequate holds. To the right was a gentle slope of snow that curved upward and out of sight behind the rocks. As we watched, Osborn ascended to the edge of the snow, stopped, and probed it with his ax. Then, apparently satisfied that it would bear his weight he stepped out on the slope.

---

chimney: vertical groove

I felt Nace's body tense. "Paul!" he cried out.

His voice was too weak and hoarse to carry. Osborn continued his ascent.

Nace cupped his hands and called his name again, and this time Osborn turned. "Wait!" cried the Englishman.

Osborn stood still, watching us, as we struggled up the few yards to the edge of the snow slope. Nace's breath came in shuddering gasps, but he climbed faster than I had ever seen him climb before.

"Come back!" he called. "Come off the snow!"

"It's all right. The crust is firm," Osborn called back.

"But it's melting. There's . . ." Nace paused, fighting for air. "There's nothing underneath!"

In a sudden sickening flash I saw what he meant. Looked at from directly below, at the point where Osborn had come to it, the slope on which he stood appeared as a harmless covering of snow over the rocks. From where we were now, however, a little to one side, it could be seen that it was in reality no covering at all, but merely a cornice or unsupported platform clinging to the side of the mountain. Below it was not rock, but ten thousand feet of blue air.

"Come back!" I cried. "Come back!"

Osborn hesitated, then took a downward step. But he never took the next. For in that same instant the snow directly in front of him disappeared. It did not seem to fall or to break away. It was just soundlessly and magically no longer there. In the spot where Osborn had been about to set his foot there was now revealed the abysmal drop of the north face of K3.

I shut my eyes, but only for a second, and when I reopened them Osborn was still, miraculously, there. Nace was shouting, "Don't move! Don't move an inch!"

"The rope—" I heard myself saying.

The Englishman shook his head. "We'd have to throw it, and the impact would be too much. Brace yourself and play it out." As he spoke, his eyes were traveling over the rocks that bordered the snow bridge. Then he moved forward.

I wedged myself into a cleft in the wall and let out the rope which extended between us. A few yards away Osborn stood in the snow, transfixed, one foot a little in front of the other. But my eyes now were on Nace. Cautiously, but with astonishing rapidity, he edged along the rocks beside the cornice. There was a moment when his only support was an inch-wide ledge beneath his feet, another where there was nothing under his feet at all, and he supported himself wholly by his elbows and hands. But he advanced steadily and at last reached a shelf wide enough for him to turn around on. At this point he was perhaps six feet away from Osborn.

"It's wide enough here to hold both of us," he said in a quiet voice. "I'm going to reach out my ax. Don't move until you're sure you have a grip on it. When I pull, jump."

He searched the wall behind him and found a hold for his left hand. Then he slowly extended his ice ax, head foremost, until it was within two feet of Osborn's shoulder. "Grip it!" he cried suddenly. Osborn's hands shot out and seized the ax. "Jump!"

There was a flash of steel in the sunlight and a hunched figure hurtled inward from the snow to the ledge. Simultaneously another figure hurtled out. The haft* of the ax jerked suddenly from Nace's hand, and he lurched forward and downward. A violent spasm convulsed his body as the rope went taut. Then it was gone. Nace did not seem to hit the snow; he simply disappeared through it, soundlessly. In the same instant the snow itself was gone. The frayed, yellow end of broken rope spun lazily in space. . . .

haft: handle

Somehow my eyes went to Osborn. He was crouched on the ledge where Nace had been a moment before, staring dully at the ax he held in his hands. Beyond his head, not two hundred feet above, the white untrodden pinnacle of K3 stabbed the sky.

Perhaps ten minutes passed, perhaps a half hour. I closed my eyes and leaned forward motionless against the rock, my face against my arm. I neither thought nor felt; my body and mind alike were enveloped in a suffocating numbness. Through it at last came the sound of Osborn moving. Looking up, I saw he was standing beside me.

"I'm going to try for the top," he said tonelessly.

I merely stared at him.

"Will you come?"

"No," I said.

Osborn hesitated; then turned and began slowly climbing the steep chimney above us. Halfway up he paused, struggling for breath.

Then he resumed his laborious upward progress and presently disappeared beyond the crest.

I stayed where I was, and the hours passed. The sun reached its zenith above the peak and sloped away behind it. And at last I heard above me the sound of Osborn returning. As I looked up, his figure appeared at the top of the chimney and began the descent. His clothing was in tatters, and I could tell from his movements that only the thin flame of his will stood between him and collapse. In another few minutes he was standing beside me.

"Did you get there?" I asked dully.

He shook his head. "I couldn't make it," he answered. "I didn't have what it takes."

We roped together silently and began the descent to the camp.

There is nothing more to be told of the sixth assault on K3—at least not from the experiences of the men who made it. Osborn and I reached Camp V in safety, and three days later the entire expedition gathered at the advance base. It was decided, in view of the tragedy that had occurred, to make no further attempt on the summit, and by the end of the week we had begun the evacuation of the mountain.

It remained for another year and other men to reveal the epilogue.

The summer following our attempt a combined English-Swiss expedition stormed the peak successfully. After weeks of hardship and struggle they attained the topmost pinnacle of the giant, only to find that what should have been their great moment of triumph was, instead, a moment of the bitterest disappointment. For when they came out at last upon the summit they saw that they were not the first. An ax stood there. Its haft was embedded in rock and ice and on its steel head were the engraved words: TO MARTIN FROM JOHN.

They were sporting men. On their return to civilization they told their story, and the name of the conqueror of K3 was made known to the world.

About the Story

1. Though this is not a true story, what about Ullman's writing makes you believe it could be?

2. Who is the central character of the story? Who opposes the central character?

3. Describe the three conflicts in the story.

4. Explain how each conflict is resolved.

5. Which of these conflicts would you say is the dominant conflict? Why?

About the Author

James Ramsey Ullman (1907–71), author and expert mountaineer, was born in New York City and attended Princeton University. As an undergraduate, Ullman took a vacation to Switzerland and scaled the Matterhorn. After graduating, he continued to climb, devoting his time between ascents to his writing career. This life-long pursuit of his three favorite activities—writing, mountain climbing, and traveling—yielded many short stories and novels rich with realistic detail.

Ullman began his career in 1929 with four years in journalism, after which he turned to writing and producing plays in New York. His most significant production there was the Pulitzer Prize winning play by Sidney Kingsley, *Men in White*. He returned to writing full-time in 1939, but his career was interrupted by his service as an ambulance driver in World War II. After the war Ullman went on to a highly successful career writing both fiction and nonfiction. His most famous works are *The White Tower* (a novel), *Banner in the Sky* (for which he won the 1955 Newbery Medal), and *Man of Everest* (Tenzing Norgay's autobiography, which he co-wrote). Five of his novels were made into major motion pictures, but to Ullman the highlight of his career was participating in the first American expedition to Mount Everest in 1963.

Through the Tunnel

Doris Lessing

In this suspenseful story, eleven-year-old Jerry attempts to test his courage and endurance by "mastering" the blue sea and its great rocks that "lay like discolored monsters under the surface." Though nature could be viewed as a type of antagonist in this story, it is better viewed as the agent that measures the central character's maturity. There is another, more dominant antagonist Jerry must deal with. Doris Lessing makes the identification of this central conflict easier through her emphasis on certain descriptive details.

Going to the shore on the first morning of the vacation, the young English boy stopped at a turning of the path and looked down at a wild and rocky bay, and then over to the crowded beach he knew so well from other years. His mother walked on in front of him, carrying a bright striped bag in one hand. Her other arm, swinging loose, was very white in the sun. The boy watched that white naked arm, and turned his eyes, which had a frown behind them, towards the bay and back again to his mother. When she felt he was not with her, she swung around. "Oh, there you are, Jerry!" she said. She looked impatient, then smiled. "Why, darling, would you rather not come with me? Would you rather—" She frowned, conscientiously worrying over what amusements he might secretly be longing for, which she had been too busy or too careless to imagine. He was very familiar with that anxious, apologetic smile. Contrition* sent him running after her. And yet, as he ran, he looked back over his shoulder at the wild bay; and all morning, as he played on the safe beach, he was thinking of it.

---

contrition: heartfelt remorse

Next morning, when it was time for the routine of swimming and sunbathing, his mother said, "Are you tired of the usual beach, Jerry? Would you like to go somewhere else?"

"Oh, no!" he said quickly, smiling at her out of that unfailing impulse of contrition—a sort of chivalry. Yet, walking down the path with her, he blurted out, "I'd like to go and have a look at those rocks down there."

She gave the idea her attention. It was a wild-looking place, and there was no one there; but she said, "Of course, Jerry. When you've had enough, come to the big beach. Or just go straight back to the villa, if you like." She walked away, that bare arm, now slightly reddened from yesterday's sun, swinging. And he almost ran after her again, feeling it unbearable that she should go by herself, but he did not.

She was thinking, Of course he's old enough to be safe without me. Have I been keeping him too close? He mustn't feel he ought to be with me. I must be careful.

He was an only child, eleven years old. She was a widow. She was determined to be neither possessive nor lacking in devotion. She went worrying off to her beach.

As for Jerry, once he saw that his mother had gained her beach, he began the steep descent to the bay. From where he was, high up among red-brown rocks, it was a scoop of moving blueish green fringed with white. As he went lower, he saw that it spread among small promontories* and inlets of rough, sharp rock, and the crisping, lapping surface showed stains of purple and darker blue. Finally, as he ran sliding and scraping down the last few yards, he saw an edge of white surf and the shallow, luminous movement of water over white sand, and, beyond that, a solid, heavy blue.

---

promontories: projecting coastal cliffs

He ran straight into the water and began swimming. He was a good swimmer. He went out fast over the gleaming sand, over a middle region where rocks lay like discoloured monsters under the surface, and then he was in the real sea—a warm sea where irregular cold currents from the deep water shocked his limbs.

When he was so far out that he could look back not only on the little bay but past the promontory that was between it and the big beach, he floated on the buoyant surface and looked for his mother. There she was, a speck of yellow under an umbrella that looked like a slice of orange peel. He swam back to shore, relieved at being sure she was there, but all at once very lonely.

On the edge of a small cape that marked the side of the bay away from the promontory was a loose scatter of rocks. Above them, some boys were stripping off their clothes. They came running . . . down to the rocks. The English boy swam towards them, but kept his distance at a stone's throw. They were of that coast; all of them were burned smooth dark brown and speaking a language he did not understand. To be with them, of them, was a craving that filled his whole body. He swam a little closer; they turned and watched him with narrowed, alert dark eyes. Then one smiled and waved. It was enough. In a minute, he had swum in and was on the rocks beside them, smiling with a desperate, nervous supplication. They shouted cheerful greetings at him; and then, as he preserved his nervous, uncomprehending smile, they understood that he was a foreigner strayed from his own beach, and they proceeded to forget him. But he was happy. He was with them.

They began diving again and again from a high point into a well of blue sea between rough, pointed rocks. After they had dived and come up, they swam around, hauled themselves up, and waited their turn to dive again. They were big boys—men, to Jerry. He dived, and they watched him; and when he swam around to take his place, they made way for him. He felt he was accepted and he dived again, carefully, proud of himself.

Soon the biggest of the boys poised himself, shot down into the water, and did not come up. The others stood about, watching. Jerry, after waiting for the sleek brown head to appear, let out a yell of warning; they looked at him idly and turned their eyes back towards the water. After a long time, the boy came up on the other side of a big dark rock, letting the air out of his lungs in a sputtering gasp and a shout of triumph.

Immediately the rest of them dived in. One moment, the morning seemed full of chattering boys; the next, the air and the surface of the water were empty. But through the heavy blue, dark shapes could be seen moving and groping.

Jerry dived, shot past the school of underwater swimmers, saw a black wall of rock looming at him, touched it, and bobbed up at once to the surface, where the wall was a low barrier he could see across. There was no one visible; under him, in the water, the dim shapes of the swimmers had disappeared. Then one, and then another of the boys came up on the far side of the barrier of rock, and he understood that they had swum through some gap or hole in it. He plunged down again. He could see nothing through the stinging salt water but the blank rock. When he came up the boys were all on the diving rock, preparing to attempt the feat again. And now, in a panic of failure, he yelled up, in English, "Look at me! Look!" and he began splashing and kicking in the water like a foolish dog.

They looked down gravely, frowning. He knew the frown. At moments of failure, when he clowned to claim his mother's attention, it was with just this grave, embarrassed inspection that she rewarded him. Through his hot shame, feeling the pleading grin on his face like a scar that he could never remove, he looked up at the group of big brown boys on the rock and shouted *"Bonjour! Merci! Au revoir! Monsieur, monsieur!"* while he hooked his fingers round his ears and waggled them.

Water surged into his mouth; he choked, sank, came up. The rock, lately weighted with boys, seemed to rear up out of the water as their weight was removed. They were flying down past him now, into the water; the air was full of falling bodies. Then the rock was empty in the hot sunlight. He counted one, two, three . . .

At fifty, he was terrified. They must all be drowning beneath him, in the watery caves of the rock! At a hundred, he stared around him at the empty hillside, wondering if he should yell for help. He counted faster, faster, to hurry them up, to bring them to the surface quickly, to drown them quickly—anything rather than the terror of counting on and on into the blue emptiness of the morning. And then, at a hundred and sixty, the water beyond the rock was full of boys blowing like brown whales. They swam back to the shore without a look at him.

He climbed back to the diving rock and sat down, feeling the hot roughness of it under his thighs. The boys were gathering up their bits of clothing and running off along the shore to another promontory. They were leaving to get away from him. He cried openly, fists in his eyes. There was no one to see him, and he cried himself out.

It seemed to him that a long time had passed, and he swam out to where he could see his mother. Yes, she was still there, a yellow spot under an orange umbrella. He swam back to the big rock, climbed up, and dived into the blue pool among the fanged and angry boulders. Down he went, until he touched the wall of rock again. But the salt was so painful in his eyes that he could not see.

He came to the surface, swam to shore and went back to the villa to wait for his mother. Soon she walked slowly up the path, swinging her striped bag, the flushed, naked arm dangling beside her. "I want some swimming goggles," he panted, defiant and beseeching.

She gave him a patient, inquisitive look as she said casually, "Well, of course, darling."

But now, now, now! He must have them this minute, and no other time. He nagged and pestered until she went with him to a shop. As soon as she had bought the goggles, he grabbed them from her hand as if she were going to claim them for herself, and was off, running down the steep path to the bay.

Jerry swam out to the big barrier rock, adjusted the goggles, and dived. The impact of the water broke the rubber-enclosed vacuum, and the goggles came loose. He understood that he must swim down to the base of the rock from the surface of the water. He fixed the goggles tight and firm, filled his lungs, and floated, face down, on the water. Now he could see. It was as if he had eyes of a different kind—fish eyes that showed everything clear and delicate and wavering in the bright water.

Under him, six or seven feet down, was a floor of perfectly clean, shining white sand, rippled firm and hard by the tides. Two greyish shapes steered there, like long, rounded pieces of wood or slate. They were fish. He saw them nose towards each other, poise motionless, make a dart forward, swerve off, and come around again. It was like a water dance. A few inches above them the water sparkled as if sequins were dropping through it. Fish again—myriads of minute fish, the length of his fingernail—were drifting through the water, and in a moment he could feel the innumerable tiny touches of them against his limbs. It was like swimming in flaked silver. The great rock the big boys had swum through rose sheer out of the white sand—black, tufted lightly with greenish weed. He could see no gap in it. He swam down to its base.

Again and again he rose, took a big chestful of air, and went down. Again and again he groped over the surface of the rock, feeling it, almost hugging it in the desperate need to find the entrance. And then, once, while he was clinging to the black wall, his knees came up and he shot his feet out forward and they met no obstacle. He had found the hole.

He gained the surface, clambered about the stones that littered the barrier rock until he found a big one, and, with this in his arms, let himself down over the side of the rock. He dropped, with the weight, straight to the sandy floor. Clinging tight to the anchor of stone, he lay on his side and looked in under the dark shelf at the place where his feet had gone. He could see the hole. It was an irregular, dark gap; but he could not see deep into it. He let go of his anchor, clung with his hands to the edges of the hole, and tried to push himself in.

He got his head in, found his shoulders jammed, moved them in sidewise, and was inside as far as his waist. He could see nothing ahead. Something soft and clammy touched his mouth; he saw a dark frond moving against the greyish rock, and panic filled him. He thought of octopuses, of clinging weed. He pushed himself out backward and caught a glimpse, as he retreated, of a harmless tentacle of seaweed drifting in the mouth of the tunnel. But it was enough. He reached the sunlight, swam to shore, and lay on the diving rock. He looked down into the blue well of water. He knew he must find his way through that cave, or hole, or tunnel, and out the other side.

First, he thought, he must learn to control his breathing. He let himself down into the water with another big stone in his arms, so that he could lie effortlessly on the bottom of the sea. He counted. One, two, three. He counted steadily. He could hear the movement of blood in his chest. Fifty-one, fifty-two. . . . His chest was hurting. He let go of the rock and went up into the air. He saw that the sun was low. He rushed to the villa and found his mother at her supper. She said only "Did you enjoy yourself?" and he said "Yes."

All night the boy dreamed of the water-filled cave in the rock, and as soon as breakfast was over he went to the bay.

That night, his nose bled badly. For hours he had been underwater, learning to hold his

breath, and now he felt weak and dizzy. His mother said, "I shouldn't overdo things, darling, if I were you."

That day and the next, Jerry exercised his lungs as if everything, the whole of his life, all that he would become, depended upon it. Again his nose bled at night, and his mother insisted on his coming with her the next day. It was a torment to him to waste a day of his careful self-training, but he stayed with her on that other beach, which now seemed a place for small children, a place where his mother might lie safe in the sun. It was not his beach.

He did not ask for permission, on the following day, to go to his beach. He went, before his mother could consider the complicated rights and wrongs of the matter. A day's rest, he discovered, had improved his count by ten. The big boys had made the passage while he counted a hundred and sixty. He had been counting fast, in his fright. Probably now, if he tried, he could get through that long tunnel, but he was not going to try yet. A curious, most unchildlike persistence, a controlled impatience, made him wait. In the meantime, he lay underwater on the white sand, littered now by stones he had brought down from the upper air, and studied the entrance to the tunnel. He knew every jut and corner of it, as far as it was possible to see. It was as if he already felt its sharpness about his shoulders.

He sat by the clock in the villa, when his mother was not near, and checked his time. He was incredulous and then proud to find he could hold his breath without strain for two minutes. The words "two minutes," authorised by the clock, brought close the adventure that was so necessary to him.

In another four days, his mother said casually one morning, they must go home. On the day before they left, he would do it. He would do it if it killed him, he said defiantly to himself. But two days before they were to leave—a day of triumph when he increased his count by fifteen—his nose bled so badly that he turned dizzy and had to lie limply over the big rock like a bit of seaweed, watching the thick red blood flow on to the rock and trickle slowly down to the sea. He was frightened. Supposing he turned dizzy in the tunnel? Supposing he died there, trapped? Supposing—his head went around, in the hot sun, and he almost gave up. He thought he would return to the house and lie down, and next summer, perhaps, when he had another year's growth in him—*then* he would go through the hole.

But even after he had made the decision, or thought he had, he found himself sitting up on the rock and looking down into the water; and he knew that now, this moment, when his nose had only just stopped bleeding, when his head was still sore and throbbing—this was the moment when he would try. If he did not do it now, he never would. He was trembling with fear that he would not go; and he was trembling with horror at that long, long tunnel under the rock, under the sea. Even in the open sunlight, the barrier rock seemed very wide and very heavy; tons of rock pressed down on where he would go. If he died there, he would lie until one day—perhaps not before next year—those big boys would swim into it and find it blocked.

He put on his goggles, fitted them tight, tested the vacuum. His hands were shaking. Then he chose the biggest stone he could carry and slipped over the edge of the rock until half of him was in the cool enclosing water and half in the hot sun. He looked up once at the empty sky, filled his lungs once, twice, and then sank fast to the bottom with the stone. He let it go and began to count. He took the edges of the hole in his hands and drew himself into it, wriggling his shoulders in sidewise as he remembered he must, kicking himself along with his feet.

Soon he was clear inside. He was in a small rock-bound hole filled with yellowish-grey water. The water was pushing him up against the roof. The roof was sharp and pained his back. He pulled himself along with his hands—fast, fast—and used his legs as levers. His head knocked against something; a sharp pain dizzied him. Fifty, fifty-one, fifty-two. . . . He was without light, and the water seemed to press upon him with the weight of rock. Seventy-one, seventy-two . . . There was no strain on his lungs. He felt like an inflated balloon, his lungs were so light and easy, but his head was pulsing.

He was being continually pressed against the sharp roof, which felt slimy as well as sharp. Again he thought of octopuses, and wondered if the tunnel might be filled with weed that could tangle him. He gave himself a panicky, convulsive kick forward, ducked his head, and swam. His feet and hands moved freely, as if in open water. The hole must have widened out. He thought he must be swimming fast, and he was frightened of banging his head if the tunnel narrowed.

A hundred, a hundred and one . . . The water paled. Victory filled him. His lungs were beginning to hurt. A few more strokes and he would be out. He was counting wildly; he said a hundred and fifteen, and then, a long time later, a hundred and fifteen again. The water was a clear jewel-green all around him. Then he saw, above his head, a crack running up through the rock. Sunlight was falling through it, showing the clean, dark rock of the tunnel, a single mussel shell, and darkness ahead.

He was at the end of what he could do. He looked up at the crack as if it were filled with air and not water, as if he could put his mouth to it to draw in air. A hundred and fifteen, he heard himself say inside his head—

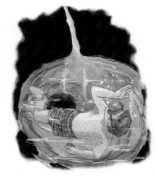

but he had said that long ago. He must go on into the blackness ahead, or he would drown. His head was swelling, his lungs cracking. A hundred and fifteen, a hundred and fifteen pounded through his head, and he feebly clutched at rocks in the dark, pulling himself forward leaving the brief space of sunlit water behind. He felt he was dying. He was no longer quite conscious. He struggled on in the darkness between lapses into unconsciousness. An immense, swelling pain filled his head, and then the darkness cracked with an explosion of green light. His hands, groping forward, met nothing; and his feet, kicking back, propelled him out into the open sea.

He drifted to the surface, his face turned up to the air. He was gasping like a fish. He felt he would sink now and drown; he could not swim the few feet back to the rock. Then he was clutching it and pulling himself up onto it. He lay face down, gasping. He could see nothing but a red-veined, clotted dark. His eyes must have burst, he thought; they were full of blood. He tore off his goggles and a gout of blood went into the sea. His nose was bleeding, and the blood had filled the goggles.

He scooped up handfuls of water from the cool, salty sea, to splash on his face, and did not know whether it was blood or salt water he tasted. After a time, his heart quieted, his eyes cleared, and he sat up. He could see the local boys diving and playing half a mile away. He did not want them. He wanted nothing but to get back home and lie down.

In a short while, Jerry swam to shore and climbed slowly up the path to the villa. He flung himself on his bed and slept, waking at the sound of feet on the path outside. His mother was coming back. He rushed to the bathroom, thinking she must not see his face with bloodstains, or tearstains, on it. He came out of the bathroom and met her as she walked into the villa, smiling, her eyes lighting up.

"Have a nice morning?" she asked, laying her hand on his warm brown shoulder a moment.

"Oh, yes, thank you," he said.

"You look a bit pale." And then, sharp and anxious, "How did you bang your head?"

"Oh, just banged it," he told her.

She looked at him closely. He was strained; his eyes were glazed-looking. She was worried. And then she said to herself, Oh, don't fuss! Nothing can happen. He can swim like a fish.

They sat down to lunch together.

"Mummy," he said, "I can stay under water for two minutes—three minutes, at least." It came bursting out of him.

"Can you, darling?" she said. "Well, I shouldn't overdo it. I don't think you ought to swim any more today."

She was ready for a battle of wills, but he gave in at once. It was no longer of the least importance to go to the bay.

About the Story

1. Does the setting of the story help portray the conflict? Why or why not?

2. What colors does the author use to describe the mother and the beach?

3. What colors are used to describe the boys swimming in the bay and the bay itself?

4. What do you think this contrast in colors implies?

5. How would you describe Jerry and his mother's relationship at the opening of the story (note paragraphs 5 and 6)? How does this relationship change when the conflict is resolved?

About the Author

Doris Lessing (b. 1919) was reared in Southern Rhodesia, where her English parents ran a farm. The people, animals, and scenery of that land deeply impressed her, not only forming a rich reservoir of detailed imagery for her writings but also shaping a social and political conscience that would surface in her work even after she left the country in 1949. Her first novel, *The Grass Is Singing*, was so effectively anti-colonialist that the government of Southern Rhodesia exiled her in 1956. Lessing's desire for social justice has led her to espouse many causes in her writing over the years, including communism (which she abandoned in disillusionment in 1954) and feminism (the subject of her most famous work, *The Golden Notebook*). For her influential literary accomplishments, she was awarded the 2007 Nobel Prize in Literature.

In her novels and short stories, Doris Lessing's underlying theme is commitment—to political causes, to love, to family, to friends, and to oneself. Personal integrity and independence rise above all other goals in the lives of many of Lessing's later characters. Although the inner conflicts of her characters are generally well drawn and realistically portrayed, they are often resolved in ways unacceptable to a Christian reader. An exception is "Through the Tunnel," in which Jerry successfully fulfills his commitment to himself without shirking his responsibility to his mother. This proving of oneself is another important theme in Lessing's writings.

One of the most important yet most overlooked building blocks of a story is the setting. Though we often think of setting simply in reference to physical space or objects, it encompasses other matters as well. **Setting** consists of the time, place, and way of life in which the action of the story occurs. In other words, an author's choice of time and place not only demands a certain landscape or type of dress, but it may also dictate the social mores the author must work with when creating believable characters and conflicts. All three aspects of setting contribute to conflicts in a story. For example, a story set in 1943 Germany inevitably addresses both the physical hardships as a result of the ongoing war and the ideological conflict that helped foster it.

Another term closely related to setting is *atmosphere*. A story's **atmosphere** denotes the mood or emotion that the reader is supposed to share with the characters. This general mood can vary widely in different works, from terror to uncertainty, even to hilarity. Authors may also use specific techniques to create atmosphere. For example, an atmosphere of anticipation can be created by use of suspense. (See the Unit 1 essay, "Conflict.") Sometimes the setting of a story contributes to its atmosphere. For example, many of Edgar Allan Poe's famous short stories are set in sinister landscapes or spooky buildings in order to reinforce the reader's sense of impending disaster. Such stories also illustrate that a story's atmosphere usually heightens the conflicts and anticipates their resolutions.

Sometimes the use of figurative language (such as similes and metaphors) can enhance setting and the atmosphere. For example, in this unit's story "Top Man," the use of personification highlights aspects of both. **Personification** is a figure of speech that assigns human characteristics to something that is not human. In "Top Man," nature (the setting) is often personified, creating a sense of deliberate opposition on the part of the mountain and the weather to the climbers' endeavors. In this respect, personification also serves to amplify the story's conflict between man and nature.

1. What are the three aspects of **setting** (time, place, and social values) as seen in "Miss Hinch"?

2. In what physical place does a great deal of "Miss Hinch" take place? List ways in which this particular choice of setting affects the story's course of events.

3. What technique creates the **atmosphere** of "Miss Hinch"?

4. Sometimes a story will emphasize one aspect of setting over another. Which aspect is most prominent in "Top Man"?

5. How would you describe the overall atmosphere of "Top Man"? In what ways does this atmosphere enhance the conflicts of the story?

6. List five examples of **personification** from "Top Man."

7. How does the setting of "Through the Tunnel" affect the conflict of the story?

8. How does time affect Jerry's internal conflict?

The Duel

Nikolai Dmitrievich Teleshov

Like the hero in "Through the Tunnel," the central character in this story faces a test of courage. Unlike Jerry, however, Ivan Golubenko does not take up his challenge willingly. How does Ivan's attitude toward conflict affect the resolution of the story?

It was early morning—

Vladimir Kladunov, a tall, graceful young man, twenty-two years of age, almost boyish in appearance, with a handsome face and thick, fair curls, dressed in the uniform of an officer and in long riding boots, minus overcoat and cap, stood upon a meadow covered with new-fallen snow, and gazed at another officer, a tall, red-faced, mustached man, who faced him at a distance of thirty paces, and was slowly lifting his hand in which he held a revolver, and aimed it straight at Vladimir.

With his arms crossed over his breast and also holding in one hand a revolver, Kladunov, almost with indifference, awaited the shot of his opponent. His handsome, young face, though a little paler than usual, was alight with courage, and wore a scornful smile. His dangerous position, and the merciless determination of his adversary, the strenuous attention of the seconds* who silently stood at one side, and the imminence of death, made the moment one of terrible intensity—mysterious, almost solemn. A question of honor was to be decided. Every one felt the importance of the question; the less they understood what they were doing, the deeper seemed the solemnity of the moment.

---

seconds: official attendants of the contestants in a duel

A shot was fired; a shiver ran through all. Vladimir threw his hands about, bent his knees, and fell. He lay upon the snow, shot through the head, his hands apart, his hair, face, and even the snow around his head covered with blood. The seconds ran toward him and lifted him; the doctor certified his death, and the question of honor was solved. It only remained to announce the news to the regiment and to inform, as tenderly and carefully as possible, the mother, who was now left alone in the world, for the boy that had been killed was her only son. Before the duel no one had given her even a thought; but now they all became very thoughtful. All knew and loved her, and recognized the fact that she must be prepared by degrees for the terrible news. At last Ivan Golubenko was chosen as most fit to tell the mother, and smooth out matters as much as possible.

· ·

Pelageia Petrovna had just risen and was preparing her morning tea when Ivan Golubenko, gloomy and confused, entered the room.

"Just in time for tea, Ivan Ivanovich!" amiably exclaimed the old lady, rising to meet her guest. "You have surely called to see Vladimir!"

"No, I—in passing by—" Golubenko stammered, abashed.

"You will have to excuse him; he is still asleep. He walked up and down his room the whole of last night, and I told the servant not to wake him, as it is a—holy day. But probably you came on urgent business?"

"No, I only stepped in for a moment in passing—"

"If you wish to see him, I will give the order to wake him up."

"No, no, do not trouble yourself!"

But Pelageia Petrovna, believing that he had called to see her son on some business or other, left the room, murmuring to herself.

Golubenko walked excitedly to and fro, wringing his hands, not knowing how to tell her the terrible news. The decisive moment was quickly approaching, but he lost control of himself, was frightened, and cursed fate that had so mixed him up with the whole business.

"Now! How can a body trust you young people!" Pelageia exclaimed good-naturedly to her guest, reentering the room. "Here I have been taking care not to make the least noise with the cups and saucers, and asking you not to wake my boy, and he has long ago departed without leaving a trace! But why do you not take a seat, Ivan Ivanovich, and have a cup of tea? You have been neglecting us terribly lately!"

She smiled as with a secret joy, and added in a low voice:

"And we have had so much news during that time!—Vladimir surely could not keep it. He must have told you all about it by this; for he is very straightforward and open-hearted, my Vladimir. I was thinking last night, in my sinful thoughts: 'Well, when my Vladimir paces the room the whole night—that means that he is dreaming of Lenochka!' That is always the case with him: if he paces the room the whole night he will surely leave to-morrow. —Ah, Ivan Ivanovich, I only ask the Lord to send me this joy in my old age. What more does an old woman need? I have but one desire, one joy—and it seems to me I shall have nothing more to pray for after Vladimir and Lenochka are married. So joyful and happy it would make me! —I do not need anything besides Vladimir; there is nothing dearer to me than his happiness."

The old lady became so affected that she had to wipe away the tears which came to her eyes.

"Do you remember," she continued, "things did not go well in the beginning—either between the two or on account of the money—you young officers are not even allowed to marry without bonds—well, now everything has been arranged; I have obtained the necessary five thousand rubles for Vladimir, and they could go to the altar even to-morrow! Yes, and Lenochka has written such a lovely letter to me—my heart is rejoicing!"

Continuing to speak, Pelageia Petrovna took a letter out of her pocket, which she showed to Golubenko, and then put back again.

"She is such a dear girl! And so good!"

Ivan Golubenko, listening to her talk, sat as if on red-hot coals. He wanted to interrupt her flow of words, to tell her that everything was at an end, that her Vladimir was dead, and that in one short hour nothing would remain to her of all her bright hopes; but he listened to her and kept silent. Looking upon her good, gentle face, he felt a convulsive gripping in his throat.

"But why are you looking so gloomy to-day?" the old lady at last asked. "Why, your face looks as black as night!"

Ivan wanted to say "Yes! And yours will be the same when I tell you!" But instead of telling her anything, he turned his head away, and began to twirl his mustaches.

Pelageia Petrovna did not notice it, and, wholly absorbed in her own thoughts, continued:

"I have a greeting for you. Lenochka writes that I should give Ivan Ivanovich her regards, and should compel him to come with Vladimir and pay her a visit—you know yourself how she likes you, Ivan Ivanovich!—No, it seems I am not able to keep it to myself. I must show you the letter. Just see for yourself how loving and sweet it is."

And Pelageia Petrovna again took out the package of letters from her pocket, took from it a thin letter-sheet, closely written, and unfolded it before Ivan Golubenko, whose face had become still gloomier, and he tried to push away with his hand the extended note, but Pelageia Petrovna had already started to read:

"Dear Pelageia Petrovna: When will the time arrive when I will be able to address you, not as above, but as my dear, sweet mother! I am anxiously awaiting the time, and hope so much that it will soon come that even now I do not want to call you otherwise than mama—"

Pelageia Petrovna lifted her head, and, ceasing to read, looked at Golubenko with eyes suffused with tears.

"You see, Ivan Ivanovich," she added; but seeing that Golubenko was biting his mustaches, and that his eyes too were moist, she rose, placed a trembling hand upon his hair, and quietly kissed him on the forehead. "Thank you, Ivan Ivanovich," she whispered, greatly moved. "I always thought that you and Vladimir were more like brothers than like simple friends—forgive me—I am so very happy, God be thanked!"

Tears streamed down her cheeks, and Ivan Golubenko was so disturbed and confused that he could only catch in his own her cold, bony hand and cover it with kisses; tears were suffocating him, and he could not utter a word, but in this outburst of motherly love he felt such a terrible reproach to himself that he would have preferred to be lying himself upon the field, shot through the head, than to hear himself praised for his friendship by this woman who would in half an hour find out the whole truth; what would she then think of him? Did not he, the friend, the almost brother, stand quietly by when a revolver was pointed at Vladimir? Did not this brother himself measure the space between the two antagonists and load the revolvers? All this he did himself, did consciously; and now this friend and brother silently sat there without having even the courage to fulfil his duty.

He was afraid; at this moment he despised himself, but could not prevail upon himself to say even one word. His soul was oppressed by a strange lack of harmony; he felt sick at heart and stifling. And in the meanwhile time flew—he knew it, and the more he knew it the less had he the courage to deprive Pelageia Petrovna of her few last happy moments. What should he say to her? How should he prepare her? Ivan Golubenko lost his head entirely.

He had had already time enough to curse in his thoughts all duels, all quarrels, every kind of heroism, and all kinds of so-called questions of honor, and he at last rose from his seat ready to confess or to run away. Silently and quickly he caught the hand of Pelageia Petrovna, and stooping over it to touch it with his lips, thus hid his face, over which a torrent of tears suddenly streamed down; impetuously, without another thought, he ran out into the corridor, snatching his great coat, and then out of the house without having said a word.

Pelageia Petrovna looked after him with astonishment, and thought:

"He also must be in love, poor fellow—well, that is their young sorrow—before happiness!" . . .

And she soon forgot him, absorbed in her dreams of the happiness which seemed to her so inviolable and entire.

About the Story

1. Who is the central character of the story?

2. Whom or what is the central character fighting against? Support your answer with specific quotations from the story.

3. How is the dominant conflict resolved?

4. What is the secondary conflict in this story?

5. Ivan Golubenko goes through a conflict similar to Jerry's in "Through the Tunnel." Compare and contrast both characters' responses to their experiences.

About the Author

Though Nikolai Dmitrievich Teleshov (1867–1957) remains relatively unknown in world literature, as a Russian writer, critic, and patron of the arts during the late nineteenth and early twentieth centuries, he had tremendous influence on the literary greats of his time. His involvement with the cultural scene of Moscow was unparalleled, though he generally chose to stay out of the limelight. Teleshov was influenced by and wrote for the famous author Maxim Gorky, "the Father of Soviet literature" and the initiator of Socialist Realism. Like Gorky, Teleshov was perceived as a radical writer during the czarist regime. His sketches and stories often depicted the plight of the Russian peasant or Siberian exile. Like many of these stories, "The Duel" is a vivid portrayal of psychological conflict. Though a supporter of the Bolshevik cause, Teleshov (like Gorky and other intellectuals of the era) was not an avid supporter of Lenin. Following Lenin's rise to power in 1917, Teleshov devoted his energies to writing reminiscences of such famous authors as Gorky, Chekov, and Andreyev, thus contributing to the literary fame of several of his contemporaries, a fame Teleshov himself was denied.

Robert Louis Stevenson Banks, aka Chimley

Ernest J. Gaines

The following story is a chapter from the novel *A Gathering of Old Men*. Told from the perspectives of many narrators, the book follows the varying responses of the black, Cajun, and white inhabitants of a rural Louisiana community to the murder of a white man by a black man. In the process, the author examines the changing state of race relations in the southern United States. Though little action takes place during this excerpt, the story is riddled with both internal and external conflicts of the past, present, and future. As you read, determine which of these conflicts is the primary focus of the chapter. Consider how the past and future conflicts affect or may be affected by the outcome of the main conflict.

Me and Mat was down there fishing. We goes fishing every Tuesday and every Thursday. We got just one little spot now. Ain't like it used to be when you had the whole river to fish on. The white people, they done bought up the river now, and you got nowhere to go but that one little spot. Me and Mat goes there every Tuesday and Thursday. Other people uses it other days, but on Tuesday and Thursday they leaves it for us. We been going to that one little spot like that every Tuesday and Thursday the last ten, 'leven years. That one little spot. Just ain't got nowhere else to go no more.

We had been down there—oh, 'bout a hour. Mat had caught eight or nine good-size perches, and me about six—throw in a couple of sackalays* there with the bunch. Me and Mat was just sitting there taking life easy, talking low. Mat was sitting on his croker* sack, I was sitting on my bucket. The fishes we had caught, we had them on a string in the water, keeping them fresh. We was just sitting there talking low, talking 'bout the old days.

---

sackalays: a freshwater fish

croker: a burlap bag

Then that oldest boy of Berto, that sissy one they called Fue, come running down the riverbank and said Clatoo said Miss Merle said that young woman at Marshall, Candy, wanted us on the place right away. She wanted us to get twelve-gauge shotguns and number five shells and she wanted us to shoot, but keep the empty shells and get there right away.

Me and Mat looked at him standing there sweating—a great big old round-face sissy-looking boy, in blue jeans and a blue gingham shirt, the shirt wet from him running.

Mat said, "All that for what?"

The boy looked like he was ready to run some more. Sweat just pouring down the side of his face. He was one of them great big old sissy-looking boys—round, smooth, sissy-looking face.

He said: "Something to do with Mathu, and something to do with Beau Boutan dead in his yard. That's all I know, all I want to know. Up to y'all now, I done done my part. Y'all can go and do like she say or y'all can go home, lock y'all doors, and crawl under the bed like y'all used to. Me, I'm leaving."

He turned.

"Where you going?" Mat called to him.

"You and no Boutan'll ever know," he called back.

"You better run out of Louisiana," Mat said to himself.

The boy had already got out of hearing reach—one of them great big old sissy boys, running hard as he could go up the riverbank.

Me and Mat didn't look at each other for a while. Pretending we was more interested in the fishing lines. But it wasn't fishing we was thinking about now. We was thinking about what happened to us after something like this did happen. Not a killing like this. I had never knowed in all my life where a black man had killed a white man in this parish. I had knowed about fights, about threats, but not killings. And now I was thinking about what happened after these fights, these threats, how the white folks rode. This what I was thinking, and I was sure Mat was doing the same. That's why we didn't look at each other for a while. We didn't want to see what the other one was thinking. We didn't want to see the fear in the other one's face.

"He works in mysterious ways, don't He?" Mat said. It wasn't loud, more like he was talking to himself, not to me. But I knowed he was talking to me. He didn't look at me when he said it, but I knowed he was talking to me. I went on looking at my line.

"That's what they say," I said.

Mat went on looking at his line awhile. I didn't have to look and see if he was looking at his line. We had been together so much, me and him, I knowed what he was doing without looking at him.

"You don't have to answer this 'less you want to, Chimley," he said. He didn't say that loud, neither. He had just jerked on the line, 'cause I could hear the line cut through the water.

"Yeah, Mat?" I said.

He jerked on the line again. Maybe it was a turtle trying to get at the bait. Maybe he just jerked on the line to do something 'stead of looking at me.

"Scared?" he asked. His voice was still low. And he still wasn't looking at me.

"Yes." I said.

He jerked on the line again. Then he pulled in a sackalay 'bout long and wide as my hand. He rebaited the hook and spit on the bait for luck and throwed the line back out in the water. He didn't look at me all this time. I didn't look at him, either. Just seen all this out the corner of my eyes.

"I'm seventy-one, Chimley," he said after the line had settled again. "Seventy-one and a half. I ain't got too much strength left to go crawling under that bed like Fue said."

"I'm seventy-two," I said. But I didn't look at him when I said it.

We sat there awhile looking out at the lines. The water was so clean and blue, peaceful and calm. I coulda sat there all day long looking out there at my line.

"Think he did it?" Mat asked.

I hunched my shoulders. "I don't know, Mat."

"If he did it, you know we ought to be there, Chimley," Mat said.

I didn't answer him, but I knowed what he was talking about. I remembered the fight Mathu and Fix had out there at Marshall store. It started over a Coke bottle. After Fix had drunk his Coke, he wanted Mathu to take the empty bottle back in the store. Mathu told him he wasn't nobody's servant. Fix told him he had to take the bottle back in the store or fight.

A bunch of us was out there, white and black, sitting on the garry* eating gingerbread and drinking pop. The sheriff, Guidry, was there, too. Mathu told Guidry if Fix started anything, he was go'n protect himself. Guidry went on eating his gingerbread and drinking pop like he didn't even hear him.

When Fix told Mathu to take the bottle back in the store again, and Mathu didn't, Fix hit him—and the fight was on. Worst fight I ever seen in my life. For a hour it was toe to toe. But when it was over, Mathu was up, and Fix was down. The white folks wanted to lynch Mathu, but Guidry stopped them. Then he walked up to Mathu, cracked him 'side the jaw, and Mathu hit the ground. He turned to Fix, hit him in the mouth, and Fix went down again. Then Guidry came back to the garry to finish his gingerbread and pop. That was the end of that fight. But that wasn't the last fight Mathu had on that river with them white people. And that's what Mat was talking about. That's what he meant when he said if Mathu did it we ought to be there. Mathu was the only one we knowed had ever stood up.

I looked at Mat sitting on the croker sack. He was holding the fishing pole with both hands, gazing out at the line. We had been

---

garry: regional term for a covered porch along the side of a building; a gallery together so much I just about knowed what he was thinking. But I asked him anyhow.

"'Bout that bed," he said. "I'm too old to go crawling under that bed. I just don't have the strength for it no more. It's too low, Chimley."

"Mine ain't no higher," I said.

He looked at me now. A fine-featured brown-skin man. I had knowed him all my life. Had been young men together. Had done our little running around together. Had been in a little trouble now and then, but nothing serious. Had never done what we was thinking about doing now. Maybe we had thought about it. Sure, we had thought about it. But we had never done it.

"What you say, Chimley?" he said.

I nodded to him.

We pulled in the lines and went up the bank. Mat had his fishes in the sack; mine was in the bucket.

"She wants us to shoot first," I said. "I wonder why."

"I don't know," Mat said. "How's that old gun of yours working?"

"Shot good last time," I said. "That's been a while, though."

"You got any number five shells?" Mat asked.

"Might have a couple round there," I said. "I ain't looked in a long time."

"Save me one or two if you got them," Mat said. "Guess I'll have to borrow a gun, too. Nothing round my house work but that twenty-gauge and that old rifle."

"How you figure on getting over there?" I asked him.

"Clatoo, I reckon," Mat said. "Try to hitch a ride with him on the truck."

"Have him pick me up, too." I said.

When we came up to my gate, Mat looked at me again. He was quite a bit taller than me, and I had to kinda hold my head back to look at him.

"You sure now, Chimley?" he said.

"If you go, Mat."

"I have to go, Chimley," he said. "This can be my last chance."

I looked him in the eyes. Lightish-brown eyes. They was saying much more than he had said. They was speaking for both of us, though, me and him.

"I'm going, too," I said.

Mat still looked at me. His eyes was still saying more than he had said. His eyes was saying: We wait till now? Now, when we're old men, we get to be brave?

I didn't know how to answer him. All I knowed, I had to go if he went.

Mat started toward his house, and I went on in the yard. Now, I ain't even stepped in the house good 'fore that old woman started fussing at me. What I'm doing home so early for? She don't like to be cleaning fishes this time of day. She don't like to clean fishes till evening when it's cool. I didn't answer that old woman. I set my bucket of fishes on the table in the kitchen; then I come back in the front room and got my old shotgun from against the wall. I looked through the shells I kept in a cigar box on top of the armoire till I found me a number five. I blowed the dust off, loaded the old gun, stuck it out the window, turnt my head just in case the old gun decided to blow up, and I shot. Here come that old woman starting right back on me again.

"What's the matter with you, old man? What you doing shooting out that window, raising all that racket for?"

"Right now, I don't know what I'm doing all this for," I told her. "But, see, if I come back from Marshall and them fishes ain't done and ready for me to eat, I'm go'n do me some more shooting around this house. Do you hear what I'm saying?"

She tightened her mouth and rolled her eyes at me, but she had enough sense not to get too cute. I got me two or three more number five shells, blowed the dust off them, and went out to the road to wait for Clatoo.

About the Story

1. How does the setting of the story influence its conflicts?

2. What is the primary conflict of the story? Is it external or internal?

3. How do the past conflicts mentioned in the story affect the primary conflict?

4. Mat and Chimley face a difficult choice. What are the possible consequences of either option?

5. Why do Mat and Chimley make the choice they do? What do they hope to accomplish?

About the Author

Ernest J. Gaines (b. 1933) was born on River Lake Plantation in Pointe Coupée Parish, Louisiana, into a fifth generation of sharecroppers. The first of twelve children, Gaines was working in the fields by age nine. At fifteen, however, Gaines moved to California to live with his mother and stepfather and to attend high school. After graduation, he served two years in the army and then enrolled in San Francisco State University. Upon graduating in 1957, he attended Stanford University on a scholarship for creative writing. Though he received favorable reviews for his early novels, his first major work was *The Autobiography of Miss Jane Pittman* (1971). Later novels receiving similar acclaim include *A Gathering of Old Men* (1983) and *A Lesson Before Dying* (1993).

Gaines's writing focuses primarily on the rural African-American culture of Louisiana. His style echoes the oral traditions of that culture as he frequently uses a first-person narrator, employs the dialects of his youth, and creates characters who give personal perspectives on the African-American past. Gaines has never been afraid to confront the continuing tensions of race relations in America in a nuanced manner. Throughout his long career as a writer and professor of writing, Gaines has earned a multitude of honors and awards, both national and international. Among the most notable are the 1994 Pulitzer Prize (for *A Lesson Before Dying*) and a 2004 nomination for the Nobel Prize in Literature. He is currently a writer-in-residence at the University of Southwestern Louisiana.

Under the Lion's Paw

Hamlin Garland

Garland's story, like Ullman's, presents all three types of conflict. It would be difficult, however, to discern the dominant conflict of "Under the Lion's Paw" without understanding the historical context in which the story was written. The story is set during a time when the Midwest was plagued by greedy land speculators. Through unethical practices these speculators swindled the tenant farmers hired to work the land. Initially the law sided with the speculators. But with the emergence of the Populist Movement, Midwestern farmers were eventually granted protection from wily, opportunistic men.

I

It was the last of autumn and first day of winter coming together. All day long the plowmen on their prairie farms had moved to and fro in their wide level fields through the falling snow, which melted as it fell, wetting them to the skin—all day, notwithstanding the frequent squalls of snow, the dripping, desolate clouds, and the muck of the furrows, black and tenacious* as tar.

---

tenacious: holding firmly together

Under their dripping harness the horses swung to and fro silently, with that marvel-ous uncomplaining patience which marks the horse. All day the wild geese, honking wildly as they sprawled sidewise down the wind, seemed to be fleeing from an enemy behind, and with neck outthrust and wings extended, sailed down the wind, soon lost to sight.

Yet the plowman behind his plow, though the snow lay on his ragged great-coat, and the cold, clinging mud rose on his heavy boots, fettering him like gyves,* whistled in the very beard of the gale. As day passed, the snow, ceasing to melt, lay along the plowed

land, and lodged in the depth of the stubble, till on each slow round the last furrow stood out black and shining as jet* between the plowed land and the gray stubble.

gyves: a shackle for legs
jet: dense black coal

When night began to fall, and the geese, flying low, began to alight invisibly in the near corn-field, Stephen Council was still at work "finishing a land." He rode on his sulky* plow when going with the wind, but walked when facing it. Sitting bent and cold but cheery under his slouch hat, he talked encouragingly to his four-in-hand.*

sulky: a lightweight two-wheel vehicle that holds one person
four-in-hand: team of four horses

"Come round there, boys!—Round agin! We got t' finish this land. Come in there, Dan! *Stiddy*, Kate,—stiddy! None o' y'r tantrums, Kittie. It's purty tuff, but got a be did. *Tchk! Tchk!* Step along, Pete! Don't let Kate git y'r single-tree on the wheel. *Once more!*"

They seemed to know what he meant, and that this was the last round, for they worked so with greater vigor than before.

"Once more, boys, an' than, sez I, oats an' a nice warm stall, an' sleep f'r all."

By the time the last furrow was turned on the land it was too dark to see the house, and the snow was changing to rain again. The tired and hungry man could see the light from the kitchen shining through the leafless hedge, and he lifted a great shout, "Supper f'r a half a dozen!"

It was nearly eight o'clock by the time he had finished his chores and started for supper. He was picking his way carefully through the mud, when the tall form of a man loomed up before him with a premonitory cough.

"Waddy ye want?" was the rather startled question of the farmer.

"Well, ye see," began the stranger, in a deprecating* tone, "we'd like t' git in f'r the night. We've tried every house f'r the last two miles, but they hadn't any room f'r us. My wife's jest about sick, 'n' the children are cold and hungry—"

deprecating: belittling

"Oh, y' want 'o stay all night, eh?"

"Yes, sir; it 'ud be a great accom—"

"Waal, I don't make it a practice t' turn anybuddy way hungry, not on sech nights as this. Drive right in. We ain't got much, but sech as it is—"

But the stranger had disappeared. And soon his steaming, weary team, with drooping heads and swinging single-trees, moved past the well to the block beside the path. Council stood at the side of the "schooner" and helped the children out—two little half-sleeping children—and then a small woman with a babe in her arms.

"There ye go!" he shouted jovially, to the children. "*Now* we're all right! Run right along to the house there, an' tell Mam' Council you wants sumpthin' t' eat. Right this way, Mis'—keep right off t' the right there. I'll go an' git a lantern. Come," he said to the dazed and silent group at his side.

"Mother," he shouted, as he neared the fragrant and warmly lighted kitchen, "here are some wayfarers an' folks who need sumpthin' t' eat an' a place t' snooze." He ended by pushing them all in.

Mrs. Council, a large, jolly, rather coarse-looking woman, took the children in her arms. "Come right in, you little rabbits. 'Most asleep, hey? Now here's a drink o' milk f'r each o' ye. I'll have s'm tea in a minute. Take off y'r things and set up t' the fire."

While she set the children to drinking milk, Council got out his lantern and went out to the barn to help the stranger about his team, where his loud, hearty voice could be heard as it came and went between the hay-mow and the stalls.

The woman came to light as a small, timid and discouraged-looking woman, but still pretty, in a thin and sorrowful way.

"Land sakes! An' you've traveled all the way from Clear Lake t'-day in this mud! Waal! waal! No wonder you're all tired out. Don't wait f'r the men, Mis'—" She hesitated, waiting for the name.

"Haskins."

"Mis' Haskins, set right up to the table an' take a good swig o' tea whilst I make y' s'm toast. It's green tea, an' it's good. I tell Council as I git older I don't seem to enjoy Young Hyson n'r Gunpowder. I want the reel green tea, jest as it comes off'n the vines. Seems t'have more heart in it, some way. Don't s'pose it has. Council says it's all in m' eye."

Going on in this easy way, she soon had the children filled with bread and milk and the woman thoroughly at home, eating some toast and sweet-melon pickles, and sipping the tea.

"See the little rats!" she laughed at the children. "They're full as they can stick now, and they want to go to bed. Now, don't git up, Mis' Haskins; set right where you are an' let me look after 'em. I know all about young ones, though I'm all alone now. Jane went an' married last fall. But, as I tell Council, it's lucky we keep our health. Set right there, Mis' Haskins; I won't have you stir a finger."

It was an unmeasured pleasure to sit there in the warm, homely kitchen, the jovial chatter of the housewife driving out and holding at bay the growl of the impotent, cheated wind.

The little woman's eyes filled with tears which fell down upon the sleeping baby in her arms. The world was not so desolate and cold and hopeless, after all.

"Now I hope Council won't stop out there and talk politics all night. He's the greatest man to talk politics an' read the *Tribune*— How old is it?"

She broke off and peered down at the face of the babe.

"Two months 'n' five days." said the mother, with a mother's exactness.

"Ye don't say! I want 'o know! The dear little pudzy-wudzy!" she went on, stirring it up in the neighborhood of the ribs with her fat forefinger.

"Pooty tough on 'oo go gallivant'n' 'cross lots this way—"

"Yes, that's so; a man can't lift a mountain," said Council, entering the door. "Mother, this is Mr. Haskins, from Kansas. He's been eat up 'n' drove out by grasshoppers."

"Glad t' see yeh!—Pa, empty that wash-basin 'n' give him a chance t' wash."

Haskins was a tall man, with a thin, gloomy face. His hair was a reddish brown, like his coat, and seemed equally faded by the wind and sun, and his sallow face, though hard and set, was pathetic somehow. You would have felt that he had suffered much by the line of his mouth showing under his thin, yellow mustache.

"Hain't Ike got home yet, Sairy?"

"Hain't seen 'im."

"W-a-a-l, set right up, Mr. Haskins; wade right into what we've got; 'tain't much, but we manage to live on it—she gits fat on it," laughed Council, pointing his thumb at his wife.

After supper, while the women put the children to bed, Haskins and Council talked on, seated near the huge cooking-stove, the steam rising from their wet clothing. In the Western fashion Council told as much of his own life as he drew from his guest. He asked but few questions, but by and by the story of

Haskins' struggles and defeat came out. The story was a terrible one, but he told it quietly, seated with his elbows on his knees, gazing most of the time at the hearth.

"I didn't like the looks of the country, anyhow," Haskins said, partly rising and glancing at his wife. "I was ust t' northern Ingyannie, where we have lots o' timber 'n' lots o' rain, 'n' I didn't like the looks o' that dry prairie. What galled me the worst was goin' s' far away acrosst so much fine land layin' all through here vacant."

"And the 'hoppers eat ye four years, hand runnin', did they?"

"Eat! They wiped us out. They chawed everything that was green. They jest set around waitin' f'r us to die t' eat us, too. I ust t' dream of 'em sittin' 'round on the bedpost, six feet long, workin' their jaws. They eet the fork-handles. They got worse 'n' worse till they jest rolled on one another, piled up like snow in winter. Well, it ain't no use. If I was t' talk all winter I couldn't help thinkin' of all that land back here that nobuddy was usin' that I ought 'o had 'stead o' bein' out there in that cussed country."

"Waal, why didn't ye stop an' settle here?" asked Ike, who had come in and was eating his supper.

"Fer the simple reason that you fellers wantid ten 'r fifteen dollars an acre fer the bare land, and I hadn't no money fer that kind o' thing."

"Yes, I do my own work," Mrs. Council was heard to say in the pause which followed. "I'm a gettin' purty heavy t' be on m'

laigs all day, but we can't afford t' hire, so I keep rackin' around somehow, like a foundered horse. S'lame—I tell Council he can't tell how lame I am, f'r I'm jest as lame in one laig as t' other." And the good soul laughed at the joke on herself as she took a handful of flour and dusted the biscuit-board to keep the dough from sticking.

"Well, I hain't *never* been very strong," said Mrs. Haskins. "Our folks was Canadians an' small-boned, and then since my last child I hain't got up again fairly. I don't like t' complain. Tim has about all he can bear now—but they was days this week when I jes wanted to lay right down an' die."

"Waal, now, I'll tell ye," said Council, from his side of the stove, silencing everybody with his good-natured roar, "I'd go down and *see* Butler, *anyway*, if I was you. I guess he'd let you have his place purty cheap; the farm's all run down. He's ben anxious t' let t' somebuddy next year. It 'ud be a good chance fer you. Anyhow, you go to bed and sleep like a babe. I've got some plowin' t' do, anyhow, an' we'll see if somethin' can't be done about your case. Ike, you go out an' see if the horses is all right, an' I'll show the folks t' bed."

When the tired husband and wife were lying under the generous quilts of the spare bed, Haskins listened a moment to the wind in the eaves, and then said, with a slow and solemn tone,

"There are people in this world who are good enough t' be angels, an' only haff t' die to *be* angels."

II

Jim Butler was one of those men called in the West "land poor." Early in the history of Rock River he had come into the town and started in the grocery business in a small way, occupying a small building in a mean part of the town. At this period of his life he

earned all he got, and was up early and late sorting beans, working over butter, and carting his goods to and from the station. But a change came over him at the end of the second year, when he sold a lot of land for four times what he paid for it. From that time forward he believed in land speculation as the surest way of getting rich. Every cent he could save or spare from his trade he put into land at forced sale, or mortgages on land, which were "just as good as the wheat," he was accustomed to say.

Farm after farm fell into his hands, until he was recognized as one of the leading land-owners of the county. His mortgages were scattered all over Cedar County, and as they slowly but surely fell in he sought usually to retain the former owner as tenant.

He was not ready to foreclose; indeed, he had the name of being one of the "easiest" men in the town. He let the debtor off again and again, extending the time whenever possible.

"I don't want y'r land," he said. "All I'm after is the int'rest on my money—that's all. Now, if y' want 'o stay on the farm, why, I'll give y' a good chance. I can't have the land layin' vacant." And in many cases the owner remained as tenant.

In the meantime he had sold his store; he couldn't spend time in it; he was mainly occupied now with sitting around town on rainy days smoking and "gassin' with the boys," or in riding to and from his farms. In fishing-time he fished a good deal. Doc Grimes, Ben Ashley, and Cal Cheatham were his cronies on these fishing excursions or hunting trips in the time of chickens or partridges. In winter they went to Northern Wisconsin to shoot deer.

In spite of all these signs of easy life Butler persisted in saying he "hadn't enough money to pay taxes on his land," and was careful to convey the impression that he was poor in spite of his twenty farms. At one time, he was said to be worth fifty thousand dollars, but land had been a little slow of sale of late, so that he was not worth so much.

A fine farm, known as the Higley place, had fallen into his hands in the usual way the previous year, and he had not been able to find a tenant for it. Poor Higley, after working

himself nearly to death on it in the attempt to lift the mortgage, had gone off to Dakota, leaving the farm and his curse to Butler.

This was the farm which Council advised Haskins to apply for; and the next day Council hitched up his team and drove down town to see Butler.

"You jest let *me* do the talkin'," he said. "We'll find him wearin' out his pants on some salt barrel somew'ers; and if he thought you *wanted* a place he'd sock it to you hot and heavy. You jest keep quiet; I'll fix 'im."

Butler was seated in Ben Ashley's store telling fish yarns when Council sauntered in casually.

"Hello, Butler; lyin' agin, hey!"

"Hellow, Steve! how goes it?"

"Oh, so-so. Too much rain these days. I thought it was goin' t' freeze up f'r good last night. Tight squeak if I get m' plowin' done. How's farmin' with *you* these days?"

"Bad. Plowin' ain't half done."

"It 'ud be a religious idee f'r you t' go out an' take a hand y'rself."

"I don't haff to," said Butler, with a wink.

"Got anybody on the Higley place?"

"No. Know of anybody?"

"Waal, no; not eggsackly. I've got a rela-tion back t' Michigan who's ben hot an' cold on the idee o' comin' West f'r sometime. *Might* come if he could get a good layout. What do you talk on the farm?"

"Well, I d'know. I'll rent it on shares or I'll rent it money rent."

"Waal, how much money, say?"

"Well, say ten per cent, on the price—two fifty."

"Waal, that ain't bad. Wait on 'im till 'e thrashes?"

Haskins listened eagerly to his important question, but Council was coolly eating a dried apple which he had speared out of a barrel with his knife. Butler studied him carefully.

"Well, knocks me out of twenty-five dollars interest."

"My relation'll need all he's got t' git his crops in," said Council, in the safe, indifferent way.

"Well, all right; *say* wait," concluded Butler.

"All right; this is the man. Haskins, this is Mr. Butler—no relation to Ben—the hardest-working man in Cedar County."

On the way home Haskins said: "I ain't much better off. I'd like that farm; it's a good farm, but it's all run down, an' so 'm I. I could make a good farm of it if I had half a show. But I can't stock it n'r seed it."

"Wall, now, don't you worry," roared Council in his ear. "We'll pull y' through somehow till next harvest. He's agreed t' hire it plowed, an' you can earn a hundred dollars plowin' an' y' e'n git the seed o' me, an' pay me back when y' can."

Haskins was silent with emotion, but at last he said, "I ain't got nothin' t' live on."

"Now, don't you worry 'bout that. You jest make your headquarters at ol' Steve Council's. Mother'll take a pile o' comfort in havin' y'r wife an' children 'round. Y' see, Jane's married off lately, an' Ike's away a good 'eal, so we'll be glad t' have y' stop with us this winter. Nex' spring we'll see if y' can't git a start agin." And he chirruped to the team, which sprang forward with the rumbling, clattering wagon.

"Say, looky here, Council, you can't do this. I never saw—" shouted Haskins in his neighbor's ear.

Council moved about uneasily in his seat and stopped his stammering gratitude by saying: "Hold on, now: don't make such a fuss over a little thing. When I see a man down, an' things all on top of 'm, I jest like t' kick 'em off an' help 'm up."

They rode the rest of the way home in silence. And when the red light of the lamp shone out into the darkness of the cold and windy night, and he thought of this refuge for his children and wife. Haskins could have put his arm around the neck of his burly companion and squeezed him. But he contented himself with saying, "Steve Council, you'll git y'r pay f'r this some day."

"Don't want any pay. My religion ain't run on such business principles."

The wind was growing colder, and the ground was covered with a white frost, as they turned into the gate of the Council farm, and the children came rushing out, shouting, "Papa's come!" They hardly looked like the same children who had sat at the table the night before. Their torpidity,* under the influence of sunshine and Mother Council, had given way to a sort of spasmodic cheerfulness, as insects in winter revive when laid on the hearth.

---

torpidity: motionlessness; numbness

III

Haskins worked like a fiend, and his wife, like the heroic woman that she was, bore also uncomplainingly the most horrible burdens. They rose early and toiled without intermission

till the darkness fell on the plain, then tumbled into bed, every bone and muscle aching with fatigue, to rise with the sun next morning to the same round of the same ferocity of labor.

The eldest boy drove a team all through the spring, plowing and seeding, milked the cows, and did chores innumerable, in most ways taking the place of a man.

An infinitely pathetic but common figure, this boy on the American farm, where there is no law against child labor. To see him in his coarse clothing, his huge boots, and his ragged cap, as he staggered with a pail of water from the well, or trudged in the cold and cheerless dawn out into the frosty field behind his team, gave the city-bred visitor a sharp pang of sympathetic pain. Yet Haskins loved his boy, and would have saved him from this if he could, but he could not.

By June the first year the result of such Herculean toil began to show on the farm. The yard was cleaned up and sown to grass, the garden plowed and planted, and the house mended.

Council had given them four of his cows.

"Take 'em an' run 'em on shares. I don't want 'o milk s' many. Ike's away s' much now, Sat'd'ys an' Sund'ys, I can't stand the bother anyhow."

Other men, seeing the confidence of Council in the newcomer, had sold him tools on time; and as he was really an able farmer, he soon had round him many evidences of his care and thrift. At the advice of Council he had taken the farm for three years, with the privilege of re-renting or buying at the end of the term.

"It's a good bargain, an' y' want 'o nail it," said Council. "If you have any kind of a crop, you c'n pay y'r debts, an' keep seed an' bread."

The new hope which now sprang up in the heart of Haskins and his wife grew great almost as a pain by the time the wide field of wheat began to wave and swirl in the wind of July. Day after day he would snatch a few moments after supper to go and look at it.

"Have ye seen the wheat t'-day, Nettie?" he asked one night as he rose from supper.

"No, Tim, I ain't had time."

"Well, take time now. Let's go look at it."

She threw an old hat on her head—Tommy's hat—and looking almost pretty in her thin, sad way, went out with her husband to the hedge.

"Ain't it grand, Nettie? Just look at it.

It was grand. Level, russet here and there, heavy-headed, wide as a lake, and full of multitudinous whispers and gleams of wealth, it stretched away before the gazers like the fabled field of the cloth of gold.

"Oh, I think—I *hope* we'll have a good crop, Tim; and, oh, how good the people have been to us!"

"Yes; I don't know where we'd be t'-day if it hadn't ben f'r Council and his wife."

"They're the best people in the world," said the little woman, with a great sob of gratitude.

"We'll be in the field on Monday, sure," said Haskins, gripping the rail on the fence as if already at the work of the harvest.

The harvest came, bounteous glorious, but the winds came and blew it into tangles, and the rain matted it here and there close to the ground, increasing the work of gathering it threefold.

Oh, how they toiled in those glorious days! Clothing dripping with sweat, arms aching, filled with briers, fingers raw and bleeding, backs broken with the weight of heavy bundles, Haskins and his man toiled on. Tommy drove the harvester, while his father and a hired man bound on the machine. In this way they cut ten acres every day, and almost every night after supper, when the hand went to bed, Haskins returned to the field shocking the bound grain in the light of the moon. Many a night he worked till his anxious wife came out at ten o'clock to call him in to rest and lunch.

At the same time she cooked for the men, took care of the children, washed and ironed, milked the cows at night, made the butter, and sometimes fed the horses and watered them while her husband kept at the shocking.

No slave in the Roman galleys could have toiled so frightfully and lived, for this man thought himself a free man, and that he was working for his wife and babes.

When he sank into his bed with a deep groan of relief, too tired to change his grimy, dripping clothing, he felt that he was getting nearer and nearer to a home of his own, and pushing the wolf of want a little farther from his door.

There is no despair so deep as the despair of a homeless man or woman. To roam the roads of the country or the streets of the city, to feel there is no rood of ground on which the feet can rest, to halt weary and hungry outside lighted windows and hear laughter and song within—these are the hungers and rebellions that drive men to crime and women to shame.

It was the memory of this homelessness, and the fear of its coming again, that spurred Timothy Haskins and Nettie his wife, to such ferocious labor during that first year.

IV

"'M, yes; 'm, yes; first-rate," said Butler, as his eye took in the neat garden, the pigpen, and the well-filled barnyard. "You're gitt'n' quite a stock around yeh. Done well, eh?

Haskins was showing Butler around the place. He had not seen it for a year, having spent the year in Washington and Boston with Ashley, his brother-in-law, who had been elected to Congress.

"Yes, I've laid out a good deal of money durin' the last three years. I've paid out three hundred dollars f'r fencin'."

"Um—h'm! I see, I see," said Butler while Haskins went on:

"The kitchen there cost two hundred: the barn ain't cost much in money, but I've put a lot o' time on it. I've dug a new well, and I—"

"Yes, yes, I see. You've done well. Stock worth a thousand dollars," said Butler, picking his teeth with a straw.

"About that," said Haskins, modestly. "We begin to feel's if we was gitt'n a home f'r ourselves; but we've worked hard. I tell you we began to feel it, Mr. Butler, and we're goin' t' begin to ease up purty soon. We've been kind o' plannin' a trip back t' *her* folks after the fall plowin's done."

"*Eggs*-actly!" said Butler, who was evidently thinking of something else. "I suppose you've kind o' calc'lated on stayin' here three years more?"

"Well, yes. Fact is, I think I c'n buy the farm this fall, if you'll give me a reasonable show."

"Um—m! What do you call a reasonable show?"

"Well, say a quarter down and three years time."

Butler looked at the huge stacks of wheat, which filled the yard, over which the chickens were fluttering and crawling, catching grasshoppers, and out of which the crickets were singing innumerable. He smiled in a peculiar way as he said, "Oh, I won't be hard on yeh. But what did you expect to pay f'r the place?"

"Why, about what you offered it for before, two thousand five hundred, or *possibly* three thousand dollars," he added quickly as he saw the owner shake his head.

"This farm is worth five thousand and five hundred dollars," said Butler, in a careless and decided voice.

"*What!*" almost shrieked the astounded Haskins. "What's that? Five thousand? Why, that's double what you offered it for three years ago."

"Of course, and it's worth it. It was all run down then; now it's in good shape. You've laid out fifteen hundred dollars in improvements, according to your own story."

"But *you* had nothin' t' do about that. It's my work an' my money."

"You bet it was; but it's my land."

"But what's to pay me for all my—"

"Ain't you had the use of 'em?" replied Butler, smiling calmly into his face.

Haskins was like a man struck on the head with a sandbag; he couldn't think; he stammered as he tried to say: "But—I never'd git the use—You'd rob me! More'n that: you agreed—you promised that I could buy or rent at the end of three years at—"

"That's all right. But I didn't say I'd let you carry off the improvements, nor that I'd go on renting the farm at two-fifty. The land is doubled in value, it don't matter how; it don't enter into the question; an' now you can pay me five hundred dollars a year rent, or take it on your own terms at fifty-five hundred, or—git out."

He was turning away when Haskins, the sweat pouring from his face, fronted him, saying again:

"But *you've* done nothing to make it so. You hain't added a cent. I put it all there myself, expectin' to buy. I worked an' sweat to improve it. I was workin' for myself an' babes—"

"Well, why didn't you buy when I offered to sell? What y' kickin' about?"

"I'm kickin' about payin' you twice f'r my own things,—my own fences, my own kitchen, my own garden."

Butler laughed. "You're too green t'eat, young feller. *Your* improvements! The law will sing another tune."

"But I trusted your word."

"Never trust anybody, my friend. Besides, I didn't promise not to do this thing. Why, man, don't look at me like that. Don't take me for a thief. It's the law. The reg'lar thing. Everybody does it."

"I don't care if they do. It's stealin' jest the same. You take three thousand dollars of my money—the work o' my hands and my wife's." He broke down at this point. He was not a strong man mentally. He could face hardship, ceaseless toil, but he could not face the cold and sneering face of Butler.

"But I don't take it," said Butler, coolly. "All you've got to do is to go on jest as you've been a-doin', or give me a thousand dollars down, and a mortgage at ten per cent on the rest."

Haskins sat down blindly on a bundle of oats near by, and with staring eyes and drooping head went over the situation. He was under the lion's paw. He felt a horrible numbness in his heart and limbs. He was hid in a mist, and there was no path out.

Butler walked about, looking at the huge stacks of grain, and pulling now and again a few handfuls out, shelling the heads in his hands and blowing the chaff away. He hummed a little tune as he did so. He had an accommodating air of waiting.

Haskins was in the midst of the terrible toil of the last year. He was walking again in the rain and the mud behind his plow; he felt the dust and dirt of the threshing. The ferocious husking-time, with its cutting wind and biting, clinging snows, lay hard upon him. Then he thought of his wife, how she had cheerfully cooked and baked, without holiday and without rest.

"Well, what do you think of it?" inquired the cool, mocking, insinuating voice of Butler.

"I think you're a thief and a liar!" shouted Haskins, leaping up. "A black-hearted houn'!" Butler's smile maddened him; with a sudden leap he caught a fork in his hands, and whirled it in the air. "You'll never rob another man!"

he grated through his teeth, a look of pitiless ferocity in his accusing eyes.

Butler shrank and quivered, expecting the blow; stood, held hypnotized by the eyes of the man he had a moment before despised— a man transformed into an avenging demon. But in the deadly hush between the lift of the weapon and its fall there came a gush of faint, childish laughter and then across the range of his vision, far away and dim, he saw the sun-bright head of his baby girl, as, with the pretty, tottering run of a two-year-old, she moved across the grass of the dooryard. His hands relaxed; the fork fell to the ground; his head lowered.

"Make out y'r deed an' mor'gage, an' git off'n my land, an' don't ye never cross my line agin; if y' do, I'll kill ye."

Butler backed away from the man in wild haste, and climbing into his buggy with trembling limbs drove off down the road, leaving Haskins seated dumbly on the sunny piles of sheaves, his head sunk into his hands.

About the Story

1. What are the different types of conflicts in the story?

2. How are the different conflicts resolved?

3. Which is the dominant conflict in the story?

4. Speculate on what Haskins thinks as he faces Butler with the pitchfork.

5. What does Council mean when he says, "Don't want any pay. My religion ain't run on such business principles"?

6. Explain the significance of the title of the story.

About the Author

The background of Hamlin Garland (1860–1940) well qualified him to write about Midwestern farmers. Born in Wisconsin, he grew up on farms in Iowa and South Dakota. These childhood experiences instilled in him a deep appreciation for the courage and self-discipline of settlers. Garland's hunger for education drove him to work his way through school, and upon graduating in 1884, he traveled east to Boston for further study.

His first success as a writer came with his book of short stories set in the Midwest, *Main-Travelled Roads* (1891). His best-known work, however, is *A Son of the Middle Border* (1917), a collection of his memoirs, which he followed with the Pulitzer Prize-winning *A Daughter of the Middle Border* (1922) and four other books based on his journal.

In his writing and in lectures, Garland advocated the techniques of local color and realism. He often traveled in the West to thoroughly research his topics, which included Native Americans and cowboys as well as farmers. As a result, his stories are rich and readable sources of information about the American West. For stories such as "Under the Lion's Paw," Garland returned to his parents' farm to regain a flavor of the countryside and to record his mother's vivid recollections of fellow settlers.

❦ THINKING ZONE ❧

You have already studied the general concept of setting in this unit, but sometimes authors emphasize setting to the extent that it becomes a defining characteristic of their writing. For example, authors who use **local color** attempt to recreate the dress, dialect, geography, social practices, and general worldview of a specific region. A famous American practitioner of local color, Samuel Clemens (Mark Twain), aptly reconstructs the worldview and ways of life that he grew up with in *Huckleberry Finn*, a story of life along the Mississippi River. He includes everything from Southern attitudes toward religion, slavery, family, and community to the inadequacies of those attitudes, as seen in conflicts involving shysters, family feuds, orphaned boys, and runaway slaves. Often, an obvious marker of local color is the use of **dialect** (dialogue written to reflect qualities of a character's speech). Dialect goes beyond the occasional use of regional words to reconstruct the overall accent and speech patterns of a region. Huck's surprise when his father shows up after hearing about Huck's newfound wealth is a fine example of dialect: "Looky here—mind how you talk to me; I'm astanding about all I can stand now—so don't gimme no sass. I've been in town two days, and I hain't heard nothing but about you bein' rich."

In two stories you have read for this unit, local color has been used as a tool within a broader purpose, persuasion. **Persuasion** is argument that motivates the listener to change not only his ideas but also his actions. Though ethical persuasion must be based on good logic, it primarily attempts to engage the audience at the emotional level; for what people feel strongly about, they will act on. For this reason, two tools (among many others) commonly used are humor and emotionally moving illustrations. Persuasive fiction also demands a high level of conflict to make readers emotionally invest in the outcome of the story. Given this emotional involvement, an author can use conflict resolution to drive home his ideas more effectively. A subcategory of persuasive writing, **propaganda**, refers to literature plainly written to persuade the reader to espouse the author's position on a significant issue of his time. Though this term currently has negative connotations, an author may write propaganda that is effective, truthful, and ethical. Indeed, for the Christian, knowing how to write such propaganda is an indispensable skill.

1. In what way does Teleshov use persuasive techniques in "The Duel"?

2. Both Gaines's and Garland's stories contain **local color**. Use the definition above to list specific examples that place each story in the category of local color.

3. Gaines uses Louisianan **dialect** freely in his story. "Translate" a sentence of dialect from the story into English that you would use for a school paper.

4. Imagine that both Gaines's and Garland's dialogues were written in Standard American English. How would your impressions of the characters change?

5. Garland's story attempts to garner sympathy for farmers swindled out of their land. Do you think that the author's use of local color supports that purpose (beyond portraying farmers accurately)? Why or why not?

6. Does Garland succeed in using conflict (as well as resolution) to gain your sympathy? Why or why not?

7. "Under the Lion's Paw" is an example of **persuasion**. Do you think it could also qualify as **propaganda**? Why or why not?

8. What do you believe to be Garland's worldview as evidenced in "Under the Lion's Paw"?

UNIT I REVIEW

REMEMBER THE TERMS

Review the following terms from the opening essay, "Conflict," and the Thinking Zone pages. Be prepared to discuss their meanings and uses.

conflict

man against a greater force

man against man

man against himself

external conflict

internal conflict

protagonist

antagonist

hero

villain

conflict resolution

suspense

foreshadowing

setting

atmosphere

personification

local color

dialect

persuasion

propaganda

APPLY THE CONCEPTS

Answer the following questions about how the literary concepts you have studied are used in this unit.

1. Of which type is the main conflict in "Miss Hinch"? Identify the participants.
2. What word best describes the atmosphere of "Miss Hinch"?
3. How is the primary conflict of "Top Man" resolved?
4. Does the character Nace experience any internal conflict?
5. In "Top Man" what figure of speech establishes setting as an antagonist?
6. What is the main conflict of "Through the Tunnel" and how is it resolved?
7. How do the two main settings in Lessing's story create differing atmospheres and mirror the main conflict?
8. Is the primary conflict of "The Duel" internal or external?
9. How would you describe the atmosphere of "The Duel"?
10. Given the way he resolves the main conflict, what does Teleshov want to say?
11. List two features of local color writing found in "Robert Louis Stevenson Banks, aka Chimley."
12. What kind of atmosphere do the setting and conflict of Gaines's story promote?
13. How might Gaines's story also fit in the category of persuasion?
14. Who are the protagonist and antagonist of "Under the Lion's Paw"?
15. In what ways might "Under the Lion's Paw" fit into the category of propaganda?

EVALUATE THE IDEAS

Identify each of the following statements as true or false. If false, rewrite the underlined portion of the statement to make it true.

16. "Miss Hinch" contains a great deal of <u>foreshadowing</u>.

17. Nace is <u>the hero</u> of "Top Man."

18. Osborn's main problem in "Top Man" is <u>that he doesn't really believe he's a good climber</u>.

19. The narrator of the story thinks Osborn is <u>too proud</u>.

20. In "Through the Tunnel" Jerry's mother lets him go to the beach because <u>she doesn't want to baby him</u>.

21. At the end of "Through the Tunnel," Jerry decides <u>to show the native boys that he can now swim through the tunnel</u>.

22. Ivan Golubenko is <u>the villain</u> of "The Duel."

23. The <u>social values of the setting</u> are especially important to the conflicts of Teleshov's story.

24. <u>The use of dialogue</u> in "Robert Louis Stevenson Banks, aka Chimley" helps identify it as local color writing.

25. The primary conflict of Gaines's story is <u>man against man</u>.

26. Gaines's conflicts and characters are inseparable from his choice of <u>setting</u>.

27. "Under the Lion's Paw" illustrates an <u>ethical</u> form of propaganda.

28. Garland's story contains <u>all three types of conflict</u>.

29. The persuasive elements of "Under the Lion's Paw" <u>appeal to the emotions of readers, often at the expense of their reason</u>.

WRITE A RESPONSE

Completely answer each of the following questions.

30. The main conflict of both "Through the Tunnel" and "The Duel" is man against himself. Compare and contrast the methods and success rates of Jerry and Ivan in dealing with their respective problems.

31. Using one of the unit stories, illustrate how the setting and atmosphere of a story can enhance the conflict.

32. Contrast the characters of Stephen Council and Jim Butler using specific quotations and incidents from "Under the Lion's Paw" to illustrate your ideas.

AMERICAN GOTHIC
Grant Wood

II

❧ CHARACTER ❧

Artist Grant Wood grew up on a farm in Iowa raising his own goats and chickens. Interested at an early age in drawing, he later studied painting for a time in Europe but returned to his roots to create a style all his own. Wood's iconic American Gothic *is a painting that for many people symbolizes the Midwest. The farmer and his daughter are modeled after Wood's family dentist and his own sister, Nan.*

✤ Wood's painting is an example of regionalism. What about *American Gothic* is characteristic of the Midwest?

✤ Why do you think Wood titled his painting as he did?

✤ What about Wood's painting might lead some critics to call the painting a satire (corrective ridicule)? What do you think?

✤ Wood himself denied that *American Gothic* was a satire but stated that it was instead a kind of tribute to that way of life. What specific details about the painting seem to show a strong work ethic?

Grant Wood, American, 1891-1942, *American Gothic*, 1930, Oil on beaver board, 30 11/16 x 25 11/16 in. (78 x 65.3 cm) unframed, Friends of American Art Collection, 1930.934, The Art Institute of Chicago. Photography © The Art Institute of Chicago.

❧ CHARACTER ❧

In our daily experience, actions come from actors. Events cannot be understood unless they are seen as deeds done by people. It is true that the world has come into existence, but we do not begin to understand the world until we affirm that *God* has brought this world into being.

So it is in literature: plot and character are inseparable. The plot—the most basic component of a story—is produced by the words and actions of the characters. If there are no characters, there is no plot. But characters are much more than plot producers. They turn a string of events into a story that challenges the mind and moves the emotions. For this reason, analyzing **character traits**—how the characters think and act—helps us appreciate a story more fully.

CHARACTER REVELATION

An author uses description, action, and dialogue to reveal character traits either directly or indirectly. **Description** tells the reader about the character's appearance or environment and may also explicitly reveal character traits. For example, the opening of the book of Job explicitly reveals Job to the reader through description. Job 1:1 summarizes Job's character, calling him "perfect and upright, . . . one that feared God, and eschewed evil." This type of description consists of straightforward details that tell the reader about the character, a technique known as **direct characterization**. Description may also provide **indirect characterization**, in which the reader must infer character traits from information shown by the author. An author may describe a character's facial appearance, body language, or dress and thereby suggest the character's state of mind or social status. Often, authors will employ description to introduce the reader to a character. The reader then finds out more about the inner lives of the characters through action and dialogue.

In Job 1:7–11 Satan approaches God and contradicts God's favorable description of Job by implying that Job's good deeds are motivated by God's gifts of favor. Attempting to prove this claim against Job, Satan predicts that Job would curse God if his family and possessions were taken from him. The Lord allows Satan to attack Job's household, killing his children and destroying his home and earthly goods. In response to this catastrophe, Job "rent his mantle, and shaved his head, and fell down upon the ground, and worshipped" (1:20). Job's **actions**, or what he does, testify to the description in Job 1:1. This indirect characterization leaves the reader to infer Job's piety and dedication to God.

Finally, **dialogue** encompasses not only what a character says but also what others say about him. In conjunction with Job's actions, the dialogue between Job and God and among Job and his three friends reveals more about all of these characters. Job's own words directly attest to his good deeds—he has been a godly father and a compassionate master; he has given shelter to orphans and protection to widows, and he has upheld the cause of the poor (29:1–16). Because his limited knowledge of God causes him to misinterpret the source of his suffering, his speeches are filled with contradictory thoughts and feelings. For example, in one passage he laments, "What is my strength, that I should hope?" (6:11). Later he proclaims, "I know that my redeemer liveth, and that he shall stand at the latter day upon the earth: And though after my skin worms destroy this body, yet in my flesh shall I see God" (19:25–26). These statements indirectly expose Job's humanity and growth. Like all of us, he is prone to doubt and fear, yet he eventually admits faith in God and His promises. In the stories of Scripture, dialogue is often the most important means of character revelation. Scripture focuses on dialogue for its character revelation because in life a person's speech reveals his heart.

CHARACTER TYPES

Job's lengthy poetic utterances make him a multifaceted or **round character**, a man as complex as the problem of pain he faces. Round characters are capable of surprising the reader, for they are complex and often undergo changes in their actions and thoughts. Unlike Job, his three friends are one-dimensional or **flat characters**. We learn nothing of their past, nor are we given any proof of their personal integrity. We know only that they believe suffering to be a result of personal sin. Because these three possess character qualities that directly oppose Job's, they may also be described as **foils**.

Job's three friends are also unchanging or **static characters**. Throughout their conversations with Job, they show no change in their attitudes or development in their thinking. On the other hand, the changes that occur in Job as a result of his growth make him a developing or **dynamic character**. His speeches reveal a man tortured by a desperate struggle, a man rushing down every avenue of reasoning in order to find an answer to his dilemma. Although Job never learns the specific reason for his suffering, he does gain a clearer view of himself and his Creator: "Then Job answered the Lord, and said, I know that thou canst do every thing, and that no thought can be withholden from thee. . . . Wherefore I abhor myself, and repent in dust and ashes" (42:1–2, 6). This growth in Job is consistent with what we have learned about his virtuous character. Dynamic characters play an important role in the stories of Scripture, as well as in literature in general. They remind the reader that people do change. In the Bible Jacob becomes Israel, Simon becomes Peter, and Saul of Tarsus becomes Paul the Apostle. One of the most blessed truths of Scripture is that in the gospel of Jesus Christ, there is dynamic power.

You can apply these same principles of character analysis while reading the selections in this unit. With each selection, notice the physical descriptions of the characters, what the characters do, and especially what the characters think and say. Be prepared to distinguish round from flat characters and static from dynamic characters. You can evaluate the author's characterization by asking and answering the following questions: Are these characters lifelike and interesting? What does the author reveal about the characters that makes me accept any change as believable?

from Treasure Island

ROBERT LOUIS STEVENSON

The exciting action and intriguing characters of Robert Louis Stevenson's *Treasure Island* have made it a beloved classic. The hero and narrator of the story is a boy, Jim Hawkins, whose parents own the Admiral Benbow Inn. In this excerpt from the novel, the inn receives a mysterious visitor whose sojourn sets off a series of dangerous adventures for Jim. How much can you learn about Jim and the other characters by studying their actions, dialogue, and descriptions? Based on that knowledge, can you identify which of the characters are flat and which are round?

CHAPTER 1
THE OLD SEA DOG AT THE "ADMIRAL BENBOW"

Squire Trelawney, Dr. Livesey, and the rest of these gentlemen having asked me to write down the whole particulars about Treasure Island, from the beginning to the end, keeping nothing back but the bearings of the island, and that only because there is still treasure not yet lifted, I take up my pen in the year of grace 17—, and go back to the time when my father kept the "Admiral Benbow" inn, and the brown old seaman with the saber cut first took up his lodging under our roof.

I remember him as if it were yesterday, as he came plodding to the inn door, his sea chest following behind him in a handbarrow; a tall, strong, heavy, nutbrown man; his tarry* pigtail falling over the shoulders of his soiled blue coat; his hands ragged and scarred, with black, broken nails; and the saber cut across one cheek, a dirty, livid

white. I remember him looking round the cove and whistling to himself as he did so, and then breaking out in that old sea song that he sang so often afterward:

"Fifteen men on the dead man's chest—
Yo-ho-ho, and a bottle of rum!"

in the high, old, tottering voice that seemed to have been tuned and broken at the capstan* bars. Then he rapped on the door with a bit of stick like a handspike that he carried, and when my father appeared, called roughly for a glass of rum. This, when it was brought to him, he drank slowly, like a connoisseur, lingering on the taste, and still looking about him at the cliffs and up at our signboard.

tarry: black, as if smeared with tar
capstan: a mechanism made of a vertical cylinder rotated manually or by motor, used for lifting weights by winding in the cable

"This is a handy cove," says he at length, "and a pleasant sittyated grogshop.* Much company, mate?"

grogshop: tavern; place where diluted rum was offered

My father told him no, very little company, the more was the pity.

"Well, then," said he, "this is the berth for me. Here you, matey," he cried to the man who trundled the barrow, "bring up alongside and help up my chest. I'll stay here a bit," he continued. "I'm a plain man; rum and bacon and eggs is what I want, and that head up there for to watch ships off. What you mought call me? You mought call me captain. Oh, I see what you're at—there," and he threw down three or four gold pieces on the threshold. "You can tell me when I've worked through that," says he, looking as fierce as a commander.

And, indeed, bad as his clothes were and coarsely as he spoke, he had none of the appearance of a man who sailed before the mast; but seemed like a mate or skipper, accustomed to be obeyed or to strike. The man who came with the barrow told us the mail* had set him down the morning before at the "Royal George"; that he had inquired what inns there were along the coast, and hearing ours well spoken of, I suppose, and described as lonely, had chosen it from the others for his place of residence. And that was all we could learn of our guest.

mail: mail coach

He was a very silent man by custom. All day he hung round the cove or upon the cliffs, with a brass telescope; all evening he sat in a corner of the parlor next to the fire, and drank rum and water very strong. Mostly he would not speak when spoken to; only look up sudden and fierce, and blow through his nose like a foghorn; and we and the people who came about our house soon learned to let him be. Every day, when he came back from his stroll, he would ask if any seafaring men had gone by along the road. At first we thought it was the want of company of his own kind that made him ask this question, but at last we began to see he was desirous to avoid them. When a seaman put up at the "Admiral Benbow" (as now and then some did, making by the coast road from Bristol), he would look in at him through the curtained door before he entered the parlor; and he was always sure to be as silent as a mouse when any such was present. For me, at least, there was no secret about the matter, for I was, in a way, a sharer in his alarms. He had taken me aside one day and promised me a silver fourpenny* on the first of every month if I would only keep my "weather eye open for a seafaring man with one leg," and let him know the moment he appeared. Often enough, when the first of the month came round, and I applied to him for my wage, he would only blow through his nose at me and stare me down; but before the week was out he was sure to think better of it, bring me my fourpenny piece, and then repeat his former orders to look out for "the seafaring man with one leg."

---

fourpenny: valued at four pence (British pennies); a token sum

---

How that personage haunted my dreams I need scarcely tell you. On stormy nights, when the wind shook the four corners of the house and the surf roared along the cove and up the cliffs, I would see him in a thousand forms and with a thousand diabolical expressions. Now the leg would be cut off at the knee, now at the hip; now he as a monstrous kind of creature who had never had but the one leg, and that in the middle of his body. To see him leap and run and pursue me over hedge and ditch was the worst of nightmares. And altogether I paid pretty dear for my monthly fourpenny piece, in the shape of these abominable fancies.

But though I was so terrified by the idea of the seafaring man with one leg, I was far less afraid of the captain himself than anybody else who knew him. There were nights when he took a deal more rum and water than his head would carry; and then he would sometimes sit and sing his wicked, old, wild sea songs, minding nobody; but sometimes he would call for glasses round and force all the trembling company to listen to his stories or bear a chorus to his singing. Often I have heard the house shaking with "Yo-ho-ho, and a bottle of rum," all the neighbors joining in for dear life, with the fear of death upon them, and each singing louder than the other to avoid remark. For in these fits he was the most overriding companion ever known; he would slap his hand on the table for silence all round; he would fly up in a passion of anger at a question, or sometimes because none was put, and so he judged the company was not following his story. Nor would he allow anyone to leave the inn till he had drunk himself sleepy and reeled off to bed.

His stories were what frightened people worst of all. Dreadful stories they were: about hanging, and walking the plank, and storms at sea, and the Dry Tortugas,* and wild deeds and places on the Spanish Main. By his own account he must have lived his life among some of the wickedest men that God ever allowed upon the sea; and the language in which he told these stories shocked our plain country people almost as much as the crimes that he described. My father was always saying the inn would be ruined, for people would soon cease coming there to be tyrannized over and put down, and sent shivering to their beds; but I really believe his presence did us good. People were frightened at the time, but on looking back they rather liked it; it was a fine excitement in a quiet country life; and there was even a party of the younger men who pretended to admire him, calling him a "true sea dog," and a "real old salt," and suchlike names, and saying there was the sort of man that made England terrible at sea.

---

the Dry Tortugas: an island group off the coast of south Florida, about sixty miles west of Key West

---

In one way, indeed, he bade fair to ruin us, for he kept on staying week after week, and at last month after month, so that all the money had been long exhausted, and still my father never plucked up the heart to insist on having more. If ever he mentioned it, the captain blew through his nose so loudly that you might say he roared, and stared my poor father out of the room. I have seen him wringing his hands after such a rebuff, and I am sure the annoyance and the terror he lived in must have greatly hastened his early and unhappy death.

All the time he lived with us the captain made no change whatever in his dress but to buy some stockings from a hawker.* One of the cocks* of his hat having fallen down, he let it hang from that day forth, though it was a great annoyance when it blew. I remember the appearance of his coat, which he patched himself upstairs in his room, and which, before the end, was nothing but patches. He never wrote or received a letter, and he never spoke with any but the neighbors, and with these, for the most part, only when drunk on rum. The great sea chest none of us had ever seen open.

hawker: peddler
cocks: points

He was only once crossed, and that was toward the end, when my poor father was far gone in a decline that took him off. Dr. Livesey came late one afternoon to see the patient, took a bit of dinner from my mother, and went into the parlor to smoke a pipe until his horse should come down from the hamlet, for we had no stabling at the old "Benbow." I followed him in, and I remember observing the contrast the neat, bright doctor, with his powder* as white as snow, and his bright, black eyes and pleasant manners, made with the coltish country-folk, and above all, with that filthy, heavy, bleared scarecrow of a pirate of ours, sitting far gone in rum with his arms on the table. Suddenly he—the captain, that is—began to pipe up his eternal song:

> "Fifteen men on the dead man's chest—
> Yo-ho-ho, and a bottle of rum!
> Drink and the devil had done for the rest—
> Yo-ho-ho, and a bottle of rum!"

powder: wig

At first I had supposed "the dead man's chest" to be that identical big box of his upstairs in the front room, and the thought had been mingled in my nightmares with that of the one-legged seafaring man. But by this time we had all long ceased to pay any particular notice to the song; it was new, that night, to nobody but Dr. Livesey, and on him I observed it did not produce an agreeable effect, for he looked up for a moment quite angrily before he went on with his talk to old Taylor, the gardener, on a new cure for the rheumatics. In the meantime, the captain gradually brightened up at his own music and at last flapped his hand upon the table before him in a way we all knew to mean—silence. The voices stopped at once, all but Dr. Livesey's; he went on as before, speaking clear and kind and drawing briskly at his pipe between every word or two. The captain glared at him for awhile, flapped his hand again, glared still harder, and at last broke out with a villainous, low oath: "Silence, there, between decks!"

"Were you addressing me, sir?" says the doctor; and when the ruffian had told him, with another oath, that this was so, "I have only one thing to say to you, sir," replied the doctor, "that if you keep on drinking rum, the world will soon be quit of a very dirty scoundrel!"

The old fellow's fury was awful. He sprang to his feet, drew and opened a sailor's clasp knife, and, balancing it open on the palm of his hand, threatened to pin the doctor to the wall.

The doctor never so much as moved. He spoke to him, as before, over his shoulder, and in the same tone of voice; rather high, so that all the room might hear, but perfectly calm and steady:

"If you do not put that knife this instant in your pocket, I promise, upon my honor, you shall hang at the next assizes."*

assizes: court sessions

Then followed a battle of looks between them; but the captain soon knuckled under, put up his weapon, and resumed his seat, grumbling like a beaten dog.

"And now, sir," continued the doctor, "since I now know there's such a fellow in my district, you may count I'll have an eye upon you day and night. I'm not a doctor only, I'm a magistrate; and if I catch a breath of complaint against you, if it's only for a piece of incivility like tonight's, I'll take effectual means to have you hunted down and routed* out of this. Let that suffice."

---
routed: driven out

Soon after, Dr. Livesey's horse came to the door and he rode away; but the captain held his peace that evening and for many evenings to come.

About the Story

1. Why does the old seaman choose this particular inn?

2. Stevenson uses all three types of characterization—description, actions, and dialogue—to better acquaint the reader with the old seaman. Find one example of each type and identify how each reveals more about the seaman's character.

3. For whom is Jim instructed to keep his "weather-eye" open?

4. What makes most people fear the old seaman?

5. Why is Jim less afraid of the old seaman than others are?

6. About what does the doctor condemn the old seaman?

Chapter 2
Black Dog Appears and Disappears

It was not very long after this that there occurred the first of the mysterious events that rid us at last of the captain, though not, as you will see, of his affairs. It was a bitter cold winter, with long, hard frosts and heavy gales; and it was plain from the first that my poor father was little likely to see the spring. He sank daily, and my mother and I had all the inn upon our hands; and were kept busy enough, without paying much regard to our unpleasant guest.

It was one January morning, very early—a pinching, frosty morning—the cove all gray with hoarfrost, the ripple lapping softly on the stones, the sun still low and only touching the hilltops and shining far to seaward. The captain had risen earlier than usual, and set out down the beach, his cutlass swinging under the broad skirts of the old blue coat, his brass telescope under his arm, his hat tilted back upon his head. I remember his breath hanging like smoke in his wake as he strode off, and the last sound I heard of him, as he turned the big rock, was a loud snort of indignation, as though his mind was still running upon Dr. Livesey.

Well, mother was upstairs with father; and I was laying the breakfast table against the captain's return, when the parlor door opened and a man stepped in on whom I had never set my eyes before. He was a pale, tallowy* creature, wanting two fingers of the left hand; and, though he wore a cutlass,* he did not look much like a fighter. I had always my eye open for seafaring men, with one leg or two, and I remember this one puzzled me. He was not sailorly, and yet he had a smack of the sea about him too.

---

tallowy: appearing as if covered with tallow, a whitish solid fat obtained from the bodies of cattle, sheep, or horses and used in some food products or to make candles

cutlass: sword

I asked him what was for his service, and he said he would take rum; but as I was going out of the room to fetch it, he sat down upon a table and motioned me to draw near. I paused where I was with my napkin in my hand.

"Come here, sonny," says he. "Come nearer here."

I took a step nearer.

"Is this here table for my mate Bill?" he asked, with a kind of leer.*

---

leer: sideways evil look

I told him I did not know his mate Bill, and this was for a person who stayed in our house, whom we called the captain.

"Well," said he, "my mate Bill would be called the captain, as like as not. He has a cut on one cheek, and a mighty pleasant way with him, particularly in drink, has my mate Bill. We'll put it, for argument like, that your captain has a cut on one cheek—and we'll put it, if you like, that that cheek's the right one. Ah, well! I told you. Now, is my mate Bill in this here house?"

I told him he was out walking.

"Which way, sonny? Which way is he gone?"

And when I had pointed out the rock and told him how the captain was likely to return, and how soon, and answered a few other questions, "Ah," said he, "this'll be as good as drink to my mate Bill."

The expression of his face as he said these words was not at all pleasant, and I had my own reasons for thinking that the stranger was mistaken, even supposing he meant what he said. But it was no affair of mine, I thought; and, besides, it was difficult to know what to do. The stranger kept hanging about just inside the inn door, peering round the corner like a cat waiting for a mouse. Once I

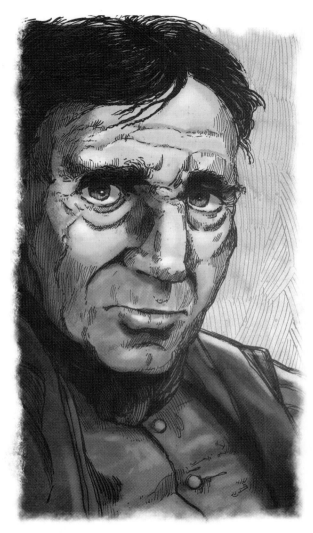

is discipline, sonny—discipline. Now, if you had sailed along of Bill, you wouldn't have stood there to be spoke to twice—not you. That was never Bill's way, nor the way of sich as sailed with him. And here, sure enough, is my mate Bill, with a spyglass under his arm, bless his 'art, to be sure. You and me'll just go back into the parlor, sonny, and get behind the door, and we'll give Bill a little surprise—bless his 'art, I say again."

fawning: seeking attention through flattery

So saying, the stranger backed along with me into the parlor, and put me behind him in the corner, so that we were both hidden by the open door. I was very uneasy and alarmed, as you may fancy, and it rather added to my fears to observe that the stranger was certainly frightened himself. He cleared the hilt of his cutlass and loosened the blade in the sheath; and all the time we were waiting there he kept swallowing as if he felt what we used to call a lump in the throat.

At last in strode the captain, slammed the door behind him, without looking to the right or left, and marched straight across the room to where his breakfast awaited him.

"Bill," said the stranger, in a voice that I thought he had tried to make bold and big.

The captain spun round on his heel and fronted us; all the brown had gone out of his face, and even his nose was blue; he had the look of a man who sees a ghost, or the evil one, or something worse, if anything can be; and, upon my word, I felt sorry to see him, all in a moment, turn so old and sick.

"Come, Bill, you know me; you know an old shipmate, Bill, surely," said the stranger.

The captain made a sort of gasp.

"Black Dog!" said he.

"And who else?" returned the other, getting more at his ease. "Black Dog as ever was, come for to see his old shipmate Billy, at the 'Admiral Benbow' inn. Ah, Bill, Bill,

stepped out myself into the road, but he immediately called me back, and, as I did not obey quick enough for his fancy, a most horrible change came over his tallowy face, and he ordered me in, with an oath that made me jump. As soon as I was back again he returned to his former manner, half fawning,* half sneering, patted me on the shoulder, told me I was a good boy, and he had taken quite a fancy to me. "I have a son of my own," said he, "as like you as two blocks, and he's all the pride of my 'art. But the great thing for boys

we have seen a sight of times, us two, since I lost them two talons,"* holding up his mutilated hand.

---
talons: claws (of animals) or fingers (of human beings)

"Now, look here," said the captain, "you've run me down; here I am; well, then, speak up: what is it?"

"That's you, Bill," returned Black Dog, "you're in the right of it, Billy. I'll have a glass of rum from this dear child here, as I've took such a liking to, and we'll sit down, if you please, and talk square, like old shipmates."

When I returned with the rum they were already seated on either side of the captain's breakfast table—Black Dog next to the door, and sitting sideways, so as to have one eye on his old shipmate and one, as I thought, on his retreat.

He bade me go, and leave the door wide open. "None of your keyholes for me, sonny," he said; and I left them together, and retired into the bar.

For a long time, though I certainly did my best to listen, I could hear nothing but a low gabbling;* but at last the voices began to grow higher, and I could pick up a word or two, mostly oaths, from the captain.

---
gabbling: rapid or senseless speech

"No, no, no, no; and an end of it!" he cried once. And again, "If it comes to swinging, swing all, say I."

Then all of a sudden there was a tremendous explosion of oaths and other noises—the chair and table went over in a lump, a clash of steel followed, and then a cry of pain, and the next instant I saw Black Dog in full flight, and the captain hotly pursuing, both with drawn cutlasses, and the former streaming blood from the left shoulder. Just at the door, the captain aimed at the fugitive one last tremendous cut, which would certainly have split him to the chin had it not been intercepted by our signboard of "Admiral Benbow." You may see the notch on the lower side of the frame to this day.

That blow was the last of the battle. Once out upon the road, Black Dog, in spite of his wound, showed a wonderful clean pair of heels, and disappeared over the edge of the hill in half a minute. The captain, for his part, stood staring at the signboard like a bewildered man. Then he passed his hand over his eyes several times, and at last turned back into the house.

"Jim," says he, "rum"; and as he spoke, he reeled a little, and caught himself with one hand against the wall.

"Are you hurt?" cried I.

"Rum," he repeated. "I must get away from here. Rum! Rum!"

I ran to fetch it; but I was quite unsteadied by all that had fallen out, and I broke one glass and fouled the tap, and while I was still getting in my own way I heard a loud fall in the parlor and, running in, beheld the captain lying full length upon the floor. At the same instant my mother, alarmed by the cries and fighting, came running downstairs to help me. Between us we raised his head. He was breathing very loud, and hard; but his eyes were closed, and his face a horrible color.

"Dear, deary me," cried my mother, "what a disgrace upon the house! And your poor father sick!"

In the meantime, we had no idea what to do to help the captain, nor any other thought but that he had got his death-hurt in the scuffle with the stranger. I got the rum, to be sure, and tried to put it down his throat, but his teeth were tightly shut and his jaws as strong as iron. It was a happy relief for us when the door opened and Dr. Livesey came in, on his visit to my father.

"Oh, doctor," we cried, "what shall we do? Where is he wounded?"

"Wounded? A fiddlestick's end!" said the doctor. "No more wounded than you or I. The man has had a stroke, as I warned him. Now, Mrs. Hawkins, just you run upstairs to your husband, and tell him, if possible, nothing about it. For my part, I must do my best to save this fellow's trebly* worthless life; and, Jim, you get me a basin."

trebly: threefold or triple

When I got back with the basin, the doctor had already ripped up the captain's sleeve, and exposed his great sinewy arm. It was tattooed in several places. "Here's luck," "A fair wind," and "Billy Bones his fancy" were very neatly and clearly executed on the forearm; and up near the shoulder there was a sketch of a gallows and a man hanging from it—done, as I thought, with great spirit.

"Prophetic," said the doctor, touching this picture with his finger. "And now, Master Billy Bones, if that be your name, we'll have a look at the color of your blood. Jim," he said, "are you afraid of blood?"

"No, sir," said I.

"Well, then," said he, "you hold the basin," and with that he took his lancet from his case and opened a vein.

A great deal of blood was taken before the captain opened his eyes and looked mistily about him. First he recognized the doctor with an unmistakable frown; then his glance fell upon me, and he looked relieved. But suddenly his color changed, and he tried to raise himself, crying:

"Where's Black Dog?"

"There is no Black Dog here," said the doctor, "except what you have on your own back. You have been drinking rum; you have had a stroke, precisely as I told you; and I have just, very much against my own will, dragged you head foremost out of the grave. Now, Mr. Bones—"

"That's not my name," he interrupted.

"Much I care," returned the doctor. "It's the name of a buccaneer of my acquaintance, and I call you by it for the sake of shortness; and what I have to say to you is this: one glass of rum won't kill you, but if you take one you'll take another and another, and I stake my wig if you don't break off short you'll die—do you understand that?—die, and go to your own place, like the man in the Bible.* Come, now, make an effort. I'll help you to your bed for once."

like the man in the Bible: Judas Iscariot, as described in Acts 1:25

Between us, with much trouble, we managed to hoist him upstairs, and laid him on his bed, where his head fell back on the pillow as if he were almost fainting.

"Now, mind you," said the doctor, "I clear my conscience—the name of rum for you is death."

And with that he went off to see my father, taking me with him by the arm.

"This is nothing," he said, as soon as he had closed the door. "I have drawn blood enough to keep him quiet awhile; he should lie for a week where he is—that is the best thing for him and you; but another stroke would settle him."

About the Story

1. Identify examples of foreshadowing at the beginning of Chapter 2.

2. Who is the old seaman's unexpected visitor?

3. Describe this visitor using quotations from the story.

4. What happens to the old seaman after the visitor leaves?

5. What is the treatment that the doctor gives Billy, the old seaman?

CHAPTER 3
THE BLACK SPOT

About noon I stopped at the captain's door with some cooling drinks and medicines. He was lying very much as we had left him, only a little higher, and he seemed both weak and excited.

"Jim," he said, "you're the only one here that's worth anything; and you know I've been always good to you. Never a month but I've given you a silver fourpenny for yourself. And now you see, mate, I'm pretty low, and deserted by all; and, Jim, you'll bring me one noggin of rum, now, won't you, matey?"

"The doctor—" I began.

But he broke in cursing the doctor, in a feeble voice but heartily. "Doctors is all swabs,"* he said; "and that doctor there, why, what do he know about seafaring men? I been in places hot as pitch, and mates dropping round with yellow jack,* and the blessed land a-heaving like the sea with earthquakes—what do the doctor know of lands like that?—and I lived on rum, I tell you. It's been meat and drink, and man and wife, to me; and if I'm not to have my rum now I'm a poor old hulk on a lee shore,* my blood'll be on you. Jim, and that doctor swab," and he ran on again for a while with curses. "Look, Jim, how my fingers fidges," he continued in the pleading tone. "I can't keep 'em still, not I. I haven't had a drop this blessed day. That doctor's a fool, I tell you. If I don't have a drain o'rum, Jim, I'll have the horrors; I seen some on 'em already. I seen old Flint in the corner there, behind you; as plain as print, I seen him; and if I get the horrors, I'm a man that has lived rough, and I'll raise Cain. Your doctor hisself said one glass wouldn't hurt me. I'll give you a golden guinea for a noggin, Jim."

swabs: awkward, stupid persons
yellow jack: yellow fever
lee shore: shore away from the wind

He was growing more and more excited, and this alarmed me for my father, who was very low that day and needed quiet; besides, I was reassured by the doctor's words, now quoted to me, and rather offended by the offer of a bribe.

"I want none of your money," said I, "but what you owe my father. I'll get you one glass, and not more."

When I brought it to him, he seized it greedily and drank it out.

"Aye, aye," said he, "that's some better, sure enough. And now, matey, did that doctor say how long I was to lie here in this old berth?"

"A week at least," said I.

"Thunder!" he cried. "A week! I can't do that; they'd have the black spot on me by then. The lubbers* is going about to get the wind of me this blessed moment; lubbers as couldn't keep what they got, and want to nail what is another's. Is that seamanly behavior, now, I want to know? But I'm a saving soul. I never wasted good money of mine, nor lost it neither; and I'll trick 'em again. I'm not afraid on 'em. I'll shake out another reef,* matey, and daddle* 'em again."

lubbers: clumsy sailors
shake out another reef: to unfurl a sail with a good shake
daddle: dawdle; trifle with

As he was thus speaking he had risen from bed with great difficulty, holding to my shoulder with a grip that almost made me cry out, and moving his legs like so much dead weight. His words, spirited as they were in meaning, contrasted sadly with the weakness of the voice in which they were uttered. He paused when he had got into a sitting position on the edge.

"That doctor's done me," he murmured. "My ears is singing. Lay me back."

Before I could do much to help him he had fallen back again to his former place, where he lay for a while silent.

"Jim," he said, at length, "you saw that seafaring man today!"

"Black Dog?" I asked.

"Ah! Black Dog," says he. "He's a bad 'un; but there's worse that put him on. Now, if I can't get away nohow, and they tip me the black spot, mind you, it's my old sea chest they're after; you get on a horse—you can, can't you? Well, then, you get on a horse, and go to—well, yes, I will!—to that eternal doctor swab, and tell him to pipe all hands—magistrates and sich—and he'll lay 'em aboard at the 'Admiral Benbow'—all old Flint's crew, man and boy, all on 'em that's left. I was first mate, I was, old Flint's first mate, and I'm the on'y one as knows the place. He gave it me at Savannah, when he lay a-dying, like as if I was to now, you see. But you won't peach* unless they get the black spot on me, or unless you see that Black Dog again, or a seafaring man with one leg, Jim—him above all."

peach: turn informer

"But what is the black spot, captain?" I asked.

"That's a summons, mate. I'll tell you if they get that. But you keep your weather eye open, Jim, and I'll share with you equals, upon my honor."

He wandered a little longer, his voice growing weaker; but soon after I had given him his medicine, which he took like a child, with the remark, "If ever a seaman wanted drugs, it's me," he fell at last into a heavy, swoonlike sleep, in which I left him. What I should have done had all gone well I do not know. Probably I should have told the whole story to the doctor; for I was in mortal fear lest the captain should repent of his confessions and make an end of me. But as things

fell out, my poor father died quite suddenly that evening, which put all other matters on one side. Our natural distress, the visits of the neighbors, the arranging of the funeral, and all the work of the inn to be carried on in the meanwhile, kept me so busy that I had scarcely time to think of the captain, far less to be afraid of him.

He got downstairs next morning, to be sure, and had his meals as usual, though he ate little, and had more, I am afraid, than his usual supply of rum, for he helped himself out of the bar, scowling and blowing through his nose, and no one dared to cross him. On the night before the funeral he was as drunk as ever; and it was shocking, in that house of mourning, to hear him singing away at his ugly old sea song; but, weak as he was, we were all in the fear of death for him, and the doctor was suddenly taken up with a case many miles away and was never near the house after my father's death. I have said the captain was weak; and indeed, he seemed rather to grow weaker than regain his strength. He clambered up and down stairs, and went from the parlor to the bar and back again, and sometimes put his nose out of doors to smell the sea, holding onto the walls as he went for support, and breathing hard and fast like a man on a steep mountain. He never particularly addressed me, and it is my belief he had as good as forgotten his confidences; but his temper was more flighty and, allowing for his bodily weakness, more violent than ever. He had an alarming way now, when he was drunk, of drawing his cutlass and laying it bare before him on the table. But, with all that, he minded people less, and seemed shut up in his own thoughts and rather wandering. Once, for instance, to our extreme wonder, he piped up to a different air, a kind of country love song, that he must have learned in his youth before he had begun to follow the sea.

So things passed until, the day after the funeral, and about three o'clock of a bitter, foggy, frosty afternoon, I was standing at the door for a moment, full of sad thoughts about my father, when I saw someone drawing slowly near along the road. He was plainly blind, for he tapped before him with a stick, and wore a great green shade over his eyes and nose; and he was hunched, as if with age or weakness, and wore a huge old tattered sea cloak with a hood, that made him appear positively deformed. I never saw in my life a more dreadful-looking figure.

He stopped a little distance from the inn, and, raising his voice in an odd singsong, addressed the air in front of him:

"Will any kind friend inform a poor blind man, who has lost the precious sight of his eyes in the gracious defense of his native country, England, and God bless King George!—where or in what part of this country he may now be?"

"You are at the 'Admiral Benbow,' Black Hill Cove, my good man," said I.

"I hear a voice," said he, "a young voice. Will you give me your hand, my kind, young friend, and lead me in?"

I held out my hand, and the horrible, soft-spoken, eyeless creature gripped it in a moment like a vise. I was so much startled that I struggled to withdraw; but the blind man pulled me close up to him with a single action of his arm.

"Now, boy," he said, "take me in to the captain."

"Sir," said I, "upon my word I dare not."

"Oh," he sneered, "that's it! Take me in straight, or I'll break your arm."

And he gave it, as he spoke, a wrench that made me cry out.

"Sir," said I, "it is for yourself I mean. The captain is not what he used to be. He sits with a drawn cutlass. Another gentleman—"

"Come, now, march," interrupted he; and I never heard a voice so cruel, and cold, and ugly as that blind man's. It cowed me more than the pain; and I began to obey him at once, walking straight in at the door and toward the parlor, where our sick old buccaneer was sitting, dazed with rum. The blind man clung close to me, holding me in one iron fist, and leaning almost more of his weight on me than I could carry. "Lead me straight up to him, and when I'm in view, cry out, 'Here's a friend for you, Bill.' If you don't, I'll do this"; and with that he gave me a twitch that I thought would have made me faint. Between this and that, I was so utterly terrified of the blind beggar that I forgot my terror of the captain, and as I opened the parlor door, cried out the words he had ordered in a trembling voice.

The poor captain raised his eyes, and at one look the rum went out of him, and left him staring sober. The expression of his face was not so much of terror as of mortal sickness. He made a movement to rise, but I do not believe he had enough force left in his body.

"Now, Bill, sit where you are," said the beggar. "If I can't see, I can hear a finger stirring. Business is business. Hold out your left hand. Boy, take his left hand by the wrist, and bring it near to my right."

We both obeyed him to the letter, and I saw him pass something from the hollow of the hand that held his stick into the palm of the captain's, which closed upon it instantly.

"And now that's done," said the blind man; and at the words he suddenly left hold of me, and, with incredible accuracy and nimbleness, skipped out of the parlor and into the road, where, as I still stood motionless, I could hear his stick go tap-tap-tapping into the distance.

It was some time before either I or the captain seemed to gather our senses; but at

length, and about at the same moment, I released his wrist, which I was still holding, and he drew in his hand and looked sharply into the palm.

"Ten o'clock!" he cried. "Six hours. We'll do them yet." And he sprang to his feet.

Even as he did so, he reeled, put his hand to his throat, stood swaying for a moment, and then, with a peculiar sound, fell from his whole height face foremost to the floor.

I ran to him at once, calling to my mother. But haste was all in vain. The captain had been struck dead by thundering apoplexy.* It is a curious thing to understand, for I had certainly never liked the man, though of late I had begun to pity him, but as soon as I saw that he was dead I burst into a flood of tears. It was the second death I had known, and the sorrow of the first was still fresh in my heart.

---

apoplexy: stroke

About the Story

1. What method or methods of characterization does Stevenson use throughout Chapter 3 to reveal Billy Bones's state of mind? Explain what each reveals about what the captain is thinking and feeling.

2. Describe the blind man that Jim sees coming up the road on the day after the funeral.

3. What action of the blind man contradicts his initial friendly greeting to Jim?

4. What is the blind man's business at the inn?

5. How many hours does the summons give Billy Bones?

CHAPTER 4
THE SEA CHEST

I lost no time, of course, in telling my mother all that I knew, and perhaps should have told her long before, and we saw ourselves at once in a difficult and dangerous position. Some of the man's money—if he had any—was certainly due to us; but it was not likely that our captain's shipmates, above all the two specimens seen by me, Black Dog and the blind beggar, would be inclined to give up their booty in payment of the dead man's debts. The captain's order to mount at once and ride for Dr. Livesey would have left my mother alone and unprotected, which was not to be thought of. Indeed, it seemed impossible for either of us to remain much longer in the house: the fall of coals in the kitchen grate, the very ticking of the clock, filled us with alarms. The neighborhood, to our ears, seemed haunted by approaching footsteps; and what between the dead body of the captain on the parlor floor and the thought of that detestable blind beggar hovering near at hand, and ready to return, there were moments when, as the saying goes, I jumped in my skin for terror. Something must speedily be resolved upon; and it occurred to us at last to go forth together and seek help in the neighboring hamlet. No sooner said than done. Bareheaded as we were, we ran out at once in the gathering evening and the frosty fog.

The hamlet lay not many hundred yards away though out of view, on the other side of the next cove; and what greatly encouraged me, it was in an opposite direction from that whence the blind man had made his appearance, and whither he had presumably returned. We were not many minutes on the road, though we sometimes stopped to lay hold of each other and hearken. But there was no unusual sound—nothing but the low wash of the ripple and the croaking of the inmates of the wood.

It was already candlelight when we reached the hamlet, and I shall never forget how much I was cheered to see the yellow shine in doors and windows; but that, as it proved, was the best of the help we were likely to get in that quarter. For—you would have thought men would have been ashamed of themselves—no soul would consent to return with us to the "Admiral Benbow." The more we told of our troubles, the more—man, woman, and child—they clung to the shelter of their houses. The name of Captain Flint, though it was strange to me, was well enough known to some there and carried a great weight of terror. Some of the men who had been to field work on the far side of the "Admiral Benbow" remembered, besides, to have seen several strangers on the road, and, taking them to be smugglers, to have bolted away; and one at least had seen a little lugger* in what we called Kitt's Hole. For that matter, anyone who was a comrade of the captain's was enough to frighten them to death. And the short and the long of the matter was that, while we could get several who were willing enough to ride to Dr. Livesey's, which lay in another direction, not one would help us to defend the inn.

lugger: small boat with two or three masts, each with a lugsail, and two or three jibs set on the bowsprit

They say cowardice is infectious, but then argument is, on the other hand, a great emboldener;* and so when each had said his say, my mother made them a speech. She would not, she declared, lose money that belonged to her fatherless boy; "if none of the rest of you dare," she said, "Jim and I dare. Back we will go, the way we came, and small thanks to you big, hulking, chickenhearted men. We'll have that chest open, if we die for it. And I'll thank you for that bag, Mrs. Crossley, to bring back our lawful money in."

emboldener: object that fosters boldness

Of course I said I would go with my mother, and of course they all cried out at our foolhardiness; but even then not a man would go along with us. All they would do was to give me a loaded pistol, lest we were attacked; and to promise to have horses ready saddled, in case we were pursued on our return; while one lad was to ride forward to the doctor's in search of armed assistance.

My heart was beating finely when we two set forth in the cold night upon this dangerous venture. A full moon was beginning to rise and peered redly through the upper edges of the fog, and this increased our haste, for it was plain that, before we came forth again, all would be as bright as day, and our departure exposed to the eyes of any watchers. We slipped along the hedges, noiseless and swift, nor did we see or hear anything to increase our terrors, till, to our relief, the door of the "Admiral Benbow" had closed behind us.

I slipped the bolt at once, and we stood and panted for a moment in the dark, alone in the house with the dead captain's body. Then my mother got a candle in the bar, and, holding each other's hands, we advanced into the parlor. He lay as we had left him, on his back, with his eyes open, and one arm stretched out.

"Draw down the blind, Jim," whispered my mother; "they might come and watch outside. And now," said she, when I had done so, "we have to get the key off that; and who's to touch it, I should like to know!" and she gave a kind of sob as she said the words.

FROM *TREASURE ISLAND*   87

I went down on my knees at once. On the floor close to his hand there was a little round of paper, blackened on the one side. I could not doubt that *this* was the *black spot*; and taking it up, I found written on the other side, in a very good clear hand, this short message: "You have till ten tonight."

"He had till ten, mother," said I; and just as I said it, our old clock began striking. This sudden noise startled us shockingly; but the news was good, for it was only six.

"Now, Jim," she said, "that key."

I felt in his pockets, one after another. A few small coins, a thimble, and some thread and big needles, a piece of pigtail tobacco bitten away at the end, his gully* with the cracked handle, a pocket compass, and a tinderbox,* were all that they contained, and I began to despair.

gully: large knife
tinderbox: metal box holding combustible material used to start a fire

"Perhaps it's round his neck," suggested my mother.

Overcoming a strong repugnance, I tore open his shirt at the neck, and there, sure enough, hanging to a bit of tarry string, which I cut with his own gully, we found the key. At this triumph we were filled with hope and hurried upstairs, without delay, to the little room where he had slept so long and where his box had stood since the day of his arrival.

It was like any other seaman's chest on the outside, the initial "B" burned on the top of it with a hot iron, and the corners somewhat smashed and broken as by long, rough usage.

"Give me the key," said my mother; and though the lock was very stiff, she had turned it and thrown back the lid in a twinkling.

A strong smell of tobacco and tar rose from the interior, but nothing was to be seen on the top except a suit of very good clothes, carelessly brushed and folded. They had never been worn, my mother said. Under that, the miscellany began—a quadrant,* a tin cannikin,* several sticks of tobacco, two brace* of very handsome pistols, a piece of bar silver, an old Spanish watch and some other trinkets of little value and mostly of foreign make, a pair of compasses mounted with brass, and five or six curious West Indian shells. I have often wondered since why he should have carried about these shells with him in his wandering, guilty, and hunted life.

quadrant: navigational instrument for measuring the altitude of stars (distance from the horizon)
cannikin: mug
brace: pair

In the meantime, we had found nothing of any value but the silver and the trinkets, and neither of these were in our way. Underneath there was an old boat cloak, whitened with sea salt on many a harbor bar. My mother pulled it up with impatience, and there lay before us, the last things in the chest, a bundle tied up in oilcloth, and looking like papers, and a canvas bag, that gave forth, at a touch, the jingle of gold.

"I'll show these rogues that I'm an honest woman," said my mother. "I'll have my dues, and not a farthing over. Hold Mrs. Crossley's bag." And she began to count over the amount of the captain's score from the sailor's bag into the one that I was holding.

It was a long, difficult business, for the coins were of all countries and sizes—doubloons, and louis d'ors, and guineas, and pieces of eight, and I know not what besides, all shaken together at random. The guineas, too, were about the scarcest, and it was with these only that my mother knew how to make her count.

When we were about halfway through, I suddenly put my hand upon her arm; for

I had heard in the silent, frosty air a sound that brought my heart into my mouth—the tap-tapping of the blind man's stick upon the frozen road. It drew nearer and nearer, while we sat holding our breath. Then it struck sharp on the inn door, and then we could hear the handle being turned, and the bolt rattling as the wretched being tried to enter; and then there was a long time of silence both within and without. At last the tapping recommenced and, to our indescribable joy and gratitude, died slowly away again until it ceased to be heard.

"Mother," said I, "take the whole and let's be going." For I was sure the bolted door must have seemed suspicious and would bring the whole hornet's nest about our ears; though how thankful I was that I had bolted it, none could tell who had never met that terrible blind man.

But my mother, frightened as she was, would not consent to take a fraction more than was due to her, and was obstinately unwilling to be content with less. It was not yet seven, she said, by a long way; she knew her rights and she would have them; and she was still arguing with me when a little low whistle sounded a good way off upon the hill. That was enough, and more than enough, for both of us.

"I'll take what I have," she said, jumping to her feet.

"And I'll take this to square the count," said I, picking up the oilskin packet.

Next moment we were both groping downstairs, leaving the candle by the empty chest; and the next we had opened the door and were in full retreat. We had not started a moment too soon. The fog was rapidly dispersing; already the moon shone quite clear on the high ground on either side; and it was only in the exact bottom of the dell and round the tavern door that a thin veil still hung unbroken to conceal the first steps of our escape. Far less than halfway to the hamlet, very little beyond the bottom of the hill, we had to come forth into the moonlight. Nor was this all; for the sound of several footsteps running came already to our ears, and as we looked back in their direction, a light tossing to and fro and still rapidly advancing showed that one of the newcomers carried a lantern.

"My dear," said my mother suddenly, "take the money and run on. I am going to faint."

This was certainly the end for both of us, I thought. How I cursed the cowardice of the neighbors; how I blamed my poor mother for her honesty and her greed, for her past foolhardiness and present weakness! We were just at the little bridge, by good fortune; and I helped her, tottering as she was, to the edge of the bank, where, sure enough, she gave a sigh and fell on my shoulder. I do not know how I found the strength to do it at all, and I am afraid it was roughly done; but I managed to drag her down the bank and a little way under the arch. Farther I could not move her, for the bridge was too low to let me do more than crawl below it. So there we had to stay—my mother almost entirely exposed and both of us within earshot of the inn.

About the Story

1. Identify at least four descriptive words or phrases from the first paragraph of Chapter 4 that create atmosphere and increase suspense.

2. Why will no one return to the inn with Jim and his mother?

3. What does Jim hear while looking through the chest?

4. What does Jim take from the chest? What does his mother take?

5. At the end of the chapter, where are Jim and his mother? Why are they there?

CHAPTER 5
THE LAST OF THE BLIND MAN

My curiosity, in a sense, was stronger than my fear; for I could not remain where I was, but crept back to the bank again, whence, sheltering my head behind a bush of broom, I might command the road before our door. I was scarcely in position ere my enemies began to arrive, seven or eight of them, running hard, their feet beating out of time along the road, and the man with the lantern some paces in front. Three men ran together, hand in hand; and I made out, even through the mist, that the middle man of this trio was the blind beggar. The next moment his voice showed me that I was right.

"Down with the door!" he cried.

"Aye, aye, sir!" answered two or three; and a rush was made upon the "Admiral Benbow," the lantern bearer following. And then I could see them pause, and hear speeches passed in a lower key, as if they were surprised to find the door open. But the pause was brief, for the blind man again issued his commands. His voice sounded louder and higher, as if he were afire with eagerness and rage.

"In, in, in!" he shouted, and cursed them for their delay.

Four or five of them obeyed at once, two remaining on the road with the formidable* beggar. There was a pause, then a cry of surprise, and then a voice shouting from the house:

formidable: fearsome

"Bill's dead!"

But the blind man swore at them again for their delay.

"Search him, some of you shirking lubbers, and the rest of you aloft and get the chest," he cried.

I could hear their feet rattling up our old stairs, so that the house must have shook with it. Promptly afterwards fresh sounds of astonishment arose; the window of the captain's room was thrown open with a slam and a jingle of broken glass; and a man leaned out into the moonlight, head and shoulders, and addressed the blind beggar on the road below him.

"Pew," he cried, "they've been before us. Someone's turned the chest out alow and aloft."*

alow and aloft: from the hold to the crow's nest (of a ship); below and above; thoroughly

"Is it there?" roared Pew.

"The money's there."

The blind man cursed the money.

"Flint's fist, I mean," he cried.

"We don't see it here nohow," returned the man.

"Here, you below there, is it on Bill?" cried the blind man again.

At that, another fellow, probably the one who had remained below to search the captain's body, came to the door of the inn. "Bill's been overhauled a'ready," said he, "nothin' left."

"It's these people of the inn—it's that boy. I wish I had put his eyes out!" cried the blind man, Pew. "They were here no time ago—they had the door bolted when I tried it. Scatter, lads, and find 'em."

"Sure enough, they left their glim* here," said the fellow from the window.

glim: source of light, such as a candle

"Scatter and find 'em! Rout the house out!" reiterated Pew, striking with his stick upon the road.

Then there followed a great to-do through all our old inn, heavy feet pounding to and fro, furniture thrown over, doors kicked in, until the very rocks re-echoed, and the men came out again, one after another, on the road, and declared that we were nowhere to be found. And just then the same whistle that had alarmed my mother and myself over the dead captain's money was once more clearly audible through the night, but this time twice repeated. I had thought it to be the blind man's trumpet, so to speak, summoning his crew to the assault; but I now found that it was a signal from the hillside toward the hamlet, and, from its effect upon the buccaneers, a signal to warn them of approaching danger.

"There's Dirk again," said one. "Twice! We'll have to budge, mates."

"Budge, you skulk!" cried Pew. "Dirk was a fool and a coward from the first—you wouldn't mind him. They must be close by; they can't be far; you have your hands on it. Scatter and look for them, dogs! Oh, shiver my soul," he cried, "if I had eyes!"

This appeal seemed to produce some effect, for two of the fellows began to look here and there among the lumber, but halfheartedly, I thought, and with half an eye to their own danger all the time, while the rest stood irresolute* on the road.

---
irresolute: undecided

"You have your hands on thousands, you fools, and you hang a leg! You'd be as rich as kings if you could find it, and you know it's here, and you stand there skulking. There wasn't one of you dared face Bill, and I did it—a blind man! And I'm to lose my chance for you! I'm to be a poor, crawling beggar, sponging for rum, when I might be rolling in a coach! If you had the pluck of a weevil in a biscuit you would catch them still."

"Hang it, Pew, we've got the doubloons!" grumbled one.

"They might have hid the blessed thing," said another. "Take the Georges,* Pew, and don't stand here squalling."

Georges: coins

Squalling was the word for it, Pew's anger rose so high at these objections; till at last, his passion completely taking the upper hand, he struck at them right and left in his blindness, and his stick sounded heavily on more than one.

These, in their turn, cursed back at the blind miscreant,* threatened him in horrid terms, and tried in vain to catch the stick and wrest it from his grasp.

---
miscreant: villain

This quarrel was the saving of us, for while it was still raging, another sound came from the top of the hill on the side of the hamlet—the tramp of horses galloping. Almost at the same time a pistol shot, flash and report, came from the hedge side. And that was plainly the last signal of danger, for the buccaneers turned at once and ran, separating in every direction, one seaward along the cove, one slant across the hill, and so on, so that in half a minute not a sign of them remained but Pew. Him they had deserted, whether in sheer panic or out of revenge for his ill words and blows, I know not; but there he remained behind, tapping up and down the road in a frenzy, and groping and calling for his comrades. Finally he took the wrong turn, and ran a few steps past me, toward the hamlet, crying:

"Johnny, Black Dog, Dirk," and other names, "you won't leave old Pew, mates—not old Pew!"

Just then the noise of horses topped the rise and four or five riders came in sight in the moonlight and swept at full gallop down the slope.

At this Pew saw his error, turned with a scream, and ran straight for the ditch, into which he rolled. But he was on his feet again in a second and made another dash, now utterly bewildered, right under the nearest of the coming horses.

The rider tried to save him, but in vain. Down went Pew with a cry that rang high into the night; and the four hoofs trampled and spurned him and passed by. He fell on his side, then gently collapsed upon his face, and moved no more.

I leaped to my feet and hailed the riders. They were pulling up, at any rate, horrified at the accident; and I soon saw what they were. One, tailing out behind the rest, was a lad that had gone from the hamlet to Dr. Livesey's; the rest were revenue officers, whom he had met by the way and with whom he had had the intelligence to return at once. Some news of the lugger in Kitt's Hole had found its way to Supervisor Dance and set him forth that night in our direction, and to that circumstance my mother and I owed our preservation from death.

Pew was dead, stone dead. As for my mother, when we had carried her up to the hamlet, a little cold water and salts very soon brought her back again, and she was none the worse for her terror, though she still continued to deplore the balance of the money. In the meantime the supervisor rode on, as fast as he could, to Kitt's Hole; but his men had to dismount and grope down the dingle,* leading, and sometimes supporting, their horses, and in continual fear of ambushes; so it was no great matter for surprise that when they got down to the Hole the lugger was already under way, though still close in. He hailed her. A voice replied, telling him to keep out of the moonlight or he would get some lead in him, and at the same time a bullet whistled close by his arm. Soon after, the lugger doubled* the point and disappeared. Mr. Dance stood there, as he said, "like a fish out of water," and all he could do was to dispatch a man to B— to warn the cutter. "And that," said he, "is just about as good as nothing. They've got off clean, and there's an end. Only," he added, "I'm glad I trod on Master Pew's corns," for by this time he had heard my story.

dingle: wooded hollow
doubled: rounded

I went back with him to the "Admiral Benbow," and you cannot imagine a house in such a state of smash; the very clock had been thrown down by these fellows in their furious hunt after my mother and myself; and though nothing had actually been taken away except the captain's moneybag and a little silver from the till, I could see at once that we were ruined. Mr. Dance could make nothing of the scene.

"They got the money, you say? Well, then, Hawkins, what in fortune were they after? More money, I suppose?"

"No, sir; not money, I think," replied I. "In fact, sir, I believe I have the thing in my breast pocket; and, to tell you the truth, I should like to get it put in safety."

"To be sure, boy; quite right," said he. "I'll take it, if you like."

"I thought, perhaps, Dr. Livesey—" I began.

"Perfectly right," he interrupted very cheerily, "perfectly right—a gentleman and a magistrate. And, now I come to think of it, I might as well ride round there myself and report to him or squire. Master Pew's dead, when all's done; not that I regret it, but he's dead, you see, and people will make it out against an officer of his majesty's revenue, if make it out they can. Now,

I'll tell you, Hawkins: if you like, I'll take you along."

I thanked him heartily for the offer, and we walked back to the hamlet where the horses were. By the time I had told mother of my purpose they were all in the saddle.

"Dogger," said Mr. Dance, "you have a good horse; take up this lad behind you."

As soon as I was mounted, holding onto Dogger's belt, the supervisor gave the word and the party struck out at a bouncing trot on the road to Dr. Livesey's house.

About the Story

1. In Chapter 5, how does Stevenson reveal Pew's character through dialogue and action? Explain, citing one example of each in the chapter.

2. What is Pew looking for in the chest?

3. What happens to Pew?

4. Based on your reading, decide which of the following characters are round characters and explain your answers.
   a. Jim
   b. Billy Bones
   c. Jim's mother
   d. Pew
   e. Dirk, Johnny, Black Dog (buccaneers)

About the Author

Robert Louis Stevenson (1850–94) is an author whose life is as rich and interesting as his writing. He was reared by strong, Protestant parents and a pious, loving nurse who instilled in him a clear sense of right and wrong and a thorough knowledge of the Scriptures, though no evidence exists of any emphasis on personal conversion in his or his parents' lives.

Though he studied law, he never practiced it, choosing rather to follow his literary ambitions. To improve his fragile health, Stevenson took walking tours in France. On this and other trips worldwide, Stevenson gathered vivid details with which he flavored his dramatic stories. The author of such classics as *Kidnapped* and *Dr. Jekyll and Mr. Hyde*, Stevenson spent his last days in a setting as exotic as any found in his works. Stevenson and his American wife, Fanny Osbourne, journeyed to the South Sea island of Samoa in a final attempt to alleviate the discomfort of his lung disease. There he died at age forty-four, and he was buried by the natives, who looked upon this man not merely as a great storyteller from a faraway country but as a noble and good friend.

Phaëthon

Ovid

translated by Edith Hamilton

Classical myths like Phaëthon (pronounced FAY uh THON) descended primarily from the Greeks and Romans. These old tales about gods and mortals were written to explain the world and man's place in it. Of course, Christians look to Scripture, not mythology, for understanding life and its purpose. Christians can, however, appreciate the literary beauty and the universal themes presented in mythology. In a limited sense, myths are profitable as moral fables, for they teach such virtues as courage, wisdom, hospitality, and constancy in love. They also warn against such vices as pride, rashness, and reckless ambition. The story of Phaëthon was told—or retold—by the master Roman storyteller Ovid. Its vivid description makes it one of his best—and makes the story come to life for the reader.

The palace of the Sun was a radiant place. It shone with gold and gleamed with ivory and sparkled with jewels. Everything without and within flashed and glowed and glittered. It was always high noon there. Shadowy twilight never dimmed the brightness. Darkness and night were unchanging brilliancy of light, but few had ever found their way thither.

Nevertheless, one day a youth, mortal on his mother's side, dared to approach. Often he had to pause and clear his dazzled eyes, but the errand which had brought him was so urgent that his purpose held fast and he pressed on, up to the palace, through the burnished doors, and into the throne-room where, surrounded by a blinding, blazing splendor, the Sun-god sat. There the lad was forced to halt. He could bear no more.

Nothing escapes the eyes of the Sun. He saw the boy instantly and he looked at him very kindly. "What brought you here?" he asked.

"I have come," the other answered boldly, "to find out if you are my father or not. My mother said you were, but the boys at school laugh when I tell them I am your son. They will not believe me. I told my mother and she said I had better go and ask you."

Smiling, the Sun took off his crown of burning light so that the lad could look at him without distress. "Come here, Phaëthon," he said. "You are my son. Clymenë told you the truth. I expect you will not doubt my word too? But I will give you a proof. Ask anything you want of me, and you shall have it. I call the Styx to be witness to my promise, the river of the oath of the gods."

No doubt Phaëthon had often watched the Sun riding through the heavens and had told himself with a feeling, half awe, half excitement, "It is my father up there." And then he would wonder what it would be like to be in that chariot, guiding the steeds along that dizzy course, giving light to the world. Now at his father's words this wild dream had become possible. Instantly he cried, "I choose to take your place, Father. That is the only thing I want. Just for a day, a single day, let me have your car to drive."

The Sun realized his own folly. Why had he taken that fatal oath and bound himself

to give in to anything that happened to enter a boy's rash young head? "Dear lad," he said, "this is the only thing I would have refused you. I know I cannot refuse. I have sworn by the Styx. I must yield if you persist. But I do not believe you will. Listen while I tell you what this is you want. You are Clymenë's son as well as mine. You are mortal, and no mortal could drive my chariot. Indeed, no god except myself can do that. The ruler of the gods cannot. Consider the road. It rises up from the sea so steeply that the horses can hardly climb it, fresh though they are in the early morning. In midheaven it is so high that even I do not like to look down. Worst of all is the descent, so precipitous that the sea-gods waiting to receive me wonder how I can avoid falling headlong. To guide the horses, too, is a perpetual struggle. Their fiery spirits grow hotter as they climb and they scarcely suffer my control. What would they do with you?

"Are you fancying that there are all sorts of wonders up there, cities of the gods full of beautiful things? Nothing of the kind. You will have to pass beasts, fierce beasts of prey, and they are all that you will see. The Bull, the Lion, the Scorpion, the great Crab, each will try to harm you. Be persuaded. Look around you. See all the goods the rich world holds. Choose from them your heart's desire and it shall be yours. If what you want is to be proved my son, my fears for you are proof enough that I am your father."

But none of all this wise talk meant anything to the boy. A glorious prospect opened before him. He saw himself proudly standing in that wondrous car, his hands triumphantly guiding those steeds which Jove himself could not master. He did not give a thought to the dangers his father detailed. He felt not a quiver of fear, not a doubt of his own powers. At last the Sun gave up trying to dissuade him. It was hopeless, as he saw. Besides, there was no time. The moment for starting was at hand. Already the gates of the east glowed purple, and Dawn had opened her courts full of rosy light. The stars were leaving the sky; even the lingering morning star was dim.

There was need for haste, but all was ready. The seasons, the gatekeepers of Olympus, stood waiting to fling the doors wide. The horses had been bridled and yoked to the car. Proudly and joyously Phaëthon mounted it, and they were off. He had made his choice. Whatever came of it he could not change now. Not that he wanted to in that first exhilarating rush through the air, so swift that the East Wind was outstripped and left far behind. The horses' flying feet went through the low-banked clouds near the ocean as through a thin sea mist and then up and up in the clear air, climbing the height of heaven. For a few ecstatic moments Phaëthon felt himself the Lord of the Sky. But suddenly there was a change. The chariot was swinging wildly to and fro; the pace was faster; he had lost control. Not he but the horses were directing the course. That light weight in the car, those feeble hands clutching the reins, had told them their own driver was not there. They were the masters then. No one else could command them. They left the road and rushed where they chose, up, down, to the right, to the left. They nearly wrecked the chariot against the Scorpion; they brought up short and almost ran into the Crab. By this time the poor charioteer was half fainting with terror, and he let the reins fall.

That was the signal for still more mad and reckless running. The horses soared up to the very top of the sky and then, plunging headlong down, they set the world on fire. The highest mountains were the first to burn, Ida and Helicon, where the Muses dwell, Parnassus, and the heaven-piercing Olympus. Down their slopes the flame ran to the low-lying valleys and the dark forest lands, until all things everywhere were ablaze. The springs turned into steam; the rivers shrank. It is said that it was then the Nile fled and hid his head, which still is hidden.

In the car Phaëthon, hardly keeping his place there, was wrapped in thick smoke and heat as if from a fiery furnace. He wanted nothing except to have this torment and terror ended. He would have welcomed death. Mother Earth, too, could bear no more. She uttered a great cry which reached up to the gods. Looking down from Olympus they saw that they must act quickly if the world was to be saved. Jove seized his thunderbolt and hurled it at the rash, repentant driver. It struck him dead, shattered the chariot, and made the maddened horses rush down into the sea.

Phaëthon all on fire fell from the car through the air to the earth. The mysterious river Eridanus, which no mortal eyes have ever seen, received him and put out the flames and cooled the body. The naiads,* in pity for him, so bold and so young to die, buried him and carved upon the tomb:

> Here Phaëthon lies
> who drove the Sun-god's car.
> Greatly he failed,
> but he had greatly dared.

---

naiads: nymphs that live in and preside over streams and brooks

His sisters, the Heliades, the daughters of Helios, the Sun, came to his grave to mourn for him. There they were turned into poplar trees, on the bank of the Eridanus,

> *Where sorrowing they weep*
> *into the stream forever.*
> *And each tear as it falls shines in the*
> *water a glistening drop of amber.*

About the Story

1. Is Phaëthon a round character or a flat character? Explain your answer.

2. What incident causes Phaëthon to visit the Sun-god?

3. Who are Phaëthon's parents?

4. Why does the Sun call his oath "folly"?

About the Translator

Edith Hamilton (1867–1963) gained her interest in learning at a young age from her father, who challenged her to read about and master any subject that interested her. Taking up this challenge, Hamilton taught herself a myriad of subjects ranging from math to classical literature. She also became proficient in Latin, Greek, French, and German. Always, however, her first love was the study of classical literature, especially Greek.

Though Hamilton was deficient in her understanding of Scripture, she did have an abundant supply of human insight and a gift for rendering the universal truths in classical literature accessible to the modern English reader. In books such as *The Greek Way*, she interpreted the thoughts and values of cultures different from our own and conveyed an appreciation for the effects of Greek thought on modern man. Certainly she brought out much that is noble and of literary merit in Greek literature.

Old Man

Ricardo Sánchez

Just as artists paint, sketch, and sculpt likenesses of individuals, writers use characterization to create mental pictures in the minds of their readers. As you read this selection, notice how Sánchez uses the three methods of characterization—description, dialogue, and action—to create this poetic sketch of an old man.

remembrance
(smiles / hurts sweetly)
October 8, 1972

old man
with brown skin
talking of past
    when being shepherd
      in utah, nevada, colorado and   5
        new mexico
was life lived freely;

old man,
    grandfather,
wise with time   10
running rivulets* on face,
deep, rich furrows,
    each one a legacy,
deep, rich memories of life . . .
"you are indio,*   15
    among other things,"
he would tell me
    during nights spent
so long ago
    amidst familial gatherings   20
in albuquerque . . .

rivulets: streams

indio: Indian or Native American

old man, loved and respected,
he would speak sometimes
of pueblos,*   pueblos: Native American towns in New Mexico
     san juan, santa clara,   25
     and even santo domingo,
and his family, he would say,
     came from there:
     some of our blood was here,
     he would say,   30
     before the coming of coronado,*   Coronado: Spaniard who became the first
other of our blood   European to explore the Southwestern
     came with los españoles,*   United States.
and the mixture   los españoles: Spanish people
was rich,   35
     though often painful . . .
old man,
who knew earth
     by its awesome aromas
and who felt   40
the heated sweetness
     of chile verde*   chile verde: green pepper
by his supple touch,
gone into dust is your body
     with its stoic* look and resolution,   45   stoic: unaffected by good or bad events
but your reality, old man, lives on
in a mindsoul touched by you . . .
Old Man . . .

About the Poem

1. An epigraph is a short statement, quotation, or phrase that is part of a work of literature yet intended to serve as a preface (or introduction) to the work. What is the epigraph to "Old Man"? What significance does the epigraph have?

2. Identify two portions of the poem that describe the old man's appearance. According to the author, what does the old man's appearance suggest?

3. What do the old man's words reveal about his view of his heritage?

4. Consider the last two lines of the third stanza. How is it possible for the old man's reality to live on?

5. How are the poet and the old man related? Aside from this relationship, for what other reason(s) does the author admire the old man?

About the Author

Ricardo Sánchez (1941–95) grew up in El Paso, Texas, where he developed a thirst for knowledge and an insatiable desire to read. As a teen, however, Sánchez was quickly absorbed into the El Paso *pachuco* subculture. This group was made up of young people who were not able to identify with either American or Mexican culture, who dressed in a distinct style and spoke *caló*, a mixture of English and Spanish phrases, and who were sometimes identified with gang influences.

Sánchez's experiences in school were far from positive. Many teachers of the 1950s lacked understanding of and appreciation for the Chicanos (Americans of Mexican heritage) in their classes. Sánchez recalls telling one of his teachers that he would like to be a poet one day. The teacher responded by saying that people like him would be only janitors. As a result of experiences like that one, Sánchez eventually quit school and joined the United States Army.

Through a disastrous series of events, Sánchez served two prison terms during which he read and wrote extensively. As an adult, Sánchez readily labeled his earlier attitudes and actions as foolish and attempted to educate young people against the lifestyle choices that landed him in prison.

In 1974 Sánchez earned a PhD in American studies and cultural linguistic theory and held a variety of positions until his death. He was a well-known professor, author, poet, and esteemed public speaker. Sánchez spoke worldwide against the kind of prejudice that he had experienced in his youth, but a passion for preserving the uniqueness of the Chicano culture remained foremost in his thinking and writing.

The Revolt of Mother

MARY E. WILKINS FREEMAN

In previous stories, you have observed both flat and round characters. In this story, the two central characters are dynamic and evidence change throughout the course of the story; however, although these changes may be considered positive, the method used to evoke the change is not necessarily the best. As you read, list specific ways in which the dynamic characters change. What are their responses to change? Do you think these responses indicate a positive change in these characters? What different methods might have been used to encourage the same results?

"Father!"

"What is it?"

"What are them men diggin' over there in the field for?"

There was a sudden dropping and enlarging of the lower part of the old man's face, as if some heavy weight had settled therein; he shut his mouth tight and went on harnessing the great bay mare. He hustled the collar on to her neck with a jerk.

"Father!"

The old man slapped the saddle upon the mare's back.

"Look here, Father, I want to know what them men are diggin' over in the field for, an' I'm goin' to know."

"I wish you'd go into the house, Mother, an' 'tend to your own affairs," the old man said then. He ran his words together, and his speech was almost as inarticulate as a growl.

But the woman understood; it was her native tongue. "I ain't goin' into the house till you tell me what them men are doin' over there in the field," said she.

Then she stood waiting. She was a small woman, short and straight-waisted like a child in her brown cotton gown. Her forehead was mild and benevolent between the smooth curves of gray hair; there were meek downward lines about her nose and mouth; but her eyes, fixed upon the old man, looked as if the meekness had been the result of her own will, never of the will of another.

They were in the barn, standing before the wide open doors. The spring air, full of the smell of growing grass and unseen blossoms, came in their faces. The deep yard in front was littered with farm wagons and piles of wood; on the edges, close to the fence and the house, the grass was a vivid green, and there were some dandelions.

The old man glanced doggedly at his wife as he tightened the last buckles on the harness. She looked as immovable to him as one of the rocks in his pasture land, bound to the earth with generations of blackberry vines. He slapped the reins over the horse, and started forth from the barn.

"*Father*!" said she.

The old man pulled up. "What is it?"

"I want to know what them men are diggin' over there in that field for."

"They're diggin' a cellar, I s'pose, if you've got to know."

"A cellar for what?"

"A barn."

"A barn? You ain't goin' to build a barn over there where we was goin' to have a house, Father?"

The old man said not another word. He hurried the horse into the farm wagon and clattered out of the yard, jouncing as sturdily on his seat as a boy.

The woman stood a moment looking after him, then she went out of the barn across a corner of the yard to the house. The house, standing at right angles with the great barn and a long reach of sheds and outbuildings, was infinitesimal compared with them. It was scarcely as commodious* for people as the little boxes under the barn eaves were for doves.

commodious: roomy

A pretty girl's face, pink and delicate as a flower, was looking out of one of the house windows. She was watching three men who were digging over in the field which bounded the yard near the road line. She turned quietly when the woman entered.

"What are they digging for, Mother?" said she. "Did he tell you?"

"They're diggin' for—a cellar for a new barn."

"Oh, Mother, he ain't going to build another barn?"

"That's what he says."

A boy stood before the kitchen glass combing his hair. He combed slowly and painstakingly, arranging his brown hair in a smooth hillock over his forehead. He did not seem to pay any attention to the conversation.

"Sammy, did you know Father was going to build a new barn?" asked the girl.

The boy combed assiduously.*

assiduously: diligently

"Sammy!"

He turned and showed a face like his father's under his smooth crest of hair. "Yes, I s'pose I did," he said reluctantly.

"How long have you known it?" asked his mother.

"'Bout three months, I guess."

"Why didn't you tell of it?"

"Didn't think 'twould do no good."

"I don't see what Father wants another barn for," said the girl, in her sweet, slow voice. She turned again to the window and stared out at the digging men in the field. Her tender, sweet face was full of gentle distress. Her forehead was as bald and innocent as a baby's, with the light hair strained back from it in a row of curl papers. She was quite large, but her soft curves did not look as if they covered muscles.

Her mother looked sternly at the boy. "Is he goin' to buy more cows?" said she.

The boy did not reply; he was tying his shoes.

"Sammy, I want you to tell me if he's goin' to buy more cows."

"I s'pose he is."

"How many?"

"Four, I guess."

His mother said nothing more. She went into the pantry, and there was a clatter of dishes. The boy got his cap from a nail behind the door, took an old arithmetic from the shelf, and started for school. He was lightly built, but clumsy. He went out of the yard with a curious spring in the hips, that made his loose homemade jacket tilt up in the rear.

The girl went to the sink and began to wash the dishes that were piled up there. Her mother came promptly out of the pantry and shoved her aside. "You wipe 'em," said she; "I'll wash. There's a good many this mornin'."

The mother plunged her hands vigorously into the water; the girl wiped the plates slowly and dreamily. "Mother," said she, "don't you think it's too bad Father's going to build that new barn, much as we need a decent house to live in?"

Her mother scrubbed a dish fiercely. "You ain't found out yet we're womenfolks, Nanny Penn," said she. "You ain't seen enough of menfolks yet to. One of these days you'll find it out, an' then you'll know that we know only what menfolks think we do, so far as any use of it goes, an' how we'd ought to reckon menfolks in with Providence an' not complain of what they do any more than we do of the weather."

"I don't care; I don't believe George is anything like that, anyhow," said Nanny. Her delicate face flushed pink, her lips pouted softly, as if she were going to cry.

"You wait an' see. I guess George Eastman ain't no better than other men. You hadn't ought to judge Father, though. He can't help it, 'cause he don't look at things jest the way we do. An' we've been pretty comfortable here, after all. The roof don't leak—ain't never but once—that's one thing. Father's kept it shingled right up."

"I do wish we had a parlor."

"I guess it won't hurt George Eastman any to come to see you in a nice clean kitchen. I guess a good many girls don't have as good a place as this. Nobody's ever heard me complain."

"I ain't complained either, Mother."

"Well, I don't think you'd better, a good father an' a good home as you've got. S'pose your father made you go out an' work for your livin'? Lots of girls have to that ain't no stronger an' better able to than you be."

Sarah Penn washed the frying pan with a conclusive air. She scrubbed the outside of it as faithfully as the inside. She was a masterly keeper of her box of a house. Her one living room never seemed to have in it any of the dust which the friction of life with inanimate matter produces. She swept, and there seemed to be no dirt to go before the broom; she cleaned, and one could see no difference. She was like an artist so perfect that he has apparently no art. Today she got out a mixing bowl and a board and rolled some pies, and there was no more flour upon her than upon her daughter who was doing finer work. Nanny was to be married in the fall, and she was sewing on some white cambric* and embroidery. She sewed industriously while her mother cooked; her soft milk-white hands and wrists showed whiter than her delicate work.

---

cambric: white linen or cotton fabric

"We must have the stove moved out in the shed before long," said Mrs. Penn. "Talk about not havin' things, it's been a real blessin' to be able to put a stove up in that shed in hot weather. Father did one good thing when he fixed that stovepipe out there."

Sarah Penn's face as she rolled her pies had that expression of meek vigor which might have characterized one of the New Testament saints. She was making mince pies. Her husband, Adoniram Penn, liked them better than any other kind. She baked twice a week. Adoniram often liked a piece of pie between meals. She hurried this morning. It had been later than usual when she began, and she wanted to have a pie baked for dinner. However deep a resentment she might be forced to hold against her husband, she would never fail in sedulous* attention to his wants.

---
sedulous: diligent

Nobility of character manifests itself at loopholes when it is not provided with large doors. Sarah Penn's showed itself today in flaky dishes of pastry. So she made the pies faithfully, while across the table she could see, when she glanced up from her work, the sight that rankled in her patient and steadfast soul—the digging of the cellar of the new barn in the place where Adoniram forty years ago had promised her their new house should stand.

The pies were done for dinner. Adoniram and Sammy were home a few minutes after twelve o'clock. The dinner was eaten with serious haste. There was never much conversation at the table in the Penn family. Adoniram asked a blessing, and they ate promptly, then rose up and went about their work.

Sammy went back to school, taking soft sly lopes out of the yard like a rabbit. He wanted a game of marbles before school and feared his father would give him some chores to do. Adoniram hastened to the door and called after him, but he was out of sight.

"I don't see what you let him go for, Mother," said he. "I wanted him to help me unload that wood."

Adoniram went to work out in the yard unloading wood from the wagon. Sarah put away the dinner dishes, while Nanny took down her curl papers and changed her dress. She was going down to the store to buy some more embroidery and thread.

When Nanny was gone, Mrs. Penn went to the door. "Father!" she called.

"Well, what is it!"

"I want to see you jest a minute, Father."

"I can't leave this wood nohow. I've got to git it unloaded an' go for a load of gravel afore two o'clock. Sammy had ought to helped me. You hadn't ought to let him go to school so early."

"I want to see you jest a minute."

"I tell ye I can't, nohow, Mother."

"Father, you come here." Sarah Penn stood in the door like a queen; she held her head as if it bore a crown; there was that patience which makes authority royal in her voice. Adoniram went.

Mrs. Penn led the way into the kitchen and pointed to a chair. "Sit down, Father," said she; "I've got somethin' I want to say to you."

He sat down heavily; his face was quite stolid, but he looked at her with restive* eyes. "Well, what is it, Mother?"

---
restive: nervous or restless

"I want to know what you're buildin' that new barn for, Father?"

"I ain't got nothin' to say about it."

"It can't be you think you need another barn?"

"I tell ye I ain't got nothin' to say about it, Mother; an' I ain't goin' to say nothin'."

"Be you goin' to buy more cows?"

Adoniram did not reply; he shut his mouth tight.

"I know you be, as well as I want to. Now, Father, look here"—Sarah Penn had not sat down; she stood before her husband in the humble fashion of a Scripture woman—"I'm goin' to talk real plain to you; I never have sence I married you, but I'm goin' to now. I ain't never complained, an' I ain't goin' to complain now, but I'm goin' to talk plain. You see this room here, Father; you look at

it well. You see there ain't no carpet on the floor, an' you see the paper is all dirty an' droppin' off the walls. We ain't had no new paper on it for ten year, an' then I put it on myself, an' it didn't cost but ninepence a roll. You see this room, Father; it's all the one I've had to work in an' eat in an' sit in sence we was married. There ain't another woman in the whole town whose husband ain't got half the means you have but what's got better. It's all the room Nanny's got to have her company in; an' there ain't one of her mates but what's got better, an' their fathers not so able as hers is. It's all the room she'll have to be married in. What would you have thought, Father, if we had had our weddin' in a room no better than this? I was married in my mother's parlor, with a carpet on the floor, an' stuffed furniture, an' a mahogany card table. An' this is all the room my daughter will have to be married in. Look here, Father!"

Sarah Penn went across the room as though it were a tragic stage. She flung open a door and disclosed a tiny bedroom, only large enough for a bed and bureau, with a path between. "There, Father," said she—

"there's all the room I've had to sleep in forty year. All my children were born there—the two that died, an' the two that's livin'. I was sick with a fever there."

She stepped to another door and opened it. It led into the small, ill-lighted pantry. "Here," said she, "is all the buttery I've got—every place I've got for my dishes, to set away my victuals in, an' to keep my milk pans in. Father, I've been takin' care of the milk of six cows in this place, an' now you're going to build a new barn, an' keep more cows, an' give me more to do in it."

She threw open another door. A narrow crooked flight of stairs wound upward from it. "There, Father," said she, "I want you to look at the stairs that go up to them two unfinished chambers that are all the places our son an' daughter have had to sleep in all their lives. There ain't a prettier girl in town nor a more ladylike one than Nanny, an' that's the place she has to sleep in. It ain't so good as your horse's stall; it ain't so warm an' tight."

Sarah Penn went back and stood before her husband. "Now, Father," said she, "I want to know if you think you're doin' right an' accordin' to what you profess. Here, when we was married, forty year ago, you promised me faithful that we should have a new house built in that lot over in the field before the year was out. You said you had money enough, an' you wouldn't ask me to live in no such place as this. It is forty year now, an' you've been makin' more money, an' I've been savin' of it for you ever sence, an' you ain't built no house yet. You've built sheds an' cow houses an' one new barn an' now you're goin' to build another. Father, I want to know if you think it's right. You're lodgin' your dumb beasts better than you are your own flesh an' blood. I want to know if you think it's right."

"I ain't got nothin' to say."

"You can't say nothin' without ownin' it ain't right, Father. An' there's another thing—I ain't complained; I've got along forty year, an' I s'pose I should forty more, if it wa'n't for that—if we don't have another house. Nanny she can't live with us after she's married. She'll have to go somewheres else to live away from us, an' it don't seem as if I could have it so, noways, Father. She wa'n't ever strong. She's got considerable color, but there wa'n't never any backbone to her. I've always took the heft of everything off her, an' she ain't fit to keep house an' do everything herself. She'll be all worn out inside of a year. Think of her doin' all the washin' an' ironin' an' bakin' with them soft white hands an' arms, an' sweepin'! I can't have it so noways, Father."

Mrs. Penn's face was burning; her mild eyes gleamed. She had pleaded her little cause like a Webster;* she had ranged from severity to pathos;* but her opponent employed that obstinate silence which makes eloquence futile with mocking echoes. Adoniram arose clumsily.

[Daniel] Webster (1782–1852): famous American speaker

pathos: a quality which arouses feelings of sympathy, pity, or sorrow

---

"Father, ain't you got nothin' to say?" said Mrs. Penn.

"I've got to go off after that load of gravel. I can't stan' here talkin' all day."

"Father, won't you think it over an' have a house built there instead of a barn?"

"I ain't got nothin' to say."

Adoniram shuffled out. Mrs. Penn went into her bedroom. When she came out, her eyes were red. She had a roll of unbleached cotton cloth. She spread it out on the kitchen table and began cutting out some shirts for her husband. The men over in the field had a team to help them this afternoon; she could hear their halloos. She had a scanty pattern for the shirts; she had to plan and piece the sleeves.

Nanny came home with her embroidery and sat down with her needlework. She had taken down her curl papers and there was a soft roll of fair hair like an aureole* over her forehead; her face was as delicately fine and clear as porcelain. Suddenly she looked up, and the tender red flamed all over her face and neck. "Mother," said she.

---

aureole: halo

"What say?"

"I've been thinking—I don't see how we're goin' to have any—wedding in this room. I'd be ashamed to have his folks come if we didn't have anybody else."

"Mebbe we can have some new paper before then; I can put it on. I guess you won't have no call to be ashamed of your belongin's."

"We might have the wedding in the new barn," said Nanny, with gentle pettishness. "Why, Mother, what makes you look so?"

Mrs. Penn had started, and was staring at her with a curious expression. She turned again to her work and spread out a pattern carefully on the cloth. "Nothin," said she.

Presently Adoniram clattered out of the yard in his two-wheeled dump cart, standing as proudly upright as a Roman charisoteer. Mrs. Penn opened the door and stood there a minute looking out; the halloos of the men sounded louder.

It seemed to her all through the spring months that she heard nothing but the halloos and the noises of saws and hammers. The new barn grew fast. It was a fine edifice for this little village. Men came on pleasant Sundays, in their meeting suits and clean shirt bosoms, and stood around it admiringly. Mrs. Penn did not speak of it, and Adoniram did not mention it to her, although sometimes, upon a return from

inspecting it, he bore himself with injured dignity.

"It's a strange thing how your mother feels about the new barn," he said, confidentially, to Sammy one day.

Sammy only grunted after an odd fashion for a boy; he had learned it from his father.

The barn was all completed ready for use by the third week in July. Adoniram had planned to move his stock in on Wednesday; on Tuesday he received a letter which changed his plans. He came in with it early in the morning. "Sammy's been to the post office," said he, "an I've got a letter from Hiram." Hiram was Mrs. Penn's brother, who lived in Vermont.

"Well," said Mrs. Penn, "what does he say about the folks?"

"I guess they're all right. He says he thinks if I come up country right off there's a chance to buy jest the kind of a horse I want." He stared reflectively out of the window at the new barn.

Mrs. Penn was making pies. She went on clapping the rolling pin into the crust, although she was very pale, and her heart beat loudly.

"I dun' know but what I'd better go," said Adoniram. "I hate to go off jest now, right in the midst of hayin', but the ten-acre lot's cut, an' I guess Rufus an' the others can git along without me three or four days. I can't get a horse round here to suit me, nohow, an' I've got to have another for all that wood haulin' in the fall. I told Hiram to watch out, an' if he got wind of a good horse to let me know. I guess I'd better go."

"I'll get out your clean shirt an' collar," said Mrs. Penn calmly.

She laid out Adoniram's Sunday suit and his clean clothes on the bed in the little bedroom. She got his shaving water and razor ready. At last she buttoned on his collar and fastened his black cravat.*

---

cravat: a fabric scarf worn as a tie

Adoniram never wore his collar and cravat except on extra occasions. He held his head high, with a rasped dignity. When he was all ready, with his coat and hat brushed, and a lunch of pie and cheese in a paper bag, he hesitated on the threshold of the door. He looked at his wife, and his manner was defiantly apologetic, "If them cows come today, Sammy can drive 'em into the new barn," said he; "an' when they bring the hay up, they can pitch it in there."

"Well," replied Mrs. Penn.

Adoniram set his shaven face ahead and started. When he had cleared the doorstep, he turned and looked back with a kind of nervous solemnity. "I shall be back by Saturday if nothin' happens," said he.

"Do be careful, Father," replied his wife.

She stood in the door with Nanny at her elbow and watched him out of sight. Her eyes had a strange, doubtful expression in them; her peaceful forehead was contracted. She went in and about her baking again. Nanny sat sewing. Her wedding day was drawing nearer, and she was getting pale and thin with her steady sewing. Her mother kept glancing at her.

"Have you got that pain in your side this mornin'?" she asked.

"A little."

Mrs. Penn's face, as she worked, changed, her perplexed forehead smoothed, her eyes were steady, her lips firmly set. She formed a maxim for herself, although incoherently with her unlettered thoughts. "Unsolicited opportunities are the guideposts of the Lord to the new roads of life," she repeated in effect, and she made up her mind to her course of action.

"S'posin' I *had* wrote to Hiram," she muttered once, when she was in the pantry—"s'posin' I had wrote an' asked him if he knew of any horse? But I didn't an' Father's goin' wa'n't none of my doin'. It looks like a providence."* Her voice rang out quite loud at the last.

---

providence: foreordained circumstance

"What you talkin' about, Mother?" called Nanny.

"Nothin'."

Mrs. Penn hurried her baking; at eleven o'clock it was all done. The load of hay from the west field came slowly down the cart track and drew up at the new barn. Mrs. Penn ran out. "Stop!" she screamed—"stop!"

The men stopped and looked; Sammy upreared from the top of the load and stared at his mother.

"Stop!" she cried out again. "Don't you put the hay in that barn; put it in the old one."

"Why, he said to put it in here," returned one of the haymakers, wonderingly. He was a young man, a neighbor's son, whom Adoniram hired by the year to help on the farm.

"Don't you put the hay in the new barn; there's room enough in the old one, ain't there?" said Mrs. Penn.

"Room enough," returned the hired man, in his thick, rustic tones. "Didn't need the new barn, nohow, far as room's concerned. Well, I s'pose he changed his mind." He took hold of the horses' bridles.

Mrs. Penn went back to the house. Soon the kitchen windows were darkened, and a fragrance like warm honey came into the room.

Nanny laid down her work. "I thought father wanted them to put the hay into the new barn?" she said wonderingly.

"It's all right," replied her mother.

Sammy slid down from the load of hay and came in to see if dinner was ready.

"I ain't goin' to get a regular dinner today, as long as Father's gone," said his mother. "I've let the fire go out. You can have some bread an' milk an' pie. I thought we could get along." She set out some bowls of milk, some bread, and a pie on the kitchen table. "You better eat your dinner now," said she. "You might jest as well get through with it. I want you to help me afterward."

Nanny and Sammy stared at each other. There was something strange in their mother's manner. Mrs. Penn did not eat anything herself. She went into the pantry, and they heard her moving dishes while they ate. Presently she came out with a pile of plates. She got the clothes basket out of the shed and packed them in it. Nanny and Sammy watched. She brought out cups and saucers and put them in with the plates.

"What you goin' to do, Mother?" inquired Nanny, in a timid voice. A sense of something unusual made her tremble, as if it were a ghost. Sammy rolled his eyes over his pie.

"You'll see what I'm goin' to do," replied Mrs. Penn. "If you're through, Nanny, I want you to go upstairs an' pack up your things; an' I want you, Sammy, to help me take down the bed in the bedroom."

"Oh, Mother, what for?" gasped Nanny.

"You'll see."

During the next few hours a feat was performed by the simple, pious New England mother which was equal in its way to Wolfe's storming of the Heights of Abraham.* It took no more genius and audacity of bravery for Wolfe to cheer his wondering soldiers up those steep precipices, under the sleeping eyes of the enemy, than for Sarah Penn, at the head of her children, to move all their little household goods into the new barn while her husband was away.

Heights of Abraham: a plain situated on top of some steep cliffs near the city of Quebec; the site where the English general Wolfe defeated the French general Montcalm in 1759

Nanny and Sammy followed their mother's instructions without a murmur; indeed, they were overawed. There is a certain un-

canny and superhuman quality about all such purely original undertakings as their mother's was to them. Nanny went back and forth with her light loads, and Sammy tugged with sober energy.

At five o'clock in the afternoon the little house in which the Penns had lived for forty years had emptied itself into the new barn.

Every builder builds somewhat for unknown purposes and is in a measure a prophet. The architect of Adoniram Penn's barn, while he designed it for the comfort of four-footed animals, had planned better than he knew for the comfort of humans. Sarah Penn saw at a glance its possibilities. Those great box stalls, with quilts hung before them, would make better bedrooms than the one she had occupied for forty years, and there was a tight carriage room. The harness room, with its chimney and shelves, would make a kitchen of her dreams. The great middle space would make a parlor, by and by, fit for a palace. Upstairs there was as much room as down. With partitions and windows, what a house would there be! Sarah looked at the row of stanchions* before the allotted space for the cows and reflected that she would have her front entry there.

---

stanchions: vertical posts

At six o'clock the stove was up in the harness room, the kettle was boiling, and the table was set for tea. It looked almost as homelike as the abandoned house across the yard had ever done. The young hired man milked, and Sarah directed him calmly to bring the milk to the new barn. He came gaping, dropping little blots of foam from the brimming pails on the grass. Before the next morning he had spread the story of Adoniram Penn's wife moving into the new barn all over the little village. Men assembled in the store and talked it over, women with shawls over their heads scuttled into each other's houses before their work was done. Any deviation from the ordinary course of life in this quiet town was enough to stop all progress in it. Everybody paused to look at the staid, independent figure on the side track. There was a difference of opinion with regard to her. Some held her to be insane; some, of a lawless and rebellious spirit.

Friday the minister went to see her. It was in the forenoon, and she was at the barn door shelling peas for dinner. She looked up and returned his salutation with dignity, then she went on with her work. She did not invite him in. The saintly expression of her face remained fixed, but there was an angry flush over it.

The minister stood awkwardly before her and talked. She handled the peas as if they were bullets. At last she looked up, and her eyes showed the spirit that her meek front had covered for a lifetime.

"There ain't no use talkin', Mr. Hersey," said she. "I've thought it all over, an' I believe I'm doin' what's right. I've made it the subject of prayer, an' it's betwixt me an' the Lord an' Adoniram. There ain't no call for nobody else to worry about it."

"Well, of course, if you have brought it to the Lord in prayer and feel satisfied that you are doing right, Mrs. Penn," said the minister, helplessly.

"I think it's right jest as much as I think it was right for our forefathers to come over from the old country 'cause they didn't have what belonged to 'em," said Mrs. Penn. She arose. The barn threshold might have been Plymouth Rock from her bearing. "I don't doubt you mean well, Mr. Hersey," said she, "but there are things people hadn't ought to interfere with. I've been a member of the church for over forty years. I've got my own mind an' my own feet, an' I'm goin' to think my own thoughts an' go my own ways, an' nobody but the Lord is goin' to dictate to me unless I've a mind to have

him. Won't you come in an' set down? How is Mis' Hersey?"

"She is well, I thank you," replied the minister. He added some more perplexed apologetic remarks; then he retreated.

He could expound the intricacies of every character study in the Scriptures, he was competent to grasp the Pilgrim Fathers and all historical innovators, but Sarah Penn was beyond him. He could deal with primal cases, but parallel ones worsted him. But, after all, although it was aside from his province, he wondered more how Adoniram Penn would deal with his wife than how the Lord would. Everybody shared the wonder. When Adoniram's four new cows arrived, Sarah ordered three to be put in the old barn, the other in the house shed where the cooking stove had stood. That added to the excitement. It was whispered that all four cows were domiciled in the house.

Toward sunset on Saturday, when Adoniram was expected home, there was a knot of men in the road near the new barn. The hired man had milked, but he still hung around the premises. Sarah Penn had supper all ready. There were brown bread and baked beans and a custard pie; it was the supper that Adoniram loved on a Saturday night. She had on a clean calico, and she bore herself imperturbably.* Nanny and Sammy kept close at her heels. Their eyes were large, and Nanny was full of nervous tremors. Still there was to them more pleasant excitement than anything else. An inborn confidence in their mother over their father asserted itself.

---

imperturbably: unshakably calmly

Sammy looked out of the harness-room window. "There he is," he announced, in an awed whisper. He and Nanny peeped around the casing. Mrs. Penn kept on about her work. The children watched Adoniram leave the new horse standing in the drive while he went to the house door. It was fastened. Then he went around to the shed. That door was seldom locked, even when the family was away. The thought how her father would be confronted by the cow flashed upon Nanny. There was a hysterical sob in her throat. Adoniram emerged from the shed and stood looking about in a dazed fashion. His lips moved. He was saying something, but they could not hear what it was. The hired man was peeping around a corner of the old barn, but nobody saw him.

Adoniram took the new horse by the bridle and led him across the yard to the new barn. Nanny and Sammy slunk close to their mother. The barn doors rolled back, and there stood Adoniram, with the long mild face of the great Canadian farm horse looking over his shoulder.

Nanny kept behind her mother, but Sammy stepped suddenly forward and stood in front of her.

Adoniram stared at the group. "What on airth you all down her for?" said he. "What's the matter over to the house?"

"We've come here to live, Father," said Sammy. His shrill voice quavered out bravely.

"What"—Adoniram sniffed—"what is it smells like cookin'?" said he. He stepped forward and looked in the open door of the harness room. Then he turned to his wife. His old bristling face was pale and frightened. "What on airth does this mean, Mother?" he gasped.

"You come in here, Father," said Sarah. She led the way into the harness room and shut the door. "Now, Father," said she, "you needn't be scared. I ain't crazy. There ain't nothin' to be upset over. But we've come here to live, an' we're goin' to live here. We've got jest as good a right here as new horses an' cows. The house wa'n't fit for us to live in any longer, an' I made up my mind I wa'n't goin' to stay there. I've done my duty by you forty year, an' I'm goin' to do it now; but I'm goin' to live here. You've got to put in some windows and partitions; an' you'll have to buy some furniture."

"Why, Mother!" the old man gasped.

"You'd better take your coat off an' get washed—there's the washbasin—and then we'll have supper."

"Why, Mother!"

Sammy went past the window, leading the new horse to the old barn. The old man saw him and shook his head speechlessly. He tried to take off his coat, but his arms seemed to lack the power. His wife helped him. She poured some water into the tin basin and put in a piece of soap. She got the comb and brush and smoothed his thin

gray hair after he had washed. Then she put the beans, hot bread, and tea on the table. Sammy came in, and the family drew up. Adoniram sat looking dazedly at his plate, and they waited.

"Ain't you goin' to ask a blessin', Father?" said Sarah. And the old man bent his head and mumbled.

All through the meal he stopped eating at intervals and stared furtively at his wife, but he ate well. The home food tasted good to him, and his old frame was too sturdily healthy to be affected by his mind. But after supper he went out and sat down on the step of the smaller door at the right of the barn, through which he had meant his Jerseys to pass in stately file, but which Sarah designed for her front house door, and he leaned his head on his hands.

After the supper dishes were cleared away and the milk pans washed, Sarah went out to him. The twilight was deepening. There was a clear green glow in the sky. Before them stretched the smooth level of field; in the distance was a cluster of haystacks like the huts of a village; the air was very cool and calm and sweet. The landscape might have been an ideal one of peace.

Sarah bent over and touched her husband on one of his thin, sinewy shoulders. "Father!"

The old man's shoulder heaved; he was weeping.

"Why, don't do so, Father," said Sarah.

"I'll—put up the—partitions, an'—everything you—want, Mother."

Sarah put her apron up to her face; she was overcome by her own triumph.

Adoniram was like a fortress whose walls had no active resistance and went down the instant the right besieging tools were used. "Why, Mother," he said, hoarsely, "I hadn't no idee you was so set on't as all this comes to."

About the Story

1. Explain why the main characters are considered round characters.

2. How does Sarah Penn get the idea of moving into the barn?

3. How does the community react to Mrs. Penn's revolt?

4. What evidence is there for calling Mr. Penn a dynamic character?

5. What character traits do Mr. and Mrs. Penn share? How are Mr. and Mrs. Penn different?

6. Peter tells us, "Yea, all of you be subject one to another, and be clothed with humility" (I Peter 5:5). In what ways do Mr. and Mrs. Penn fail to apply this principle in the story. In what ways do they succeed?

About the Author

Mary E. Wilkins Freeman (1852–1930) was born in Massachusetts and lived her whole life in New England. Her work reflects her intimate knowledge of the countryside and the people of that region. Her greatest talent was not in constructing plots but in creating characters. Many of Freeman's characters resemble her in that they bear quietly a great deal of heartache. By the time she was thirty-one, all Freeman's immediate family had died. After these losses, she lived with a childhood friend for many years, writing stories to help support herself and her aunt. Although she had been too sickly as a child to attend school regularly, she had read and learned to appreciate good literature.

She eventually married at fifty, but the marriage was an unhappy one, for her husband drank heavily, and she struggled with a hearing loss. She wrote little after her marriage, but among her life's accomplishments are her long employment as secretary to Oliver Wendell Holmes and her acquisition of several literary awards, one of which placed her among the first four women in the National Institute of Arts and Letters.

❧ THINKING ZONE ❧

Within a work of fiction, the descriptions, actions, and dialogue of well-drawn characters will always coax a response from the reader. The extent to which an author encourages a reader to respond favorably or unfavorably toward a character will lend support to the message that the author wishes to communicate. Characters that a reader favors or identifies with are known as **sympathetic characters**, while characters for whom the reader feels disdain are known as **unsympathetic characters**. Some authors encourage readers to find wicked characters sympathetic or virtuous characters unsympathetic; therefore, the Christian reader should thoughtfully examine each author's attitude toward the actions and attitudes of his characters.

While one may assume that flawed characters will always appear unsympathetic to the reader, this is not necessarily true. Within literary works known as **tragedies**, the protagonist's flaws cause him tremendous suffering that eventually results in a catastrophe, or disastrous conclusion. Consequently, though the protagonist in such works may not be a likable character, we nevertheless are led to sympathize with him because of the universality of his flaws and the severity of his woes. In these literary works, the protagonist is also the **tragic hero**, and his **tragic flaw**, or most significant flaw—often pride (known as hubris)—triggers his downfall. According to critics, tragedies not only cause us to feel pity for the protagonist but also instill the reader or viewer with a sense of fear. We take pity on the tragic hero because he suffers terribly, yet we also fear that the same unchecked weaknesses in our own lives may lead us to a similar fate. The true story of Samson from Judges 13–16 illustrates characteristics of the basic tragic plot, with the protagonist facing a ruinous end because of his flaw (lust) yet finally realizing his fallibility. Though Samson's initial hubris and rashness detract significantly from our sympathy, we eventually pity him because he suffers greatly because of his flaw.

1. Identify each of the following characters from *Treasure Island* as either sympathetic or unsympathetic: Jim Hawkins, Pew, Jim's mother, and Black Dog. Explain your answer for each character, identifying the traits that make each either **sympathetic** or **unsympathetic**.

2. Do you find Phaëthon sympathetic or unsympathetic? Explain.

3. How does Freeman encourage the reader to sympathize with Mrs. Penn in "The Revolt of Mother"?

4. Is the reader ever encouraged by Freeman to sympathize with Adoniram Penn?

5. Would it ever be morally permissible for an author to render a flawed character sympathetic to the reader? Can you think of any examples from the Bible?

6. Which of the four selections that you have read thus far in this unit best fits the definition of a **tragedy**? What is the catastrophe in that selection?

7. For the story you identified in the previous question, who is the **tragic hero**? What is his **tragic flaw**?

Neighbour Rosicky

Willa Cather

The characters in "Neighbour Rosicky" are based on a Bohemian family whom Cather knew. While reading this story, pay close attention to what Rosicky says, what others say about him, and what he does. What does this information reveal about his character? What are some qualities in Rosicky's character that make his influence on others believable?

I

When Doctor Burleigh told neighbour Rosicky he had a bad heart, Rosicky protested.

"So? No, I guess my heart was always pretty good. I got a little asthma, maybe. Just a awful short breath when I was pitchin' hay last summer, dat's all."

"Well now, Rosicky, if you know more about it than I do, what did you come to me for? It's your heart that makes you short of breath, I tell you. You're sixty-five years old, and you've always worked hard, and your heart's tired. You've got to be careful from now on, and you can't do heavy work any more. You've got five boys at home to do it for you."

The old farmer looked up at the Doctor with a gleam of amusement in his queer triangular-shaped eyes. His eyes were large and lively, but the lids were caught up in the middle in a curious way, so that they formed a triangle. He did not look like a sick man. His brown face was creased but not wrinkled; he had a ruddy colour in his smooth-shaven cheeks and in his lips, under his long brown moustache. His hair was thin and ragged around his ears, but very little gray. His forehead, naturally high and crossed by deep parallel lines, now ran all the way up to his pointed crown. Rosicky's face had the habit of looking interested—suggested a contented disposition and a reflective quality that was gay rather than grave. This gave him a certain detachment, the easy manner of an onlooker and observer.

"Well, I guess you ain't got no pills for a bad heart, Doctor Ed. I guess the only thing is fur me to git me a new one."

Doctor Burleigh swung round in his desk chair and frowned at the old farmer. "I think if I were you I'd take a little care of the old one, Rosicky."

Rosicky shrugged. "Maybe I don't know how. I expect you mean fur me not to drink my coffee no more."

"I wouldn't, in your place. But you'll do as you choose about that. I've never yet been able to separate a Bohemian from his coffee or his pipe. I've quit trying. But the sure thing is you've got to cut out farm work. You can feed the stock and do chores about the barn, but you can't do anything in the fields that makes you short of breath."

"How about shelling corn?"

"Of course not!"

Rosicky considered with puckered brows.

"I can't make my heart go no longer'n it wants to, can I, Doctor Ed?"

"I think it's good for five or six years yet, maybe more, if you'll take the strain off it. Sit around the house and help Mary. If I had a good wife like yours, I'd want to stay around the house."

His patient chuckled. "It ain't no place fur a man. I don't like no old man hanging round the kitchen too much. An' my wife, she's a awful hard worker her own self."

"That's it; you can help her a little. Rosicky, you are one of the few men I know who has a family he can get some comfort out of; happy dispositions, never quarrel among themselves, and they treat you right. I want to see you live a few years and enjoy them."

"Oh, they're good kids, all right," Rosicky assented.

The Doctor wrote him a prescription and asked him how his oldest son, Rudolph, who had married in the spring, was getting on. Rudolph had struck out for himself, on rented land. "And how's Polly? I was afraid Mary mightn't like an American daughter-in-law, but it seems to be working out all right."

"Yes, she's a fine girl. Dat widder woman bring her daughters up very nice. Polly got lots of spunk, an' she got some style, too. Da's nice, for young folks to have some style." Rosicky inclined his head gallantly. His voice and his twinkly smile were an affectionate compliment to his daughter-in-law.

"It looks like a storm, and you'd better be getting home before it comes. In town in the car?" Doctor Burleigh rose.

"No, I'm in de wagon. When you got five boys, you ain't got much chance to ride round in de Ford. I ain't much for cars, noway."

"Well, it's a good road out to your place; but I don't want you bumping around in a wagon much. And never again on a hay-rake, remember!"

Rosicky placed the Doctor's fee delicately behind the desk-telephone, looking the other way, as if this were an absent-minded gesture. He put on his plush cap and his corduroy jacket with a sheepskin collar, and went out.

The Doctor picked up his stethoscope and frowned at it as if he were seriously annoyed with the instrument. He wished it had been telling tales about some other man's heart, some old man who didn't look the Doctor in the eye so knowingly, or hold out such a warm brown hand when he said good-bye. Doctor Burleigh had been a poor boy in the country before he went away to medical school; he had known Rosicky almost ever since he could remember, and he had a deep affection for Mrs. Rosicky.

Only last winter he had had such a good breakfast at Rosicky's, and that when he needed it. He had been out all night on a long, hard confinement case at Tom Marshall's—a big rich farm where there was plenty of stock and plenty of feed and a great deal of expensive farm machinery of the newest model, and no comfort whatever. The woman had too many children and too much work, and she was no manager. When the baby was born at last, and handed over to the assisting neighbour woman, and the mother was properly attended to, Burleigh refused any breakfast in that slovenly house, and drove his buggy—the snow was too deep for a car—eight miles to Anton Rosicky's place. He didn't know another farm-house where a man could get such a warm welcome, and such good strong coffee with rich cream. No wonder the old chap didn't want to give up his coffee!

He had driven in just when the boys had come back from the barn and were washing up for breakfast. The long table, covered with a bright oilcloth,* was set out with dishes waiting for them, and the warm kitchen was full of the smell of coffee and hot biscuits and sausage. Five big handsome boys, running from twenty to twelve, all with what Burleigh called natural good manners—they hadn't a bit of the painful self-consciousness he himself had to struggle with when he was a lad. One ran to put his horse away, another helped him off with his fur coat and hung it up, and Josephine, the youngest child and the only daughter, quickly set another place under her mother's direction.

---

oilcloth: a material treated with clay, oil, and pigments to make the material waterproof

---

With Mary, to feed creatures was the natural expression of affection—her chickens, the calves, her big hungry boys. It was a rare pleasure to feed a young man whom she seldom saw and of whom she was as proud as if he belonged to her. Some country housekeepers would have stopped to spread a white cloth over the oilcloth, to change the thick cups and plates for their best china, and the wooden-handled knives for plate ones. But not Mary.

"You must take us as you find us, Doctor Ed. I'd be glad to put out my good things for you if you was expected, but I'm glad to get you any way at all."

He knew she was glad—she threw back her head and spoke out as if she were announcing him to the whole prairie. Rosicky hadn't said anything at all; he merely smiled his twinkling smile and put some more coal on the fire. When they were all seated, he watched his wife's face from his end of the table and spoke to her in Czech. Then, with the instinct of politeness which seldom failed him, he turned to the Doctor and said slyly: "I was just tellin' her not to ask you no questions about Mrs. Marshall till you eat some breakfast. My wife, she's terrible fur to ask questions."

The boys laughed, and so did Mary. She watched the Doctor devour her biscuit and sausage, too much excited to eat anything herself. She drank her coffee and sat taking in everything about her visitor. She had known him when he was a poor country boy, and was boastfully proud of his success, always saying: "What do people go to Omaha for, to see a doctor, when we got the best one in the State right here?" If Mary liked people at all, she felt physical pleasure in the sight of them, personal exultation in any good fortune that came to them. Burleigh didn't know many women like that, but he knew she was like that.

When his hunger was satisfied, he did, of course, have to tell them about Mrs. Marshall, and he noticed what a friendly interest the boys took in the matter.

Rudolph, the oldest one (he was still living at home then), said: "The last time I was over there, she was lifting them big heavy milkcans, and I knew she oughtn't to be doing it."

"Yes, Rudolph told me about that when he come home, and I said it wasn't right," Mary put in warmly. "It was all right for me to do them things up to the last, for I was terrible strong, but that woman's weakly. And do you think she'll be able to nurse it, Ed?"

She sometimes forgot to give him the title she was so proud of. "And to think of your being up all night and then not able to get a decent breakfast! I don't know what's the matter with such people."

"I wish I'd been in practice when these were getting born." The doctor looked down the row of close-clipped heads. "I missed some good breakfasts by not being."

The boys began to laugh at their mother because she flushed so red, but she stood her ground and threw up her head. "I don't care, you wouldn't have got away from this house without breakfast. No doctor ever did. I'd have had something ready fixed that Anton could warm up for you."

The boys laughed harder than ever, and exclaimed at her: "I'll bet you would!" "She would, that!"

"Father, did you get breakfast for the doctor when we were born?"

"Yes, and he used to bring me my breakfast, too, mighty nice. I was always awful hungry!" Mary admitted with a guilty laugh.

While the boys were getting the Doctor's horse, he went to the window to examine the house plants. "What do you do to your geraniums to keep them blooming all winter, Mary? I never pass this house that from the road I don't see your windows full of flowers."

She snapped off a dark red one, and a ruffled new green leaf, and put them in his button hole. "There, that looks better. You look too solemn for a young man, Ed. Why don't you git married? I'm worried about you. Settin' at breakfast, I looked at you real hard, and I seen you've got some grey hairs already."

"Oh, yes! They're coming. Maybe they'd come faster if I married."

"Don't talk so. You'll ruin your health eating at the hotel. I could send your wife a nice loaf of nut bread, if you only had one. I don't like to see a young man getting grey. I'll tell you something, Ed; you make some strong black tea and keep it handy in a bowl, and every morning just brush it into your hair, an' it'll keep the grey from showin' much. That's the way I do!"

Sometimes the Doctor heard the gossipers in the drug-store wondering why Rosicky didn't get on faster. He was industrious, and so were his boys, but they were rather free and easy, weren't pushers, and they didn't always show good judgment. They were comfortable, they were out of debt, but they didn't get much ahead. Maybe, Doctor Burleigh reflected, people as generous and warm-hearted and affectionate as the Rosickys never got ahead much; maybe you couldn't enjoy your life and put it into the bank, too.

II

When Rosicky left Doctor Burleigh's office, he went into the farm-implement store to light his pipe and put on his glasses and read over the list Mary had given him. Then he went into the general merchandise place next door and stood about until the pretty girl with the plucked eyebrows, who always waited on him, was free. Those eyebrows, two thin India-ink strokes, amused him, because he remembered how they used to be. Rosicky always prolonged his shopping by a little joking; the girl knew the old fellow admired her, and she liked to chaff with him.

"Seems to me about every other week you buy ticking, Mr. Rosicky, and always the best quality," she remarked as she measured off the heavy bolt with red stripes.

"You see, my wife is always makin' goose-fedder pillows, an' de thin stuff don't hold in dem little down-fedders."

"You must have lots of pillows at your house."

"Sure. She makes quilts of dem, too. We sleeps easy. Now she's makin' a fedder quilt for my son's wife. You know Polly, that married my Rudolph. How much my bill, Miss Pearl?"

"Eight eighty-five."

"Chust make it nine, and put in some candy fur de women."

"As usual. I never did see a man buy so much candy for his wife. First thing you know, she'll be getting too fat."

"I'd like dat. I ain't much fur all dem slim women like what de style is now."

"That's one for me, I suppose, Mr. Bohunk!"* Pearl sniffed and elevated her India-ink strokes.

---

*Bohunk: slang term (now considered offensive) for a laborer from east-central Europe

---

When Rosicky went out to his wagon, it was beginning to snow—the first snow of the season, and he was glad to see it. He rattled out of town and along the highway through a wonderfully rich stretch of country, the finest farms in the county. He admired this High Prairie, as it was called, and always liked to drive through it. His own place lay in a rougher territory, where there was some clay in the soil and it was not so productive. When he bought his land, he hadn't the money to buy on High Prairie; so he told his boys, when they grumbled, that if their land hadn't some clay in it, they wouldn't own it at all. All the same, he enjoyed looking at these fine farms, as he enjoyed looking at a prize bull.

After he had gone eight miles, he came to the graveyard, which lay just at the edge of his own hay-land. There he stopped his horses and sat still on his wagon seat, looking about at the snowfall. Over yonder on the hill he could see his own house, crouching low, with the clump of orchard behind and the windmill before, and all down the gentle hill-slope the rows of pale gold cornstalks stood out against the white field. The snow was falling over the cornfield and the pasture and the hay-land, steadily, with very little wind—a nice dry snow. The graveyard had only a light wire fence about it and was all overgrown with long red grass. The fine snow, settling into this red grass and upon the few little evergreens and the headstones, looked very pretty.

It was a nice graveyard, Rosicky reflected, sort of snug and homelike, not cramped or mournful—a big sweep all round it. A man could lie down in the long grass and see the complete arch of the sky over him, hear the wagons go by; in summer the mowing-machine rattled right up to the wire fence. And it was so near home. Over there across the cornstalks his own roof and windmill looked so good to him that he promised himself to mind the Doctor and take care of himself. He was awful fond of his place, he admitted. He wasn't anxious to leave it. And it was a comfort to think that he would never have to go farther than the edge of his own hayfield. The snow, falling over his barnyard and the graveyard, seemed to draw things together like. And they were all old neighbours in the graveyard, most of them friends; there was nothing to feel awkward or embarrassed about. Embarrassment was the most disagreeable feeling Rosicky knew. He didn't often have it—only with certain people whom he didn't understand at all.

Well, it was a nice snowstorm; a fine sight to see the snow falling so quietly and graciously over so much open country. On his cap and shoulders, on the horses' backs and manes, light, delicate, mysterious it fell; and with it a dry cool fragrance was released into the air. It meant rest for vegetation and men and beasts, for the ground itself; a season of long nights for sleep, leisurely breakfasts, peace by the fire. This and much more went through Rosicky's mind, but he merely told himself that winter was coming, clucked to his horses, and drove on.

When he reached home, John, the youngest boy, ran out to put away his team for him, and he met Mary coming up from the outside cellar with her apron full of carrots. They went into the house together. On the table, covered with oilcloth figured with clusters of blue grapes, a place was set, and he smelled hot coffee-cake of some kind. Anton never lunched in town; he thought that extravagant, and anyhow he didn't like the food. So Mary always had something ready for him when he got home.

After he was settled in his chair, stirring his coffee in a big cup, Mary took out of the oven a pan of *kolache** stuffed with apricots, examined them anxiously to see whether they had got too dry, put them beside his plate, and then sat down opposite him.

kolache: a rich pastry with a fruit or poppyseed filling

Rosicky asked her in Czech if she wasn't going to have any coffee.

She replied in English, as being somehow the right language for transacting business: "Now what did Doctor Ed say, Anton? You tell me just what."

"He said I was to tell you some compliments, but I forgot 'em." Rosicky's eyes twinkled.

"About you, I mean. What did he say about your asthma?"

"He says I ain't got no asthma." Rosicky took one of the little rolls in his broad brown fingers. The thickened nail of his right thumb told the story of his past.

"Well, what is the matter? And don't try to put me off."

"He don't say nothing much, only I'm a little older, and my heart ain't so good like it used to be."

Mary started and brushed her hair back from her temples with both hands as if she were a little out of her mind. From the way she glared, she might have been in a rage with him.

"He says there's something the matter with your heart? Doctor Ed says so?"

"Now don't yell at me like I was a hog in de garden, Mary. You know I always did like to hear a woman talk soft. He didn't say anything de matter wid my heart, only it ain't so young like it used to be, an' he tell me not to pitch hay or run de corn-sheller."

Mary wanted to jump up, but she sat still. She admired the way he never under any circumstances raised his voice or spoke roughly. He was city-bred, and she was country-bred; she often said she wanted her boys to have their papa's nice ways.

"You never have no pain there, do you? It's your breathing and your stomach that's been wrong. I wouldn't believe nobody but Doctor Ed about it. I guess I'll go see him myself. Didn't he give you no advice?"

"Chust to take it easy like, an' stay round de house dis winter. I guess you got some carpenter work for me to do. I kin make some new shelves for you, and I want dis long time to build a closet in de boys room and make dem two little fellers keep dere clo'es hung up."

Rosicky drank his coffee from time to time, while he considered. His moustache was of the soft long variety and came down over his mouth like the teeth of a buggy-rake over a bundle of hay. Each time he put down his cup, he ran his blue handkerchief over his lips. When he took a drink of water, he managed very neatly with the back of his hand.

Mary sat watching him intently, trying to find any change in his face. It is hard to see anyone who has become like your own body to you. Yes, his hair had got thin, and his high forehead had deep lines running from left to right. But his neck, always clean shaved except in the busiest seasons, was not loose or baggy. It was burned a dark reddish brown, and there were deep creases in it, but it looked firm and full of blood. His cheeks had a good colour. On either side of his mouth there was a half-moon down the length of his cheek, not wrinkles, but two lines that had come there from his habitual expression. He was shorter and broader than when she married him; his back had grown broad and curved, a good deal like the shell of an old turtle, and his arms and legs were short.

He was fifteen years older than Mary, but she had hardly ever thought about it before. He was her man, and the kind of man she liked. She was rough, and he was gentle—city-bred, as she always said. They had been shipmates on a rough voyage and had stood by each other in trying times. Life had gone well with them because, at bottom, they had the same ideas about life. They agreed, without discussion, as to what was most important and what was secondary. They didn't often exchange opinions, even in Czech—it was as if they had thought the same thought together. A good deal had to be sacrificed and thrown overboard in a hard life like theirs, and they had never disagreed as to the things that could go. It had been a hard life, and a soft life, too. There wasn't anything brutal in the short, broad-backed man with the three-cornered eyes and the forehead that went on to the top of his skull. He was a city man, a gentle man, and though he had married a rough farm girl, he had never touched her without gentleness.

They had been at one accord not to hurry through life, not to be always skimping and saving. They saw their neighbours buy more land and feed more stock than they did, without discontent. Once when the creamery agent came to the Rosickys to persuade them to sell him their cream, he told them how much money the Fasslers, their nearest neighbours, had made on their cream last year.

"Yes," said Mary, "and look at them Fassler children! Pale, pinched little things, they look like skimmed milk. I'd rather put some colour into my children's faces than put money into the bank."

The agent shrugged and turned to Anton.

"I guess we'll do like she says," said Rosicky.

III

Mary very soon got into town to see Doctor Ed, and then she had a talk with her boys and set a guard over Rosicky. Even John, the youngest, had his father on his mind. If Rosicky went to throw hay down from the loft, one of the boys ran up the ladder and took the fork from him. He sometimes complained that though he was getting to be an old man, he wasn't an old woman yet.

That winter he stayed in the house in the afternoons and carpentered, or sat in the chair between the window full of plants and the wooden bench where the two pails of drinking-water stood. This spot was called "Father's corner," though it was not a corner at all. He had a shelf there, where he kept his Bohemian papers and his pipes and tobacco, and his shears and needles and thread and tailor's thimble. Having been a tailor in his youth, he couldn't bear to see a woman patching at his clothes, or at the boys'. He liked tailoring, and always patched all the overalls

and jackets and work shirts. Occasionally he made over a pair of pants one of the older boys had outgrown, for the little fellow.

While he sewed, he let his mind run back over his life. He had a good deal to remember, really; life in three countries. The only part of his youth he didn't like to remember was the two years he had spent in London, in Cheapside, working for a German tailor who was wretchedly poor. Those days, when he was nearly always hungry when his clothes were dropping off him for dirt, and the sound of a strange language kept him in continual bewilderment, had left a sore spot in his mind that wouldn't bear touching.

He was twenty when he landed at Castle Garden in New York, and he had a protector who got him work in a tailor shop in Vesey Street, down near the Washington Market. He looked upon that part of his life as very happy. He became a good workman, he was industrious, and his wages were increased from time to time. He minded his own business and envied nobody's good fortune. He went to night school and learned to read English. He often did overtime work and was well paid for it, but somehow he never saved anything. He couldn't refuse a loan to a friend, and he was self-indulgent. He often stood through an opera on Saturday nights; he could get standing-room for a dollar. Those were the great days of opera in New York, and it gave a fellow something to think about for the rest of the week. Rosicky had a quick ear, and a childish love of all the stage splendour; the scenery, the costumes, the ballet. It was a fine life; for the first five years or so it satisfied him completely. He was never hungry or cold or dirty, and everything amused him: a fire, a dog fight, a parade, a storm, a ferry ride. He thought New York the finest, richest, friendliest city in the world.

Moreover, he had what he called a happy home life. Very near the tailor shop was a small furniture-factory, where an old Austrian, Loeffler, employed a few skilled men and made unusual furniture, most of it to order, for the rich German housewives up-town. The top floor of Loeffler's five-storey factory was a loft, where he kept his choice lumber and stored the odd pieces of furniture left on his hands. One of the young workmen he employed was a Czech, and he and Rosicky became fast friends. They persuaded Loeffler to let them have a sleeping-room in one corner of the loft. They bought good beds and bedding and had their pick of the furniture kept up there. The loft was low-pitched, but light and airy, full of windows, and good-smelling by reason of the fine lumber put up there to season. Old Loeffler used to go down to the docks and buy wood from South America and the East from the sea captains. The young men were as foolish about their house as a bridal pair. Zichec, the young cabinet-maker, devised every sort of convenience, and Rosicky kept their clothes in order. At night and on Sundays, when the quiver of machinery underneath was still, it was the quietest place in the world, and on summer nights all the sea winds blew in. Zichec often practiced on his flute in the evening. They were both fond of music and went to the opera together. Rosicky thought he wanted to live like that for ever.

But as the years passed, all alike, he began to get a little restless. When spring came round, he would begin to feel fretted. He never had time to figure out what ailed him, though he knew something did. When the grass turned green in Park Place, and the lilac hedge at the back of Trinity churchyard put out its blossoms, he was tormented by a longing to run away.

Rosicky, the old Rosicky, could remember as if it were yesterday the day when the young Rosicky found out what was the matter with him. It was on a Fourth of July afternoon, and he was sitting in Park Place in the sun. The lower part of New York was empty. Wall Street, Liberty Street, Broadway, all empty. So much stone and asphalt with nothing going on, so many empty windows. The emptiness was intense, like the stillness in a great factory when the machinery stops and the belts and bands cease running. It was too great a change, it took all the strength out of one. Those blank buildings, without the stream of life pouring through them, were like empty jails. It struck young Rosicky that this was the trouble with big cities; they built you in from the earth itself, cemented you away from any contact with the ground. You lived in an unnatural world, like the fish in an aquarium, who were probably much more comfortable than they ever were in the sea.

On that very day he began to think seriously about the articles he had read in the Bohemian papers, describing prosperous Czech farming communities in the West. He believed he would like to go out there as a farm hand; it was hardly possible that he could ever have land of his own. His people had always been workmen; his father and grandfather had worked in shops. His mother's parents had lived in the country, but they rented their farm and had a hard time to get along. Nobody in his family had ever owned any land—that belonged to a different station of life altogether. Anton's mother died when he was little, and he was sent into the country to her parents. He stayed with them until he was twelve, and formed those ties with the earth and the farm animals and growing things which are never made at all unless they are made early. After his grandfather died, he went back to live with his father and stepmother, but she was very hard on him and his father helped him to get passage to London.

After that Fourth of July day in Park Place, the desire to return to the country never left him. To work on another man's farm would be all he asked; to see the sun rise and set and to plant things and watch them grow. He was a very simple man. He was like a tree that has not many roots, but one tap-root that goes down deep. He subscribed for a Bohemian paper printed in Chicago, then for one printed in Omaha. His mind got farther and farther west. He began to save a little money to buy his liberty. When he was thirty-five, there was a great meeting in New York of Bohemian athletic societies, and Rosicky left the tailor shop and went home with the Omaha delegates to try his fortune in another part of the world.

IV

Perhaps the fact that his own youth was well over before he began to have a family was one reason why Rosicky was so fond of his boys. He had almost a grandfather's indulgence for them. He had never had to worry about any of them—except, just now, a little about Rudolph.

On Saturday night the boys always piled into the Ford, took little Josephine, and went to town. One Saturday morning they were talking at the breakfast table about starting early that evening, so that they would have an hour or so to see the Christmas things in the stores. Rosicky looked down the table.

"I hope you boys ain't disappointed, but I want you to let me have de car tonight. Maybe some of you go in with de neighbours."

Their faces fell. They worked hard all week, and they were still like children. A new jackknife or a box of candy pleased the older ones as much as the little fellow.

"If you and Mother are going to town," Frank said, "maybe you could take a couple of us along with you, anyway."

"No, I want to take de car down to Rudolph's, and let him an' Polly go in. She don't git into town enough, an' I'm afraid she's gettin' lonesome, an' he can't afford no car yet."

That settled it. The boys were a good deal dashed. Their father took another piece of apple-cake and went on: "Maybe next Saturday night de two little fellers can go along wid dem."

"Oh, is Rudolph going to have the car every Saturday night?"

Rosicky did not reply at once; then he began to speak seriously: "Listen, boys; Polly ain't lookin' so good. I don't like to see nobody lookin' sad. It comes hard fur a town girl to be a farmer's wife. I don't want no trouble to start in Rudolph's family. When it starts, it ain't so easy to stop. An American girl don't git used to our ways all at once. I like to tell Polly she and Rudolph can have the car every Saturday night till after New Year's, if it's all right with you boys."

"Sure it's all right, Papa," Mary cut in. "And it's good you thought about that. Town girls is used to more than country girls. I lay awake nights, scared she'll make Rudolph discontented with the farm."

The boys put as good a face on it as they could. They surely looked forward to their Saturday nights in town. That evening Rosicky drove the car the half-mile down to Rudolph's new, bare little house.

Polly was in a short-sleeved gingham dress, clearing away the supper dishes. She was a trim, slim little thing, with blue eyes and shingled yellow hair, and her eyebrows were reduced to a mere brush-stroke, like Miss Pearl's.

"Good evening, Mr. Rosicky. Rudolph's at the barn, I guess." She never called him father, or Mary mother. She was sensitive about having married a foreigner. She never in the world would have done it if Rudolph hadn't been such a handsome, persuasive fellow and such a gallant lover. He had graduated in her class in the high school in town, and their friendship began in the ninth grade.

Rosicky went in, though he wasn't exactly asked. "My boys ain't goin' to town tonight, an' I brought de car over fur you two to go."

Polly, carrying dishes to the sink, looked over her shoulder at him. "Thank you. But I'm late with my work tonight, and pretty tired. Maybe Rudolph would like to go in with you."

"You won't feel so tired after you ride in de air a ways. It's a nice clear night, an' it ain't cold. You go an' fix yourself up, Polly, an' I'll wash de dishes an' leave everything nice fur you."

Polly blushed and tossed her bob. "I couldn't let you do that, Mr. Rosicky. I wouldn't think of it."

Rosicky said nothing. He found a bib apron on a nail behind the kitchen door. He slipped it over his head and then took Polly by her two elbows and pushed her gently toward the door of her own room. "I washed up de kitchen many times for my wife, when de babies was sick or somethin'. You go an' make yourself look nice. I like you to look prettier'n any of dem town girls when you go in. De young folks must have some fun, an' I'm goin' to look out fur you, Polly."

That kind, reassuring grip on her elbows, the old man's funny bright eyes, made Polly want to drop her head on his shoulder for a second. She restrained herself, but she lingered in his grasp at the door of her room, murmuring tearfully: "You always lived in the city when you were young, didn't you? Don't you ever get lonesome out here?"

As she turned round to him, her hand fell naturally into his, and he stood holding it and smiling into her face with his peculiar, knowing, indulgent smile without a shadow of reproach in it. "Dem big cities is all right fur de rich, but dey is terrible hard fur de poor."

"I don't know. Sometimes I think I'd like to take a chance. You lived in New York, didn't you?"

"An' London. Da's bigger still. I learned my trade dere. Here's Rudolph comin', you better hurry."

"Will you tell me about London sometime?"

"Maybe. Only I ain't no talker, Polly. Run an' dress yourself up."

The bedroom door closed behind her, and Rudolph came in from the outside, looking anxious. He had seen the car and was sorry any of his family should come just then. Supper hadn't been a very pleasant occasion. Halting in the doorway, he saw his father in a kitchen apron, carrying dishes to the sink. He flushed crimson and something flashed in his eye. Rosicky held up a warning finger.

"I brought de car over fur you an' Polly to go into town an' I made her let me finish here so you won't be late. You go put on a clean shirt, quick!"

"But don't the boys want the car, Father?"

"Not tonight dey don't." Rosicky fumbled under his apron and found his pants pocket. He took out a silver dollar and said in a hurried whisper: "You go an' buy dat girl some ice cream an' candy tonight, like you was courtin'. She's awful good friends wid me."

Rudolph was very short of cash, but he took the money as if it hurt him. There had been a crop failure all over the county. He had more than once been sorry he'd married this year.

In a few minutes the young people came out, looking clean and a little stiff. Rosicky hurried them off, and then he took his own time with the dishes. He scoured the pots and pans and put away the milk and swept the kitchen. He put some coal in the stove and shut off the draughts, so the place would be warm for them when they got home late at night. Then he sat down and had a pipe and listened to the clock tick.

Generally speaking, marrying an American girl was certainly a risk. A Czech should marry a Czech. It was lucky that Polly was the daughter of a poor widow woman; Rudolph was proud, and if she had a prosperous family to throw up at him, they could never make it go. Polly was one of four sisters, and they all worked; one was bookkeeper in the bank, one taught music, and Polly and her younger sister had been clerks, like Miss Pearl. All four of them were musical, had pretty voices, and sang in the Methodist choir, which the eldest sister directed.

Polly missed the sociability of a store position. She missed the choir, and the company of her sisters. She didn't dislike housework, but she disliked so much of it. Rosicky was a little anxious about this pair. He was afraid Polly would grow so discontented that Rudy would quit the farm and take a factory job in Omaha. He had worked for a winter up there, two years ago, to get money to marry on. He had done very well, and they would always take him back at the stockyards. But to Rosicky that meant the end of everything for his son. To be a landless man was to be a wage-earner, a slave, all your life; to have nothing, to be nothing.

Rosicky thought he would come over and do a little carpentering for Polly after the New Year. He guessed she needed jollying. Rudolph was a serious sort of chap, serious in love and serious about his work.

Rosicky shook out his pipe and walked home across the fields. Ahead of him the lamplight shone from his kitchen windows. Suppose he were still in a tailor shop on Vesey Street, with a bunch of pale, narrow-chested sons working on machines, all coming home tired and sullen to eat supper in a kitchen that was a parlour also; with another crowded, angry family quarrelling just across the dumbwaiter shaft, and squeaking pulleys at the windows where dirty washings hung on dirty lines above a court full of old brooms and mops and ash-cans . . . .

He stopped by the windmill to look up at the frosty winter stars and draw a long breath before he went inside. That kitchen with the shining windows was dear to him; but the sleeping fields and bright stars and the noble darkness were dearer still.

About the Story

1. Judging from the title of the story, what sort of person would you believe Rosicky to be?

2. What does the description of Rosicky on page 117 suggest about his character?

3. In what ways are Anton (Rosicky) and Mary the same? In what ways are they different?

4. Is Mary a round or flat character? Is she sympathetic or unsympathetic? Explain your answer.

5. Explain the following description of Mary and Anton's life together: "It had been a hard life, and a soft life, too" (p. 124). How does this seemingly contradictory statement make sense when read in the context of this story?

V

On the day before Christmas the weather set in very cold; no snow, but a bitter, biting wind that whistled and sang over the flat land and lashed one's face like fine wires. There was baking going on in the Rosicky kitchen all day, and Rosicky sat inside, making over a coat that Albert had outgrown into an overcoat for John. Mary had a big red geranium in bloom for Christmas, and a row of Jerusalem cherry trees, full of berries. It was the first year she had ever grown these; Doctor Ed brought her the seeds from Omaha when he went to some medical convention. They reminded Rosicky of plants he had seen in England; and all afternoon, as he stitched, he sat thinking about those two years in London, which his mind usually shrank from even after all this while.

He was a lad of eighteen when he dropped down into London, with no money and no connections except the address of a cousin who was supposed to be working at a confectioner's. When he went to the pastry shop, however, he found that the cousin had gone to America. Anton tramped the streets for several days, sleeping in doorways and on the Embankment, until he was in utter despair. He knew no English, and the sound of the strange language all about him confused him. By chance he met a poor German tailor who had learned his trade in Vienna, and could speak a little Czech. This tailor, Lifschnitz, kept a repair shop in a Cheapside basement, underneath a cobbler. He didn't much need an apprentice, but he was sorry for the boy and took him in for no wages but his keep and what he could pick up. The

brick court, four flights down. There were bugs in the place, and multitudes of fleas, though the poor woman did the best she could. Rosicky knew she often went empty to give another potato or a spoonful of dripping to the two hungry, sad-eyed boys who lodged with her. He used to think he would never get out of there, never get a clean shirt to his back again. What would he do, he wondered, when his clothes actually dropped to pieces and the worn cloth wouldn't hold patches any longer?

It was still early when the old farmer put aside his sewing and his recollections. The sky had been a dark grey all day, with not a gleam of sun, and the light failed at four o'clock. He went to shave and change his shirt while the turkey was roasting. Rudolph and Polly were coming over for supper.

After supper they sat round in the kitchen, and the younger boys were saying how sorry they were it hadn't snowed. Everybody was sorry. They wanted a deep snow that would lie long and keep the wheat warm, and leave the ground soaked when it melted.

"Yes, sir!" Rudolph broke out fiercely; "if we have another dry year like last year, there's going to be hard times in this country."

Rosicky filled his pipe. "You boys don't know what hard times is. You don't owe nobody, you got plenty to eat an' keep warm, an' plenty of water to keep clean. When you got them, you can't have it very hard."

Rudolph frowned, opened and shut his big right hand, and dropped it clenched upon his knee. "I've got to have a good deal more than that, Father, or I'll quit this farming gamble. I can always make good wages railroading, or at the packing house and be sure of my money."

"Maybe so," his father answered dryly.

Mary, who had just come in from the pantry and was wiping her hands on the roller towel, thought Rudy and his father

pickings were supposed to be coppers given you when you took work home to a customer. But most of the customers called for their clothes themselves, and the coppers that came Anton's way were very few. He had, however, a place to sleep. The tailor's family lived upstairs in three rooms; a kitchen, a bedroom, where Lifschnitz and his wife and five children slept, and a living-room. Two corners of this living-room were curtained off for lodgers; in one Rosicky slept on an old horsehair sofa, with a feather quilt to wrap himself in. The other corner was rented to a wretched, dirty boy, who was studying the violin. He actually practiced there. Rosicky was dirty, too. There was no way to be anything else. Mrs. Lifschnitz got the water she cooked and washed with from a pump in a

were getting too serious. She brought her darning-basket and sat down in the middle of the group.

"I ain't much afraid of hard times, Rudy," she said heartily. "We've had a plenty, but we've always come through. Your father wouldn't never take nothing very hard, not even hard times. I got a mind to tell you a story on him. Maybe you boys can't hardly remember the year we had that terrible hot wind that burned everything up on the Fourth of July? All the corn an' the gardens. An' that was in the days when we didn't have alfalfa yet—I guess it wasn't invented.

"Well, that very day your father was out cultivatin' corn, and I was here in the kitchen makin' plum preserves. We had bushels of plums that year. I noticed it was terrible hot, but it's always hot in the kitchen when you're preservin', an' I was too busy with my plums to mind. Anton come in from the field about three o'clock, an' I asked him what was the matter.

"'Nothin',' he says, 'but it's pretty hot, an' I think I won't work no more today.' He stood round for a few minutes, an' then he says: 'Ain't you near through? I want you should git up a nice supper for us tonight. It's Fourth of July.'

"I told him to git along, that I was right in the middle of preservin', but the plums would taste good on hot biscuit. 'I'm goin' to have fried chicken, too,' he says, and he went off an' killed a couple. You three oldest boys was little fellers, playin' round outside, real hot an' sweaty, an' your father took you to the horse tank down by the windmill an' took off your clothes an' put you in. Them two box-elder trees was little then, but they made shade over the tank. Then he took off all his own clothes, an' got in with you. While he was playin' in the water with you, the Methodist preacher drove into our place to say how all the neighbours was goin' to meet at the schoolhouse that night, to pray for rain. He drove right to the windmill, of course, and there was your father and you three with no clothes on. I was in the kitchen door, an' I had to laugh, for the preacher acted like he ain't never seen a naked man before. He surely was embarrassed, an' your father couldn't git to his clothes; they was all hangin' up on the windmill to let the sweat dry out of 'em. So he laid in the tank where he was, an' put one of you boys on top of him to cover him up a little, an' talked to the preacher.

"When you got through playin' in the water, he put clean clothes on you and a clean shirt on himself, an' by that time I'd begun to get supper. He says: 'It's too hot in here to eat comfortable. Let's have a picnic in the orchard. We'll eat our supper behind the mulberry hedge, under them linden trees.'

"So he carried our supper down, an' everything tasted good, I can tell you. The wind got cooler as the sun was goin' down, and it turned out pleasant, only I noticed how the leaves was curled up on the linden trees. That made me think, an' I asked your father if that hot wind all day hadn't been terrible hard on the gardens an' the corn.

"'Corn,' he says, 'there ain't no corn.'

"'What you talkin' about?' I said. 'Ain't we got forty acres?'

"'We ain't got an ear,' he says, 'nor nobody else ain't got none. All the corn in this country was cooked by three o'clock today, like you'd roasted it in an oven.'

"'You mean you won't get no crop at all?' I asked him. I couldn't believe it, after he'd worked so hard.

"'No crop this year,' he says. 'That's why we're havin' a picnic. We might as well enjoy what we got.'

"An' that's how your father behaved, when all the neighbours was so discouraged they couldn't look you in the face. An' we enjoyed ourselves that year, poor as we was, an' our neighbours wasn't a bit better off for bein' miserable. Some of 'em grieved till they got poor digestions and couldn't relish what they did have."

The younger boys said they thought their father had the best of it. But Rudolph was thinking that, all the same, the neighbours had managed to get ahead more, in the fifteen years since that time. There must be something wrong about his father's way of doing things. He wished he knew what was going on in the back of Polly's mind. He knew she liked his father, but he knew, too, that she was afraid of something. When his mother sent over coffee-cake or prune tarts or a loaf of fresh bread, Polly seemed to regard them with a certain suspicion. When she observed to him that his brothers had nice manners, her tone implied that it was remarkable they should have. With his mother she was stiff and on her guard. Mary's hearty frankness and gusts of good humor irritated her. Polly was afraid of being unusual or conspicuous in any way, of being "ordinary," as she said!

When Mary had finished her story, Rosicky laid aside his pipe.

"You boys like me to tell you about some of dem hard times I been through in London?" Warmly encouraged, he sat rubbing his forehead along the deep creases. It was bothersome to tell a long story in English (he nearly always talked to the boys in Czech), but he wanted Polly to hear this one.

"Well, you know about dat tailor shop I worked in in London? I had one Christmas dere I ain't never forgot. Times was awful bad before Christmas; de boss ain't got much work, an' have it awful hard to pay his rent. It ain't so much fun, bein' poor in a big city like London, I'll say! All de windows is full of good t'ings to eat, an' all de pushcarts in de streets is full, an' you smell 'em all de time, an' you ain't got no money—not a bit. I

didn't mind de cold so much, though I didn't have no overcoat, chust a short jacket I'd outgrowed so it wouldn't meet on me, an' my hands was chapped raw. But I always had a good appetite, like you all know, an' de sight of dem pork pies in de windows was awful fur me!

"Day before Christmas was terrible foggy dat year, an' dat fog gits into your bones and makes you all damp like. Mrs. Lifschnitz didn't give us nothin' but a little bread an' drippin' for supper, because she was savin' to try for to give us a good dinner on Christmas Day. After supper de boss say I can go an' enjoy myself, so I went into de streets to listen to de Christmas singers. Dey sing old songs an' make very nice music, an' I run round after dem a good ways, till I got awful hungry. I t'ink maybe if I go home, I can sleep till morning an' forgit my belly.

"I went into my corner real quiet, and roll up in my fedder quilt. But I ain't got my head down, till I smell somet'ing good. Seem like it git stronger an' stronger, an' I can't git to sleep noway. I can't understand dat smell. Dere was a gas light in a hall across de court, dat always shine in at my window a little. I got up an' look around. I got a little wooden box in my corner fur a stool, 'cause I ain't got no chair. I picks up dat box, and under it dere is a roast goose on a platter! I can't believe my eyes. I carry it to de window where de light comes in, an' touch it and smell it to find out, an' den I taste it to be sure. I say, I will eat chust one little bite of dat goose, so I can go to sleep, and tomorrow I won't eat none at all. But I tell you, boys, when I stop, one half of dat goose was gone!

The narrator bowed his head, and the boys shouted. But little Josephine slipped behind his chair and kissed him on the neck beneath his ear.

"Poor little Papa, I don't want him to be hungry!"

"Da's long ago, child. I ain't never been hungry since I had your mudder to cook fur me."

"Go on and tell us the rest, please," said Polly.

"Well, when I come to realize what I done, of course, I felt terrible. I felt better in de stomach, but very bad in de heart. I set on my bed wid dat platter on my knees, an' it all come to me; how hard dat poor woman save to buy dat goose, and how she get some neighbour to cook it dat got more fire, an' how she put it in my corner to keep it away from dem hungry children. Dey was a old carpet hung up to shut my corner off, an' de children wasn't allowed to go in dere. An' I know she put it in my corner because she trust me more'n she did de violin boy. I can't stand it to face her after I spoil de Christmas. So I put on my shoes and go out into de city. I tell myself I better throw myself in de river; but I guess I ain't dat kind of a boy.

"It was after twelve o'clock, an terrible cold, an' I start out to walk about London all night. I walk along de river awhile, but dey was lots of drunks all along; men, and women too. I chust move along to keep away from de police. I git onto de Strand, an' den over to New Oxford Street, where dere was a big German restaurant on de ground floor, wid big windows all fixed up fine, an' I could see de people havin' parties inside. While I was lookin' in, two men and two ladies come out, laughin' and talkin' and feelin' happy about all dey been eatin' and drinkin', and dey was speakin' Czech,—not like de Austrians, but like de home folks talk it.

"I guess I went crazy, an' I done what I ain't never done before nor since. I went right up to dem gay people an' begun to beg dem. 'Fellow-countrymen, give me money enough to buy a goose!'

"Dey laugh, of course, but de ladies speak awful kind to me, an dey take me back into de

restaurant and give me hot coffee and cakes, an' make me tell all about how I happened to come to London, an what I was doin' dere. Dey take my name and where I work down on paper, an' both of dem ladies give me ten shillings.

"De big market at Covent Garden ain't very far away, an' by dat time it was open. I go dere an' buy a big goose an' some pork pies, an' potatoes and onions, an' cakes an' oranges fur de children,—all I could carry! When I git home, everybody is still asleep. I pile all I bought on de kitchen table, an' go in an' lay down on my bed, an' I ain't waken up till I hear dat woman scream when she comes out into her kitchen. My goodness, but she was surprise! She laugh an' cry at de same time, an' hug me and waken all de children. She ain't stop fur no breakfast; she git de Christmas dinner ready dat morning, and we all sit down an' eat all we can hold. I ain't never seen dat violin boy have all he can hold before.

"Two three days after dat, de two men come to hunt me up, an' dey ask my boss, and he give me a good report an' tell dem I was a steady boy all right. One of dem Bohemians was very smart an' run a Bohemian newspaper in New York, an' de odder was a rich man, in de importing business, an' dey been traveling togedder. Dey told me how t'ings was easier in New York, an' offered to pay my passage when dey was goin' home soon on a boat. My boss say to me: 'You go. You ain't got no chance here, an' I like to see you git ahead, fur you always been a good boy to my woman, and fur dat fine Christmas dinner you give us all.' An' da's how I got to New York."

That night when Rudolph and Polly, arm in arm, were running home across the fields with the bitter wind at their backs, his heart leaped for joy when she said she thought they might have his family come over for supper on New Year's Eve. "Let's get up a nice supper, and not let your mother help at all; make her be company for once."

"That would be lovely of you, Polly," he said humbly. He was a very simple, modest boy, and he, too, felt vaguely that Polly and her sisters were more experienced and worldly than his people.

VI

The winter turned out badly for farmers. It was bitterly cold, and after the first light snows before Christmas there was no snow at all—and no rain. March was as bitter as February. On those days when the wind fairly punished the country, Rosicky sat by his window. In the fall he and the boys had put in a big wheat planting, and now the seed had frozen in the ground. All that land would have to be ploughed up and planted over again, planted in corn. It had happened before, but he was younger then, and he never worried about what had to be. He was sure of himself and of Mary; he knew they could bear what they had to bear, that they would always pull through somehow. But he was not so sure about the young ones, and he felt troubled because Rudolph and Polly were having such a hard start.

Sitting beside his flowering window while the panes rattled and the wind blew in under the door, Rosicky gave himself to reflection as he had not done since those Sundays in the loft of the furniture-factory in New York, long ago. Then he was trying to find what he wanted in life for himself; now he was trying to find what he wanted for his boys, and why it was he so hungered to feel sure they would be here, working this very land, after he was gone.

They would have to work hard on the farm, and probably they would never do much more than make a living. But if he could think of them as staying here on the land, he wouldn't have to fear any great unkindness for them. Hardships, certainly; it was a hardship to have the wheat freeze in the ground when seed was so high; and to have to sell your stock because you had no feed. But there would be other years when everything came along right, and you caught up. And what you had was your own. You didn't have to do with dishonest and cruel people. They were the only things in his experience he had found terrifying and horrible; the look in the eyes of a dishonest and crafty man, of a scheming and rapacious woman.

In the country, if you had a mean neighbour, you could keep off his land and make him keep off yours. But in the city, all the foulness and misery and brutality of your neighbours was part of your life. The worst things he had come upon in his journey through the world were human—depraved and poisonous specimens of man. To this day he could recall certain terrible faces in the London streets. There were mean people everywhere, to be sure, even in their own country town here. But they weren't tempered, hardened, sharpened, like the treacherous people in cities who live by grinding or cheating or poisoning their fellow-men. He had helped to bury two of his fellow-workmen in the tailoring trade, and he was distrustful of the organized industries that see one out of the world in big cities. Here, if you were sick, you had Doctor Ed to look after you; and if you died, fat Mr. Haycock, the kindest man in the world, buried you.

It seemed to Rosicky that for good, honest boys like his, the worst they could do on the farm was better than the best they would be likely to do in the city. If he'd had a mean boy, now, one who was crooked and sharp and tried to put anything over on his brothers, then town would be the place for him. But he had no such boy. As for Rudolph, the discontented one, he would give the shirt off his back to anyone who touched his heart. What Rosicky really hoped for his boys was that they could get through the world without ever knowing much about the cruelty of human beings. "Their mother and me ain't prepared them for that," he sometimes said to himself.

These thoughts brought him back to a grateful consideration of his own case. What an escape he had had, to be sure! He, too, in his time, had had to take money for repair work from the hand of a hungry child who let it go so wistfully; because it was money due his boss. And now, in all these years, he had never had to take a cent from anyone in bitter need—never had to look at the face of a woman become like a wolf's from struggle and famine. When he thought of these things, Rosicky would put on his cap and jacket and slip down to the barn and give his work-horses a little extra oats, letting them eat it out of his hand in their slobbery fashion. It was his way of expressing what he felt, and made him chuckle with pleasure.

The spring came warm, with blue skies—but dry, dry as a bone. The boys began ploughing up the wheat-fields to plant them over in corn. Rosicky would stand at the fence corner and watch them, and the earth was so dry it blew up in clouds of brown dust that hid the horses and the sulky plough and the driver. It was a bad outlook.

The big alfalfa field that lay between the home place and Rudolph's came up green, but Rosicky was worried because during that open windy winter a great many Russian thistle plants had blown in there and lodged. He kept asking the boys to rake them out; he was afraid their seed would root and "take the alfalfa." Rudolph said that was nonsense.

The boys were working so hard planting corn, their father felt he couldn't insist about the thistles, but he set great store by that big alfalfa field. It was a feed you could depend on—and there was some deeper reason, vague, but strong. The peculiar green of that clover woke early memories in old Rosicky, went back to something in his childhood in the old world. When he was a little boy, he had played in fields of that strong blue-green colour.

One morning, when Rudolph had gone to town in the car, leaving a work-team idle in his barn, Rosicky went over to his son's place, put the horses to the buggy-rake, and set about quietly raking up those thistles. He behaved with guilty caution, and rather enjoyed stealing a march on Doctor Ed, who was just then taking his first vacation in seven years of practice and was attending a clinic in Chicago. Rosicky got the thistles raked up, but did not stop to burn them. That would take some time, and his breath was pretty short, so he thought he had better get the horses back to the barn.

He got them into the barn and to their stalls, but the pain had come on so sharp in his chest that he didn't try to take the harness off. He started for the house, bending lower with every step. The cramp in his chest was shutting him up like a jack-knife. When he reached the windmill, he swayed and caught at the ladder. He saw Polly coming down the hill, running with the swiftness of a slim greyhound. In a flash she had her shoulder under his armpit.

"Lean on me, Father, hard! Don't be afraid. We can get to the house all right." Somehow they did, though Rosicky became blind with pain; he could keep on his legs, but he couldn't steer his course. The next thing he was conscious of was lying on Polly's bed, and Polly bending over him wringing out bath towels in hot water and putting them on

his chest. She stopped only to throw coal into the stove, and she kept the tea-kettle and the black pot going. She put these hot applications on him for nearly an hour, she told him afterwards, and all that time he was drawn up stiff and blue, with the sweat pouring off him.

As the pain gradually loosed its grip, the stiffness went out of his jaws, the black circles round his eyes disappeared, and a little of his natural colour came back. When his daughter-in-law buttoned his shirt over his chest at last, he sighed.

"Da's fine, de way I feel now, Polly. It was a awful bad spell, an' I was so sorry it all come on you like it did."

Polly was flushed and excited. "Is the pain really gone? Can I leave you long enough to telephone over to your place?"

Rosicky's eyes fluttered. "Don't telephone, Polly. It ain't no use to scare my wife. It's nice and quiet here, an' if I ain't too much trouble to you, just let me lay still till I feel like myself. I ain't got no pain now. It's nice here."

Polly bent over him and wiped the moisture from his face. "Oh, I'm so glad it's over!" she broke out impulsively. "It just broke my heart to see you suffer so, Father."

Rosicky motioned her to sit down on the chair where the tea-kettle had been, and looked up at her with that lively affectionate gleam in his eyes. "You was awful good to me, I won't never forget dat. I hate it to be sick on you like dis. Down at de barn I say to myself, dat young girl ain't had much experience in sickness, I don't want to scare her, an' maybe she's got a baby comin' or somet'ing."

Polly took his hand. He was looking at her so intently and affectionately and confidingly; his eyes seemed to caress her face, to regard it with pleasure. She frowned with her funny streaks of eyebrows, and then smiled back at him.

"I guess maybe there is something of that kind going to happen. But I haven't told anyone yet, not my mother or Rudolph. You'll be the first to know."

His hand pressed hers. She noticed that it was warm again. The twinkle in his yellow-brown eyes seemed to come nearer.

"I like mighty well to see dat little child, Polly," was all he said. Then he closed his eyes and lay half-smiling. But Polly sat still, thinking hard. She had a sudden feeling that nobody in the world, not her mother, not Rudolph, or anyone, really loved her as much as old Rosicky did. It perplexed her. She sat frowning and trying to puzzle it out. It was as if Rosicky had a special gift for loving people, something that was like an ear for music or an eye for colour. It was quiet, unobtrusive; it was merely there. You felt it in his hands, too. After he dropped off to sleep, she sat holding his warm, broad, flexible brown hand. She had never seen another in the least like it. She wondered if it wasn't a kind of gypsy hand, it was so alive and quick and light in its communications—very strange in a farmer. Nearly all the farmers she knew had huge lumps of fists, like mauls, or they were knotty and bony and uncomfortable-looking, with stiff fingers. But Rosicky's was like quicksilver, flexible, muscular, about the colour of a pale cigar, with deep, deep creases across the palm. It wasn't nervous, it wasn't a stupid lump; it was a warm brown human hand, with some cleverness in it, a great deal of generosity, and something else which Polly could only call "gypsy-like,"— something nimble and lively and sure, in the way that animals are.

Polly remembered that hour long afterwards; it had been like an awakening to her. It seemed to her that she had never learned so much about life from anything as from old

Rosicky's hand. It brought her to herself; it communicated some direct and untranslatable message.

When she heard Rudolph coming in the car, she ran out to meet him.

"Oh, Rudy, your father's been awful sick! He raked up those thistles he's been worrying about, and afterwards he could hardly get to the house. He suffered so I was afraid he was going to die."

Rudolph jumped to the ground. "Where is he now?"

"On the bed. He's asleep. I was terribly scared, because, you know, I'm so fond of your father." She slipped her arm through his and they went into the house. That afternoon they took Rosicky home and put him to bed, though he protested that he was quite well again.

The next morning he got up and dressed and sat down to breakfast with his family. He told Mary that his coffee tasted better than usual to him, and he warned the boys not to bear any tales to Doctor Ed when he got home. After breakfast he sat down by his window to do some patching and asked Mary to thread several needles for him before she went to feed her chickens—her eyes were better than his, and her hands steadier. He lit his pipe and took up John's overalls. Mary had been watching him anxiously all morning, and as she went out of the door with her bucket of scraps, she saw that he was smiling. He was thinking, indeed, about Polly, and how he might never have known what a tender heart she had if he hadn't got sick over there. Girls nowadays didn't wear their heart on their sleeve. But now he knew Polly would make a fine woman after the foolishness wore off. Either a woman had that sweetness at her heart or she hadn't. You couldn't always tell by the look of them; but if they had that, everything came out right in the end.

After he had taken a few stitches, the cramp began in his chest, like yesterday. He put his pipe cautiously down on the window-sill and bent over to ease the pull. No use—he had better try to get to his bed if he could. He rose and groped his way across the familiar floor, which was rising and falling like the deck of a ship. At the door he fell. When Mary came in, she found him lying there, and the moment she touched him she knew that he was gone.

Doctor Ed was away when Rosicky died, and for the first few weeks after he got home he was hard driven. Every day he said to himself that he must get out to see that family that had lost their father. One soft, warm moonlight night in early summer he started for the farm. His mind was on other things, and not until his road ran by the graveyard did he realize that Rosicky wasn't over there on the hill where the red lamplight shone, but here, in the moonlight. He stopped his car, shut off the engine, and sat there for a while.

A sudden hush had fallen on his soul. Everything here seemed strangely moving and significant, though signifying what, he did not know. Close by the wire fence stood Rosicky's mowing-machine, where one of the boys had been cutting hay that afternoon; his own work-horses had been going up and down there. The new-cut hay perfumed all the night air. The moonlight silvered the long, billowy grass that grew over the graves and hid the fence; the few little evergreens stood out black in it, like shadows in a pool. The sky was very blue and soft, the stars rather faint because the moon was full.

For the first time it struck Doctor Ed that this was really a beautiful graveyard. He thought of city cemeteries; acres of shrubbery and heavy stone, so arranged and lonely and unlike anything in the living world. Cities of the dead, indeed; cities of the forgotten, of the

"put away." But this was open and free, this little square of long grass which the wind for ever stirred. Nothing but the sky overhead, and the many-coloured fields running on until they met that sky. The horses worked here in summer; the neighbours passed on their way to town; and over yonder, in the cornfield, Rosicky's own cattle would be eating fodder as winter came on. Nothing could be more undeathlike than this place; nothing could be more right for a man who had helped to do the work of great cities and had always longed for the open country and had got to it at last. Rosicky's life seemed to him complete and beautiful.

About the Story

1. Why do you think the author includes several anecdotes (or very short stories) about Anton Rosicky's past? What character traits do these highlight? Name at least three.

2. What does Rosicky value most for his children?

3. Why does Rosicky like country life better than city life? Do you agree with Rosicky or disagree? Explain why.

4. Does Polly develop throughout the story? If so, how does she develop? If not, explain why she is a static character.

5. Explain the following sentence that describes the field where Rosicky was buried: "Nothing could be more undeathlike than this place" (p. 141). Why does this seem like an appropriate place for Anton Rosicky?

6. How do Mr. and Mrs. Rosicky compare with Mr. and Mrs. Penn in "The Revolt of Mother"?

— About the Author —

As a young girl growing up on the plains of Nebraska, Willa Cather (1873–1947) was a vibrant, imaginative tomboy who read voraciously, loved adventure, and dreamed of becoming a medical doctor. The inspirations for most of Cather's writing came from the impressions and experiences of her childhood and youth. When her family moved from the gently rolling hills of Virginia to the unbroken plains of Nebraska, Cather was only ten years old, yet the extreme change powerfully affected her. Especially influential were the numerous immigrants from Europe who became neighbors and friends. They introduced Cather to European culture, language, and literature, and they appeared later as characters in her works. The dreams and frustrations of such people are a favorite theme of Cather's, as is the conflict between the need to make a living and the need for the purely pleasurable rewards of being artistic and creative. Many of Cather's characters have lives that are full of hard work and duties yet are richly rewarding.

from Don Quixote

MIGUEL DE CERVANTES

translated by John Ormsby

Few literary characters have entertained and delighted readers around the world as much as the misguided adventurer Don Quixote, the title character of Miguel de Cervantes' timeless novel. Drawing from the works of chivalry and romance that had become popular in his day, Cervantes composed this parody (humorous imitation) of these high-toned yet often badly written stories. Today, *Don Quixote* remains one of the most important contributions to world literature, having inspired countless imitations as well as subsequent novels, plays, and works of art.

CHAPTER 1
WHICH TREATS OF THE CHARACTER AND PURSUITS OF THE FAMOUS GENTLEMAN DON QUIXOTE OF LA MANCHA

In a village of La Mancha, the name of which I have no desire to call to mind, there lived not long since one of those gentlemen that keep a lance in the lance-rack, an old buckler,* a lean hack,* and a greyhound for coursing.* An olla* of rather more beef than mutton, a salad on most nights, scraps on Saturdays, lentils on Fridays, and a pigeon or so extra on Sundays, made away with three-quarters of his income. The rest of it went in a doublet of fine cloth and velvet breeches and shoes to match for holidays, while on week-days he made a brave figure in his best homespun. He had in his house a housekeeper past forty, a niece under twenty, and a lad for the field and market-place, who used to saddle the hack as well as handle the bill-hook.* The age of this gentleman of ours was bordering on fifty; he was of a hardy habit, spare,* gaunt-featured, a very early riser and a great sportsman. They will have it his surname was Quixada or Quesada (for here there is some difference of opinion among the authors who write on the subject), although from reasonable conjectures it seems plain that he was called Quexana. This, however, is of but little importance to our tale; it will be enough not to stray a hair's breadth from the truth in the telling of it.

buckler: a small shield

hack: a horse used for riding

coursing: hunting

olla: a round pot or jar

bill-hook: a long instrument with a blade at the end, used for pruning and clearing brush

spare: lean

You must know, then, that the above-named gentleman whenever he was at leisure (which was mostly all the year round) gave himself up to reading books of chivalry with such ardor* and avidity* that he almost entirely neglected the pursuit of his field-sports, and even the management of his property; and to such a pitch did his eagerness and infatuation go that he sold many an acre of tillageland* to buy books of chivalry to read, and brought home as many of

them as he could get. But of all there were none he liked so well as those of the famous Feliciano de Silva's* composition, for their lucidity* of style and complicated conceits* were as pearls in his sight, particularly when in his reading he came upon courtships and cartels,* where he often found passages like *"the reason of the unreason with which my reason is afflicted so weakens my reason that with reason I murmur at your beauty;"* or again, *"the high heavens, that of your divinity divinely fortify you with the stars, render you deserving of the desert* your greatness deserves."* Over conceits of this sort the poor gentleman lost his wits, and used to lie awake striving to understand them and worm the meaning out of them; what Aristotle himself could not have made out or extracted had he come to life again for that special purpose. He commended, however, the author's way of ending his book with the promise of that interminable* adventure, and many a time was he tempted to take up his pen and finish it properly as is there proposed, which no doubt he would have done, and made a successful piece of work of it too, had not greater and more absorbing thoughts prevented him.

---

ardor: intensity

avidity: enthusiastic interest

tillageland: cultivated land

Feliciano de Silva: popular sixteenth-century Spanish writer whose works of chivalry Cervantes mocks throughout his story

lucidity: ability to be understood

conceits: exaggerated or fanciful thoughts or ideas

cartels: letters of challenge

desert: noun form of *deserve*

interminable: seemingly endless

In short, he became so absorbed in his books that he spent his nights from sunset to sunrise, and his days from dawn to dark, poring over them; and what with little sleep and much reading his brains got so dry that he lost his wits. His fancy grew full of what he used to read about in his books, enchantments, quarrels, battles, challenges, wounds, wooings, loves, agonies, and all sorts of impossible nonsense; and it so possessed his mind that the whole fabric of invention and fancy he read of was true, that to him no history in the world had more reality in it.

In short, his wits being quite gone, he hit upon the strangest notion that ever madman in this world hit upon, and that was that he fancied it was right and requisite,* as well for the support of his own honour as for the service of his country, that he should make a knight-errant* of himself, roaming the world over in full armour and on horseback in quest of adventures, and putting in practice himself all that he had read of as being the usual practices of knights-errant; righting every kind of wrong, and exposing himself to peril and danger from which, in the issue, he was to reap eternal renown and fame. Already the poor man saw himself crowned by the might of his arm Emperor of Trebizond* at least; and so, led away by the intense enjoyment he found in these pleasant fancies, he set himself forthwith to put his scheme into execution.

---

requisite: necessary

knight-errant: wandering or roving knight

Trebizond: Greek empire that existed from 1204–1461

The first thing he did was to clean up some armour that had belonged to his great-grandfather, and had been for ages lying forgotten in a corner eaten with rust and covered with mildew. He scoured and polished it as best he could, but he perceived one great defect in it, that it had no closed helmet, nothing but a simple morion.* This deficiency, however, his ingenuity supplied, for he contrived a kind of half-helmet of pasteboard which, fitted on to the morion, looked like a whole one. It is true that, in order to see if it was strong and fit to stand a cut, he drew his sword and gave it a couple of slashes, the first of which undid in an instant what had taken him a week to do. The ease with which he had knocked it to pieces disconcerted him somewhat, and to guard against that danger he set to work again, fixing bars of iron on the inside until he was satisfied with its strength; and then, not caring to try any more experiments with it, he passed it and adopted it as a helmet of the most perfect construction.

---

morion: a triangular metal helmet with a curved brim often worn by soldiers in the sixteenth and seventeenth centuries

---

He next proceeded to inspect his hack. Four days were spent in thinking what name to give him, because (as he said to himself) it was not right that a horse belonging to a knight so famous, and one with such merits of his own, should be without some distinctive name, and he strove to adapt it so as to indicate what he had been before belonging to a knight-errant, and what he then was; for it was only reasonable that, his master taking a new character, he should take a new name, and that it should be a distinguished and full-sounding one, befitting the new order and calling he was about to follow. And so, after having composed, struck out, rejected, added to, unmade, and remade a multitude of names out of his memory and fancy, he decided upon calling him Rocinante,* a name, to his thinking, lofty, sonorous,* and significant of his condition as a hack before he became what he now was, the first and foremost of all the hacks in the world.

Rocinante: From the Spanish *rocín*, meaning "nag" or "low-quality horse," and *-ante*, meaning "before, previously." The implication is that the horse was a nag until becoming Quixote's hack.
sonorous: producing a rich sound

Having got a name for his horse so much to his taste, he was anxious to get one for himself, and he was eight days more pondering over this point, till at last he made up his mind to call himself "Don Quixote,"* whence, as has been already said, the authors of this veracious history have inferred that his name must have been beyond a doubt Quixada, and not Quesada as others would have it. [H]e, like a good knight, resolved to add on the name of his, and to style himself Don Quixote of La Mancha, whereby, he considered, he described accurately his origin and country, and did honour to it in taking his surname from it.

Quixote: pronounced kee-HO-tay

So then, his armour being furbished, his morion turned into a helmet, his hack christened, and he himself confirmed, he came to the conclusion that nothing more was needed now but to look out for a lady to be in love with; for a knight-errant without love was like a tree without leaves or fruit, or a body without a soul. As he said to himself, "If, for my sins, or by my good fortune, I come across some giant hereabouts, a common occurrence with knights-errant, and overthrow him in one onslaught, or cleave him asunder to the waist, or, in short, vanquish and subdue him, will it not be well to have some one I may send him to as a present, that he may come in and fall on his knees before my sweet lady, and in a humble, submissive voice say, 'I am the giant Caraculiambro, lord of the island of Malindrania, vanquished in single combat by the never sufficiently extolled knight Don Quixote of La Mancha, who has commanded me to present myself before your Grace, that your Highness dispose of me at your pleasure'?" Oh, how our good gentleman enjoyed the delivery of this speech, especially when he had thought of some one to call his Lady! There was, so the story goes, in a village near his own a very good-looking farm-girl with whom he had been at one time in love, though, so far as is known, she never knew it nor gave a thought to the matter. Her name was Aldonza Lorenzo, and upon her he thought fit to confer the title of Lady of his Thoughts; and after some search for a name which should not be out of harmony with her own, and should suggest and indicate that of a princess and great lady, he decided upon calling her Dulcinea del Toboso—she being of El Toboso—a name, to his mind, musical, uncommon, and significant, like all those he had already bestowed upon himself and the things belonging to him.

Not long after embarking upon his adventures, Quixote meets local peasant Sancho Panza. Don Quixote promises Sancho the governorship of an island in exchange for his services as a squire. Sancho agrees and rides alongside Don Quixote for the rest of his "quest," serving as the voice of realism and practicality.

CHAPTER 8
OF THE GOOD FORTUNE WHICH THE VALIANT DON QUIXOTE HAD IN THE TERRIBLE AND UNDREAMT-OF ADVENTURE OF THE WINDMILLS, WITH OTHER OCCURRENCES WORTHY TO BE FITLY RECORDED

At this point they came in sight of thirty or forty windmills that there are on that plain, and as soon as Don Quixote saw them he said to his squire, "Fortune is arranging matters for us better than we could have shaped our desires ourselves, for look there, friend Sancho Panza, where thirty or more monstrous giants present themselves, all of whom I mean to engage in battle and slay, and with whose spoils we shall begin to make our fortunes; for this is righteous warfare, and it is God's good service to sweep so evil a breed from off the face of the earth."

"What giants?" said Sancho Panza.

"Those thou seest there," answered his master, "with the long arms, and some have them nearly two leagues long."

"Look, your worship," said Sancho; "what we see there are not giants but windmills, and what seem to be their arms are the sails that turned by the wind make the millstone go."

"It is easy to see," replied Don Quixote, "that thou art not used to this business of adventures; those are giants; and if thou art afraid, away with thee out of this and betake thyself to prayer while I engage them in fierce and unequal combat."

So saying, he gave the spur to his steed Rocinante, heedless of the cries his squire Sancho sent after him, warning him that most certainly they were windmills and not giants he was going to attack. He, however, was so positive they were giants that he neither heard the cries of Sancho, nor perceived, near as he was, what they were, but made at them shouting, "Fly not, cowards and vile beings, for a single knight attacks you."

A slight breeze at this moment sprang up, and the great sails began to move, seeing which Don Quixote exclaimed, "Though ye flourish more arms than the giant Briareus,* ye have to reckon with me."

Briareus: a giant mentioned throughout Greek mythology and in Homer's *Iliad*. Briareus possessed one hundred arms and fifty legs.

So saying, and commending himself with all his heart to his lady Dulcinea, imploring her to support him in such a peril, with lance in rest and covered by his buckler, he charged at Rocinante's fullest gallop and fell upon the first mill that stood in front of him; but as he drove his lance-point into the sail the wind whirled it round with such force that it shivered the lance to pieces, sweeping with it horse and rider, who went rolling over on the plain, in a sorry condition. Sancho hastened to his assistance as fast as his donkey could go, and when he came up found him unable to move, with such a shock had Rocinante fallen with him.

Said Sancho, "did I not tell your worship to mind what you were about, for they were only windmills? and no one could have made any mistake about it but one who had something of the same kind in his head."

"Hush, friend Sancho," replied Don Quixote, "the fortunes of war more than any other are liable to frequent fluctuations; and moreover I think, and it is the truth, that that same sage Friston* who carried off my study and books, has turned these giants into mills in order to rob me of the glory of vanquishing them, such is the enmity he bears me; but in the end his wicked arts will avail but little against my good sword."

Friston: a magician whom Quixote imagines to be his arch nemesis

"God order it as he may," said Sancho Panza, and helping him to rise got him up again on Rocinante, whose shoulder was half out; and then, discussing the late adventure, they followed the road to Puerto Lápice, for there, said Don Quixote, they could not fail to find adventures in abundance and variety, as it was a great thoroughfare. For all that, he was much grieved at the loss of his lance, and saying so to his squire, he added, "I remember having read how a Spanish knight, Diego Perez de Vargas by name, having broken his sword in battle, tore from an oak a ponderous bough or branch, and with it did such things that day, and pounded so many Moors, that he got the surname of Machuca, and he and his descendants from that day forth were called Vargas y Machuca. I mention this

because from the first oak I see I mean to rend such another branch, large and stout like that, with which I am determined and resolved to do such deeds that thou mayest deem thyself very fortunate in being found worthy to come and see them, and be an eye-witness of things that will with difficulty be believed."

"Be that as God will," said Sancho, "I believe it all as your worship says it; but straighten yourself a little, for you seem all on one side, may be from the shaking of the fall."

"That is the truth," said Don Quixote, "and if I make no complaint of the pain it is because knights-errant are not permitted to complain of any wound, even though their bowels be coming out through it."

"If so," said Sancho, "I have nothing to say; but I would rather your worship complained when anything ailed you. For my part, I confess I must complain however small the ache may be; unless this rule about not complaining extends to the squires of knights-errant also."

Don Quixote could not help laughing at his squire's simplicity, and he assured him he might complain whenever and however he chose, just as he liked, for, so far, he had never read of anything to the contrary in the order of knighthood.

Sancho bade him remember it was dinner-time, to which his master answered that he wanted nothing himself just then, but that he might eat when he had a mind. With this permission Sancho settled himself as comfortably as he could on his beast, and taking out of the *alforjas** what he had stowed away in them, he jogged along behind his master munching deliberately, and from time to time taking a pull at the *bota** with a relish that the thirstiest tapster* in Malaga might have envied; and while he went on in this way, gulping down draught after draught, he never gave a thought to any of the promises his master had made him, nor did he rate it as hardship but rather as recreation going in quest of adventures, however dangerous they might be. Finally they passed the night among some trees, from one of which Don Quixote plucked a dry branch to serve him after a fashion as a lance, and fixed on it the head he had removed from the broken one.

alforjas: leather or canvas saddlebags
bota: winebag
tapster: one who serves wine

All that night Don Quixote lay awake thinking of his lady Dulcinea, in order to conform to what he had read in his books, how many a night in the forests and deserts knights used to lie sleepless supported by the memory of their mistresses. Not so did Sancho Panza spend it, for having his stomach full of something stronger than chicory water* he made but one sleep of it, and, if his master had not called him, neither the rays of the sun beating on his face nor all the cheery notes of the birds welcoming the approach of day would have had power to waken him. On getting up he tried the bota and found it somewhat less full than the night before, which grieved his heart because they did not seem to be on the way to remedy the deficiency readily. Don Quixote did not care to break his fast, for, as has been already said, he confined himself to savoury recollections for nourishment.

chicory water: a beverage made from the roots of the chicory plant, often used as a substitute for coffee

About the Story

1. The term *farce* refers to a work (usually a play or film) that contains comically absurd situations and characters. From what we read in these two chapters, how is it possible to call *Don Quixote* a farce? Explain, citing at least two examples from the text.

2. Based on what you have read in these chapters, is Don Quixote a round or flat character? Explain.

3. Explain how Sancho Panza functions as a foil to Don Quixote in Chapter 8.

4. In the chapters that you read, do you find Don Quixote a sympathetic or an unsympathetic character? Do you sympathize with Sancho? Explain.

5. Gifted authors develop narratives that entertain readers to the extent that they overlook fanciful, ridiculous elements for the sake of enjoying the story. Samuel Taylor Coleridge coined the term *suspension of disbelief* to refer to this willingness of the reader to accept the unbelievable as true. What techniques does Cervantes employ that encourage you to suspend your disbelief?

About the Author

Miguel de Cervantes (1547–1616) was born to noble parents in a town near Madrid, Spain. Although his father was a surgeon, Cervantes still had to search for work. When Cervantes was about six years old, his father was imprisoned for bad debts. The family endured great hardship as a result of this situation.

After serving in the Spanish army and being captured by pirates, Cervantes was able to study abroad and pursue a literary career. He too failed to provide adequately for his family and was, at times, imprisoned for bad debts. After the publication of the first part of *Don Quixote* in 1605, Cervantes' life became easier. Although he never became rich, he gained recognition and was able to devote more time to writing. In 1615 he published the second part of *Don Quixote*. Cervantes continued to write many plays, short stories, novels, and poems.

In the year of its publication, *Don Quixote*, Part I, went through six editions. *Don Quixote* was soon translated into both English and French and was considered the first European novel.

❦ THINKING ZONE ❧

As we have already seen, authors communicate and persuade through their characters. Using the three basic methods of characterization (description, dialogue, and action), the author encourages reader sympathy for some characters and discourages it for others, thereby attempting to convince the reader to adopt the author's moral point of view. But sometimes an author will disclose his moral standards more explicitly by including a character who acts as his "mouthpiece." The **normative character**, sometimes called simply "the norm," models and articulates the author's ethics throughout the story. This fixed set of values that the normative character personifies generally causes the character to be static rather than dynamic, for he evidences little change in perspective throughout the story. This character usually retains our sympathy because he exhibits few significant character flaws, remaining steadfast even though the other characters may experience lapses in moral judgment.

Also affecting our sympathies, however, may be our understanding of any **character's motivation** (or reason) for how he behaves. For example, a character's actions and dialogue might lead us to sympathize with him, but the revelation of the character's impure motives might serve to alienate him from us. Knowing the motivation for a character's behavior also makes the character more real to us, because real people speak and act for specific reasons. Understanding those reasons helps us to understand the character's behavior, making the character and the overall story more applicable to real-life scenarios.

1. How does understanding **character motivation** help to make a character more believable?

2. How might knowing a character's motives affect our sympathy for the character?

3. What is the doctor's motivation for limiting Anton Rosicky's activity?

4. What is Rosicky's motivation for letting Rudolph and Polly have the car on Saturday evenings? What does knowing Rosicky's motivation tell us about him as a character?

5. Explain Don Quixote's motivations for his imaginary quest.

6. What is Sancho Panza's motivation for trying to stop Don Quixote from attacking the "giants"?

7. How might Anton Rosicky in "Neighbour Rosicky" be considered a **normative character**? Explain.

My Last Duchess

ROBERT BROWNING

Though Robert Browning wrote extensively, the form of poetry for which he became most famous was the dramatic monologue, in which a single character speaks either to himself or to another character. In this dramatic monologue the speaker is the Duke of Ferrara, an Italian Renaissance nobleman. The Duke is describing a painting of his last Duchess to an envoy of the count whose daughter the Duke now wishes to wed. Browning does a masterful job of creating a well-rounded character through one simple speech. What does the Duke's speech reveal about how he views himself and his former wife? What do you think of the Duke by the end of the poem?

Leonardo da Vinci (1452–1519). *Le belle ferronniere.*
Portrait of a lady from the court of Milan. Oil on wood,
63 × 45 cm. Inv 778. Photo: Herve' Lewandowski.
Louvre, Paris, France.

That's my last Duchess painted on the wall,
Looking as if she were alive; I call
That piece a wonder, now; Fra Pandolf's* hands
Worked busily a day, and there she stands.
Will't please you sit and look at her? I said   5
"Fra Pandolf" by design, for never read
Strangers like you that pictured countenance,
The depth and passion of its earnest glance,
But to myself they turned (since none puts by
The curtain I have drawn for you, but I)   10
And seemed as they would ask me, if they durst,
How such a glance came there; so, not the first
Are you to turn and ask thus. Sir, 'twas not
Her husband's presence only, called that spot
Of joy into the Duchess' cheek: perhaps   15
Fra Pandolf chanced to say, "Her mantle laps
Over my lady's wrist too much," or, "Paint
Must never hope to reproduce the faint
Half flush that dies along her throat"; such stuff
Was courtesy, she thought, and cause enough   20
For calling up that spot of joy. She had
A heart . . . how shall I say? . . . too soon made glad,
Too easily impressed; she liked whate'er
She looked on, and her looks went everywhere.
Sir, 'twas all one! My favor at her breast,   25
The dropping of the daylight in the West,

Fra Pandolf: Brother Pandolf, an imaginary monk
   and painter of the Italian Renaissance period

The bough of cherries some officious* fool
Broke in the orchard for her, the white mule
She rode with round the terrace—all and each
Would draw from her alike the approving speech, 30
Or blush, at least. She thanked men—good; but thanked
Somehow . . . I know not how . . . as if she ranked
My gift of a nine-hundred-year-old name
With anybody's gift. Who'd stoop to blame
This sort of trifling? Even had you skill 35
In speech—which I have not—to make your will
Quite clear to such an one, and say, "Just this
Or that in you disgusts me; here you miss
Or there exceed the mark"—and if she let
Herself be lessoned so, nor plainly set 40
Her wits to yours, forsooth, and made excuse
—E'en then would be some stooping, and I choose
Never to stoop. Oh, sir, she smiled, no doubt,
Whene'er I passed her; but who passed without
Much the same smile? This grew; I gave commands; 45
Then all smiles stopped together. There she stands
As if alive. Will 't please you rise? We'll meet
The company below, then. I repeat,
The Count your Master's known munificence*
Is ample warrant that no just pretense* 50
Of mine for dowry will be disallowed;
Though his fair daughter's self, as I avowed
At starting, is my object. Nay, we'll go
Together down, sir! Notice Neptune,* though,
Taming a sea horse, thought a rarity, 55
Which Claus of Innsbruck* cast in bronze for me!

officious: extremely forward in offering one's services to other people

munificence: liberality in giving

pretense: claim

Neptune: the Greek god of the sea

Claus of Innsbruck: an imaginary sculptor

About the Poem

1. Who is speaking in the poem? To whom is he speaking?

2. What does the title of the poem suggest about the Duke's attitude toward his late wife?

3. Notice the words of the Duke. What do his own words reveal about his character?

4. By the end of the poem do you like or dislike the Duke? Explain.

5. What is your overall impression of the Duchess? Explain your answer with at least two passages from the poem.

About the Author

Robert Browning (1812–89) was born in London into a well-to-do, happy family who appreciated and encouraged his natural talent. Browning's father was a man of letters and himself a poet. His mother was a devout woman whose religious outlook powerfully colored her son's work. From her, Browning inherited a profound spiritual optimism that permeated his writing. As William Lyon Phelps, one of Browning's biographers, states, "He always tried to see what was good."

Browning was largely self-educated. His father's vast library helped develop an early love of reading and writing. His reading was far-reaching, but he thoroughly learned the subjects he studied. In his writing, he did not strive to please his readers but rather to teach them, to show them his observations and beliefs about mankind. Browning's insight into human character is valuable for the Christian reader, for he shows how people reveal their hearts, whether they intend to or not. "My Last Duchess" is an exquisite example of Browning's ability to expose the true character of a man.

UNIT II REVIEW

REMEMBER THE TERMS

Review the following terms from the opening essay, "Character," and the Thinking Zone pages. Be prepared to discuss their meanings and uses.

character trait	round character	unsympathetic character
description	flat character	tragedy
direct characterization	foil	tragic hero
indirect characterization	static character	tragic flaw
action	dynamic character	normative character
dialogue	sympathetic character	character motivation

APPLY THE CONCEPTS

Answer the following questions about how the literary concepts you have studied are used in this unit.

1. In Chapter 1 of *Treasure Island*, what is Billy Bones's motivation for choosing to stay at the Admiral Benbow?
2. What is the source of the conflict between Dr. Livesey and Billy Bones in Chapter 1?
3. What method or methods of characterization does Stevenson use at the beginning of Chapter 3 to reveal Billy Bones's state of mind?
4. In Chapter 3 how do Pew's actions contradict his initial dialogue with Jim?
5. Identify each of the following characters as round or flat: Jim Hawkins, Jim's mother, Billy Bones, Black Dog. Explain your answers.
6. In "Phaëthon" what is Phaëthon's motivation for visiting the sun-god?
7. Is Phaëthon a round character or a flat character? Explain.
8. In "Old Man" what do the old man's words reveal about his view of his heritage?
9. Is Sarah Penn from "The Revolt of Mother" a round or flat character?
10. Which story in the first half of the unit contains a tragic hero? What is his tragic flaw?
11. In "Neighbour Rosicky," how does the description of Anton Rosicky's appearance suggest his character?
12. Is Mary Rosicky a sympathetic character or an unsympathetic character? Explain.
13. Is Polly a dynamic character or a static character? Explain.
14. How does Sancho Panza function as a foil to Don Quixote?
15. What does the title "My Last Duchess" suggest concerning the Duke's viewpoint toward his late wife?

EVALUATE THE IDEAS

Identify each of the following statements as true or false. If false, rewrite the underlined portion of the sentence to make it true.

16. The description of a character's appearance <u>sometimes</u> qualifies as indirect characterization.

17. Job's friends are examples of <u>round</u> characters.

18. Billy Bones from *Treasure Island* is a <u>dynamic</u> character.

19. In *Treasure Island*, because Dr. Livesey reprimands Billy Bones, the reader finds the doctor <u>unsympathetic</u>.

20. <u>Pride</u> is a common flaw found in tragic heroes.

21. <u>Dynamic</u> characters undergo changes within themselves in a story.

22. The <u>norm</u> is the character whose traits emphasize opposing traits in the main character.

23. <u>Nanny</u> Penn from "The Revolt of Mother" is a flat character.

24. One difference between round and flat characters is that <u>flat</u> characters are more likely to be dynamic characters.

25. Rudolph from "Neighbour Rosicky" is a <u>static</u> character.

26. Most tragedies end in a <u>catastrophe</u>.

27. We sympathize with the <u>duchess</u> in "My Last Duchess."

28. Cervantes uses <u>description</u> in Chapter 1 of *Don Quixote* to tell the reader about the main character.

29. Tragic heroes are generally <u>unsympathetic</u>.

WRITE A RESPONSE

Completely answer each of the following questions.

30. Throughout *Treasure Island* how does Robert Louis Stevenson use description, action, and dialogue to reveal the character of Billy Bones to the reader?

31. How does the character of Anton Rosicky from "Neighbour Rosicky" contrast with Adoniram Penn in "The Revolt of Mother"?

32. What is the Duke's main character flaw in "My Last Duchess"? How do his words reveal this flaw?

FUNERAL PROCESSION
Ellis Wilson

III

❧ THEME ❧

Kentucky artist Ellis Wilson (1899–1977) traveled often to study and to paint African Americans in ordinary settings. Despite several awards for his work, a Guggenheim fellowship, and a number of exhibitions, Wilson's work was not exceptionally popular during his lifetime—a problem that many black artists of the time experienced. He attended the School of the Art Institute in Chicago, where at times he was unable to attend classes because of racial tensions in the city. Following his death, Wilson's simple, spirited paintings gained renewed popularity when the painting Funeral Procession *was featured on the long-running television series* The Cosby Show.

⚜ The setting for Wilson's *Funeral Procession* is Haiti. What evidence can you find of the Haitian influence?

⚜ Setting includes not only place but also time and way of life. What can you tell about the time period of this painting? the way of life?

⚜ What impression do you think Wilson wanted to evoke from *Funeral Procession*?

c.1950s, Aaron Douglas Collection, *Funeral Procession* by Ellis Wilson, used by permission of Amistad Research Center.

❧ THEME ❧

We live in a world filled not just with conflict and "characters" but also with meaning. Everything we see and experience has come into existence because God—a Being of infinite intelligence and wisdom—has spoken (Gen. 1:3). He declares that what He ordains is filled with meaning because all things contribute to accomplishing His good purposes. Though we are often unable to discern why people are the way they are or why things happen as they do, we can be confident that God is in control and that through every event He is working out His will (Eph. 1:11).

Since we are made in the image of God, humans reflect, however poorly, His nature. It should not surprise us then, that whether creating or hearing stories, we instinctively seek to convey or find meaning behind them. The goal of interpreting story elements such as conflict, character, setting, and plot is to discern that meaning, or theme. Specifically, **theme** refers to the recurring or emerging ideas about the world that are found in a work of literature. Some themes are the author's statements on very specific issues of his time. But most long-lasting works contain **universal themes**, or ideas about life that are found throughout world literature because they can be understood by people of all times and places. For example, several stories in this unit show that appearances do not always reflect the true nature of people or things. The truth of this statement can be understood by readers of all backgrounds. But whether universal or specific, themes are an author's attempt to communicate to the reader a message that he believes to be important.

ORIGINS OF THEME

Usually, an author creates a work with a specific purpose in mind. He may hope to correct an injustice, to motivate an audience to action, or simply to illustrate a particular truth. Whatever the reason, the **authorial intent** behind well-crafted literature forms the basis for theme, dictating everything from the form of a work to its characters and conflict resolutions. Because themes are the expression of an author's ideas about the world, even literature written primarily for entertainment can contain them. Through the characters and situations a reader is supposed to sympathize with, an author inevitably communicates his views of what is right or fair and of how people really think, feel, and behave. In any type of literature, ascertaining the author's view of conflicts, characters, setting, and plot is where finding theme begins.

EXPLICIT THEMES

A writer may choose to reveal a theme explicitly by stating it directly for the reader, whether through the characters' words or through the narration. A **moral**, the simplest form of theme, does the latter: much like a proverb, morals are short, pithy, and overt statements by a narrator that teach broad life lessons from simple stories such as fables. For example, "a bird in the hand is worth two in the bush" (Aesop) is a moral that means it is better to be content with what is than to seek what might be. In narratives with more complex plotlines, characters, and conflicts, theme may also be explicitly stated at some point in the story. However, these statements are usually less direct than the statement of the moral, summarizing an insight the story's elements have already revealed. Consider "Neighbour Rosicky." In Doctor Ed's final statement, he notes what the story has already shown through the characters (Rosicky and Polly in particular) and their settings—that "nothing could be more undeathlike than this place" (the country). There the characters are free to live life as the author believes it should be lived, in selfless love for others.

IMPLICIT THEMES

Many times, themes are never openly stated in a story. Instead the author relies on the reader to infer the meaning implied in the details of the story. A familiar story relying on implicit theme is that of the Prodigal Son (Luke 15:11–32). Unlike many of Christ's parables, this story relies solely on the story elements to communicate theme. First, the conflicts reveal the theme. The prodigal son's conflict with his father begins the story, but in dealing with the consequences of his choice, the son must battle his own pride and guilt. The older brother, though he complies with his father's will, resents his father's choice to forgive the younger son, falling prey to his own pride. Throughout the story, the father deals with conflict correctly, exhibiting compassion for both of his sons. Second, the characters who gain our approval through the story indicate what Christ values. The father consistently shows love and wisdom, making his decisions ones we can sympathize with. In contrast, the elder brother, though dutiful, loses our support through his uncompassionate and unforgiving response. Meanwhile, the prodigal, though initially corrupt, proud, and rebellious, chooses the better path of repentance, humility, and obedience. Together, these characters and conflicts clearly reveal the messages Christ meant to convey—that the Father's love is always waiting and that forgiveness and repentance are far better than pleasures, duty, or pride. Because these story elements are well-developed, we can grasp the central message without an explicit statement of theme. More important, integrating the theme into the elements of the narrative results in a story at once more sophisticated in structure and more poignant in effect.

Most of the selections you have read thus far have used the implicit approach to revealing theme. Many selections in this unit do likewise. As you read, ask yourself the following questions: Do the details of the selections help you discern the theme? What idea do the conflict, characters, and resolution support? Does the title of the story give any hints about the author's intent? Once you can summarize these ideas in one or two sentences, you will have mastered the selection's theme.

The Silver Mine

Selma Lagerlöf

translated by Velma Swanston Howard

For this story, Selma Lagerlöf drew on the folklore of her native Sweden. "The Silver Mine," though fictional, has an actual geographical and historical setting. The narrative is laid in Dalecarlia, a region of west central Sweden, during the reign of Gustaf III (1771–92).

"The Silver Mine" is a story within a story. This narrative is the frame for the parson's tale about the discovery of a silver mine and its effects on the villagers.

King Gustaf III was traveling through Dalecarlia. He was pressed for time, and all the way he wanted to drive like lightning. Although they drove with such speed that the horses were extended like stretched rubber bands and the coach cleared the turns on two wheels, the king poked his head out of the window and shouted to the postilion,* "Why don't you go ahead? Do you think you are driving over eggs?"

---

postilion: rider on a leading horse of a coach team

Since they had to drive over poor country roads at such a mad pace, it would have been almost a miracle had the harness and wagon held together! And they didn't, either; for at the foot of a steep hill the pole broke— and there the king sat! The courtiers sprang from the coach and scolded the driver, but this did not lessen the damage done. There was no possibility of continuing until the coach was mended.

When the courtiers looked around to try to find something with which the king could amuse himself while he waited, they noticed a church spire looming high above the trees in a grove a short distance ahead. They intimated to the king that he might step into one of the coaches in which the attendants were riding and drive up to the church. It was a Sunday, and the king might attend services to pass the time until the royal coach was ready.

The king accepted the proposal and drove toward the church. He had been traveling for hours through dark forest regions; but here it looked more cheerful, with fairly large meadows and villages, and with the Dal River gliding on light and pretty, between thick rows of alder bushes.

But the king had ill luck to this extent: the bell ringer took up the recessional chant just as the king was stepping from the coach on the church knoll and the people were coming out from the service. But when they came walking past him, the king remained standing, with one foot in the wagon and the other on the footstep. He did not move from the spot—only stared at them. They were the finest lot of folk he had ever seen. All the men were above the average height, with intelligent and earnest faces, and the women were dignified and stately, with an air of Sabbath peace about them.

The whole of the preceding day the king had talked only of the desolate tracts he was passing through, and had said to his courtiers again and again, "Now I am certainly driving through the very poorest part of my kingdom!" But now, when he saw the people, garbed in the picturesque dress of this section of the country, he forgot to think of their poverty; instead his heart warmed, and he remarked to himself, "The king of Sweden is not so badly off as his enemies think. So long as my subjects look like this,

I shall probably be able to defend both my faith and my country."

He commanded the courtiers to make known to the people that the stranger who was standing among them was their King and that they should gather around him, so he could talk to them.

And then the king made a speech to the people. He spoke from the high steps outside the vestry,* and the narrow step upon which he stood is there even today.

---

vestry: wardrobe room in churches whose clergy wear vestments

---

The king gave an account of the sad plight in which the kingdom was placed. He said that the Swedes were threatened with war by both Russians and Danes. Under ordinary circumstances it would not be such a serious matter; but now the army was filled with traitors, and he did not dare depend upon it. Therefore there was no other course for him to take than to go himself into the country settlements and ask his subjects if they would be loyal to their king and help him with men and money, so he could save the fatherland.

The peasants stood quietly while the king was speaking to them, and when he had finished they gave no sign either of approval or disapproval.

The king himself thought that he had spoken well. The tears had sprung to his eyes several times while he was speaking. But when the peasants stood there all the while, troubled and undecided, and could not make up their minds to answer him, the king frowned and looked displeased.

The peasants understood that it was becoming monotonous for the king to wait, and finally one of them stepped out from the crowd.

"Now, you must know, King Gustaf, that we were not expecting a royal visit in the parish today," said the peasant, "and therefore we are not prepared to answer you at once. I advise you to go into the vestry and speak with our pastor, while we discuss among ourselves this matter which you have laid before us."

When he came into the vestry, he found no one there but a man who looked like a peasant. He was tall and rugged, with big hands toughened by labor, and he wore neither cassock* nor collar but leather breeches and a long white homespun coat like all the other men.

---

cassock: clerical robe

He rose and bowed to the king when the latter entered.

"I thought I should find the parson in here," said the king.

The man grew somewhat red in the face. He thought it annoying to mention the fact that he was the parson of this parish, when he saw that the king had mistaken him for a peasant. "Yes," said he, "the parson is usually on hand in here."

The king dropped into a large armchair which stood in the vestry at that time and which stands there today, looking exactly like itself, with this difference: the congregation has had a gilded crown attached to the back of it.

"Have you a good parson in this parish?" asked the king, who wanted to appear interested in the welfare of the peasants.

When the king questioned him in this manner, the parson felt that he couldn't possibly tell who he was. "It's better to let him go on believing that I'm only a peasant," thought he, and replied that the parson was good enough. He preached a pure and clear gospel and tried to live as he taught.

The king thought that this was a good commendation, but he had a sharp ear and marked a certain doubt in the tone. "You sound as if you were not quite satisfied with the parson," said the king.

"He's a bit arbitrary," said the man, thinking that, if the king should find out later who he was, he would not think that the parson had been standing here and blowing his own horn; therefore he wished to come out with a little faultfinding also. "There are some, no doubt, who say the parson wants to be the only one to counsel and rule in this parish," he continued.

"Then, at all events, he has led and managed in the best possible way," said the king. He didn't like it that the peasant complained of one who was placed above him. "To me it appears as though good habits and old-time simplicity were the rule here."

"The people are good enough," said the curate,* "but then they live in poverty and isolation. Human beings here would certainly be no better than others if this world's temptations came closer to them."

---

curate: clergyman in charge of a parish district served by a church

---

"But there's no fear of anything of the sort happening," said the king, with a shrug.

He said nothing further but began thrumming on the table with his fingers. He thought he had exchanged a sufficient number of gracious words with this peasant and wondered when the others would be ready with their answer.

"These peasants are not very eager to help their king," thought he. "If I only had my coach, I would drive away from them and their palaver!"*

---

palaver: tedious talk

The pastor sat there troubled, debating with himself as to how he should decide an important matter which he must settle. He was beginning to feel happy because he had not told the king who he was. Now he felt that he could speak with him about matters which otherwise he could not have placed before him.

After a while the parson broke the silence and asked the king if it was an actual fact that enemies were upon them and that the kingdom was in danger.

The king thought this man ought to have sense enough not to trouble him further. He simply glared at him and said nothing.

"I ask because I was standing in here and could not hear very well," said the parson. "But if this is really the case, I want to say to you that the pastor of this congregation might perhaps be able to procure for the king as much money as he will need."

"I thought that you said just now that everyone here was poor," said the king,

thinking that the man did not know what he was talking about.

"Yes, that's true," replied the rector,* "and the parson has no more than any of the others. But if the king would condescend to listen to me for a moment, I will explain how the pastor happens to have the power to help him."

---

rector: clergyman in charge of a parish

"You may speak," said the king. "You seem to find it easier to get the words past your lips than your friends and neighbors out there, who never will be ready with what they have to tell me."

"It is not so easy to reply to the king! I'm afraid that, in the end, it will be the parson who must undertake this on behalf of the others."

The king crossed his legs, folded his arms, and let his head sink down upon his breast. "You may begin now," he said, in the tone of one already asleep.

"Once upon a time there were five men from this parish who were out on a moose hunt," began the clergyman. "One of them was the parson of whom we are speaking. Two of the others were soldiers, named Olaf and Eric Svärd; the fourth man was the innkeeper in this settlement, and the fifth was a peasant named Israel Per Persson."

"Don't go to the trouble of mentioning so many names," muttered the king, letting his head droop to one side.

"Those men were good hunters," continued the parson, "who usually had luck with them, but that day they had wandered long and far without getting anything. Finally they gave up the hunt altogether and sat down on the ground to talk. They said there was not a spot in the whole forest fit for cultivation; all of it was only mountain and swampland. 'Our Lord has not done right by us in giving us such a poor land to live in,' said one.

'In other localities people can get riches for themselves in abundance, but here, with all our toil and drudgery we can scarcely get our daily bread.'"

The pastor paused a moment, as if uncertain that the king heard him, but the latter moved his little finger to show that he was awake.

"Just as the hunters were discussing this matter, the parson saw something that glittered at the base of the mountain where he had kicked away a moss tuft. 'This is a queer mountain,' he thought, as he kicked off another moss tuft. He picked up a sliver of stone that came with the moss and which shone exactly like the other. 'It can't be possible that this stuff is lead,' said he.

"Then the others sprang up and scraped away the turf with the butt ends of their rifles. When they did this, they saw plainly that a broad vein of ore followed the mountain.

"'What do you think this might be?' asked the parson.

"The men chipped off bits of stone and bit into them. 'It must be lead or zinc, at least,' said they.

"'And the whole mountain is full of it,' added the innkeeper."

When the parson had got thus far in his narrative, the king's head was seen to straighten up a little and one eye opened. "Do you know if any of these persons knew anything about ore and minerals?" he asked.

"They did not," replied the parson.

Then the king's head sank and both eyes closed.

"The clergyman and his companions were very happy," continued the speaker, without letting himself be disturbed by the king's indifference; "they fancied that now they had found that which would give them and their descendants wealth. 'I'll never have to do any more work,' said one. 'Now I can afford to do nothing at all the whole week through,

and on Sundays I shall drive to church in a golden chariot!' They were otherwise sensible men, but the great find had gone to their heads, and they talked like children. Still they had enough presence of mind to put back the moss tufts and conceal the vein of ore. Then they carefully noted the place where it was and went home. Before they parted company, they agreed that the parson should travel to Falun and ask the mining expert what kind of ore this was. He was to return as soon as possible, and until then they promised one another on oath not to reveal to a soul where the ore was to be found."

The king's head was raised again a trifle, but he did not interrupt the speaker with a word. It appeared as though he was beginning to believe that the man actually had something of importance he wished to say to him, since he didn't allow himself to be disturbed by his indifference.

"Then the parson departed with a few samples of ore in his pocket. He was just as happy in the thought of becoming rich as were the others. He was thinking of rebuilding the parsonage, which at present was no better than a peasant's cottage, and then he would marry a dean's daughter whom he liked. He had thought that he might have to wait for her many years. He was poor and obscure and knew that it would be a long while before he should get any post that would enable him to marry.

"The parson drove over to Falun in two days, and there he had to wait another whole day because the mining expert was away. Finally he ran across him and showed him the bits of ore. The mining expert took them in his hand. He looked at them first, then at the parson. The parson related how he had found them in a mountain at home in his parish and wondered if it might not be lead.

"'No, it's not lead,' said the mining expert.

"'Perhaps it is zinc then?' asked the parson.

"'Nor is it zinc,' said the mineralogist.

"The parson thought that all the hope within him sank. He had not been so depressed in many a long day.

"'Have you many stones like this in your parish?' asked the mineralogist.

"'We have a whole mountainful,' said the parson.

"Then the mineralogist came up closer, slapped the parson on the shoulder, and said, 'Let us see that you make such good use of this that it will prove a blessing both to yourselves and to the country, for this is silver.'

"'Indeed?' said the parson, feeling his way. 'So it is silver.'

"The mineralogist began telling him how he should go to work to get legal rights to the mine and gave him many valuable suggestions; but the parson stood there dazed and did not listen to what the mineralogist was saying. He was thinking how wonderful it was that at home in his poor parish stood a whole mountain of silver ore, waiting for him."

The king raised his head so suddenly that the parson stopped short in his narrative. "It turned out, of course, that when he got home and began working the mine, he saw that the mineralogist had only been fooling him," said the king.

"Oh, no, the mineralogist had not fooled him," said the parson.

"You may continue," said the king as he settled himself more comfortably in the chair to listen.

"When the parson was at home again and was driving through the parish," continued the clergyman, "he thought that first of all he should inform his partners of the value of their find. And as he drove alongside the innkeeper Sten Stensson's place, he intended to drive up to the house to tell him they had found silver. But when he stopped outside the gate, he noticed that a broad path of evergreen was strewn all the way up to the doorstep.

"'Who had died in this place?' asked the parson of a boy who stood leaning against the fence.

"'The innkeeper himself,' answered the boy. Then he let the clergyman know that the innkeeper had drunk himself full every day for a week. 'Oh, so much brandy, so much brandy, has been drunk here!'

"'How can that be?' asked the parson. 'The innkeeper used never to drink himself full.'

"'Oh,' said the boy, 'he drank because he said he had found a mine. He was very rich. He should never have to do anything now but drink, he said. Last night he drove off, full as he was, and the wagon turned over and he was killed.'

"When the parson heard this, he drove homeward, distressed over what he had heard. He had come back so happy, rejoicing because he could tell the great news.

"When the parson had driven a few paces, he saw Israel Per Persson walking along. He looked about as usual, and the parson thought it was well that fortune had not gone to his head too. Him he would cheer at once with the good news that he was a rich man.

"'Good day!' said Per Persson. 'Do you come from Falun now?'

"'I do,' said the parson. 'And now I must tell you that it has turned out even better than we had imagined. The mineralogist said it was silver ore that we had found.'

"That instant Per Persson looked as though the ground had opened under him. 'What are you saying, what are you saying? Is it silver?'

"'Yes,' answered the parson. 'We'll all be rich men now, all of us, and can live like gentlemen.'

"'Oh, is it silver?' said Per Persson, looking more and more mournful.

"'Why, of course it is silver,' replied the parson. 'You mustn't think that I want to deceive you. You mustn't be afraid to be happy.'

"'Happy!' said Per Persson. 'Should I be happy? I believed it was only glitter that we had found, so I thought it would be better to take the certain for the uncertain; I have sold my share in the mine to Olaf Svärd for a hundred dollars.' He was desperate and, when the parson drove away from him, he stood on the highway and wept.

"When the clergyman got back to his home, he sent a servant to Olaf Svärd and his brother to tell them that it was silver they had found. He thought that he had had quite enough of driving around and spreading the good news.

"But in the evening, when the parson sat alone, his joy asserted itself again. He went out in the darkness and stood on a hillock upon which he contemplated building the new parsonage. It should be imposing, of course, as fine as a bishop's palace. He stood there long that night, nor did he content himself with rebuilding the parsonage! It occurred to him that, since there were such riches to be found in the parish, throngs of people would pour in and, finally, a whole city would be built around the mine. And then he would have to erect a new church in place of the old one. Toward this object a large portion of his wealth would probably go. And he was not content with this, either, but fancied that, when his church was ready, the king and many bishops would come to the dedication. Then the king would be pleased with the church; but he would remark that there was no place where a King might put up, and then he would have to erect a castle in the new city."

Just then one of the king's courtiers opened the door of the vestry and announced that the big royal coach was mended.

At the first moment the king was ready to withdraw, but on second thought he changed his mind. "You may tell your story to the end," he said to the parson. "But you can hurry it a bit. We know all about how the man thought and dreamed. We want to know about how he acted."

"But while the parson was still lost in his dreams," continued the clergyman, "word came to him that Israel Per Persson had made away with himself. He had not been able to bear the disappointment of having sold his share in the mine. He had thought, no doubt, that he could not endure to go about every day seeing another enjoying the wealth that might have been his."

The king straightened up a little. He kept both eyes open. "Upon my word," he said, "if I had been that parson, I should have had enough of the mine!"

"The king is a rich man," said the parson. "He has quite enough, at all events. It is not the same thing with a poor curate who possesses nothing. The unhappy wretch thought instead, when he saw that God's blessing was not with his enterprise, 'I will dream no more of bringing glory and profit to myself with these riches, but I can't let the silver lie buried in the earth! I must take it out, for the benefit of the poor and needy. I will work the mine, to put the whole parish on its feet.'

"So one day the parson went out to see Olaf Svärd, to ask him and his brother as to what should be done immediately with the silver mountain. When he came in the vicinity of the barracks he met a cart surrounded by armed peasants, and in the cart sat a man with his hands tied behind him and a rope around his ankles.

"When the parson passed by, the cart stopped and he had time to regard the prisoner, whose head was tied up so it was not easy to see who he was. But the parson thought he recognized Olaf Svärd. He heard the prisoner beg those who guarded him to let him speak a few words with the parson.

"The parson drew nearer, and the prisoner turned toward him. 'You will soon be the only one who knows where the silver mine is,' said Olaf.

"'What are you saying, Olaf?' asked the parson.

"'Well, you see, parson, since we have learned that it was a silver mine we had found, my brother and I could no longer be as good friends as before. We were continually quarreling. Last night we got into a controversy over which one of us five it was who first discovered the mine. It ended in strife between us, and we came to blows. I have killed my brother and he has left me with a souvenir across the forehead to remember him by. I must hang now, and then you will be the only one who knows about the mine; therefore I wish to ask something of you.'

"'Speak out!' said the parson. 'I'll do what I can for you.'

"'You know that I am leaving several little children behind me,' began the soldier, but the parson interrupted him.

"'As regards this, you can rest easy. That which comes to your share in the mine they shall have, exactly as if you yourself were living.'

"'No,' said Olaf Svärd, 'it was another thing I wanted to ask of you. Don't let them have any portion of that which comes from the mine!'

"The parson staggered back a step. He stood there dumb and could not answer.

"'If you do not promise me this, I cannot die in peace,' said the prisoner.

"'Yes,' said the parson slowly and painfully. 'I promise you what you ask of me.'

"Thereupon the murderer was taken away, and the parson stood on the highway thinking how he should keep the promise he had given him. On the way home he thought of the wealth which he had been so happy over. What if it really were true that the people in this community could not stand riches? Already four were ruined who hitherto had been dignified and excellent men. He seemed to see the whole community before him, and he pictured to himself how this silver mine would destroy one after another. Was it befitting that he, who had been appointed to watch over these poor human beings' souls, should let loose upon them that which would be their destruction?"

All of a sudden the king sat bolt upright in his chair. "I declare!" said he, "you'll make me understand that a parson in this isolated settlement must be every inch a man."

"Nor was it enough with what had already happened," continued the parson, "for as soon as the news about the mine spread among the parishioners, they stopped working and went about in idleness, waiting for the time when great riches should pour in on them. All the ne'er-do-wells there were in this section streamed in, and drunkenness and fighting were what the parson heard talked of continually. A lot of people did nothing but tramp round in the forest searching for the mine, and the parson marked that as soon as he left the house people followed him stealthily to find out if he wasn't going to the silver mountain and to steal the secret from him.

"When matters were come to this pass, the parson called the peasants together to vote. To start with he reminded them of all the misfortunes which the discovery of the mountain had brought upon them, and he

asked them if they were going to let themselves be ruined or if they would save themselves. Then he told them that they must not expect him, who was their spiritual adviser, to help on their destruction. Now he had declared not to reveal to anyone where the silver mine was, and never would he himself take riches from it. And then he asked the peasants how they would have it henceforth. If they wished to continue their search for the mine and wait upon riches, then he would go so far away that no word of their misery could reach him; but if they would give up thinking about the silver mine and be as heretofore, he would remain with them. 'Whichever way you may choose,' said the parson, 'remember this, that from me no one shall ever know anything about the silver mountain.'"

"Well," said the king, "how did they decide?"

"They did as their pastor wished," said the parson. "They understood that he meant well by them when he wanted to remain poor for their sakes. And they commissioned him to go to the forest and conceal the vein of ore with evergreen and stone, so that no one would be able to find it—neither they nor their posterity."

"And ever since the parson has been living here just as poor as the rest?"

"Yes," answered the curate, "he has lived here just as poor as the rest."

"He has married, of course, and built a new parsonage?" said the king.

"No, he couldn't afford to marry and he lives in the old cabin."

"It's a pretty story that you have told me," said the king. After a few seconds he resumed, "Was it of the silver mountain that you were thinking when you said that the parson here would be able to procure for me as much money as I need?"

"Yes," said the other.

"But I can't put the thumbscrews on him," said the king. "Or how would you advise that I get such a man to show me the mountain—a man who has renounced his sweetheart and the allurements of life?"

"Oh, that's a different matter," said the parson. "But if it's the fatherland that is in need of the fortune, he will probably give in."

"Will you answer for that?" asked the king.

"Yes, that I will answer for," said the clergyman.

"Doesn't he care, then, what becomes of his parishioners?"

"That can rest in God's hands."

The king rose from his chair and walked over to the window. He stood for a moment and looked upon the group of people outside. The longer he looked, the clearer his large eyes shone; and his figure seemed to grow. "You may greet the pastor of this congregation and say that for Sweden's king there is no sight more beautiful than to see a people such as this!"

Then the king turned from the window and looked at the clergyman. He began to smile. "Is it true that the pastor of this parish is so poor that he removes his black clothes as soon as the service is over and dresses himself like a peasant?" asked the king.

"Yes, so poor is he," said the curate, and a crimson flush leaped into his rough-hewn face.

The king went back to the window. One could see that he was in his best mood. All that was noble and great within him had been quickened into life. "You must let that mine lie in peace," said the king. "Inasmuch as you have labored and starved a lifetime to make this people such as you would have it, you may keep it as it is."

"But if the kingdom is in danger?" said the parson.

"The kingdom is better served with men than with money," remarked the king. When he had said this, he bade the clergyman farewell and went out from the vestry.

Without stood the group of people, as quiet and taciturn as they were when he went in. As the king came down the steps, a peasant stepped up to him.

"Have you had a talk with our pastor?" said the peasant.

"Yes," said the king. "I have."

"Then of course you have our answer," said the peasant. "We asked you to go in and talk with our parson, that he might give you an answer from us."

"I have the answer," said the king.

About the Story

1. How are the stories of the parson and parishioners and of the king and his army different?

2. Why do you think the parson told the story to the king?

3. What character in the story is a sort of companion for you, the reader, one with whom you can identify and with whom you can progressively learn?

4. In one sentence, state what you think is the central theme of the story.

About the Author

Selma Lagerlöf (1858–1940) had a special gift for creative storytelling. Throughout her life she shared modern versions of old Swedish folktales and delightful creations of her own vivid imagination. Her works were infused with childlike optimism and a deep appreciation of the value of integrity, honesty, and selflessness. One recurrent theme in her literature is the reconciliation of the desire to be happy with the need to be virtuous and noble. Her short story "The Silver Mine" is an excellent example of her approach to storytelling and her method of expressing truth to make it appealing to the reader.

Although she had the honor of being both the first woman to receive the Nobel Prize in Literature and Sweden's foremost storyteller, Lagerlöf lived a quiet and uneventful life. Her imagination, however, was always active, sustained from childhood by the wealth of Swedish folklore that she knew well. She grew up on a farm in Sweden, and as an adult she purchased the estate and ran it with the help of Swedish peasants. The Swedish school system commissioned Lagerlöf to write a reader for use in grade schools. The resulting two books, *The Wonderful Adventures of Nils* and *The Further Adventures of Nils*, tell of the escapades of a young boy who magically flies about Sweden. These enchanting stories richly portray the country and customs of the Swedish countryside.

Beauty and the Beast

Suzanne Barbot de Villeneuve

(retold by Andrew Lang)

The French vogue of fairy-tale writing began in the court of Louis XIV (1638–1715) and continued until the Revolution (1789). In 1697 a lawyer connected with the court, Charles Perrault, offered for publication a volume of fairy tales containing "The Sleeping Beauty," "Red Riding Hood," "Blue Beard," "Puss in Boots," "Cinderella," and several others that have become world classics. Efforts by later participants in the vogue produced little that is noteworthy. An exception is "Beauty and the Beast." This story gives classic form to the theme of love's power to see through outward appearances. The heroine is named Beauty. Is her name appropriate in more ways than one?

Once upon a time, in a very far-off country, there lived a merchant who had been so fortunate in all his undertakings that he was enormously rich. As he had, however, six sons and six daughters, he found that his money was not too much to let them all have everything they fancied, as they were accustomed to do.

But one day a most unexpected misfortune befell them. Their house caught fire and was speedily burnt to the ground, with all the splendid furniture, the books, pictures, gold, silver, and precious goods it contained; and this was only the beginning of their troubles. Their father, who had until this moment prospered in all ways, suddenly lost every ship he had upon the sea, either by dint of* pirates, shipwreck, or fire. Then he heard that his clerks in distant countries, whom he trusted entirely, had proved unfaithful; and at last from great wealth he fell into the direst poverty.

by dint of: by force of

All that he had left was a little house in a desolate place at least a hundred leagues* from the town in which he had lived, and to this he was forced to retreat with his children, who were in despair at the idea of leading such a different life. Indeed, the daughters at first hoped that their friends, who had been so numerous while they were rich, would insist on their staying in their houses now they no longer possessed one. But they soon found that they were left alone, and that their former friends even attributed their misfortunes to their own extravagance, and showed no intention of offering them any help. So nothing was left for them but to take their departure to the cottage, which stood in the midst of a dark forest, and seemed to be the most dismal place upon the face of the earth. As they were too poor to have any servants, the girls had to work hard, like peasants, and the sons, for their part, cultivated the fields to earn their living. Roughly clothed, and living in the simplest way, the girls regretted unceasingly the luxuries and amusements of their former life; only the youngest tried to be brave and cheerful. She had been as sad as anyone when misfortune first overtook her father, but, soon recovering her natural gaiety, she set to work to make the best of things, to amuse her father and brothers as well as she could, and to try to persuade her sisters to join her in dancing and singing. But they would do nothing of the sort, and, because she was not as doleful* as themselves, they declared that this miserable life was all she was fit for. But she was really far prettier and cleverer than they were; indeed, she was so lovely that she was always called Beauty. After two years, when they were all beginning to get used to their new life, something happened to disturb their tranquility. Their father received the news that one of his ships, which he had believed to be lost, had come safely into port with a rich cargo. All the sons and daughters at once thought that their poverty was at an end, and wanted to set out directly for the town; but their father, who was more prudent, begged them to wait a little, and, though it was harvest-time, and he could ill be spared, determined to go himself first, to make inquiries. Only the youngest daughter had any doubt but that they would soon again be as rich as they were before, or at least rich enough to live comfortably in some town where they would find amusement and gay companions once more. So they all loaded their father with commissions for jewels and dresses which it would have taken a fortune to buy; only Beauty, feeling sure that it was of no use, did not ask for anything. Her father, noticing her silence, said: "And what shall I bring for you, Beauty?"

---

a hundred leagues: three hundred miles
doleful: melancholy

"The only thing I wish for is to see you come home safely," she answered.

But this reply vexed her sisters, who fancied she was blaming them for having asked for such costly things. Her father, however, was pleased, but as he thought that at her age she certainly ought to like pretty presents, he told her to choose something.

"Well, dear father," she said, "as you insist upon it, I beg that you will bring me a rose. I have not seen one since we came here, and I love them so much."

So the merchant set out and reached the town as quickly as possible, but only to find that his former companions, believing him to be dead, had divided between them the goods which the ship had brought; and after six months of trouble and expense he found himself as poor as when he started, having been able to recover only just enough to pay the cost of his journey. To make matters worse, he was obliged to leave the town in the most terrible weather, so that by the time he was within a few leagues of his home he was almost exhausted with cold and fatigue. Though he knew it would take some hours to get through the forest, he was so anxious to be at his journey's end that he resolved to go on; but night overtook him, and the deep snow and bitter frost made it impossible for his horse to carry him any farther. Not a house was to be seen; the only shelter he could get was the hollow trunk of a great tree, and there he crouched all the night, which seemed to him the longest he had ever known. In spite of his weariness the howling of the wolves kept him awake, and even when at last the day broke he was not much better off, for the falling snow had covered up every path, and he did not know which way to turn.

At length he made out some sort of track, and though at the beginning it was so rough and slippery that he fell down more than once, it presently became easier, and led him into an avenue of trees which ended in

whom he could ask to give him something to eat. Deep silence reigned everywhere, and at last, tired of roaming through empty rooms and galleries, he stopped in a room smaller than the rest, where a clear fire was burning and a couch was drawn up cosily close to it. Thinking that this must be prepared for someone who was expected, he sat down to wait till he should come, and very soon fell into a sweet sleep.

agate: a fine-grained variety of grayish quartz with colored bands

When his extreme hunger wakened him after several hours, he was still alone; but a little table, upon which was a good dinner, had been drawn up close to him, and, as he had eaten nothing for twenty-four hours, he lost no time in beginning his meal, hoping that he might soon have an opportunity of thanking his considerate entertainer, whoever it might be. But no one appeared, and even after another long sleep, from which he awoke completely refreshed, there was no sign of anybody, though a fresh meal of dainty cakes and fruit was prepared upon the little table at his elbow. Being naturally timid, the silence began to terrify him, and he resolved to search once more through all the rooms; but it was of no use. Not even a servant was to be seen; there was no sign of life in the palace! He began to wonder what he should do, and to amuse himself by pretending that all the treasures he saw were his own, and considering how he would divide them among his children. Then he went down into the garden, and though it was winter everywhere else, here the sun shone, and the birds sang, and the flowers bloomed, and the air was soft and sweet. The merchant, in ecstasies with all he saw and heard, said to himself:

"All this must be meant for me. I will go this minute and bring my children to share all these delights."

a splendid castle. It seemed to the merchant very strange that no snow had fallen in the avenue, which was entirely composed of orange trees, covered with flowers and fruit. When he reached the first court of the castle he saw before him a flight of agate* steps, and went up them, and passed through several splendidly furnished rooms. The pleasant warmth of the air revived him, and he felt very hungry; but there seemed to be nobody in all this vast and splendid palace

In spite of being so cold and weary when he reached the castle, he had taken his horse to the stable and fed it. Now he thought he would saddle it for his homeward journey, and he turned down the path which led to the stable. This path had a hedge of roses on each side of it, and the merchant thought he had never seen or smelt such exquisite flowers. They reminded him of his promise to Beauty, and he stopped and had just gathered one to take to her when he was startled by a strange noise behind him. Turning round, he saw a frightful Beast, which seemed to be very angry and said, in a terrible voice:

"Who told you that you might gather my roses? Was it not enough that I allowed you to be in my palace and was kind to you? This is the way you show your gratitude, by stealing my flowers! But your insolence shall not go unpunished."

The merchant, terrified by these furious words, dropped the fatal rose, and, throwing himself on his knees, cried: "Pardon me, noble sir. I am truly grateful to you for your hospitality, which was so magnificent that I could not imagine that you would be offended by my taking such a little thing as a rose." But the Beast's anger was not lessened by this speech.

"You are very ready with excuses and flattery," he cried; "but that will not save you from the death you deserve."

"Alas!" thought the merchant, "if my daughter Beauty could only know what danger her rose has brought me into!"

And in despair he began to tell the Beast all his misfortunes, and the reason of his journey, not forgetting to mention Beauty's request.

"A king's ransom would hardly have procured all that my other daughters asked," he said; "but I thought that I might at least take Beauty her rose. I beg you to forgive me, for you see I meant no harm."

The Beast considered for a moment, and then he said, in a less furious tone:

"I will forgive you on one condition—that is, that you will give me one of your daughters."

"Ah!" cried the merchant, "if I were cruel enough to buy my own life at the expense of one of my children's, what excuse could I invent to bring her here?"

"No excuse would be necessary," answered the Beast. "If she comes at all she must come willingly. On no other condition will I have her. See if any one of them is courageous enough, and loves you well enough to come and save your life. You seem to be an honest man, so I will trust you to go home. I give you a month to see if either of your daughters will come back with you and stay here, to let you go free. If neither of them is willing, you must come alone, after bidding them good-bye forever, for then you will belong to me. And do not imagine that you can hide from me, for if you fail to keep your word I will come and fetch you!" added the Beast grimly.

The merchant accepted this proposal, though he did not really think any of his daughters would be persuaded to come. He promised to return at the time appointed, and then, anxious to escape from the presence of the Beast, he asked permission to set off at once.

But the Beast answered that he could not go until the next day. "Then you will find a horse ready for you," he said. "Now go and eat your supper, and await my orders."

The poor merchant, more dead than alive, went back to his room, where the most delicious supper was already served on the little table which was drawn up before a blazing fire. But he was too terrified to eat, and tasted only a few of the dishes, for fear the Beast should be angry if he did not obey his orders. When he had finished he heard a great noise in the next room, which he knew meant that the Beast was coming. As he could do nothing to escape his visit, the only thing that remained was to seem as little afraid as possible; so when the Beast appeared and asked roughly if he had supped well, the merchant answered humbly that he had, thanks to his host's kindness. Then the Beast warned him to remember their agreement, and to prepare his daughter exactly for what she had to expect.

"Do not get up tomorrow," he added, "until you see the sun and hear a golden bell ring. Then you will find your breakfast waiting for you here, and the horse you are to ride will be ready in the courtyard. He will also bring you back again when you come with your daughter a month hence. Farewell. Take a rose to Beauty, and remember your promise!"

The merchant was only too glad when the Beast went away, and though he could not sleep for sadness, he lay down until the sun rose. Then, after a hasty breakfast, he went to gather Beauty's rose, and mounted his horse, which carried him off so swiftly that in an instant he had lost sight of the palace, and he was still wrapped in gloomy thoughts when it stopped before the door of the cottage.

His sons and daughters, who had been very uneasy at his long absence, rushed to meet him, eager to know the result of his journey, which, seeing him mounted upon a splendid horse and wrapped in a rich mantle, they supposed to be favorable. But he hid the truth from them at first, only saying sadly to Beauty as he gave her the rose:

"Here is what you asked me to bring you; you little know what it has cost."

But this excited their curiosity so greatly that presently he told them his adventures from beginning to end, and then they were all very unhappy. The girls lamented loudly over their lost hopes, and the sons declared that their father should not return to this terrible castle, and began to make plans for killing the Beast if it should come to fetch him. But he reminded them that he had promised to go back. Then the girls were very angry with Beauty, and said it was all her fault, and that if she had asked for something sensible this would never have happened, and complained bitterly that they should have to suffer for her folly.

Poor Beauty, much distressed, said to them:

"I have indeed caused this misfortune, but I assure you I did it innocently. Who could have guessed that to ask for a rose in the middle of summer would cause so much misery? But as I did the mischief it is only just that I should suffer for it. I will therefore go back with my father to keep his promise."

At first nobody would hear of this arrangement, and her father and brothers, who loved her dearly, declared that nothing should make them let her go; but Beauty was firm. As the time drew near she divided all her little possessions between her sisters, and said good-bye to everything she loved, and when the fatal day came she encouraged and cheered her father as they mounted together the horse which had brought him back. It seemed to fly rather than gallop, but so smoothly that Beauty was not frightened; indeed, she would have enjoyed the journey if she had not feared what might happen to her at the end of it. Her father still tried to persuade her to go back, but in vain. While they were talking the night fell, and then, to their great surprise, wonderful colored lights began to shine in all directions, and splendid fireworks blazed out before them; all the forest was illuminated by them, and even felt pleasantly warm, though it had been bitterly cold before.

This lasted until they reached the avenue of orange trees, where were statues holding flaming torches, and when they got nearer to the palace they saw that it was illuminated from the roof to the ground, and music sounded softly from the courtyard. "The Beast must be very hungry," said Beauty, trying to laugh, "if he makes all this rejoicing over the arrival of his prey."

But, in spite of her anxiety, she could not help admiring all the wonderful things she saw.

The horse stopped at the foot of the flight of steps leading to the terrace; and when they had dismounted, her father led her to the little room he had been in before, where they found a splendid fire burning and the table daintily spread with a delicious supper.

The merchant knew that this was meant for them, and Beauty, who was rather less frightened now that she had passed through so many rooms and seen nothing of the Beast, was quite willing to begin, for her long ride had made her very hungry. But they had hardly finished their meal when the noise of the Beast's footsteps was heard approaching and Beauty clung to her father in terror, which became all the greater when she saw how frightened he was. But when the Beast really appeared, though she trembled at the sight of him, she made a great effort to hide her horror, and saluted him respectfully.

This evidently pleased the Beast. After looking at her he said, in a tone that might have struck terror into the boldest heart, though he did not seem to be angry:

"Good evening, old man. Good evening, Beauty."

The merchant was too terrified to reply, but Beauty answered sweetly:

"Good evening, Beast."

"Have you come willingly?" asked the Beast. "Will you be content to stay here when your father goes away?"

Beauty answered bravely that she was quite prepared to stay.

"I am pleased with you," said the Beast. "As for you, old man," he added, turning to the merchant, "at sunrise tomorrow you will take your departure. When the bell rings, get up quickly and eat your breakfast, and you will find the same horse waiting to take you home; but remember that you must never expect to see my palace again."

Then turning to Beauty, he said:

"Take your father into the next room, and help him to choose everything you think your brothers and sisters would like to have. You will find two traveling-trunks there; fill them as full as you can. It is only just that you should send them something very precious as a remembrance of yourself."

Then he went away, after saying, "Good-bye, Beauty; good-bye, old man"; and though Beauty was beginning to think with great dismay of her father's departure, she was afraid to disobey the Beast's orders; and they went into the next room, which had shelves and cupboards all round it. They were greatly surprised at the riches it contained. There were splendid dresses fit for a queen, with all the ornaments that were to be worn with them; and when Beauty opened the cupboards she was quite dazzled by gorgeous jewels that lay in heaps upon every shelf. After choosing a vast quantity, which she divided between her sisters—for she had made a heap of the wonderful dresses for each of them—she opened the last chest, which was full of gold.

"I think, father," she said, "that, as the gold will be more useful to you, we had better take out the other things again, and fill the trunks with it." So they did this; but the more they put in, the more room there seemed to be, and at last they put back all the jewels and dresses they had taken out, and Beauty even added as many more of the jewels as she could carry at once; and then the trunks were not too full, but they were so heavy that an elephant could not have carried them!

"The Beast was mocking us," cried the merchant; "he must have pretended to give us all these things, knowing that I could not carry them away."

"Let us wait and see," answered Beauty. "I cannot believe that he meant to deceive us. All we can do is to fasten them up and leave them ready."

So they did this and returned to the little room, where, to their astonishment, they found breakfast ready. The merchant ate his with a good appetite, as the Beast's generosity made him believe that he might perhaps venture to come back soon and see Beauty. But she felt sure that her father was leaving her forever, so she was very sad when the bell rang sharply for the second time and warned them that the time was come for them to part. They went down into the courtyard, where two horses were waiting, one loaded with the two trunks, the other for him to ride. They were pawing the ground in their impatience to start, and the merchant was forced to bid Beauty a hasty farewell; and as soon as he was mounted he went off at such a pace that she lost sight of him in an instant. Then Beauty began to cry, and wandered sadly back to her own room. But she soon found that she was very sleepy, and as she had nothing better to do she lay down and instantly fell asleep. And then she dreamed that she was walking by a brook bordered with trees, and lamenting her sad fate, when a young prince, handsomer than anyone she had ever seen, and with a voice that went straight to her heart, came and said to her, "Ah, Beauty! you are not so unfortunate as you suppose. Here you will be rewarded for all you have suffered elsewhere. Your every wish shall be gratified. Only try to find me out, no matter how I may be disguised, as I love you dearly, and in making me happy you will find your own happiness. Be as true hearted as you are beautiful, and we shall have nothing left to wish for."

"What can I do, Prince, to make you happy?" said Beauty.

"Only be grateful," he answered, "and do not trust too much to your eyes. And, above all, do not desert me until you have saved me from my cruel misery."

After this she thought she found herself in a room with a stately and beautiful lady, who said to her:

"Dear Beauty, try not to regret all you have left behind you, for you are destined to a better fate. Only do not let yourself be deceived by appearances."

Beauty found her dreams so interesting that she was in no hurry to awake, but presently the clock roused her by calling her name softly twelve times, and then she got up and found her dressing table set out with everything she could possibly want; and when her toilette* was finished she found dinner was waiting in the room next to hers. But dinner does not take very long when you are all by yourself, and very soon she sat down cozily in the corner of a sofa and began to think about the charming Prince she had seen in her dream.

---

toilette: grooming

"He said I could make him happy," said Beauty to herself. "It seems, then, that this horrible Beast keeps him a prisoner. How can I set him free? I wonder why they both told me not to trust to appearances? I don't understand it. But, after all, it was only a dream, so why should I trouble myself about it? I had better go and find something to do to amuse myself."

So she got up and began to explore some of the many rooms of the palace.

The first she entered was lined with mirrors, and Beauty saw herself reflected on every side, and thought she had never seen such a charming room. Then a bracelet which was hanging from a chandelier caught her

eye, and on taking it down she was greatly surprised to find that it held a portrait of her unknown admirer, just as she had seen him in her dream. With great delight she slipped the bracelet on her arm, and went on into a gallery of pictures, where she soon found a portrait of the same handsome Prince, as large as life, and so well painted that as she studied it he seemed to smile kindly at her. Tearing herself away from the portrait at last, she passed through into a room which contained every musical instrument under the sun, and here she amused herself for a long while in trying some of them, and singing until she was tired. The next room was a library, and she saw everything she had ever wanted to read, as well as everything she had read, and it seemed to her that a whole lifetime would not be enough even to read the names of the books, there were so many. By this time it was growing dusk, and wax candles in diamond and ruby candlesticks were beginning to light themselves in every room.

Beauty found her supper served just at the time she preferred to have it, but she did not see anyone or hear a sound; and, though her father had warned her that she would be alone, she began to find it rather dull.

But presently she heard the Beast coming, and wondered tremblingly if he meant to eat her up now.

However, as he did not seem at all ferocious, and only said gruffly: "Good evening, Beauty," she answered cheerfully and managed to conceal her terror. Then the Beast asked her how she had been amusing herself, and she told him all the rooms she had seen.

Then he asked if she thought she could be happy in his palace; and Beauty answered that everything was so beautiful that she would be very hard to please if she could not be happy. And after about an hour's talk Beauty began to think that the Beast was not nearly so terrible as she had supposed at first. Then he got up to leave her, and said in his gruff voice:

"Do you love me, Beauty? Will you marry me?"

"Oh! what shall I say?" cried Beauty, for she was afraid to make the Beast angry by refusing.

"Say 'yes' or 'no' without fear," he replied.

"Oh! no, Beast," said Beauty hastily.

"Since you will not, good-night, Beauty," he said. And she answered: "Good-night, Beast," very glad to find that her refusal had not provoked him. And after he was gone she was very soon in bed and asleep, and dreaming of her unknown Prince. She thought he came and said to her:

"Ah, Beauty! why are you so unkind to me? I fear I am fated to be unhappy for many a long day still."

And then her dreams changed, but the charming Prince figured in them all; and when morning came her first thought was to look at the portrait and see if it was really like him, and she found that it certainly was.

This morning she decided to amuse herself in the garden, for the sun shone, and all the fountains were playing; but she was astonished to find that every place was familiar to her, and presently she came to the brook where the myrtle trees were growing where she had first met the Prince in her dream, and that made her think more than ever that he must be kept a prisoner by the Beast. When she was tired she went back to the palace, and found a new room full of materials for every kind of work—ribbons to make into bows, and silks to work into flowers. Then there was an aviary full of rare birds, which were so tame that they flew to Beauty as soon as they saw her, and perched upon her shoulders and her head.

"Pretty little creatures," she said, "how I wish that your cage was nearer to my room that I might often hear you sing!"

So saying she opened a door, and found to her delight that it led into her own room, though she had thought it was quite the other side of the palace.

There were more birds in a room farther on, parrots and cockatoos that could talk, and they greeted Beauty by name; indeed, she found them so entertaining that she took one or two back to her room, and they talked to her while she was at supper; after which the Beast paid her his usual visit, and asked the same questions as before, and then with a gruff "good-night" he took his departure, and Beauty went to bed to dream of her mysterious Prince. The days passed swiftly in different amusements, and after a while Beauty found out another strange thing in the palace, which often pleased her when she was tired of being alone. There was one room which she had not noticed particularly; it was empty, except that under each of the windows stood a very comfortable chair; and the first time she had looked out of the window it had seemed to her that a black curtain prevented her from seeing anything outside. But the second time she went into the room, happening to be tired, she sat down in one of the chairs, when instantly the curtain was rolled aside, and a most amusing pantomime was acted before her; there were dances, and colored lights, and music, and pretty dresses, and it was all so gay that Beauty was in ecstasies. After that she tried the other seven windows in turn, and there was some new and surprising entertainment to be seen from each of them, so that Beauty never could feel lonely any more. Every evening after supper the Beast came to see her, and always before saying good-night asked her in his terrible voice:

"Beauty, will you marry me?"

And it seemed to Beauty, now she understood him better, that when she said, "No, Beast," he went away quite sad. But her happy dreams of the handsome young prince soon made her forget the poor Beast, and the only thing that at all disturbed her was to be constantly told to distrust appearances, to let her heart guide her, and not her eyes, and many other equally perplexing things, which, consider as she would, she could not understand.

So everything went on for a long time, until at last, happy as she was, Beauty began to long for the sight of her father and her brothers and sisters; and one night, seeing her look very sad, the Beast asked her what was the matter. Beauty had quite ceased to be afraid of him. Now she knew that he was really gentle in spite of his ferocious looks and his dreadful voice.

So she answered that she was longing to see her home once more. Upon hearing this the Beast seemed sadly distressed, and cried miserably.

"Ah! Beauty, have you the heart to desert an unhappy Beast like this? What more do you want to make you happy? Is it because you hate me that you want to escape?"

"No, dear Beast," answered Beauty softly, "I do not hate you, and I should be very sorry never to see you anymore, but I long to see my father again. Only let me go for two months, and I promise to come back to you and stay for the rest of my life."

The Beast, who had been sighing dolefully while she spoke, now replied:

"I cannot refuse you anything you ask, even though it should cost me my life. Take the four boxes you will find in the room next to your own, and fill them with everything you wish to take with you. But remember your promise and come back when the two months are over, or you may have cause to repent it, for if you do not come in good time, you will find your faithful Beast dead. You will not need any chariot to bring you back. Only say good-bye to all your brothers and sisters the night before you come away, and when you have gone to bed, turn this ring round upon your finger and say firmly: 'I wish to go back to my palace and see my Beast again.' Good-night, Beauty. Fear nothing, sleep peacefully, and before long you shall see your father once more."

As soon as Beauty was alone she hastened to fill the boxes with all the rare and precious things she saw about her, and only when she was tired of heaping things into them did they seem to be full.

Then she went to bed, but could hardly sleep for joy. And when at last she did begin to dream of her beloved prince she was grieved to see him stretched upon a grassy bank sad and weary, and hardly like himself.

"What is the matter?" she cried.

But he looked at her reproachfully, and said:

"How can you ask me, cruel one? Are you not leaving me to my death perhaps?"

"Ah! don't be so sorrowful," cried Beauty; "I am only going to assure my father that I am safe and happy. I have promised the Beast faithfully that I will come back, and he would die of grief if I did not keep my word!"

"What would that matter to you?" said the prince. "Surely you would not care?"

"Indeed I should be ungrateful if I did not care for such a kind Beast," cried Beauty indignantly. "I would die to save him from pain. I assure you it is not his fault that he is so ugly."

Just then a strange sound woke her—someone was speaking not very far away; and opening her eyes she found herself in a room she had never seen before, which was certainly not nearly so splendid as those she was used to in the Beast's palace. Where could she be? She got up and dressed hastily, and then saw that the boxes she had packed the night before were all in the room. While she was wondering by what magic the Beast had transported them and her to this strange place, she suddenly heard her father's voice and rushed out and greeted him joyfully. Her brothers and sisters were all astonished at her appearance, since they had never expected to see her again, and there was no end to the questions they asked her. She had also much to hear about what had happened to them while she was away, and of her father's journey home. But when they heard that she had only come to be with them for a short time, and then must go back to the Beast's palace forever, they lamented loudly. Then Beauty asked her father what he thought could be the meaning of her strange dreams, and why the Prince constantly begged her not to trust to appearances. After much consideration he answered: "You tell me yourself that the Beast, frightful as he is, loves you dearly, and deserves your love and gratitude for his gentleness and kindness; I think the prince must mean you to understand that you ought to reward him by doing as he wishes you to, in spite of his ugliness."

Beauty could not help seeing that this seemed very probable; still, when she thought of her dear prince who was so handsome, she did not feel at all inclined to marry the Beast. At any rate, for two months she need not decide but could enjoy herself with her sisters. But though they were rich now, and lived in a town again, and had plenty of acquaintances, Beauty found that nothing amused her very much; and she often thought of the palace, where she was so happy, especially as at home she never once dreamed of her dear Prince, and she felt quite sad without him.

Then her sisters seemed to have got quite used to being without her, and even found her rather in the way, so she would not have been sorry when the two months were over, but for her father and brothers, who begged her to stay and seemed so grieved at the thought of her departure that she had not the courage to say good-bye to them. Every day when she got up she meant to say it at night, and when night came she put it off again, until at last she had a dismal dream which helped her to make up her mind. She thought she was wandering in a lonely path in the palace gardens when she heard groans which seemed to come from some bushes hiding the entrance of a cave, and running quickly to see what could be the matter, she found the Beast stretched out upon his side, apparently dying. He reproached her faintly with being the cause of his distress, and at the same moment a stately lady appeared, and said very gravely:

"Ah! Beauty, you are only just in time to save his life. See what happens when people do not keep their promises! If you had delayed one day more, you would have found him dead."

Beauty was so terrified by this dream that the next morning she announced her intention of going back at once, and that very night she said good-bye to her father and all her brothers and sisters, and as soon as she was in bed she turned her ring round upon her finger, and said firmly:

"I wish to go back to my palace and see my Beast again," as she had been told to do.

Then she fell asleep instantly, and only woke up to hear the clock saying, "Beauty, Beauty," twelve times in its musical voice, which told her at once that she was really in the palace once more. Everything was just as before, and her birds were so glad to see her! But Beauty thought she had never known such a long day, for she was so anxious to see the Beast again that she felt as if supper time would never come.

But when it did come and no Beast appeared, she was really frightened; so, after listening and waiting for a long time, she ran down into the garden to search for him. Up and down the paths and avenues ran poor Beauty, calling him in vain, for no one answered, and not a trace of him could she find; until at last, quite tired, she stopped for a minute's rest, and saw that she was standing opposite the shady path she had seen in her dream. She rushed down it, and sure enough, there was the cave, and in it lay the Beast— asleep, as Beauty thought. Quite glad to have found him, she ran up and stroked his head, but to her horror he did not move or open his eyes.

"Oh! He is dead; and it is all my fault," said Beauty, crying bitterly.

But then, looking at him again, she fancied he still breathed, and, hastily fetching some water from the nearest fountain, she sprinkled it over his face, and to her great delight he began to revive.

"Oh! Beast, how you frightened me!" she cried. "I never knew how much I loved you until just now, when I feared I was too late to save your life."

"Can you really love such an ugly creature as I am?" said the Beast faintly. "Ah! Beauty, you only came just in time. I was dying because I thought you had forgotten your promise. But go back now and rest, I shall see you again by and by."

Beauty, who had half expected that he would be angry with her, was reassured by his gentle voice and went back to the palace, where supper was awaiting her; and afterwards the Beast came in as usual, and talked about the time she had spent with her father, asking if she had enjoyed herself, and if they had all been very glad to see her.

Beauty answered politely, and quite enjoyed telling him all that had happened to her. And when at last the time came for him to go, and he asked, as he had so often asked before:

"Beauty, will you marry me?" She answered softly: "Yes, dear Beast."

As she spoke a blaze of light sprang up before the windows of the palace; fireworks crackled and guns banged, and across the avenue of orange trees, in letters all made of fire-flies, was written: "Long Live the Prince and His Bride."

Turning to ask the Beast what it could all mean, Beauty found that he had disappeared, and in his place stood her long-loved prince! At the same moment the wheels of a chariot were heard upon the terrace, and two ladies entered the room. One of them Beauty recognized as the stately lady she had seen in her dreams; the other was also so grand and queenly that Beauty hardly knew which to greet first.

But the one she already knew said to her companion:

"Well, Queen, this is Beauty, who has had the courage to rescue your son from the terrible enchantment. They love one another, and only your consent to their marriage is wanting to make them perfectly happy."

"I consent with all my heart," cried the Queen. "How can I ever thank you enough, charming girl, for having restored my dear son to his natural form?"

And then she tenderly embraced Beauty and the Prince, who had meanwhile been greeting the Fairy and receiving her congratulations.

"Now," said the Fairy to Beauty, "I suppose you would like me to send for all your brothers and sisters to dance at your wedding?"

And so she did, and the marriage was celebrated the very next day with the utmost splendor, and Beauty and the Prince lived happily ever after.

About the Story

1. What two types of beauty are described in this selection?

2. Which type does the author portray as more enduring and valuable?

3. How does Beauty differ from her sisters?

4. What characteristics of true beauty are found in the following passages of Scripture?

   1 Chronicles 16:29
   Psalm 90:17
   Proverbs 20:29
   1 Peter 3:4

5. What is the theme of the story? Is it explicit or implicit? What is the basis for your answer?

6. Do you think this theme qualifies as universal? Why or why not?

About the Editor

Andrew Lang (1844–1912) wrote on such a wide range of topics that he acquired the nickname "editor-in-chief" (of Great Britain). The title was well deserved because Lang's scholarly interests were diverse and his sense of the flow and beauty of language was keen.

An expert in historical research, Lang developed a number of concepts concerning the ultimate sources of fairy tales and folk literature. Regrettably he presents Scripture as myth and categorizes the God of the Bible with false gods such as Apollo and Hyperion. In addition, Lang's anthropological works evidence his habitual twisting of Scripture in an attempt to make it agree with Darwinism.

Apart from his anthropological work, however, Lang's accomplishments as a scholar are admirable. For many years he enjoyed great respect as a journalist. He also edited and translated Greek literature such as Homer's works and fairy tales from many sources. These enchanting stories were not just a scholarly pursuit for Lang; a genuine love of their literary beauty inspired him to repopularize the genre in a series of fairy-tale collections. Each volume is designated by a different color, such as *The Blue Fairy Book* and *The Red Fairy Book*. Lang is best known, not for his own writing, but for his story collections that continue to delight adults and children alike.

Go Down, Death

(A Funeral Sermon)

JAMES WELDON JOHNSON

For his 1927 collection, *God's Trombones: Seven Negro Sermons in Verse*, African-American poet James Weldon Johnson drew on folk sermons he had heard in his youth, sermons that had been passed in similar form from preacher to preacher. As a result, these poems reflect some of the major themes of the Bible, including "The Creation," "The Crucifixion," and "The Judgment Day." The following poem from Johnson's collection depicts how to deal with the reality of death in a fallen world. According to the speaker in this poem, what is God's attitude toward death and what should be the Christian's attitude toward death?

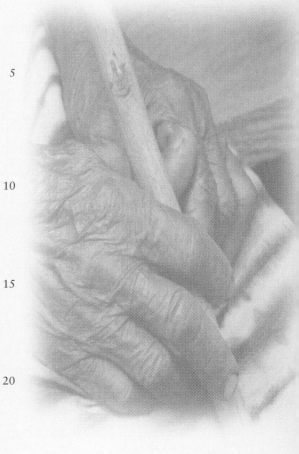

Weep not, weep not,
She is not dead;
She's resting in the bosom of Jesus.
Heart-broken husband—weep no more;
Grief-stricken son—weep no more; 5
Left-lonesome daughter—weep no more;
She's only just gone home.

Day before yesterday morning,
God was looking down from his great,
    high heaven,
Looking down on all his children, 10
And his eye fell on Sister Caroline,
Tossing on her bed of pain.
And God's big heart was touched with pity,
With the everlasting pity.

And God sat back on his throne, 15
And he commanded that tall, bright angel
    standing at his right hand:
Call me Death!
And that tall, bright angel cried in a voice
That broke like a clap of thunder:
Call Death!—Call Death! 20
And the echo sounded down the streets of heaven
Till it reached away back to that shadowy place,
Where Death waits with his pale, white horses.

And Death heard the summons,
And he leaped on his fastest horse, 25
Pale as a sheet in the moonlight.
Up the golden street Death galloped,
And the hoofs of his horse struck fire from
    the gold,
But they didn't make no sound.
Up Death rode to the Great White Throne, 30
And waited for God's command.

And God said: Go down, Death, go down,
Go down to Savannah, Georgia,
Down in Yamacraw,
And find Sister Caroline. 35
She's borne the burden and heat of the day,
She's labored long in my vineyard,
And she's tired—
She's weary—
Go down, Death, and bring her to me. 40

And Death didn't say a word,
But he loosed the reins on his pale, white horse,
And he clamped the spurs to his bloodless sides,
And out and down he rode,
Through heaven's pearly gates, 45
Past suns and moons and stars;
On Death rode,
And the foam from his horse was like a comet
    in the sky;
On Death rode,
Leaving the lightning's flash behind; 50
Straight on down he came.

While we were watching round her bed,
She turned her eyes and looked away,
She saw what we couldn't see;
She saw Old Death. She saw Old Death 55
Coming like a falling star.
But Death didn't frighten Sister Caroline;
He looked to her like a welcome friend.
And she whispered to us: I'm going home,
And she smiled and closed her eyes. 60

And Death took her up like a baby,
And she lay in his icy arms,

But she didn't feel no chill.
And Death began to ride again—
Up beyond the evening star,   65
Out beyond the morning star,
Into the glittering light of glory,
On to the Great White Throne.
And there he laid Sister Caroline
On the loving breast of Jesus.   70

And Jesus took his own hand and wiped away
    her tears,
And he smoothed the furrows from her face,
And the angels sang a little song,
And Jesus rocked her in his arms,
And kept a-saying: Take your rest,   75
Take your rest, take your rest.

Weep not—weep not,
She is not dead;
She's resting in the bosom of Jesus.

About the Author

Born in Florida into a middle-class family, James Weldon Johnson (1871–1938) was a Renaissance man whose titles include professor, lawyer, songwriter, anthologist, poet, novelist, diplomat, and civil rights activist. Upon graduation from Atlanta University in 1894, he took the job of principal at Stanton School and while teaching, became the first African American to pass the bar exam in Florida. He and his brother then moved to New York City to collaborate as Broadway songwriters. Most notably, they coauthored "Lift Every Voice and Sing," known today as the "Negro National Hymn." Unsatisfied by this career, Johnson entered public service, acting as an American consul in Venezuela and Nicaragua for six years before returning to New York. There, writing became his full-time occupation, and his poetry as well as his editorials in favor of racial equality attracted attention. Meanwhile, in 1916 Johnson joined the NAACP and by 1920 had become its first African-American executive secretary, a post he held with distinction until 1930.

Johnson is most famous for his many literary accomplishments. A noted anthologist and critic of African-American literature, he recognized and promoted around the world the literary and cultural value of black folk songs, sermons, and stories. Moreover, he encouraged contemporary black artists to create and publish high-caliber literature reflecting the African-American experience. In this role, he is considered one of the founders of the Harlem Renaissance. Upon retirement, he taught at Fisk University as a professor of creative writing. His three best-known works are his first novel, *An Autobiography of an Ex-Colored Man* (1912); the first anthology of African-American literature, *The Book of American Negro Poetry* (1922); and his collection of poetry, *God's Trombones: Seven Negro Sermons in Verse* (1927).

Do not go gentle into that good night

Dylan Thomas

Like many poems, "Go Down, Death" is the statement of a fictional person. In contrast, the following poem is actually a direct statement by the poet, who wrote it to his dying father. What is Thomas's message to his father? What does that message reveal about the poet's attitude toward death? How does his attitude compare with that of the preacher in Johnson's poem?

Do not go gentle into that good night,
Old age should burn and rave at close of day;
Rage, rage against the dying of the light.

Though wise men at their end know dark is right,
Because their words had forked no lightning they   5
Do not go gentle into that good night.

Good men, the last wave by, crying how bright
Their frail deeds might have danced in a green bay,
Rage, rage against the dying of the light.

Wild men who caught and sang the sun in flight,   10
And learn, too late, they grieved it on its way,
Do not go gentle into that good night.

Grave men, near death, who see with blinding sight
Blind eyes could blaze like meteors and be gay,
Rage, rage against the dying of the light.   15

And you, my father, there on the sad height,
Curse, bless, me now with your fierce tears, I pray.
Do not go gentle into that good night.
Rage, rage against the dying of the light.

About the Author

Welsh poet Dylan Thomas (1914–53) is considered by many to be one of the greatest lyric poets of the English language, with nearly unparalleled expertise in using its sounds and rhythms. His father an English teacher, Thomas read the greats of literature from childhood and excelled at the study of English in school. He left school at age sixteen and by age twenty had published his *18 Poems* to resounding success. While publishing more poetry and short stories, the poet also earned money by writing scripts and broadcasting for the BBC.

With the 1946 publication of *Deaths and Entrances* (his fourth volume of poems) and after three tours reading his poetry throughout the United States, Thomas became known internationally. His rich and well-trained voice captivated audiences, but his deliberately showy persona and scandalous personal life led some critics to downplay his talent. In 1953, Thomas's drama depicting life in small town Wales, *Under Milk Wood*, successfully debuted in America. After celebrating by drinking heavily, Thomas collapsed and died several days later, most likely from complications of longtime alcoholism. Though his poetry is sprinkled liberally with allusions to the Bible, a book he grew up listening to, by his own admission and the evidence in his poetry, Dylan Thomas never embraced Christianity. He struggled with the meaning of life and the inevitability of death, seeing little hope for the future. As a result, his beautiful and powerful poetry often reflects the hollowness of life without the hope found in Christ.

About the Poems

1. In these two poems, how do the people who are dying respond to that fact?

2. How do the main speakers of the poems approach the certainty of death?

3. All of the men in Thomas's poem share a similar emotion as they approach death. What is it?

4. It is unlikely that Dylan Thomas believed that death could be avoided. Why do you think he still wanted people to fight it?

5. Given your answers to the previous questions, briefly state what you think the theme of each poem is.

6. Which theme aligns itself better with Scripture? Explain your answer.

In expressing a theme, an author uses various tools to help add layers of meaning. One of the more complex and comprehensive methods is **allegory**, a type of extended metaphor that forms a story with two levels of meaning. In true allegory, the characters of a story (and often the places, institutions, people groups, etc.) represent a real-life situation about which the author wishes to speak. While the story unfolds on a fictional level, where characters are no more than what they seem, the action also conveys the author's opinions about the nonfictional ideas or people represented. Allegory is used for many purposes, from satirizing political situations to explaining broad truths about life. As you might imagine, creating a story that is both believable on the fictional level and true to the reality it represents is rather complicated. But when done well, allegory enables the author to express his themes more directly than a normal narrative will allow.

For example, the most famous allegory, *The Pilgrim's Progress*, may at first seem to be only a story about the perilous journey of the protagonist, Christian. But as Christian encounters characters such as Mr. Worldly Wiseman, places such as Vanity Fair, and enemies such as the Giant Despair, the reader quickly realizes that the author had more in mind than creating a riveting story. Instead, he is chronicling the spiritual journey of all Christians, including both their struggles and triumphs. Of course, not all allegories tie all aspects of the literal story so directly or so obviously to the metaphorical meaning, but a careful reader can learn to discern through context what the author of an allegory wants his story to portray.

Another tool authors use to infuse meaning into a story is that of symbol. At its most basic, a **symbol** is a person, place, thing, or idea that means something in addition to itself. While the meaning represented in an allegory is specific and limited, the meanings of symbols can be harder to pin down. A symbol gains its meaning by cultural associations, by the way an author uses it in a story, or by a combination of both. For example, many cultures associate the sun with life because of its function in agriculture, and this connotation appears often in literature. In contrast, a symbol specific to a particular work is the New Testament's use of water to signify the Holy Spirit. Both approaches are combined in Ullman's "Top Man," where the mountain serves both as a universal symbol of obstacles to be overcome and a specific symbol of the internal and external conflicts that Nace and Osborn must conquer.

1. Given the theme of "The Silver Mine," what object from the story might qualify as a **symbol**? Explain your reasoning.

2. The story "Beauty and the Beast" qualifies as an **allegory**, teaching several truths about life. What do you think the characters of Beauty and the Beast stand for in the story? What lesson do these characters help us understand?

3. What does Beauty ask her father for? How does it symbolize Beauty's nature? Does the Beast's reaction to the same object reinforce that symbolic meaning?

Quality

John Galsworthy

The details of both conflict and character are important in helping crystallize a story's theme. An author, however, may choose to emphasize one of these elements above the other. In Galsworthy's story, conflict is subservient to character. The intriguing characters of the Gessler brothers create the conflict. They are the embodiment of a particular set of values, values that can find no place in a world of growing industrialization and materialism.

As you read, try to discern what the author's attitude is toward the central characters he creates. Does he sympathize with the Gessler brothers? Or does he view them as old-fashioned and eccentric? What elements of the story help you discern Galsworthy's attitude toward his characters? Does the title of the story give you a clue?

I knew him from the days of my extreme youth, because he made my father's boots; inhabiting with his elder brother two little shops let into one, in a small by-street—now no more, but then most fashionably placed in the West End.

That tenement had a certain quiet distinction; there was no sign upon its face that he made for any of the Royal Family—merely his own German name of Gessler Brothers; and in the window a few pairs of boots. I remember that it always troubled me to account for those unvarying boots in the window, for he made only what was ordered, reaching nothing down, and it seemed so inconceivable that what he made could ever have failed to fit. Had he bought them to put there? That, too, seemed inconceivable. He would never have tolerated in his house leather on which he had not worked himself. Besides, they were too beautiful—the pair of pumps, so inexpressibly slim; the patent leathers with cloth tops, making water come into one's mouth; the tall brown riding boots with marvelous sooty glow, as if, though new, they had been worn a hundred years. Those pairs could have been made only by one who saw before him the Soul of Boot—so truly were they prototypes incarnating the very spirit of all footgear. These thoughts, of course, came to me later, though even when I was promoted to him, at the age of perhaps fourteen, some inkling haunted me of the dignity of himself and his brother. For to make boots—such boots as he made—seemed to me then, and still seems to me, mysterious and wonderful.

I remember well my shy remark, one day, while stretching out to him my youthful foot.

"Isn't it awfully hard to do, Mr. Gessler?"

And his answer, given with a sudden smile from out of the sardonic* redness of his beard: "Id is an ardt!"

---

sardonic: mocking with scorn

Himself, he was a little as if made from leather, with his yellow crinkly face, and crinkly reddish hair and beard, and neat folds slanting down his cheeks to the corners of his mouth, and his guttural and one-toned voice, for leather is a sardonic substance, and stiff and slow of purpose. And that was the character of his face, save that his eyes, which were grey-blue, had in them the simple gravity of one secretly possessed by the Ideal. His elder brother was so very like him—though watery, paler in every way, with a great industry—that sometimes in early days I was not quite sure of him until the interview was over. Then I knew that it was he, if the words, "I will ask my brudder," had not been spoken; and that if they had, it was his elder brother.

When one grew old and wild and ran up bills, one somehow never ran them up with Gessler Brothers. It would not have seemed becoming to go in there and stretch out one's foot to that blue iron-spectacled glance, owing him for more than—say—two pairs, just the comfortable reassurance that one was still his client.

For it was not possible to go to him very often—his boots lasted terribly, having something beyond the temporary—some, as it were, essence of boot stitched into them.

One went in, not as into most shops, in the mood of: "Please serve me, and let me go!" but restfully, as one enters a church; and, sitting on the single wooden chair, waited—for there was never anybody there. Soon, over the top edge of that sort of well—rather dark, and smelling soothingly of leather—which formed the shop, there would be seen his face, or that of his elder brother, peering down. A guttural sound, and the narrow wooden stairs, and he would stand before one without coat, a little bent, in leather apron, with sleeves turned back, blinking—as if awakened from some dream of boots, or like an owl surprised in daylight and annoyed at this interruption.

And I would say: "How do you do, Mr. Gessler? Could you make me a pair of Russian leather boots?"

Without a word he would leave me, retiring whence he came, or into the other portion of the shop, and I would continue to rest in the wooden chair, inhaling the incense of his trade. Soon he would come back, holding in his thin, veined hand a piece of gold-brown leather. With eyes fixed on it, he would remark: "What a beaudiful biece!" When I, too, had admired it, he would speak again. "When do you wand dem?" And I would answer: "Oh! As soon as you conveniently can." And he would say: "Tomorrow fordnighd?"* Or if he were his elder brother: "I will ask my brudder!"

---

fordnighd (fortnight): two weeks

Then I would murmur: "Thank you! Good morning, Mr. Gessler." "Goot morning!" He would reply, still looking at the leather in his hand. And as I moved to the door, I would hear the tip-tap of his bast* slippers restoring him, up the stairs, to his dream of boots. But if it were some new kind of footgear that he had not yet made me, then indeed he would observe ceremony—divesting me of my boot and holding it long in his hand, looking at it with eyes at once critical and loving, as if recalling the glow with which he had created it, and rebuking the way in which one had disorganized this masterpiece. Then placing my foot on a thin piece of paper, he would two or three times tickle the outer edges with a pencil and pass his nervous fingers over my toes, feeling himself into the heart of my requirements.

---

bast: flexible fibrous material used to make textiles

I cannot forget that day on which I had occasion to say to him: "Mr. Gessler, that last pair of town walking-boots creaked, you know."

He looked at me for a time without replying, as if expecting me to withdraw or qualify the statement, then said:

"Id shouldn't 'ave greaked."

"It did, I'm afraid."

"You god dem wed before dey found demselves?"

"I don't think so."

At that he lowered his eyes, as if hunting for memory of those boots, and I felt sorry I had mentioned this grave thing.

"Zend dem back!" he said; "I will look at dem."

A feeling of compassion for creaking boots surged up in me, so well could I imagine the sorrowful long curiosity of regard which he would bend on them.

"Zome boods," he said slowly, "are bad from birdt. If I can do noding wid dem, I dake dem off your bill."

Once (once only) I went absent-mindedly into his shop in a pair of boots bought in an emergency at some large firm. He took my order without showing me any leather, and I could feel his eyes penetrating the inferior covering of my foot. At last he said:

"Dose are nod my boods."

The tone was not one of anger, nor of sorrow, not even of contempt, but there was in it something quiet that froze the blood. He put his hand down and pressed a finger on the place where the left boot, endeavoring to be fashionable, was not quite comfortable.

"Id 'urds you dere," he said. "Dose big virms 'ave no self-respect. Drash!" And then as if something had given way within him, he spoke long and bitterly. It was the only time I ever heard him discuss the conditions and hardships of his trade.

"Dey ged id all," he said, "dey ged id by adverdisement, nod by work. Dey dake id away from us, who lofe our boods. Id gomes to dis—bresently I haf no work. Every year id gets less—you will see." And looking at his lined face I saw things I had never noticed before, bitter things and bitter struggle—and what a lot of grey hairs there seemed suddenly in his red beard!

As best I could, I explained the circumstances of the purchase of those ill-omened boots. But his face and voice made so deep an impression that during the next few minutes I ordered many pairs. Nemesis* fell! They lasted more terribly than ever. And I was not able conscientiously to go to him for nearly two years.

---

nemesis: retributive justice

When at last I went I was surprised to find that outside one of the two little windows of his shop another name was painted, also that of a boot-maker—making, of course, for the Royal Family. The old familiar boots, no longer in dignified isolation, were huddled in the single window. Inside, the now contracted well of the one little shop was more scented and darker than ever. And it was longer than usual, too, before a face peered down, and the tip-tap of the bast slippers began. At last he stood before

me, and, gazing through those rusty iron spectacles, said:

"Mr. —, isn'd id?"

"Ah, Mr. Gessler," I stammered. "But your boots are really *too* good, you know! See, these are quite decent still!" And I stretched out to him my foot. He looked at it.

"Yes," he said, "beoble do nod wand good boods, id seems."

To get away from his reproachful eyes and voice I hastily remarked: "What have you done to your shop?"

He answered quietly. "Id was too exbensif. Do you wand some boods?"

I ordered three pairs, though I had wanted only two, and quickly left. I had, I do not know quite what feeling of being part, in his mind, of a conspiracy against him; or not perhaps so much against him as against his idea of boot. One does not, I suppose, care to feel like that; for it was again many months before my next visit to his shop, paid, I remember, with the feeling: "Oh, well, I can't leave the old boy—so here goes! Perhaps it will be his elder brother!"

For his elder brother, I knew, had not character enough to reproach me, even dumbly.

And, to my relief, in the shop there did appear to be his elder brother, handling a piece of leather.

"Well, Mr. Gessler," I said, "How are you?"

He came close and peered at me.

"I am breddy well," he said slowly; "but my elder brudder is dead."

And I saw that he was indeed himself—but how aged and wan! And never before had I heard him mention his brother. Much shocked, I murmured: "Oh! I am sorry!"

"Yes," he answered, "he was a good man, he made a good bood; but he is dead." And he touched the top of his head, where the hair had suddenly gone as thin as it had been on that of his poor brother, to indicate, I suppose, the cause of death. "He could nod ged over losing de oder shop. Do you wand any boods?" And he held up the leather in his hand: "Id's a beaudiful biece."

I ordered several pairs. It was not very long before they came—but they were better than ever. One simply could not wear them out. And soon after that I went abroad.

It was over a year before I was again in London. And the first shop I went to was my old friend's. I had left a man of sixty; I came back to one of seventy-five, pinched and worn and tremulous, who genuinely, this time, did not at first know me.

"Oh! Mr. Gessler," I said, sick at heart; "how splendid your boots are! See, I've been wearing this pair nearly all the time I've been abroad; and they're not half worn out, are they?"

He looked long at my boots—a pair of Russian leather, and his face seemed to regain steadiness. Putting his hand on my instep, he said:

"Do dey vid you here? I 'ad drouble wid dat bair; I remember."

I assured him that they had fitted beautifully.

"Do you wand any boods?" he said. "I can make dem quickly; id is a slack dime."

I answered: "Please, please! I want boots all around—every kind!"

"I will make a vresh model. Your foot must be bigger." And with utter slowness, he traced round my foot, and felt my toes, only once looking up to say:

"Did I dell you my brudder was dead?"

To watch him was painful, so feeble had he grown; I was glad to get away.

I had given those boots up, when one evening they came. Opening the parcel, I set the four pairs in a row. Then one by one I tried them on. There was no doubt about it. In shape and fit, in finish and quality of leather, they were the best he had ever made me. And in the mouth of one of the town walking-boots I found his bill. The amount was the same as usual, but it gave me quite a shock. He had never before sent it till quarter day*. I flew downstairs, and wrote a cheque and posted it at once with my own hand.

---

quarter day: traditionally in England, any of one of four dates in the financial year on which payments become due

---

A week later, passing the little street, I thought I would go in and tell him how splendidly the new boots fitted. But when I came to where his shop had been, his name was gone. Still there, in the window, were the slim pumps, the patent leathers with cloth tops, the sooty riding boots.

I went in, very much disturbed. In the two little shops—again made into one—was a young man with an English face:

"Mr. Gessler in?" I said.

He gave me a strange, ingratiating look.

"No, sir," he said, "no, but we can attend to anything with pleasure. We've taken the shop over. You've seen our name, no doubt, next door. We make for some very good people."

"Yes, yes," I said, "but Mr. Gessler?"

"Oh!" he answered; "dead."

"Dead! But I received these boots from him last Wednesday week."

"Ah! he said, "a shockin' go. Poor old man starved 'imself."

"What! You mean—!"

"Slow starvation, the doctor called it! You see, he went to work in such a way! Would keep the shop on; wouldn't have a soul touch his boots except himself. When he got an order, it took him such a time. People won't wait. He lost everybody. And there he'd sit, goin' on and on—I will say that for him—not a man in London made a better boot! But look at the competition! He never advertised! Would 'ave the best leather, too, and do it all 'imself. Well, there it is. What could you expect with his ideas?"

"But starvation—!"

"That may be a bit flowery, as the sayin' is—but I know myself he was sittin' over his boots day and night, to the very last. You see, I used to watch him. Never gave himself time to eat; never had a penny in the house. All went in rent and leather. How he lived so long I don't know. He regular let his fire go out. He was a character. But he made good boots."

"Yes," I said, "he made good boots."

And I turned and went out quickly, for I did not want that youth to know that I could hardly see.

About the Story

1. What clue does the title of the story give you about the theme? Is the theme an explicit or implicit one?

2. Who embodies the characteristic of quality? How is this shown in the story?

3. What is the main conflict of the story?

4. How does quality determine the action of the story?

5. What consequences occur because of the Gessler brothers' strong belief in quality?

6. How is the conflict resolved?

7. How does the author feel about the Gessler brothers? How do we know his feelings?

About the Author

John Galsworthy (1867–1933), with his monocle and his ability to keep a "stiff upper lip," appeared to be the epitome of the stereotypical Englishman. His upper-middle-class family was steeped in conventional English values, tastes, and attitudes; however, Galsworthy was markedly openhearted toward children and young people, especially those aspiring to be writers. Throughout his life, Galsworthy displayed a compassion for the underdog. Although he always enjoyed the benefits of prosperity, he criticized any improper use of social position to advantage.

Educated at Oxford and trained to practice law, Galsworthy was inspired by his wife, Ada, and by his acquaintance with influential men such as Joseph Conrad and Edward Garnett to turn from that profession to writing. In his numerous short stories and novels, Galsworthy discusses the conflicts that troubled his generation: the restrictions of tradition-bound English society, the tension between social classes, and the detrimental consequences of the rising materialism of his day. His writings reflect his deepest feelings, and his characters often verbalize his own convictions about society's values and morals. His short story "Quality" illustrates Galsworthy's concerns. Here he shows that in an industrialized society, avarice may prohibit the reward of excellence and the encouragement of "quality." Galsworthy's works have always been more popular with readers than with critics. His stories have enjoyed enduring popularity in England and America.

Dr. Heidegger's Experiment

Nathaniel Hawthorne

"Dr. Heidegger's Experiment" is a rare blend of the somber and the fanciful, of the simple and the complex. Through the setting and characters of this story, Hawthorne focuses on universal themes, asking whether human nature is inherently flawed, whether old age always brings wisdom, and whether fulfilling fleshly appetites is ever really satisfying in the long run. The characters' responses to their "second-chance" opportunity show you Hawthorne's answer to these questions.

That very singular man, old Dr. Heidegger, once invited four venerable friends to meet him in his study. There were three white-bearded gentlemen, Mr. Medbourne, Colonel Killigrew, and Mr. Gascoigne, and a withered gentlewoman, whose name was the Widow Wycherly. They were all melancholy old creatures, who had been unfortunate in life, and whose greatest misfortune it was that they were not long ago in their graves. Mr. Medbourne, in the vigor of his age, had been a prosperous merchant, but had lost his all by a frantic speculation, and was now little better than a mendicant.* Colonel Killigrew had wasted his best years, and his health and substance, in the pursuit of sinful pleasures which had given birth to a brood of pains, such as the gout, and divers other torments of soul and body. Mr. Gascoigne was a ruined politician, a man of evil fame, or at least had been so, till time had buried him from the knowledge of the present generation, and made him obscure instead of infamous. As for the Widow Wycherly, tradition tells us that she was a great beauty in her day; but, for a long while past, she had lived in deep seclusion, on account of certain scandalous stories which had prejudiced the gentry of the town against her. It is a circumstance worth mentioning, that each of these three old gentlemen, Mr. Medbourne, Colonel Killigrew, and Mr. Gascoigne, were early lovers of the Widow Wycherly, and had once been on the point of cutting each other's throats for her sake. And before proceeding further, I will merely hint that Dr. Heidegger and all his four guests were sometimes thought to be a little beside themselves, as is not unfrequently the case with old people, when worried either by present troubles or woeful recollections.

mendicant: a beggar

"My dear old friends," said Dr. Heidegger, motioning them to be seated, "I am desirous of your assistance in one of those little experiments with which I amuse myself here in my study."

If all stories were true, Dr. Heidegger's study must have been a very curious place. It was a dim, old-fashioned chamber, festooned with cobwebs, and besprinkled with antique dust. Around the walls stood several oaken bookcases, the lower shelves of which were filled with rows of gigantic folios* and black-letter quartos,* and the upper with little parchment-covered duodecimos.* Over the central bookcase was a bronze bust of Hippocrates, with which, according to some authorities, Dr. Heidegger was accustomed

to hold consultations in all difficult cases of his practice. In the obscurest corner of the room stood a tall and narrow oaken closet, with its door ajar, within which doubtfully appeared a skeleton. Between two of the bookcases hung a looking glass, presenting its high and dusty plate within a tarnished gilt frame. Among many wonderful stories related of this mirror, it was fabled that the spirits of all the doctor's deceased patients dwelt within its verge, and would stare him in the face whenever he looked thitherward. The opposite side of the chamber was ornamented with the full-length portrait of a young lady, arrayed in the faded magnificence of silk, satin, and brocade, and with a visage as faded as her dress. Above half a century ago, Dr. Heidegger had been on the point of marriage with this young lady; but, being affected with some slight disorder, she had swallowed one of her lover's prescriptions, and died on the bridal evening. The greatest curiosity of the study remains to be mentioned; it was a ponderous folio volume, bound in black leather, with massive silver clasps. There were no letters on the back, and nobody could tell the title of the book. But it was well known to be a book of magic; and once, when a chambermaid had lifted it, merely to brush away the dust, the skeleton had rattled in its closet, the picture of the young lady had stepped one foot upon the floor, and several ghastly faces had peeped forth from the mirror, while the brazen head of Hippocrates frowned, and said—"Forbear!"

folios: books about 15 inches in height
quartos: books wherein the page is obtained by folding a whole sheet into four leaves
duodecimos: books with each page being 5 by 7 3/4 inches

Such was Dr. Heidegger's study. On the summer afternoon of our tale, a small round table, as black as ebony, stood in the center of the room, sustaining a cut-glass vase of beautiful form and elaborate workmanship. The sunshine came through the window, between the heavy festoons* of two faded damask* curtains, and fell directly across this vase; so that a mild splendor was reflected from it on the ashen visages of the five old people who sat around. Four glasses were also on the table.

festoons: strings or garlands draped in a curve between two points
damask: a rich patterned fabric of cotton or other material

"My dear old friends," repeated Dr. Heidegger, "may I reckon on your aid in performing an exceedingly curious experiment?"

Now Dr. Heidegger was a very strange old gentleman, whose eccentricity had become the nucleus for a thousand fantastic stories. Some of these fables, to my shame be it spoken, might possibly be traced back to mine own veracious* self; and if any passages of the present tale should startle the reader's faith, I must be content to bear the stigma of a fiction-monger.

veracious: truthful

When the doctor's four guests heard him talk of his proposed experiment, they anticipated nothing more wonderful than the murder of a mouse in an air pump, or the examination of a cobweb by the microscope, or some similar nonsense, with which he was constantly in the habit of pestering his intimates. But without waiting for a reply, Dr. Heidegger hobbled across the chamber, and returned with the same ponderous folio, bound in black leather, which common report affirmed to be a book of magic. Undoing the silver clasps, he opened the volume, and took from among its black-letter* pages a rose, or what was once a rose, though now the green leaves and crimson petals had assumed one brownish hue, and the ancient flower seemed ready to crumble to dust in the doctor's hands.

black-letter: a heavy type style used in European typesetting up to the time of World War II

"This rose," said Dr. Heidegger, with a sigh, "this same withered and crumbling flower, blossomed five and fifty years ago. It was given me by Sylvia Ward, whose portrait hangs yonder; and I meant to wear it in my bosom at our wedding. Five and fifty years it has been treasured between the leaves of this old volume. Now, would you deem it possible that this rose of half a century could ever bloom again?"

"Nonsense!" said the Widow Wycherly, with a peevish toss of her head. "You might as well ask whether an old woman's wrinkled face could ever bloom again."

"See!" answered Dr. Heidegger.

He uncovered the vase, and threw the faded rose into the water which it contained. At first it lay lightly on the surface of the fluid, appearing to imbibe none of its moisture. Soon, however, a singular change began to be visible. The crushed and dried petals stirred, and assumed a deepening tinge of crimson, as if the flower were reviving from a deathlike slumber; the slender stalk and twigs of foliage became green; and there was the rose of half a century, looking as fresh as when Sylvia Ward had first given it to her lover. It was scarcely full blown; for some of its delicate red leaves curled modestly around its moist bosom, within which two or three dewdrops were sparkling.

"That is certainly a very pretty deception," said the doctor's friends; carelessly, however, for they had witnessed greater miracles at a conjurer's show; "pray how was it effected?"

"Did you never hear of the 'Fountain of Youth'?" asked Dr. Heidegger, "which Ponce de Leon, the Spanish adventurer, went in search of, two or three centuries ago?"

"But did Ponce de Leon ever find it?" said the Widow Wycherly.

"No," answered Dr. Heidegger, "for he never sought it in the right place. The famous Fountain of Youth, if I am rightly informed, is situated in the southern part of the Floridian peninsula, not far from Lake Macaco. Its source is overshadowed by several gigantic magnolias, which, though numberless centuries old, have been kept as fresh as violets by the virtues of this wonderful water. An acquaintance of mine, knowing my curiosity in such matters, has sent me what you see in the vase."

"Ahem!" said Colonel Killigrew, who believed not a word of the doctor's story; "and what may be the effect of this fluid on the human frame?"

"You shall judge for yourself, my dear colonel," replied Dr. Heidegger; "and all of you, my respected friends, are welcome to so much of this admirable fluid as may restore to you the bloom of youth. For my own part, having had much trouble in growing old, I am in no hurry to grow young again. With your permission, therefore, I will merely watch the progress of the experiment."

While he spoke, Dr. Heidegger had been filling the four glasses with the water of the Fountain of Youth. It was apparently impregnated with an effervescent gas, for little bubbles were continually ascending from the depths of the glasses, and bursting in silvery spray at the surface. As the liquor diffused a pleasant perfume, the old people doubted not that it possessed cordial and comfortable properties; and, though utter skeptics as to its rejuvenescent power, they were inclined to swallow it at once. But Dr. Heidegger besought them to stay a moment.

"Before you drink, my respectable old friends," said he, "it would be well that, with the experience of a lifetime to direct you, you should draw up a few general rules for your guidance, in passing a second time through the perils of youth. Think what a sin and a shame it would be, if with your peculiar advantages, you should not become patterns of virtue and wisdom to all the young people of the age!"

The doctor's four venerable friends made him no answer, except by a feeble and tremulous laugh; so very ridiculous was the idea, that, knowing how closely repentance treads behind the steps of error, they should ever go astray again.

"Drink, then," said the doctor, bowing; "I rejoice that I have so well selected the subjects of my experiment."

With palsied hands they raised the glasses to their lips. The liquid, if it really possessed such virtues as Dr. Heidegger imputed to it, could not have been bestowed on four human beings who needed it more woefully. They looked as if they had never known what youth or pleasure was, but had been the offspring of Nature's dotage,* and always the gray, decrepit, sapless, miserable creatures, who now sat stooping round the doctor's table, without life enough in their souls or

bodies to be animated even by the prospect of growing young again. They drank off the water, and replaced their glasses on the table.

---

dotage: a feeble-minded condition caused by mental deterioration

---

Assuredly, there was an almost immediate improvement in the aspect of the party, with a sudden glow of cheerful sunshine, brightening over all their visages at once. There was a healthful suffusion on their cheeks, instead of the ashen hue that had made them look so corpselike. They gazed at one another, and fancied that some magic power had really begun to smooth away the deep and sad inscription which Father Time had been so long engraving on their brows. The Widow Wycherly adjusted her cap, for she felt almost like a woman again.

"Give us more of this wondrous water!" cried they eagerly. "We are younger—but we are still too old! Quick—give us more!"

"Patience, patience!" quoth Dr. Heidegger, who sat watching the experiment with philosophic coolness. "You have been a long time growing old. Surely you might be content to grow young in half an hour! But the water is at your service."

Again he filled their glasses with the water of youth, enough of which still remained in the vase to turn half the old people in the city to the age of their own grandchildren. While the bubbles were yet sparkling on the brim, the doctor's four guests snatched their glasses from the table, and swallowed the contents at a single gulp. Was it delusion? Even while the draught was passing down their throats, it seemed to have wrought a change on their whole systems. Their eyes grew clear and bright; a dark shade deepened among their silvery locks; they sat around the table, three gentlemen of middle age, and a woman hardly beyond her buxom prime.

"My dear widow, you are charming!" cried Colonel Killigrew, whose eyes had been fixed upon her face, while the shadows of age were flitting from it like darkness from the crimson daybreak.

The fair widow knew, of old, that Colonel Killigrew's compliments were not always measured by sober truth; so she started up and ran to the mirror, still dreading that the ugly visage of an old woman would meet her gaze. Meanwhile, the three gentlemen behaved in such a manner as proved that the water of the Fountain of Youth possessed some intoxicating qualities; unless, indeed, their exhilaration of spirits were merely a lightsome dizziness, caused by the sudden removal of the weight of years. Mr. Gascoigne's mind seemed to run on political topics, but whether relating to the past, present, or future, could not easily be determined, since the same ideas and phrases have been in vogue these fifty years. Now he rattled forth full-throated sentences about patriotism, national glory, and the people's rights; now he muttered some perilous stuff or other, in a sly and doubtful whisper, so cautiously that even his own conscience could scarcely catch the secret; and now again he spoke in measured accents, and a deeply deferential tone, as if a royal ear were listening to his well-turned periods.* Colonel Killigrew all this time had been trolling forth a jolly bottle song, and ringing his glass in symphony with the chorus, while his eyes wandered towards the figure of the Widow Wycherly. On the other side of the table, Mr. Medbourne was involved in a calculation of dollars and cents, with which was strangely intermingled a project for supplying the East Indies with ice, by harnessing a team of whales to the polar icebergs.

---

well-turned periods: clever phrases or sentences

As for the Widow Wycherly, she stood before the mirror curtsying and simpering to her own image, and greeting it as the friend whom she loved better than all the world beside. She thrust her face close to the glass, to see whether some long-remembered wrinkle or crow's-foot had indeed vanished. She examined whether the snow had so entirely melted from her hair, that the venerable* cap could be safely thrown aside. At last, turning briskly away, she came with a sort of dancing step to the table.

---

venerable: worthy of respect because of character, position, or age

---

"My dear old doctor," cried she, "pray favor me with another glass!"

"Certainly, my dear madam, certainly!" replied the complaisant doctor; "See! I have already filled the glasses."

There, in fact, stood the four glasses, brimful of this wonderful water, the delicate spray of which, as it effervesced from the surface, resembled the tremulous glitter of diamonds. It was now so nearly sunset that the chamber had grown duskier than ever; but a mild and moonlike splendor gleamed from within the vase, and rested alike on the four guests, and on the doctor's venerable figure. He sat in a high-backed, elaborately carved, oaken armchair, with a gray dignity of aspect that might have well befitted that very Father Time whose power had never been disputed save by this fortunate company. Even while quaffing the third draught of the Fountain of Youth, they were almost awed by the expression of his mysterious visage.

But, the next moment, the exhilarating gush of young life shot through their veins. They were now in the happy prime of youth. Age, with its miserable train of cares, and sorrows, and diseases, was remembered only as the trouble of a dream from which they had joyously awoke. The fresh gloss of the soul, so early lost, and without which the world's successive scenes had been but a gallery of faded pictures, again threw its enchantment over all their prospects. They felt like new-created beings, in a new-created universe.

"We are young! We are young!" they cried, exultingly.

Youth, like the extremity of age, had effaced* the strongly marked characteristics of middle life, and mutually assimilated them all. They were a group of merry youngsters, almost maddened with the exuberant frolicsomeness of their years. The most singular effect of their gaiety was an impulse to mock the infirmity and decrepitude of which they had so lately been the victims. They laughed loudly at their old-fashioned attire, the wide-skirted coats and flapped waistcoats of the young men, and the ancient cap and gown of the blooming girl. One limped across the floor, like a gouty grandfather; one set a pair of spectacles astride of his nose, and pretended to pore over the black-letter pages of the book of magic; a third seated himself in an armchair, and strove to imitate the venerable dignity of Dr. Heidegger. Then all shouted mirthfully, and leaped about the room. The Widow Wycherly—if so fresh a damsel could be called a widow—tripped up to the doctor's chair, with a mischievous merriment in her rosy face.

---

effaced: erased

"Doctor, you dear old soul," cried she, "get up and dance with me!" And then the four young people laughed louder than ever, to think what a queer figure the poor old doctor would cut.

"Pray excuse me," answered the doctor quietly. "I am old and rheumatic, and my dancing days were over long ago. But either of these gay young gentlemen will be glad of so pretty a partner."

"Dance with me, Clara!" cried Colonel Killigrew.

"No, no, I will be her partner!" shouted Mr. Gascoigne.

"She promised me her hand, fifty years ago!" exclaimed Mr. Medbourne.

They all gathered round her. One caught both her hands in his passionate grasp—another threw his arm about her waist—the third buried his hand among the glossy curls that clustered beneath the widow's cap. Blushing, panting, struggling, chiding, laughing, her warm breath fanning each of their faces by turns, she strove to disengage herself, yet still remained in their triple embrace. Never was there a livelier picture of youthful rivalship, with bewitching beauty for the prize. Yet, by a strange deception, owing to the duskiness of the chamber, and the antique dresses which they still wore, the tall mirror is said to have reflected the figures of the three old, gray, withered grandsires, ridiculously contending for the skinny ugliness of a shriveled grandam.

But they were young: their burning passions proved them so. Inflamed to madness by the coquetry of the girl-widow, who neither granted nor quite withheld her favors, the three rivals began to interchange threatening glances. Still keeping hold of the fair prize, they grappled fiercely at one another's throats. As they struggled to and fro, the table was overturned, and the vase dashed into a thousand fragments. The precious Water of Youth flowed in a bright stream across the floor, moistening the wings of a butterfly, which, grown old in the decline of summer, had alighted there to die. The insect fluttered

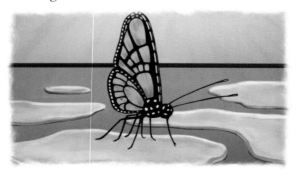

lightly through the chamber, and settled on the snowy head of Dr. Heidegger.

"Come, come, gentlemen!—come, Madam Wycherly," exclaimed the doctor, "I really must protest against this riot."

They stood still, and shivered; for it seemed as if gray Time were calling them back from their sunny youth, far down into the chill and darksome vale of years. They looked at old Dr. Heidegger, who sat in his carved armchair, holding the rose of half a century, which he had rescued from among the fragments of the shattered vase. At the motion of his hand, the four rioters resumed their seats; the more readily, because their violent exertions had wearied them, youthful though they were.

"My poor Sylvia's rose!" ejaculated Dr. Heidegger, holding it in the light of the sunset clouds; "it appears to be fading again."

And so it was. Even while the party were looking at it, the flower continued to shrivel up, till it became as dry and fragile as when the doctor had first thrown it into the vase. He shook off the few drops of moisture which clung to its petals.

"I love it as well thus as in its dewy freshness," observed he, pressing the withered rose to his withered lips. While he spoke, the butterfly fluttered down from the doctor's snowy head, and fell upon the floor.

His guests shivered again. A strange chillness, whether of the body or spirit they could not tell, was creeping gradually over them all. They gazed at one another, and fancied that each fleeting moment snatched away a charm, and left a deepening furrow where none had been before. Was it an illusion? Had the changes of a lifetime been crowded into so brief a space, and were they now four aged people, sitting with their old friend, Dr. Heidegger?

"Are we grown old again, so soon?" cried they dolefully.

In truth, they had. The Water of Youth possessed merely a virtue more transient than that of wine. The delirium which it created had effervesced away. Yes! they were old again. With a shuddering impulse that showed her a woman still, the widow clasped her skinny hands before her face, and wished that the coffin lid were over it, since it could be no longer beautiful.

"Yes, friends, ye are old again," said Dr. Heidegger; "and lo! the Water of Youth is all lavished on the ground. Well—I bemoan it not; for if the fountain gushed at my very doorstep, I would not stoop to bathe my lips in it—no, though its delirium were for years instead of moments. Such is the lesson ye have taught me!"

But the doctor's four friends had taught no such lesson to themselves. They resolved forthwith to make a pilgrimage to Florida, and quaff at morning, noon, and night, from the Fountain of Youth.

About the Story

1. What do you think is the main theme of the story?

2. Notice the doctor's advice to his companions before they drink the liquid (page 204). How would you describe their reactions to his advice?

3. Now look at their nonphysical characteristics after the experiment (pages 206–7). Have they changed as a result of drinking the Water of Youth? How do they act?

4. After the experiment, how does each character respond?

5. Which of the following best describes the central conflict?

    man *vs.* man
    man *vs.* a force greater than himself
    man *vs.* himself

6. How is the conflict resolved?

7. What does Dr. Heidegger learn from his experiment?

About the Author

Nathaniel Hawthorne (1804–64) was born in Salem, Massachusetts, and acquired his love of books as a boy. After attending college, Hawthorne returned to Salem and began his literary career while working at a number of jobs, including one as surveyor of Salem's port. Although never a rich man, Hawthorne enjoyed an especially happy family life. He enjoyed reading the Bible and works on theology but maintained that *The Pilgrim's Progress* was his favorite book.

Hawthorne's timeless stories and novels reflect his heritage. His acute consciousness of his Puritan background pervades his writings. Because of his insight into the human heart, Hawthorne is regarded as one of the greatest moralistic writers in American literature. Among his masterpieces are *The Scarlet Letter*, a classic allegory of human sin and suffering, and *The House of Seven Gables*, both of which draw heavily on Hawthorne's rich family history and life in nineteenth-century New England. Fellow-writer Herman Melville greatly admired Hawthorne for maintaining a depth and balance in his viewpoint of man. Hawthorne did not give in to the groundless optimism of contemporary Romantic writers. While he did not condone the flaws of his Puritan forefathers, neither did he condemn their concern with morality and the consequences of man's fallen nature.

When You Are Old

William Butler Yeats

Among other themes, two universal themes have been cited in this unit:
the wisdom age can bring and the power of love to see true beauty. Yeats
uses both themes to frame the message of his poem "When You Are Old."

When you are old and gray and full of sleep,
And nodding by the fire, take down this book,
And slowly read, and dream of the soft look
Your eyes had once, and of their shadows deep;

How many loved your moments of glad grace,　　5
And loved your beauty with love false or true;
But one man loved the pilgrim soul in you,
And loved the sorrows of your changing face.

And bending down beside the glowing bars,
Murmur, a little sadly, how Love fled　　10
And paced upon the mountains overhead
And hid his face amid a crowd of stars.

About the Poem

1. Describe the speaker in "When You Are Old."

2. Whom is the speaker addressing?

3. According to the poem, what does the speaker love about the person addressed?

4. What do you think was the author's purpose for this speech?

5. Do the prince in "Beauty and the Beast" and the speaker in this poem have anything in common? If so, what?

6. What is the implicit theme of "When You Are Old"?

About the Author

William Butler Yeats (1865–1939) was born in Dublin, Ireland, and his lifelong love for his native country provided the inspiration for much of his work. As a boy, Yeats showed more interest in his bug collection than in his books; in fact, literature proved to be his worst subject. His family, nevertheless, was convinced of his creative abilities and felt certain that he would someday write.

While he was an art student in Dublin, Yeats's interest in the literary world grew, and at twenty-one he decided to make literature his profession. In addition to his work as a writer and editor, Yeats contributed to the Irish cultural revival by writing and promoting drama. As a young man, Yeats fell deeply in love with Maude Gonne, a strong-willed and elegant actress who was preoccupied with the Irish nationalist movement and other prevalent political and social causes. Yeats's devotion was unreturned, and their relationship remained purely platonic. Still, her influence on the young poet and future Irish statesman was considerable. Along with his continuing interest in Irish folklore and politics, Yeats's unrequited love for the beautiful Maude Gonne strongly influenced his writing.

In the poem "When You Are Old," Yeats demonstrates his ability to create the beautiful lyric poetry for which he is famous. Much of his poetry reflects his study of Celtic folklore and Irish fairy tales. By his generous use of symbolic imagery, Yeats sought to express his thoughts and feelings as a means of expressing reality.

A Black Man Talks of Reaping

Arna Bontemps

In the following poem, Bontemps, an African-American poet, uses an extended metaphor to portray the racial situation in 1920s America. To what did he liken the state of affairs? What does he see as the source of the conditions? Note how his presentation of theme fulfills the purpose of persuasion.

I have sown beside all waters in my day.
I planted deep, within my heart the fear
That wind or fowl would take the grain away.
I planted safe against this stark, lean year.

I scattered seed enough to plant the land   5
In rows from Canada to Mexico,
But for my reaping only what the hand
Can hold at once is all that I can show.

Yet what I sowed and what the orchard yields
My brother's sons are gathering stalk and root,   10
Small wonder then my children glean in fields
They have not sown, and feed on bitter fruit.

Share Croppers, c1939. Watercolor by Robert Gwathmey / The Granger Collection, New York

About the Poem

1. Why is the speaker's harvest ironic?

2. What metaphor is Bontemps using?

3. What is Bontemps's theme in this poem? Is it implicit or explicit?

4. What response do you think Bontemps wanted from readers?

About the Author

Arna Wendell Bontemps (1902–73) was born in Alexandria, Louisiana. His father was a bricklayer and his mother a teacher. When Bontemps was very young, his family moved to California, where he lived until he graduated from Pacific Union College. Bontemps then taught in New York City and anticipated completing a doctorate in English. Instead, he put his studies on hold to become involved in the Harlem Renaissance of the 1930s and began writing. His first poems appeared in two literary magazines: *Crisis* and *Opportunity*. In addition to his poetry, Bontemps wrote a number of children's books.

Bontemps received a master's degree in library science and was appointed librarian at the Fisk Library in Chicago. One of Bontemps's most enduring contributions was his work as a chronicler and preserver of writings of black cultural heritage.

Irony is the use of language to convey meaning other than what is stated. It can also be a contradiction in what is expected to happen and what actually happens. Humor, fear, or suspense is the result. Often an author uses irony to emphasize a point he is trying to make. Consider these lines from Coleridge's "The Rime of the Ancient Mariner": "Water, water, every where, / Nor any drop to drink." Note the irony: surrounded by a vast body of water, the mariner cannot quench his thirst because the water is undrinkable.

The broad term *irony* covers three more specific kinds of irony: situational irony, verbal irony, and dramatic irony. The closing of Galsworthy's story "Quality" demonstrates **situational irony**, an irony that occurs when a story's events violate the normal expectations. The narrator is surprised that a bill accompanies the shoes that he receives from Mr. Gessler. "He [Mr. Gessler] had never before sent it [the bill] till quarter day." Unknown to the narrator is Mr. Gessler's dire need for money.

Verbal irony occurs when an author's or character's meaning differs from what he expresses in words. For example, perhaps your mother has said, "Oh, that's beauti-ful!" when she sees your room in shambles. Certainly her meaning is different from her words. (Specifically, your mother is using sarcasm, verbal irony in the form of mock praise.) **Dramatic irony** allows the reader to be aware of a plot development of which the characters are unaware. O. Henry's short story "The Gift of the Magi" capitalizes on dramatic irony. The reader is aware of the actions each character conceals from the other: Della cuts and sells her hair to buy a chain for Jim's watch while Jim sells his watch to buy combs for Della's hair.

Irony, then, is a tool the author uses to reveal something subtly, sometimes without the reader's realizing what is happening. Ultimately, the reader thinks about what he has read and responds. Situational irony, for example, can be a corrective for readers, reminding us that our expectations and our sense of what is reasonable are often in error. Christ's incarnation demonstrates situational irony. Although He is the King of kings, Jesus was born in a stable in the small town of Bethlehem. This supreme example of situational irony reminds us that greatness is not found in the trappings of greatness but rather in what a person is and does.

1. What is **ironic** about the title of the story "Quality"?

2. Love has been an element of the themes for the stories in this unit. How is love evident in "Quality"?

3. Although Dr. Heidegger's friends think themselves young during Hawthorne's tale, what circumstance does the narrator note that creates **dramatic irony**?

4. What element of **situational irony** do you find in stanza 2 of "When You Are Old"?

5. In "A Black Man Talks of Reaping," what is ironic about the man's hard work and his harvest yield? Identify the type of irony.

UNIT III REVIEW

REMEMBER THE TERMS

Review the following terms from the opening essay, "Theme," and the Thinking Zone pages. Be prepared to discuss their meanings and uses.

theme   explicit theme   irony
universal theme   implicit theme   situational irony
authorial intent   allegory   verbal irony
moral   symbol   dramatic irony

APPLY THE CONCEPTS

Answer the following questions about how the literary concepts you have studied are used in this unit.

1. In "The Silver Mine," what does the king decide is most important to his kingdom?

2. How does the parson and his friends' early opinion of wealth become ironic?

3. What is the main theme of "The Silver Mine"?

4. In "Beauty and the Beast," what does Beauty's request of her father when he leaves to check on his ships reveal about her?

5. What does the prince mean by the advice he gives Beauty in her dream: "Do not trust too much to your eyes"?

6. Does the theme of "Beauty and the Beast" qualify as universal? Why or why not?

7. What is the type of conflict in "Go Down, Death"? Explain your answer briefly.

8. Which two lines from "Do not go gentle into that good night" explicitly state the theme of the poem?

9. How does the title "Quality" reveal authorial intent?

10. In "Dr. Heidegger's Experiment," what object acts as a symbol of lost youth?

11. In "When You Are Old," does Yeats state his theme explicitly? Explain.

12. In "A Black Man Talks of Reaping," the author focuses on what theme?

13. According to Bontemps's poem, the grain is taken away by whom or what?

EVALUATE THE IDEAS

Identify each of the following statements as true or false. If false, rewrite the underlined portion of the statement to make it true.

14. In "The Silver Mine" the king discovered the parishioners to be <u>downtrodden, desperately unhappy, and eager to leave the villages.</u>

15. The parishioners' land was difficult to farm, and they could barely supply a livelihood for their families.

16. "Beauty and the Beast" is an example of allegory.

17. When the Beast allows her to visit her family, Beauty stays longer than planned because she does not want to return to the Beast.

18. In "Go Down, Death" the preacher tells the mourners not to cry because Sister Caroline's death was peaceful.

19. The men in "Do not go gentle into that good night" fight death because they regret leaving behind the possible future accomplishments and experiences.

20. The primary conflict in "Quality" is man against a power greater than himself: the Gessler brothers against a growing industrial society.

21. The authorial intent in writing "Quality" is to reveal the hardships of the trade and working conditions.

22. According to "Dr. Heidegger's Experiment," the guests who participated in the experiment gained wisdom from their experience.

23. One theme of "Dr. Heidegger's Experiment" is man's desire to perpetually enjoy the pleasures of youth.

24. "When You Are Old" highlights the value of inner beauty.

25. In "A Black Man Talks of Reaping," Bontemps presents African Americans as having the opportunity to fulfill the American dream.

26. The last stanza of Bontemps's poem gives an example of situational irony.

Write a Response

Completely answer each of the following questions.

27. In "The Silver Mine," how do the king and the parson differ both in character and in how they learn the lesson of true riches? Explain your answer.

28. In "Beauty and the Beast," is Beauty's first impression of the Beast accurate? Why or why not?

29. What emotion do the characters described by the speakers of "Do not go gentle into that good night" and "When You Are Old" have in common?

30. Choose one theme from these Unit 3 themes and illustrate its presence in one of the unit selections you have read: (1) Love has the power to change the thinking, behavior, or perspectives of those who experience it. (2) Maintaining integrity and avoiding moral pitfalls demand strong character. (3) Though it seems to answer many problems, wealth often has a strong corrupting influence.

BOATERS ON THE YERRES
Gustave Caillebotte

❧ POINT OF VIEW ❧

Gustave Caillebotte (1848–1894) was born into a wealthy Parisian family and probably began drawing at his family's riverside home in Yerres, a few miles outside of Paris. He studied at the École des Beaux-Arts and was acquainted with several well-known painters of his time, including Renoir and Degas. Many of the subjects of his paintings were his brothers, parents, and family friends. Caillebotte's style is an interesting blend of Impressionism (emphasis on movement, angles, and light, with loose, visible brushstrokes) and Realism (showing subjects as they are, without artistic interpretation, sometimes with an emphasis on the sordid). His style is often at the same time soft and rich.

* ✤ From what point of view is Caillebotte's work painted?
* ✤ From your perspective, in what direction is the boat moving?
* ✤ Based on Caillebotte's use of light and dark, what do you think is the time of day?
* ✤ What kind of atmosphere does Caillebotte create in his painting?
* ✤ What do you suppose is Caillebotte's purpose for this painting?

❧ POINT OF VIEW ❧

In life, our individual knowledge of the people and conflicts around us is limited. As a result, we are prone to misunderstanding others' thoughts and motives and can rarely determine the true significance of life's events, much less predict their outcome. Furthermore, as sinful humans, our understanding of our own hearts is fatally flawed as well (Jer. 17:9). Our limited perspective could lead us to despair, but God has faithfully provided us with the answers we need through His Word. The Bible tempers our limited knowledge with God's eternal, all-knowing perspective: it serves as a window of truth into the inner workings of our hearts, the consequences of our actions, and the true priorities of life. In short, through God's perspective we gain true wisdom and certain hope, knowing His overarching meaning for our lives.

In literature, as in life, the perspective from which we see people or events greatly influences our understanding of them. We have all heard such comments as "That's not the way I remember it!" or "That's not how he told the story." A person's perspective, whether physical or psychological, influences his account of a story, and our experience confirms that a single incident can be viewed in several ways. Moreover, how much the storyteller knows and how much he reveals determine what we learn from a narrative and how we interpret what we learn. An essential technique of storytelling, literary **point of view** refers to the perspective from which an author presents the conflicts, characters, and events of a story.

To construct a particular perspective, authors create a persona or a personality that narrates the story. **Personas** can be anything from impersonal narrators who remain unnamed to characters in the story who have their own highly-developed personalities. Usually, varying points of view are organized according to how much a narrator, and thus the reader, knows about the thoughts and actions of a story's characters. Under this system, three main points of view exist.

THIRD-PERSON POINTS OF VIEW

Two points of view are written as third-person narratives, stories in which the narrator speaks about the characters using third-person pronouns such as *he*, *she*, and *they*. Of these two, the **omniscient viewpoint** is the more versatile. From this point of view, the storyteller "knows all." He can tell us not only what all the characters do but also how they think and feel. "Beauty and the Beast" (pp. 173–85) provides a good illustration of the omniscient viewpoint. Look, for example, at the following excerpt:

"'The only thing I wish for is to see you come home safely,' she answered.

"*But this reply vexed her sisters, who fancied she was blaming them for having asked for such costly things. Her father, however, was pleased, but as he thought that at her age she certainly ought to like pretty presents, he told her to choose something."*

The italicized portion shows that the narrator does not simply record what characters say and do; he also reveals the thoughts that prompt their actions and the contradictory feelings that arise from those actions. He may also comment on *why* the characters are as they are or behave as they do.

The second kind of third-person narrative is the **limited-omniscient viewpoint**. Though still using third person, the narrator "gets inside" only one of the characters, usually the protagonist. Look again at the excerpt from "Beauty and the Beast," this time rewritten from the limited-omniscient point of view.

"'The only thing I wish for is to see you come home safely,' she answered.

She felt this reply would vex her sisters, who would fancy she was blaming them for having asked for such costly things. Her father, however, seemed pleased, for he told her to choose something. 'At your age,' he said, 'you ought to like pretty things.'"

The revised portion narrows the scope somewhat. Beauty's inner life is still revealed, but references to her sisters' and father's thoughts and feelings are now phrased as speculations. Though the narrator gives no reason to doubt Beauty's opinions, we know these statements are now just that—opinion. The advantage to this viewpoint is that it draws us more completely into Beauty's world by focusing our attention on her feelings about characters or situations. In other words, we have exchanged some breadth of knowledge for greater understanding of a single character.

FIRST-PERSON POINT OF VIEW

The last point of view forms a first-person narrative (narrator uses "I" and "we") in which the narrator drops the outsider perspective and *becomes* one of the characters. This **first-person viewpoint** relates only what the narrator character can reasonably know of the events and people around him. The narrator is most often a major character in the story, giving the reader a closer view of the main action. You may notice that the Bible only rarely uses the first-person viewpoint as it does in Nehemiah. Usually when the first person is used, the author switches between the third and first person as in Ezra, Acts, and Daniel.

As the following rewritten excerpt illustrates, first-person viewpoint provides an even more intimate perspective than either the omniscient or limited-omniscient point of view.

"'The only thing I wish for is to see you come home safely,' *I answered.*

I knew my sisters would be vexed, thinking I was blaming them for having asked for such costly things. But I could tell my father was pleased.

He said, 'Choose something, Beauty, for at your age you ought to like pretty things.'"

Beauty, the central character, tells us the story. We see only what she sees, feel only what she feels, and think only as she thinks. We have gained an even greater sense of familiarity. At the same time, however, we have narrowed our scope considerably by removing other characters' perceptions and the author's third-person commentary.

Authors use one or a combination of the three viewpoints. To discover the point of view an author chose, ask the following questions: Who is telling the story? How much does the storyteller know and reveal about the characters' thoughts and actions? Once you have determined the point of view, ask two final questions: How does the perspective affect my opinion of characters and events? As a result, how does the author's viewpoint clarify or enhance the story's message?

The Forty Thieves

ARABIAN FOLKTALE

retold by Andrew Lang

"The Forty Thieves" is one of many stories from *The Thousand and One Nights,* also called *The Arabian Nights.* References to the tales by such noted literary figures as Alfred, Lord Tennyson, William Wordsworth, and Edgar Allan Poe indicate the popularity of these stories throughout the Western world from the 1780s onward. The tales are intertwined with the story of the Sultan Shahriyar, who customarily executes each of his brides on the morning after their wedding. The beautiful and clever Scheherazade volunteers to marry him with the hope that she can convince him to end this cruel practice. On the evening of her wedding day, she charms the sultan with a tale of marvels but leaves the tale unfinished. Shahriyar grants Scheherazade a one-day's stay of execution to finish her story. She finishes the tale the next night but immediately begins another, again breaking off at the climax of the story. Again she is granted a reprieve. By the time he grants 1001 such reprieves, Shahriyar is in love with Scheherazade, who has won the sultan's heart by first capturing his imagination.

As you read, take note of how much information the storyteller reveals. Judging from the details you are given about the characters and their thoughts, can you identify the story's point of view? Also be sure to note plot points and themes that contradict a Christian worldview.

In a town in Persia there dwelt two brothers, one named Cassim, the other Ali Baba. Cassim was married to a rich wife and lived in plenty, while Ali Baba had to maintain his wife and children by cutting wood in a neighboring forest and selling it in the town. One day, when Ali Baba was in the forest, he saw a troop of men on horseback, coming towards him in a cloud of dust. He was afraid they were robbers, and climbed into a tree for safety. When they came up to him and dismounted, he counted forty of them. They unbridled their horses and tied them to trees. The finest man among them, whom Ali Baba took to be their captain, went a little way among some bushes, and said: "Open, Sesame!" so plainly that Ali Baba heard him. A door opened in the rocks, and having made the troop go in, he followed them, and the door shut again of itself. They stayed some time inside, and Ali Baba, fearing they might come out and catch him, was forced to sit patiently in the tree. At last the door opened again, and the Forty Thieves came out. As the Captain went in last he came out first, and made them all pass by him; he then closed the door, saying: "Shut, Sesame!" Every man bridled his horse and mounted, the Captain put himself at their head, and they returned as they came.

Then Ali Baba climbed down and went to the door concealed among the bushes, and said: "Open, Sesame!" and it flew open. Ali Baba, who expected a dull, dismal place, was greatly surprised to find it large and well lighted, and hollowed by the hand of man in the form of a vault, which received the light from an opening in the ceiling. He saw rich bales of merchandise—silk, stuff-brocades, all piled together, and gold and silver in heaps, and money in leather purses. He went in and the door shut behind him. He did not look at the silver, but brought out as many bags of gold as he thought his asses, which were browsing outside, could carry, loaded them with the bags, and hid it all with fagots.* Using the words: "Shut, Sesame!" he closed the door and went home.

---

fagots: a bundle of branches or twigs

Then he drove his asses into the yard, shut the gates, carried the money bags to his wife, and emptied them out before her. He bade her keep the secret, and he would go and bury the gold. "Let me first measure it," said his wife. "I will go borrow a measure of someone, while you dig the hole." So she ran to the wife of Cassim and borrowed a measure. Knowing Ali Baba's poverty, the sister was curious to find out what sort of grain his wife wished to measure, and artfully put some suet* at the bottom of the measure. Ali Baba's wife went home and set the measure on the heap of gold, and filled it and emptied it often, to her great content. She then carried it back to her sister, without noticing that a piece of gold was sticking to it, which Cassim's wife perceived directly* her back was turned. She grew very curious, and said to Cassim when he came home: "Cassim, your brother is richer than you. He does not count his money, he measures it." He begged her to explain this riddle, which she did by showing him the piece of money and telling him where she found it. Then Cassim grew so envious that he could not sleep, and went to his brother in the morning before sunrise. "Ali Baba," he said showing him the gold piece, "you pretend to be poor and yet you measure gold." By this Ali Baba perceived that through his wife's folly Cassim and his wife knew their secret, so he confessed all and offered Cassim a share. "That I expect," said Cassim; "but I must know where to find the treasure, otherwise I will discover all, and you will lose all." Ali Baba, more out of kindness than fear, told him of the cave, and the very words to use. Cassim left Ali Baba, meaning to be beforehand with him and get the treasure for himself. He rose early next morning, and set out with ten mules loaded with great chests. He soon found the place, and the door in the rock. He said: "Open, Sesame!" and the door opened and shut behind him. He could have feasted his eyes all day on the treasures, but he now hastened to gather together as much of it as possible; but when he was ready to go he could not remember what to say for thinking of his great riches. Instead of "Sesame," he said: "Open, Barley!" and the door remained fast. He named several different sorts of grain, all but the right one, and the door still stuck fast. He was so frightened at the danger he was in that he had as much forgotten the word as if he had never heard it.

---

suet: hard fatty tissues from cattle or sheep, used in cooking or making tallow

directly: as soon as

About noon the robbers returned to their cave, and saw Cassim's mules roving about with great chests on their backs. This gave them the alarm; they drew their sabers, and went to the door, which opened on their Captain's saying: "Open, Sesame!" Cassim, who heard the trampling of their horses' feet, resolved to sell his life dearly, so when the door opened he leaped out and threw the Captain down. In vain, however, for the robbers with their sabers soon killed him. On entering the cave they saw all the bags laid ready, and could not imagine how anyone had got in without knowing their secret. They cut Cassim's body into four quarters, and nailed them up inside the cave, in order to frighten anyone who should venture in, and went away in search of more treasure.

As night drew on Cassim's wife grew very uneasy, and ran to her brother-in-law, and told him where her husband had gone. Ali Baba did his best to comfort her, and set out to the forest in search of Cassim. The first thing he saw on entering the cave was his dead brother. Full of horror, he put the body on one of his asses, and bags of gold on the other two, and, covering all with some fagots, returned home. He drove the two asses laden with gold into his own yard, and led the other to Cassim's house. The door was opened by the slave Morgiana, whom he knew to be both brave and cunning. Unloading the ass, he said to her: "This is the body of your master, who has been murdered, but whom we must bury as though he had died in his bed. I will speak with you again, but now tell your mistress I am come." The wife of Cassim, on learning the fate of her husband, broke out into cries and tears, but Ali Baba offered to take her to live with him and his wife if she would promise to keep his counsel and leave everything to Morgiana; whereupon she agreed, and dried her eyes.

Morgiana, meanwhile, sought an apothecary and asked him for some lozenges. "My poor master," she said, "can neither eat nor speak, and no one knows what his distemper is." She carried home the lozenges and returned next day weeping, and asked for an essence only given to those just about to die. Thus, in the evening, no one was surprised to hear the wretched shrieks and cries of Cassim's wife and Morgiana, telling everyone that Cassim was dead. The day after

Morgiana went to an old cobbler near the gates of the town who opened his stall early, put a piece of gold in his hand, and bade him follow her with his needle and thread. Having bound his eyes with a handkerchief, she took him to the room where the body lay, pulled off the bandage, and bade him sew the quarters together, after which she covered his eyes again and led him home. Then they buried Cassim, and Morgiana his slave followed him to the grave, weeping and tearing her hair, while Cassim's wife stayed at home uttering lamentable cries. Next day she went to live with Ali Baba, who gave Cassim's shop to his eldest son.

The Forty Thieves, on their return to the cave, were much astonished to find Cassim's body gone and some of their money-bags. "We are certainly discovered," said the Captain, "and shall be undone if we cannot find out who it is that knows our secret. Two men must have known it; we have killed one, we must now find the other. To this end one of you who is bold and artful must go into the city dressed as a traveller, and discover whom we have killed, and whether men talk of the strange manner of his death. If the messenger fails he must lose his life, lest we be betrayed." One of the thieves started up and offered to do this, and after the rest had highly commended him for his bravery he disguised himself, and happened to enter the town at daybreak, just by Baba Mustapha's stall. The thief bade him good-day, saying: "Honest man, how can you possibly see to stitch at your age?" "Old as I am," replied the cobbler, "I have very good eyes, and you will believe me when I tell you that I sewed a dead body together in a place where I had less light than I have now." The robber was overjoyed at his good fortune, and, giving him a piece of gold, desired to be shown the house where he stitched up the dead body. At first Mustapha refused, saying that he had been blindfolded; but when the robber gave him another piece of gold he began to think he might remember the turnings if blindfolded as before. This means succeeded; the robber partly led him, and was partly guided by him, right in front of Cassim's house, the door of which the robber marked with a piece of chalk. Then, well pleased, he bade farewell to Baba Mustapha and returned to the forest. By-and-by Morgiana, going out, saw the mark the robber had made, quickly guessed that some mischief was brewing, and fetching a piece of chalk marked two or three doors on each side, without saying anything to her master or mistress.

The thief, meantime, told his comrades of his discovery. The Captain thanked him, and bade him show him the house he had marked. But when they came to it they saw that five or six of the houses were chalked in the same manner. The guide was so confounded that he knew not what answer to make, and when they returned he was at once beheaded for having failed. Another robber was dispatched, and, having won over Baba Mustapha, marked the house in red chalk; but Morgiana being again too clever for them, the second messenger was put to death also. The Captain now resolved to go himself, but, wiser than the others, he did not mark the house, but looked at it so closely that he could not fail to remember it. He returned, and ordered his men to go into the neighboring villages and buy nineteen mules, and thirty-eight leather jars, all empty, except one which was full of oil. The Captain put one of his men, fully armed, into each, rubbing the outside of the jars with oil from the full vessel. Then the nineteen mules were loaded with thirty-seven robbers in jars, and the jar of oil, and reached the town by dusk. The Captain stopped his mules in front of Ali Baba's house, and said to Ali Baba, who was sitting outside for coolness: "I have brought some oil from a distance to sell at to-morrow's market, but it is now so late that I know not where to pass the night, unless you will do me the favor to take me in." Though Ali Baba had seen the Captain of the robbers in the forest, he did not recognize him in the disguise of an oil merchant. He bade him welcome, opened his gates for the mules to enter, and went to Morgiana to bid her prepare a bed and supper for his guest. He brought the stranger into his hall, and after they had supped went again to speak to Morgiana in the kitchen, while the Captain went into the yard under pretense of seeing after his mules, but really to tell his men what to do. Beginning at the first jar and ending at the last, he said to each man: "As soon as I throw some stones from the window of the chamber where I lie, cut the jars open with your knives and come out, and I will be with you in a trice."* He returned to the house, and Morgiana led him to his chamber. She then told Abdallah, her fellow-slave, to set on the pot to make some broth for her master, who had gone to bed. Meanwhile her lamp went out, and she had no more oil in the house. "Do not be uneasy," said Abdallah; "go into the yard and take some out of one of those jars." Morgiana thanked him for his advice, took the oil pot, and went into the yard. When she came to the first jar the robber inside said softly: "Is it time?"

---

trice: short period of time

Any other slave but Morgiana, on finding a man in the jar instead of the oil she wanted, would have screamed and made a noise; but she, knowing the danger her master was in, bethought herself of a plan, and answered quietly: "Not yet, but presently." She went to all the jars, giving the same answer, till she came to the jar of oil. She now saw that her master, thinking to entertain an oil merchant, had let thirty-eight robbers

into his house. She filled her oil pot, sent back to the kitchen, and, having lit her lamp, went again to the oil jar and filled a large kettle full of oil. When it boiled she went and poured enough oil into every jar to stifle and kill the robber inside. When this brave deed was done she went back to the kitchen, put out the fire and the lamp, and waited to see what would happen.

In a quarter of an hour the Captain of the robbers awoke, got up, and opened the window. As all seemed quiet he threw down some little pebbles which hit the jars. He listened, and as none of his men seemed to stir he grew uneasy, and went down into the yard. On going to the first jar and saying: "Are you asleep?" he smelt the hot boiled oil, and knew at once that his plot to murder Ali Baba and his household had been discovered. He found all the gang were dead, and, missing the oil out of the last jar, became aware of the manner of their death. He then forced the lock of a door leading into a garden, and climbing over several walls made his escape. Morgiana heard and saw all this, and, rejoicing at her success, went to bed and fell asleep.

At daybreak Ali Baba arose, and, seeing the oil jars there still, asked why the merchant had not gone with his mules. Morgiana bade him look in the first jar and see if there was any oil. Seeing a man, he started back in terror. "Have no fear," said Morgiana; "the man cannot harm you: he is dead." Ali Baba, when he had recovered somewhat from his astonishment, asked what had become of the merchant. "Merchant!" said she, "He is no more a merchant than I am!" and she told him the whole story, assuring him that it was a plot of the robbers of the forest, of whom only three were left, and that the white and red chalk marks had something to do with it. Ali Baba at once gave Morgiana her freedom, saying that he owed her his life. They then buried the bodies in Ali Baba's garden, while the mules were sold in the market by his slaves.

The Captain returned to his lonely cave, which seemed frightful to him without his lost companions, and firmly resolved to avenge them by killing Ali Baba. He dressed himself carefully, and went into town, where he took lodgings in an inn. In the course of a great many journeys to the forest he carried away many rich stuffs and much fine linen, and set up a shop opposite that of Ali Baba's son. He called himself Cogia Hassan, and as he was both civil and well dressed he soon made friends with Ali Baba's son, and through him with Ali Baba, whom he was continually asking to sup with him. Ali Baba, wishing to return his kindness, invited him into his house and received him smiling, thanking him for his kindness to his son. When the merchant was about to take his leave Ali Baba stopped him, saying: "Where are you going, sir, in such haste? Will you not stay and sup with me?" The merchant refused, saying that he had a reason; and, on Ali Baba's asking him what that was, he replied: "It is, sir, that I can eat no victuals that have any salt in them." "If that is all," said Ali Baba, "let me tell you that there shall be no salt in either the meat or the bread that we eat tonight." He went to give this order to Morgiana, who was much surprised. "Who is this man," she said, "who eats no salt with his meat?" "He is an honest man, Morgiana," returned her master; "therefore do as I bid you." But she could not withstand a desire to see this strange man, so she helped Abdallah to carry up the dishes, and saw in a moment that Cogia Hassan was the robber Captain, and carried a dagger under his garment. "I am not surprised," she said to herself, "that this wicked man, who intends to kill my master, will eat no salt* with him; but I will hinder his plans."

eat no salt: make no tacit pledge of friendship

She sent up the supper by Abdallah, while she made ready for one of the boldest acts that could be thought on. When the dessert had been served, Cogia Hassan was left alone with Ali Baba and his son, whom he thought to make drunk and then to murder them. Morgiana, meanwhile, put on a headdress like a dancing-girl's, and clasped a girdle round her waist, from which hung a dagger with a silver hilt, and said to Abdallah: "Take your tabor,* and let us go and divert* our master and his guest." Abdallah took his tabor and played before Morgiana until they came to the door, where Abdallah stopped playing and Morgiana made a low courtesy. "Come in, Morgiana," said Ali Baba, and, turning to Cogia Hassan, he said: "She's my slave and my housekeeper." Cogia Hassan was by no means pleased, for he feared that his chance of killing Ali Baba was gone for the present; but he pretended great eagerness to see Morgiana, and Abdallah began to play and Morgiana to dance. After she had performed several dances she drew her dagger and made passes with it, sometimes pointing it at her own breast, sometimes at her master's, as if it were part of the dance. Suddenly, out of breath, she snatched the tabor from Abdallah with her left hand, and, holding the dagger in her right, held out the tabor to her master. Ali Baba and his son put a piece of gold into it, and Cogia Hassan, seeing that she was coming to him, pulled out his purse to make her a present, but while he was putting his hand into it Morgiana plunged the dagger into his heart.

---

tabor: small drum

divert: entertain

"Unhappy girl!" cried Ali Baba and his son, "what have you done to ruin us?" "It was to preserve you, master, not to ruin you," answered Morgiana. "See here," opening the false merchant's garment and showing the dagger; "see what an enemy you have entertained! Remember, he would eat no salt with you, and what more would you have? Look at him! he is both the false oil merchant and the Captain of the Forty Thieves."

Ali Baba was so grateful to Morgiana for thus saving his life that he offered her to his son in marriage, who readily consented, and a few days after the wedding was celebrated with great splendor. At the end of the year Ali Baba, hearing nothing of the two remaining robbers, judged they were dead, and set out to the cave. The door opened on his saying: "Open, Sesame!" He went in, and saw that nobody had been there since the Captain left it. He brought away as much gold as he could carry, and returned to town. He told his son the secret of the cave, which his son handed down in his turn, so the children and grandchildren of Ali Baba were rich to the end of their lives.

About the Story

1. Does the author desire you to have more sympathy for Cassim or Ali Baba?

2. Identify the point of view from which the story is written and explain the role of point of view in guiding the reader's sympathies.

3. After analyzing each character's actions, can you say that any of them are really noble? Why or why not?

4. Although the resolution of the story is in some ways satisfying, it is not completely acceptable from a moral standpoint. Explain why.

5. Could a Christian draw a biblically based, moral lesson from the events of this story? Are there any aspects of the resolution that conflict with the Christian worldview?

After the Battle

Joseph A. Altsheler

Consider the viewpoint from which Altsheler tells this tale of two men caught in the crossfire of the Civil War. In the previous story, the perspective of the storyteller toward the conflict and toward the characters' actions and motivations enhanced the story's suspense. As you read this story, decide whether the point of view is the same as or different from the point of view of the previous story. Does point of view serve the same purpose in this story, or does it emphasize a different aspect? Be prepared to discuss the importance and benefits of the story's point of view.

The falling dusk quenched the fury of the battle. The cannon glimmered but feebly on the dim horizon like the sputter of a dying fire. The shouts of combatants were unheard, and Dave Joyce concluded that the fighting was over for that day at least. In his soul he was glad of it.

"Pardner," he said to the wounded man, "the battle has passed on an' left us here like a canoe stuck on a sand bank. I think the fightin' is over, but if it ain't we're out of it anyhow, an' I don't know any law why we shouldn't make ourselves as comf'table as things will allow."

"If there's anythin' done," said the wounded man, "you'll have to do it, for I can't walk, an' I can't move, except when there's a bush for me to grab hold of and pull myself along by."

"That's mighty bad," said Joyce, sympathetically. "Where did you say that bullet took you?"

"I got it in my right leg here," the other replied, "an' I think it broke the bone. Leastways the leg ain't any more use to me than if it was dead, though it hurts like tarnation sometimes. I guess it'll be weeks before I walk again."

"Maybe I could do somethin' for you," said Joyce, " if there was a little more light. I guess I'll take a look, anyhow. I haven't been two years in the army not to know anythin' about bullet wounds."

He bent down and with his pocket-knife cut away a patch of the faded blue cloth from the wounded man's leg.

"I guess I'd better not fool with that," he said, looking critically at the wound. "The bullet's gone all the way through, but the blood's clotted up so thick over the places that the bleedin' has stopped. You won't die if you don't move too much an' start that wound to bleedin' again."

"That's consolin'," said the wounded man; "but, since I can't move, I don't know what's to become of me but to lay here on the field an' die anyway."

"Don't you fret," said Joyce, cheerfully. "I'll take care of you. You're Fed. and I'm Confed., but you're hurt an' I ain't, an' if the case was the other way I'd expect you to do as much for me. Besides, I've lost my regiment in the shuffle, and the chances are if I tried to find it again to-night I'd run right into the middle of the Yankee army, and that would mean Camp Chase for your humble servant, which is a bunk he ain't covetin' very bad just now. So I guess it'll be the safe as well as the right thing for me to do to stick by you. Listen to that! Just hear them crickets chirpin', will you!"

There was a blaze of light in the west, followed by a crash which seemed to roll around the horizon and set all the trees of the forest to trembling. When the echoes were lost beyond the hills the silence became heavy and portentous. The night was hot and sticky, and the powdery vapor that still hung over the field crept into Joyce's throat and made him cough for breath.

"Thunderation!" he said at length, still looking in the direction in which the light had blazed up. "I guess at least a dozen of the big cannon must have been fired at once then. Can't some fellows get enough fightin' in the daytime, without pluggin' away in the nighttime too? Now I come of fightin' stock myself—I'm from Kentucky—but twelve hours out of the twenty-four always 'peared to me to be enough for that sort of thing. Besides, it's awful hot to-night, too."

"It was hotter than this for me a while ago." said the wounded man.

"So it was, so it was," said Joyce, apologetically, "an' I mustn't forget you, either. Let 'em fight over there if they want to, an' if they're big enough fools to spile a night that way when they might be restin'. What you need just now is water. I think there's a spring runnin' out of the side of that hill there. If you'll listen you'll hear it tricklin' away, so cool and refreshin' like. I guess it was tricklin' that same way, just as calm an' peaceful as Sunday mornin', while the battle was goin' on round here. Don't you feel as if a little water would help you mightily, pardner?"

"'Twould so," said the wounded man. "I'm burnin' up inside, an' if you'd get a big drink of it I'd think you were mighty nigh good enough to be one of the twelve apostles."

"It's easy enough for me to do it," said Joyce. "I'll be back in a minute."

He took off his big slouch hat and walked toward the source of the trickling sound. From beneath an overhanging rock in the side of the hill near by a tiny stream of water flowed. After a fall of five feet it plunged into a little basin which it had hallowed out for itself in the rock, and formed a deep and cool little pool. Around the edge of the pool the tender green grass grew. The overflow from it wandered away in a little rill through the woods.

"Thunder, but ain't this purty?" exclaimed Joyce, forgetting that the wounded man was out of hearing. "It's just like our springhouse back in old Kentuck. I've put out butter-crocks an' milk-buckets a hundred times to cool in our pool when I was a boy. Wish I had some of them things now!"

The stirring of peaceful memories caused Joyce to linger a little, in forgetfulness of the wounded man. It was cool in the shadow of the hill, and the gay little stream tinkled merrily in his ears. He would have liked to remain there, but he pulled himself together with an impatient jerk, filled the crown of his hat with the limpid water, and started back to the relief of the wounded man.

He followed the channel of the stream for a little way, and as he turned to step across it he noticed the increasing depth of its waters.

"It's dammed up," he muttered. "I wonder what's done that."

Then he started back shuddering and spilled half the water from his hat, for he had almost stepped on the body of a man that had fallen across the channel of the poor little rivulet, checking the flow of its waters and deepening the stream.

The body lay face downward, and Joyce could not see the wound that had caused death. But as he stooped down he saw again the broad red flash in the west, and heard the heavy crash of the cannon.

"Will them cannon always be hungry?" he muttered. "But I guess I must give this poor little stream which 'ain't done no harm to anybody the right of way again."

He stooped and pulled the body to one side. With a thankful rush and gurgle the waters of the recent pool sped on in their natural channel, and Joyce returned to the fountain-head to fill his hat again.

He found the wounded man waiting with patience.

"I was gone longer than I ought to have been. Did you think I had left you, pardner?" asked Joyce.

"No," said the man. "I didn't believe you'd play that kind of a trick on me."

"An' so I haven't," said Joyce, "an' for your faith in me I've brought you a hatful of the nicest an' freshest an' coolest water you ever put your lips to in all your born days. Raise your head up, there, an' drink."

The wounded man drank and drank, and then when the hat was emptied he laid his head back in the grass and sighed as if he were in heaven.

"I must say that you 'pear to like water, pardner," said Joyce.

"Like it?" said the wounded man. "Wait till you've been wounded, an' then you'll know what it is to want water. Why, till you brought it I felt as if my inside was full of hot coals an' I'd burn all up if I didn't get something mighty quick to put the fire out."

"Then I reckon I've stopped a whole conflagration," said Joyce, "an' with mighty little trouble to myself, too. But I don't wonder that you get thirsty on a night like this. Thunderation, but ain't it clammy!"

He sat down on the fallen tree and drew his coat-sleeve across his brow. Then he held up the sleeve: it was wet with sweat. There was no wind. The night had brought no coolness. The thick and heavy atmosphere hung close to the earth and coiled the throats and nostrils of the two men.

"I wish I was at home sleepin' on the hall floor," said Joyce. "I'll bet it would be cool there."

The wounded man made no answer, but turned his face up to the sky and drew in great mouthfuls of the warm air.

"Them fools over yonder 'pear to have their dander up yet," said Joyce, pointing to the west, where the alternate flashing and rumbling showed that the battle still lingered. "I thought the battle was over long ago, but I guess it ain't. I've knowed some fools in my time, but the fellows that would

temper as a little lamb friskin' about in our field at home. I hope that there fightin' won't come our way; at least not to-night. How are you feelin', pardner?"

"Pretty well for a wounded man," replied the other; "but I'd like to have some more water."

"Then I'm the man to get it for you," said Joyce, springing up. "An' I'm goin' to see if I can't get somethin' to eat, too, for my innards are cryin' cupboard mighty loud. There's dead men layin' aroun' here, an' there may be somethin' in their haversacks.* I hate to rob the dead, but if they've got grub we need it more'n they do."

---

haversacks: bags slung over the shoulder used to carry supplies

---

He returned with another hatful of water, which the wounded man drank eagerly, gratefully. Then he went back and searched in the grass and bushes for the fallen. Presently he came in great glee, and triumphantly held up two haversacks.

"Luck, pardner!" he exclaimed. "Great luck! Bully luck! One of these I got off a dead Fed. and t'other off a dead Confed., and both must have been boss foragers,* for in one haversack there's a roast chicken an' in t'other there's half a b'iled ham, an' in both there's plenty of bread. I haven't had such luck before in six months. You're a Yank, pardner, and a Northerner, an' maybe you don't know much about the vanities of roast chicken an' cold b'iled ham. But it's time you did know. I've come from the field at home when I'd been plowin' all day, an' my appetite was as sharp as a razor an' as big as our barn. I'd put up old Pete, our black mule that I'd been plowin' with, an' feed him; then I'd go to the house an' kinder loosen my waist-ban', an' mother would say to me, 'Come in the kitchen, Dave; your supper's ready for you.' Say, pardner, you ought to see me then. There'd be a pitcher of cold

keep on fightin' on a hot night like this must be the biggest fools."

Then the two lay quite still for a while, watching the uneasy rising and falling of the night battle. Had they not known so much of war, they might have persuaded themselves that the flashes they saw were flashes of heat-lightning and the rumbling but the rumbling of summer thunder. But they knew better. They knew it was men and not the elements that fought.

"It's mighty curious," said Joyce, "how the sand's all gone out of me for the time. Today I felt as if I could whip the whole Yankee army all by myself. To-night I don't want to fight anythin'. I'm as peaceful in

buttermilk from the spring-house, and one dish of roast chicken, an' another of cold ham, an' all for me, too. An' say, pardner, I can taste that ham now. When you eat one piece you want another, an' then another, an' you keep on till there ain't any left on the dish, an' then you lean back in your chair an' wish that when you come to die you'd feel as happy as you do then. Pardner, I wish them times was back again."

---

forager: one who collects or looks for food

"I wish so too," said the wounded man.

"We can't have 'em back, at least not now," said Joyce, cheerily, "but we can make believe, an' it'll be mighty good make-believe, too, for we've got the ham an' the chicken, an' we can get cold water to take the place of cold milk. I guess you can use your arms all right; so you can spread this ham an' chicken out on the grass an' I'll see if I can't find a canteen to keep the water in. Say pardner, we'll have a banquet, you an' me, that's what we'll have."

The stalwart young fellow, full of boyish delight at the idea that the thought of home had suggested to him, swung off in search of the canteen. He found not one alone, but two. Then he returned clanking them together to indicate his success. As he came up he called out, in his hearty voice:

"Pardner, is the supper-table ready? Have you got the knives an' forks? You needn't min' about the napkins. I guess we can get along without 'em just this once."

"All ready," said the wounded man; "an' I guess I can keep you company at this ham an' chicken an' bread, for I'm gettin' a mighty sharp edge on my appetite too."

"So much the better," said Joyce. "There's plenty for both, an' it wouldn't be good manners for me to eat by myself."

He sat down on the grass in front of the improvised repast, and placed one canteen beside the wounded man and the other beside himself.

"Now, pardner," he said, "we'll drink to each other's health, an' then we'll charge the ham an' chicken with more vim than either of us ever charged a breastwork."

They drank from the canteens; and then they made onslaught upon the provisions. Joyce ate for a while in deep and silent content, forgetting the heat and the battle which still lowered in the west. But presently, when his appetite was dulled, he remembered the cannonade.

"There they go again!" he said. "Boom! Boom! Boom! Won't them fellows ever get enough? I thought I was hungry, but the cannon over there 'pear to be hungrier. I suppose there ain't men enough in all this country to stop up their iron throats. But bang away! They don't bother us, do they, pardner? They can't spile this supper, for all their boomin' an' flashin'."

The wounded man bowed assent and took another piece of the ham.

Joyce leaned back on the grass, held up a chicken leg in his hand, and looked contemplatively at it.

"Ain't it funny, pardner," he said, "that you a Tommy Yank, an' me, a Johnny Reb, are sittin' here, eatin' grub together, as friendly as two brothers, when we ought to be killin' each other? I don't know what Jeff Davis an' old Abe Lincoln will say about it when they hear of the way you an' me are doin'."

The wounded man laughed.

"You can say that I was your prisoner," he said, "when they summon you before the courtmartial. An' so I am, if you choose to make me. I can't resist."

"I'm thinkin' more about gettin' back safe to our army than makin' prisoners," said Joyce, as he flung the chicken bone, now bare, into the bushes.

"That may be hard to do," said the wounded man; "for neither you nor me can tell which way the armies will go. Listen to that boomin'! Wasn't it louder than before? That fightin' must be movin' round nearer to us."

"Let it move," said Joyce. "I tell you I've had enough of fightin' for one day. That battle can take care of itself. I won't let it bother me. I don't want to shoot anybody."

"Is that the way you feel when you go into battle?" asked the wounded man.

"I can't say exactly," replied Joyce. "Of course when I go out in a charge with my regiment I want to beat the other fellows, but I don't hate 'em, no, not a bit. I've got nothin' against the Yanks. I've knowed some of 'em that was mighty good fellows. There ain't any of 'em that I want to kill. No, I'll take that back; there is one, just one, a bloody villain that I'd like to draw a bead on an' send a bullet through his skulkin' body."

"Who is that?" asked the wounded man; "an' why do you make an exception of him?"

Joyce remained silent for a moment or two and drew a long blade of grass restlessly through his fingers.

"It's not a pleasant story," he said at last, "an' it hurts me to tell it, but I made you ask the question, an' I guess I might as well tell you, 'cause I feel friendly toward you, pardner, bein' as we are together in distress, like two Robinson Crusoes, so to speak."

The wounded man settled himself in the grass like one who is going to listen comfortably to a story.

"It's just a yarn of the Kentuck hills," said Joyce, "an' a bad enough one, too. We're a good sort of people up there, but we're hot-blooded, an' when we get into trouble, as we sometimes do, kinfolks stan' together. I guess you're from Maine, or York State, or somewhere away up North, an' you can't understand us. But it's just as

I say. Sometimes two men up in our hills fight, an' one kills the other. Then the dead man's brothers, an' sons if he's got any old enough, an' cousins, an' so on, take up their guns an' go huntin' for the man that killed him. An' the livin' man's brothers an' sons' an' cousins an' so on take up their guns an' come out to help him. An' there you've got your feud, an' there's no tellin' how many years it'll run on, an' how many people will get killed in it.—Thunderation, but wasn't them cannon loud that time! The battle is movin' round toward us sure!"

Joyce listened a moment, but heard nothing more except the echoes.

"Our family got into one of them feuds," he said. "It was the Joyces and the Ryders. I's Dave Joyce, the son of Henry Joyce. I don't remember how the feud started; about nothin' much, I guess; but it was a red-hot one, I can tell you, pardner. It was fought fair for a long time, but at last Bill Ryder shot father from ambush and killed him. Father hadn't had much to do with the feud, either; he didn't like that sort of thing—didn't think it was right. I said right then that if I ever found the chance when I got big enough I'd kill Bill Ryder."

"Did you get the chance?" asked the wounded man.

"No," replied Joyce. "Country got too hot for Ryder, and he went away. He came back after a while, an' I was big enough to go gunnin' for him then, but the war broke out, an' off he went into the Union army before I could get a chance to draw a bead on him. I ain't heard of him since. Maybe he's been killed in battle an' his bones are bleachin' somewhere in the woods."

"Most likely," said the wounded man.

"There's no tellin'," said Joyce. "Still, some day when we're comin' up against the Yanks face to face I may see him before me, an' then I'll hold my gun steady an' shoot straight at him, instead of whoopin' like mad an' firin' lickety-split into the crowd, aimin' at nothin', as I generally do."

"It's a sad story, very sad for you," said the wounded man.

"Yes," said Joyce. "You don't have such things as feuds up North, do you?"

"No," replied the other, "an' we're well off without 'em. Hark, there's the cannon again!"

"Yes, an' they keep creepin' round toward us with their infernal racket," said Joyce. "Cannon love to chaw up people an' then brag about it. But if them fellows are bent on fightin' all night I guess we'll have to give 'em room for it. What do you say to movin'? I've eat all I want, an' I guess you have too, an' we can take what's left with us."

"I don't know," said the wounded man. "My leg's painin' me a good deal, an' the grass is soft an' long here where I'm layin'. It makes a good bed, an' maybe I'd better stay where I am."

"I think not," said Joyce, decidedly. "That night fight's still swingin' down on us, an' if we stay too long them cannon'll feed on us too. We'd better move, pardner. Let me take a look at your wound. It's gettin' lighter, an' I can see better now. The moon's up, an' she's shinin' for all she's worth through them trees. Besides, them cannon-flashes help. Raise your head, pardner, an' we'll take a look at your wound together."

"I don't think you can do any good," said the wounded man. "It would be better not to disturb it."

"But we must be movin', pardner," said Joyce, a little impatiently. "See, the fight's warmin' up, an' it's still creepin' down on us. Seems to me I can almost hear the tramp of the men an' the rollin' of the cannon-wheels. What a blaze that was! I say, it's time for us to be goin'. If we stay here we're likely to be ground to death under the cannon-wheels, if

we ain't shot first. Just let me get a grip under your shoulders, pardner, an' I'll take you out of this."

The cannon flamed up again, and the deep thunder filled all the night.

"Listen how them old iron throats are growlin' an' mutterin'," said Joyce; "an' they're sayin' 'it's time for us to be travelin'.'"

"I believe," said the wounded man, "that I would rather stay where I am an' take my chances. If I move I'm afraid I'll break open my wound. Besides, I think you're mistaken. It seems to me that the fight's passin' round to the right of us."

"Passin' to the right of us nothin'," said Joyce. "It's comin' straight this way, with no more respect for our feelin's than if you an' me was a couple of field-mice."

The wounded man made no answer.

"Do you think, pardner," asked Joyce, slight offence showing in his voice, "that the Yanks may come this way an' pick you up an' then you won't be a prisoner? Is that your game?"

As his companion made no answer, Joyce continued:

"You don't think, pardner, that I want to hold you a prisoner, do you? an' you a wounded man, too, that I picked up on the battle-field and that I've eat and drank with? Why, that ain't my style."

He waited for an answer and as none came he was seized with a sudden alarm.

"You ain't dead, pardner?" he cried. "What if he's dead while I've been standin' here talkin' an' wastin' time!"

He bent over to take a look at the other's face, but the wounded man, with a sudden and convulsive movement, writhed away from him and struck at him with his open hand.

"Keep away!" he cried. "Don't touch me! Don't come near me! I won't have it! I won't have it!"

"Thunderation, pardner!" exclaimed Joyce; "what do you mean? I ain't goin' to harm you. I want to help you." Then he added, pityingly, "I guess he's got the fever an' gone out of his head. So I'll take him along whether he wants to go or not."

He bent over again, seized the wounded man by the shoulders, and forcibly raised him up. At the same moment the cannonade burst out afresh and with increased violence. A blaze of light played over the face of the wounded man, revealing and magnifying every line.

Joyce uttered no exclamation, but he dropped the man as if he had been a coiling serpent in his hands, and looked at him, an expression of hate and loathing creeping over his face.

"So," he said, at last, "this is the way I have found you?"

The wounded man lay as he had fallen, with his face to the earth.

"No wonder," said Joyce, "you wanted to keep your face hid in the grass! No wonder you hide it there now!"

"Oh, Dave! Dave!" exclaimed the man, springing to his knees with sudden energy, "Don't kill me! Don't kill me, Dave!"

"Why shouldn't I kill you?" asked Joyce, scornfully. "What reason can you give why I shouldn't do it?"

"There ain't any. There ain't any. Oh, I know there ain't any," cried the wounded man. "But don't do it, Dave! Don't do it!"

"You murderer! You sneakin', ambushin' murderer!" said Joyce. "It's right for you to beg for your life an' then not get it! Hear them cannon! Hear how they growl, an' see the flash from their throats! They'd like to feed on you, but they won't. That sort of death is too good for the likes of you. The death for you is to be shot like a ravin' cur."

He drew the loaded pistol from his belt and cocked it with deliberate motion.

"Dave! Dave!" the man cried, dragging himself to Joyce's feet, "you won't do that! You can't! It would be murder, Dave, to shoot me here, me a wounded man that can't help myself!"

"You done it, an' worse," said Joyce. "Of all the men unburnt in hell I think the one who deserves to be there most is the man who hid in ambush and shot another in the back that had never harmed him."

"I know it, Dave, I know it!" cried the wounded man, grasping Joyce's feet with both hands; "it was an awful thing to do, an' I've been sorry a thousand times that I done it, but all the sorrow in the world an' everythin' else that's in the world can't undo it now."

"That's so," said Joyce, "but it don't make any reason why the murderer ought to be kept on livin'."

"It don't, Dave; you're right, I know; but I don't want to die!" cried the man. "I'm a coward, Dave, and I don't want to die by myself here in the woods an' in the dark!"

"You'll soon have light enough," said Joyce, "an' I won't shoot you."

He let down the hammer of his pistol and replaced the weapon in his belt.

"Oh, Dave! Dave!" exclaimed the man, kissing Joyce's foot. "I'm so glad you'll let me have my life. I know I ain't fit to live, but I want to live anyhow."

"I said I wouldn't shoot you," said Joyce, "but I never said I'd spare your life. See that blaze in the trees up there."

A few hundred yards away the forest had burst into flame. Sparks fell upon a tree and blazed up. Long red spirals coiled themselves around the trunk and boughs until the tree became a mass of fire, and then other tongues of flame leaped forward and seized other trees. There was a steady crackling and roaring, and the wind that had sprung up drove smoke and ashes and fiery particles before it.

"That," said Joyce, "is the wood on fire. Them cannon that's been makin' so much fuss done it. I've seen it often in battle when the cannon have been growlin'. The fire grows an' it grows, an' it burns up everythin' in its way. The army is still busy fightin', an' the wounded, them that's hurt too bad to help theirselves, have to lay there on the ground an' watch the fire comin', an' sure to get 'em. By an' by it sweeps down on 'em, an' they shriek an' shriek, but that don't do you no good, for before long the fire goes on, an' there they are, dead an' burnt to a coal. I tell you it's an awful death!"

The wounded man was silent now. He had drawn himself up a little, and was watching the fire as it leaped from tree to tree and devoured them one after another.

"That fire is comin' for us, an' the wind is bringin' it along fast," said Joyce, composedly, "but it's easy enough for me to get out of its way. All I've got to do is to go up the hill, an' the clearin's run for a long way beyond. I can stay up there an' watch the fire pass, an' you'll be down here right in its track."

"Dave!" cried the man, "you ain't goin' to let me burn to death right before your eyes?"

"That's what I mean to do," said Joyce. "I don't like to shoot a wounded man that can't help himself, an' I won't do it, but I ain't got no call to save you from another death."

"I'd rather be shot than burned to death," cried the man, in a frenzy.

"It's just the death for you," said Joyce.

Then the wounded man again dragged himself to the feet of Joyce.

"Don't do it, Dave!" he cried. "Don't leave me here to burn to death! Oh, I tell you, Dave, I ain't fit to die!"

"Take your hands off my feet," said Joyce. "I don't want 'em to touch me. There's too much blood on 'em."

"Don't leave me to the fire!" continued the man. "You've been kind to me to-night. Help me a little more, Dave, an' you'll be glad you done it when you come to die yourself!"

"I must be goin'," said Joyce, repulsing the man's detaining hands. "It's gettin' hot here now, an' that fire will soon be near enough to scorch my face. Good-by."

"For the sake of your own soul, Dave Joyce," cried the man, beating the ground with his hands, "don't leave me to be burned to a coal! Think, Dave, how we eat an' drank together to-night, like two brothers, an' how you waited on me an' brought the water an' the grub. You'll remember them things, Dave, when you come to die yourself!"

The fire increased in strength and violence. The flames ran up the trees, and whirled far above them in red coils that met and twined with each other, and then whirled triumphantly on in search of fresh fuel. A giant oak, burned through at the base and swept of all its young boughs and foliage, fell with a rending crash, a charred and shattered trunk. The flames roared, and the burning trees maintained an incessant crackling like a fire of musketry. The smoke through which the sparks of fire were sown in millions grew stifling.

"What a sight!" cried Joyce.

"Dave, you won't leave me to that?" cried Ryder.

Joyce drew down his hat over his eyes to shield them from the smoke. Then he stooped, lifted the wounded man upon his powerful shoulders, and went on over the hill.

About the Story

1. From what point of view is the story told?

2. Why do you think the author chose to tell the story using this viewpoint?

3. How do Dave Joyce and Bill Ryder differ?

4. How is the conflict resolved?

5. What does the resolution to the conflict reveal about the character of Dave Joyce?

6. If Joyce had been the wounded man, how do you think Ryder would have treated him? Support your answer with examples from the story's text.

About the Author

At the turn of the twentieth century, Joseph A. Altsheler (1862–1919) was the most popular author of adventure stories for boys. He maintained this popularity well into the 1920s. Altsheler's stories gave his youthful readers drama, humor, and reliable history while improving their literary tastes. His well-constructed plots and skillful characterization raised the standard of children's literature.

Altsheler's first story was written while he was editor of the New York *World*, a well-known magazine published three times weekly. One day, Altsheler needed a boy's adventure story to include in the magazine. Because none was forthcoming, Altsheler took it upon himself to fill the need. Although he had been working in journalism successfully, Altsheler found his true talent as an author of historical romances for young readers. His adventures dealt with the American West, American Indians, the Civil War, and World War I. Although Altsheler had no intention of becoming a children's author when he wrote his first story, his subsequent output (usually one or two books annually) helped him become one of America's favorite children's authors.

The Open Window

SAKI (H. H. MUNRO)

Known as Saki, a pseudonym taken from the cupbearer in *The Rubaiyat of Omar Khayyam,* H. H. Munro has a unique ability to entertain his readers with witty, ironic tales. Saki's stories often contain a strange mixture of emotions. "The Open Window" is a good example of this quality in Saki's work.

In this brief tale Saki manipulates the story's viewpoint to amuse the reader. Unlike the previous stories, however, the author narrates much of the story from one viewpoint and then shifts to another. Be prepared to explain why the author shifts viewpoints and how it is effective in this case.

"My aunt will be down presently, Mr. Nuttel," said a very self-possessed young lady of fifteen; "in the meantime you must try and put up with me."

Framton Nuttel endeavored to say the correct something which should duly flatter the niece of the moment without unduly discounting the aunt that was to come. Privately he doubted more than ever whether these formal visits on a succession of total strangers would do much toward helping the nerve cure which he was supposed to be undergoing.

"I know how it will be," his sister had said when he was preparing to migrate to this rural retreat; "you will bury yourself down there and not speak to a living soul, and your nerves will be worse than ever from moping. I shall just give you letters of introduction to all the people I know there. Some of them, as far as I can remember, were quite nice."

Framton wondered whether Mrs. Sappleton, the lady to whom he was presenting one of the letters of introduction, came into the nice division.

"Do you know many of the people round here?" asked the niece, when she judged that they had had sufficient silent communion.

"Hardly a soul," said Framton. "My sister was staying here, at the rectory, you know, some four years ago, and she gave me letters of introduction to some of the people here."

He made the last statement in a tone of distinct regret.

"Then you know practically nothing about my aunt?" pursued the self-possessed young lady.

"Only her name and address," admitted the caller. He was wondering whether Mrs. Sappleton was in the married or widowed state. An undefinable something about the room seemed to suggest masculine habitation.

"Her great tragedy happened just three years ago," said the child; "that would be since your sister's time."

"Her tragedy?" asked Framton; somehow in this restful country spot tragedies seemed out of place.

"You may wonder why we keep that window wide open on an October afternoon," said the niece, indicating a large French window that opened on to a lawn.

"It is quite warm for the time of the year," said Framton; "but has that window got anything to do with the tragedy?"

"Out through that window, three years ago to a day, her husband and her two young brothers went off for their day's shooting. They never came back. In crossing the moor to their favorite snipeshooting ground they were all three engulfed in a treacherous piece of bog. It had been that dreadful wet summer, you know, and places that were safe in other years gave way suddenly without warning. Their bodies were never recovered. That was the dreadful part of it." Here the child's voice lost its self-possessed note and became falteringly human. "Poor aunt always thinks that they will come back some day, they and the little brown spaniel that was lost with them, and walk in at that window just as they used to do. That is why the window is kept open every evening till it is quite dusk. Poor dear aunt, she has often told me how they went out, her husband with his white waterproof coat over his arm, and Ronnie, her youngest brother, singing, 'Bertie, why do you bound?' as he always did to tease her, because she said it got on her nerves. Do you know, sometimes on still, quiet evenings like this, I almost get a creepy feeling that they will all walk in through that window—"

She broke off with a little shudder. It was a relief to Framton when the aunt bustled into the room with a whirl of apologies for being late in making her appearance.

"I hope Vera has been amusing you?" she said.

"She has been very interesting," said Framton.

"I hope you don't mind the open window," said Mrs. Sappleton briskly; "my husband and brothers will be home directly from shooting, and they always come in this way. They've been out for snipe in the marshes today, so they'll make a fine mess over my poor carpets. So like you men-folk, isn't it?"

She rattled on cheerfully about the shooting and the scarcity of birds, and the pros-pects for duck in the winter. To Framton it was all purely horrible. He made a desperate but only partially successful effort to turn the talk on to a less ghastly topic; he was conscious that his hostess was giving him only a fragment of her attention, and her eyes were constantly straying past him to the open window and the lawn beyond. It was certainly an unfortunate coincidence that he should have paid his visit on this tragic anniversary.

"The doctors agree in ordering me complete rest, an absence of mental excitement, and avoidance of anything in the nature of violent physical exercise," announced Framton, who labored under the tolerably wide-spread delusion that total strangers and chance acquaintances are hungry for the least detail of one's ailments and infirmities, their cause and cure. "On the matter of diet they are not so much in agreement," he continued.

"No?" said Mrs. Sappleton, in a voice which only replaced a yawn at the last moment. Then she suddenly brightened into alert attention—but not to what Framton was saying.

"Here they are at last!" she cried. "Just in time for tea, and don't they look as if they were muddy up to the eyes!"

Framton shivered slightly and turned toward the niece with a look intended to convey sympathetic comprehension. The child was staring out through the open window with dazed horror in her eyes. In a chill shock of nameless fear Framton swung around in his seat and looked in the same direction.

In the deepening twilight three figures were walking across the lawn toward the window; they all carried guns under their arms, and one of them was additionally burdened with a white coat hung over his shoulders. A tired brown spaniel kept close at their heels. Noiselessly they neared the house, and then a

hoarse young voice chanted out of the dusk: "I said, Bertie, why do you bound?"

Framton grabbed wildly at his stick and hat; the hall-door, the gravel-drive, and the front gate were dimly noted stages in his headlong retreat. A cyclist coming along the road had to run into the hedge to avoid imminent collision.

"Here we are, my dear," said the bearer of the white mackintosh, coming in through the window; "fairly muddy, but most of it's dry. Who was that who bolted out as we came up?"

"A most extraordinary man, a Mr. Nuttel," said Mrs. Sappleton; "could only talk about his illnesses, and dashed off without a word of good-bye or apology when you arrived. One would think he had seen a ghost."

"I expect it was the spaniel," said the niece calmly; "he told me he had a horror of dogs. He was once hunted into a cemetery somewhere on the banks of the Ganges by a pack of pariah* dogs, and had to spend the night in a newly dug grave with the creatures snarling and grinning and foaming just above him. Enough to make anyone lose their nerve."

pariah: outcast

Romance at short notice was her specialty.

About the Story

1. Identify at least one example of foreshadowing at the beginning of the story that hints at the character of Vera, Mrs. Sappleton's niece.

2. "The Open Window" uses the limited omniscient point of view through most of the story. Which character does Saki use to view the events?

3. At what point do you begin to suspect that Vera was making up her story?

4. In the last four paragraphs of the story, Saki changes point of view. What is the point of view of these last four paragraphs? Explain, using the definitions given to you earlier.

5. Why do you think the author chose to alter the story's viewpoint near the ending?

About the Author

Hector Hugh Munro (1870–1916) was born in Akyab, Union of Myanmar, while his father served in the British armed forces. After the death of Munro's mother, his father left Munro and his older brother and sister in the care of a grandmother and two severe, complaining aunts and returned to India. The three children, cloistered in a stuffy English country house, were reared in a stifling atmosphere with no encouragement to be imaginative. Nevertheless, the three of them created their own little world and made their own adventures.

Munro adopted the pen name Saki and began writing for publication. Many of his characters and situations were taken from childhood memories. His upbringing affected his writing profoundly, especially his characterization and moral tone. Children in Saki's writing often deal cruelly with some oppressive adult figure, and they display a studied indifference to wrongdoing. The moral tone of Saki's writing is considered by some to be the result of the eccentricity and mental cruelty of his aunts. Saki's greatest skill, however, seems to be his ability to present life's little miseries with ironic humor, without losing a hint of childish enjoyment.

In 1893 Saki returned to Myanmar as a part of the British military police force there. His short stay (a year and one month) furnished him with more creative fuel for his imaginative stories. During this time Saki was more adept at drawing than at writing; however, only a few years after his return to England, he decided to make writing his career. His first works were political satires (*Not So Stories*, 1902). Saki then began to travel widely as a newspaper correspondent in Eastern Europe. His *Reginald* sketches (1904) are humorous short stories recounting the adventures and opinions of a young Englishman. His output of short stories was enormous.

Saki readily enlisted when World War I broke out, and he displayed great character and concern for others while serving in France. He was killed there by enemy fire in 1916.

❧ THINKING ZONE ❧

Sometimes a story's point of view may be influenced by its genre. **Genre** refers to categories or types of literature. The three standard genre divisions in literature are prose, poetry, and drama. These divisions acknowledge the differences in structure that distinguish such compositions from one another. Within these broad categories, many other genres exist as well. They can be described primarily by content (e.g., fiction and nonfiction), by structure (e.g., short stories and novels), or even by a combination of both (e.g., sonnets and epic poems). Often a work fits into several different categories at once. For example, a Sherlock Holmes mystery belongs to four progressively smaller divisions of genre—prose, fiction, short story, and detective story. The special conventions of the final category make it the most likely to influence the writer's viewpoint.

In this unit, you have already encountered three highly specific prose genres. First, **frame stories** contain a second story set within the opening and closing narrative. "The Silver Mine" from Unit 3 is an example of a frame tale: it opens and closes with the king's story but contains the parson's story in the middle. The frame story is told from an omniscient point of view, but the second story is told by a character from the frame tale (the parson) using the limited-omniscient point of view. Second, an **anecdote** is a short narrative of a single interesting or amusing incident. A good anecdote generally focuses on action and has a definite point. Most anecdotes concern one main character's experience (often the narrator's); thus, they are usually told from the limited-omniscient or the first-person point of view. The final genre, historical fiction, is much broader, being based purely on content. **Historical fiction** encompasses any fictional story employing real characters and settings from a time period other than the one it was written in. Because of the genre's wide-ranging nature, historical fiction can be easily written from any point of view. However, if an author writes of a historical time or place that is very remote from his readers, he may choose the omniscient viewpoint since it provides more opportunities for the author to explore the differing customs, mindsets, and histories that form the backgrounds of the characters and events.

1. Based on the definition of *frame story*, which of the selections in this unit is part of a frame story? Why does the story fit into that **genre**?

2. Which story best fits the definition of *historical fiction*? How does it fit that description?

3. Which of the three selections fits the definition of *anecdote*? How does it fulfill those requirements?

4. In "The Open Window," the narrator uses the limited-omniscient viewpoint for most of the story, focusing on Nuttel's perspective. How does that point of view aid the author in accomplishing the purposes of the genre he is using?

By Any Other Name

Santha Rama Rau

In this autobiographical essay, the author recalls her first day at school. But her first day is not like that of most children. Notice the effectiveness of the author's point of view as you learn about the headmistress, the school, and the other children. As you read, picture yourself in a similar situation and consider how you would have reacted.

At the Anglo-Indian day school in Zorinabad* to which my sister and I were sent when she was eight and I was five and a half, they changed our names. On the first day of school, a hot, windless morning of a north Indian September, we stood in the headmistress's study and she said, "Now you're the *new* girls. What are your names?"

Zorinabad: town in northern India

My sister answered for us. "I am Premila, and she"—nodding in my direction—"is Santha."

The headmistress had been in India, I suppose, fifteen years or so, but she still smiled her helpless inability to cope with Indian names. Her rimless half-glasses glittered, and the precarious bun on the top of her head trembled as she shook her head. "Oh, my dears, those are much too hard for me. Suppose we give you pretty English names. Wouldn't that be more jolly? Let's see, now— Pamela for you, I think." She shrugged in a baffled way at my sister. "That's as close as I can get. And for *you*" she said to me, "how about Cynthia? Isn't that nice?"

My sister was always less easily intimidated than I was, and while she kept a stubborn silence, I said, "Thank you," in a very tiny voice.

We had been sent to that school because my father, among his responsibilities as an officer of the civil service, had a tour of duty to perform in the villages around that

steamy little provincial town, where he had his headquarters at that time. He used to make his shorter inspection tours on horseback, and a week before, in the stale heat of a typically postmonsoon* day, we had waved goodbye to him and a little procession—an assistant, a secretary, two bearers, and the man to look after the bedding rolls and luggage. They rode away through our large garden, still bright green from the rains, and we turned back into the twilight of the house and the sound of fans whispering in every room.

---
postmonsoon: referring to the dry spell that generally follows the rainy season, when ocean winds called monsoons bring rain to India

---

Up to then, my mother had refused to send Premila to school in the British-run establishments of that time, because, she used to say, "you can bury a dog's tail for seven years and it still comes out curly, and you can take a Britisher away from his home for a lifetime and he still remains insular."* The examinations and degrees from entirely Indian schools were not, in those days, considered valid. In my case, the question had never come up, and probably never would have come up if Mother's extraordinary good health had not broken down. For the first time in my life, she was not able to continue the lessons she had been giving us every morning. So our Hindi* books were put away, the stories of the Lord Krishna* as a little boy were left in midair, and we were sent to the Anglo-Indian school.

insular: narrow-minded, as if an island

Hindi: an Indo-European language that is now considered the official language of India

Lord Krishna: in the Hindu religion, human form taken by the god Vishnu; many Hindu stories recount episodes in the life of Lord Krishna

That first day at school is still, when I think of it, a remarkable one. At that age, if one's name is changed, one develops a curious form of dual personality. I remember having a certain detached and disbelieving concern in the actions of "Cynthia," but certainly no responsibility. Accordingly, I followed the thin, erect back of the headmistress down the veranda to my classroom feeling, at most, a passing interest in what was going to happen to me in this strange, new atmosphere of School.

The building was Indian in design, with wide verandas opening onto a central courtyard, but Indian verandas are usually white-washed, with stone floors. These, in the tradition of British schools, were painted dark brown and had matting on the floors. It gave a feeling of extra intensity to the heat.

I suppose there were about a dozen Indian children in the school—which contained perhaps forty children in all—and four of them were in my class. They were all sitting at the back of the room, and I went to join them. I sat next to a small, solemn girl who didn't smile at me. She had long, glossy black braids and wore a cotton dress, but she still kept on her Indian jewelry—a gold chain around her neck, thin gold bracelets, and tiny ruby studs in her ears. Like most Indian children, she had a rim of black kohl* around her eyes. The cotton dress should have looked strange, but all I could think of was that I should ask my mother if I couldn't wear a dress to school, too, instead of my Indian clothes.

kohl: dark powder used as eye makeup

I can't remember too much about the proceedings in class that day, except for the beginning. The teacher pointed to me and asked me to stand up. "Now, dear, tell the class your name."

I said nothing.

"Come along," she said, frowning slightly. "What's your name, dear?"

"I don't know," I said, finally.

The English children in the front of the class—there were about eight or ten of them—giggled and twisted around in their chairs to look at me. I sat down quickly and opened my eyes very wide, hoping in that way to dry them off. The little girl with the braids put out her hand and very lightly touched my arm. She still didn't smile.

Most of that morning I was rather bored. I looked briefly at the children's drawings pinned to the wall, and then concentrated on a lizard clinging to the ledge of the high, barred window behind the teacher's head. Occasionally it would shoot out its long yellow tongue for a fly, and then it would rest, with its eyes closed and its belly palpitating, as though it were swallowing several times quickly. The lessons were mostly concerned with reading and writing and simple numbers—things that my mother had already taught me—and I paid very little attention. The teacher wrote on the easel blackboard

words like "bat" and "cat," which seemed babyish to me; only "apple" was new and incomprehensible.

When it was time for the lunch recess, I followed the girl with braids out onto the veranda. There the children from the other classes were assembled. I saw Premila at once and ran over to her, as she had charge of our lunchbox. The children were all opening packages and sitting down to eat sandwiches. Premila and I were the only ones who had Indian food—thin wheat chapatties,* some vegetable curry, and a bottle of buttermilk. Premila thrust half of it into my hand and whispered fiercely that I should go and sit with my class, because that was what the others seemed to be doing.

chapatties: thin unleavened fried bread

The enormous black eyes of the little Indian girl from my class looked at my food longingly, so I offered her some. But she only shook her head and plowed her way solemnly through her sandwiches.

I was very sleepy after lunch, because at home we always took a siesta. It was usually a pleasant time of day, with the bedroom darkened against the harsh afternoon sun, the drifting off into sleep with the sound of Mother's voice reading a story in one's mind, and, finally, the shrill, fussy voice of the ayah* waking one for tea.

ayah: nanny in India

At school, we rested for a short time on low, folding cots on the veranda, and then we were expected to play games. During the hot part of the afternoon we played indoors, and after the shadows had begun to lengthen and the slight breeze of the evening had come up we moved outside to the wide courtyard.

I had never really grasped the system of competitive games. At home, whenever we played tag or guessing games, I was always allowed to "win"—"because," Mother used to tell Premila, "she is the youngest, and we have to allow for that." I had often heard her say it, and it seemed quite reasonable to me, but the result was that I had no clear idea of what "winning" meant.

When we played twos-and-threes* that afternoon at school in accordance with my training, I let one of the small English boys catch me, but was naturally rather puzzled when the other children did not return the courtesy. I ran about for what seemed like hours without ever catching anyone, until it was time for school to close. Much later I learned that my attitude was called "not being a good sport," and I stopped allowing myself to be caught, but it was not for years that I really learned the spirit of the thing.

twos-and-threes: game similar to tag

When I saw our car come up to the school gate, I broke away from my classmates and rushed toward it yelling, "Ayah! Ayah!" It seemed like an eternity since I had seen her that morning—a wizened, affectionate figure in her white cotton sari,* giving me dozens of urgent and useless instructions on how to be a good girl at school. Premila followed more sedately, and she told me on the way home never to do that again in front of the other children.

sari: a long piece of cloth wrapped around the body to form a skirt and mantle; the main form of dress worn by Hindu women

When we got home we went straight to Mother's high, white room to have tea with her, and I immediately climbed onto the bed and bounced gently up and down on the springs. Mother asked how we had liked our first day in school. I was so pleased to be home and to have left that peculiar Cynthia behind that I had nothing whatever to say about school, except to ask what "apple" meant. But Premila told Mother about the classes, and added that in her class they had weekly tests to see if they had learned their lessons well.

I asked, "What's a test?"

Premila said, "You're too small to have them. You won't have them in your class for donkey's years."* She had learned the expression that day and was using it for the first time. We all laughed enormously at her wit. She also told Mother, in an aside, that we should take sandwiches to school the next day. Not, she said, that *she* minded. But they would be simpler for me to handle.

donkey's years: British expression meaning "a long time"

That whole lovely evening I didn't think about school at all. I sprinted barefoot across the lawns with my favorite playmate, the cook's son, to the stream at the end of the garden. We quarreled in our usual way, waded in the tepid water under the lime trees, and waited for the night to bring out the smell of the jasmine.* I listened with fascination to his stories of ghosts and demons, until I was too frightened to cross the garden alone in the semidarkness. The ayah found me, shouted at the cook's son, scolded me, hurried me in to supper—it was an entirely usual, wonderful evening.

jasmine: tropical shrub with fragrant flowers

It was a week later, the day of Premila's first test, that our lives changed rather abruptly. I was sitting at the back of my class, in my usual inattentive way, only half listening to the teacher. I had started a rather guarded

friendship with the girl with the braids, whose name turned out to be Nalini (Nancy in school). The three other Indian children were already fast friends. Even at that age it was apparent to all of us that friendship with the English or Anglo-Indian children was out of the question. Occasionally, during the class, my new friend and I would draw pictures and show them to each other secretly.

The door opened sharply and Premila marched in. At first, the teacher smiled at her in a kindly and encouraging way and said, "Now, you're little Cynthia's sister?"

Premila didn't even look at her. She stood with her feet planted firmly apart and her

shoulders rigid, and addressed herself directly to me. "Get up," she said. "We're going home."

I didn't know what had happened, but I was aware that it was a crisis of some sort. I rose obediently and started to walk toward my sister.

"Bring your pencils and your notebook," she said.

I went back for them, and together we left the room. The teacher started to say something just as Premila closed the door, but we didn't wait to hear what it was.

In complete silence we left the school grounds and started to walk home. Then I asked Premila what the matter was. All she would say was "We're going home for good."

It was a very tiring walk for a child of five and a half, and I dragged along behind Premila with my pencils growing sticky in my hand. I can still remember looking at the dusty hedges, and the tangles of thorns in the ditches by the side of the road, smelling the faint fragrance from the eucalyptus trees and wondering whether we would ever reach home. Occasionally a horse-drawn tonga* passed us, and the women, in their pink or green silks, stared at Premila and me trudging along on the side of the road. A few coolies* and a line of women carrying baskets of vegetables on their heads smiled at us. But it was nearing the hottest time of the day, and the road was almost deserted. I walked more and more slowly, and shouted to Premila, from time to time, "Wait for me!" with increasing peevishness. She spoke to me only once, and that was to tell me to carry my notebook on my head, because of the sun.

tonga: two-wheeled carriage
coolies: manual laborers

When we got to our house the ayah was just taking a tray of lunch into Mother's room. She immediately started a long, worried questioning about what are you children doing back here at this hour of the day.

Mother looked very startled and very concerned, and asked Premila what had happened.

Premila said, "We had our test today, and she made me and the other Indians sit at the back of the room, with a desk between each one."

Mother said, "Why was that, darling?"

"She said it was because Indians cheat," Premila added. "So I don't think we should go back to that school."

Mother looked very distant, and was silent a long time. At last she said, "Of course not, darling." She sounded displeased.

We all shared the curry she was having for lunch, and afterward I was sent off to the beautifully familiar bedroom for my siesta. I could hear Mother and Premila talking through the open door.

Mother said, "Do you suppose she understood all that?"

Premila said, "I shouldn't think so. She's a baby."

Mother said, "Well, I hope it won't bother her."

Of course, they were both wrong. I understood it perfectly, and I remember it all very clearly. But I put it happily away, because it had all happened to a girl called Cynthia, and I never was really particularly interested in her.

About the Essay

1. Consider closely the descriptions of the girls' home (p. 245) and the school (p. 243). How does the atmosphere of each differ? What does this say about Rau's attitude toward each?

2. Why does the girl with the braids touch Santha's arm?

3. From what point of view is the essay written? How can you tell?

4. What would you say is the main theme of Rau's account? How does the essay's point of view strengthen the theme?

5. What do Premila's actions on the first day of school and on the day of the test reveal about her? How does she seem to differ from Santha?

6. The title of Rau's essay comes from William Shakespeare's classic play *Romeo and Juliet*. The character Juliet states, "That which we call a rose / By any other name would smell as sweet," meaning that the identity of a person or thing cannot be determined exclusively by its name. How, then, might the title "By Any Other Name" relate to the theme of Rau's essay?

About the Author

Santha Rama Rau (1923–2009) was born in Madras, India, at a time when India was under British rule. She attended school in England for her pre-college education and was the first Indian student to be accepted at Wellesley College in Massachusetts, where she graduated with honors. During her career she was both a writer and a teacher.

Rau is most famous for her travel books; she had, however, compiled autobiographical sketches into a collection from which this selection comes. Throughout her writings, a reader recognizes her deep love for her country and for her heritage.

The Age of Miracles

Melville Davisson Post

Like Doyle's signature character and sleuth, Sherlock Holmes, Post's Uncle Abner is a keen observer of detail and an avid student of human nature. Unlike Holmes, however, Abner is not eccentric, and his motive for unraveling complex problems is different from Holmes's. It is a sense of moral responsibility, not the stimulation of a mental challenge, that motivates Abner. He is not a professional who simply enjoys his work; he is, rather, a moral man who desires justice.

As you read this detective story, note the viewpoint from which the narrator tells the story and the advantages of that point of view. Be prepared to discuss some of the difficulties the author would have faced if he had told the story from another point of view.

The girl was standing apart from the crowd in the great avenue of poplars that led up to the house. She seemed embarrassed and uncertain what to do, a thing of April emerging into summer.

Abner and Randolph marked her as they entered along the gravel road.

They had left their horses at the gate, but she had brought hers inside, as though after some habit unconsciously upon her.

But half-way to the house she had remembered and got down. And she stood now against the horse's shoulder. It was a black hunter, big and old, but age marred no beauty of his lines. He was like a horse of ebony, enchanted out of the earth by some Arabian magic, but not yet by that magic awakened into life.

The girl wore a long, dark riding-skirt, after the fashion of the time, and a coat of hunter's pink. Her dark hair was in a great wrist-thick plait. Her eyes, too, were big and dark, and her body firm and lithe from the out-of-doors.

"Ah!" cried Randolph, making his characteristic gesture, "Prospero has been piping in this grove. Here is a daughter of the immortal morning! We grow old, Abner, and it is youth that the gods love."

My uncle, his hands behind him, his eyes on the gravel road, looked up at the bewitching picture.

"Poor child," he said; "the gods that love her must be gods of the valleys and not gods of the hills."

"Ruth amid the alien corn! Is it a better figure, Abner? Well, she has a finer inheritance than these lands; she has youth!"

"She ought to have both," replied my uncle. "It was sheer robbery to take her inheritance."

"It was a proceeding at law," replied the Justice. "It was the law that did the thing, and we cannot hold the law in disrespect."

"But the man who uses the law to accomplish a wrong, we can so hold," said Abner. "He is an outlaw, as the highwayman and the pirate are."

He extended his arm toward the great house sitting at the end of the avenue.

"In spite of the sanction of the law, I hold this dead man for a robber. And I would have wrested these lands from him, if I could. But your law, Randolph, stood before him."

"Well," replied the Justice, "he takes no gain from it; he lies yonder waiting for the grave."

"But his brother takes," said Abner, "and this child loses."

The Justice, elegant in the costume of the time, turned his ebony stick in his fingers.

"One should forgive the dead," he commented in a facetious note; "it is a mandate of the Scripture."

I am not concerned about the dead," replied Abner. "The dead are in God's hands. It is the living who concern me."

"Then," cried the Justice, "you should forgive the brother who takes."

"And I shall forgive him," replied Abner, "when he returns what he has taken."

"Returns what he has taken!" Randolph laughed. "Why, Abner, the devil could not filch* coins out of the clutches of old Benton Wolf."

---

filch: to take in a furtive manner; snitch

"The devil," said my uncle, "is not an authority that I depend on."

"A miracle of Heaven, then," said the Justice. "But, alas, it is not the age of miracles."

"Perhaps," replied Abner, his voice descending into a deeper tone, "but I am not so certain."

They had come now to where the girl stood, her back against the black shoulder of the horse. The morning air moved the yellow leaves about her feet. She darted out to meet them, her face aglow.

"How do you do, Julia?" cried Randolph. "I have hardly seen you since you were no taller than my stick, and told me that your name was 'Pete-George,' and that you were a circus-horse, and offered to do tricks for me."

"I remember," she said. "it was up there on the porch!"

"And so it was!" cried Randolph, embarrassed.

He kissed the tips of the girl's fingers and the shadow in her face fled.

For the man's heart was good, and he had the manner of a gentleman. But it was Abner that she turned to in her dilemma.

"I forgot," she said, "and almost rode into the house. Do you think I could leave the horse here? He will stand if I drop the rein."

Then she went on to make her explanation. She wanted to see the old house that had been so long her home. This was the only opportunity, to-day, when all the countryside came to the dead man's burial. She thought she might come, too, although her motive was no tribute of respect.

She put her hand through Abner's arm and he looked down upon her, grave and troubled.

"My child," he said, "leave the horse where he stands and come with me, for my motive, also, is no tribute of respect; and you go with a better right than I do."

"I suppose," the girl hesitated, "that one ought to respect the dead, but this man—these men—I cannot."

"Nor can I," replied my uncle. "If I do not respect a man when he is living, I shall not pretend to when he is dead. One does not make a claim upon my honor by going out of life."

They went up the avenue among the yellow poplar leaves and the ragweed and fennel springing up along the unkept gravel.

It was a crisp and glorious morning. The frost lay on the rail fence. The spider-webs stretched here and there across the high grasses of the meadows in intricate and bewildering lace-work. The sun was clear and bright, but it carried no oppressive heat as it drew on in its course toward noon.

The countryside had gathered to see Adam Wolf buried. It was a company of tenants, the idle and worthless mostly, drawn by curiosity. For in life the two old men who had seized upon this property by virtue of a defective acknowledgment to a deed, permitted no invasion of their boundary.

Everywhere the lands were posted; no urchin fished and no schoolboy hunted. The green perch, fattened in the deep creek that threaded the rich bottom lands, no man disturbed. But the quail, the pheasant, the robin and the meadow-lark, old Adam pursued with his fowling-piece. He trampled about with it at all seasons. One would have believed that all the birds of heaven had done the creature some unending harm and in revenge he had declared a war. And so the accident by which he met his death was a jeopardy of the old man's habits, and to be looked for when one lived with a fowling-piece in one's hands and grew careless in its use.

The two men lived alone and thus all sorts of mystery sprang up around them, gaining in grim detail at every story-teller's hand. It had the charm and thrilling interest of an adventure, then, for the countryside to get this entry.

The brothers lived in striking contrast. Adam was violent, and his cries and curses, his hard and brutal manner were the terror of the poor man who passed at night that way, or the urchin overtaken by darkness on his road home. But Benton got about his affairs in silence, with a certain humility of manner, and a mild concern for the opinion of his fellows. Still, somehow, the poor man and the urchin held him in a greater terror. Perhaps because he had got his coffin made and kept it in his house, together with his clothes for burial. It seemed uncanny thus to prepare against his dissolution and to bargain for the outfit, with anxiety to have his shilling's worth.

And yet, with this gruesome furniture at hand, the old man, it would seem, was in no contemplation of his death. He spoke sometimes with a marked savor and an unctuous kneading of the hands of that time when he should own the land, for he was the younger and by rule should have the expectancy of life.

There was a crowd about the door and filling the hall inside, a crowd that elbowed and jostled, taken with a quivering interest, and there to feed its maw* of curiosity with every item.

maw: jaws

The girl wished to remain on the portico, where she could see the ancient garden and the orchard and all the paths and byways that had been her wonderland of youth, but Abner asked her to go in.

Randolph turned away, but my uncle and the girl remained some time by the coffin. The rim of the dead man's forehead and his jaw were riddled with bird-shot, but his eyes and an area of his face below them, where the thin nose came down and with its lines and furrows made up the main identity of features, were not disfigured. And these preserved the hard stamp of his violent nature, untouched by the accident that had dispossessed him of his life.

He lay in the burial clothes and the coffin that Benton Wolf had provided for himself, all except the gloves upon his hands. These the old man had forgot. And now when he came to prepare his brother for a public burial, for no other had touched the man, he must needs take what he could find about the house, a pair of old, knit gloves with every rent and moth-hole carefully darned, as though the man had sat down there with pains to give his brother the best appearance that he could.

This little touch affected the girl to tears, so strange is a woman's heart. "Poor thing!" she said. And for this triviality she would forget the injury that the dead man and his brother had done to her, the loss they had inflicted, and her long distress.

She took a closer hold upon Abner's arm, and dabbed her eyes with a tiny kerchief.

"I am sorry for him," she said, "for the living brother. It is so pathetic."

And she indicated the old, coarse gloves so crudely darned and patched together.

But my uncle looked down at her, strangely, and with a cold, inexorable* face.

---

inexorable: incapable of being persuaded by entreaty

"My child," he said, "there is a curious virtue in this thing that moves you. Perhaps it will also move the man whose handiwork it is. Let us go up and see him."

Then he called the Justice.

"Randolph," he said, "come with us."

The Justice turned about. "Where do you go?" he asked.

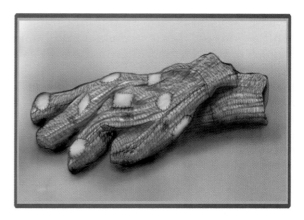

"Why, sir," Abner answered, "this child is weeping at the sight of the dead man's gloves, and I thought, perhaps, that old Benton might weep at them too, and in the softened mood return what he has stolen."

The Justice looked upon Abner as upon one gone mad.

"And be sorry for his sins! And pluck out his eye and give it to you for a bauble! Why, Abner, where is your common sense? This thing would take a miracle of God."

My uncle was undisturbed.

"Well," he said, "come with me, Randolph, and help me to perform that miracle."

He went out into the hall and up the wide old stairway, with the girl, in tears, upon his arm. And the Justice followed, like one who goes upon a patent and ridiculous fool's errand.

They came into an upper chamber, where a great bulk of a man sat in a padded chair looking down upon his avenue of trees. He looked with satisfaction. He turned his head about when the three came in and then his eyes widened in among the folds of fat.

"Abner and Mr. Randolph and Miss Julia Clayborne!" he gurgled. "You come to do honor to the dead!"

"No, Wolf," replied my uncle, "we come to do justice to the living."

The room was big, and empty but for chairs and an open secretary of some English make. The pictures on the wall had been turned about as though from lack of interest in the tenant. But there hung in a frame above the secretary—with its sheets of foolscap,* its iron ink-pot and quill pens—a map in detail, and the written deed for the estate that these men had taken in their lawsuit. It was not the skill of any painter that gave pleasure to this mountain of a man; not fields or groves imagined or copied for their charm, but the fields and groves that he possessed and mastered. And he would be reminded at his ease of them and of no other.

---

foolscap: a large sheet of writing paper

The old man's eyelids fluttered an instant as with some indecision, then he replied, "It was kind to have this thought of me. I have been long neglected. A little justice of recognition, even now, does much to soften the sorrow at my brother's death." Randolph caught at his jaw to keep in the laughter. And the huge old man, his head crouched into his billowy shoulders, his little reptilian eye shining like a crum of glass, went on with his speech.

"I am the greater moved," he said, "because you have been aloof and distant with me. You, Abner, have not visited my house, nor you, Randolph, although you live at no great distance. It is not thus that one gentleman should treat another. And especially when I

and my dead brother, Adam, were from distant parts and came among you without a friend to take us by the hand and bring us to your door."

He sighed and put the fingers of his hands together.

"Ah, Abner," he went on, "it was a cruel negligence, and one from which I and my brother Adam suffered. You, who have a hand and a word at every turning, can feel no longing for this human comfort. But to the stranger, alone, and without the land of his nativity, it is a bitter lack."

He indicated the chairs about him.

"I beg you to be seated, gentlemen and Miss Clayborne. And overlook that I do not rise. I am shaken at Adam's death."

Randolph remained planted on his feet, his face now under control. But Abner put the child into a chair and stood behind it, as though he were some close and masterful familiar.

"Wolf," he said, "I am glad that your heart is softened."

"My heart—softened!" cried the man. "Why, Abner, I have the tenderest heart of any of God's creatures. I cannot endure to kill a sparrow. My brother Adam was not like that. He would be for hunting the wild creatures to their death with firearms. But I took no pleasure in it."

"Well," said Randolph, "the creatures of the air got their revenge of him. It was a foolish accident to die by."

"Randolph," replied the man, "it was the very end and extreme of carelessness. To look into a fowling-piece, a finger on the hammer, a left hand holding the barrel halfway up, to see if it was empty. It was a foolish and simple habit of my brother, and one that I abhorred and begged him to forego, again and again, when I have seen him do it.

"But he had no fear of any firearms, as though by use and habit he had got their spirit tamed—as trainers, I am told, grow careless of wild beasts, and jugglers of the fangs and poison of their reptiles. He was growing old and would forget if they were loaded."

He spoke to Randolph, but he looked at Julia Clayborne and Abner.

The girl sat straight and composed, in silence. The body of my uncle was to her a great protecting presence. He stood with his broad shoulders above her, his hands on the back of the chair, his face lifted. And he was big and dominant, as painters are accustomed to draw Michael in Satan's wars.

The pose held the old man's eyes, and he moved in his chair; then he went on, speaking to the girl.

"It was kind of you, Abner, and you, Randolph, to come in to see me in my distress, but it was fine and noble in Miss Julia Clayborne. Men will understand the justice of the law and by what right it gives and takes. But a child will hardly understand that. It would be in nature for Miss Clayborne in her youth, to hold the issue of this lawsuit against me and my brother Adam, to feel that we had wronged her; had by some unfairness taken what her father bequeathed to her at his death, and always regarded as his own. A child would not see how the title had never vested, as our judges do. How possession is one thing, and the title in fee simple another and distinct. And so I am touched by this consideration."

Abner spoke then.

"Wolf," he said, "I am glad to find you in this mood, for now Randolph can write his deed, with consideration of love and affection instead of the real one I came with."

The old man's beady eye glimmered and slipped about.

"I do not understand, Abner. What deed?"

"The one Randolph came to write," replied my uncle.

"But, Abner," interrupted the Justice, "I did not come to write a deed." And he looked at my uncle in amazement.

"Oh yes," returned Abner, "that is precisely what you came to do."

He indicated the open secretary with his hand.

"And the grantor, as it happens, has got everything ready for you. Here are foolscap and quill pens and ink. And here, exhibited for your convenience, is a map of the lands with all the metes* and bounds. And here," he pointed to the wall, "in a frame, as though it were a work of art with charm, is the court's deed. Sit down, Randolph, and write." And such virtue is there in a dominant command, that the Justice sat down before the secretary and began to select a goose quill.

---

metes: a boundary line

Then he realized the absurdity of the direction and turned about.

"What do you mean, Abner?" he cried.

"I mean precisely what I say," replied my uncle. "I want you to write a deed."

"But what sort of deed," cried the astonished Justice, "and by what grantor, and to whom, and for what lands?"

"You will draw a conveyance," replied Abner, "in form, with covenants of general warranty for the manor and lands set out in the deed before you and given in the plat. The grantor will be Benton Wolf, esquire, and the grantee Julia Clayborne, infant, and mark you, Randolph, the consideration will be love and affection, with a dollar added for the form."

The old man was amazed. His head, bedded into his huge shoulders, swung about; his pudgy features worked; his expression and his manner changed; his reptilian eyes hardened; he puffed with his breath in gusts.

"Not so fast, my fine gentleman!" he gurgled. "There will be no such deed."

"Go on, Randolph," said my uncle, "let us get this business over."

"But, Abner," returned the Justice, "it is fool work, the grantor will not sign."

"He will sign," said my uncle, "when you have finished, and seal and acknowledge—go on!"

"But, Abner, Abner!" the amazed Justice protested.

"Randolph," cried my uncle, "will you write, and leave this thing to me?"

And such authority was in the man to impose his will that the bewildered Justice spread out his sheet of foolscap, dipped his quill into the ink and began to draw the instrument, in form and of the parties, as my uncle said. And while he wrote, Abner turned back to the gross old man.

"Wolf," he said, "must I persuade you to sign the deed?"

"Abner," cried the man, "do you take me for a fool?"

He had got his unwieldy body up and defiant in the chair.

"I do not," replied my uncle, "and therefore I think that you will sign."

The obese old man spat violently on the floor, his face a horror of great folds.

"Sign!" he sputtered. "Fool, idiot, madman! Why should I sign away my lands?"

"There are many reasons," replied Abner calmly. "The property is not yours. You got it by a legal trick; the Judge who heard you was bound by the technicalities of language. But you are old, Wolf, and the next Judge will go behind the record. He will be hard to face. He has expressed Himself on these affairs. 'If the widow and the orphan cry to me, I will surely hear their cry.' Sinister words, Wolf, for one who comes with a case like yours into the court of Final Equity."

"Abner," cried the old man, "begone with your little sermons!"

My uncle's big fingers tightened on the back of the chair.

"Then, Wolf," he said, "if this thing does not move you, let me urge the esteem of men and this child's sorrow, and our high regard."

The old man's jaw chattered and he snapped his fingers.

"I would not give that for the things you name," he cried, and he set off a tiny measure on his index-finger with the thumb.

"Why, sir, my whim, idle and ridiculous, is a greater power to move me than this drivel."

Abner did not move, but his voice took on depth and volume.

"Wolf," he said, "a whim is sometimes a great lever to move a man. Now, I am taken with a whim myself. I have a fancy, Wolf, that your brother Adam ought to go out of the world barehanded as he came into it."

The old man twisted his great head, as though he would get Abner wholly within the sweep of his reptilian eye.

"What?" he gurgled. "What is that?"

"Why, this," replied my uncle. "I have a whim—'idle and ridiculous,' did you say, Wolf? Well, then, idle and ridiculous, if you like, that your brother ought not to be buried in his gloves."

Abner looked hard at the man and, although he did not move, the threat and menace of his presence seemed somehow to advance him. And the effect upon the huge old man was like some work of sorcery. The whole mountain of him began to quiver and the folds of his face seemed spread over with thin oil. He sat piled up in the chair and the oily sweat gathered and thickened on him. His jaw jerked and fell into a baggy gaping and the great expanse of him shook.

Finally, out of the pudgy, undulating mass, a voice issued, thin and shaken.

"Abner," it said, "has any other man this fancy?"

"No," replied my uncle, "but I hold it, Wolf, at your decision."

"And, Abner," his thin voice trembled, "you will let my brother be buried as he is?"

"If you sign!" said my uncle.

The man reeked and grew wet in terror on him, and one thought that his billowy body would never be again at peace. "Randolph," he quavered, "bring me the deed."

Outside, the girl sobbed in Abner's arms. She asked for no explanation. She wished to believe her fortune a miracle of God, forever—to the end of all things. But Randolph turned on my uncle when she was gone.

"Abner! Abner!" he cried "Why in the name of the Eternal was the old creature so shaken at the gloves?"

"Because he saw the hangman behind them," replied my uncle. "Did you notice how the rim of the dead man's face was riddled by the bird-shot and the center of it clean? How could that happen, Randolph?"

"It was a curious accident of gun-fire," replied the Justice.

"It was no accident at all," said Abner. "That area of the man's face is clean because it was protected. Because the dead man put up his hands to cover his face when he saw that his brother was about to shoot him.

"The backs of old Adam's hands, hidden by the gloves, will be riddled with bird-shot like the rim of his face."

About the Story

1. How does Abner's view of justice differ from Randolph's?

2. What specific, significant details does Abner notice that the other characters overlook?

3. At what point in the story does Post let you know the real reason that Wolf consents to sign the deed?

4. From what point of view is the story told?

5. How does this point of view aid in building suspense?

About the Author

Melville Davisson Post (1869–1930) was a skilled defense lawyer who turned his observations of the inner workings of justice into short stories and novels. In his stories Post includes a character called Uncle Abner, a country squire who solves mysteries through intuition and close attention to detail. Abner's sense of God's justice, though, helps him to realize that the judicial system does not always produce true justice. In addition to Uncle Abner, Post's stories include the character Randolph Mason, a product of Post's advanced studies in criminology.

Unlike many writers of detective fiction, however, Post did not create a spokesman for the glorification of human reasoning. Through the character of Uncle Abner, Post really presents reason as a God-given ability by which feeble man might come to know and realize the truth and thereby obey it.

THINKING ZONE

One of the most famous and beloved genres, the detective story began with Edgar Allen Poe's 1841 short story, "The Murders in the Rue Morgue." The "whodunit" genre reached new heights at the turn of the twentieth century with Arthur Conan Doyle's peerless detective, Sherlock Holmes, and later with Agatha Christie's relentless investigator, Hercule Poirot. The enduring popularity of the genre illustrates our fascination with logical puzzles and the labyrinth of human motivations and behavior. **Detective fiction** may be simply defined as fiction in which a recurring character (not necessarily a professional detective by trade) investigates and solves crimes. Usually these detectives possess unusual powers of deduction and a deep understanding of the human heart. Many detective stories are narrated by another character, using the first-person point of view. This perspective increases the story's suspense because the readers share the narrator's ignorance of what the detective is thinking. Often the author reveals important information to us, but without the main character's skills of deduction, we can rarely predict the outcome. Typically, not until the end does the detective divulge his solution and explain his investigation process.

The genres we have discussed so far in this unit have all dealt with fictional works. Nonfiction, however, encompasses a great many genres, too, including essays, biographies, journal articles, travelogues, speeches, and much more. Like fiction genres, some are described by content, some by form, and some by a combination of the two. One perennially popular category of nonfiction is biographical writing. While the biography (an account and analysis of a person's life) is probably the best known of this group, biographical writing also includes diaries, memoirs, and journals, among other types of works. The **autobiographical essay** is one form of biographical writing: it is a short essay written by the author about himself, usually focused on a particular event in his life and not on mere biographical facts. The author recounts experiences that helped to form his opinions, opinions that he now wants to communicate to his readers. Naturally, the essay is written from the first-person point of view. One example of autobiographical writing in the Bible is the story in Daniel 4. Since the story is Nebuchadnezzar's own record of his humiliation by Yahweh, the account could be considered an inspired autobiographical essay. When you read of the biblical king's pathetic plight, what do you think Nebuchadnezzar wanted to communicate to you?

1. How does "The Age of Miracles" qualify as **detective fiction**?
2. Name an advantage to an author's using either limited-omniscient or first-person point of view for a detective story.
3. Cite two reasons that "By Any Other Name" qualifies as an **autobiographical essay**.
4. In "By Any Other Name," Rau combines her adult perspective on this past event with her initial impressions as a child. How do you think this variation on point of view aids in showing how the author's opinions of certain things were formed?

UNIT IV REVIEW

REMEMBER THE TERMS

Review the following terms from the opening essay, "Point of View," and the Thinking Zone pages. Be prepared to discuss their meanings and uses in class.

point of view

persona

third-person point
 of view

omniscient viewpoint

limited-omniscient
 viewpoint

first-person viewpoint

genre

frame story

anecdote

historical fiction

detective fiction

autobiographical essay

APPLY THE CONCEPTS

Answer the following questions about how the literary concepts you have studied are used in this unit.

1. Which viewpoint or viewpoints allow the reader to "get inside" all of the characters?

2. In which viewpoint or viewpoints does one of the characters serve as the narrator?

3. From what two viewpoints are anecdotes generally told?

4. Which story in Unit 4 best fits the definition of an autobiographical essay?

5. Most of "The Open Window" is told from which character's perspective?

6. From what viewpoint is "After the Battle" told? How can you tell?

7. Poetry is one of the three standard literary genres. Name the other two.

8. In what longer work would one find the story "The Forty Thieves"?

9. From what viewpoint is the story of "The Forty Thieves" told? How can you tell?

10. Identify the literary genre of "The Age of Miracles."

11. From whose perspective is "The Age of Miracles" told?

12. From this unit, which selection is identified as historical fiction?

13. How is an autobiography different from a biography?

14. From what viewpoint is "By Any Other Name" told? How can you tell?

15. How does Rau's use of point of view strengthen the theme of her account?

EVALUATE THE IDEAS

Identify each of the following statements as true or false. If false, rewrite the underlined portion of the statement to make it true.

16. Historical fiction can easily be written from any point of view.

17. Anecdotes are generally longer than autobiographical essays.

18. Frame stories usually contain a second story within them.

19. "The Open Window" contains a point-of-view shift near its ending.

20. In "By Any Other Name," the author's attitude toward her surroundings helps the reader identify the genre of the piece.

21. Because the reader understands the characters' motivations, the author of "The Forty Thieves" wants the reader to sympathize with Cassim and his wife.

22. The conflict of "After the Battle" is resolved when Bill Ryder carries Dave Joyce to safety.

23. Nonfiction is often written from the first-person point of view.

24. When Vera in "The Open Window" asks her visitor whether he knows anything about her aunt, the author is using a type of frame story.

WRITE A RESPONSE

Completely answer the following question.

25. Why would an author use the first-person point of view of a secondary character to narrate a mystery story?

RELATIVITY
M.C. Escher

❦ STRUCTURE ❧

Maurits Cornelius Escher (1898–1972) was a master of the lithographic style of printing. Simply put, a lithograph is an image drawn on a smooth plate and treated chemically to retain ink. Ink applied to the plate adheres only to the treated portion. Many of Escher's works are in-depth studies of symmetry, geometric planes, and architecture. His fascination with perspective led him to complete numerous drawings of objects up close and far away—often simultaneously and with seemingly impossible results.

- ⚜ After studying *Relativity,* what do you consider to be "impossible" about the print?

- ⚜ In the print, each gravitational plane is at right angles to the other two. The people in each plane adhere to that plane's rules of gravity. Keeping that in mind, discuss the people climbing the various stairways.

- ⚜ Which part of the world of *Relativity* is most mystifying to you?

- ⚜ How does the style of Escher's lithograph contribute to its effectiveness?

☙ STRUCTURE ☙

Conflict, character, and theme provide the core of a story, whereas point of view controls the perspective from which the reader perceives these elements. An author's effectiveness in communicating a story, however, also depends on the structure of the composition. Structure provides the framework on which the basic three elements are realized, lending order and purpose to the content. Though there are many legitimate structural approaches, we will focus on analyzing those of narrative prose and of poetry.

STRUCTURE IN NARRATIVE PROSE

In most prose narratives, the plot, or action, of the story determines the structure. Simply defined, **plot** is a series of events arranged to produce a definite sense of movement toward a specific goal. In this sense, plot covers not just a list of incidents, but also how those incidents relate to each other and to the overall effect the author is trying to create. In addition, one or more **subplots,** which are lesser in significance, may complement the main plot. As readers, we attempt to grasp the intentions of an author for his story, and we will often anticipate a certain resolution based on our assumptions. Understanding this tendency, some authors use **plot twists** (a plot development that violates the reader's expectations) or **surprise endings** (a plot twist at the end of a story) to highlight their message.

Plot is often broken down into seven primary steps. The opening **exposition** introduces us to the setting, the characters, and the situation. The exposition often leads to the **inciting incident** of the plot, an event that sets the conflict in motion. Next, the **rising action** describes the events leading up to the crisis of the story. At this stage, the author further develops the story's conflict and characters, often creating various complications for the central character to face. Encountering these obstacles helps build toward the story's **crisis,** the major turning point for the main character or the point at which something happens that affects the outcome of the story, determining the future of the main character. A plot point similar to the crisis but varying in its position in the story is the climax. The **climax** refers to the plot's moment of highest emotional intensity: it has no set position in the plotline and can come before the crisis, such as when the protagonist encounters the main problem to be solved, or after the crisis, perhaps when the implications of crucial changes become evident. An example from the Bible may help illustrate the difference between these two stages. The crisis, or turning point, of Scripture (of human history, in fact) is the death, burial, and resurrection of Christ. The climax, or point of highest emotional intensity, will be Christ's return and the establishment of His kingdom on earth (Rev. 19). Next, the step following the crisis is the **falling action**, the events that unfold the results of the crisis and lead to the conclusion. Lastly, the **dénouement** (DAY-noo-MAHN: from the French for "an untying"), or plot resolution, presents the final outcome of the story in which the major complications are explained or settled. Six of these stages can be outlined on a diagram as follows.

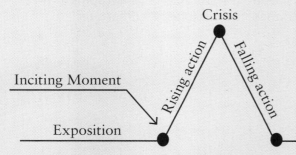

Plots may not always fall neatly into this order, however. For example, the descriptions of the various elements are based on **chronological** order. But an author may sometimes begin *in medias res* (in the middle of events) in order to plunge the reader straight into the main action of the story, thus switching the normal pattern. In these cases an author may also use the technique of **flashback**, a reference either to events that occurred before the main action of the story or to action that occurred before the time in which the narrator is speaking. This technique is helpful in revealing essential information or background that would otherwise be left out.

STRUCTURE IN POETRY

Like prose, poetry must be carefully structured if it is to communicate a message effectively. Indeed, by its definition (artfully compressed thought resulting in the elevated expression of ideas), poetry demands an even more precisely calculated framework than prose. Poetic structures vary widely, including ancient forms as well as constantly evolving new forms, yet certain basic concepts remain the same.

Rhyme, meter, and form are three foundational aspects of poetic structure that will be specifically explored and illustrated as you read the poems in this unit. Though the first two are not absolutely indispensable to great poetry, they are widely used methods of imposing structure on a poet's thoughts. Broadly defined, rhyme refers to two or more words having identical sounds in the last stressed vowel and all of the sounds following that vowel. Next, meter refers to the regular arrangement of stressed and unstressed syllables in a poem. **Verse forms** refer to specific combinations of rhyme and meter. Finally, you will study some traditional forms of poetry that use a broad spectrum of techniques and patterns to organize poetic lines.

As you read each selection, the information in the headnotes and end questions will guide your understanding of the structure of the piece. As you read the prose selections, ask yourself the following questions: What are the most important events of the story? What do the arrangement of events and their effects on the protagonist say about the author's goals? Note that these questions involve your ability to identify a story's main conflict and theme and to understand the main characters' development. Then, as you learn the basics of poetic structure, analyze the meter, rhyme, or sound devices the author has chosen. How do those choices contribute to the poem's overall effect or message? If the poet uses a particular traditional form, what does that mean for the content and purpose of the poem?

John 9

JESUS AND THE MAN BORN BLIND

The concise stories of Scripture are an excellent starting point for discerning plot structure. Indeed, the following account from Christ's ministry clearly illustrates how one incident can initiate a series of events. As you read, note Christ's part in the story. Both of His appearances have a profound effect on the protagonist's life and the story's plot. What spiritual lesson does He teach to the blind man, His disciples, the Pharisees, and to us?

And as Jesus passed by, he saw a man which was blind from his birth.

And his disciples asked him, saying, Master, who did sin, this man, or his parents, that he was born blind?

Jesus answered, Neither hath this man sinned, nor his parents: but that the works of God should be made manifest* in him.

---

manifest: clearly apparent

I must work the works of him that sent me, while it is day: the night cometh, when no man can work.

As long as I am in the world, I am the light of the world.

When he had thus spoken, he spat on the ground, and made clay of the spittle, and he anointed the eyes of the blind man with the clay.

And said unto him, Go, wash in the pool of Si-lo´am, (which is by interpretation, Sent.) He went his way therefore, and washed, and came seeing.

The neighbours therefore, and they which before had seen him that he was blind, said, Is not this he that sat and begged?

Some said, This is he: others said, He is like him: but he said, I am he.

Therefore said they unto him, How were thine eyes opened?

He answered and said, A man that is called Jesus made clay, and anointed mine eyes, and said unto me, Go to the pool of Si-lo´am, and wash: and I went and washed, and I received sight.

Then said they unto him, Where is he? He said, I know not.

They brought to the Pharisees him that aforetime was blind.

And it was the sabbath day when Jesus made the clay, and opened his eyes.

Then again the Pharisees also asked him how he had received his sight. He said unto them, He put clay upon mine eyes, and I washed, and do see.

Therefore said some of the Pharisees, This man is not of God, because he keepeth not the sabbath day. Others said, How can a man that is a sinner do such miracles? And there was a division among them.

They say unto the blind man again, What sayest thou of him, that he hath opened thine eyes? He said, He is a prophet.

But the Jews did not believe concerning him, that he had been blind, and received his sight, until they called the parents of him that had received his sight.

And they asked them, saying, Is this your son, who ye say was born blind? how then doth he now see?

His parents answered them and said, We know that this is our son, and that he was born blind:

But by what means he now seeth, we know not; or who hath opened his eyes, we know not: he is of age; ask him: he shall speak for himself.

These words spake his parents, because they feared the Jews: for the Jews had agreed already, that if any man did confess that he was Christ, he should be put out of the synagogue.

Therefore said his parents, He is of age; ask him.

Then again called they the man that was blind, and said unto him, Give God the praise: we know that this man is a sinner.

He answered and said, Whether he be a sinner or no, I know not: one thing I know, that, whereas I was blind, now I see.

Then said they to him again, What did he to thee? how opened he thine eyes?

He answered them, I have told you already, and ye did not hear: wherefore would ye hear it again? will ye also be his disciples?

Then they reviled him, and said, Thou art his disciple; but we are Moses' disciples.

We know that God spake unto Moses: as for this fellow, we know not from whence he is.

The man answered and said unto them, Why herein is a marvelous* thing, that ye know not from whence he is, and yet he hath opened mine eyes.

---

marvelous: causing wonder or astonishment

Now we know that God heareth not sinners: but if any man be a worshipper of God, and doeth his will, him he heareth.

Since the world began was it not heard that any man opened the eyes of one that was born blind.

If this man were not of God, he could do nothing.

They answered and said unto him, Thou wast altogether born in sins, and dost thou teach us? And they cast him out.

Jesus heard that they had cast him out; and when he had found him, he said unto him, Dost thou believe on the Son of God?

He answered and said, Who is he, Lord, that I might believe on him?

And Jesus said unto him, Thou hast both seen him, and it is he that talketh with thee.

And he said, Lord, I believe. And he worshipped him.

And Jesus said, For judgment I am come into this world, that they which see not might see; and that they which see might be made blind.

And some of the Pharisees which were with him heard these words, and said unto him, Are we blind also?

Jesus said unto them, If ye were blind, ye should have no sin: but now ye say, We see; therefore your sin remaineth.

About the Story

1. Identify the **inciting moment, crisis,** and **resolution** (dénouement) of the story.

2. How do Christ's actions frame the story? What might have happened had He not followed up on His initial action?

3. What do you believe the climax of the story to be? Explain your choice.

4. The story centers on blindness, both physical and spiritual. What do you think Christ meant to tell the Pharisees by His final statement?

5. Name another Bible story that follows the plot pyramid structure.

The Necklace

Guy de Maupassant

The structure of this classic short story is a common variation on the typical pyramid plot structure. As you read through this story that so clearly displays the dangers of selfishness, see whether you can discover how the shape of the plot is different from the standard diagram. See too whether you can discover what Mathilde Loisel and her husband should have done differently.

She was one of those pretty and charming girls, born, as if by an accident of fate, into a family of clerks. With no dowry, no prospects, no way of any kind of being met, understood, loved, and married by a man both prosperous and famous, she was finally married to a minor clerk in the Ministry of Education.

She dressed plainly because she could not afford fine clothes, but was as unhappy as a woman who has come down in the world; for women have no family rank or social class. With them, beauty, grace, and charm take the place of birth and breeding. Their natural poise, their instinctive good taste, and their mental cleverness are the sole guiding principles which make daughters of the common people the equals of ladies in high society.

She grieved incessantly,* feeling that she had been born for all the little niceties and luxuries of living. She grieved over the shabbiness of her apartment, the dinginess of the walls, the worn-out appearance of the chairs, the ugliness of the draperies. All these things, which another woman of her class would not even have noticed, gnawed at her and made her furious. The sight of the little Breton* girl who did her humble housework roused in her disconsolate* regrets and wild daydreams.

incessantly: without interruption
Breton: a native of Brittany
disconsolate: unable to be consoled

She would dream of silent chambers, draped with Oriental tapestries and lighted by tall bronze floor lamps, and of two handsome butlers in knee breeches, who, drowsy from the heavy warmth cast by the central stove, dozed in large over-stuffed armchairs.

She would dream of great reception halls hung with old silks, of fine furniture filled with priceless curios,* and of small, stylish, scented sitting rooms just right for the four o'clock chat with intimate friends, with distinguished and sought-after men whose attention every woman envies and longs to attract.

curios: unusual objects of art or bric-a-brac

When dining at the round table, covered for the third day with the same cloth, opposite her husband who would raise the cover of the soup tureen, declaring delightedly, "Ah! a good stew! There's nothing I like better . . ." she would dream of fashionable dinner parties, of gleaming silverware, of tapestries making the walls alive with characters out of history and strange birds in a fairyland forest; she would dream of delicious dishes served on wonderful china, of gallant compliments whispered and listened to with a sphinxlike* smile as one eats the rosy flesh of a trout or nibbles at the wings of a grouse.

sphinxlike: mysterious

She had no evening clothes, no jewels, nothing. But those were the things she wanted; she felt that was the kind of life for her. She so much longed to please, be envied, be fascinating and sought after.

She had a well-to-do friend, a classmate of convent-school days whom she would no longer go to see, simply because she would feel so distressed on returning home. And she would weep for days on end from vexation, regret, despair, and anguish.

Then one evening, her husband came home proudly holding out a large envelope.

"Look," he said, "I've got something for you."

She excitedly tore open the envelope and pulled out a printed card bearing these words:

"The Minister of Education and Mme. Georges Ramponneau beg M. and Mme.* Loisel to do them the honor of attending an evening reception at the ministerial mansion on Friday, January 18."

M. and Mme: Monsieur and Madame

Instead of being delighted, as her husband had hoped, she scornfully tossed the invitation on the table, murmuring, "What good is that to me?"

"But, my dear, I thought you'd be thrilled to death. You never get a chance to go out, and this is a real affair, a wonderful one! I had an awful time getting a card. Everybody wants one; it's much sought after, and not many clerks have a chance at one. You'll see all the most important people there."

She gave him an irritated glance and burst out impatiently, "What do you think I have to go in?"

He hadn't given that a thought. He stammered, "Why, the dress you wear when we go to the theater. That looks quite nice, I think."

He stopped talking, dazed and distracted to see his wife burst out weeping. Two large tears slowly rolled from the corners of her eyes to the corners of her mouth; he gasped, "Why, what's the matter? What's the trouble?"

By sheer will power she overcame her outburst and answered in a calm voice while wiping the tears from her wet cheeks:

"Oh, nothing. Only I don't have an evening dress and therefore I can't go to that affair. Give the card to some friend at the office whose wife can dress better than I can."

He was stunned. He resumed, "Let's see, Mathilde. How much would a suitable outfit cost—one you could wear for other affairs too—something very simple?"

She thought it over for several seconds, going over her allowance and thinking also of the amount she could ask for without bringing an immediate refusal and an exclamation of dismay from the thrifty clerk.

Finally, she answered hesitatingly, "I'm not sure exactly, but I think with four hundred francs I could manage it."

He turned a bit pale, for he had set aside just that amount to buy a rifle so that, the following summer, he could join some friends who were getting up a group to shoot larks on the plain near Nanterre.

However, he said, "All right. I'll give you four hundred francs. But try to get a nice dress."

As the day of the party approached, Mme. Loisel seemed sad, moody, and ill at ease. Her outfit was ready, however. Her husband said to her one evening, "What's the matter? You've been all out of sorts for three days."

And she answered, "It's embarrassing not to have a jewel or a gem—nothing to wear on my dress. I'll look like a pauper: I'd almost rather not go to that party."

He answered, "Why not wear some flowers? They're very fashionable this season. For ten francs you can get two or three gorgeous roses."

She wasn't at all convinced. "No. . . . There's nothing more humiliating than to look poor among a lot of rich women."

But her husband exclaimed, "My, but you're silly! Go see your friend Mme. Forestier and ask her to lend you some jewelry. You and she know each other well enough for you to do that."

She gave a cry of joy, "Why, that's so! I hadn't thought of it."

The next day she paid her friend a visit and told her of her predicament.

Mme. Forestier went toward a large closet with mirrored doors, took out a large jewel box, brought it over, opened it, and said to Mme. Loisel: "Pick something out, my dear."

At first her eyes noted some bracelets, then a pearl necklace, then a Venetian cross, gold and gems, of marvelous workmanship. She tried on these adornments in front of the mirror, but hesitated, unable to decide which to part with and put back. She kept on asking, "Haven't you something else?"

"Oh, yes, keep on looking. I don't know just what you'd like."

All at once she found, in a black satin box, a superb diamond necklace; and her pulse beat faster with longing. Her hands trembled as she took it up. Clasping it around her throat, outside her high-necked dress, she stood in ecstasy looking at her reflection.

Then she asked, hesitatingly, pleading, "Could I borrow that, just that and nothing else?"

"Why, of course."

She threw her arms around her friend, kissed her warmly, and fled with her treasure.

The day of the party arrived. Mme. Loisel was a sensation. She was the prettiest one there, fashionable, gracious, smiling, and wild with joy. All the men turned to look at her, asked who she was, begged to be introduced. All the cabinet officials wanted to waltz with her. The minister took notice of her.

She danced madly, wildly, drunk with pleasure, giving no thought to anything in the triumph of her beauty, the pride of her success, in a kind of happy cloud composed of all the adulation,* of all the admiring glances, of all the awakened longings, of a sense of complete victory that is so sweet to a woman's heart.

---

adulation: excessive flattery

She left around four o'clock in the morning. Her husband, since midnight, had been dozing in a small empty sitting room with three other gentlemen whose wives were having too good a time.

He threw over her shoulders the wraps he had brought for going home, modest garments of everyday life whose shabbiness clashed with the stylishness of her evening clothes. She felt this and longed to escape, unseen by the other women who were draped in expensive furs.

Loisel held her back.

"Hold on! You'll catch cold outside. I'll call a cab."

But she wouldn't listen to him and went rapidly down the stairs. When they were on the street, they didn't find a carriage; and they set out to hunt for one, hailing drivers whom they saw going by at a distance.

They walked toward the Seine, disconsolate and shivering. Finally on the docks they found one of those carriages that one sees in Paris only after nightfall, as if they were ashamed to show their drabness during daylight hours.

It dropped them at their door in the Rue des Martyrs, and they climbed wearily up to their apartment. For her, it was all over. For him, there was the thought that he would have to be at the ministry at ten o'clock.

Before the mirror, she let the wraps fall from her shoulders to see herself once again in all her glory. Suddenly she gave a cry. The necklace was gone.

Her husband, already half undressed, said, "What's the trouble?"

She turned toward him despairingly, "I . . . I . . . I don't have Mme. Forestier's necklace."

"What! You can't mean it! It's impossible!"

They hunted everywhere, through the folds of the dress, through the folds of the coat, in the pockets. They found nothing.

He asked, "Are you sure you had it when leaving the dance?"

"Yes, I felt it when I was in the hall of the ministry."

"But if you had lost it on the street we'd have heard it drop. It must be in the cab."

"Yes, Quite likely. Did you get its number?"

"No. Didn't you notice it either?"

"No."

They looked at each other aghast. Finally Loisel got dressed again.

"I'll retrace our steps on foot," he said, "to see if I can find it."

And he went out. She remained in her evening clothes, without the strength to go

to bed, slumped in a chair in the unheated room, her mind a blank.

Her husband came in about seven o'clock. He had had no luck.

He went to the police station, to the newspapers to post a reward, to the cab companies, everywhere the slightest hope drove him.

That evening Loisel returned, pale, his face lined; still he had learned nothing.

"We'll have to write your friend," he said, "to tell her you have broken the catch and are having it repaired. That will give us a little time to turn around."

She wrote to his dictation.

At the end of a week, they had given up all hope.

And Loisel, looking five years older, declared, "We must take steps to replace that piece of jewelry."

The next day they took the case to the jeweler whose name they found inside. He consulted his records. "I didn't sell that necklace, madame," he said. "I only supplied the case."

Then they went from one jeweler to another hunting for a similar necklace, going over their recollections, both sick with despair and anxiety.

They found, in a shop in Palais Royal, a string of diamonds which seemed exactly like the one they were seeking. It was priced at forty thousand francs. They could get it for thirty-six.

They asked the jeweler to hold it for them for three days. And they reached an agreement that he would take it back for thirty-four thousand if the lost one was found before the end of February.

Loisel had eighteen thousand francs he had inherited from his father. He would borrow the rest.

He went about raising the money, asking a thousand francs from one, four hundred from another, a hundred here, sixty there. He signed notes, made ruinous deals, did business with loan sharks,* ran the whole gamut* of moneylenders. He compromised the rest of his life, risked his signature without knowing if he'd be able to honor it, and then, terrified by the outlook for the future, by the blackness of despair about to close around him, by the prospect of all the privations of the body and tortures of the spirit, he went to claim the new necklace with the thirty-six thousand francs which he placed on the counter of the shopkeeper.

---

loan sharks: moneylenders using excessive interest rates
gamut: complete range

When Mme. Loisel took the necklace back, Mme. Forestier said to her frostily, "You should have brought it back sooner; I might have needed it."

She didn't open the case, an action her friend was afraid of. If she had noticed the substitution, what would she have thought? What would she have said? Would she have thought her a thief?

Mme. Loisel experienced the horrible life the needy live. She played her part, however, with sudden heroism. That frightful debt had to be paid. She would pay it. She dismissed her maid; they rented a garret under the eaves.

She learned to do the heavy housework, to perform the hateful duties of cooking. She washed dishes, wearing down her shell-pink nails scouring the grease from pots and pans; she scrubbed dirty linen, shirts, and cleaning rags which she hung on a line to dry; she took the garbage down to the street each morning and brought up water, stopping on each landing to get her breath. And, clad like a peasant woman, basket on arm, guarding sou by sou her scanty allowance, she bargained with the fruit dealers, the grocer, the butcher, and was insulted by them.

Each month notes had to be paid, and others renewed to give more time.

Her husband labored evenings to balance a tradesman's accounts, and at night, often, he copied documents at five sous a page.

And this went on for ten years.

Finally, all was paid back, everything including the exorbitant rates of the loan sharks and accumulated compound interest.

Mme. Loisel appeared an old woman, now. She became heavy, rough, harsh, like one of the poor. Her hair untended, her skirts askew, her hands red, her voice shrill, she even slopped water on her floors and scrubbed them herself. But, sometimes, while her husband was at work, she would sit near the window and think of that long-ago evening when, at the dance, she had been so beautiful and admired.

What would have happened if she had not lost that necklace? Who knows? Who can say? How strange and unpredictable life is! How little there is between happiness and misery!

Then one Sunday when she had gone for a walk on the Champs Élysées* to relax a bit from the week's labors, she suddenly noticed a woman strolling with a child. It was Mme. Forestier, still young-looking, still beautiful, still charming.

Champs Élysées: famous street in Paris leading to the Arc de Triomphe

---

Mme. Loisel felt a rush of emotion. Should she speak to her? Of course. And now that everything was paid off, she would tell her the whole story. Why not?

She went toward her. "Hello, Jeanne."

The other, not recognizing her, showed astonishment at being spoken to so familiarly by this common person. She stammered, "But . . . madame . . . I don't recognize . . . You must be mistaken."

"No, I'm Mathilde Loisel."

Her friend gave a cry, "Oh, my poor Mathilde, how you've changed!"

"Yes, I've had a hard time since last seeing you. And plenty of misfortunes—and all on account of you!"

"Of me . . . How do you mean?"

"Do you remember that diamond necklace you loaned me to wear to the dance at the ministry?"

"Yes, but what about it?"

"Well, I lost it."

"You lost it! But you returned it."

"I brought you another just like it. And we've been paying for it for ten years now. You can imagine that wasn't easy for us who had nothing. Well, it's over now, and I am glad of it."

Mme. Forestier stopped short. "You mean to say you bought a diamond necklace to replace mine?"

"Yes. You never noticed, then? They were quite alike."

And she smiled with proud and simple joy.

Mme. Forestier, quite overcome, clasped her by the hands, "Oh, my poor Mathilde.

But mine was only paste.* Why, at most it was worth only five hundred francs!"

paste: gems made of glass

About the Story

1. Identify the inciting moment, crisis, and dénouement in this story.

2. How is the plot pyramid for this story different from the pyramid for the first story in this unit?

3. How does that difference affect the story for the reader?

4. What mistakes do Mathilde and her husband make?

5. What should they have done when they realized the necklace was not to be found?

6. Who is more at fault for what happened, Mathilde or her husband?

7. What term from the unit introduction does the ending of this story illustrate? Explain briefly.

About the Author

Acknowledged as the greatest French short-story writer, Guy de Maupassant (1850–93) created works of international and timeless appeal. He was a Naturalist, one of a group who thought that life can be known only through what can be perceived through the physical senses. As a result, his short stories generally portray life as hopelessly bleak and disappointing. The despair of many Maupassant characters is usually a direct result of some sin or combination of sinful tendencies. As in "The Necklace," covetousness and lying are two of the more common vices that destroy the lives and hopes of his characters.

Maupassant was born at the château de Miromesnil, France, but moved to Normandy with his mother at age eleven. As a young boy, he was exposed to all types and classes of French society, collecting many mental images of the people he met. He found, though, in the middle class, or bourgeoisie, his greatest interest. While working in the government bureaucracy as an adult, Maupassant honed his writing skills through long years of literary apprenticeship to the famous French writer (and his godfather) Flaubert. Though he achieved great financial and literary success, Maupassant gradually became reclusive because of a severe physical ailment resulting in mental instability. After attempting suicide in 1892, he was committed to an asylum and died there in June of 1893.

The Possibility of Evil

Shirley Jackson

Like Maupassant in "The Necklace," Jackson uses the exposition of her story to establish the central character. The rest of her plot structure uses specific events to reveal and confront the protagonist's worldview. As you read, note how Jackson uses plot to explore the following questions: What is the protagonist's underlying opinion of herself and of people in general? How do those attitudes affect those around her? What does the author think of this mindset? Does the protagonist change her way of thinking?

Miss Adela Strangeworth stepped daintily along Main Street on her way to the grocery. The sun was shining, the air was fresh and clear after the night's heavy rain, and everything in Miss Strangeworth's little town looked washed and bright. Miss Strangeworth took deep breaths, and thought that there was nothing in the world like a fragrant summer day.

She knew everyone in town, of course; she was fond of telling strangers—tourists who sometimes passed through the town and stopped to admire Miss Strangeworth's roses—that she had never spent more than a day outside this town in all her long life. She was seventy-one, Miss Strangeworth told the tourists, with a pretty little dimple showing by her lip, and she sometimes found

herself thinking that the town belonged to her. "My grandfather built the first house on Pleasant Street," she would say, opening her blue eyes wide with the wonder of it. "This house, right here. My family has lived here for better than a hundred years. My grandmother planted these roses, and my mother tended them, just as I do. I've watched my town grow; I can remember when Mr. Lewis, Senior, opened the grocery store, and the year the river flooded out the shanties on the low road, and the excitement when some young folks wanted to move the park over to the space in front of where the new post office is today. They wanted to put up a statue of Ethan Allen"*—Miss Strangeworth would frown a little and sound stern—"but it should have been a statue of my grandfather. There wouldn't have been a town here at all if it hadn't been for my grandfather and the lumber mill."

Ethan Allen: Revolutionary War hero from Vermont

Miss Strangeworth never gave away any of her roses, although the tourists often asked her. The roses belonged on Pleasant Street, and it bothered Miss Strangeworth to think of people wanting to carry them away, to take them into strange towns and down strange streets. When the new minister came, and the ladies were gathering flowers to decorate the church, Miss Strangeworth sent over a great basket of gladioli; when she picked the roses at all, she set them in bowls and vases around the inside of the house her grandfather had built.

Walking down Main Street on a summer morning, Miss Strangeworth had to stop every minute or so to say good morning to someone or to ask after someone's health. When she came into the grocery, half a dozen people turned away from the shelves and the counters to wave at her or call out good morning.

"And good morning to you, too, Mr. Lewis," Miss Strangeworth said at last. The Lewis family had been in the town almost as long as the Strangeworths; but the day young Lewis left high school and went to work in the grocery, Miss Strangeworth had stopped calling him Tommy and started calling him Mr. Lewis, and he had stopped calling her Addie and started calling her Miss Strangeworth. They had been in high school together, and had gone to picnics together, and to high school dances and basketball games; but now Mr. Lewis was behind the counter in the grocery, and Miss Strangeworth was living alone in the Strangeworth house on Pleasant Street.

"Good morning," Mr. Lewis said, and added politely, "lovely day."

"It is a very nice day," Miss Strangeworth said as though she had only just decided that it would do after all. "I would like a chop, please, Mr. Lewis, a small, lean veal chop. Are those strawberries from Arthur Parker's garden? They're early this year."

"He brought them in this morning," Mr. Lewis said.

"I shall have a box," Miss Strangeworth said. Mr. Lewis looked worried, she thought, and for a minute she hesitated, but then she decided that he surely could not be worried over the strawberries. He looked very tired indeed. He was usually so chipper, Miss Strangeworth thought, and almost commented, but it was far too personal a subject to be introduced to Mr. Lewis, the grocer, so she only said, "And a can of cat food and, I think, a tomato."

Silently, Mr. Lewis assembled her order on the counter and waited. Miss Strangeworth looked at him curiously and then said, "It's Tuesday, Mr. Lewis. You forgot to remind me."

"Did I? Sorry."

"Imagine your forgetting that I always buy my tea on Tuesday," Miss Strangeworth said gently. "A quarter pound of tea, please, Mr. Lewis."

"Is that all, Miss Strangeworth?"

"Yes, thank you, Mr. Lewis. Such a lovely day, isn't it?"

"Lovely," Mr. Lewis said.

Miss Strangeworth moved slightly to make room for Mrs. Harper at the counter. "Morning Adela," Mrs. Harper said, and Miss Strangeworth said, "Good morning, Martha."

"Lovely day," Mrs. Harper said, and Miss Strangeworth said, "Yes, lovely," and Mr. Lewis, under Mrs. Harper's glance, nodded.

"Ran out of sugar for my cake frosting," Mrs. Harper explained. Her hand shook slightly as she opened her pocketbook. Miss Strangeworth wondered, glancing at her quickly, if she had been taking proper care of herself. Martha Harper was not as young as she used to be, Miss Strangeworth thought. She probably could use a good, strong tonic.*

---
tonic: a medication to invigorate or strengthen

"Martha," she said, "you don't look well."

"I'm perfectly all right," Mrs. Harper said shortly. She handed her money to Mr. Lewis, took her change and her sugar, and went out without speaking again. Looking after her, Miss Strangeworth shook her head slightly. Martha definitely did *not* look well.

Carrying her little bag of groceries, Miss Strangeworth came out of the store into the bright sunlight and stopped to smile down on the Crane baby. Don and Helen Crane were really the two most infatuated* young parents she had ever known, she thought indulgently, looking at the delicately embroidered baby cap and the lace-edged carriage cover.

---
infatuated: marked by foolish or unreasoning fondness

"That little girl is going to grow up expecting luxury all her life," she said to Helen Crane.

Helen laughed. "That's the way we want her to feel," she said. "Like a princess."

"A princess can be a lot of trouble sometimes," Miss Strangeworth said dryly. "How old is her highness now?"

"Six months next Tuesday," Helen Crane said, looking down with rapt wonder at her child. "I've been worrying, though, about her. Don't you think she ought to move around more? Try to sit up, for instance?"

"For plain and fancy worrying," Miss Strangeworth said, amused, "give me a new mother every time."

"She just seems—slow," Helen Crane said.

"Nonsense. All babies are different. Some of them develop much more quickly than others."

"That's what my mother says." Helen Crane laughed, looking a little bit ashamed.

"I suppose you've got young Don all upset about the fact that his daughter is already six months old and hasn't yet begun to learn to dance?"

"I haven't mentioned it to him. I suppose she's just so precious that I worry about her all the time."

"Well, apologize to her right now," Miss Strangeworth said. "*She* is probably worrying about why you keep jumping around all the time." Smiling to herself and shaking her old head, she went on down the sunny street, stopping once to ask little Billy Moore why he wasn't out riding in his daddy's shiny new car, and talking for a few minutes outside the library with Miss Chandler, the librarian, about the new novels to be ordered, and paid for by the annual library appropriation.* Miss Chandler seemed absentminded and very much as though she was thinking about something else. Miss Strangeworth noticed that Miss Chandler had not taken much trouble with her hair that morning, and sighed. Miss Strangeworth hated sloppiness.

appropriation: money set aside for a particular purpose

Many people seemed disturbed recently, Miss Strangeworth thought. Only yesterday the Stewarts' fifteen-year-old Linda had run crying down her own front walk and all the way to school, not caring who saw her. People around town thought she might have had a fight with the Harris boy, but they showed up together at the soda shop after school as usual, both of them looking grim and bleak. Trouble at home, people concluded, and sighed over the problems of trying to raise kids right these days.

From halfway down the block Miss Strangeworth could catch the heavy accent of her roses, and she moved a little more quickly. The perfume of roses meant home, and home meant the Strangeworth House on Pleasant Street. Miss Strangeworth stopped at her own front gate, as she always did, and looked with deep pleasure at her house, with the red and pink and white roses massed along the narrow lawn, and the rambler going up along the porch; and the neat, the unbelievably trim lines of the house itself, with its slimness and its washed white look. Every window sparkled, every curtain hung stiff and straight, and even the stones of the front walk were swept and clear. People around town wondered how old Miss Strangeworth managed to keep the house looking the way it did, and there was a legend about a tourist once mistaking it for the local museum and going all through the place without finding out about his mistake. But the town was proud of Miss Strangeworth and her roses and her house. They had all grown together. Miss Strangeworth went up her front steps, unlocked her front door with her key, and went into the kitchen to put away her groceries. She debated having a cup of tea and then decided that it was too close to midday dinnertime; she would not have the appetite for her little chop if she had tea now. Instead she went into the light, lovely sitting room, which still glowed from the hands of her mother and her grandmother, who had covered the chairs with bright chintz and hung the curtains. All the furniture was spare and shining, and the round hooked rugs on the floor had been the work of Miss Strangeworth's grandmother and her mother. Miss Strangeworth had put a bowl of her red roses on the low table before the window, and the room was full of their scent.

Miss Strangeworth went to the narrow desk in the corner, and unlocked it with her key. She never knew when she might feel like writing letters, so she kept her notepaper inside, and the desk locked. Miss Strangeworth's usual stationery was heavy and cream-colored, with "Strangeworth House" engraved across the top, but, when she felt like writing her other letters, Miss Strangeworth used a pad of various-colored paper, bought from the local newspaper shop. It was almost a town joke, that colored paper, layered in pink and green and blue and yellow; everyone in town bought it and used it for odd, informal notes and shopping lists. It was usual to remark, upon receiving a note written on a blue page, that so-and-so would be needing a new pad soon—here she was, down to the blue already. Everyone used the matching envelopes for tucking away recipes, or keeping odd little things in, or even to hold cookies in the school lunch boxes. Mr. Lewis sometimes gave them to the children for carrying home penny candy.

Although Miss Strangeworth's desk held a trimmed quill pen, which had belonged to her grandfather, and a gold-frost fountain pen, which had belonged to her father, Miss Strangeworth always used a dull stub of pen-

cil when she wrote her letters, and she printed them in a childish block print. After thinking for a minute, although she had been phrasing the letter in the back of her mind all the way home, she wrote on a pink sheet: *Didn't you ever see an idiot child before? Some people just shouldn't have children, should they?*

She was pleased with the letter. She was fond of doing things exactly right. When she made a mistake, as she sometimes did, or when the letters were not spaced nicely on the page, she had to take the discarded page to the kitchen stove and burn it at once. Miss Strangeworth never delayed when things had to be done.

After thinking for a minute, she decided that she would like to write another letter, perhaps to go to Mrs. Harper, to follow up the ones she had already mailed. She selected a green sheet this time and wrote quickly: *Have you found out yet what they were all laughing about after you left the bridge club on Thursday? Or is the wife really always the last one to know?*

Miss Strangeworth never concerned herself with facts; her letters all dealt with the more negotiable stuff of suspicion. Mr. Lewis would never have imagined for a minute that his grandson might be lifting petty cash* from the store register if he had not had one of Miss Strangeworth's letters. Miss

Chandler, the librarian, and Linda Stewart's parents would have gone unsuspectingly ahead with their lives, never aware of possible evil lurking nearby, if Miss Strangeworth had not sent letters to open their eyes. Miss Strangeworth would have been genuinely shocked if there *had* been anything between Linda Stewart and the Harris boy, but, as long as evil existed unchecked in the world, it was Miss Strangeworth's duty to keep her town alert to it. It was far more sensible for Miss Chandler to wonder what Mr. Shelley's first wife had really died of than to take a chance on not knowing. There were so many wicked people in the world and only one Strangeworth left in town. Besides, Miss Strangeworth liked writing her letters.

---

petty cash: a small sum of money for incidental expenses

She addressed an envelope to Don Crane after a moment's thought, wondering curiously if he would show the letter to his wife, and using a pink envelope to match the pink paper. Then she addressed a second envelope, green, to Mrs. Harper. Then an idea came to her and she selected a blue sheet and wrote: *You never know about doctors. Remember they're only human and need money like the rest of us. Suppose the knife slipped accidentally. Would Doctor Burns get his fee and a little extra from that nephew of yours?*

She addressed the blue envelope to old Mrs. Foster, who was having an operation next month. She had thought of writing one more letter, to the head of the school board, asking how a chemistry teacher like Billy Moore's father could afford a new convertible, but all at once she was tired of writing letters. The three she had done would do for one day. She could write more tomorrow; it was not as though they all had to be done at once.

She had been writing her letters—sometimes two or three every day for a week, sometimes no more than one in a month—for the past year. She never got any answers, of course, because she never signed her name. If she had been asked, she would have said that her name, Adela Strangeworth, a name honored in the town for so many years, did not belong on such trash. The town where she lived had to be kept clean and sweet, but people everywhere were lustful and evil and degraded, and needed to be watched; the world was so large, and there was only one Strangeworth left in it. Miss Strangeworth sighed, locked her desk, and put the letters into her big, black leather pocketbook, to be mailed when she took her evening walk.

She broiled her little chop nicely, and had a sliced tomato and good cup of tea ready when she sat down to her midday dinner at the table in her dining room, which could be opened to seat twenty-two, with a second table, if necessary, in the hall. Sitting in the warm sunlight that came through the tall windows of the dining room, seeing her roses massed outside, handling the heavy, old silverware and the fine, translucent* china, Miss Strangeworth was pleased; she would not have cared to be doing anything else. People must live graciously, after all, she thought, and sipped her tea. Afterward, when her plate and cup and saucer were washed and dried and put back onto the shelves where they belonged, and her silverware was back in the mahogany silver chest, Miss Strangeworth went up the graceful staircase and into her bedroom, which was the front room overlooking the roses, and had been her mother's and her grandmother's. Their Crown Derby dresser set and furs had been kept here, their fans and silver-backed brushes and their own bowls of roses; Miss Strangeworth kept a bowl of white roses on the bed table.

translucent: allowing light to pass through but not distinct images; semitransparent

She drew the shades, took the rose-satin spread from the bed, slipped out of her dress and her shoes, and lay down tiredly. She knew that no doorbell or phone would ring; no one in town would dare to disturb Miss Strangeworth during her afternoon nap. She slept, deep in the rich smell of roses.

After her nap she worked in her garden for a little while, sparing herself because of the heat; then she went in to her supper. She ate asparagus from her own garden, with sweet-butter sauce, and a soft-boiled egg, and, while she had her supper, she listened to a late-evening news broadcast and then to a program of classical music on her small radio. After her dishes were done and her kitchen set in order, she took up her hat—Miss Strangeworth's hats were proverbial* in the town; people believed that she had inherited them from her mother and her grandmother—and, locking the front door of her house behind her, set off on her evening walk, pocketbook under her arm. She nodded to Linda Stewart's father, who was washing his car in the pleasantly cool evening. She thought that he looked troubled.

proverbial: well-known, famous (as if referred to in a proverb)

There was only one place in town where she could mail her letters, and that was the new post office, shiny with red brick and silver letters. Although Miss Strangeworth

had never given the matter any particular thought, she had always made a point of mailing her letters very secretly; it would, of course, not have been wise to let anyone see her mail them. Consequently, she timed her walk so she could reach the post office just as darkness was starting to dim the outlines of the trees and the shapes of people's faces, although no one could ever mistake Miss Strangeworth, with her dainty walk and her rustling skirts.

There was always a group of young people around the post office, the very youngest roller-skating upon its driveway, which went all the way around the building and was the only smooth road in town; and the slightly older ones already knowing how to gather in small groups and chatter and laugh and make great, excited plans for going across the street to the soda shop in a minute or two. Miss Strangeworth had never had any self-consciousness before the children. She did not feel that any of them were staring at her unduly or longing to laugh at her; it would have been most reprehensible* for their parents to permit their children to mock Miss Strangeworth of Pleasant Street. Most of the children stood back respectfully as Miss Strangeworth passed, silenced briefly in her presence, and some of the older children greeted her, saying soberly, "Hello, Miss Strangeworth."

reprehensible: deserving rebuke or censure

Miss Strangeworth smiled at them and quickly went on. It had been a long time since she had known the name of every child in town. The mail slot was in the door of the post office. The children stood away as Miss Strangeworth approached it, seemingly surprised that anyone should want to use the post office after it had been officially closed up for the night and turned over to the children. Miss Strangeworth stood by the door, opening her black pocketbook to take out the letters, and heard a voice which she knew at once to be Linda Stewart's. Poor little Linda was crying again, and Miss Strangeworth listened carefully. This was, after all, her town, and these were her people; if one of them was in trouble, she ought to know about it.

"I can't tell you, Dave," Linda was saying—so she *was* talking to the Harris boy, as Miss Strangeworth had supposed—"I just *can't*. It's just *nasty*."

"But why won't your father let me come around anymore? What on earth did I do?"

"I can't tell you. I just wouldn't tell you for *any*thing. You've got to have a dirty dirty mind for things like that."

"But something's happened. You've been crying and crying, and your father is all upset. Why can't *I* know about it, too? Aren't I like one of the family?"

"Not anymore, Dave, not anymore. You're not to come near our house again; my father said so. He said he'd horsewhip you. That's all I can tell you: You're not to come near our house anymore."

"But I didn't *do* anything."

"Just the same, my father said . . ."

Miss Strangeworth sighed and turned away. There was so much evil in people. Even in a charming little town like this one, there was still so much evil in people.

She slipped her letters into the slot, and two of them fell inside. The third caught on the edge and fell outside, onto the ground at Miss Strangeworth's feet. She did not notice it because she was wondering whether a letter to the Harris boy's father might not be of some service in wiping out this potential badness. Wearily Miss Strangeworth turned to go home to her quiet bed in her lovely house, and never heard the Harris boy calling to her to say that she had dropped something.

"Old lady Strangeworth's getting deaf," he said, looking after her and holding in his hand the letter he had picked up.

"Well, who cares?" Linda said. "Who cares anymore, anyway?"

"It's for Don Crane," the Harris boy said, "this letter. She dropped a letter addressed to Don Crane. Might as well take it on over. We pass his house anyway." He laughed. "Maybe it's got a check or something in it and he'd be just as glad to get it tonight instead of tomorrow."

"Catch old lady Strangeworth sending anybody a check," Linda said. "Throw it in the post office. Why do anyone a favor?" She sniffed. "Doesn't seem to me anybody around here cares about us," she said. "Why should we care about them?"

"I'll take it over, anyway," the Harris boy said. "Maybe it's good news for them. Maybe they need something happy tonight, too. Like us."

Sadly, holding hands, they wandered off down the dark street, the Harris boy carrying Miss Strangeworth's pink envelope in his hand.

Miss Strangeworth awakened the next morning with a feeling of intense happiness and, for a minute, wondered why, and then remembered that this morning three people would open her letters. Harsh, perhaps, at first, but wickedness was never easily banished, and a clean heart was a scoured heart. She washed her soft, old face and brushed her teeth, still sound in spite of her seventy-one years, and dressed herself carefully in her sweet, soft clothes and buttoned shoes. Then, going downstairs, reflecting that perhaps a little waffle would be agreeable for breakfast in the sunny dining room, she found the mail on the hall floor, and bent to pick it up. A bill, the morning paper, a letter in a green envelope that looked oddly familiar. Miss Strangeworth stood perfectly still for a minute, looking down at the green envelope with the penciled printing, and thought: It looks like one of my letters. Was one of my letters sent back? No, because no one would know where to send it. How did this get here?

Miss Strangeworth was a Strangeworth of Pleasant Street. Her hand did not shake as she opened the envelope and unfolded the sheet of green paper inside. She began to cry silently for the wickedness of the world when she read the words: *Look out at what used to be your roses.*

About the Story

1. Why does Miss Strangeworth think of the town as belonging to her?

2. In the first part of the story, how does Miss Strangeworth's life contrast with the lives of the townspeople?

3. Once you learn about Miss Strangeworth's letters, what seems odd about her previous reactions to the troubles of those around her?

4. Given Miss Strangeworth's attitude toward Dave, what is ironic about his choice to personally deliver the letter?

5. Why do you think the person who attacks Miss Strangeworth decides to do so by destroying her roses? Were you surprised by this ending? Why or why not?

6. Do you think that Miss Strangeworth has learned anything by the end of the story? Why or why not?

7. Identify the crisis and the climax of the story.

About the Author

Shirley Jackson (1916–65) was born in San Francisco, California, but during her high school years, she and her family moved to New York. She attended Syracuse University, graduating in 1940. While in college, she became interested in literature and also met her future husband, Stanley Hyman, who later became a famous literary critic. Married in 1940, the couple lived in Bennington, Vermont, where her husband taught at a small college. She worked in her home, rearing four children while writing numerous stories and novels.

Many details of her personal life are unknown because Jackson was reluctant to reveal such information, but her fiction reflects dissatisfaction with the frequently rigid rules and harsh judgments of society. Her stories usually focus on the characters' psychological condition, contain elements of the supernatural, and generate a great deal of suspense. Though Jackson's works include novels, short stories, and children's books, as well as her own memoirs, her most famous piece is "The Lottery," a short story. *The Haunting of Hill House* (1959) and *We Have Always Lived in the Castle* (1962) are her best-known novels. "The Possibility of Evil" was published after her death in 1965 and won the 1966 Mystery Writers of America Edgar Award for Best Short Story.

In the Ring with Jack Dempsey

PAUL GALLICO

The American journalist and short-story writer Paul Gallico (1894–1976) began as a sportswriter. Like other writers, he wanted firsthand experience in the subjects he was writing about. His autobiographical essay, "The Feel," from which this excerpt is taken, tells of his participation in various sports he was assigned to cover. Notice that this excerpt is organized both chronologically as a narrative and logically as a cause-effect essay.

It all began back in 1922 when I was a cub* sportswriter and consumed with more curiosity than was good for my health. I had seen my first professional prizefights and wondered at the curious behavior of men under the stress of blows, the sudden checking and the beginning of a little fall forward after a hard punch, the glazing of eyes and the loss of locomotor control,* the strange actions of men on the canvas after a knockdown as they struggled to regain their senses and arise on legs that seemed to have turned into rubber. I had never been in any bad fist fights as a youngster, though I had taken a little physical punishment in football, but it was not enough to complete the picture. Could one think under those conditions?

cub: novice

locomotor control: ability to control one's movements

I had been assigned to my first training-camp coverage, Dempsey's at Saratoga Springs, where he was preparing for his famous fight with Luis Firpo. For days I watched him sag a spar boy with what seemed to be no more than a light cuff on the neck, or pat his face with what looked like no more than a caressing stroke of his arm, and the fellow would come all apart at the seams and collapse in a useless heap, grinning vacuously* or twitching strangely. My burning curiosity got the better of prudence and a certain reluctance to expose myself to physical pain. I asked Dempsey to permit me to box a round with him. I had never boxed before, but I was in good physical shape, having just completed a four-year stretch as a galley slave in the Columbia eight-oared shell.*

vacuously: stupidly, without meaning

Columbia eight-oared shell: a long narrow racing boat

When it was over and I escaped through the ropes, shaking, bleeding a little from the mouth, with rosin dust on my pants and a vicious throbbing in my head, I knew all that there was to know about being hit in the prize-ring. It seems that I had gone to an expert for tuition. I knew the sensation of being stalked and pursued by a relentless, truculent* professional destroyer whose trade and business it was to injure men. I saw the quick flash of the brown forearm that precedes the stunning shock as a bony, leather-bound fist lands on cheek or mouth. I learned more (partly from photographs of the lesson, viewed afterwards, one of which shows me ducked under a vicious left hook, an act of which I never had the slightest recollection) about instinctive ducking and blocking than I could have in ten years of looking at prizefights, and I learned, too, that as the soldier never hears the bullet that kills him, so does the fighter rarely, if ever, see the punch that tumbles blackness over him like a mantle, with a tearing rip as

though the roof of his skull were exploding, and robs him of his senses.

truculent: savage, cruel

There was just that—a ripping in my head and then sudden blackness, and the next thing I knew, I was sitting on the canvas covering of the ring floor with my legs collapsed under me, grinning idiotically. How often since have I seen that same silly, goofy look on the faces of dropped fighters—and understood it. I held onto the floor with both hands, because the ring and the audience outside were making a complete clockwise revolution, came to a stop, and then went back again counterclockwise. When I struggled to my feet, Jack Kearns, Dempsey's manager, was counting over me, but I neither saw nor heard him and was only conscious that I was in a ridiculous position and that the thing to do was to get up and try to fight back. The floor swayed and rocked beneath me like a fishing dory* in an off-shore swell,* and it was a welcome respite when Dempsey rushed into a clinch,* held me up, and whispered into my ear: "Wrestle around a bit, son, until your head clears." And then it was that I learned what those little lovetaps to the back of the neck and the short digs to the ribs can mean to the groggy pugilist* more than half knocked out. It is a murderous game, and the fighter who can escape after having been felled by a lethal blow has my admiration. And there, too, I learned that there can be no sweeter sound than the bell that calls a halt to hostilities.

dory: a small, narrow, flatbottom boat
swell: long, deep wave from the open sea
clinch: in boxing, a hold obstructing the opponent's punches
pugilist: boxer

From that afternoon, also, dated my antipathy* for the spectator at prizefights who yells: "Come on, you bum, get up and fight! Oh, you big quitter! Yah yellow, yah yellow!" Yellow, eh? It is all a man can do to get up after being stunned by a blow, much less fight back. But they do it. And how a man is able to muster any further interest in a combat after being floored with a blow to the pit of the stomach will always remain to me a miracle of what the human animal is capable of under stress.

antipathy: extreme dislike

About the Essay

1. Though Gallico's piece is an essay rather than a short story, is there an incident that could serve as an inciting moment?

2. List several misconceptions Gallico held about fighting before he entered the ring with Dempsey.

3. How did Gallico's attitude as a spectator change after his encounter in the ring?

4. Gallico compares his experience in the ring to that of a man being stalked by a professional destroyer and that of a soldier in his last battle. Why do you think Gallico chose these two specific comparisons? Which of these comparisons did you think was stronger? Why?

5. Through vivid description, Gallico makes you almost feel Dempsey's blows. List three specific phrases that were especially effective in making you empathize with Gallico.

About the Author

Paul Gallico (1897–1976) developed an interest in sports during his college days and distinguished himself as a college cheerleader and captain of the crewing (rowing) team. Following a tour of duty as a sailor in World War I, Gallico finished his college work and took a position with the New York *Daily News*. After working as sports editor for that newspaper for twelve years, Gallico decided to limit himself to freelance work. His short stories and novels became popular. Later, he served as a war correspondent during World War II.

Gallico's greatest gift was his keen observance of minute detail and his ability to transfer his careful study of people and places into well-narrated stories. In his first-person narration "In the Ring with Jack Dempsey," Gallico uses his gifts to help the reader "feel" the rigors of prizefighting. It is not only Gallico who, through his experience with a professional boxer, has learned lessons about human determination and bravery. His readers too have been "in the ring," thanks to his storytelling ability.

The Adventure of the Beryl Coronet

Sir Arthur Conan Doyle

As a hero, Doyle's master detective Sherlock Holmes has ample physical courage, strength, and agility. But he relies mainly on his brainpower: his ability to see significance in details that everyone else overlooks and to reason accurately from them. He is also a student of human nature and can construct hypotheses on the basis of people's actions. Notice that his interpretations of certain characters' actions often oppose the interpretations of others. What moral lessons are hinted at in these differences?

Keep in mind that detective stories often rely heavily on dialogue and exposition as characters relate their version of an incident or as the narrator relates the details of a setting or a character's reactions. As a result, the events of the plot can appear out of sequence or even overlap.

"Holmes," said I, as I stood one morning in our bow-window* looking down the street, "here is a madman coming along. It seems rather sad that his relatives should allow him to come out alone."

bow-window: curved bay window

My friend rose lazily from his arm-chair and stood with his hands in the pockets of his dressing-gown, looking over my shoulder. It was a bright, crisp February morning, and the snow of the day before still lay deep upon the ground, shimmering brightly in the wintry sun. Down the center of Baker Street it had been plowed in a brown crumbly band by the traffic, but at either side and on the heaped-up edges of the foot-paths it still lay as white as when it fell. The gray pavement

had been cleaned and scraped, but was still dangerously slippery, so that there were fewer passengers than usual. Indeed, from the direction of the Metropolitan Station no one was coming save the single gentleman whose eccentric conduct had drawn my attention.

He was a man of about fifty, tall, portly,* and imposing, with a massive, strongly marked face and a commanding figure. He was dressed in a sombre yet rich style, in black frock-coat, shining hat, neat brown gaiters,* and well-cut pearl-gray trousers. Yet his actions were in absurd contrast to the dignity of his dress and features, for he was running hard, with occasional little springs, such as a weary man gives who is little accustomed to set any tax* upon his legs. As he ran he jerked his hands up and down, waggled his head, and writhed his face into the most extraordinary contortions.

---

portly: stout

gaiters: buttoned coverings for instep and ankle

tax: strain

"What on earth can be the matter with him?" I asked. "He is looking up at the numbers of the houses."

"I believe that he is coming here," said Holmes, rubbing his hands.

"Here?"

"Yes; I rather think he is coming to consult me professionally. I think that I recognize the symptoms. Ha! did I not tell you?" As he spoke, the man, puffing and blowing, rushed at our door and pulled at our bell until the whole house resounded with clanging.

A few moments later he was in our room, still puffing, still gesticulating, but with so fixed a look of grief and despair in his eyes that our smiles were turned in an instant to horror and pity. For a while he could not get his words out, but swayed his body and plucked at his hair like one who has been driven to the extreme limits of his reason.

Then, suddenly springing to his feet, he beat his head against the wall with such force that we both rushed upon him and tore him away to the center of the room. Sherlock Holmes pushed him down into the easy-chair, and, sitting beside him, patted his hand, and chatted with him in the easy, soothing tones which he knew so well how to employ.

"You have come to me to tell your story, have you not?" said he. "You are fatigued with your haste. Pray wait until you have recovered yourself, and then I shall be most happy to look into any little problem which you may submit to me."

The man sat for a minute or more with a heaving chest, fighting against his emotion. Then he passed his handkerchief over his brow, set his lips tight, and turned his face towards us.

"No doubt you think me mad?" said he.

"I see that you have had some great trouble," responded Holmes.

"I have!—a trouble which is enough to unseat my reason, so sudden and so terrible is it. Public disgrace I might have faced, although I am a man whose character has never yet borne a stain. Private affliction also is the lot of every man; but the two coming together, and in so frightful a form, have been enough to shake my very soul. Besides, it is not I alone. The very noblest in the land may suffer, unless some way be found out of this horrible affair."

"Pray compose yourself, sir," said Holmes, "and let me have a clear account of who you are, and what it is that has befallen you."

"My name," answered our visitor, "is probably familiar to your ears. I am Alexander Holder, of the banking firm of Holder & Stevenson, of Threadneedle Street."

The name was indeed well known to us as belonging in the senior partner in the second largest private banking concern in the City of London. What could have happened, then, to bring one of the foremost citizens of London to this most pitiable pass? We waited, all curiosity, until with another effort he braced himself to tell his story.

"I feel that time is of value," said he; "that is why I hastened here when the police inspector suggested that I should secure your cooperation. I came to Baker Street by the Underground,* and hurried from there on foot, for the cabs go slowly through this snow. That is why I was so out of breath, for I am a man who takes very little exercise. I feel better now, and I will put the facts before you as shortly and yet as clearly as I can.

Underground: subway

"It is, of course, well known to you that in a successful banking business as much depends upon our being able to find remunerative* investments for our funds as upon our increasing our connection and the number of our depositors. One of our most lucrative means of laying out money is in the shape of loans, where the security is unimpeachable.* We have done a good deal in this direction during the last few years, and there are many noble families to whom we have advanced large sums upon the security of their pictures, libraries, or plate.*

remunerative: well-paying
unimpeachable: unquestionable
plate: silver

"Yesterday morning I was seated in my office at the bank when a card was brought in to me by one of the clerks. I started* when I saw the name, for it was that of none other than—well, perhaps even to you I had better say no more than that it was a name which is a household word all over the earth—one of the highest, noblest, most exalted names in England. I was overwhelmed by the honor, and attempted, when he entered, to say so, but he plunged at once into business with the

air of a man who wishes to hurry quickly through a disagreeable task.

started: jumped

"'Mr. Holder,' said he, 'I have been informed that you are in the habit of advancing money.'

"'The firm does so when the security is good,' I answered.

"'It is absolutely essential to me,' said he, 'that I should have £50,000 at once. I could of course borrow so trifling a sum ten times over from my friends, but I much prefer to make it a matter of business, and to carry out that business myself. In my position you can readily understand that it is unwise to place one's self under obligations.'

"'For how long, may I ask, do you want this sum?' I asked.

"'Next Monday I have a large sum due to me, and I shall then most certainly repay what you advance, with whatever interest you think it right to charge. But it is very essential to me that the money should be paid at once.'

"'I should be happy to advance it without further parley from my own private purse,' said I, 'were it not that the strain would be rather more than it could bear. If, on the other hand, I am to do it in the name of the firm, then in justice to my partner I must insist that, even in your case, every businesslike precaution should be taken.'

"'I should much prefer to have it so,' said he, raising up a square, black morocco case which he had laid beside his chair. 'You have doubtless heard of the Beryl Coronet?'"

"'One of the most precious public possessions of the empire,'" said I.

"'Precisely.' He opened the case, and there, imbedded in soft, flesh-colored velvet, lay the magnificent piece of jewelry which he had named. 'There are thirty-nine enormous beryls,'* said he, 'and the price of the gold chasing* is incalculable. The lowest estimate

would put the worth of the coronet at double the sum which I have asked. I am prepared to leave it with you as my security.'

---

beryl: a clear mineral valued as a gemstone

chasing: decorated metal

"I took the precious case into my hands and looked in some perplexity from it to my illustrious client.

"'You doubt its value?' he asked.

"'Not at all. I only doubt—'

"'The propriety of my leaving it. You may set your mind at rest about that. I should not dream of doing so were it not absolutely certain that I should be able in four days to reclaim it. It is a pure matter of form. Is the security sufficient?'

"'Ample.'

"'You understand, Mr. Holder, that I am giving you a strong proof of the confidence which I have in you, founded upon all that I have heard of you. I rely upon you not only to be discreet and to refrain from all gossip upon the matter, but, above all, to preserve this coronet with every possible precaution, because I need not say that a great public scandal would be caused if any harm were to befall it. Any injury to it would be almost as serious as its complete loss, for there are no beryls in the world to match these, and it would be impossible to replace them. I leave it with you, however, with every confidence, and I shall call for it in person on Monday morning.'

"Seeing that my client was anxious to leave, I said no more; but, calling for my cashier, I ordered him to pay over fifty £1000 notes. When I was alone once more, however, with the precious case lying upon the table in front of me, I could not but think with some misgivings of the immense responsibility which it entailed upon me. There could be no doubt that, as it was a national possession, a horrible scandal would ensue if any misfortune should occur to it. I already regretted having

ever consented to take charge of it. However, it was too late to alter the matter now, so I locked it up in my private safe, and turned once more to my work.

"When evening came I felt that it would be an imprudence to leave so precious a thing in the office behind me. Bankers' safes had been forced before now, and why should not mine be? If so, how terrible would be the position in which I should find myself! I determined, therefore, that for the next few days I would always carry the case backward and forward with me, so that it might never be really out of my reach. With this intention, I called a cab, and drove out to my house at Streatham, carrying the jewel with me. I did not breathe freely until I had taken it upstairs and locked it in the bureau of my dressing-room.

"And now a word as to my household, Mr. Holmes, for I wish you to thoroughly understand the situation. My groom and my page sleep out of the house, and may be set aside altogether. I have three maid-servants who have been with me a number of years, and whose absolute reliability is quite above suspicion. Another, Lucy Parr, the second waiting-maid, has only been in my service a few months. She came with an excellent character, however, and has always given me satisfaction. She is a very pretty girl, and has attracted admirers who have occasionally hung about the place. That is the only drawback which we have found to her, but we believe her to be a thoroughly good girl in every way.

"So much for the servants. My family itself is so small that it will not take me long to describe it. I am a widower, and have an only son, Arthur. He has been a disappointment to me, Mr. Holmes—a grievous disappointment. I have no doubt that I am myself to blame. People tell me that I have spoiled him. Very likely I have. When my dear wife died I felt that he was all I had to love. I could not bear to see the smile fade even for a moment from his face. I have never denied him a wish. Perhaps it would have been better for both of us had I been sterner, but I meant it for the best.

"It was naturally my intention that he should succeed me in my business, but he was not of a business turn. He was wild, wayward, and, to speak the truth, I could not trust him in the handling of large sums of money. When he was young he became a member of an aristocratic club, and there, having charming manners, he was soon the intimate of a number of men with long purses and expensive habits. He learned to play heavily at cards and to squander money on the turf,* until he had again and again to come to me and implore me to give him an advance upon his allowance, that he might settle his debts of honor. He tried more than once to break away from the dangerous company which he was keeping, but each time the influence of his friend Sir George Burnwell was enough to draw him back again.

turf: horseracing

"And, indeed, I could not wonder that such a man as Sir George Burnwell should gain an influence over him, for he has frequently brought him to my house, and I have found myself that I could hardly resist the fascination of his manner. He is older than Arthur, a man of the world to his finger-tips, one who had been everywhere, seen everything, a brilliant talker, and a man of great personal beauty. Yet when I think of him in cold blood, far away from the glamor of his presence, I am convinced from his cynical speech, and the look which I have caught in his eyes, that he is one who should be deeply distrusted. So I think, and so, too, thinks my little Mary, who has a woman's quick insight into character.

"And now there is only she to be described. She is my niece; but when my brother died five years ago and left her alone in the world I adopted her, and have looked upon her ever since as my daughter. She is a sunbeam in my house—sweet, loving, beautiful, a wonderful manager and housekeeper, yet as tender and quiet and gentle as a woman could be. She is my right hand. I do not know what I could do without her. In only one matter has she ever gone against my wishes. Twice my boy has asked her to marry him, for he loves her devotedly, but each time she has refused him. I think that if any one could have drawn him into the right path it would have been she, and that his marriage might have changed his whole life; but now, alas! it is too late—for ever too late!

"Now, Mr. Holmes, you know the people who live under my roof, and I shall continue with my miserable story.

"When we were taking coffee in the drawing-room that night, after dinner, I told Arthur and Mary my experience, and of the precious treasure which we had under our roof, suppressing only the name of my client. Lucy Parr, who had brought in the coffee, had, I am sure, left the room; but I cannot swear that the door was closed. Mary and Arthur were much interested, and wished to see the famous coronet, but I thought it better not to disturb it.

"'Where have you put it?' asked Arthur.

"'In my own bureau.'

"'Well, I hope to goodness the house won't be burgled during the night,' said he.

"'It is locked up,' I answered.

"'Oh, any old key will fit that bureau. When I was a youngster I have opened it myself with the key of the box-room* cupboard.'

box-room: storeroom

"He often had a wild way of talking, so that I thought little of what he said. He followed me to my room, however, that night with a very grave face.

"'Look here, Dad,' said he, with his eyes cast down, 'can you let me have £200?'

"'No, I cannot!' I answered sharply. 'I have been far too generous with you in money matters.'

"'You have been very kind,' said he: 'but I must have this money, or else I can never show my face inside the club again.'

"'And a very good thing, too!' I cried.

"'Yes, but you would not have me leave it a dishonored man,' said he. 'I could not bear the disgrace. I must raise the money in some way, and if you will not let me have it, then I must try other means.'

"I was very angry, for this was the third demand during the month. 'You shall not have a farthing from me,' I cried; on which he bowed and left the room without another word.

"When he was gone I unlocked my bureau, made sure that my treasure was safe, and locked it again. Then I started to go round the house to see that all was secure— a duty which I usually leave to Mary, but which I thought it well to perform myself that night. As I came down the stairs I saw Mary herself at the side window of the hall, which she closed and fastened as I approached.

"'Tell me, Dad,' said she, looking, I thought, a little disturbed, 'did you give Lucy, the maid, leave to go out tonight?'

"'Certainly not.'

"'She came in just now by the back door. I have no doubt that she has only been to the side gate to see someone; but I think that it is hardly safe, and should be stopped.'

"'You must speak to her in the morning, or I will, if you prefer it. Are you sure that everything is fastened?'

"'Quite sure, Dad.'

"'Then, good-night.' I kissed her, and went up to my bedroom again, where I was soon asleep.

"I am endeavoring to tell you everything, Mr. Holmes, which may have any bearing upon the case, but I beg that you will question me upon any point which I do not make clear."

"On the contrary, your statement is singularly lucid."

"I come to a part of my story now in which I should wish to be particularly so. I am not a very heavy sleeper, and the anxiety in my mind tended, no doubt, to make me even less so than usual. About two in the morning, then, I was awakened by some sound in the house. It had ceased ere I was wide awake, but it had left an impression behind it as though a window had gently closed somewhere. I lay listening with all my ears. Suddenly, to my horror, there was a distinct sound of footsteps moving softly in the next room. I slipped out of bed, all palpitating with fear, and peeped round the corner of my dressing-room door.

"'Arthur!' I screamed, 'you villain! you thief! How dare you touch that coronet?'

"The gas was half up, as I had left it, and my unhappy boy, dressed only in his shirt and trousers, was standing beside the light, holding the coronet in his hands. He appeared to be wrenching at it, or bending it with all his strength. At my cry he dropped it from his grasp, and turned as pale as death. I snatched it up and examined it. One of the gold corners, with three of the beryls in it, was missing.

"'You blackguard!'* I shouted, beside myself with rage. 'You have destroyed it! You have dishonored me for ever! Where are the jewels which you have stolen?'

---

blackguard: villain

"'Stolen!' he cried.

"'Yes, you thief!' I roared, shaking him by the shoulder.

"'There are none missing. There cannot be any missing,' said he.

"'There are three missing. And you know where they are. Must I call you a liar as well as a thief? Did I not see you trying to tear off another piece?'

"'You have called me names enough,' said he; 'I will not stand it any longer. I shall not say another word about this business since you have chosen to insult me. I will leave your house in the morning and make my own way in the world.'

"'You shall leave it in the hands of the police!' I cried, half-mad with grief and rage. 'I shall have this matter probed to the bottom.'

"'You shall learn nothing from me,' said he, with a passion such as I should not have thought was in his nature. 'If you choose to call the police, let the police find what they can.'

"By this time the whole house was astir, for I had raised my voice in my anger. Mary was the first to rush into my room, and, at the sight of the coronet and of Arthur's face, she read the whole story, and, with a scream, fell down senseless on the ground. I sent the housemaid for the police, and put the investigation into their hands at once. When the inspector and a constable entered the house, Arthur, who had stood sullenly with his arms folded, asked me whether it was my intention to charge him with theft. I answered that it had ceased to be a private matter, but had become a public one, since the ruined coronet was national property. I was determined that the law should have its way in everything.

"'At least,' said he, 'you will not have me arrested at once. It would be to your advantage as well as mine if I might leave the house for five minutes.'

"'That you may get away, or perhaps that you may conceal what you have stolen,' said I. And then realizing the dreadful position in which I was placed, I implored him to re-member that not only my honor, but that of one who was far greater than I was at stake; and that he threatened to raise a scandal which would convulse the nation. He might avert* it all if he would but tell me what he had done with the three missing stones.

---

avert: avoid

"'You may as well face the matter,' said I; 'you have been caught in the act, and no confession could make your guilt more heinous.* If you but make reparation as is in your power, by telling us where the beryls are, all shall be forgiven and forgotten.'

---

heinous: evil

"'Keep your forgiveness for those who ask for it,' he answered, turning away from me, with a sneer. I saw that he was too hardened for any words of mine to influence him. There was but one way for it. I called in the inspector, and gave him into custody. A search was made at once, not only of his person, but of his room, and of every portion of the house where he could possibly have concealed the gems; but no trace of them could be found, nor would the wretched boy open his mouth for all our persuasions and our threats. This morning he was removed to a cell, and I, after going through all the police formalities, have hurried round to you, to implore you to use your skill in unraveling the matter. The police have openly confessed that they can at present make nothing of it. You may go to any expense which you think necessary. I have already offered a reward of £1000. What shall I do! I have lost my honor, my gems, and my son in one night. Oh, what shall I do!"

He put a hand on either side of his head, and rocked himself to and fro, droning to himself like a child whose grief has got beyond words.

Sherlock Holmes sat silent for some few minutes, with his brows knitted and his eyes fixed upon the fire.

"Do you receive much company?" he asked.

"None, save my partner with his family, and an occasional friend of Arthur's. Sir George Burnwell has been several times lately. No one else, I think."

"Do you go out much in society?"

"Arthur does. Mary and I stay at home. We neither of us care for it."

"That is unusual in a young girl."

"She is of a quiet nature. Besides, she is not so very young. She is four and twenty."

"This matter, from what you say, seems to have been a shock to her also."

"Terrible! She is even more affected than I."

"You have neither of you any doubt as to your son's guilt?"

"How can we have, when I saw him with my own eyes with the coronet in his hands."

"I hardly consider that a conclusive proof. Was the remainder of the coronet at all injured?"

"Yes, it was twisted."

"Do you not think, then, that he might have been trying to straighten it?"

"God bless you! You are doing what you can for him and for me. But it is too heavy a task. What was he doing there at all? If his purpose were innocent, why did he not say so?"

"Precisely. And if it were guilty, why did he not invent a lie? His silence appears to me to cut both ways. There are several singular points about the case. What did the police think of the noise which awoke you from your sleep?"

"They considered that it might be caused by Arthur's closing his bedroom door."

"A likely story! As if a man bent on felony would slam his door so as to wake a house-hold. What did they say, then, of the disappearance of these gems?"

"They are still sounding the planking and probing the furniture in the hope of finding them."

"Have they thought of looking outside the house?"

"Yes, they have shown extraordinary energy. The whole garden has already been minutely examined."

"Now, my dear sir," said Holmes, "is it not obvious to you now that this matter really strikes very much deeper than either you or the police were at first inclined to think? It appeared to you to be a simple case; to me it seems exceedingly complex. Consider what is involved by your theory. You suppose that your son came down from his bed, went, at great risk, to your dressing-room, opened your bureau, took out your coronet, broke off by main force a small portion of it, went off to some other place, concealed three gems out of the thirty-nine, with such skill that nobody can find them, and then returned with the other thirty-six into the room in which he exposed himself to the greatest danger of being discovered. I ask you now, is such a theory tenable?"*

---

tenable: reasonable

"But what other is there?" cried the banker, with a gesture of despair. "if his motives were innocent, why does he not explain them?"

"It is our task to find that out," replied Holmes; "so now, if you please, Mr. Holder, we will set off for Streatham together, and devote an hour to glancing a little more closely into details."

My friend insisted upon my accompanying them in their expedition, which I was eager enough to do, for my curiosity and sympathy were deeply stirred by the story to which we had listened. I confess that the guilt

of the banker's son appeared to me to be as obvious as it did to his unhappy father, but still I had such faith in Holmes's judgment that I felt that there must be some grounds for hope as long as he was dissatisfied with the accepted explanation. He hardly spoke a word the whole way out to the southern suburb, but sat with his chin upon his breast and his hat drawn over his eyes, sunk in the deepest thought. Our client appeared to have taken fresh heart at the little glimpse of hope which had been presented to him, and he even broke into a desultory* chat with me over his business affairs. A short railway journey and a shorter walk brought us to Fairbank, the modest residence of the great financier.

desultory: rambling

Fairbank was a good-sized square house of white stone, standing back a little from the road. A double carriage-sweep,* with a snow-clad lawn, stretched down in front to two large iron gates which closed the entrance.

On the right side was a small wooden thicket, which led into a narrow path between two neat hedges stretching from the road to the kitchen door, and forming the tradesmen's entrance. On the left ran a lane which led to the stables, and was not itself within the grounds at all, being a public, though little used, thoroughfare. Holmes left us standing at the door, and walked slowly all round the house, across the front, down the tradesmen's path, and so round by the garden behind into the stable lane. So long was he that Mr. Holder and I went into the dining-room and waited by the fire until he should return. We were sitting there in silence when the door opened and a young lady came in. She was rather above the middle height, slim, with dark hair and eyes, which seemed the darker against the absolute pallor of her skin. I do not think that I have ever seen such deadly paleness in a woman's face. Her lips, too, were bloodless, but her eyes were flushed with crying. As she swept silently into the room she impressed me with a greater sense of grief than the banker had done in the morning, and it was the more striking in her as she was evidently a woman of strong character, with immense capacity for self-restraint. Disregarding my presence, she went straight to her uncle, and passed her hand over his head with a sweet womanly caress.

double carriage-sweep: circular drive

"You have given orders that Arthur should be liberated, have you not, Dad?" she asked.

"No, no, my girl, the matter must be probed to the bottom."

"But I am so sure that he is innocent. You know what women's instincts are. I know that he has done no harm and that you will be sorry for having acted so harshly."

"Why is he silent, then, if he is innocent?"

"Who knows? Perhaps because he was so angry that you should suspect him."

"How could I help suspecting him, when I actually saw him with the coronet in his hand?"

"Oh, but he had only picked it up to look at it. Oh do, do take my word for it that he is innocent. Let the matter drop and say no more. It is so dreadful to think of our dear Arthur in prison!"

"I shall never let it drop until the gems are found—never, Mary! Your affection for Arthur blinds you as to the awful consequences to me. Far from hushing the thing up, I have brought a gentleman down from London to inquire more deeply into it."

"This gentleman?" she asked, facing round to me.

"No, his friend. He wished us to leave him alone. He is round in the stable lane now."

"The stable lane?" She raised her dark eyebrows. "What can he hope to find there? Ah! this, I suppose, is he. I trust, sir, that you will succeed in proving, what I feel sure is the truth, that my cousin Arthur is innocent of this crime."

"I fully share your opinion, and I trust, with you, that we may prove it," returned Holmes, going back to the mat to knock the snow from his shoes. "I believe I have the honor of addressing Miss Mary Holder. Might I ask you a question or two?"

"Pray do, sir, if it may help to clear this horrible affair up."

"You heard nothing yourself last night?"

"Nothing, until my uncle began to speak loudly. I heard that, and I came down."

"You shut up the windows and doors the night before. Did you fasten all the windows?"

"Yes."

"Were they all fastened this morning?"

"Yes."

"You have a maid who has a sweetheart? I think that you remarked to your uncle last night that she had been out to see him?"

"Yes, and she was the girl who waited in the drawing-room, and who may have heard uncle's remarks about the coronet."

"I see. You infer that she may have gone out to tell her sweetheart, and that the two may have planned the robbery."

"But what is the good of all these vague theories," cried the banker, impatiently, "when I have told you that I saw Arthur with the coronet in his hands?"

"Wait a little, Mr. Holder. We must come back to that. About this girl, Miss Holder. You saw her return by the kitchen door, I presume?"

"Yes; when I went to see if the door was fastened for the night I met her slipping in. I saw the man, too, in the gloom."

"Do you know him?"

"Oh yes; he is the green-grocer* who brings our vegetables round. His name is Francis Prosper."

green-grocer: produce man

"He stood," said Holmes, "to the left of the door—that is to say, farther up the path than is necessary to reach the door?"

"Yes, he did."

"And he is a man with a wooden leg?"

Something like fear sprang up in the young lady's expressive black eyes. "Why, you are like a magician," said she. "How do you know that?" She smiled, but there was no answering smile in Holmes's thin, eager face.

"I should be very glad now to go upstairs," said he. "I shall probably wish to go over the outside of the house again. Perhaps I had better take a look at the lower windows before I go up."

He walked swiftly round from one to the other, pausing only at the large one which looked from the hall onto the stable lane. This he opened, and made a very careful examination of the sill with his powerful magnifying lens. "Now we shall go upstairs," said he, at last.

The banker's dressing-room was a plainly furnished little chamber, with a gray carpet, a large bureau, and a long mirror. Holmes went to the bureau first and looked hard at the lock.

"Which key was used to open it?" he asked.

"That which my son himself indicated—that of the cupboard of the lumber-room."*

---

lumber-room: storeroom

"Have you it here?"

"That is it on the dressing-table."

Sherlock Holmes took it up and opened the bureau.

"It is a noiseless lock," said he. "It is no wonder that it did not wake you. This case, I presume, contains the coronet. We must have a look at it." He opened the case, and, taking out the diadem, he laid it upon the table. It was a magnificent specimen of the jeweler's

art, and the thirty-six stones were the finest that I have ever seen. At one side of the coronet was a cracked edge, where a corner holding three gems had been torn away.

"Now, Mr. Holder," said Holmes, "here is the corner which corresponds to that which has been so unfortunately lost. Might I beg that you will break it off."

The banker recoiled in horror. "I should not dream of trying." said he.

"Then I will." Holmes suddenly bent his strength upon it, but without result. "I feel it give a little," said he; "but, though I am exceptionally strong in the fingers, it would take me all my time to break it. An ordinary man could not do it. Now, what do you think would happen if I did break it, Mr. Holder? There would be a noise like a pistol shot. Do you tell me that all this happened within a few yards of your bed, and that you heard nothing of it?"

"I do not know what to think. It is all dark to me."

"But perhaps it may grow lighter as we go. What do you think, Miss Holder?"

"I confess that I still share my uncle's perplexity."

"Your son had no shoes or slippers on when you saw him?"

"He had nothing on save only his trousers and shirt."

"Thank you. We have certainly been favored with extraordinary luck during this inquiry, and it will be entirely our own fault if we do not succeed in clearing the matter up. With your permission, Mr. Holder, I shall now continue my investigations outside."

He went alone, at his own request, for he explained that any unnecessary footmarks might make his task more difficult. For an hour or more he was at work, returning at last with his feet heavy with snow and his features as inscrutable* as ever.

---

inscrutable: unrevealing of his thought

"I think that I have seen now all that there is to see, Mr. Holder," said he; "I can serve you best by returning to my rooms."

"But the gems, Mr Holmes. Where are they?"

"I cannot tell."

The banker wrung his hands. "I shall never see them again!" he cried. "And my son? You give me hopes?"

"My opinion is in no way altered."

"Then, what was this dark business which was acted in my house last night?"

"If you can call upon me at my Baker Street rooms tomorrow morning between nine and ten I shall be happy to do what I can to make it clearer. I understand that you give me *carte blanche** to act for you, provided only that I get back the gems, and that you place no limit on the sum I may draw."

carte blanche: unrestricted power

"I would give my fortune to have them back."

"Very good. I shall look into the matter between this and then. Good-bye; it is just possible that I may have to come over here again before evening."

It was obvious to me that my companion's mind was now made up about the case, although what his conclusions were was more than I could even dimly imagine. Several times during our homeward journey I endeavored to sound* him upon the point, but he always glided away to some other topic, until at last I gave it over in despair. It was not yet three when we found ourselves in our room once more. He hurried to his chamber, and was down again in a few minutes dressed as a common loafer.* With his collar turned up, his shiny, seedy coat, his red cravat,* and his worn boots, he was a perfect sample of the class.

sound: probe

loafer: tramp or beggar

cravat: necktie

"I think that this should do," said he, glancing into the glass above the fireplace. "I only wish that you could come with me, Watson, but I fear that it won't do. I may be on the trail in this matter, or I may be following a will-of-the-wisp,* but I shall soon know which it is. I hope that I may be back in a few hours." He cut a slice of beef from the joint upon the sideboard,* sandwiched it between two rounds of bread, and, thrusting this rude* meal into his pocket, he started off upon his expedition.

will-of-the-wisp: false hope

sideboard: buffet

rude: simple

I had just finished my tea when he returned, evidently in excellent spirits, swinging an old elastic-sided boot in his hand. He chucked it down into a corner and helped himself to a cup of tea.

"I only looked in as I passed," said he. "I am going right on."

"Where to?"

"Oh, to the other side of the West End. It may be some time before I get back. Don't wait up for me in case I should be late."

"How are you getting on?"

"Oh, so-so. Nothing to complain of. I have been out to Streatham since I saw you last, but I did not call at the house. It is a very sweet little problem, and I would not have missed it for a good deal. However, I must not sit gossiping here, but must get these disreputable clothes off and return to my highly respectable self."

I could see for his manner that he had stronger reasons for satisfaction than his words alone would imply. His eyes twinkled, and there was even a touch of color upon his sallow cheeks. He hastened upstairs, and a few minutes later I heard the slam of the hall door, which told me he was off once more upon his congenial hunt.

I waited until midnight, but there was no sign of his return, so I retired to my room. It was no uncommon thing for him to be away for days and nights on end when he was hot upon a scent, so that his lateness caused me no surprise. I do not know at what hour he came in, but when I came down to breakfast in the morning, there he was with a cup of coffee in one hand and the paper in the other, as fresh and trim as possible.

"You will excuse my beginning without you, Watson," said he; "but you remember that our client has rather an early appointment this morning."

"Why, it is after nine now," I answered. "I should not be surprised if that were he. I thought I heard a ring."

It was, indeed, our friend the financier. I was shocked by the change which had come over him, for his face, which was naturally of a broad and massive mould, was now pinched and fallen in, while his hair seemed to me at least a shade whiter. He entered with a weariness and lethargy* which was even more painful than his violence of the morning before, and he dropped heavily into the armchair which I pushed forward for him.

lethargy: dullness

"I do not know what I have done to be so severely tried," said he. "Only two days ago I was a happy and prosperous man, without a care in the world. Now I am left to a lonely and dishonored age. One sorrow comes close upon the heels of another. My niece, Mary, has deserted me."

"Deserted you?"

"Yes, Her bed this morning had not been slept in, her room was empty, and a note for me lay upon the hall table. I had said to her last night, in sorrow and not in anger, that if she had married my boy all might have been well with him. Perhaps it was thoughtless of me to say so. It is to that remark that she refers in this note:

"'My Dearest Uncle,

I feel that I have brought trouble upon you, and that if I had acted differently this terrible misfortune might never have occurred. I cannot, with this thought in my mind, ever again be happy under your roof, and I feel that I must leave you for ever. Do not worry about my future, for that is provided for; and, above all, do not search for me, for it will be fruitless labor and an ill-service to me. In life or in death, I am ever your loving

Mary.'

"What could she mean by that note, Mr. Holmes? Do you think it points to suicide?"

"No, no, nothing of the kind. It is perhaps the best possible solution. I trust, Mr. Holder, that you are nearing the end of your troubles."

"Ha! You say so! You have heard something, Mr. Holmes; you have learned something! Where are the gems?"

"You would not think £1000 apiece an excessive sum for them?"

"I would pay ten."

"That would be unnecessary. Three thousand will cover the matter. And there is a little reward, I fancy. Have you your checkbook? Here is a pen. Better make it out for £3000."

With a dazed face the banker made out the required check. Holmes walked over to his desk, took out a little triangular piece of gold with three gems in it, and threw it down upon the table.

With a shriek of joy our client clutched it up.

"You have it!" he gasped. "I am saved! I am saved!"

The reaction of joy was as passionate as his grief had been, and he hugged his recovered gems to his bosom.

"There is one other thing you owe, Mr. Holder," said Sherlock Holmes, rather sternly.

"Owe!" He caught up a pen. "Name the sum, and I will pay it."

"No, the debt is not to me. You owe a very humble apology to that noble lad, your son, who has carried himself in this matter as I should be proud to see my own son do, should I ever chance to have one."

"Then it was not Arthur who took them?"

"I told you yesterday, and I repeat today, that it was not."

"You are sure of it! Then let us hurry to him at once, to let him know that the truth is known."

"He knows already. When I had cleared it all up I had an interview with him, and, finding that he would not tell me the story, I told it to him, on which he had to confess that I was right, and to add the very few details which were not yet quite clear to me. Your news of this morning, however, may open his lips."

"For Heaven's sake, tell me, then, what is this extraordinary mystery!"

"I will do so, and I will show you the steps by which I reached it. And let me say to you, first, that which it is hardest for me to say and for you to hear: there has been an understanding between Sir George Burnwell and your niece Mary. They have now fled together."

"My Mary? Impossible!"

"It is, unfortunately, more than possible; it is certain. Neither you nor your son knew the true character of this man when you admitted him into your family circle. He is one of the most dangerous men in England—a ruined gambler, an absolutely desperate villain, a man without heart or conscience. Your niece knew nothing of such men. When he breathed his vows to her, as he had done to a hundred before her, she flattered herself that she alone had touched his heart. The devil knows best what he said, but at least she became his tool, and was in the habit of seeing him nearly every evening."

"I cannot, and I will not, believe it!" cried the banker, with an ashen face.

"I will tell you, then, what occurred in your house last night. Your niece, when you had, as she thought, gone to your room, slipped down and talked to her lover through the window which leads into the stable lane. His footmarks had pressed right through the snow, so long had he stood there. She told him of the coronet. His wicked lust for gold kindled at the news, and he bent her to his will. I have no doubt that she loved you, but there are women in whom the love of a lover extinguishes all other loves, and I think that she must have been one. She had hardly listened to his instructions when she saw you coming downstairs, on which she closed the window rapidly, and told you about one of the servants' escapade with her wooden-legged lover, which was all perfectly true.

"Your boy, Arthur, went to bed after his interview* with you, but he slept badly on account of his uneasiness about his club debts. In the middle of the night he heard a soft tread pass his door, so he rose, and looking out, was surprised to see his cousin walking very stealthily along the passage, until she disappeared into your dressing-room. Petrified with astonishment, the lad slipped on some clothes, and waited there in the dark to see what would come of this strange affair. Presently she emerged from the room again, and in the light of the passage-lamp your son saw that she carried the precious coronet in her hands. She passed down the stairs, and he, thrilling* with horror, ran along and slipped behind the curtain near your door, whence he could see what passed in the hall beneath. He saw her stealthily open the window, hand out the coronet to some one in the gloom, and then closing it once more hurry back to her room, passing quite close to where he stood hid behind the curtain.

interview: conversation

thrilling: shuddering

As long as she was on the scene he could not take any action without a horrible exposure of the woman whom he loved. But the instant that she was gone he realized how crushing a misfortune this would be for you, and how all-important it was to set

it right. He rushed down, just as he was, in his bare feet, opened the window, sprang out into the snow, and ran down the lane, where he could see a dark figure in the moonlight. Sir George Burnwell tried to get away, but Arthur caught him, and there was a struggle between them, your lad tugging at one side of the coronet, and his opponent at the other. In the scuffle, your son struck Sir George, and cut him over the eye. Then something suddenly snapped, and your son, finding that he had the coronet in his hands, rushed back, closed the window, ascended to your room, and had just observed that the coronet had been twisted in the struggle and was endeavoring to straighten it when you appeared upon the scene."

"Is it possible?" gasped the banker.

"You then roused his anger by calling him names at a moment when he felt that he had deserved your warmest thanks. He could not explain the true state of affairs without betraying one who certainly deserved little enough consideration at his hands. He took the more chivalrous view, however, and preserved her secret."

"And that was why she shrieked and fainted when she saw the coronet," cried Mr. Holder. "Oh, what a blind fool I have been! And his asking to be allowed to go out for five minutes! The dear fellow wanted to see if the missing piece were at the scene of the struggle. How cruelly I have misjudged him!"

"When I arrived at the house," continued Holmes, "I at once went very carefully round it to observe if there were any traces in the snow which might help me. I knew that none had fallen since the evening before, and also that there had been a strong frost to preserve impressions. I passed along the tradesmen's path, but found it all trampled down and indistinguishable. Just beyond it, however, at the far side of the kitchen door, a woman had stood and talked with a man, whose round impressions on one side showed that he had a wooden leg. I could even tell that they had been disturbed, for the woman had run back swiftly to the door, as was shown by the deep toe and light heel marks, while Wooden-Leg had waited a little, and then had gone away. I thought at the time that this might be the maid and her sweetheart of whom you had already spoken to me, and inquiry showed it was so. I passed round the garden without seeing anything more than random tracks, which I took to be the police; but when I got into the stable lane a very long and complex story was written in the snow in front of me.

"There was a double line of tracks of a booted man, and a second double line which I saw with delight belonged to a man with naked feet. I was at once convinced from what you had told me that the latter was your son. The first had walked both ways, but the other had run swiftly, and, as his tread was marked in places over the depression of the

boot, it was obvious that he had passed after the other. I followed them up, and found that they led to the hall window, where Boots had worn all the snow away while waiting. Then I walked to the other end, which was a hundred yards or more down the lane. I saw where Boots had faced round, where the snow was cut up as though there had been a struggle, and, finally, where a few drops of blood had fallen, to show me that I was not mistaken. Boots had then run down the lane, and another little smudge of blood showed that it was he who had been hurt. When he came to the highroad at the other end, I found that the pavement had been cleared, so there was an end to that clue.

"On entering the house, however, I examined, as you remember, the sill and framework of the hall window with my lens, and I could at once see that someone had passed out. I could distinguish the outline of an instep where the wet foot had been placed in coming in. I was then beginning to be able to form an opinion as to what had occurred. A man had waited outside the window, someone had brought the gems; the deed had been overseen by your son, he had pursued the thief, had struggled with him, they had each tugged at the coronet, their united strength causing injuries which neither alone could have effected. He had returned with the prize, but had left a fragment in the grasp of his opponent. So far I was clear. The question now was, who was the man, and who was it brought him the coronet?

"It is an old maxim of mine that when you have excluded the impossible, whatever remains, however improbable, must be the truth. Now, I knew that it was not you who had brought it down, so there only remained your niece and the maids. But if it were the maids, why should your son allow himself to be accused in their place? There could be no possible reason. As he loved his cousin, however, there was an excellent explanation why he should retain her secret—the more so as the secret was a disgraceful one. When I remembered that you had seen her at that window, and how she had fainted on seeing the coronet again, my conjecture became a certainty.

"And who could it be who was her confederate? A lover evidently, for who else could outweigh the love and gratitude which she must feel to you? I knew that you went out little, and that your circle of friends was a very limited one. But among them was Sir George Burnwell. I had heard of him before as being a man of evil reputation among women. It must have been he who wore those boots and retained the missing gems. Even though he knew that Arthur had discovered him, he might still flatter himself that he was

safe, for the lad could not say a word without compromising* his own family.

---
compromising: implicating

"Well, your own good sense will suggest what measures I took next. I went in the shape of a loafer to Sir George's house, managed to pick up an acquaintance with his valet, learned that his master had cut his head the night before, and, finally, at the expense of six shillings, made all sure by buying a pair of his cast-off shoes. With these I journeyed down to Streatham, and saw that they exactly fitted the tracks."

"I saw an ill-dressed vagabond in the lane yesterday evening," said Mr. Holder.

"Precisely. It was I. I found that I had my man, so I came home and changed my clothes. It was a delicate part which I had to play then, for I saw that a prosecution must be avoided to avert scandal, and I knew that so astute a villain would see that our hands were tied in the matter. I went and saw him. At first, of course, he denied everything. But when I gave him every particular that had occurred, he tried to bluster, and took down a life-preserver* from the wall. I knew my man, however, and I clapped a pistol to his head before he could strike. Then he became a little more reasonable. I told him that we would give him a price for the stones he held— £1000 apiece. That brought out the first signs of grief that he had shown. 'Why, dash it all!' said he, 'I've let them go at six hundred for the three!' I soon managed to get the address of the receiver who had them, on promising him that there would be no prosecution. Off I set to him, and after much chaffering* I got our stones at £1000 a piece. Then I looked in upon your son, told him that all was right, and eventually got to my bed about two o'clock, after what I may call a really hard day's work."

life-preserver: blackjack

chaffering: haggling

"A day which has saved England from a great public scandal," said the banker, rising. "Sir, I cannot find words to thank you, but you shall not find me ungrateful for what you have done. Your skill has indeed exceeded all that I have heard of it. And now I must fly to my dear boy to apologize to him for the wrong which I have done him. As to what you tell me of poor Mary, it goes to my very heart. Not even your skill can inform me where she is now."

"I think that we may safely say," returned Holmes, "that she is wherever Sir George Burnwell is. It is equally certain, too, that whatever her sins are, they will soon receive a more than sufficient punishment."

About the Story

1. When Watson first sees Mr. Holder on Baker Street, what does he deduce about the man? Does Holmes agree?

2. What is the cause of Mr. Holder's frenzied condition?

3. What specific details of Mr. Holder's story convince Holmes that Mr. Holder's son is innocent?

4. When does Doyle typically use the technique of flashback in the story, and what does his use of the technique accomplish?

5. What incident brings the story to a crisis?

6. Was the resolution satisfying? Why or why not?

About the Author

Sir Arthur Conan Doyle (1859–1930), the creator of the fictional detective Sherlock Holmes, was an amateur sleuth himself. Though Doyle solved several intricate cases, he did not make a profession of detective work. He was rather like the famous Watson in his stories, a medical doctor who also became a respected author. Finding that his fledgling medical practice was slow to develop, the young Doyle took to writing stories to fill spare time and bring in much-needed income. The popularity of the Holmes stories surprised and encouraged Doyle. He had viewed the stories as entertaining and profitable but unimportant compared to his more serious writing, which includes several

fine historical novels such as the enduringly popular *The White Company* (1891).

Doyle proved his reputation for being a man of great character and honor throughout his life, especially in his work as a military doctor. For his loyal service, which also included the writing of a pamphlet and several historical works, King Edward VII knighted Doyle in 1902. Sir Arthur Conan Doyle's popularity, both personal and literary, remains high today. His unforgettable Holmes, accompanied by the faithful Watson, is recognized worldwide as the epitome of the private detective, even by those who have never actually read a Sherlock Holmes story.

Rhyme

Perhaps the most recognized feature of poetry, rhyme is actually not a compulsory element of the genre. However, most poets utilize the tool of rhyme often and in a variety of ways. **Rhyme,** or **perfect rhyme** (the type most frequently used), consists of two or more words having identical sounds in the last stressed vowel and all of the sounds following that vowel (e.g., imagin*ation* and agit*ation*). However, poets also employ rhymes that are not exact matches. For example, **slant rhyme** is a common variant in which two words with similar but slightly mismatched sounds are paired (e.g., *star* and *door*). Likewise, **eye rhyme** refers to word pairs that are spelled alike but pronounced differently (e.g., *cough* and *bough*).

Rhyme can also be labeled according to its placement in a line of poetry. **End rhyme**, which falls at the end of corresponding poetic lines, is the standard form of rhyme; but **internal rhyme**, or rhyme occurring within a single line of poetry, is often used to good effect as well. End rhyme is common enough that some poetic forms even require a specific **rhyme scheme** (the poem's pattern of end rhyme). To find the rhyme scheme of a poem, each new end rhyme sound is labeled with a letter of the alphabet, beginning with *a*. The same letter is used again for every subsequent occurrence of that particular sound as end rhyme. Thus the rhyme scheme of the first stanza of "Allen-a-Dale" would be *aabbcc*. We will further examine rhyme scheme during our study of poetic forms later in this unit.

Allen-a-Dale

Sir Walter Scott

Allen-a-Dale has no fagot* for burning,
Allen-a-Dale has no furrow for turning,
Allen-a-Dale has no fleece for the spinning,
Yet Allen-a-Dale has red gold for the winning.
Come, read me my riddle! come, hearken my tale!   5
And tell me the craft of bold Allen-a-Dale.

The Baron of Ravensworth prances in pride,
And he views his domains upon Arkindale side.
The mere* for his net and the land for his game,   10
The chase for the wild and the park for the tame;
Yet the fish of the lake and the deer of the vale
Are less free to Lord Dacre than Allen-a-Dale!

fagot: bundle of twigs or sticks tied together

mere: a small lake

Allen-a-Dale was ne'er belted* a knight,
Though his spur be as sharp and his blade be as
   bright;
Allen-a-Dale is no baron or lord,   15
Yet twenty tall yeomen* will draw at his word;
And the best of our nobles his bonnet will vail*,
Who at Rere-cross on Stanmore meets Allen-a-Dale!

Allen-a-Dale to his wooing is come,
The mother, she asked of his household and home: 20
'Though the castle of Richmond stand fair on the hill,
"My hall," quoth bold Allen, "shows gallanter still;
'Tis the blue vault of heaven, with its crescent so pale
And with all its bright spangles!" said Allen-a-Dale.

The father was steel and the mother was stone;   25
They lifted the latch, and they bade him begone;
But loud, on the morrow, their wail and their cry!
He had laughed on the lass with his bonny black eye,
And she fled to the forest to hear a love-tale,
And the youth it was told by was Allen-a-Dale!

belted: made a knight

yeomen: *archaic*, a commoner who owns land

vail: remove in respect

About the Author

From the time he was a small boy, Scottish writer Sir Walter Scott (1771–1832) liked nothing better than to listen to stories of the turbulent times in Scotland's history. Encouraged at school by an excellent and capable teacher, Scott worked hard at his history lessons and even learned to read foreign languages so that he could enjoy the stories of different countries. Although he later became an apprentice to his father and continued in an uneventful law career, Scott's interest in literature became his true occupation. He traveled extensively in Scotland, gathering traditional songs and stories, and eventually published *The Minstrelsy of the Scottish Border*, a collection of Scottish ballads with Scott's commentary. His next book, a collection of traditional-style ballads, was, unlike the first, wholly original and launched Scott's professional career.

His more influential contribution was his single-handed invention and popularization of the historical novel. Admired throughout the world as well as in Britain, his anonymously written *Waverley* novels brought him a steady income and the nickname "Wizard of the North." They also set a new literary standard for the English novel. Some of Scott's historical novels take for their settings places other than Scotland. Two of his more popular novels were set in Europe: *Quentin Durward* in France and *Ivanhoe* in England during the reign of Richard the Lion-Hearted. Scott's stories have continued to enthrall audiences. In particular, *Ivanhoe* has been revived as an opera, two films, and numerous television adaptations.

Futility

Wilfred Owen

Move him into the sun—
Gently its touch awoke him once,
At home, whispering of fields unsown.
Always it woke him, even in France,
Until this morning and this snow.
If anything might rouse him now
The kind old sun will know.

Think how it wakes the seeds—
Woke once the clays of a cold star.
Are limbs, so dear-achieved, are sides
Full-nerved, still warm, too hard to stir?
Was it for this the clay grew tall?
—O what made fatuous* sunbeams toil
To break earth's sleep at all?

fatuous: unconsciously foolish

About the Author

The product of middle-class British society and a relatively unremarkable childhood, Wilfred Owen (1893–1918) nonetheless came to be recognized as the greatest poet of World War I. Owen became interested in writing poetry early in his life, but his family's straitened finances kept him from university studies. Determined to pursue his goal through self-education, Owen left England in 1913 to tutor in France. While there, he saw the outbreak of World War I and eventually enlisted in the British armed forces in 1915.

Diagnosed with shell shock and sent home in 1917, Owen met the poet Siegfried Sassoon during his hospital stay. Sassoon introduced Owen to other fine poets and encouraged him to write what he knew.

What Owen termed "war, and the pity of war" became his subject. He produced such poems as "Anthem for Doomed Youth" and *"Dulce et Decorum Est,"* which flouted the hypernationalistic fervor of many of his contemporaries. Though he became the voice of a generation scarred by war, Owen also reaches audiences untouched by the fighting because his poetry relates universal truths about humanity's condition. Unfortunately, the poet never knew of his success. After returning to duty in 1918, he was awarded the Military Cross for bravery at Amiens, only to be killed on November 4, seven days before the armistice. His works were published posthumously in 1920 as *Poems of Wilfred Owen.*

About the Poems

1. Allen-a-Dale wants to marry the woman he loves. Why do her parents object?

2. What does the poet seem to think of Allen-a-Dale? What mood does he convey?

3. What types of rhyme does "Allen-a-Dale" exhibit?

4. In "Futility," to whom do you think the "him" refers and from what does he need awakening?

5. In the poem "Futility," the speaker's attitude toward the sun seems to alter. How does it change, and what deeper change of heart does this process indicate?

6. In the final three lines of "Futility," what are *earth* and *clay* metaphors for?

7. Without repeating answers, identify in "Futility" an example of each of the following types of rhyme: end rhyme, perfect rhyme, slant rhyme, eye rhyme.

8. Taking into account the different types of rhyme you've learned, identify the rhyme scheme of Owen's poem.

In literature of a high caliber, artfulness becomes as important as precision in expressing ideas. A great writer can create artful (aesthetically pleasing) yet clear communication using a variety of techniques, such as imagery, figurative language, and sentence structure, to emphasize his message. Well-crafted writing begins with careful word choice. Writers may choose particular words not only for their meanings but also for their appeals to the senses, including the sounds and rhythm they evoke alone or in combination. For example, rhyme comprises individual words chosen for their combined visual or audio effect, whereas **onomatopoeia** employs words sounding like what they mean (e.g., *buzz* or *sip*). The following similar sound devices are utilized most often in poetry, but they may also surface in well-written prose.

Related to rhyme, **assonance** is the repetition of similar vowel sounds in a series of words. This device can evoke several effects. Writers often use it to emphasize the rhythm of a line or the importance of a word. For example, in Poe's "The Raven," assonance often appears in the stressed syllables of a line, in words that generally carry more significance. The following lines from the poem illustrate this practice through the repetition of the long *i* and *o* as well as the short *e* and *o* sounds.

> Ah, distinctly *I* remember, it was in the bleak December,
> And each separate dying ember wrought its ghost upon the floor.

Certain vowels are also thought to affect the mood of a poem. As a result, throughout "The Raven" Poe repeatedly used the long *o* sound in order to reinforce the poem's melancholy atmosphere.

> Eagerly I wished the morrow;—vainly I had sought to borrow
> From my books surcease of sorrow— sorrow for the lost Lenore.

Two additional devices utilize the consonant sounds of a word. **Alliteration**, the repetition of initial consonant sounds, appears often in prose as well as poetry. For example, the main points of outlines or speeches are often alliterated to help the audience retain ideas. **Consonance**, the repetition of terminal consonant sounds, and more rarely of internal consonants, also creates extra emphasis on the words involved. Like the vowel sounds of assonance, these repeated consonant sounds can create an almost onomatopoetic effect to the reader's ear. For example, the repeated use of "f" ("Fee! Fi! Fo! Fum!") creates a harsh sound whereas a repeated "s" or "l" ("She sells sea shells") is softer and smoother to the ear. A writer can thus use alliteration or consonance to elicit the reader reaction he wants. In repetition, these techniques can also provide unity and forward motion to a poem as their application often extends through more than one line. As you read through the remaining poems of the unit, take note of each poet's use of these devices; you will gain insight into the poet's intentions for the poem.

1. You have already examined Paul Gallico's use of effective imagery. Does he use any **onomatopoetic** words in his descriptions?

2. Can you find any examples of **alliteration** in "Allen-a-Dale"?

3. "Futility" incorporates **assonance** to create a certain mood. Which vowel is used repeatedly in prominent places throughout stanza one, and what mood do you think it communicates?

4. Reread stanza one of "Futility" and find three examples of word pairs in one line that use the same vowel.

5. Line 3 of "Futility" illustrates **consonance**. Explain how.

   Line 3—"At home, whispering of fields unsown"

Meter

In poetry, **meter**—the regular arrangement of stressed and unstressed syllables—creates the rhythm of a poem. **Scansion** refers to the process of identifying the two major features of meter in a particular poem. First, the **poetic foot** of a poem refers to the specific combination of two or three stressed (′) and/or unstressed syllables (⌣) that repeats throughout the poem's lines. There are six common metrical feet, the most common of which is the **iambic foot**, consisting of one unstressed and one stressed syllable, in that order. The rest are as follows: **trochaic foot** combines a stressed then an unstressed syllable; **anapestic foot** contains two unstressed then one stressed syllable; **dactylic foot** has one stressed then two unstressed syllables; **spondaic foot** repeats two stressed syllables; and **pyrrhic foot**, two unstressed syllables. A poet may vary the poetic foot in isolated instances in a metered poem, but one type should predominate. Second, the type of metrical line also conveys how many times the specific poetic foot repeats in each line. One foot per line is labeled monometer; two feet are called dimeter; three, trimeter; four, tetrameter; and so on. Thus, if there are five iambs in each line of a poem, that poem's meter is **iambic pentameter**. Though not all poems have regular rhythm, many traditional forms do demand a specific meter.

Meter not only gives structure to a poem but also can reinforce its content. For example, scanning "The Charge of the Light Brigade," Tennyson's poem about a famous cavalry charge, reveals a poetic foot that mimics the gallop of horses combined with a short line length to evoke a feeling of speed and urgency.

The Charge of the Light Brigade

Alfred, Lord Tennyson

Half a league, half a league,
Half a league onward,
All in the valley of Death
   Rode the six hundred.
"Forward the Light Brigade!   5
Charge for the guns!" he said.
Into the valley of Death
   Rode the six hundred.

"Forward, the Light Brigade!"
Was there a man dismay'd?   10
Not tho' the soldier knew
   Some one had blunder'd.
Theirs not to make reply,
Theirs not to reason why,
Theirs but to do and die.   15
Into the valley of Death
   Rode the six hundred.

Cannon to right of them,
Cannon to left of them,
Cannon in front of them   20
   Volley'd and thunder'd;
Storm'd at with shot and shell,
Boldly they rode and well,
Into the jaws of Death,
Into the mouth of hell   25
   Rode the six hundred.

Flash'd all their sabres bare,
Flash'd as they turn'd in air
Sabring the gunners there,
Charging an army, while   30
   All the world wonder'd.
Plunged in the battery-smoke
Right thro' the line they broke;
Cossack and Russian
Reel'd from the sabre-stroke   35
   Shatter'd and sunder'd.

Then they rode back, but not,
  Not the six hundred.

Cannon to right of them,
Cannon to left of them,   40
Cannon behind them
  Volley'd and thunder'd;
Storm'd at with shot and shell,
While horse and hero fell,
They that had fought so well   45
Came thro' the jaws of Death,
Back from the mouth of hell,
All that was left of them,
  Left of six hundred.

When can their glory fade?   50
O the wild charge they made!
  All the world wonder'd.
Honor the charge they made!
Honor the Light Brigade,
  Noble six hundred!   55

About the Author

Alfred, Lord Tennyson (1809–92) was born into a large family of noble descent but straitened circumstances. His father's mental instability produced a very volatile family life that Alfred was able to escape by entering the University of Cambridge. At college, Tennyson met many other men interested in literature and the arts and joined the Apostles, a club of intellectuals who gathered to discuss their ideas and enjoy good company. There he became close friends with Arthur H. Hallam. In 1833, harsh criticism of his first book of poetry added to the shock of Hallam's unexpected death led Tennyson to stop publishing for the next decade. The inner struggles resulting from Hallam's tragic death also eventually formed the foundation of Tennyson's masterpiece, *In Memoriam*, published in 1850.

In 1842, Tennyson finally began publishing poetry again, receiving much public acclaim. His resulting popularity earned him the coveted position of poet laureate of England when he was only forty-one years old. Four years later, he wrote the poem "The Charge of the Light Brigade," which reflects the Victorian high esteem for the virtues of duty, patriotism, and unquestioning obedience. Though some of his poetry reflects ideas and ideals admired by Christians, Tennyson rejected several essential Christian doctrines in favor of an optimistic faith in man's moral and scientific progress.

The Destruction of Sennacherib

GEORGE GORDON, LORD BYRON

The Assyrian* came down like a wolf on the fold,
And his cohorts* were gleaming in purple and gold;
And the sheen of their spears was like stars on the sea,
When the blue wave rolls nightly on deep Galilee.

Like the leaves of the forest when Summer is green,   5
That host with their banners at sunset were seen:
Like the leaves of the forest when Autumn hath
   blown,
That host on the morrow lay withered and strown.*

For the Angel of Death spread his wings on the blast,
And breathed in the face of the foe as he passed;   10
And the eyes of the sleepers waxed deadly and chill,
And their hearts but once heaved, and for ever grew still!

And there lay the steed with his nostril all wide,
But through it there rolled not the breath of his pride:
And the foam of his gasping lay white on the turf,   15
And cold as the spray of the rock-beating surf.

And there lay the rider distorted and pale,
With the dew on his brow, and the rust on his mail;
And the tents were all silent, the banners alone,
The lances unlifted, the trumpet unblown.   20

And the widows of Ashur* are loud in their wail,
And the idols are broke in the temple of Baal;*
And the might of the Gentile,* unsmote by the sword,
Hath melted like snow in the glance of the Lord!

The Assyrian: Sennacherib, ruler of Assyria in
  the seventh century BC
cohort: a division of an army
strown: scattered
Ashur: noted Assyrian city on the Tigris River
Baal: a major god in many ancient Near Eastern
  religions
Gentile: a non-Jew, used in reference here to
  Sennacherib

About the Author

George Gordon, Lord Byron (1788–1824) led a life as romantic as his poetry. When he was only ten years old, he inherited a Gothic mansion and the title of baron. Unfortunately, little wealth accompanied the title, and Byron and his mother struggled with poverty for many years. In addition to financial worries, Byron was self-conscious about his lame right leg.

Byron published his first book of verse, *Hours of Idleness*, when he was nineteen. This work was so poorly received that he composed a satire against his critics, which garnered more attention than his original book. After this attempt at writing, Byron traveled to the Near East with a friend. Inspired by the exotic foreign countries, Byron wrote a narrative poem entitled *Childe Harold's Pilgrimage*, the publication of which launched his social and literary career. Unfortunately, Byron's popularity was not a measure of his moral uprightness. His mistreatment of his wife, who eventually fled to her parents, combined with many other scandals, left Byron facing the growing disapproval of British society. In 1816 he left England permanently to escape public outrage.

Byron traveled to Switzerland, Italy, and Greece. He first turned his interests to Italian politics and the struggles of the Italian revolutionaries, but when this cause ceased to interest him, Byron promoted the cause of the Greek freedom fighters. Unhappily, before he had the opportunity to lend them his aid, he died of a fever at the age of thirty-six.

About the Poems

1. Although both Tennyson's and Byron's poems are serious narratives about specific historical events, which one would you say builds greater tension? Which one presents a mood of grandeur or awe?

2. What type of meter is used in "The Charge of the Light Brigade"? Why do you think Tennyson chose this meter?

3. What is the meter of "The Destruction of Sennacherib"? How does the effect of this meter differ from that of Tennyson's poem?

4. After Byron describes the stunning devastation of Sennacherib's forces for three stanzas, he concludes by mentioning God in the final line. What does this final line suggest about God?

Verse Forms

Verse refers broadly to compositions written in meter. The following three basic verse forms predominate in poetry and are defined by their use of both rhyme and meter. "The Eagle" by Tennyson is standard **rhymed verse**, having end rhyme and regular meter. The second poem, an excerpt from Shakespeare's *Julius Caesar*, illustrates the popular **blank verse**, unrhymed iambic pentameter. Blank verse is most like the natural rhythms of our speech; thus, Shakespeare could use this verse form in his drama and still maintain a conversational quality in his dialogue. The last poem in the group illustrates **free verse**: Sandburg's free verse poem has neither regular meter nor rhyme. Its rhythm, however, is more controlled, and the line length is shorter than it would be in ordinary prose.

The Eagle

ALFRED, LORD TENNYSON

He clasps the crag with crooked hands.
Close to the sun in lonely lands,
Ringed with the azure* world, he stands.

The wrinkled sea beneath him crawls,
He watches from his mountain walls,   5
And like a thunderbolt he falls.

azure: purplish blue

from *Julius Caesar*

WILLIAM SHAKESPEARE*

*For biographical information, see p. 321.

Cowards die many times before their deaths;
The valiant never taste of death but once.
Of all the wonders that I yet have heard,
It seems to me most strange that men should fear;
Seeing that death, a necessary end,   5
Will come when it will come.

Splinter

Carl Sandburg

The voice of the last cricket
across the first frost
is one kind of good-by.
It is so thin a splinter of singing.

About the Author

Carl August Sandburg (1878–1967) is internationally recognized for his free verse poetry celebrating America. Trained in the school of experience, Sandburg could express the dreams and desires of everyday people, having fought in the Spanish-American war, worked as an itinerant laborer and journalist in Chicago, and participated in Socialist causes supporting workers. Sandburg's career took off with the publication of his *Chicago Poems* in 1916. In addition to poetry, he went on to produce successful novels (for both adults and children), biographies, reports on important social issues, and collections of American music and folklore. Sandburg was twice awarded the Pulitzer Prize, in 1939 for his *Abraham Lincoln: The War Years* and in 1950 for his *Complete Poems*.

After achieving popularity as a writer, Sandburg traveled the country widely as a singer and guitarist, reciting his own poetry and becoming an American symbol in the process. His writing reveals his three great passions: faith in democracy and the working class, delight in nature and all honest beauty, and an affinity for realism. Unfortunately, Sandburg's firmly humanistic view of life led him to place his faith in people's innate goodness and capacity to adapt and succeed. Although Sandburg himself claimed affiliation with no particular religious view, he spoke against what he defined as "intolerance," viewing God as the father of all men.

About the Poems

1. How does Tennyson's description of the eagle differ from the description you may find in an encyclopedia?

2. The first five lines of Tennyson's poem are simple description. Line 6, however, adds action to the description. What does the simile "like a thunderbolt he falls" in line 6 convey?

3. In Shakespeare's excerpt from *Julius Caesar*, what is the meaning of Caesar's first line, "Cowards die many times before their deaths"?

4. Evaluate what Caesar says about death from the perspective of Hebrews 2:14–15.

5. Why do you think Sandburg chose to compare "voice of the last cricket" to "one kind of good-by"? What do you think could be the setting for the "good-by" Sandburg is describing in his poem?

Traditional Forms

Because of poetry's compressed nature, the overall structure of a poem is generally used to help convey meaning. As we have seen, the entire structure or form of a poem can comprise a number of features, such as meter and rhyme scheme. Over the centuries, specific poetic templates have evolved that restrict practitioners of those templates to a particular type of content as well as to a specific verse or stanza type.

Stanzas are divisions of a poem based on thought, meter, or rhyme and are usually recognized by the number of lines they contain. The most popular stanza forms are the couplet (two lines), the quatrain (four lines), the sestet (six lines), and the octave (eight lines). A poetic form may utilize one stanza type or combine several and may even specify a particular rhyme scheme for each. The poems in the following section will illustrate a number of traditional forms.

First, "Bonnie George Campbell" is a **ballad,** a narrative poem often derived from folklore and originally intended to be sung or recited. Ballads typically use quatrains (probably the most common stanza form), written in iambic trimeter or tetrameter and having an *abcb* rhyme scheme. "Bonnie George Campbell," like many ballads, also contains a **refrain,** a line or group of lines repeated throughout a poem.

Donne's "Holy Sonnet 10" and Shakespeare's "Sonnet 29" represent the sonnet form. A **sonnet** is a lyric (songlike) poem of fourteen lines. The two most common types of sonnets are the Italian (or Petrarchan) and the English (or Shakespearean). In an **Italian sonnet** the first eight lines (an octave, rhyming *abbaabba*) form a distinct unit of thought, and the last six lines (a sestet, rhyming variously with two or three new rhymes) form another. In an **English sonnet** the thought is usually distributed over three quatrains with a concluding couplet, the whole rhyming *ababcdcdefefgg*.

The next two poems in this group are haiku. **Haiku** is a Japanese form of poetry written to create vivid imagery that touches the reader's heart and/or enlightens his mind. Any significance to the image created is not stated but must be inferred by the reader. Traditional haiku comprises three lines, the first and last having five syllables and the middle, seven. The tone is often serious but can vary to playfulness.

Created in the style of Japanese haiku and tanka (a five-line poem), the **cinquain** ("November Night") is a quintet also focused on evocative imagery. The first line contains one stressed syllable; the second, two; the third, three; and the fourth, four. The fifth line, like the first, has only one stressed syllable. This form demands careful selection and placement of words to keep the rhythmic guidelines as well as the flow of the desired mental picture.

Two poems in the unit are shaped poems. In a **shaped poem** the author has, in addition to the normal challenges of writing poetry, the problem of arranging the sentences on the page to form a specific picture. As a result, these poems rarely follow any specific stanza or verse form. However, each poet's shaped image supports the subject of his poem.

As the traditional forms in this section illustrate, when using multiple elements of form, a poet accomplishes two main purposes: he can both organize his thoughts and intensify his poem's intended effect on or message to the reader.

Bonnie George Campbell

High upon Highlands*
And low upon Tay,*
Bonnie George Campbell
Rade out on a day.

Saddled and bridled   5
And gallant rade he:
Hame* cam his guid horse,
But never cam he.

Out cam his auld mither,
Greeting fu' sair,*   10
And out cam his bonnie bride,
Riving* her hair.

Saddled and bridled
And booted rade he:
Toom* hame cam the saddle,   15
But never cam he.

"My meadow lies green,
And my corn is unshorn,*
My barn is to build,
And my babe is unborn."   20

Saddled and bridled
And booted rade he:
Toom hame cam the saddle,
But never cam he.

Highlands: northern Scotland

Tay: a long river in the Scottish Highlands emptying into the North Sea

Hame: home

Greeting fu' sair: weeping greatly

Riving: tearing

Toom: empty

unshorn: grains unharvested

Holy Sonnet 10

JOHN DONNE

Death be not proud, though some have calléd thee
Mighty and dreadful, for thou art not so;
For those whom thou think'st thou dost overthrow
Die not, poor Death, nor yet canst thou kill me.
From rest and sleep, which but thy pictures be,   5
Much pleasure; then from thee much more must flow,
And soonest our best men with thee do go,
Rest of their bones, and soul's delivery.
Thou art slave to fate, chance, kings, and desperate
   men,
And dost with poison, war, and sickness dwell,   10
And poppy* or charms can make us sleep as well
And better than thy stroke; why swell'st thou* then?
One short sleep past, we wake eternally
And death shall be no more; Death, thou shalt die.

poppy: opium; in Donne's time, commonly used
   to cure insomnia

why swell'st thou: why do you become proud

— About the Author —

John Donne (1572–1631), a contemporary of William Shakespeare, was for most of his life a passionate, impetuous man. Born a Catholic in Protestant England, Donne was denied the social advancement he desired. Despite his sometimes profligate lifestyle, he did achieve a measure of success in government, only to earn society's censure by secretly marrying a girl without the consent of her father. The resulting loss of his position as well as the subsequent birth of twelve children (only seven of whom survived) kept Donne and his wife poverty-stricken for the next decade.

Nevertheless, these years solidified Donne's conversion to the Anglican Church and provided inspiration for new poetry as well as pamphlets on religious and social issues. Eventually, Donne took orders in the Church and became one of the most famous preachers of the day, eventually being appointed Dean of St. Paul's in London.

Donne's poetry is of the metaphysical school, using highly disparate comparisons and imagery to illuminate ideas. His central concerns were love and death. Though the poet's preoccupation with the latter probably sprang from the numerous deaths among his family and close friends, Donne did acknowledge death as the door through which one comes to God, an idea firmly grounded in his faith in Christ's atonement.

Sonnet 29

William Shakespeare

When, in disgrace with fortune and men's eyes,
I all alone beweep my outcast state,
And trouble deaf heaven with my bootless* cries,
And look upon myself, and curse my fate,
Wishing me like to one more rich in hope,   5
Featured like him, like him with friends possessed,
Desiring this man's art and that man's scope,
With what I most enjoy contented least;
Yet in these thoughts myself almost despising,
Haply I think on thee—and then my state,   10
Like to the lark at break of day arising
From sullen earth, sings hymns at heaven's gate;
For thy sweet love remembered such wealth brings
That then I scorn to change my state with kings.

bootless: useless

About the Author

Nearly four hundred years after his death, English poet and playwright William Shakespeare (1564–1616) remains beloved by audiences and readers around the world. Moreover, he is still considered one of the finest (if not the finest) English language writers of all time. Details of his life remain sketchy, but a few facts are clear. Born in the English town of Stratford-upon-Avon, Shakespeare was reared in an upper middle class family. He likely entered a "grammar school," receiving a solid education in Latin language and literature, a knowledge his poems and dramas would later reflect. At age eighteen, he married Anne Hathaway, with whom he had three children.

Shakespeare traveled to London sometime in his early twenties, eventually joining a theatrical company known as the Lord Chamberlain's Men. For nearly three decades, he served as an actor and writer for the company and was a stockholder in it. Among his most famous plays are *Hamlet*, *King Lear*, and *Romeo and Juliet*. In addition, he wrote 154 sonnets dealing with topics such as love, friendship, and death. Though Shakespeare was perhaps not a Christian himself, his works are based on an intellectually Christian worldview and reflect many biblical truths. His continuing popularity with people of many cultures attests to his works' bases in universal situations and themes.

A Haiku

Matsuo Bashō

TWO TRANSLATIONS

The lightning flashes!
And slashing through the darkness,
A night-heron's screech.

A lightning gleam:
into darkness travels
a night heron's scream.

About the Author

Matsuo Bashō (1644–94) is undoubtedly Japan's most highly revered poet of haiku. He was, in fact, instrumental in developing this unusual form. His writing is not limited to poetry, however. He also wrote literary criticism, numerous essays, and travelogues. In his travel diaries Bashō includes haiku written during lengthy trips he made throughout his native Japan.

Matsuo Bashō's father was a samurai, a member of the military class in ancient Japan. Bashō initially wanted to become a samurai like his father. But while he was still young, he became the personal servant of a young noble who inspired him to write poetry. After the death of his master, Bashō spent several years in the capital of Kyoto and then in Edo (Tokyo). While there he decided to make writing and the teaching of writing his vocation. Between teaching stints there, he set out on wandering journeys throughout the country. Bashō was a thoughtful, meditative, and upright person. His reputation as a teacher and a poet was well established during his lifetime and remains so today.

November Night

Adelaide Crapsey

Listen.
With faint dry sound,
Like steps of passing ghosts,
The leaves, frost-crisp'd, break from the trees
And fall.

About the Author

The contribution of Adelaide Crapsey (1878–1914) to poetry, though small in volume, is significant because of her invention of the cinquain, a compact yet highly expressive verse form. Instead of explicitly presenting her emotions on themes such as life, death, and change, Crapsey chose to organize sensory images into a compressed verse form that expresses her worldview.

Born in Rochester, New York, Adelaide Crapsey led a life as brief and concise as her poetry. She died when only thirty-six years old, after having taught English literature and history at a girls' school and also at Smith College. She followed her interests in archeology and English poetry until tuberculosis made these hobbies impossible. She devoted her later years to writing her own highly personalized cinquains. Most of these have been included in the first collection of her poems entitled *Verse*, which was published after her death. She also left an unfinished scholarly work, *Analysis of English Metrics*.

About the Poems

1. The ballad of "Bonnie George Campbell" is about the powerful Campbell clan of the western highlands. The Campbells were hated by all other clans; thus, they had to be fighters as well as tillers of the soil. This ballad shows clan rivalry from a woman's point of view. The facts are few but eloquently expressive. Notice the careful organization and the use of repetition with variation. What effect is produced by the repetition of the second stanza?

2. What is the rhyme scheme of Donne's "Holy Sonnet 10"? Based on your answer, which type of sonnet is it?

3. "Sonnet 29" is one of the many sonnets in which Shakespeare extols a friendship. As you learned in the introduction to Traditional Forms (p.318), the thought in an English sonnet is usually distributed over three quatrains and a concluding couplet. Sometimes, however, as in "Sonnet 29," a major break occurs after the eighth line, much like the manner of the Italian form. What prompts this sudden shift in thought and feeling? How is it an evidence of the power of love and a compliment to his friend?

4. Two different translators have interpreted Bashō's haiku comparing lightning and a night heron's cry. Which translation do you like better and why?

5. Which syllables are stressed in each line of Crapsey's cinquain?

6. Adelaide Crapsey took the Japanese ideal of concisely presented evocative images as inspiration for her cinquain form. In "November Night" did she succeed in creating a vivid image? What serious topic might she have meant to evoke with this image?

Having examined some artistic techniques that writers employ with individual words, you can now study some creative ways to structure word groups. Many of these techniques are based on some form of repetition. For example, **anaphora** is the repetition of specific words or phrases at the beginnings of lines or grammatical units. This practice emphasizes the repeated words and can allow a writer to extend a statement without losing audience comprehension. Dickens's famous beginning to *A Tale of Two Cities*—"*It was the* best of times, *it was the* worst of times, *it was the* age of wisdom, *it was the* age of foolishness, *it was the* epoch of belief, *it was the* epoch of incredulity"—is an excellent example of a long sentence using anaphora for clarity as well as for emphasis. Also, in both poetry and prose, anaphora can be used to enhance rhythm. For instance, Tennyson's "The Charge of the Light Brigade" employs anaphora in every stanza. In this context, the technique creates not only emphasis but also a rhythmic effect, combining with the short lines to create a driving beat of sound evoking an actual charge.

Another technique for arranging word groups is **parallelism**, or similarity in the structure of two or more phrases, clauses, or sentences. The main appeal of parallelism is its symmetry, which both satisfies readers' aesthetic senses and attracts attention to the content. Writers can exhibit parallelism in both grammar and thought. In fact, the Dickens quotation provides a fine example of grammatical parallelism as well as anaphora: each clause follows the same sentence pattern of subject ("it"), verb ("was"), article ("the"), predicate noun ("best"), prepositional phrase ("of times"). Parallelism of thought is less common in English language poetry. However, Hebrew poetry makes good use of this form, as the Bible clearly illustrates. Verses such as Proverbs 10:1—"A wise son maketh a glad father: but a foolish son is the heaviness of his mother"—display parallelism of two precisely contrasted ideas, whereas many like Proverbs 22:1—"A good name is rather to be chosen than great riches, and loving favour rather than silver and gold"—rephrase an idea for emphasis. An alternate form of parallelism is chiasmus. **Chiasmus** inverts the parallel structure, keeping the elements of the original phrase, clause, or sentence but reversing them in the following unit. For example, in Shakespeare's line from "Sonnet 29"—"With what I most enjoy contented least"—the final four words display chiasmus on a small scale (adverb, verb, verb, adverb).

1. According to the description in your text, what common feature of ballads exhibits repetition?

2. In this unit, two poems besides Tennyson's employ **anaphora**. Name one and explain what effect the anaphora might contribute to the poem.

3. Aside from the refrain, what parallel structures exist in "Bonnie George Campbell"? Cite an example and tell what effect **parallelism** might create in the poem.

4. The haiku form requires parallelism. What must be parallel?

5. You have already seen an example of **chiasmus** from "Sonnet 29." Line 6 contains another. Explain how this line shows chiasmus.

400-Meter Freestyle

Maxine Kumin

The gun full swing the swimmer catapults and cracks

s
i
x

     feet away onto that perfect glass he catches at

a
n
d

throws behind him scoop after scoop cunningly moving

t
h
e

water back to move him forward. Thrift is his wonderful

s
e
c

ret; he has schooled out all extravagance. No muscle

r
i
p

ples without compensation wrist cock to heel snap to

h
i
s

mobile mouth that siphons in the air that nurtures

h
i
m

at half an inch above sea level so to speak.

T
h
e

  astonishing whites of the soles of his feet rise

a
n
d

salute us on the turns. He flips, converts, and is gone

a
l
l
in one. We watch him for signs. His arms are steady at

t
h
e
catch, his cadent* feet tick in the stretch, they know

cadent: rhythmic

t
h
e
lesson well. Lungs know, too; he does not list for

a
i
r
he drives along on little sips carefully expended

b
u
t
 that plum red heart pumps hard cries hurt how soon

i
t
s
near one more and makes its final surge TIME: 4:25:9

About the Author

Maxine Kumin (b. 1925) is a contemporary American poet noted especially for her clear style and use of realistic imagery. Kumin generally frames her poetry with imagery of everyday life, emphasizing unsensational yet ever-present subjects such as personal relationships, nature, life, and death.

Kumin was born in Philadelphia, Pennsylvania, and attended Radcliffe College, Cambridge, Massachusetts. She has three children and lives in New Hampshire. Active in many scholarly and educational organizations, she has years of experience as a teacher and lecturer at some of the most prestigious American institutions. Although she has enjoyed success as a novelist and an author of children's books, her greatest achievements have been as a poet. In 1973 she won a Pulitzer Prize for *Up Country*, a collection of poetry. Since then she has continued to garner awards and recognition for her work, including a position as Consultant in Poetry to the Library of Congress (1981–82) and as poet laureate of New Hampshire (1989–1994).

The Altar

George Herbert

A broken altar, Lord, thy servant rears,
Made of a heart and cemented with tears;

Whose parts are as thy hand did frame;
No workman's tool hath touched the same

      A   heart   alone   5
      Is   such   a   stone
      As   nothing   but
      Thy power doth cut.
      Wherefore each part
      Of   my   hard   heart   10
      Meets in this frame
      To praise thy name;

That if I chance to hold my peace,
These stones to praise thee may not cease.

Oh, let thy blessed sacrifice be mine,   15
And sanctify this altar to be thine.

About the Author

George Herbert (1593–1633) was born into an aristocratic English family well known for its literary patronage. After earning two degrees at Cambridge, he received the prestigious position of public orator at age twenty-seven. From there, he entered Parliament and served for two years under the guidance of James I. Upon the king's death, Herbert revived his first ambition and entered a career in the Anglican Church in 1630. He devoted the last three years of his life to this calling, serving in the small parish of Bemerton. Although Herbert died at thirty-nine, he was already well beloved by his parishioners for his faithful ministry.

After Herbert's death a friend privately published *The Temple*, a volume of Herbert's verse. Its simple, musical style, originality in meter and form, and brilliant use of elaborate metaphor quickly attracted attention. Herbert's poems touch every area of Christian life, especially the surrender of the individual's will to God, reflecting his own surrender of personal ambition and the peace that resulted. This selection is taken from *The Temple*. Its twin themes are God's love and mercy and the proper human responses of contrition and sanctification.

About the Poems

1. In Kumin's poem, what is the arrangement of the lines on the page meant to show?

2. In addition to a swimming race, what might the title "400-Meter Freestyle" refer to?

3. What is the theme of Herbert's poem "The Altar"?

4. Herbert's poem is obviously shaped, but does he use any other methods of structure as well (such as rhyme, meter, etc.)? If so, identify them.

5. How are the last two lines of Herbert's poem emphasized by the poet? What do you think the purpose of this emphasis is?

Freedom to Breathe

Aleksandr Solzhenitsyn

translated by Michael Glenny

Prose poems unite the two most basic literary forms, drawing on both the meterless structure of prose and the sensory images, sound devices, and compressed speech of poetry. The following prose poem was written by Russian author Aleksandr Solzhenitsyn some time after his nearly decade-long imprisonment and internal exile by the Soviet government. As you read, examine the text closely to identify characteristics of both types of literature within this selection.

A shower fell in the night and now dark clouds drift across the sky, occasionally sprinkling a fine film of rain.

I stand under an apple tree in blossom and I breathe. Not only the apple tree but the grass round it glistens with moisture; words cannot describe the sweet fragrance that pervades the air. I inhale as deeply as I can, and the aroma invades my whole being; I breathe with my eyes open. I breathe with my eyes closed—I cannot say which gives me the greater pleasure.

This, I believe, is the single most precious freedom that prison takes away from us: the freedom to breathe freely, as I now can. No food on earth, no wine, not even a woman's kiss is sweeter to me than this air steeped in the fragrance of flowers, of moisture and freshness.

No matter that this is only a tiny garden, hemmed in by five-story houses like cages in a zoo. I cease to hear the motorcycles backfiring, radios whining, the burble of loudspeakers. As long as there is fresh air to breathe under an apple tree after a shower, we may survive a little longer.

About the Poem

1. What "single most precious freedom" does the poet say prison takes from the individual? Explain how prison takes away this freedom.

2. Identify three sensory images in the poem and the senses that each appeals to. How does the author use this imagery to communicate how the speaker feels?

3. Analyze the sound devices (assonance, alliteration, or consonance) appearing in this translation of the poem. Explain two of them.

4. What aspect of poetic form (pp. 318–19) can you find in "Freedom to Breathe"?

5. In the final paragraph, identify the simile that the poet uses to describe the place where he stands. What is ironic about this simile? According to the author, what signifies his freedom?

About the Author

Aleksandr Solzhenitsyn (1918–2008) was perhaps the most famous Russian author of the twentieth century. He was reared in poverty by his widowed mother; yet he eventually studied mathematics at Rostov State University while taking correspondence courses in literature at Moscow State University. During World War II he served as an officer and was twice decorated, but in 1945 he was imprisoned for writing a letter criticizing the wartime policies of dictator Joseph Stalin.

Until 1953 Solzhenitsyn remained in various Soviet prisons and labor camps and was then exiled to Kazakhstan for three years. During this time, Solzhenitsyn abandoned Marxism and began writing. In 1962 during a short period of loosened restrictions under Khrushchev, Solzhenitsyn published his first novel, *One Day in the Life of Ivan Denisovich*. Based on his experiences, the novel alerted the world to the reality of the extensive Soviet prison system.

As political repression continued to grow, Solzhenitsyn was harassed for his sustained criticism of government policies. Upon receiving the Nobel Prize for Literature in 1970, he declined to accept the prize personally, fearing he would be denied readmission to Russia. In 1973 Solzhenitsyn began to publish *The Gulag Archipelago*, his work narrating the history of the Soviet prison system from 1917 on. Its publication led to his deportation for treason in 1974. While settled in the United States and continuing his criticism of Soviet policies, the author also sharply denounced Western culture as decadent and spiritually empty. His citizenship restored in 1990, Solzhenitsyn and his wife returned to Russia in 1994. He wrote of his time in the West in a series of prose poems, *The Grain Between the Millstones*. In 2007, Russian President Vladimir Putin conferred on Solzhenitsyn the State Prize of the Russian Federation for his humanitarian work.

UNIT V REVIEW

REMEMBER THE TERMS

Review the following terms from the opening essay, "Structure," the poetry introductory paragraphs, and the Thinking Zone pages. Be prepared to discuss their meanings and uses.

plot
subplot
plot twist
surprise ending
exposition
inciting incident
rising action
crisis
climax
falling action
dénouement
chronological order
flashback
verse form
rhyme
perfect rhyme
slant rhyme
eye rhyme
end rhyme
internal rhyme
rhyme scheme
onomatopoeia
assonance
alliteration
consonance
meter

scansion
poetic foot
iambic foot
trochaic foot
anapestic foot
dactylic foot
spondaic foot
pyrrhic foot
iambic pentameter
verse
rhymed verse
blank verse
free verse
stanza
ballad
refrain
sonnet
Italian sonnet
English sonnet
haiku
cinquain
shaped poem
anaphora
parallelism
chiasmus

APPLY THE CONCEPTS

Answer the following questions about how the literary concepts you have studied are used in this unit.

1. Which character creates both the inciting incident and the resolution of John 9's plot?

2. In "The Necklace," which stage of the plot is left for the reader to infer?

3. Where does the crisis occur in "The Possibility of Evil"?

4. How does Gallico choose to arrange his essay "In the Ring with Jack Dempsey"?

5. Which story in the unit does not follow strict chronological order?

6. In "The Adventure of the Beryl Coronet," Holmes's examination of Holder's home takes place during what phase of the plot?

7. What technique is Doyle using when he has characters in "The Adventure of the Beryl Coronet" relate their previous experiences?

8. What common form of rhyme does "Allen-a-Dale" use exclusively?

9. What type of rhyme does Owen use most in "Futility"?

10. The first two lines of Tennyson's "The Charge of the Light Brigade" exhibit what specific type of parallelism?

11. Identify the meter of "The Charge of the Light Brigade" and define your terms.

12. In the following line from Byron's poem, what sound devices studied in the unit are present? Explain your answer.

    "And the sheen of their spears was like stars on the sea."

13. Which type of verse is Sandburg's "Splinter" written in? Explain your answer.

14. Like many ballads, "Bonnie George Campbell" repeats what element of form?

15. What difference in form exists between "Holy Sonnet 10" and "Sonnet 29"? Explain your answer.

16. What technique does line 8 of "Sonnet 29" illustrate?

    "With what I most enjoy contented least."

17. Though "Freedom to Breathe" is written in prose style (no meter, rhyme, or poetic lines), it still shows certain features of poetry. List two techniques Solzhenitsyn used that generally have more in common with poetry than with prose.

EVALUATE THE IDEAS

Identify each of the following statements as true or false. If false, rewrite the underlined portion of the sentence to make it true.

18. Plot refers <u>simply to the order in which a story's incidents occur</u>.

19. Subplots are <u>secondary plots of lesser importance than the main plot</u>.

20. The rising action of the plot <u>introduces us to the setting, the characters, and the situation</u>.

21. The crisis of the plot is <u>the point at which the plot reaches the moment of highest emotional intensity</u>.

22. Plot twists are <u>plot developments that violate the reader's expectations</u>.

23. The words *enough* and *though* are an example of <u>slant rhyme</u>.

24. The rhyme scheme of a poem refers to <u>its pattern of end rhyme</u>.

25. The repetition of initial consonant sounds in nearby words is known as <u>consonance</u>.

26. Sound devices are often used <u>to elicit certain emotional responses from the reader</u>.

27. Scanning a poem refers to finding its <u>rhyme scheme</u>.

28. The poetic foot most commonly used is the <u>spondaic</u>.

29. Poetry written in <u>unrhymed iambic tetrameter</u> is called blank verse.

30. Stanzas are <u>divisions of a poem based on thought, meter, or rhyme</u>.

31. A sonnet is <u>a dramatic poem of fourteen lines</u>.

32. The structure of both a haiku and a cinquain <u>is defined partly by syllables</u>.

33. Chiasmus could be called <u>inverted parallelism</u>.

34. The repetition of specific words or phrases <u>at the ends of lines or grammatical units</u> is known as anaphora.

35. Two common types of parallelism are <u>those of thought and of grammar</u>.

WRITE A RESPONSE

Completely answer each of the following questions.

36. In "The Necklace," the exposition of the plot is very important in establishing Mathilde's character. How did Maupassant relate Mathilde's defining characteristics?

37. "In the Ring with Jack Dempsey" could be called a cause-effect essay. What causes the main events described in the essay and what are the eventual effects of those events?

38. Like Doyle's mystery, Shirley Jackson's "The Possibility of Evil" is quite suspenseful; but in Jackson's story, the suspense begins, rather than ends, with the discovery of Miss Strangeworth's secret. After this revelation, why do we still feel uncertain until the story's end? Why does the ending still defy our expectations?

39. In both "The Charge of the Light Brigade" and "The Destruction of Sennacherib," armies prepare to battle. But while the first poem is full of action, in the second, the army is entirely passive save for the first stanza. How did the poets use the structural elements of their poems to reflect the presence or absence of action?

THE STARRY NIGHT

Vincent van Gogh

VI

❦ TONE ❦

Considered one of the world's greatest and most popular painters, Dutch artist Vincent van Gogh (1853–90) lived most of his short life in obscurity, supported financially by his brother and battling fits of depression and mental illness. Van Gogh was part of a group of postimpressionist painters, whose ranks included Paul Cézanne, Georges Seurat, Henri de Toulouse-Lautrec, and Paul Gauguin. The postimpressionists sought to communicate raw emotion by using fluid geometric shapes, expressive lines, and vibrant colors. Of his roughly eight hundred paintings, many critics consider The Starry Night *to be van Gogh's finest, a painting that showcases the striking colors and bold, prominent brushstrokes so typical of the artist's style.*

- ⚜ What part of the painting is your eye first drawn toward? Why?

- ⚜ Identify the dark object on the left of the painting. What mood does it seem to convey? What mood is conveyed by the village? How do these moods compare or contrast?

- ⚜ Van Gogh painted *The Starry Night* while confined to a mental asylum. What about the technique and the colors that van Gogh uses might suggest his tortured mental state?

The Starry Night, June 1889 (oil on canvas) by Vincent van Gogh (1853-90) © Museum of Modern Art, New York, USA/ The Bridgeman Art Library Nationality / copyright status: Dutch / out of copyright.

❧ TONE ❧

By now you have learned five of the fundamental elements that compose the study of literature: conflict, character, theme, point of view, and structure. Once defined, all of these elements become relatively easy to identify within a work; however, the sixth and final element, tone, requires careful reading and thoughtful analysis, for tone often presents itself indirectly and subtly to the reader. This essay will attempt to define tone and discuss its importance when studying a work of literature.

How Tone and Mood Differ

When discussing **tone** in literature, we are referring to the attitude of an author toward his or her subject. This aspect of literary study may sound very similar to the study of atmosphere, or mood, which was discussed in Unit 1. But it must be remembered that *atmosphere* describes the emotion that the reader is intended to share with the story's characters. While in some cases the two may be described in similar terms (especially in works with a first-person narrator), they do not refer to the same outlook.

To illustrate the difference, we can look at Tennyson's "The Charge of the Light Brigade" (p. 312). When considering the characters and their situation in combination with Tennyson's description of the troop bravely riding into fierce conflict, the *atmosphere* is one of suspense and impending doom. Tennyson's *tone* as he relates their story in poetic form, however, is one of admiration (he refers to them as the "noble six hundred"), albeit mixed with sadness for their having to make such a sacrifice.

How Tone Affects the Other Elements of Literature

Readers may arrive at an accurate idea of the author's tone by closely analyzing two aspects of the fundamental elements of literature: conflict and character. First, a reader should examine the conflict between the protagonist and antagonist and where each stands in the author's estimation. Re-examine the conflict in Hamlin Garland's "Under the Lion's Paw" (p. 52). The harsh conflicts that arise between Haskins and Butler and between Haskins and his land (man vs. man, man vs. nature) reflect Garland's pessimistic tone toward life and toward the policies guiding the ethics of United States landowners in this time in history.

Secondly, the extent to which a reader is led to sympathize with a character will reveal much about the author's tone. For example, consider "Neighbour Rosicky" from Unit 2 (p. 117). The author's depiction of a simple, selfless, peaceful man develops reader sympathy toward Rosicky and his lifestyle and is evidence of her compassionate tone toward him and what he stands for. If, for example, Cather had suddenly revealed at the end of the story that Rosicky is guilty of unspeakable crimes, the reader would be encouraged to view such a character as a hypocrite, and Cather's tone toward Rosicky's outwardly simple life would have been critical and possibly mocking.

How Word Choice Affects Tone

Tone is also affected by the words that an author chooses to tell his story. The use of certain figures of speech may also determine whether the tone of a piece is lighthearted or scathing. Some writers, for example, choose to employ a type of **overstatement** known as hyperbole in their writing. When using **hyperbole**, a writer obviously overstates a condition to make a point. Writers often use hyperbole for humorous purposes and to convey a lighter tone, although hyperbole may also be used to mock or criticize harshly. Arna Bontemps uses a form of condemning hyperbole when he states in his poem "A Black Man Talks of Reaping" that the sower has sown the entire United States with grain to no avail. On the other hand, a writer may also use **understatement** skillfully and subtly in order to lend significance to a statement or episode. Ironically, understatement often provides more emphasis than if one were to articulate explicitly the importance of a certain concept.

Another popular type of writing is satire. **Satire** may be defined as corrective ridicule. In satirical writing, the object of the scorn is usually someone or something outside of the literature itself.

Worldview and Moral Tone

The tone of a work is greatly affected by the author's worldview. (You read about worldview on pp. xiv–xv.) In brief, worldview is a person's perspective on life and the universe, consisting of a set of beliefs about where the world came from, what it means to be human, what the difference between good and evil is, and what reality is. An author's worldview will color his attitude toward his subject (tone), and this tone will influence how he presents his story to the reader. A discerning reader always attempts to discover an author's worldview so that he can make informed decisions about how to interpret the author's writing.

One important way to discern elements of an author's worldview is to consider moral tone. **Moral tone** (as different from tone) is the author's attitude toward matters of morality. To determine moral tone, think about how an author develops a story. What actions, attitudes, and events are rewarded in the plot? What kinds of characters are round, dynamic, and sympathetic? Becoming skilled at determining moral tone and worldview will enable you not just to read but also to interpret and critique what you read.

As you read the selections in this final unit, think about the manner in which the writers express themselves. How do they depict characters and conflicts? What are the word choices they employ in their descriptions? Carefully consider the authors' attitudes toward ethical questions, analyzing how these attitudes align with Scripture. Taking into account the attitudes toward the characters and the conflict, how might the moral tones of the various pieces be described?

The Crime

Sir Max Beerbohm

In this satirical essay Max Beerbohm hopes to make a point by poking fun at a certain type of person. What is the point that Beerbohm is trying to make? In conveying this message to the reader, what tone does Beerbohm adopt toward himself and toward the subject of his essay? Is it sharply critical, or is it lighthearted?

On a bleak wet stormy afternoon at the outset of last year's Spring, I was in a cottage, all alone, and knowing that I must be all alone till evening. It was a remote cottage, in a remote county, and had been "let furnished" by its owner. My spirits are easily affected by weather, and I hate solitude. And I dislike to be master of things that are not mine. "Be careful not to break us," say the glass and china. "You'd better not spill ink on *me*," growls the carpet. "None of your dog's-earing, thumb-marking, back-breaking tricks *here!*" snarl the books.

The books in this cottage looked particularly disagreeable—horrid little upstarts of this and that scarlet or cerulean* "series" of "standard" authors. Having gloomily surveyed them, I turned my back on them, and watched the rain streaming down the latticed window, whose panes seemed likely to be shattered at any moment by the wind. I have known men who constantly visit the Central Criminal Court, visit also the scenes where famous crimes were committed, form their own theories of those crimes, collect souvenirs of those crimes, and call themselves Criminologists. As for me, my interest in crime is, alas, merely morbid.* I did not know, as those others would doubtless have known, that the situation in which I found myself was precisely of the kind most conducive to the darkest deeds. I did but bemoan it, and think of Lear in the hovel on the heath.*

The wind howled in the chimney, and the rain had begun to sputter right down it, so that the fire was beginning to hiss in a very sinister manner. Suppose the fire went out! It looked as if it meant to. I snatched the pair of bellows that hung beside it. I plied them vigorously. "Now mind!—not *too* vigorously. We aren't yours!" they wheezed. I handled them more gently. But I did not release them till they had secured me a steady blaze. I sat down before that blaze. Despair had been warded off. Gloom, however, remained; and gloom grew. I felt that I should prefer any one's thoughts to mine. I rose, I returned to the books. A dozen or so of those which were on the lowest of the three shelves were full-sized, were octavo, looked as though they had been bought to be read. I would exercise my undoubted right to read one of them. Which of them? I gradually decided on a novel by a well-known writer whose works, though I had several times had the honor of meeting her, were known to me only by repute.

---

cerulean: sky blue

morbid: given to interest in disturbing subject matter, such as death or disease

Lear in the hovel on the heath: an allusion to Shakespeare's *King Lear*, in which Lear, self-exiled and on the verge of madness, takes refuge from a storm in a small, miserable dwelling in the wilderness

---

I knew nothing of them that was not good. The lady's "output" had not been at all huge, and it was agreed that her "level" was high. I had always gathered that the chief characteristic of her work was its great "vitality." The book in my hand was a third edition of her latest novel, and at the end of it were numerous press-notices, at which I glanced for conformation. "Immense vitality," yes, said one critic. "Full," said another, "of an intense vitality." "A book that will live," said a third. How on earth did he know that? I was, however, very willing to believe in the vitality of this writer for all present purposes. Vitality was a thing in which she herself, her talk, her glance, her gestures, abounded. She and they had been, I remembered, rather too much for me. The first time I met her, she said something that I lightly and mildly disputed. On no future occasion did I stem any opinion of hers. Not that she had been rude. Far from it. She had but in a sisterly, brotherly way, and yet in a way that was filially* eager too, asked me to explain my point. I did my best. She was all attention. But I was conscious that my best, under her eye, was not good. She was quick to help me: she said for me just what I had tried to say, and proceeded to show me just why it was wrong. I smiled the gallant smile of a man who regards women as all the more adorable because logic is *not* their strong point, bless them! She asked— not aggressively, but strenuously, as one who dearly loves a joke—what I was smiling at. Altogether, a chastening encounter; and my memory of it was tinged with a feeble resentment. How she had scored. No man likes to be worsted in argument by a woman. And I fancy that to be vanquished by a feminine writer is the kind of defeat least of all agreeable to a man who writes. A "sex war," we are often told, is to be one of the features of the world's future—women demanding the right to do men's work, and men refusing, resisting, counter-attacking. It seems likely

enough. One can believe anything of the world's future. Yet one conceives that not all men, if this particular evil come to pass, will stand packed shoulder to shoulder against all women. One does not feel that the dockers will be very bitter against such women as want to be miners, or the plumbers frown much upon the would-be steeple-jills. I myself have never had my sense of fitness jarred, nor a spark of animosity roused in me, by a woman practicing any of the fine arts—except the art of writing. That she should write a few little poems or *pensées,** or some impressions of a trip in a dahabieh* as far as (say) Biskra,* or even a short story or two, seems to me not wholly amiss, even though she do such things for publication. But that she should be an habitual, professional author, with a passion for her art, and a fountainpen and an agent, and sums down in advance of royalties on sales in Canada and Australia, and a profound knowledge of human character, and an essentially sane outlook, is somehow incongruous with my notions—my mistaken notions, if you will— of what she ought to be.

filially: in the manner of a child to a parent
pensées: maxims; proverbs
dahabieh: large sailing boat used by travelers on the Nile
Biskra: a city in northeast Algeria

"Has a profound knowledge of human character, and an essentially sane outlook" said one of the critics quoted at the end of the book I had chosen. The wind and the rain in the chimney had not abated, but the fire was bearing up bravely. So would I. I would read cheerfully and without prejudice. I poked the fire and, pushing my chair slightly back, lest the heat should warp the book's covers, began Chapter I. A woman sat writing in a summer-house at the end of a small garden that overlooked a great valley in Surrey. The description of her was calculated to make her very admirable—a thorough *woman,* not strictly beautiful, but likely to be thought beautiful by those who knew her well; not dressed as though she gave much heed to her clothes, but dressed in a fashion that exactly harmonised with her special type. Her pen "travelled" rapidly across the foolscap, and while it did so she was described in more and more detail. But at length she came to a "knotty point" in what she was writing. She paused, she pushed back the hair from her temples, she looked forth at the valley; and now the landscape was described, but not at all exhaustively, for the writer soon overcame her difficulty, and her pen travelled faster than ever, till suddenly there was a cry of "Mammy!" and in rushed a seven-year-old child, in conjunction with whom she was more than ever admirable; after which the narrative skipped back across eight years, and the woman became a girl giving as yet no token of future eminence in literature, but—I had an impulse which I obeyed almost before I was conscious of it.

Nobody could have been more surprised than I was at what I had done—done so neatly, so quietly and gently. The book stood closed, upright, with its back to me, just as on a book-shelf, behind the bars of the grate. There it was. And it gave forth, as the flames crept up the blue cloth sides of it, a pleasant though acrid* smell. My astonishment had passed, giving place to an exquisite satisfaction. How pottering* and fumbling a thing was even the best kind of written criticism! I understood the contempt felt by the man of action for the man of words. But what pleased me most was that at last, actually, I, at my age, I of all people, had committed a crime— was guilty of a crime. I had power to revoke it. I might write to my bookseller for an unburnt copy, and place it on the shelf where this one had stood—this gloriously glowing one. I would do nothing of the sort. What I had done I had done. I would wear forever on my conscience the white rose of theft and the red rose of arson. If hereafter the owner of this cottage happened to miss that volume— let him! If he were fool enough to write me about it, would I share my grand secret with him? No. Gently, with his poker, I prodded that volume further among the coals. The all-but-consumed binding shot forth little tongues of bright colour—flamelets of sapphire, amethyst, emerald. Charming! Could even the author herself not admire them? Perhaps. Poor woman!—I had scored now, scored so perfectly that I felt myself to be almost a brute while I poked off the loosened black outer pages and led the fire on to pages that were but pale brown.

acrid: strong, harsh

pottering: variant of *puttering*

These were quickly devoured. But it seemed to me whenever I left the fire to forage for itself it made little headway. I pushed the book over on its side. The flames closed on it, but presently, licking their lips, fell back, as though they had had enough. I took the tongs and put the book upright again, and raked it fore and aft. It seemed almost as thick as ever. With poker and tongs I carved it into two, three sections—the inner pages flashing white as when they were sent to the binders. Strange! Aforetime, a book was burnt now and again in the market-place by the common hangman. Was he, I wondered, paid by the hour? I had always supposed the thing quite easy for him—a bright little, brisk little conflagration, and so home. Perhaps other books were less resistant than this one? I began to feel that the critics were more right than they knew. Here was a book that had indeed an intense vitality, and an immense vitality. It was a book that would live—do what one might. I vowed it should not. I sub-divided it, spread it, redistributed

it. Ever and anon my eye would be caught by some sentence or fragment of a sentence in the midst of a charred page before the flames crept over it. "lways loathed you, but," I remember; and "ning. Tolstoi was right." Who had always loathed whom? And what, what, had Tolstoi been right about? I had an absurd but genuine desire to know. Too late! Confound the woman!—she was scoring again. I furiously drove her pages into the yawning crimson jaws of the coals. Those jaws had lately been golden. Soon, to my horror, they seemed to be growing grey. They seemed to be closing—on nothing. Flakes of black paper, full-sized layers of paper brown and white, began to hide them from me altogether. I sprinkled a boxful of wax matches. I resumed the bellows. I lunged with the poker. I held a newspaper over the whole grate. I did all that inspiration could suggest, or skill accomplish. Vainly. The fire went out—darkly, dismally, gradually, quite out.

How she had scored again! But she did not know it. I felt no bitterness against her as I lay back in my chair, inert, listening to the storm that was still raging. I blamed only myself. I had done wrong. The small room became very cold. Whose fault was that but my own? I had done wrong hastily, but had done it and been glad of it. I had not remembered the words a wise king wrote long ago, that the lamp of the wicked shall be put out, and that the way of transgressors is hard.

About the Essay

1. Whom or what is Beerbohm satirizing in his essay? Explain.

2. What clues does Beerbohm give you that helped you discern that his tone is humorous?

3. Identify one example of hyperbole and one example of understatement in the essay. How do these figures of speech affect Beerbohm's tone?

4. What do you believe to be Beerbohm's true attitude toward women writers? Support your answer with specific passages from the essay.

5. Why do you think the author chose to write the essay in first rather than third person?

About the Author

As a youth, Max Beerbohm (1872–1956) delighted in sitting by the window observing people and noting their unique characteristics. This youthful pastime later provided valuable material for his humorous caricatures of important people. His skill in exaggerating the peculiarities of public figures and his parodies of various literary styles were to make him famous. Though he was a drama critic for over a decade, it was as a witty artist and essayist that he achieved renown, both in his native England and in America.

Well-loved for his sophisticated manners and wry humor, Beerbohm moved in social and literary circles that included such avant-garde figures as Oscar Wilde and George Bernard Shaw. He himself, however, lived an uneventful and scandal-free life; in fact, unlike the narrator of "The Crime," Beerbohm was a homebody who enjoyed solitude. He was a moralist who kept his homilies well-mixed with humor. As the preceding essay illustrates, his most insightful criticisms were always the funniest; he was at his best when laughing at himself.

We Real Cool

GWENDOLYN BROOKS

Brooks has said that her inspiration for this poem came when passing a pool hall during school hours and seeing several teens inside. Watching them, she wondered how they felt about themselves. After you have read Brooks's poem, be prepared to discuss how Brooks manages to adopt a critical yet sympathetic tone toward her subjects. How does her tone affect the reader's response to her theme?

**The Pool Players.
Seven at The Golden Shovel.**

We real cool. We
Left school. We

Lurk late. We
Strike straight. We

Sing sin. We
Thin gin. We

Jazz June. We
Die soon.

About the Poem

1. What is unique about the poet's use of rhyme in this poem?

2. Identify one example of assonance and one example of alliteration within the poem.

3. Examine the poet's tone toward her subject. Does Brooks support the actions that she writes about or does she condemn them? Explain.

4. What emotion does Brooks feel toward these young people? How does her tone differ from Max Beerbohm's in his essay?

5. How may we say that "We Real Cool" demonstrates a positive moral tone?

About the Author

From the time she was young, Gwendolyn Brooks (1917–2000) expressed a keen interest in reading and writing. Her parents encouraged her pursuits, and her first poem, "Eventide," was published in *American Childhood* when she was only thirteen. Throughout her teenage years, Brooks periodically contributed poems to the *Chicago Defender*, a newspaper for African Americans living in the Chicago area.

After high school, Brooks enrolled in Wilson Junior College in Chicago and graduated in 1936; she then attended poetry workshops to sharpen her talents. Her first collection of poetry, *A Street in Bronzeville*, was published in 1945. Another volume of poems followed in 1949. *Annie Allen*, about a young black woman's formative years in Chicago, is the book that made her the first African-American writer to win the Pulitzer Prize. Her most popular poem, "We Real Cool," was published in

a magazine in the late 1950s and was featured in a collection entitled *The Bean Eaters*, published in 1960. Since then, the poem has been featured in many poetry collections and literature anthologies.

Much of Brooks's work deals with the lives and experiences of poor urban blacks. Her contemporaries have praised her attention to realistic detail and emotion in her portrayals of African-American urban life. Brooks continued to publish poetry collections throughout the rest of the twentieth century while earning multiple awards and accolades. In 1968 she was honored with the title of poet laureate of Illinois, and from 1985 to 1986 she served as the Library of Congress consultant in poetry. She taught extensively in colleges throughout the United States and received more than seventy-five honorary doctorates from distinguished universities before her death from cancer in 2000.

❧ THINKING ZONE ❧

As you read at the beginning of this unit, an author's choice of words will strengthen the overall tone that he intends for his writing to convey to the reader. Often, an author will make use of a figure of speech known as an **analogy**, or a comparison of one thing to another. You have already learned about two types of analogies—similes and metaphors—both of which help the reader to visualize what the author is trying to convey. Another type of implied analogy is the **allusion**, a reference within one work to something else, usually another work of art (such as a work of literature, a painting, or a film). Throughout the history of Western literature, the most common allusions have been to classical literature (Greek and Roman) and to the Bible. You have most likely noticed a number of biblical allusions as you have studied the stories in this book. When used appropriately, this type of analogy can help the reader to better understand what the writer is trying to convey. Rather than simply telling the reader the details, an author may use an allusion to artfully suggest what something is like. For instance, in the story "After the Battle," the character of Dave Joyce compares his and the wounded man's situation to that of Robinson Crusoe, a literary character stranded on an island who eventually meets and befriends a native named Friday. This allusion serves to further clarify how Joyce viewed the situation. An author may also use an allusion in a joking manner, such as commenting to a friend that he looks so serious as to be a model for *Amercian Gothic*.

Regardless of how a writer uses an allusion, he should always be careful to consider his audience when choosing works to reference. If the allusions are too obscure, the author may cloud rather than clarify his meaning. For an audience of individuals who are not native English speakers, for example, the meanings of allusions to certain works of English literature would be lost. Well-chosen allusions, however, may help the author to illustrate his point or simply enhance the pleasure of the work.

1. How might an author use **allusions** to clarify a message?

2. Why is it important for a writer to choose appropriate **analogies**?

3. To what Shakespearean work does Beerbohm allude in his satire "The Crime"? How does this allusion add to the humor of his piece?

4. What biblical allusions appear at the end of "The Crime"? Explain the significance of these allusions to the rest of the essay.

5. How is the tone of "We Real Cool" different from that of "The Crime"?

Cyrano de Bergerac

EDMOND ROSTAND

translated from the French
by Gladys Thomas and Mary F. Guillemard

Edmond Rostand's heroic comedy *Cyrano de Bergerac* (1897) is based partly on historical fact. The real Cyrano (1619–55) was a native of Paris, educated in Bergerac, Gascony. A soldier for ten years, twice severely wounded, Cyrano turned to a literary career. As a writer he showed extraordinary gifts. From one of his two plays, the great Molière (1622–73), a playwright widely known for his comedies, borrowed heavily. Cyrano's swaggering Bohemian lifestyle, imaginative genius, and oversized nose are the main historical ingredients of Rostand's heroic character.

Rostand's Cyrano retains these characteristics but also excels as poet, critic, fighter, and friend. He has no equal with either sword or pen, and his poetic elegance is spontaneous. His one physical defect—his ridiculously large nose—he regards with extreme sensitivity and, it would seem, with genuine pride. In only one area of his life does he let his weakness dishearten him. Because of his face he hesitates to woo the only woman he has ever loved—his cousin, the beautiful, witty Roxane. As you read this drama, examine it closely to see what tone the author adopts toward his characters, based on how he portrays their behavior and on the responses of other characters toward them.

Characters

Primary

Cyrano de Bergerac: (SEE-rah-no duh BARE-zhur-AHK)	*admired and feared Gascon, poet, and soldier*
Roxane: (rok SAN)	*Cyrano's beautiful cousin*
Duenna: (DWEH nuh)	*servant, companion, and chaperon to Roxane*
Christian de Neuvillette: (kree-STYAHN duh NUH-vee-LET)	*a cadet in love with Roxane*
Le Bret: (luh BREH)	*Cyrano's truest friend*
Ragueneau: (RAG-uh-NOH)	*poet, pastry cook, and friend of Cyrano*
Lignière: (lee NYARE)	*Christian's friend*
Count de Guiche: (KOUNT duh GEESH)	*nephew of Richelieu, rival to Christian, and enemy of Cyrano*
Viscount de Valvert: (VY-kount duh vahl-VARE)	*friend of de Guiche*
Montfleury: (MON flur EE)	*actor despised by Cyrano and in love with Roxane*
Lise: (LEEZ)	*wife of Ragueneau*
Carbon de Castel-Jaloux: (kar-BON duh kas-TEL-zha-LOO)	*Captain of Cyrano and Christian's regiment*

Secondary

Actors	Crowd	Officers
Actresses	Cuigy (KWEE zhee)	Pages
Apprentice	Friar	Pastry Cooks
Bellerose	Guardsman	Pickpockets
Bertrand the Fifer	Intellectuals	Pikemen
Bore	Jodelet (zho DLEH)	Poets
Boy	Lackeys	Porter
Brissaille (bree SAH yuh)	Lady	Sentinel
Buffet-Girl	Lord	Sister Claire
Burgher	Man of Letters	Sister Martha
Cadets	Marquises (mar KEEZ)	Troopers
Children	Mother Marguerite	Violinists
Citizen	(MAR gare EET)	Voice
Cooks	Musketeer	Woman

Act I

A Representation at the Hôtel de Bourgogne

The hall of the Hôtel de Bourgogne in 1640. A sort of tennis court arranged and decorated for a theatrical performance. As the curtain rises, the hall is in semidarkness and still empty. The chandeliers are lowered in the middle of the pit, ready to be lighted. A confusion of loud voices is heard outside the door. A TROOPER enters hastily.

SCENE i

PORTER   *(Following him)*
Hello there! Your money!

FIRST TROOPER   I enter gratis.*

gratis: free

PORTER   Why?

FIRST TROOPER   I am of the King's Household Cavalry.

PORTER   *(To a* SECOND TROOPER *who enters)*
You?

SECOND TROOPER   I pay nothing.

PORTER   How so?

SECOND TROOPER   I am a musketeer.

FIRST TROOPER   *(To the* SECOND TROOPER*)*
The play begins at two. The pit is empty.
Come, a bout with the foils to pass the time.   5
(They fence with the foils they have brought, while others also enter and engage in various types of revelry.)

CITIZEN   *(Enters, speaking with his son)*
A man might think he had fallen in a bad house here!
(He points with his cane to a drunkard.)
What with drunkards!
(One of the fencers, in breaking off, jostles him.)
       brawlers!
(He stumbles in the midst of some card players.)
       gamblers!

(He hurriedly pulls his son away.)
And this, my boy,
Is the theater where they played
Rotrou.*

BOY   Ay, and Corneille!*   10

PAGES   *(Dance in, holding hands and singing)*
               Tra, la, la, la, la, la, la, la . . .

PORTER   You pages there, none of your tricks!

FIRST PAGE   *(With wounded dignity)*
                                                    Oh, sir!
               Such a suspicion!
               (To the SECOND PAGE *the moment the* PORTER's *back is
               turned)*
                              Have you string?

SECOND PAGE   We can angle for wigs, then, up there i' th' gallery.

FIRST PAGE   *(Calling up to other* PAGES *in the top galleries)*
               You there! Have you peashooters?   15

THIRD PAGE   *(From above)*
               Ay, we do, and peas as well!
               (He blows and peppers them with peas.)

BOY   *(To his father)*
               What play do they give us?

CITIZEN   "Clorise."

BOY   Who may the author be?

CITIZEN   Master Balthazar Baro.
               (He goes arm in arm with his son.)
               Ah! You shall presently see some renowned actors.
               Montfleury . . .

VOICE   *(Shouting from the upper gallery)*
                              Light up, below there!   20

CITIZEN   Bellerose, Jodelet . . .

Rotrou: a major French neoclassical playwright of the seventeenth century
Corneille: French playwright who shared with Rotrou responsibility for increased prestige and respectability of the theater

PAGE	*(In the pit)* Here comes the buffet-girl!
BUFFET-GIRL	*(Taking her place behind the buffet)* Oranges, milk, Raspberry-water— *(A hubbub outside the door is heard. Enter a band of young* MARQUISES.*)*

FIRST MARQUIS	*(Seeing that the hall is half empty)*
	                              What now! So we make our entrance
	Like a pack of tradesmen—peaceably,
	Without disturbing the folk, or treading on 25
	Their toes! Oh, fie! Fie!
	(Recognizing some other gentlemen who have entered a little before him)
	                              Cuigy! Brissaille!
	(Greetings and embraces)

CUIGY	True to our word! We are here before the candles are lit.
SECOND MARQUIS	Nay, see, for your consolation, Marquis, they are coming to light up!
AUDIENCE	*(Welcoming the entrance of the lighter)* Ah! 30 *(The crowd forms into groups around the chandeliers as they are lit. Some people have taken their seats in the galleries.* LIGNIÈRE, *a disheveled but distinguished-looking person, enters arm in arm with* CHRISTIAN DE NEUVILLETTE. CHRISTIAN, *who is dressed elegantly but rather behind the fashion, seems preoccupied and keeps looking at the boxes.)*
CUIGY	Lignière!

LIGNIÈRE	*(Aside to* CHRISTIAN*)*
	May I introduce you?
	*(*CHRISTIAN *nods in assent)*
	                              Baron de Neuvillette.
	(Bows. To CUIGY*)*
	                                             This gentleman
	Comes from Touraine.

CHRISTIAN
                              Yes, I have scarce
Been twenty days in Paris; tomorrow I join
The Guards.

FIRST MARQUIS   *(Watching the people who are coming into the boxes)*
                         The wife of the
Chief justice!

BUFFET-GIRL
                              Oranges, milk . . .

VIOLINISTS   *(Tuning up)*
                              La—la—

CUIGY   *(To* CHRISTIAN, *pointing to the hall, which is filling fast)*
                              'Tis crowded.   5

CHRISTIAN   Yes, indeed.

FIRST MARQUIS
                         All the great world!
*(They recognize and name the elegantly dressed ladies
who enter the boxes, bowing low to them. The ladies
send smiles in answer.)*

BRISSAILLE   Madame de Chavigny . . .

CITIZEN   Boissat—Porcheres—Colomby—all names that will live!
'Tis fine!

LIGNIÈRE   *(Drawing* CHRISTIAN *aside)*
                    Friend, I but came here to give you pleasure.
The lady comes not. I will take my leave.

CHRISTIAN   *(Persuasively)*
                              No, no!   10
You, who are ballad-maker to court and city alike,
Can tell me better than any
Who the lady is for whom I die of love.
Stay yet awhile.
I, who am so poor of wit,   15
How dare I speak to her—how address her?
This language that they speak to-day—ay, and write—
     confounds me;
I am but an honest soldier, and timid withal. She has ever
     her place,
There, on the right—the empty box, see you!

LIGNIÈRE	*(Making as if to go)*
	<div style="text-align:right">I must go.</div>
CHRISTIAN	*(Detaining him)* Nay, stay.
LIGNIÈRE	*(Resigned)* I will remain awhile.
VOICES	*(From all the audience, joyously excited, at the entrance of a plump little man)*
	<div style="text-align:right">Ah! Ragueneau! 20</div>
LIGNIÈRE	*(To CHRISTIAN)* 'Tis the famous Ragueneau.
RAGUENEAU	*(Dressed in the Sunday clothes of a pastry cook, advances quickly to LIGNIÈRE)* Sir, have you seen Monsieur de Cyrano?
LIGNIÈRE	*(Introducing him to CHRISTIAN)* Ragueneau—the pastry-cook of the actors and the poets!
RAGUENEAU	*(Overcome)* You do me too great honour . . .
LIGNIÈRE	Nay, hold your peace, Maecenas that you are! 25
RAGUENEAU	True, these gentlemen employ me . . .
LIGNIÈRE	On credit! He is himself a poet of a pretty talent . . .
RAGUENEAU	So they tell me. 'Tis true that, for a little ode . . . 30
LIGNIÈRE	You give a tart . . .
RAGUENEAU	Oh!—a tartlet!
LIGNIÈRE	And as for the theatre, which you love?
RAGUENEAU	Oh! to distraction!

LIGNIÈRE	How pay you your tickets, ha?—with cakes. 35
	Your place, tonight, come tell me in my ear, what did it
	cost you?
RAGUENEAU	Four custards, and fifteen cream-puffs.
	(Looking around)
	Monsieur de Cyrano is not here? 'Tis strange.
LIGNIÈRE	Why so?
RAGUENEAU	Montfleury plays!
LIGNIÈRE	Ay, 'tis true
	That that hippopotamus is to take Phedon's part tonight; 40
	But what is that to Cyrano?
RAGUENEAU	How? Know you not? He has got a hot hate
	For Montfleury, and so has forbidden him strictly
	To show his face on the stage for one whole month.
LIGNIÈRE	Well?
RAGUENEAU	Montfleury will play!
CUIGY	He cannot hinder that. 45
RAGUENEAU	Oh! that I have come to see!
FIRST MARQUIS	Who is this Cyrano?
CUIGY	A fellow well skilled in all tricks of fencing.
SECOND MARQUIS	Is he of noble birth?
CUIGY	Ay, noble enough.
	He is a cadet in the Guards.
	(Pointing to a gentleman who is going up and down the
	hall as if searching for someone)
	But 'tis his friend Le Bret, yonder, who can best tell you. 50
	(He calls him.)
	Le Bret!
	(LE BRET comes toward them.)
	Seek you for de Bergerac?
LE BRET	Ay, I am uneasy . . .

CUIGY	Is it not true that he is the most excellent of men?
LE BRET	True that he is the choicest of earthly beings!
RAGUENEAU	Poet!
CUIGY	Soldier!
BRISSAILLE	Philosopher!
LE BRET	Musician!
LIGNIÈRE	And how fantastic a presence! 55

RAGUENEAU

Whimsical, wild, the maddest fighter
Of all the Gascon crew—with his triple-plumed hat
And six-pointed doublet*—
The sword-point sticking up 'neath
His mantle* like an insolent cocktail!* 60
And above his ruff he carries a nose!
Ah, good my lords, what a nose is his!
When one sees it one is fain to cry aloud,
"Nay! 'tis too much! He plays a joke on us!"
Then one laughs, says, "He will soon take it off." 65
But no! Monsieur de Bergerac always keeps it on.

doublet: a close-fitting jacket worn by European men between the fifteenth and seventeenth centuries

mantle: a cloak

cocktail: a horse of racing quality but not thoroughbred; its tail was often cut short

LE BRET

(Grimly)
He keeps it on—and cleaves in two
Any man who dares remark on it!

RAGUENEAU

His sword—'tis one half of the Fate's shears!*

Fate's shears: that which cuts the thread of life

FIRST MARQUIS

(Shrugging his shoulders)
He will not come!

RAGUENEAU

I say he will! 70
And I wager a fowl—à la Ragueneau.

MARQUIS

(Laughing)
Good!
(Murmurs of admiration in hall. ROXANE *has just appeared in her box. She seats herself in front, the* DUENNA* *at the back.* CHRISTIAN, *who is paying the* BUFFET-GIRL, *does not see her enter.)*

Duenna: elderly female companion, protector of a young woman

CHRISTIAN	*(Raising his head, sees* ROXANE, *and catches* LIGNIÈRE *by the arm)*
	'Tis she!
LIGNIÈRE	Ah! Is it she?
CHRISTIAN	Ay, tell me quick—I am afraid!
LIGNIÈRE	Madeleine Robin—Roxane, so called. Sophisticated, Of a subtle wit.
CHRISTIAN	Woe is me!
LIGNIÈRE	Unmarried, An orphan. The cousin of Cyrano, Of whom we were now speaking. *(At this moment an elegant nobleman, with a blue ribbon across his breast, enters the box and talks with* ROXANE, *standing.)*
CHRISTIAN	*(Starting)* Who is yonder man?
LIGNIÈRE	Ha! Ha! Count de Guiche. Enamored of her. Would fain marry Roxane! She will none of that; but de Guiche is powerful, And can persecute the daughter of a plain untitled gentleman. I have exposed this cunning plan of his, In a song which—Ho! he must rage at me! The end hits home. Listen! *(He gets up.)*
CHRISTIAN	No. Good night.
LIGNIÈRE	Where go you?
CHRISTIAN	To Monsieur de Guiche!
LIGNIÈRE	Have a care! It is he who will kill you. *(Nods toward* ROXANE, *who is watching* CHRISTIAN*)*
	Wait!
	She is looking at you.

75

80

85

CHRISTIAN
It is true!
(He stands looking at her. A group of PICKPOCKETS, *seeing him thus, draws near to him.)*

LIGNIÈRE
'Tis I who am going.
(He goes out.)

LE BRET
(Who has been all round the hall, coming back to RAGUENEAU *reassured)*
No sign of Cyrano.

RAGUENEAU
(Incredulously)
All the same . . .

LE BRET
A hope is left to me—
That he has not seen the playbill!

AUDIENCE
Begin! Begin!   90

FIRST MARQUIS
(Watching DE GUICHE, *who comes down from* ROXANE's *box and crosses the pit, surrounded by obsequious* NOBLE-MEN, *among them the* VISCOUNT DE VALVERT)
He pays a fine court, your de Guiche!

SECOND MARQUIS
Bah!
Another Gascon!

FIRST MARQUIS
Ay, but the cold, calculating Gascon—
That is the stuff success is made of!
Believe me, we had best make our bow to him.
(They go toward DE GUICHE.)*

CHRISTIAN
(Who is watching and listening, starts on hearing this name)
De Guiche! Ah! I will throw full in his face my . . .   5
(He puts his hand in his pocket, and finds there the hand of a PICKPOCKET *who is about to rob him. He turns round.)*
Hey? I was looking for a glove.

PICKPOCKET
(Smiling piteously)
And you find a hand.
(Changing his tone, quickly and in a whisper)
Let me but go, and I will deliver you a secret.

CHRISTIAN
(Still holding him)
What is it?

PICKPOCKET	Lignière . . . he who has just left you . . .
CHRISTIAN	*(Same play)*
	Well?
PICKPOCKET	His life is in peril. A song writ by him has given offense in high places— 10 And a hundred men—I am of them—are posted tonight . . .
CHRISTIAN	A hundred men! By whom posted?
PICKPOCKET	I may not say—a secret . . .
CHRISTIAN	Oh!
PICKPOCKET	*(With great dignity)* Of the profession.
CHRISTIAN	Where are they posted?
PICKPOCKET	At the Porte de Nesle. On his way homeward. Warn him. 15
CHRISTIAN	*(Starts for the door)* Good—I fly! Ah, the scoundrels! A hundred men 'gainst one! *(Looking lovingly at* ROXANE*)* Ah, to leave her! *(Looking with rage at* DE GUICHE*)* And him! But save Lignière I must! *(He hurries out.* DE GUICHE, *the* VISCOUNT, *and the* MARQUISES *have disappeared behind the curtain to take their places on the benches placed on the stage. The pit is quite full; the galleries and boxes are also crowded.)*
AUDIENCE	Begin the play!
CITIZEN	*(Whose wig is drawn up on the end of a string by a page in the upper gallery)* My wig!
AUDIENCE	He is bald! Bravo, pages—ha! ha! ha!

VOICE	Silence! 20
	(Three raps on the stage. The curtains part. THE MARQUISES *seated on their chairs to right and left of the stage, insolently posed. Backdrop representing a pastoral scene, bluish in tone. Four little crystal chandeliers light up the stage. The violins play softly.)*
LE BRET	*(In a low voice to* RAGUENEAU*)* Montfleury comes on the scene?
RAGUENEAU	*(Also in a low voice)* Ay, 'tis he who begins.
LE BRET	Cyrano is not here.
RAGUENEAU	I have lost my wager.
LE BRET	'Tis all The better! *(An air on the drone-pipes* is heard and* MONTFLEURY *enters, enormously stout, in shepherd's dress, a hat wreathed with roses drooping over one ear, blowing into ribboned drone-pipes.)* **drone-pipes:** bagpipes
AUDIENCE	*(Applauding)* Bravo, Montfleury! Montfleury!
MONTFLEURY	*(After bowing low, begins the part of Phédon)* "Happy are those who are far from the courts, In a solitary place, 25 Choosing for themselves a voluntary exile, And who—"
VOICE	*(From the middle of the pit)* Villain! Did I not forbid you To show your face here for a month? *(General stupor. Everyone turns round. Murmurs.)*
DIFFERENT VOICES	Hey? . . . What? . . . What is't?
CUIGY	'Tis he!
LE BRET	*(Terrified)* Cyrano!

VOICE	King of clowns! Leave the stage this instant!
AUDIENCE	Oh!
MONTFLEURY	But— 30
VOICE	Do you dare defy me?
DIFFERENT VOICES	*(From the pit and the boxes)* Peace! Enough! Play on, Montfleury—fear nothing!
MONTFLEURY	*(In a trembling voice)* "Happy are those who are far from the courts—"
VOICE	*(More fiercely)* Well? Chief of all the blackguards, must I come And give you a taste of my cane? 35 *(A hand holding a cane starts up over the heads of the spectators.)*
MONTFLEURY	*(In a voice that trembles more and more)* "Happy are those—" *(The cane is shaken.)*
VOICE	Off the stage!
AUDIENCE	Oh!
CYRANO	*(Appearing suddenly in the pit, standing on a chair, his arms crossed, his hat cocked fiercely, his mustache bristling, his nose terrible to see)* Ah! I shall be angry in a minute! *(Sensation)*
MONTFLEURY	*(To the* MARQUISES*)* Come to my help, my lords!
MARQUIS	*(Carelessly)* Go on! Go on!
CYRANO	Fat man, take warning! If you go on, I Shall feel myself constrained to cuff your face!

SCENE iv

MARQUIS	Have done!
CYRANO	And if these lords hold not their tongue, 5 Shall feel constrained to make them taste my cane!
MARQUISES	*(Rising)* Enough! Montfleury—
CYRANO	If he goes not quick I will cut off his ears and slit him up!
AUDIENCE	Montfleury! Montfleury! Come—Baro's play!
CYRANO	*(To those who are calling out)* I pray you have a care! If you go on 10 My scabbard soon will render up its blade! *(The circle round him widens.)*
AUDIENCE	*(Drawing back)* Take care!
CYRANO	*(To* MONTFLEURY*)* Be gone!
AUDIENCE	*(Chanting)* "La Clorise! La Clorise!"
CYRANO	Let me but hear once more that foolish rhyme, I slaughter every man of you.
CITIZEN	Oh! Samson?
CYRANO	Yes, Samson! 15 Will you lend your jawbone,* sir?
LADY	*(In the boxes)* Outrageous!
LORD	Scandalous!
CITIZEN	'Tis most annoying!
PAGE	Fair good sport!

Samson . . . jawbone: an allusion to Judges 15:15, which tells of Samson's killing of a thousand Philistines with the jawbone of an ass

AUDIENCE	Kss!* Montfleury . . . Kss: an onomatopoeic word for hissing
	Cyrano!
CYRANO	I order silence, all!

And challenge the whole pit collectively!
I write your names! Approach, young heroes, here!   20
Each in his turn! I cry the numbers out!
Now which of you will come to start the lists—
You, sir? No! You? No! The first duelist
Shall be dispatched by me with honors due!
Let all who long for death hold up their hands!   25
(A silence)
Modest? You fear to see my naked blade?
Not one name? Not one hand? Good, I proceed!
(Turning toward the stage, where MONTFLEURY *waits in an agony)*
The theater's too full, congested—I
Would clear it out. If not,
(Puts his hand on his sword)
The knife must act!

MONTFLEURY   I—

CYRANO   *(Leaves his chair, and settles himself in the middle of the circle which has formed)*
                    I will clap my hands thrice,   30
Thus, full moon! At the third clap, eclipse
Yourself!

AUDIENCE   *(Amused)*
                    Ah!

CYRANO   *(Clapping his hands)*
                    One!

MONTFLEURY   I—

VOICE   *(In the boxes)*
            Stay!

AUDIENCE   He stays . . . he goes . . . he stays . . .

MONTFLEURY   I think,
            Gentlemen—

CYRANO   Two!

MONTFLEURY   I think 'twere wisest—

CYRANO   Three!
                         (MONTFLEURY *disappears as through a trap. Tempest of*
                         laughs, whistling cries, etc.)

AUDIENCE   Coward! Come back!

CYRANO   *(Delighted, sits back in his chair, arms crossed)*
                                              Come back an' if you dare!   35

BOY   *(To* CYRANO*)*
                         But pray, sir, for what reason, say,
                         Hate you Montfleury?

CYRANO   *(Graciously, still seated)*
                                              Youthful gander, know
                         I have two reasons—either will suffice.
                         Primo.* An actor villainous! who mouths,   **primo:** first
                         And heaves up like a bucket from a well   40
                         The verses that should, bird-like, fly! Secundo*—   **secundo:** second
                         That is my secret.

CITIZEN   *(Behind him)*
                                              Shameful! You deprive us
                         Of the "Clorise"! I must insist—

CYRANO   *(Turning his chair toward the* CITIZEN, *respectfully)*
                                              Sir, the verses of
                         Old Baro are not worth a thought! I'm glad
                         To interrupt . . .

INTELLECTUALS   *(In the boxes)*
                                              Our Baro!   45
                         My dear! How dare he venture!

CYRANO   *(Turning his chair toward the boxes gallantly)*
                         Fairest ones, radiate, bloom, hold to our lips the cup
                         Of dreams intoxicating, Hebe-like!*   **Hebe-like (HEE bee-like):**
                         Or, when death strikes, charm death with your sweet   like the goddess of youth and
                             smiles;   spring; also like the cupbearer
                         Inspire our verse, but criticize it not!   50   to the Olympian gods

BELLEROSE   We must give back the entrance fees!

CYRANO	*(Turning his chair toward the stage)*
	Bellerose,
	You make the first intelligent remark!
	Would I rend Thespis'* sacred mantle? Nay!
	Catch then the purse I throw,
	(He rises and throws a bag on the stage.)
	And hold your peace!

Thespis (THES pis): Greek poet who originated Greek tragedy

AUDIENCE	*(Dazzled)*
	Ah! Oh!
JODELET	*(Catching the purse dexterously and weighing it)*
	At this price, you've authority 55
	To come each night, and stop "Clorise," sir!
AUDIENCE	Ho! Ho!
JODELET	E'en if you chase us in a pack!
BELLEROSE	Clear out the hall!
JODELET	Get you all gone at once!
	(The people begin to go out, while CYRANO *looks on with satisfaction. But the people soon stop on hearing the following scene and remain where they are. The women, who, with their mantles on, are already standing up in the boxes, stop to listen and finally reseat themselves.)*
LE BRET	*(To* CYRANO*)*
	'Tis mad!

SCENE V

BORE	*(Coming up to* CYRANO*)*
	The actor Montfleury! 'Tis shameful!
	Why, he's protected by the Duke of Candale!
	Have you a patron?
CYRANO	No!
BORE	No patron? But—
CYRANO	None!
BORE	What! No great lord to shield you with his name. . .

CYRANO	No, 5 I have told you twice! Must I repeat? Show your heels now! Or tell me why you stare so at my nose!
BORE	*(Staggered)* I . . .
CYRANO	*(Walking straight up to him)* Well, what is there strange?
BORE	*(Drawing back)* Your Grace Mistakes!
CYRANO	How now? 10 Is't soft and dangling, like a trunk?
BORE	*(Same play)* I never . . .
CYRANO	Is it crook'd, like an owl's beak?
BORE	I . . .
CYRANO	Do you see A wart upon the tip?
BORE	Nay . . .
CYRANO	Or a fly, that takes the air there? What is there to stare at? 15
BORE	But I was careful not to look—knew better.
CYRANO	And why not look at it, If you please?
BORE	I was . . .
CYRANO	Oh! It disgusts you!
BORE	Sir!

CYRANO	Its hue Unwholesome seems to you?
BORE	Sir!
CYRANO	Or its shape?　　　20
BORE	No, on the contrary!
CYRANO	Why then that air Disparaging?* Perchance you think it large?

disparaging: belittling

BORE	No, Small, quite small—minute!
CYRANO	Minute! What now? Accuse me of a thing ridiculous! Small—my nose?
BORE	Oh, no!
CYRANO	'Tis enormous!　　　25 Old flathead, empty-headed meddler, Know that I am proud to possess such an appendage. 'Tis well known, a big nose is indicative Of a soul affable, and kind, and courteous, Liberal, brave, just like myself, and such　　　30 As you can never dare to dream yourself, Rascal contemptible! For that witless face That my hand soon will come to cuff—is all As empty— *(He cuffs him.)*
BORE	Aie!
CYRANO	Of pride, of aspiration, Of feeling, poetry, of godlike spark,　　　35 Of all that appertains to my big nose, *(He turns him by the shoulders, suiting the action to the word)* As what my boot will shortly come and kick!
BORE	*(Running away)* Help! Call the Guard!

CYRANO	Take notice all
	Who find my visage's center ornament
	A thing to jest at, that it is my wont— 40
	An' if the jester's noble—ere we part
	To let him taste my steel, and not my boot!

DE GUICHE *(Who, with the* MARQUISES, *has come down from the stage)*

But he
Becomes a nuisance!

VISCOUNT *(Shrugging his shoulders)*
Swaggerer!

DE GUICHE Will no one put him down?

VISCOUNT No one? But wait!
I'll treat him to one of my quips! See here! 45
(He goes up to CYRANO, *who is watching him. With a conceited air)*
Sir, your nose is . . . hmm . . . it is . . . very big!

CYRANO *(Gravely)*
Very!

VISCOUNT *(Laughing)*
Ha!

CYRANO *(Coolly)*
Is that all?

VISCOUNT What do you mean?

CYRANO Ah no, young blade! That was a trifle short!
You might have said at least a hundred things
By varying the tone like this, suppose— 50
Aggressive: "Sir, if I had such a nose
I'd amputate it!" *Friendly:* "When you sup
It must annoy you, dipping in your cup;
You need a drinking-bowl of special shape!"
Descriptive: " 'Tis a rock! a peak! a cape! 55
A cape, forsooth! 'Tis a peninsula!"
Curious: "How serves that oblong capsular?
For scissor-sheath? Or pot to hold your ink?"
Gracious: "You love the little birds, I think?

I see you've managed with a fond research 60
To find their tiny claws a roomy perch!
Emphatic: "No wind, O majestic nose,
Can give THEE cold!—Save when the mistral blows!"
Dramatic: "When it bleeds, what a Red Sea!"
Admiring: "Sign for a perfumery!" 65
Such, my dear sir, is what you might have said,
Had you of wit or letters the least jot
And—had you had the necessary wit,
To serve me all the pleasantries I quote
Before this noble audience, e'en so 70
You would not have been let to utter one—
Nay, not the half or quarter of such jest!
I take them from myself all in good part,
But not from any other man that breathes!

DE GUICHE   *(Trying to draw away the dismayed* VISCOUNT*)*
Come away, Viscount!

VISCOUNT   *(Choking with rage)*
                              Hear his arrogance! 75
A country lout who . . . who . . . has got no gloves!
Who goes out without sleeve-knots, ribbons, lace!

CYRANO   True; all my elegances are within.
I do not prank* myself out, puppy-like;   **prank:** to decorate or
My toilet is more thorough, if less gay;   80   dress gaudily
I would not sally forth, a half-washed-out
Affront upon my cheek, a conscience
Yellow-eyed, bilious,* from its sodden sleep,   **bilious:** having a yellowish
A ruffled honor, scruples grimed and dull!   color because of a liver
I show no bravery of shining gems.   85   disorder; ill-tempered
Truth and Independence are my fluttering plumes.
'Tis not my form I lace to make me slim,
But brace my soul with efforts as with stays,
Covered with exploits, not with ribbon-knots.
My spirit bristling high like your mustaches, 90
I, traversing the crowds and chattering groups,
Make Truth ring bravely out like clash of spurs!

VISCOUNT   But, sir—

CYRANO   I wear no gloves? And what of that?
I had one, remnant of an old worn pair,
And, knowing not what else to do with it, 95
I threw it in the face of some young fool.

VISCOUNT	Base scoundrel! Rascally flat-footed lout!
CYRANO	*(Taking off his hat and bowing as if the* VISCOUNT *had introduced himself)* Ah? And I—Cyrano-Savinien-Hercule De Bergerac. *(Laughter)*
VISCOUNT	*(Angrily)* Buffoon!*
CYRANO	*(Calling out as if he had been seized with the cramp)* Aie! Aie!
VISCOUNT	*(Who was going away, turns back)* What on earth is the fellow saying now?
CYRANO	*(With grimaces of pain)* It must be moved—it's getting stiff, I vow— This comes of leaving it in idleness! Aie!
VISCOUNT	What ails you?
CYRANO	The cramp! Cramp in my sword!
VISCOUNT	*(Drawing his sword)* Good!
CYRANO	You shall feel a charming little stroke!
VISCOUNT	*(Contemptuously)* Poet!
CYRANO	Ay, poet, sir! In proof of which, While we fence, presto! All extempore I will compose a ballade.
VISCOUNT	A ballade?
CYRANO	Perhaps you know not what a ballade is.
VISCOUNT	But . . .

buffoon: clown

100

105

CYRANO	(Reciting, as if repeating a lesson)
	Know then that the ballade should contain
	Three eight-versed couplets—

| VISCOUNT | (Stamping) |
| | Oh! |

| CYRANO | (Still reciting) |
| | And a envoi* of four lines— |

envoi: concluding remarks that explain a poem or other work of literature

| VISCOUNT | You— | 110 |

| CYRANO | I'll make one while we fight |
| | And touch you at the final line. |

| VISCOUNT | No! |

CYRANO	No?
	(Declaiming)
	The duel in Hotel of Burgundy—fought
	By de Bergerac and a good-for-naught!

VISCOUNT	What may that be, if you please?
CYRANO	The title. 115

(A circle of curious spectators in the pit, the MARQUISES *and* OFFICERS *mingled with the common people, the* PAGES *climbing on each other's shoulders to see better. All the women standing up in the boxes. To the right,* DE GUICHE *and his retinue. Left,* LE BRET, RAGUENEAU, CYRANO, *etc.)*

CYRANO

(Shutting his eyes for a second)
Wait while I choose my rhymes. . . . I have them now!
(He suits the action to each word)
I gaily doff my plumed hat low,
And, freeing hand and heel,
My heavy mantle off I throw,
And I draw my polished steel;   120
Graceful as Phoebus,* round I wheel,
Alert as Scaramouch,*
A word in your ear, sir, I steal—
At the refrain's end, I touch!
(They engage.)
Better for you had you lain low;   125
Where skewer* my cock? In the heel?
In the heart, your ribbon blue below?
In the hip, and make you kneel?
Ho for the music of clashing steel!
What now? A hit? Not much!   130
'Twill be in the paunch the stroke I steal,
When, at the end, I touch.
Oh, for a rhyme, a rhyme in o?
You wriggle, starch-white, my eel?
A rhyme! A rhyme! The white feather you SHOW!   135
Tac! I parry* the point of your steel—
The point you hoped to make me feel;
I open the line, now clutch
Your spit*, Sir Scullion*—show your zeal!
At the envoi's end, I touch.   140
(He declaims solemnly.)
Envoi.
Prince, pray Heaven for your soul's weal!*
I move a pace—lo, such! And such!
Cut over—feint!* *(Thrusting)* What, ho! You reel?
(The VISCOUNT *staggers.* CYRANO *salutes.)*

Phoebus: (FEE bus): the Greek sun god; also named Apollo

Scaramouch (SKAR uh moosh): a character in Italian comedy who is a cowardly and foolish boaster

skewer: pierce with a metal pin

parry: evade

spit: a long rod used to impale and cook meat and vegetables
Scullion: a menial kitchen cook

weal: well-being

feint: a blow or thrust aimed at something other than the real object of the attack

At the envoi's end, I touch!
(*Acclamations. Applause in the boxes. Flowers and hand-
kerchiefs are thrown down. The* OFFICERS *surround*
CYRANO, *congratulating him.* RAGUENEAU *dances for joy.*
LE BRET *is happy but anxious. The* VISCOUNT'S *friends
hold him up and bear him away.*)

AUDIENCE   (*With one long shout*)
                    Ah!

TROOPER   'Tis superb!

WOMAN   A pretty stroke!

RAGUENEAU   A marvel!   145

MARQUIS   A novelty!

LE BRET   O madman!

AUDIENCE   (*Presses round* CYRANO. *Chorus of*)
                                Compliments!
                    Bravo! Let me congratulate! . . . Quite unsurpassed!

WOMAN'S VOICE   There is a hero for you!

MUSKETEER   (*Advancing to* CYRANO *with outstretched hand*)
                                Sir, permit;
                    Naught could be finer—I'm a judge I think;
                    I stamped, i' faith! to show my admiration!   150
                    (*He goes away.*)

CYRANO   (*To* CUIGY)
                    Who is that gentleman?

CUIGY   Why—D'Artagnan!*   **D'Artagnan:** one of the king's
                                                                  musketeers; main character in
                                                                  The Three Musketeers

LE BRET   (*To* CYRANO, *taking his arm*)
                    A word with you!

CYRANO   Wait; let the rabble go!
                    (*To* BELLEROSE)
                    May I stay?

BELLEROSE	*(Respectfully)*
	Without doubt!
	(Cries are heard outside.)
JODELET	*(Who has looked out)*
	They hoot Montfleury!
BELLEROSE	*(Solemnly)*
	Sic transit gloria!*
	(To the PORTERS*)*
	Sweep—close all, but leave the lights. 155
	We eat, but later on we must return
	For a rehearsal of tomorrow's farce.*
	*(*JODELET *and* BELLEROSE *go out, bowing low to* CYRANO*.)*
PORTER	*(To* CYRANO*)*
	You do not dine, sir?
CYRANO	No.
	(The PORTER *goes out.)*
LE BRET	Because? 160
CYRANO	*(Proudly)*
	Because . . .
	(Changing his tone as the PORTER *goes away)*
	I have no money!
LE BRET	*(With the action of throwing a bag)*
	How! The bag of crowns?
CYRANO	Paternal* bounty,
	In a day, thou'rt sped!
LE BRET	How much
	Till next month?
CYRANO	I have nothing left.
LE BRET	Folly!
CYRANO	But what a graceful action! Think!
BUFFET-GIRL	*(Coughing, behind her counter)*
	Hum!

sic transit gloria (Latin): "thus the glory passes away"

farce: a humorous play with exaggerated plot and characters

paternal: from a father

(CYRANO *and* LE BRET *turn. She comes timidly forward.*)
Sir, my heart mislikes to know you fast.
(*Showing the buffet*)
                                                    See,   165
All you need. Serve yourself!

CYRANO   (*Taking off his hat*)
                                        Gentle child,
Although my Gascon pride would else forbid
To take the least bestowal from your hands,
My fear of wounding you outweighs that pride,
And bids accept . . .
(*He goes to the buffet.*)
                            A trifle! These few grapes.   170
(*She offers him the whole bunch. He takes a few.*)
Nay, but this bunch!
(*She tries to give him wine, but he stops her.*)
                            A glass of water fair!
And half a macaroon!
(*He gives back the other half.*)

LE BRET   What foolery!

BUFFET-GIRL   Take something else!

CYRANO   I take your hand to kiss.
(*He kisses her hand as though she were a princess.*)

BUFFET-GIRL   Thank you, kind sir!
(*She curtsies.*)
                          Good night.
(*She goes out.*)

CYRANO   (*To* LE BRET)
                                        Now talk—I listen.

LE BRET   These fops, would-be belligerent,*   175   **belligerent:** hostile or
Will, if you heed them only, turn your head!   aggressive
Ask people of good sense if you would know
The effect of your fine insolence—

CYRANO   (*Finishing his macaroon*)
                                        Enormous!

LE BRET	You make too many enemies by far!
CYRANO	*(Eating his grapes)* How many think you I have made tonight?
LE BRET	Forty, no less, 180 Not counting ladies.
CYRANO	Count!
LE BRET	Montfleury first, The bourgeois, then de Guiche, The Viscount, Baro, the Academy* . . .
CYRANO	Enough! I am O'erjoyed!
LE BRET	But these strange ways, Where will they lead you, at the end?
CYRANO	I in a labyrinth* 185 Was lost—too many different paths to choose; I took one . . .
LE BRET	Which?
CYRANO	Oh! By far the simplest path. Decided to be admirable in all!
LE BRET	*(Shrugging his shoulders)* So be it! But the motive of your hate 190 To Montfleury—come, tell me!
CYRANO	*(Rising)* This Silenus,* Big-bellied, coarse, still deems himself a peril— A danger to the love of lovely ladies, And, while he sputters out his actor's part, Makes sheep's eyes at their boxes—goggling frog! 195 I hate him since the evening he presumed To raise his eyes to hers. . . . Meseemed I saw A slug crawl slavering o'er a flower's petals!

Academy: prestigious organization of French writers, churchmen, and military heroes who governed literary effort. The Academy had forty members. When one died, a new member would be elected to replace him.

185 **labyrinth:** a maze

Silenus (suh LAY nus): mythological satyr, jovial, fat, and drunken

LE BRET	*(Stupefied)*
	How now?
	What? Can it be . . . ?

CYRANO	*(Laughing bitterly)*
	That I should love?
	(Changing his tone, gravely)
	I love.

LE BRET   And may I know? You never said . . .   200

CYRANO Come now! bethink you! The fond hope to be
Beloved, e'en by some poor graceless lady,
Is, by this nose of mine for aye bereft me—
This lengthy nose which, go where'er I will,
Pokes yet a quarter-mile ahead of me;   205
But I may love—and who? 'Tis Fate's decree
I love the fairest—how were't otherwise?

LE BRET The fairest?

CYRANO   Ay, the fairest in the world,
Most brilliant—most refined—most golden-haired!

LE BRET Who is this lady?

CYRANO   She's a mortal danger,   210
All unsuspicious—full of charms unconscious,
Like a sweet perfumed rose—a snare of nature,
Within whose petals Cupid lurks in ambush!
He who has seen her smile has known perfection—
Instilling into trifles grace's essence,   215
Divinity in every careless gesture.

LE BRET All is clear!

CYRANO   As spider webs!

LE BRET Your cousin, Madeleine Robin?

CYRANO   Roxane!

LE BRET Well, but so much the better! Tell her so!
She saw your triumph here this very night!   220

CYRANO	Look well at me—then tell me, with what hope
	This vile protuberance* can inspire my heart!
	I do not lull me with illusions—yet
	At times I'm weak. In evening hours dim
	I enter some fair pleasance, perfumed sweet; 225
	With my poor ugly devil of a nose
	I scent spring's essence—in the silver rays
	I see some knight—a lady on his arm,
	And think, "To saunter thus 'neath the moonshine,
	I were fain to have my lady, too, beside!" 230
	Thought soars to ecstasy—O sudden fall!
	The shadow of my profile on the wall!

protuberance: something that is bulging or swollen

LE BRET	*(Tenderly)*
	My friend!

CYRANO	My friend, at times 'tis hard, 'tis bitter,
	To feel my loneliness—my own ill-favor . . .

LE BRET	*(Taking his hand)*
	You weep?

CYRANO	No, never! Think how vilely suited 235
	Adown this nose a tear its passage tracing!
	I never will, while of myself I'm master,
	Let the divinity of tears—their beauty
	Be wedded to such common ugly grossness.
	Nothing more solemn than a tear, sublimer; 240
	And I would not by weeping turn to laughter
	The grave emotion that a tear engenders!

LE BRET	What's love? A chance of Fortune!

CYRANO	*(Shaking his head)*
	Look I a Caesar to woo Cleopatra?*
	A Tito to aspire to Berenice?* 245

Cleopatra: queen of ancient Egypt
Berenice: the mistress of the Roman emperor Titus (Tito)

LE BRET	Your courage and your wit!
	The little maid who offered you
	Refreshment even now,
	Her eyes did not abhor you—you saw well!

CYRANO	*(Impressed)*
	True!

LE BRET	Well, how then? I saw Roxane herself Was death-pale as she watched the duel.	250
CYRANO	Pale?	
LE BRET	Her heart, her fancy, are already caught! Put it to th' touch!	
CYRANO	That she may mock my face? That is the one thing on this earth I fear!	
PORTER	*(Introducing someone to* CYRANO) Sir, someone asks for you . . .	
CYRANO	*(Seeing the* DUENNA) Her duenna!	255

SCENE vi

DUENNA	*(Curtsying)* I was bid ask you where a certain lady Could see her valiant cousin—but in secret.	
CYRANO	*(Overwhelmed)* See me?	
DUENNA	Ay, sir! She has somewhat to tell. Tomorrow, at the early blush of dawn, We go to hear mass at St. Roch. After—what place for a few minutes' speech?	5
CYRANO	*(Confused)* Where? Ah! At—the pastry-house of Ragueneau On the Rue St. Honore!	
DUENNA	*(Going)* Good. Be you there at seven.	
CYRANO	Without fail. *(The* DUENNA *goes out.)*	

SCENE vii

CYRANO	*(Falling into* LE BRET'S *arms)* A rendezvous—from her!	
LE BRET	You're sad no more!	

CYRANO	Ah! Let the world go burn!
	She knows I live!
LE BRET	Now you'll be calm, I hope?
CYRANO	*(Beside himself for joy)*
	Calm? I now calm?
	I'll be frenetic, frantic—raving mad! 5
	Oh, for an army to attack! A host!
	I've ten hearts in my breast; a score of arms;
	No dwarfs to cleave in twain!
	(Wildly)
	No! Giants now!
	(For a few moments the shadows of the ACTORS have been moving on the stage; whispers are heard—the rehearsal is beginning. The violinists are in their places.)
VOICE	*(From the stage)*
	Hollo there! Silence! We rehearse!
CYRANO	*(Laughing)*
	We go!
	(He moves away. By the big door enter CUIGY, BRISSAILLE, some OFFICERS, and LIGNIÈRE.)
CUIGY	Cyrano!
CYRANO	Well, what now?
CUIGY	A lusty thrush 10
	They're bringing you!
CYRANO	*(Recognizing him)*
	Lignière! What has chanced?
CUIGY	He seeks you!
BRISSAILLE	He dare not go home!
CYRANO	Why not?
LIGNIÈRE	*(In a husky voice, showing him a crumpled letter)*
	This letter warns me . . . that a hundred men . . .
	Revenge that threatens me . . . that song, you know—
	At the Porte de Nesle. To get to my own house 15

I must pass there . . . I dare not! Give me leave
To sleep tonight beneath your roof! Allow—

CYRANO

A hundred men? You'll sleep in your own bed!

LIGNIÈRE

(Frightened)
But—

CYRANO

*(In a terrible voice, showing him the lighted lantern held
by the Porter, who is listening curiously)*
　　　Take the lantern.
(Lignière seizes it.)
　　　　　　　Let us start! I swear
That I will make your bed tonight myself!　　　　　20
(To the Officers)
Follow; some stay behind, as witnesses!

CUIGY

A hundred!

CYRANO

　　　　　Less tonight would be too few!
March!
(To the Officers)
　　　Gentlemen, when you shall see me charge,
Bear me no succor, none, whate'er the odds.
*(The Actors and Actresses in their costumes have come
down from the stage and are listening.)*

ACTRESS

(To the others)
　　　　　　　　　　　But why
A hundred men 'gainst one poor rhymer?　　　　25

ALL

To the Porte de Nesle!

CYRANO

(Standing on the threshold)
　　　　　Ay, to the Porte de Nesle!
(Turning to the Actress)
Did you not ask, young lady, for what cause
Against this rhymer fivescore men were sent?
(He draws his sword; then, calmly)
　　　　　　　　　'Twas that
They knew him for a friend of mine!
*(He goes out. LIGNIÈRE first after him, then the ACTRESSES
on the OFFICERS' arms, and then the ACTORS. The proces-
sion starts to the sound of the violins and in the faint light
of the candles.)*
　　　Curtain

About the Drama

1. What is Rostand's tone toward the activity that occurs early in the play? Explain. How does his tone toward the revelers differ from his tone toward Cyrano?

2. How do the following characters describe de Guiche?
   Lignière (p. 357)
   First Marquis (p. 358)

3. How do the following characters describe Cyrano?
   Lignière (p. 356)
   Ragueneau (pp. 356)
   Le Bret (pp. 356)

4. How do de Guiche and Cyrano differ?

5. Read Cyrano's speech about Roxane on page 377. How does his love for Roxane differ from Christian's?

Act II

The Poets' Eating-House

RAGUENEAU'S cook and pastry shop. The street, seen vaguely through the glass panes in the door at the back, is gray in the first light of dawn. Tables are covered with trays of cakes and rolls; others with chairs placed about them are set for guests. A small table in a corner is covered with papers. As the curtain rises, RAGUENEAU is seated there. He is writing poetry.

RAGUENEAU	*(Ceasing to write and raising his head)*	**SCENE i**
	Aurora's silver rays begin to glint e'en now on the copper pans,	
	And thou, O Ragueneau! must perforce stifle in thy breast the God of Song!	
	Anon shall come the hour of the lute!	
	Now 'tis the hour of the oven!	
	(He rises. To a COOK*)*	
	You, make that sauce longer, 'tis too short! 5	
COOK	How much too short?	
RAGUENEAU	Three feet.	
	(He passes on farther.)	

COOK	What means he?

RAGUENEAU	(Before the fire)
	My muse,* retire, lest thy bright eyes be reddened by the
	    fagot's blaze!
	(To a COOK, showing him some loaves)
	You have put the cleft o' th' loaves in the wrong place;
	Know you not that the caesura* should be between the
	    hemistiches?*
	(To another, showing him an unfinished pastry)
	To this palace of paste you must add the roof.
	(To a young APPRENTICE holding a dish covered by a napkin)
	And you?

APPRENTICE	(Advances) Master, I thought of your tastes, and made this, Which will please you, I hope.
RAGUENEAU	A lyre!
APPRENTICE	'Tis of brioche pastry.
RAGUENEAU	With conserved fruits.
APPRENTICE	The strings, see, are of sugar. (LISE enters; RAGUENEAU shows the lyre to LISE, with a languid air.)
RAGUENEAU	Is it not beautiful?
LISE	'Tis passing silly! (She puts a pile of paper bags on the counter.)
RAGUENEAU	Bags? Good. I thank you. (He looks at them.) Heavens! my cherished leaves! The poems of my friends! Torn, dismembered, To make bags for holding biscuits and cakes! Ah, 'tis the old tale again— Orpheus* and the Bacchantes!
LISE	And am I not free to turn at last to some use the sole thing that your silly scribblers of halting lines leave behind them by way of payment?

Line numbers (right margin): 10, 15, 20, 25

Glossary notes (right margin):

muse: a writer's source of inspiration

caesura: pause

hemistiches: lines of verse shorter than normal lines

Orpheus (OR fee us): mythological singer whose music calmed beasts and even rocks and trees; according to myth, Orpheus was torn to pieces by the Bacchantes, the priestesses of Bacchus.

| RAGUENEAU | Meddling ant! Insult not the divine Grasshoppers, the sweet singers. |

| LISE | Before you were the sworn comrade of all that crew, my friend, you did not call your wife ant and Bacchant! |

| RAGUENEAU | To turn fair verse to such a use! 30 |

| LISE | Faith, 'tis all it's good for. |

| RAGUENEAU | Pray then, madam, to what use would you degrade prose?
(Two children enter.) |

| RAGUENEAU | What would you, little ones? |

SCENE ii

| FIRST CHILD | Three pies. |

| RAGUENEAU | *(Serving them)*
See, hot and well browned. |

| SECOND CHILD | If it please you, sir, will you wrap them up for us? |

RAGUENEAU	*(Aside, distressed)* Alas! one of my bags! What? Must I wrap them up? 5 *(He takes a bag, and just as he is about to put in the pies,* *he reads.)* "Ulysses* thus, on leaving fair Penelope* . . ." Not that one! *(Takes another bag; reads)* "The gold-locked Phoebus* . . ." Nay, nor that one!
LISE	What are you dallying for?
RAGUENEAU	Here! here! Here—the sonnet to Phyllis* . . . 10 But 'tis hard to part with it!
LISE	By good luck he has made up his mind at last! Nicodemus!
RAGUENEAU	*(When she turns her back, calls back the children, who* *are already at the door)* Hist! children! render me back the sonnet to Phyllis, and you Shall have six pies instead of three. 15 *(The children give him back the bag, seize the cakes* *quickly, and go out. Smoothing out the paper, begins to* *declaim)* "Phyllis! . . ." On that sweet name a smear of butter! "Phyllis! . . ."
CYRANO	*(Enters hurriedly)* What's o'clock?
RAGUENEAU	*(Bowing low)* Six o'clock.
CYRANO	One Hour's time!
RAGUENEAU	Bravo! I saw . . .
CYRANO	Well, what saw you, then?
RAGUENEAU	Your combat!

Ulysses: heroic king of Ithaca in Greek legend

Penelope: Ulysses' faithful wife

Phoebus: god of the sun

Phyllis: a country girl addressed in Virgil's *Eclogues*

SCENE iii

CYRANO	Which?
RAGUENEAU	That in the Burgundy Hotel!
CYRANO	*(Contemptuously)* <div align="right">Ah! the duel!</div>
RAGUENEAU	*(Fencing and thrusting with a spit, which he snatches up from the hearth)* Ay! the duel in verse!
LISE	He can talk of naught else! 5 *(Noticing CYRANO's hand)* What's wrong with your hand?
CYRANO	<div align="right">Naught; a slight cut.</div>
RAGUENEAU	*(Suddenly stops his shadow fencing)* Have you been in some danger?
CYRANO	<div align="right">None in the world.</div>
LISE	Methinks you speak not the truth in saying that!
CYRANO	Did you see my nose quiver when I spoke? It must have been a monstrous lie that should move it! 10 *(Changing his tone; to RAGUENEAU)* I wait someone here. Leave us alone, And disturb us for naught an it were Not for crack of doom!
RAGUENEAU	But 'tis impossible; My poets are coming.
LISE	Oh, ay, for their first meal o' the day! 15
CYRANO	Prithee, take them aside when I shall make you a sign to do so. What's o'clock?
RAGUENEAU	<div align="right">Ten minutes after six.</div>
CYRANO	<div align="right">A pen!</div>
RAGUENEAU	Here—a swan's quill.

CYRANO	*(Taking up the pen, and motioning* RAGUENEAU *away)* I will write, fold it, give it her, and fly! *(Throws down the pen)* Coward! But strike me dead if I dare to speak to her, 20 Ay, even one single word! Ay—a single word of all those here! But writing, 'tis easier done. *(Takes up the pen)* Go to, I will write it, That love letter! Oh! I have writ it 25 And rewrit it in my own mind so oft that it lies there Ready for pen and ink; and if I lay My soul by my letter-sheet, 'Tis naught to do but to copy from it. *(He writes. Through the glass of the door the silhouettes of figures move uncertainly and hesitatingly. The* POETS *enter, dressed in black, their stockings ungartered and covered with mud.)*

LISE	*(To* RAGUENEAU*)* Here they come, your mud-bespattered friends!
FIRST POET	*(Entering, to* RAGUENEAU*)* Brother in art!
SECOND POET	*(To* RAGUENEAU, *shaking his hands)* Dear brother!
THIRD POET	High soaring eagle among pastry-cooks! *(He sniffs.)*
FOURTH POET	Apollo among master-cooks—
RAGUENEAU	*(Whom they surround and embrace)* Ah! How quick a man feels at his ease with them! 5
FIRST POET	We were stayed by the mob; They are crowded all round the Porte de Nesle!
SECOND POET	Eight bleeding brigand carcasses strew the pavements there— All slit open with sword-gashes!

CYRANO	*(Raising his head a minute)* Eight? hold, methought seven.

10

RAGUENEAU	Know you who might be the hero of the fray?

CYRANO	Not I.

LISE	*(To* RAGUENEAU*)* And you? Know you?

RAGUENEAU	Maybe!

FIRST POET	'Twas one man, single-handed, Put the whole band to the rout!

SECOND POET	'Twas a strange sight!—pikes* and cudgels* Strewed thick upon the ground.

15 **pikes:** spearheads
   cudgels: clubs

CYRANO	*(Writing)* "Thine eyes . . . thy lips . . ."

FIRST POET	'Twas a parlous fearsome giant That was the author of such exploits!

CYRANO	"And when I see thee come, I faint for fear."

20

SECOND POET	What hast rhymed of late, Ragueneau?

CYRANO	"Who worships thee . . ." No need I sign, since I give it her myself.

RAGUENEAU	I have put a recipe into verse.

THIRD POET	Go to! Let us hear these verses!

25

FOURTH POET	This roll, its cap is all a' one side! *(He takes one bite off the top.)*

FIRST POET	See this gingerbread With its almond eyes, and its eyebrows of angelica!*

angelica: an herb that is
sometimes candied for use
in pastries

RAGUENEAU	*(Who has put himself ready for reciting, cleared his throat, settled his cap, struck an attitude)* A recipe in verse!

SECOND POET	*(To first, nudging him)* You are breakfasting?
FIRST POET	And you dining, methinks.

RAGUENEAU	*(Declaims)*
	How almond tartlets are made. 30
	Beat your eggs up, light and quick;
	    Froth them thick;
	Mingle with them while you beat
	Juice of lemon, essence fine;
	    Then combine
	The burst milk of almonds sweet.
	Circle with a custard paste
	    The slim waist 35
	Of your tartlet-molds; the top
	With a skillful finger print,
	    Nick and dint,
	Round their edge, then, drop by drop,
	In its little dainty bed
	    Your cream shed
	In the oven place each mold 40
	Reappearing, softly browned,
	    The renowned
	Almond tartlets you behold!

POETS	Exquisite! Delicious!
POET	*(Choking)* Homph!
CYRANO	*(To RAGUENEAU)* Lulled by your voice, did you see How they were stuffing themselves?
RAGUENEAU	Oh, ay! 45 I never look, fearing to distress them; I gain a double pleasure when I recite to them my poems; And leave those poor fellows free to eat, While I gratify myself, see you? *(ROXANE and the DUENNA appear outside the door.)*
CYRANO	*(Clapping him on the shoulder)* Be off with you!

RAGUENEAU	*(To the* POETS*)*	
	We shall be more private there.	50
	To read poetry, 'tis better here.	
	(He leads the POETS *into an inner room. They go out.)*	

CYRANO	Ah! if I see but the faint glimmer of hope,	**SCENE V**
	Then I draw out my letter!	
	(He opens the door quickly.)	
	Enter!	
	(Walking up to the DUENNA*)*	
	Two words with you, Duenna.	

DUENNA	Four, sir, if you want to.	

CYRANO	Are you fond of sweet things?	5

DUENNA	Ay, I could eat myself sick on them!	

CYRANO	Good. See you these two sonnets of Monsieur Benserade*?	**Benserade:** seventeenth-century French poet

DUENNA	Hey?

CYRANO	Which I fill for you with cream cakes!

DUENNA	Ha.

CYRANO	Pleasure me then; go eat them all in the street.

DUENNA	But—	10

CYRANO	And come not back till the very last crumb be eaten!
	(He shuts the door, comes down toward ROXANE, *and, removing his hat, stands at a respectful distance from her.)*

CYRANO	Blessed be the moment when you condescended—	**SCENE vi**
	Remembering that humbly I exist—	
	To come to meet me, and to say . . . to tell?	

ROXANE	*(Who has unmasked)*	
	To thank you first of all. That dandy count,	
	Whom you checkmated in brave swordplay	5
	Last night, . . . his patron is a great lord,	
	Desirous of my favor . . .	

CYRANO	Ha, de Guiche?
ROXANE	*(Casting down her eyes)* Who seeks to impose on me . . . for husband . . .
CYRANO	Then I fought, happy chance! sweet lady, not For my ill favor—but your favors fair! 10
ROXANE	Confession next! But, before I confess, You must be again that brother and friend With whom I used to play by the lakeside!
CYRANO	Ay, You would come each spring to Bergerac!
ROXANE	Mind you the reeds you cut to make your swords? 15
CYRANO	While you wove corn-straw plaits for your dolls' hair!
ROXANE	Those were the days of games!
CYRANO	And blackberries!
ROXANE	In those days you did everything I bid!
CYRANO	Roxane, in her short frock, was Madeleine . . .
ROXANE	Was I fair then?
CYRANO	You were not ill to see!
ROXANE	Ofttimes, 20 With hands all bloody from a fall, You'd run to me! Then—aping mother-ways— I, in a voice would-be severe, would chide, *(Taking his hand)* "What is this scratch, again, that I see here?" *(She starts, surprised.)* Oh! 'Tis too much! What's this? 25 No, let me see! At your age, fie! Where did you get that scratch?
CYRANO	I got it— Playing at the Porte de Nesle.

ROXANE   (Seating herself by the table, and dipping her handker-
            chief in a glass of water)
            Give here!

CYRANO   So soft! so gay maternal-sweet!

ROXANE   And tell me, while I wipe away the blood,   30
            How many 'gainst you?

CYRANO   Oh! A hundred—near.

ROXANE   Come, tell me!

CYRANO   No, let be. But you, come tell
            The thing, just now, you dared not . . .

ROXANE   (Keeping his hand)
                                    Now, I dare!
            The scent of those old days emboldens me!
            Yes, now I dare. Listen. I am in love.

CYRANO	Ah! 35
ROXANE	But with one who knows not.
CYRANO	Ah!
ROXANE	Not yet.
CYRANO	Ah!
ROXANE	But who, if he knows not, Soon shall learn.
CYRANO	Ah!
ROXANE	A poor youth who all this time has loved Timidly, from afar, and dares not speak—
CYRANO	Ah! 40
ROXANE	Leave your hand; why, it is fever-hot! But I have seen love trembling on his lips.
CYRANO	Ah!
ROXANE	*(Bandaging his hand with her handkerchief)* And to think of it—he, by chance— Yes, cousin, he is of your regiment!
CYRANO	Ah!
ROXANE	Is a cadet in your own company!
CYRANO	Ah! 45
ROXANE	On his brow he bears the genius-stamp; He is proud, noble, young, intrepid,* fair—
CYRANO	*(Rising suddenly, very pale)* Fair!
ROXANE	Why, what ails you?
CYRANO	*(Smiling)* Nothing; 'tis . . . This scratch!

intrepid: fearless; brave

ROXANE	I love him; all is said. But you must know
	I have only seen him at the Comedy. 50
CYRANO	How? You have never spoken?
ROXANE	Eyes can speak.
CYRANO	How know you then that he . . . ?
ROXANE	Oh! people talk
	'Neath the limes in the Place Royale.
	Gossips' chat has let me know . . .
CYRANO	He is a cadet? 55
	His name?
ROXANE	Baron Christian de Neuvillette.
CYRANO	How now? He is not of the Guards!
ROXANE	Today
	He has now joined your ranks, under Captain
	Carbon de Castel-Jaloux.
CYRANO	Ah, how quick,
	How quick the heart has flown! But, my poor child— 60
DUENNA	*(Opening the door)*
	The cakes are eaten, Monsieur Bergerac!
CYRANO	Then read the verses printed on the bags!
	(She goes out.)
	But my poor child, you who love but flowing words,
	Bright wit—what if he be a lout unskilled?
ROXANE	No, his bright locks, like d'Urfe's heroes— 65
CYRANO	Ah! A well-curled pate, and witless tongue, perchance!
ROXANE	Ah no! I guess—I feel—his words are fair!
CYRANO	All words are fair that lurk 'neath fair mustache!
	Suppose he were a fool!
ROXANE	Then bury me!

CYRANO	*(After a pause)* Was it to tell me this you brought me here? 70 I fail to see what use this serves, madame.
ROXANE	Nay, but I felt a terror, here, in the heart— All of your company are Gascons* . . .
CYRANO	And we provoke All beardless sprigs that favor dares admit 'Midst us pure Gascons? 75 They told you that as well?
ROXANE	Ah! Think how I Trembled for him!
CYRANO	*(Between his teeth)* Not causelessly!
ROXANE	But when Last night I saw you, brave, invincible, Punish that dandy, fearless hold your own Against those brutes, I thought—I thought, if he 80 Whom all fear, all—if he would only—
CYRANO	Good— I will befriend your little baron.
ROXANE	Ah! You'll promise me you will do this for me? I've always held you as a tender friend.
CYRANO	Ay, ay.
ROXANE	Then you will be his friend?
CYRANO	I swear! 85
ROXANE	And he shall fight no duels, promise!
CYRANO	None.
ROXANE	You are kind, cousin! Now I must be gone. You have not told me of your last night's fray. Ah, but it must have been a hero-fight! Bid him to write. *(She sends him a kiss with her fingers.)* How good you are!

Gascons: people of Gascony, reputed to be assertive and boastful

CYRANO	<div align="center">Ay! Ay!</div> 90
ROXANE	A hundred men against you? Now, farewell. We are great friends?
CYRANO	<div align="center">Ay, ay!</div>
ROXANE	<div align="right">Oh, bid him write!</div>You'll tell me all one day—a hundred men— How brave—
CYRANO	*(Bowing to her)*<div align="center">I have fought better since.</div>*(She goes out.* CYRANO *stands motionless, with eyes on the ground. A silence. The door [right] opens.* RAGUENEAU *looks in.)*
RAGUENEAU	Can we come in?
CYRANO	*(Without stirring)*<div align="center">Yes.</div>*(*RAGUENEAU *signs to his friends, and they come in. At the same time, by door at back, enters* CARBON DE CASTEL-JALOUX, *in captain's uniform. He makes gestures of surprise on seeing* CYRANO*.)*
CARBON	<div align="center">Here he is!</div>
CYRANO	*(Raises his head and salutes)* Captain!
CARBON	<div align="center">Our hero! We heard all! Thirty or more</div>Of my cadets are there!
CYRANO	*(Shrinking back)*<div align="center">But . . .</div>
CARBON	*(Trying to draw him away)*<div align="right">Come with me!</div>They will not rest until they see you!
CYRANO	<div align="center">No!</div>
CARBON	They're across the street.

SCENE vii

CYRANO   I . . .   5

CARBON   *(Going to the door and calling across the street in a voice
                of thunder)*
                He won't come! The hero's in the sulks!
                *(Tumult outside. Noise of boots and swords is heard
                approaching; the* CADETS *enter noisily.)*

RAGUENEAU   *(Drawing back startled)*
                Gentlemen, are you all from Gascony?

CADETS   All!

FIRST CADET   *(To* CYRANO*)*
                                                Bravo!

SECOND CADET   *(Shaking his hands)*
                                            Vivat!*   **vivat (Latin):** "May you live
                                                                (long)!"

LE BRET   *(Entering, and running up to* CYRANO*)*
                They're looking for you! Here's a crazy mob
                Led by the men who followed you last night.

CYRANO   What!
                Have you told them where to find me?   10

LE BRET   *(Rubbing his hands)*
                Yes!

BURGHER   *(Entering, followed by a group of men)*
                    Sir, all the Marais* is a-coming here!   **Marais (French, MARSH):**
                *(Outside the street has filled with people. Chaises and   a middle class neighborhood
                carriages have drawn up.)*   in Paris

LE BRET   *(In a low voice, smiling, to* CYRANO*)*
                And Roxane?

CYRANO   *(Quickly)*
                            Hush!

CROWD   *(Calling outside)*
                                Cyrano!
                *(A crowd rush into the shop, pushing one another.
                Acclamations)*

RAGUENEAU	(Standing on a table) Lo! my shop invaded! They break all! Magnificent!
CROWD	(Crowding round CYRANO) My friend! . . . my friend!
CYRANO	It seems that yesterday 15 I had not all these friends!
LE BRET	Success!
FIRST MARQUIS	(Hurrying up with his hands held out) My friend, didst thou but know—
CYRANO	Thou! thou! Pray when Did we herd swine together, you and I!
SECOND MARQUIS	I would present you, 20 Sir, to some fair dames Who in my carriage yonder—
CYRANO	(Coldly) Ah! and who Will first present you, sir, to me?
LE BRET	(Astonished) What's wrong?
CYRANO	Hush!
MAN OF LETTERS	(With writing-board) A few details? 25
CYRANO	No.
LE BRET	(Nudging his elbow) 'Tis Theophrast, Renaudet, Of the "Court Gazette"!
CYRANO	Who cares? (A movement in the crowd. DE GUICHE appears, escorted by OFFICERS, CUIGY, BRISSAILLE, and the OFFICERS who went with CYRANO the night before.)

CUIGY	*(Goes up to* CYRANO*)* Monsieur de Guiche! 30 *(A murmur—everyone makes way.)* He comes from the Marshal de Gassion!
DE GUICHE	*(Bowing to* CYRANO*)* Who would express his admiration, sir, For your new exploit noised so loud abroad.
CROWD	Bravo!
CYRANO	*(Bowing)* The marshal is a judge of valor.
DE GUICHE	He could not have believed the thing, unless 35 These gentlemen had sworn they witnessed it.
CUIGY	With our own eyes!
LE BRET	*(Aside to* CYRANO, *who has an absent air)* But . . . you . . .
CYRANO	Hush!
LE BRET	But . . . you suffer?
CYRANO	*(Starting)* Before this rabble? I? *(He draws himself up, twirls his mustache, and throws back his shoulders.)* Wait! You shall see! 40
DE GUICHE	*(To whom* CUIGY *has spoken in a low voice)* In feats of arms, already your career Abounded. You serve with those crazy pates Of Gascons?
CYRANO	Ay, with the Cadets In the Guards.
CADET	*(In a terrible voice)* With us!

DE GUICHE	Ah!
	All these gentlemen of haughty mien, 45
	Are they the famous?
CARBON	Cyrano!
CYRANO	Ay, captain!
CARBON	Since all my company's assembled here,
	Pray favor me—present them to my lord!
CYRANO	*(Making two steps toward* DE GUICHE*)*
	My lord de Guiche, permit that I present
	The bold Cadets of Gascony, 50
	Of Carbon of Castel-Jaloux!
	Brawling and swaggering boastfully,
	The bold Cadets of Gascony!
	Spouting of armory, heraldry,
	Their veins a-brimming with blood so blue, 55
	The bold Cadets of Gascony,
	Of Carbon of Castel-Jaloux!
DE GUICHE	*(Seated with haughty carelessness in an armchair)*
	A poet! 'Tis the fashion of the hour!
	Will you be mine?
CYRANO	No, sir—no man's!
DE GUICHE	Last night 60
	Your fancy pleased my uncle Richelieu.
	I'll gladly say a word to him for you.
LE BRET	Oh my!
DE GUICHE	I imagine you have rhymed
	Five acts, or so?
LE BRET	*(In* CYRANO'S *ear)*
	Your play! your "Agrippine"!
	You'll see it staged at last!
DE GUICHE	Take them to him. 65
CYRANO	*(Tempted)*
	In sooth, I would . . .

DE GUICHE	He is a critic skilled. He may correct a line or two, at most.
CYRANO	*(Whose face stiffens at once)* Impossible! My blood congeals to think That other hand should change a comma's dot. 70
DE GUICHE	But when a verse approves itself to him He pays it dear, good friend.
CYRANO	He pays less dear Than I myself; when a verse pleases me I pay myself, and sing it to myself!
DE GUICHE	You are proud. 75
CYRANO	Really? You have noticed that?
CADET	*(Entering, with a string of old battered plumed hats, full of holes, slung on his sword)* See, Cyrano— This morning, on the quay What strange bright-feathered game we caught— The plumed hats o' the fugitives!
CARBON	Spolia opima!*
ALL	*(Laughing)* Ah! ah! ah! 80
CUIGY	He who laid that ambush, 'faith! Must curse and swear!
BRISSAILLE	Who was it?
DE GUICHE	I myself. *(The laughter stops.)* I charged them—work too dirty for my sword, To punish and chastise an old poet. *(Constrained silence)*
CADET	*(To CYRANO)* What do with them? 85 They're full of grease!—a stew?

spolia opima (Latin): "the victor's spoils"

CYRANO   *(Taking the sword and, with a salute, dropping the hats at* DE GUICHE's *feet)*
Sir, pray be good enough to render them
Back to your friends.

DE GUICHE   My chair there—quick!—I go!
(To CYRANO, *passionately)*
As to you, sirrah!—

VOICE   *(In the street)*
                            Porters   90
For my lord de Guiche!

DE GUICHE   *(Who has controlled himself—smiling)*
Have you read *Don Quixote?*

CYRANO   I have! And doff my hat
At th' mad knight-errant's name.

DE GUICHE   I counsel you to study—

PORTER   *(Appearing at back)*
                            My lord's chair!   95

DE GUICHE   The windmill chapter!

CYRANO   *(Bowing)*
                           Chapter the Thirteenth.

DE GUICHE   For when one tilts 'gainst windmills, it may chance—

CYRANO   Tilt I 'gainst those who change with every breeze?

DE GUICHE   That windmill sails may sweep you with their arms
Down—in the mire!

CYRANO   Or upward—to the stars!   100
(DE GUICHE *goes out and mounts into his chair. The other lords go away whispering together.* LE BRET *goes to the door with them. The crowd disperses.)*

CYRANO   *(Bowing mockingly to those who go out without daring to salute him)*
Gentlemen . . . gentlemen . . .

SCENE viii

| LE BRET | *(Coming back, despairingly)* |
| | Now you've done it! |

| CYRANO | Oh! scold away! |

LE BRET	At least, you will agree
	That to annihilate each chance of Fate 5
	Exaggerates—

| CYRANO | Yes! I exaggerate! |

| LE BRET | *(Triumphantly)* |
| | Ah! |

| CYRANO | But for principle—example too— |
| | I think 'tis well thus to exaggerate. |

| LE BRET | Oh! lay aside that pride of musketeer, |
| | Fortune and glory wait you! |

CYRANO

                              Ay, and then? 10
Seek a protector, choose a patron out,
And like the crawling ivy round a tree
That licks the bark to gain the trunk's support,
Climb high by creeping ruse instead of force?
No, thank you! What! I, like all the rest 15
Dedicate verse to bankers? Play buffoon
In cringing hope to see, at last, a smile
Not disapproving, on a patron's lips?
Thank you, no! What! Learn to swallow toads?
With frame aweary climbing stairs? A skin 20
Grown grimed and horny—here, about the knees?
And, acrobat-like, teach my back to bend?
No, thank you! Or—double-faced and sly—
Run with the hare, while hunting with the hounds;
And, oily-tongued, to win the oil of praise, 25
Flatter the great man to his very nose?
No, thank you! Steal soft from lap to lap,
A little great man in a circle small,
Or navigate, with madrigals for sails,
Blown gently windward by old ladies' sighs? 30
No, thank you! Bribe kindly editors
To spread abroad my verses? No, thank you!
Or try to be elected as the pope
Of tavern-councils held by imbeciles?

No, thank you! Toil to gain reputation   35
By one small sonnet, 'stead of making many?
No, thank you! Or flatter sorry bunglers?
Be terrorized by every prating paper?
Say ceaselessly, "Oh, had I but the chance
Of a fair notice in the 'Mercury'!"   40
Thank you, no! Grow pale, fear, calculate?
Prefer to make a visit to a rhyme?
Seek introductions, draw petitions up?
No, thank you! and no! and no again! But—sing?
Dream, laugh, go lightly, solitary, free,   45
With eyes that look straightforward—fearless voice!
To cock your plumed hat just the way you choose—
For "yes" or "no" show fight, or turn a rhyme!
To work without one thought of gain or fame,
To realize that journey to the moon!   50
Never to pen a line that has not sprung
Straight from the heart within. Embracing then
Modesty, say to oneself, "Good my friend,
Be thou content with flowers—fruit—nay, leaves,
But pluck them from no garden but thine own!"   55
And then, if glory come by chance your way,
To pay no tribute unto Caesar,* none,   **pay no tribute unto Caesar:** an
But keep the merit all your own! In short,   allusion to Matthew 22:21
Disdaining tendrils of the parasite,
To be content, if neither oak nor elm—   60
Not to mount high, perchance, but mount alone!

LE BRET   Alone, an if you will! But not with hand
                 'Gainst every man! Lunacy!

CYRANO   Well, what if it be my vice,
                 My pleasure to displease—to love men hate me!
                 Ah, friend of mine, believe me, I march better   65
                 'Neath the crossfire of glances inimical!*   **inimical:** unfriendly or hostile
                 How droll the stains one sees on fine-laced doublets,
                 From gall* of envy, or the poltroon's drivel!   **gall:** bitterness
                 The enervating friendship which enfolds you
                 Is like an open-laced Italian collar,   70
                 Floating around your neck in woman's fashion;
                 One is at ease thus—but less proud the carriage.
                 The forehead, free from mainstay or coercion,
                 Bends here, there, everywhere. But me, embracing
                 Hatred, she lends—forbidding, stiffly fluted—   75
                 The ruff's* starched folds that hold the head so rigid;   **ruff:** frilled collar

Each enemy another fold, a frill,
Who adds constraint and adds a ray of glory;
For Hatred, like the ruff worn by the Spanish,
Grips like a vice, but frames you like a halo!   80

Le Bret   *(After a silence, taking his arm)*
Speak proud aloud, and bitter! In my ear
Whisper me simply this—She loves thee not!

Cyrano   *(Vehemently)*
Hush!
*(Christian has just entered and mingled with the Cadets,
who do not speak to him; he has seated himself at a table,
where Lise serves him.)*

First Cadet   *(Seated at a table, glass in hand)*
Cyrano!
(Cyrano turns round.)
            The story!

Cyrano   In its time!
(He goes up on Le Bret's arm. They talk in low voices.)

First Cadet   The story of the fray! 'Twill lesson well   5
(He stops before the table where Christian is seated.)
This timid young apprentice!

Christian   *(Raising his head)*
                        'Prentice! Who?

Second Cadet   This sickly northern greenhorn!

Christian   Sickly!

First Cadet   *(Mockingly)*
                        Hark!
Monsieur de Neuvillette, this in your ear—
There's somewhat here, one no more dares to name,
Than to say "rope" to one whose sire was hanged!   10

Christian   What may that be?

Third Cadet   *(In a terrible voice)*
                See here!
(He puts his finger three times, mysteriously, on his nose.)
Do you understand?

CHRISTIAN	Oh! 'tis the—
ANOTHER	Hush! oh, never breathe that word, Unless you'd reckon with him yonder! *(He points to* CYRANO, *who is talking with* LE BRET.*)*
ANOTHER	Hark! He put two snuffling men to death, in rage, 15 For the sole reason they spoke through their nose!
ANOTHER	*(In a hollow voice, darting on all fours from under the table, where he had crept)* And if you would not perish in flower o' youth, Oh, mention not the fatal cartilage!
ANOTHER	*(Clapping him on the shoulder)* A word? A gesture! For the indiscreet His handkerchief may prove his winding-sheet!* *(Silence. All, with crossed arms, look at* CHRISTIAN. *He rises and goes over to* CARBON DE CASTEL-JALOUX, *who is talking to an officer, and feigns to see nothing.)*
CHRISTIAN	Captain!
CARBON	*(Turning and looking at him from head to foot)* Sir!
CHRISTIAN	Pray, what skills it best to do To southerners who swagger?
CARBON	Give them proof That one may be a northerner, yet brave! *(He turns his back on him.)*
CHRISTIAN	I thank you.
FIRST CADET	*(To* CYRANO*)* Now the tale!
ALL	The tale!
CYRANO	*(Coming toward them)* The tale? *(All bring their stools up, and group round him, listening eagerly.* CHRISTIAN *is astride a chair.)*

20 **winding-sheet:** cloth in which a corpse is wrapped

Well! I went all alone to meet the band.   25
The moon was shining, clock-like, full i' th' sky,
When, suddenly, some careful clockwright passed
A cloud of cotton-wool across the case
That held this silver watch. And, presto! heigh!
The night was inky black, and all the quays   30
Were hidden in the murky dark.
One could see nothing further—

CHRISTIAN

                    Than one's nose!
(Silence. All slowly rise, looking in terror at CYRANO, *who has stopped dumbfounded. Pause.)*

CYRANO   Who on the earth is that?

CADET   *(Whispering)*
                  It is a man
Who joined today.

CYRANO   *(Making a step toward* CHRISTIAN*)*
          Today?

CARBON	*(In a low voice)* Yes . . . his name is 35 The Baron de Neuvil—

CYRANO	*(Checking himself)*
	 Good! It is well . . .
	 (He turns pale, flushes, makes as if to fall on CHRISTIAN.*)*
	                I . . .
	 (He controls himself.)
	 What said I?
	 (With a burst of rage)
	           PERILOUS!
	 (Then continues calmly)
	                That it was dark.
	 (Astonishment. The CADETS *reseat themselves, staring at him.)*
	 On I went, thinking, "For a knavish cause
	 I may provoke some great man, some great prince, 40
	 Who certainly could break—"

CHRISTIAN	My nose! *(Everyone starts up.* CHRISTIAN *balances on his chair.)*
CYRANO	*(In a choked voice)* "My teeth! Who would break my teeth, and I, imprudent-like, Was poking—"
CHRISTIAN	My nose!
CYRANO	"My finger in the crack Between the tree and bark! He may prove strong And rap me—"
CHRISTIAN	Over the nose!
CYRANO	*(Wiping his forehead)* "O' th' knuckles! Ay," 45 But I cried, "Forward, Gascon! Duty calls! On, Cyrano!" And thus I ventured on, When, from the shadow, came—
CHRISTIAN	A crack o' th' nose.
CYRANO	I parry it—find myself—

CHRISTIAN	Nose to nose.

CYRANO

(Bounding on to him. All the Gascons leap up to see, but when he is close to CHRISTIAN *he controls himself and continues.)*
With a hundred brawling sots,   50
Who stank—

CHRISTIAN   A noseful!

CYRANO

(Bursting out)
                    GET OUT! all of you!
(The CADETS *rush to the doors.)*

FIRST CADET   The tiger wakes!

CYRANO   Every man, out!
Leave me alone with him!

SECOND CADET   We shall find him minced fine, minced into hash
In a big pasty!   55
(All have gone out by different doors, some by the stair-case. CYRANO *and* CHRISTIAN *are face to face, looking at each other for a moment.)*

CYRANO   Embrace me now!

CHRISTIAN   Sir?

CYRANO   You are brave.

CHRISTIAN   Oh! But—

CYRANO   Nay, I insist.

CHRISTIAN   Pray tell me—

CYRANO   Come, embrace! I am her brother.

CHRISTIAN   Whose brother?

CYRANO   Hers, i' faith! Roxane's!

CHRISTIAN   *(Rushing up to him)*
O my! Her brother?   5

CYRANO	Cousin—brother! The same thing!
CHRISTIAN	And she has told you . . . ?
CYRANO	All!
CHRISTIAN	She loves me?
CYRANO	Maybe!
CHRISTIAN	*(Taking his hands)* How glad I am to meet you, sir!
CYRANO	That may be called a sudden sentiment!
CHRISTIAN	I ask your pardon—
CYRANO	*(Looking at him, with his hand on his shoulder)* True, he's fair, the villain!
CHRISTIAN	Ah, sir! If you but knew My admiration—
CYRANO	But all those *noses*—
CHRISTIAN	Oh! I take them back!
CYRANO	Roxane expects a letter.
CHRISTIAN	Woe the day!
CYRANO	How?
CHRISTIAN	I am lost if I but ope my lips!
CYRANO	Why so?
CHRISTIAN	I am a fool— Could die for shame!
CYRANO	None is a fool who knows himself a fool. And you did not attack me like a fool.
CHRISTIAN	Bah! One finds battle cry to lead th' assault! I have a certain military wit,

10

15

20

	But, before women, can but hold my tongue.
	Their eyes! True, when I pass, their eyes are kind . . .
CYRANO	And, when you stay, their hearts, methinks, are kinder? 25
CHRISTIAN	No! for I am one of those men—tongue-tied,
	I know it—who can never tell their love.
CYRANO	If I could be a musketeer, with handsome face!
CHRISTIAN	Roxane is clever. I'm sure to prove
	A disappointment to her! 30
CYRANO	*(Looking at him)*
	Had I but such an interpreter to speak my soul!
CHRISTIAN	*(With despair)*
	Eloquence! Where to find it?
CYRANO	*(Abruptly)*
	That I lend,
	If you lend me your handsome victor-charms;
	Blended, we make a hero of romance!
CHRISTIAN	How so?
CYRANO	Think you can repeat what things 35
	I daily teach your tongue?
CHRISTIAN	What do you mean?
CYRANO	Roxane shall never have a disillusion!
	Say, wilt thou that we woo her, double-handed?
	Wilt thou that we two woo her, both together?
	Feel'st thou, passing from my leather doublet, 40
	Through thy laced doublet, all my soul inspiring?
CHRISTIAN	But, Cyrano—
CYRANO	Will you, I say?
CHRISTIAN	I fear!
CYRANO	Since, by yourself, you fear to chill her heart,
	Will you—to kindle all her heart to flame—
	Wed into one my phrases and your lips? 45

CHRISTIAN	Will it please you so? Give you such pleasure?

CYRANO	*(Madly)*
	              It—
	(Then calmly, business-like)
	                     It would amuse me!
	It is an enterprise to tempt a poet.
	Will you complete me, and let me complete you?
	You march victorious—I go in your shadow;
	Let me be wit for you, be you my beauty!

CHRISTIAN	The letter, that she waits for even now! I never can—
CYRANO	*(Taking out the letter he had written)* See! Here it is—your letter!
CHRISTIAN	What?
CYRANO	Take it! Look, it wants but the address.
CHRISTIAN	But I—
CYRANO	Fear nothing. Send it. It will suit.
CHRISTIAN	But why have you . . . ?
CYRANO	Oh! We have our pockets full, We poets, of love-letters, writ to Chloes, Daphnes—creations of our noddle-heads. Our lady-loves—phantasms of our brains, Dream-fancies blown into soap bubbles! Come! Take it, and change feigned love-words into true. I breathed my sighs and moans haphazard-wise. Call all these wandering lovebirds home to nest. You'll see that I was in these lettered lines Eloquent all the more, the less sincere! Take it, and make an end!
CHRISTIAN	Were it not well to change some words? Written haphazard-wise, Will it fit Roxane?
CYRANO	'Twill fit like a glove!

50

55

60

65

70

CHRISTIAN	But—
CYRANO	Ah, credulity of love! Roxane Will think each word inspired by herself!
CHRISTIAN	My friend! (*He throws himself into* CYRANO's *arms. They remain thus.*)
CADET	(*Half opening the door*) Naught here. The silence of the grave . . . I dare not look— (*He puts his head in*) Why?
ALL THE CADETS	(*Entering, and seeing* CYRANO *and* CHRISTIAN *embracing*) Oh! (*Consternation*)
CADET	This passes all!
MUSKETEER	(*Mockingly*) Ho, ho! Then we may speak about his nose, henceforth! Ah, see here! (*Sniffing ostentatiously*) O my! what a stink! 5 (*Going up to* CYRANO) You, sir, without a doubt have sniffed it up! What is the smell I notice here?
CYRANO	(*Cuffing his head*) Clove-heads. (*General delight. The* CADETS *have found the old* CYRANO *again! They turn somersaults.*)

SCENE XI

            Curtain

About the Drama

1. How does Cyrano react to the excessive praise and attention given to him by his fellow cadets when they hear of his victory over the hundred men? What does this tell us about Cyrano's character?

2. The central conflict of the drama is clearly revealed in Act II. (See especially pp. 394–96, 400–401, 407–9.) Would you describe the central conflict as an external one or an internal one? Name two instances that illustrate the conflict.

3. Cyrano compliments Roxane by saying that she "was not ill to see" when they were young. How is Cyrano's compliment an example of understatement?

4. How does Christian describe himself to Cyrano (pp. 410–11)? Is this an accurate assessment?

5. What does Cyrano's willingness to help Christian with Roxane's love tell us about him?

6. Though Christian presents himself a rival to Cyrano in the play, what is Rostand's tone toward him in Act II? How can you tell?

Act III

Roxane's Kiss

A small square in the old Marais. Old houses. A perspective of little streets. On the right ROXANE's house and the wall of her garden overhung with thick foliage. Window and balcony over the door. A bench in front. From the bench and the stones jutting out of the wall it is easy to climb to the balcony. In front of an old house in the same style of brick and stone. The knocker of this door is bandaged with linen like a sore thumb. At the rising of the curtain the DUENNA is seated on the bench. The window on ROXANE's balcony is wide open.

DUENNA	*(Rising, and calling up to the open window)* Roxane, are you ready? They wait for us!	SCENE i
ROXANE'S VOICE	*(From the window)* I will but put me on a cloak!	

DUENNA	*(Calling up to the window)*

DUENNA   *(Calling up to the window)*
Roxane,
If you come not down quickly, we shall miss the discourse
On the Tender Passion!*

Tender Passion: the title of a lecture to which the Duenna and Roxane are going for entertainment and education

ROXANE'S VOICE   I come!
I come!   5
(A sound of stringed instruments approaching)

CYRANO'S VOICE   *(Behind the scenes, singing)*
La, la, la, la!

DUENNA   *(Surprised)*
They serenade us?

CYRANO   *(Followed by two* PAGES *with arch-lutes)*
I tell you
They are demi-semi-quavers, demi-semi-fool!

FIRST PAGE   *(Ironically)*
You know then, sir, to distinguish between
Semi-quavers* and demi-semi-quavers?*   10

semi-quaver, demi-semi-quaver: sixteenth notes and thirty-second notes

CYRANO   Is not every disciple of Gassendi* a musician?
*(*CYRANO *snatches the lute from the First Page and goes on with the phrase.)*

Gassendi: French seventeenth-century mathematician, musician, and philosopher

ROXANE   *(Appearing on the balcony)*
What? 'Tis you? Wait, I am coming down!
(She leaves the balcony.)

DUENNA   *(Pointing to the* PAGES)
How come these two virtuosi* here?

virtuosi: masters of technique

CYRANO   'Tis for a wager I won of d'Assoucy.
We were disputing a nice point in grammar;   15
When he shows me these two long-shanks,
Whom he takes about with him as an escort,
And who are skillful in scratching lute-strings with their
     skinny claws!
"I will wager you a day's music," says he!—And lost it!
Thus, see you, till tomorrow,   20
These lute-twangers are at my heels,
Seeing all I do, hearing all I say, and
Accompanying all with melody.

'Twas pleasant at the first, but i' faith,
I begin to weary of it already!   25
(To the PAGES)
Ho there! go serenade Montfleury for me!
Play a dance to him!
(The PAGES *go toward the door. To the* DUENNA)
I have come, as is my wont, nightly,
To ask Roxane whether—
(To the PAGES, *who are going out)*
      Play a long time—
And play out of tune!   30
(To the DUENNA)
Whether her soul's elected is ever the same, ever faultless!

ROXANE   *(Coming out of the house)*
       Ah! How handsome he is, how brilliant a wit!
       And—how well I love him!

CYRANO   *(Smiling)*
       Christian has so brilliant a wit?

ROXANE   Brighter than even your own, cousin!   35

CYRANO   Be it so, with all my heart!

ROXANE   Ah! methinks 'twere impossible
       That there could breathe a man on this earth
       Skilled to say as sweetly as he
       All the pretty nothings that mean so much—   40
       That mean all! At times his mind seems far away,
       The Muse says naught—and then,
       Presto! he speaks—bewitchingly! enchantingly!

CYRANO   *(Incredulously)*
       No, no!

ROXANE   Fie! That is ill said! But lo! men are ever thus!
       Because he is fair to see, you think he must be dull of
        speech.   45

CYRANO   He hath an eloquent tongue in telling his love?

ROXANE   In telling his love? Why, 'tis not simple telling, 'tis
       Dissertation, 'tis analysis!

CYRANO	How is he with the pen?

ROXANE   Still better! Listen—here—
(Reciting)
"The more of my poor heart you take   50
The larger grows my heart!"
(Triumphantly to CYRANO*)*
How like you those lines?

CYRANO   Pooh!

ROXANE   And thus it goes on—
"And, since some target I must show
For Cupid's cruel dart,   55
Oh, if mine own you deign to keep,
Then give me your sweet heart!"

CYRANO   First he has too much, then anon not enough!
How much heart does the fellow want?

ROXANE   You would vex a saint!   60
But 'tis your jealousy.

CYRANO   *(Starting)*
                      What mean you?

ROXANE   Ay, your poet's jealousy! Hark now, if this again
Be not tender-sweet—

CYRANO   Then you have his letters by heart?

ROXANE   Every one of them!   65

CYRANO   By all oaths that can be sworn—'tis flattering!

ROXANE   They are the lines of a master!

CYRANO   Come—nay!

ROXANE   Ay, I say it—a master!

CYRANO   *(Bowing)*
                   Good—be it so.

DUENNA   *(Coming down quickly)*
Here comes Monsieur De Guiche!

	(To CYRANO, *pushing him toward the house)*
	In with you! 'twere best he see you not; 70
	It might perchance put him on the scent—
ROXANE	*(To* CYRANO*)*
	Ay, of my own dear secret! He loves me,
	And is powerful, and, if he knew, then all were lost!
	He could well deal a deathblow to my love!
CYRANO	*(Entering the house)*
	Good, good!
ROXANE	*(Curtsying to* DE GUICHE*)*
	I was going out. 75
DE GUICHE	I come to take my leave.
ROXANE	Whither go you?
DE GUICHE	To the war.
ROXANE	Ah!
DE GUICHE	Ay, tonight.
ROXANE	Oh!
DE GUICHE	I am ordered away. We are to besiege Arras.
ROXANE	Ah—to besiege?
DE GUICHE	Ay. My going moves you not, meseems.
ROXANE	Nay—
DE GUICHE	I am grieved to the core of the heart. 5
	Shall I again behold you? When? I know not.
	Heard you that I am named commander?
ROXANE	*(Indifferently)*
	Bravo!
DE GUICHE	Of the Guards regiment.
ROXANE	*(Startled)*
	What? The Guards?

DE GUICHE	Ay, where serves your cousin,
	The swaggering boaster. I will find a way 10
	To revenge myself on him at Arras.
ROXANE	*(Choking)*
	What mean you? The Guards go to Arras?
DE GUICHE	*(Laughing)*
	Bethink you, is it not my own regiment?
ROXANE	*(Falling seated on the bench—aside*)*
	Christian!
DE GUICHE	What ails you?
ROXANE	*(Moved deeply)*
	Oh—I am in despair!
	The man one loves—at the war! 15
DE GUICHE	*(Surprised and delighted)*
	You say such sweet words to me!
	'Tis the first time—and just when I must quit you!
ROXANE	*(Collected, and fanning herself)*
	Thus—you would fain revenge
	Your grudge against my cousin?
DE GUICHE	My fair lady is on his side? 20
ROXANE	Nay—against him!
DE GUICHE	Do you see him often?
ROXANE	But very rarely.
DE GUICHE	He is ever to be met now in company
	With one of the cadets—de New— 25
	Neuvillen—viller—
ROXANE	*(Coolly)*
	Of high stature?
DE GUICHE	Fair-haired!
ROXANE	Ay, a red-cheeked fellow!

aside: an expression of which the play's other characters are unaware, often made directly to the audience

DE GUICHE	Handsome!
ROXANE	Tut!
DE GUICHE	But dull-witted.
ROXANE	One would think so, to look at him! *(Changing her tone)* How mean you to play your revenge on Cyrano? 30 Perchance you think to put him i' the thick of the shots? Nay, believe me, that were a poor vengeance—he Would love such a post better than aught else! I know the way to wound his pride far more keenly!
DE GUICHE	What? 35
ROXANE	If, when the regiment march to Arras, He were left here with his beloved Cadets, To sit with crossed arms so long as the war lasted! Thus would you enrage a man of his kind; cheat him Of his chance of mortal danger, 40 And you punish him right fiercely.
DE GUICHE	What a brilliant idea from such a woman!
ROXANE	See you not how he will eat out his heart, While his friends gnaw their thick fists For that they are deprived of the battle? 45 So are you best avenged.
DE GUICHE	You love me, then, a little? *(She smiles.)* I would fain— Seeing you thus espouse my cause, Roxane— Believe it a proof of love!
ROXANE	'Tis a proof of love!
DE GUICHE	*(Showing some sealed papers)* Here are the marching orders; 50 They will be sent instantly to each company— Except— *(He detaches one.)* This one! 'Tis that of the Cadets. This I keep. Ha! ha! ha! Cyrano!

420   TONE

(To ROXANE*)*
So you can play tricks—you, of all ladies!

ROXANE   Sometimes!

DE GUICHE *(Coming close to her)*
Oh how I love you! to distraction! Listen!   55
In the Rue d'Orleans is a convent founded
By Father Athanasius, the syndic of the Capuchins.*   **Capuchins:** those who wear
True that no layman may enter—but   hooded cloaks, i.e., priests
Their habit sleeves are wide enough to hide me in.
'Tis they who serve Richelieu's private chapel   60
And from respect to the uncle, fear the nephew.
All will deem me gone. I will come to you, masked.
Give me leave to wait till tomorrow!

ROXANE   But, if this be rumored,
Your glory—

DE GUICHE   Bah!

ROXANE   But the siege—Arras—   65

DE GUICHE 'Twill take its chance. Grant but permission.

ROXANE   No!

DE GUICHE   Give me leave!

ROXANE   *(Tenderly)*
It were my duty to forbid you!

DE GUICHE Ah!

ROXANE   You must go!
(Aside)
                    Christian stays here.
(Aloud)
I would have you heroic—Antoine!

DE GUICHE   O heavenly word!   70
You love, then, him—

ROXANE   For whom I trembled.

DE GUICHE   (*In an ecstasy*)
                   Ah! I go then!
                   (*He kisses her hand.*)
                   Are you content?

ROXANE   Yes, my friend!
                   (*He goes out.*)

DUENNA   (*As* DE GUICHE *disappears, making behind his back a
                   mocking curtsy and imitating* ROXANE's *intense tone*)
                   Yes, my friend!

ROXANE   (*To the* DUENNA)
                                 Not a word of what I have done.
                   Cyrano would never pardon me for stealing   75
                   His fighting from him!
                   (*She calls toward the house.*)
                                 Cousin!

                   (CYRANO *comes out.*)

ROXANE   We are going to Clomire's house.
                   (*She points to the door opposite.*)
                   Alcandre and Lysimon are to discourse!
                   (*They have come to Clomire's door. Seeing the door open*)
                   Let us enter!
                   (*On the threshold, to* CYRANO)
                                 If Christian comes, bid him wait!
CYRANO   (*Quickly, as she is going in*)
                   Listen!
                   (*She turns.*)
                                 What mean you to question him on tonight?

ROXANE   Oh—

CYRANO   (*Eagerly*)
                   Well, say.

ROXANE   But you will be mute?

CYRANO   Mute as a fish.   5

ROXANE   I shall not question him at all,
                   But say "Speak to me of love;
                   Speak splendidly! Give rein to your fancy!"

CYRANO	*(Smiling)* Very good!
ROXANE	But secret!
CYRANO	Secret.
ROXANE	Not a word! *(She enters and shuts the door.)*
CYRANO	*(When the door is shut, bowing to her)* A thousand thanks! 10 *(The door opens again, and* ROXANE *puts her head out.)*
ROXANE	Lest he prepare himself!
CYRANO	No, no!
BOTH TOGETHER	Secret. *(The door shuts.)*
CYRANO	*(Calling)* Christian!

SCENE iv

CYRANO	I know all that is needful. Here's occasion For you to deck yourself with glory. Come, Lose no time; put away those sulky looks, Come to your house with me, I'll teach you—
CHRISTIAN	No!
CYRANO	Why?
CHRISTIAN	I will wait 5 For Roxane here.
CYRANO	How? Crazy! Come quick with me and learn—
CHRISTIAN	No, no! I say. I am aweary of these borrowed letters, Borrowed lovemakings! Thus to act a part, And tremble all the time! 'Twas well enough 10 At the beginning!—but now I know she loves! I fear no longer! I will speak myself.

CYRANO	Mercy!
CHRISTIAN	And how know you I cannot speak? I am not such a fool when all is said! I've by your lessons profited. You'll see 15 I shall know how to speak alone! I know at least to clasp her in my arms! *(Seeing* ROXANE *come out from Clomire's house)* It is she! Cyrano, no! Leave me not!
CYRANO	*(Bowing)* Speak for yourself, my friend, and take your chance. *(He disappears behind the garden wall.)*
ROXANE	*(Coming out of Clomire's house, with a company of friends, whom she leaves. Bows and good-byes)* Bon soir . . . Adieu!
DUENNA	*(Bitterly disappointed)* We've missed the speech upon the Tender Passion! *(Goes into* ROXANE's *house.)*
ROXANE	Adieu! *(All leave, going up different streets.* ROXANE *suddenly seeing* CHRISTIAN*)* You! *(She goes to him.)* Evening falls. Let's sit. Speak on—I listen. 5
CHRISTIAN	*(Sits by her on the bench. A silence)* Oh! I love you!
ROXANE	*(Shutting her eyes)* Ay, speak to me of love.
CHRISTIAN	I love thee!
ROXANE	That's the theme! But vary it.
CHRISTIAN	I love you so!
ROXANE	Oh! without doubt!—and then?
CHRISTIAN	And then—I should be—oh— So glad—so glad if you would love me! 10 Roxane, tell me so!

ROXANE   *(With a little grimace)*
                                I hoped for cream—
                You give me gruel! Say how love possesses you?

CHRISTIAN   Oh utterly!

ROXANE   Come, come!—unknot those tangled sentiments!

CHRISTIAN   Your neck—I'd kiss it!

ROXANE   Christian!

CHRISTIAN   I love thee!   15

ROXANE   *(Half-rising)*
                Again!

CHRISTIAN	*(Eagerly, detaining her)* No, no! I love thee not!
ROXANE	*(Reseating herself)* 'Tis well!
CHRISTIAN	But I adore thee!
ROXANE	*(Rising, and going further off)* Oh!
CHRISTIAN	I am grown stupid!
ROXANE	*(Dryly)* And that displeases me, As much as if you grew ill favored.
CHRISTIAN	But—
ROXANE	Rally your poor eloquence that's flown!
CHRISTIAN	I—
ROXANE	Yes, you love me; that I know. Adieu. *(She goes toward her house.)*
CHRISTIAN	Oh, go not yet! I'd tell you—
ROXANE	*(Opening the door)* You adore me? I've heard it very oft. No! Go away!
CHRISTIAN	But I would fain— *(She shuts the door in his face.)*
CYRANO	*(Who has reentered unseen)* I' faith! It is successful!
CHRISTIAN	Come to my aid!
CYRANO	Not I!
CHRISTIAN	But I shall die, unless at once I win back her fair favor.

20

SCENE vi

CYRANO   And how can I, at once,
              Lesson you in—

CHRISTIAN   *(Seizing his arm)*
                        Oh, she is there!
              (The window of the balcony is now lighted up.)

CYRANO   Her window!

CHRISTIAN   Oh! I shall die!

CYRANO   Speak lower!

CHRISTIAN   I shall die!

CYRANO   The night is dark—

CHRISTIAN   Well!   5

CYRANO — All can be repaired, although you merit not.
Stand there, poor wretch!
Fronting the balcony! I'll go beneath
And prompt your words to you.

CHRISTIAN — But—

CYRANO — Hold your tongue!

PAGES — *(Reappearing at back—to* CYRANO*)*
Ho!

CYRANO — Hush!
(He signs to them to speak softly.)

FIRST PAGE — *(In a low voice)*
We've played the serenade you bade
To Montfleury!

CYRANO — Go! lurk in ambush there,
One at this street corner, and one at that;
And if a passer-by should here intrude,
Play you a tune!

SECOND PAGE — What tune, Sir Gassendist?

CYRANO — Gay, if a woman comes—for a man, sad!
(The PAGES *disappear, one at each street corner. To* CHRISTIAN*)*
Call her!

CHRISTIAN — Roxane!

CYRANO — *(Picking up stones and throwing them at the window)*
Some pebbles!

ROXANE — *(Half-opening the casement)*
Who calls me?

CHRISTIAN — I!

ROXANE — Who's that?
(Disdainfully)
Oh, you!

CHRISTIAN	I would speak with you.
CYRANO	*(Under the balcony—to* CHRISTIAN*)* Good. Speak soft and low.
ROXANE	No, you speak stupidly! 20
CHRISTIAN	Oh, pity me!
ROXANE	No! You love me no more!
CHRISTIAN	*(Prompted by* CYRANO*)* You say— I love no more?—when—I—love more and more!
ROXANE	*(Who was about to shut the casement, pausing)* Hold! 'Tis a trifle better!
CHRISTIAN	*(Same play)* Love grew apace, rocked by the anxious beating . . . Of this poor heart, which the cruel wanton boy . . . 25 Took for a cradle!
ROXANE	*(Coming out on to the balcony)* That is better! But if you deem that Cupid be so cruel You should have stifled baby-love in's cradle!
CHRISTIAN	*(Same play)* Ah, madame, I assayed, but all in vain . . . This . . . new-born babe is a young . . . Hercules!* 30
ROXANE	Still better!
CHRISTIAN	*(Same play)* Thus he strangled in my heart The . . . serpents twain, of . . . Pride . . . and Doubt!
ROXANE	*(Leaning over the balcony)* Well said! But why so faltering? Has mental palsy Seized on your faculty imaginative?
CYRANO	*(Drawing* CHRISTIAN *under the balcony, and slipping into his place)* Give place! This waxes critical!

Hercules: mythical figure renowned for great feats of strength and endurance, including killing snakes in his cradle

ROXANE	Today 35 Your words are hesitating.
CYRANO	*(Imitating* CHRISTIAN—*in a whisper)* Night has come— In the dusk they grope their way to find your ear.
ROXANE	But my words find no such impediment.
CYRANO	They find their way at once? Small wonder that! For 'tis within my heart they find their home; 40 Bethink how large my heart, how small your ear! And—from fair heights descending, words fall fast, But mine must mount, madame, and that takes time!
ROXANE	Meseems that your last words have learned to climb.
CYRANO	With practice such gymnastic grows less hard! 45
ROXANE	In truth, I seem to speak from distant heights!
CYRANO	True, far above; at such a height 'twere death if a Hard word from you fell on my heart.
ROXANE	*(Moving)* I will come down . . .
CYRANO	*(Hastily)* No!
ROXANE	*(Showing him the bench under the balcony)* Mount then on the bench!
CYRANO	*(Starting back alarmed)* No!
ROXANE	How, you will not?
CYRANO	*(More and more moved)* Stay awhile! 'Tis sweet— 50 The rare occasion, when our hearts can speak, Our selves unseen, unseeing!
ROXANE	Why unseen?

CYRANO

Ay, it is sweet! Half hidden—half revealed—
You see the dark folds of my shrouding cloak,
And I, the glimmering whiteness of your dress,   55
I but a shadow—you a radiance fair!

Know you what such a moment holds for me?
If ever I were eloquent . . .

ROXANE
                                              You were!

CYRANO

Yet never till tonight my speech has sprung
Straight from my heart as now it springs.   60

ROXANE

Why not?

CYRANO
                              Till now I spoke haphazard . . .

ROXANE
                                                        What?

CYRANO
                                                                          Your eyes
Have beams that turn men dizzy! But tonight
Methinks I shall find speech for the first time!

ROXANE

'Tis true, your voice rings
With a tone that's new.

CYRANO

(Coming nearer, passionately)
                              Ay, a new tone!   65
In the tender, sheltering dusk
I dare to be myself for once—at last!
(He stops, falters)
What say I? I know not!—Oh, pardon me—
It thrills me—'tis so sweet, so novel . . .

ROXANE
                                                        How so novel?

CYRANO

(Off his balance, trying to find the thread of his sentence)
Ay—to be at last sincere;   70
Till now, my chilled heart, fearing to be mocked . . .

ROXANE

Mocked, and for what?

CYRANO
                              For its mad beating!—Ay,
My heart has clothed itself with witty words,
To shroud itself from curious eyes. Impelled

	At times to aim at a star, I stay my hand,	75
	And, fearing ridicule—cull a wild flower!	
ROXANE	A wild flower's sweet.	
CYRANO	Ay, but tonight—the star!	
ROXANE	Oh! never have you spoken thus before!	
CYRANO	If, leaving Cupid's arrows, quivers, torches,	
	We turned to seek for sweeter—fresher things!	80
	Instead of sipping in a pygmy glass	
	Dull fashionable waters—did we try	
	How the soul slakes its thirst in fearless draught	
	By drinking from the river's flooding brim!	
ROXANE	But wit?	
CYRANO	In love 'tis crime—'tis hateful!	85
	Turning frank loving into subtle fencing!	
	At last the moment comes, inevitable—	
	Oh, woe for those who never know that moment!	
	When feeling love exists in us, ennobling,	
	Each well-weighed word is futile and soul saddening!	90
ROXANE	Well, if that moment's come for us—suppose it!	
	What words would serve you?	
CYRANO	All, all, all, whatever	
	That came to me, e'en as they came, I'd fling them	
	In a wild cluster, not a careful bouquet.	
	I love thee! I am mad! I love, I stifle!	95
	Thy name is in my heart as in a sheep-bell,	
	And as I ever tremble, thinking of thee,	
	Ever the bell shakes, ever thy name ringeth!	
ROXANE	*(Agitated)*	
	Why, this is love indeed!	
CYRANO	Ay, true the feeling	
	Which fills me, terrible and jealous, truly	100
	Love—which is ever sad amid its transports! Love—	
	And yet, strangely, not a selfish passion!	
	I for your joy would gladly lay mine own down,	
	E'en though you never were to know it—never!—	

If but at times I might—far off and lonely—   105
Hear some gay echo of the joy I bought you!
Each glance of thine awakes in me a virtue—
A novel, unknown valor. Dost begin, sweet,
To understand? Feel'st thou my soul,
Here, through the darkness mounting?   110
Too fair the night! Too fair, too fair the moment!
That I should speak thus, and that you should hearken!

ROXANE   Ay! I am trembling, weeping!—I am thine!
Thou hast conquered all of me!

CYRANO   Then let death come!
'Tis I, 'tis I myself, who conquered thee!
               One thing, 115
But one, I dare to ask—

CHRISTIAN *(Under the balcony)*
          A kiss!

ROXANE   *(Drawing back)*
            What?

CYRANO   Oh!

ROXANE   You ask . . . ?

CYRANO   I—
    (To CHRISTIAN, *whispering)*
   Fool, you go too quick!

CHRISTIAN Since she is moved thus—I will profit by it!

CYRANO   *(To* ROXANE*)*
    My words sprang thoughtlessly, but now I see—
    Shame on me!—I was too presumptuous.   120

ROXANE   *(A little chilled)*
    How quickly you withdraw.

CYRANO   Yes, I withdraw
    Without withdrawing! Hurt I modesty?
    If so—the kiss I asked—oh, grant it not.

CHRISTIAN *(To* CYRANO, *pulling him by his cloak)*
          Why?

CYRANO	Silence, Christian! Hush!
ROXANE	*(Leaning over)*
	What whisper you?
CYRANO	I chide myself for my too bold advances; 125 I say, "Silence, Christian!"
CHRISTIAN	Oh! win for me that kiss . . .
CYRANO	No!
CHRISTIAN	Sooner or later!
CYRANO	'Tis true! The moment of intoxication— Of madness—when your mouths are sure to meet Thanks to your fair mustache—and her rose lips! 130 *(To himself)* I'd fainer it should come thanks to . . .
ROXANE	Still there? We spoke of a . . .

CYRANO	A kiss, when all is said, what is it? An oath that's ratified, a sealed promise, A heart's avowal claiming confirmation, Communion perfumed like the spring's wild flowers, The heart's relieving in the heart's outbreathing, When to the lips the soul's flood rises, brimming!	**SCENE vii**
		5
ROXANE	Hush! hush!	
CYRANO	A kiss, madame, is honorable. The queen of France* to a most favored lord* Did grant a kiss—the queen herself!	**queen of France:** Anne of Austria **most favored lord:** George Villiers, duke of Buckingham (1592–1628), who, while on a mission to Paris, carried on a flirtation with the queen of France
ROXANE	What then?	
CYRANO	Buckingham suffered dumbly—so have I— Adored his queen as loyally as I— Was sad, but faithful—so am I . . .	10
ROXANE	And you are fair as Buckingham!	
CYRANO	*(Aside—suddenly cooled)* True—I forgot!	

ROXANE	Must I then bid thee mount to cull this flower?
CYRANO	*(To* CHRISTIAN*)* Mount!
ROXANE	This heart-breathing!
CYRANO	Go!
ROXANE	This brush of bee's wing! 15
CYRANO	Climb!
CHRISTIAN	*(Hesitating)* But I feel now, as though 'twere ill done!
CYRANO	*(Still pushing him)* Come, blockhead, mount! *(*CHRISTIAN *springs forward, and by means of the bench, the branches, and the pillars, climbs to the balcony and strides over it.)*
CYRANO	Ah, Roxane! The kiss, love's feast, so near! I, Lazarus, lie at the gate in darkness. Yet to me Falls still a crumb or two from the rich man's board— 20 Ay, 'tis my heart receives thee, Roxane—mine! For on the lips you press you kiss as well The words I spoke just now!—my words—my words! *(The lutes play.)* A sad air—a gay air—the Friar! *(He begins to run as if he came from a long way off, and cries out)* Hola!
ROXANE	Who is it?
CYRANO	I—I was but passing by . . . 25 Is Christian there?
CHRISTIAN	*(Astonished)* Cyrano!
ROXANE	Good day, cousin!
CYRANO	Cousin, good day!

ROXANE	I'm coming! *(She disappears into the house. At the back enter the* FRIAR.*)*
CHRISTIAN	*(Seeing the* FRIAR*)* Oh—not now . . .
FRIAR	'Tis here, I'm sure of it— Madame Madeleine Robin.
ROXANE	*(Appearing on the threshold, followed by* RAGUENEAU, *who carries a lantern, and* CHRISTIAN*)* What is't?
FRIAR	A letter.
CHRISTIAN	What?
FRIAR	*(To* ROXANE*)* Oh, it can boot but a holy business! 'Tis from a worthy lord . . .

ROXANE	*(To* CHRISTIAN*)* De Guiche!
CHRISTIAN	He dares . . . 5
ROXANE	Oh, he will not importune me forever! I love you, therefore— *(She reads the letter in a low voice)* "Lady, the drums beat; My regiment buckles its harness on And starts; but I stay here in convent walls. 10 I have dared to disobey your mandate. I come to you tonight. By this poor monk— A simple fool—I send this message to your ears. Your lips erewhile have smiled on me, too sweet. I go not ere I've seen them once again! 15 Receive alone him whose great boldness you Have deigned, I hope, to pardon . . ."—et cetera. *(To the* FRIAR*)* Father, this is the matter of the letter— *(All come near her, and she reads aloud.)* "Lady, the Cardinal's wish is law; albeit It be to you unwelcome. For this cause 20 I send these lines—to your fair ear addressed— By a holy man, discreet, intelligent. It is our will that you receive from him, In your own house, the marriage . . . *(She turns the page.)* benediction Straightway, this night. Unknown to all the world 25 Christian becomes your husband. Him we send. He is abhorrent to your choice. Let be. Resign yourself, and this obedience Will be by Heaven well recompensed. Receive, Fair lady, all assurance of respect, 30 From him who ever was, and still remains, Your humble and obliged"—et cetera.
FRIAR	*(With great delight)* O worthy lord! I knew naught was to fear; It could be but holy business!
ROXANE	*(To* CHRISTIAN, *in a low voice)* Am I not apt at reading letters? 35

CHRISTIAN	Hum!
ROXANE	*(Aloud, with despair)*
	But this is horrible!
FRIAR	*(Who has turned his lantern on CYRANO)*
	'Tis you?
CHRISTIAN	'Tis I!
FRIAR	*(Turning the light on to him, and as if a doubt struck him on seeing his beauty)*
	But . . .
ROXANE	*(Quickly)*
	I have overlooked the postscript—see—
	"Give twenty pistoles* for the convent."

pistoles: European gold coins

FRIAR	Oh! Most worthy lord! 40
	(To ROXANE)
	Submit you?
ROXANE	*(With a martyr's look)*
	I submit!
	(While RAGUENEAU opens the door and CHRISTIAN invites the FRIAR to enter, she whispers to CYRANO.)
	Oh, keep de Guiche at bay! He will be here!
	Let him not enter till . . .
CYRANO	I understand!
	(To the FRIAR)
	What time need you to tie the marriage-knot?
FRIAR	A quarter of an hour.
CYRANO	*(Pushing them all toward the house)*
	Go! I stay.
ROXANE	*(To CHRISTIAN)*
	Come! 45
	(They enter.)
CYRANO	Now, how to detain de Guiche so long?
	(He jumps on the bench, climbs to the balcony by the wall.)

Come! up I go! I have my plan!
(The lutes begin to play a very sad air.)
                                                    What, ho!
(The tremolo grows more and more weird.)
It is a man! ay! 'tis a man this time!
(He is on the balcony, pulls his hat over his eyes, takes off his sword, wraps himself in his cloak, then leans over.)
'Tis not too high!
(He strides across the balcony, and drawing to him a long branch of one of the trees that are by the garden wall, he hangs on to it with both hands, ready to let himself fall.)
I'll shake this atmosphere!   50

DE GUICHE   *(Who enters, masked, feeling his way in the dark)*
               What can that cursed friar be about?

CYRANO   Doomed if he knows my voice!
               (Letting go with one hand, he pretends to turn an invisible key. Solemnly)
                                              Cric! Crac!
               Assume thou, Cyrano, to serve the turn,
               The accent of thy native Bergerac!

DE GUICHE   *(Looking at the house)*
               'Tis there. I see dim—this mask hinders me!   5
               (He is about to enter, when CYRANO *leaps from the balcony, holding on to the branch, which bends, dropping him between the door and* DE GUICHE; *he pretends to fall heavily, as from a great height, and lies flat on the ground, motionless, as if stunned.* DE GUICHE *starts back.)*
               What's this?
               (When he looks up, the branch has sprung back into its place. He sees only the sky and is lost in amazement.)
               Where fell that man from?

CYRANO   *(Sitting up, and speaking with a Gascon accent)*
               From the moon!

DE GUICHE   From . . . ?

CYRANO   *(In a dreamy voice)*
                                        What's o'clock?

DE GUICHE   He's lost his mind, for sure!

CYRANO	What hour? What country this? What month? What day? 10
DE GUICHE	But . . .
CYRANO	I am stupefied!
DE GUICHE	Sir!
CYRANO	Like a bomb I fell from the moon!
DE GUICHE	*(Impatiently)* Come now!
CYRANO	*(Rising, in a terrible voice)* I say—the moon!
DE GUICHE	*(Recoiling)* Good, good! let it be so! He's raving mad! 15
CYRANO	*(Walking up to him)* I say from the moon! I mean no metaphor!
DE GUICHE	But . . .
CYRANO	Was't a hundred years—a minute, since? I cannot guess what time that fall embraced That I was in that saffron-colored ball!
DE GUICHE	*(Shrugging his shoulders)* Good! Let me pass!
CYRANO	*(Intercepting him)* Where am I? 20 Tell the truth! Fear not to tell! Oh, spare me not! Where? where have I fallen like a shooting star?
DE GUICHE	Move!
CYRANO	The fall was lightning-quick! no time to choose Where I should fall—I know not where it be! 25 Oh, tell me! Is it on a moon or earth, That my posterior weight has landed me?

DE GUICHE	I tell you, sir—
CYRANO	*(Screeching in terror, making* DE GUICHE *start back)*
DE GUICHE	*(Who has remembered his mask)* This mask of mine . . .
CYRANO	*(Pretending to be reassured)* In Venice? ha!—or Rome?
DE GUICHE	*(Trying to pass)* A lady waits . . .
CYRANO	*(Quite reassured)* Oh-ho! I am in Paris!

30

DE GUICHE	*(Smiling in spite of himself)* The fool is comical!
CYRANO	You laugh?

DE GUICHE	I laugh, but would get by!
CYRANO	*(Beaming with joy)*
	I have shot back to Paris!
	(Quite at ease, laughing, dusting himself, bowing)
	Come—pardon me—by the last waterspout,
	Covered with ether—accident of travel! 35
	My eyes still full of stardust, and my spurs
	Encumbered by the planets' filaments!
	(Picking something off his sleeve)
	Ha! on my doublet?—ah, a comet's hair!
	(He puffs as if to blow it away.)
DE GUICHE	*(Beside himself)*
	Sir!
CYRANO	*(Just as he is about to pass, holds out his leg as if to show him something and stops him.)*
	In my leg—the calf—there is a tooth 40
	Of the Great Bear,* and, passing Neptune close,
	I would avoid his trident's point, and fell,
	Thus sitting, plump, right in the Scales.* My weight
	Is marked, still registered, up there in heaven!
	(Hurriedly preventing DE GUICHE *from passing, and detaining him by the button of his doublet)*
	I swear to you that if you squeezed my nose 45
	It would spout milk!
DE GUICHE	Milk?
CYRANO	From the Milky Way!
DE GUICHE	Heavens!
CYRANO	*(Crossing his arms)*
	I fall, sir, out of heaven!
	Now, would you credit it, that as I fell
	I saw that Sirius* wears a nightcap? True!
	(Confidentially)
	The other Bear* is still too small to bite.
	(Laughing)
	I went through the Lyre,* but I snapped a cord;
	(Proudly)
	I mean to write the whole thing in a book;
	The small gold stars, that, wrapped up in my cloak,

Great Bear: constellation Ursa Major

Scales: constellation Libra

Sirius: the brightest star

50 **The other Bear:** constellation Ursa Minor

Lyre: constellation Lyra

	I carried safe away at no small risks,	
	Will serve for asterisks i' the printed page! 55	
DE GUICHE	Come, make an end! I want . . .	
CYRANO	Oh-ho! You are sly!	
DE GUICHE	Sir!	
CYRANO	You would worm all out of me!—the way	
	The moon is made, and if men breathe and live	
	In its rotund cucurbita?*	cucurbita (Latin): gourd
DE GUICHE	*(Angrily)*	
	No, no! I want . . . 60	
CYRANO	Ha, ha!—to know how I got up?	
	Hark, it was by a method all my own.	
DE GUICHE	*(Wearied)*	
	He's mad!	
CYRANO	*(Contemptuously)*	
	Not for me the stupid eagle	
	Of Regiomontanus,* nor the timid	Regiomontanus: a fifteenth-
	Pigeon of Archytas*—neither of those! 65	century German astronomer
		Archytas: an ancient philosopher
DE GUICHE	Ay, 'tis a fool! But 'tis a learned fool!	
CYRANO	No imitator I of other men!	
	Six novel methods, all, this brain invented!	
	(DE GUICHE *has succeeded in getting by, and goes toward*	
	ROXANE's *door.* CYRANO *follows him, ready to stop him*	
	by force.)	
DE GUICHE	*(Turning round)*	
	Six?	
CYRANO	*(Volubly)*	
	First, with body naked as your hand, 70	
	Festooned about with crystal flacons, full	
	O' the early morning dew;	
	My body to the sun's fierce rays exposed	
	To let it suck me up, as 't sucks the dew!	

DE GUICHE	(*Surprised, making one step toward* CYRANO)
	Ah! that makes one!	75

CYRANO	(*Stepping back, and enticing him further away*)
	And then, the second way,
	To generate wind—for my impetus*—
	To rarefy* air, in a cedar case,
	By mirrors placed icosahedron-wise.*

impetus: energy or force

rarefy: make less dense

icosahedron-wise: like a twenty-sided formation

DE GUICHE	(*Making another step*)
	Two!

CYRANO	(*Still stepping backward*)
	Or—	80
	For I have some mechanic skill—
	To make a grasshopper, with springs of steel,
	And launch myself by quick succeeding fires
	Saltpetre*-fed to the stars' pastures blue!

saltpetre: the mineral potassium nitrate, that is, rock salt

DE GUICHE	(*Unconsciously following him and counting on his fingers*)
	Three!

CYRANO	Or (since fumes have property to mount)
	To charge a globe with fumes, sufficiently
	To carry me aloft!

DE GUICHE	(*Same play, more and more astonished*)
	Well, that makes four!	85

CYRANO	Or smear myself with marrow from a bull,
	Since, at the lowest point of Zodiac,
	Phoebus well loves to suck that marrow up!

DE GUICHE	(*Amazed*)
	Five!

CYRANO	(*Who, while speaking, had drawn him to the other side of the square near a bench*)
	Sitting on an iron platform—thence
	To throw a magnet in the air. This is	90
	A method well conceived—the magnet flown,
	Infallibly the iron will pursue.
	Then quick! relaunch your magnet, and you thus
	Can mount and mount unmeasured distances!

DE GUICHE	Here are six excellent expedients! 95 Which of the six chose you?
CYRANO	Why, none! a seventh!
DE GUICHE	Astonishing! What was it?
CYRANO	I'll recount.
DE GUICHE	This wild eccentric becomes interesting!
CYRANO	*(Making a noise like the waves, with weird gestures)* Houuh! Houuh!
DE GUICHE	Well.
CYRANO	You have guessed?
DE GUICHE	Not I!
CYRANO	The tide! 100 I' th' witching hour when the moon woos the wave, I laid me, fresh from a sea-bath, on the shore— And, failing not to put head foremost—for The hair holds the seawater in its mesh— I rose in air, straight! straight! like angel's flight, 105 And mounted, mounted, gently, effortless, When lo! a sudden shock! Then . . .
DE GUICHE	*(Overcome by curiosity, sitting down on the bench)* Then?
CYRANO	Oh! then . . . *(Suddenly returning to his natural voice)* The quarter's gone—I'll hinder you no more. The marriage-vows are made.

DE GUICHE	*(Springing up)*
	               What? Am I mad?
	That voice?
	(The house-door opens. Lackeys appear carrying lighted candelabra. Light. CYRANO *gracefully uncovers.)*
	       That nose—Cyrano?

CYRANO	*(Bowing)* <div align="center">Cyrano . . . 110</div>While we were chatting, they have said their vows.
DE GUICHE	Who? *(He turns round. Behind the lackeys appear* ROXANE *and* CHRISTIAN, *holding each other by the hand. The* FRIAR *follows them, smiling.* RAGUENEAU *also holds a candlestick. The* DUENNA *closes the rear, bewildered.)* <div align="center">Heavens!</div>*(To* ROXANE*)* <div align="center">You?</div>*(Recognizing* CHRISTIAN, *in amazement)* <div align="center">He?</div>*(Bowing, with admiration, to* ROXANE*)* <div align="center">Cunningly contrived!</div>*(To* CYRANO*)* My compliments—Sir Apparatus-maker! Your story would arrest at Peter's gate Saints eager for their paradise! Note well The details. 'Faith! They'd make a stirring book! 5
CYRANO	*(Bowing)* I shall not fail to follow your advice.
FRIAR	*(Showing with satisfaction the two lovers to* DE GUICHE*)* A handsome couple, son, made one by you!
DE GUICHE	*(With a freezing look)* <div align="right">Ay!</div>*(To* ROXANE*)* Bid your bridegroom, Madame, fond farewell.
ROXANE	<div align="center">Why so?</div>
DE GUICHE	*(To* CHRISTIAN*)* Even now the regiment departs. 10 Join it!
ROXANE	<div align="center">It goes to battle?</div>
DE GUICHE	<div align="center">Without doubt.</div>

SCENE X

ROXANE	But the Cadets—
	They go not?
DE GUICHE	Oh, ay! they go.
	(Drawing out the paper he had put in his pocket)
	Here is the order.
	(To CHRISTIAN*)*
	Baron, bear it, quick!
ROXANE	*(Throwing herself in* CHRISTIAN's *arms)*
	Christian!
DE GUICHE	*(Sneeringly to* CYRANO*)*
	The wedding night is far, methinks!
CYRANO	*(Aside)*
	He thinks to give me pain of death by this!
CHRISTIAN	*(To* ROXANE*)*
	Oh! once again! Your lips!
CYRANO	Come, come, enough!
CHRISTIAN	*(Still kissing* ROXANE*)*
	'Tis hard to leave her, you know not . . .
CYRANO	*(Trying to draw him away)*
	I know.
	(Sound of drums beating a march in the distance)
DE GUICHE	The regiment starts!
ROXANE	*(To* CYRANO, *holding back* CHRISTIAN, *whom* CYRANO *is drawing away)*
	Oh! I trust him you!
	Promise me that no risks shall put his life
	In danger!
CYRANO	I will try my best, but promise—
	That I cannot!
ROXANE	But swear he shall be prudent?
CYRANO	Again,
	I'll do my best, but . . .

15

20

ROXANE	In the siege Let him not suffer!
CYRANO	All that man can do, I . . .
ROXANE	Promise that he Shall be faithful!
CYRANO	Doubtless, but . . .
ROXANE	Make sure that 25 He writes oft?
CYRANO	*(Pausing)* *That* I promise you!

Curtain

About the Drama

1. List several lines from the play that reveal the character of de Guiche. What tone does the author seem to take toward him? Explain.

2. Why does Christian desire to "speak for himself"? What happens when he does?

3. What does Roxane's response to Christian's "words of love" tell us about her?

4. Reread Cyrano's speeches on pages 432–33. What do these speeches tell us about Cyrano's view of love? What does Cyrano's view of love tell us about him?

5. How do Cyrano's dealings with Roxane and Christian demonstrate both a positive and negative moral tone?

6. Name two elements of the plot in Act III that reinforce one of the play's major themes—the contrast of appearances with reality.

ACT IV

The Cadets of Gascony

Post occupied by company of CARBON DE CASTEL-JALOUX at the siege of Arras. Tents, scattered weapons, drums, et cetera. It is near daybreak, and the east is yellow with approaching dawn. Sentries at intervals. Campfires.

The curtain rise discovers the CADETS asleep, rolled in their cloaks. CARBON DE CASTEL-JALOUX and LE BRET keep watch. They are both very thin and pale. CHRISTIAN is asleep among the others, wrapped in his cloak, in the foreground, his face lighted by the flickering fire. Silence.

LE BRET	'Tis terrible.
CARBON	Not a morsel left.
LE BRET	Frightful!

CARBON	(Making a sign that he should speak lower)
	Speak quietly. You will awake them.
	(To the CADETS)
	                Hush!
	Sleep on.
	(To LE BRET)
	    He who sleeps, dines!

LE BRET	But that is sorry comfort for the sleepless! What starvation! (Firing is heard in the distance.)
CARBON	Oh, plague take their firing! 'Twill wake my sons. 5
SENTINEL	(From without) Hark! Who goes there?
CYRANO	Bergerac.
SENTINEL	Who goes there?
CYRANO	(Appearing at the top) Bergerac, idiot!
LE BRET	(Advances anxiously to meet him) Cyrano!

CYRANO	*(Making signs that he should not awake the others)* Hush!
LE BRET	Wounded?
CYRANO	No! you know it has become their custom To shoot at me every morning and to miss me. 10
LE BRET	This passes all! To take letters at each day's dawn. To risk—

CYRANO	*(Stopping before* CHRISTIAN*)*
	    I promised he should write often.
	(He looks at him.)
	He sleeps. How pale he is, but how handsome still.
	If his poor little ladylove knew that he is dying of
	    hunger . . .

LE BRET	Get you quick to bed.
CYRANO	Nay, never scold, Le Bret. 15 I ran but little risk. I have found me a spot To pass the Spanish lines, where each night They lie drunk.
LE BRET	You should try To bring us back provision.
CYRANO	A man must carry no weight 20 Who would get by there! But there will be A surprise for us this night. The French will eat or die If I mistake not!
LE BRET	Oh! tell me!
CYRANO	Nay, I am not certain. You will see!
CARBON	It is disgraceful That we should starve while we're besieging!
LE BRET	Alas, 25 How complicated is this siege of Arras! To think that while We are besieging, we should ourselves be besieged by the Cardinal Infante of Spain.

CYRANO	It were well done if *he* should be besieged.
LE BRET	I am in earnest.
CYRANO	Oh! indeed!
LE BRET	To think 30 You risk a life so precious for the sake of a letter. Where are you going?
CYRANO	*(At the door of the tent)* I am going to write another.

(CYRANO goes into the tent. The day is breaking in a rosy light. The town of Arras is golden in the horizon. The report of cannon is heard in the distance, followed immediately by the beating of drums far away to the left. Other drums are heard much nearer. Sounds of stirring in the camp. Voices of officers in the distance.)

SCENE ii

CARBON	*(Sighing)* The reveille! Nourishing sleep, thou art at an end! *(The CADETS move and stretch themselves.)* I know well what will be their first cry!
FIRST CADET	*(Sitting up)* I am so hungry!
SECOND CADET	I am dying of hunger.
TOGETHER	Oh!
CARBON	Up with you!
THIRD CADET	Cannot move a limb.
FOURTH CADET	Nor can I.
FIRST CADET	*(Looking at himself in a bit of armor)* My tongue is yellow. 5 The air at this season of the year is hard to digest.
FIFTH CADET	My coronet for a bit of cheese!

SIXTH CADET	If none can furnish to my stomach, I shall retire to my tent—like Achilles!*
CARBON	*(Going to the tent and calling softly)* Cyrano! Come to my aid, you who have the art 10 Of quick retort and gay jest. Come, hearten them up.
CYRANO	*(Appearing from the tent, very calm, with a pen stuck behind his ear and a book in his hand. To the* FIRST CADET*)* Why drag you your legs so sorrowfully?
FIRST CADET	I have something in my heels which weighs them down.
CYRANO	And what may that be?
FIRST CADET	My stomach!
CYRANO	So have I, 'faith!
FIRST CADET	It must be in your way?
CYRANO	Nay, I am all the taller.
THIRD CADET	My stomach's hollow. 5
CYRANO	'Faith, 'twill make a fine drum to sound the assault.
FOURTH CADET	I have a ringing in my ears.
CYRANO	'Tis false; a hungry stomach has no ears.
SIXTH CADET	What can we devour?
CYRANO	*(Throwing him the book that he is carrying)* How about the *Iliad*?*
SEVENTH CADET	The first minister in Paris has his four meals a day! 10
CYRANO	'Twere courteous if he sent you some salad!
SIXTH CADET	And why not? with oil, too!

Achilles: Greek hero in Homer's *Iliad* who removes himself from war, shutting himself in his tent

SCENE iii

Iliad: Homer's epic poem about the Trojan War

CYRANO	A little salad, Richelieu, s'il vous plait!*

s'il vous plait (SEEL VOO PLAY): "if you please"

FIRST CADET	*(Shrugging his shoulders)* Always your pointed word!

CYRANO

       Ay, pointed words!
I would fain die thus, some soft summer eve,   15
Making a pointed word for a good cause.
To make a soldier's end by soldier's sword,
Wielded by some brave adversary—die
On blood-stained turf, not on a fever-bed,
A point upon my lips, a point within my heart.   20

ALL

We're hungry!

CYRANO

      All your thoughts
Of meat and drink! Bertrand the fifer!
You were shepherd once—draw out your fife,
Play to these greedy, guzzling soldiers.
Play old country airs with plaintive rhythm recurring, 25
Where lurk sweet echoes of the dear home voices,
Each note of which calls like a little sister,
Those airs slow, slow ascending, as the smoke wreaths
Rise from our native hamlets,*

hamlet: a small village

Their music strikes the ear in the Gascon tongue!   30
On your flute your fingers are a-dancing
A birdlike minuet! O flute!
Make us a music pastoral days recalling—
The soul-time of your youth, in country pastures!
(The old man begins to play.)
Hark to the music, Gascons! 'Tis no longer   35
The piercing fife of camp—but 'neath his fingers
The flute of the woods! No more the call to combat,
'Tis now the love-song of the wandering goat-herds!
Hark! 'tis the valley, the wetlands, the forest,
The sunburnt shepherd boy with scarlet beret,   40
The dusk of evening on the Dordogne River—
'Tis Gascony! Hark, Gascons, to the music!
(The CADETS sit with bowed heads; their eyes have a far-off look as if dreaming, and they surreptitiously wipe away their tears with their cuffs and the corner of their cloaks.)

CARBON	*(To CYRANO in a whisper)* But you make them weep!

CYRANO	Ay, for homesickness.
	Nobler pain than hunger,—'tis of the soul, not of
	The body! Heartache is better than stomachache. 45
CARBON	But you weaken their courage
	By playing thus on their heart strings!
CYRANO	*(Making a sign to a drummer to approach)*
	Not I.
	The hero that sleeps in Gascon blood Is ever ready to
	awake in them.
	'Twould suffice—
	(He makes a signal; the drum beats.)
CADETS	*(Standing up and rushing to take arms)*
	What? What is it?
CYRANO	*(Smiling)*
	You see! 50
	One roll of the drum is enough!
	Good-bye dreams, regrets, native land, love—
	All that the pipe called forth the drum has chased away!
THIRD CADET	*(Looking toward the back of the stage)*
	Ho! here comes Monsieur de Guiche!
CADETS	*(Muttering)*
	Ugh! . . . Ugh!
CYRANO	*(Smiling)*
	Flattering welcome! 55
FIRST CADET	We are sick to death of him!
SECOND CADET	With his lace collar over his armor,
	Playing the fine gentleman!
THIRD CADET	As if one wore linen over steel!
SECOND CADET	Another plotting courtier! 60
THIRD CADET	His uncle's own nephew!
CARBON	For all that—a Gascon.

FIRST CADET	Ay, false Gascon! Trust him not. Gascons should ever be crack-brained. Naught more dangerous than a rational Gascon. 65
LE BRET	How pale he is!
FOURTH CADET	Oh! he is hungry, Just like us poor devils; but under his cuirass, With its fine gilt nails, his stomachache Glitters brave in the sun.
CYRANO	*(Hurriedly)* Let us not seem to suffer either! 70 *(ALL begin spreading out the games on the drums, the stools, the ground, and on their cloaks and begin lighting long pipes. CYRANO walks up and down, reading a little book that he has drawn from his pocket. Enter DE GUICHE. ALL appear absorbed and happy. He is very pale. He goes up to CARBON.)*
DE GUICHE	*(To CARBON)* Good day! *(They examine each other. Aside, with satisfaction)* He's green.
CARBON	*(Aside)* He has nothing left but eyes.
DE GUICHE	*(Looking at the CADETS)* Sirs, on all sides I hear that in your Ranks you scoff at me; the mountain-bred, Poor country squires scarce find for me—their colonel— A disdain sufficient! call me plotter, wily courtier! 5 It does not please their mightiness to see A point-lace collar on my steel cuirass, They enrage, because a man may be not Ragged, yet a Gascon! *(Silence. All play)* Shall I command Your captain punish you? No.
CARBON	I am free, 10 Moreover, will not punish.
DE GUICHE	Ah!

CARBON   I have paid my company—'tis mine.
                      I bow but to headquarters.

DE GUICHE   So?—in faith!
                      That will suffice.
                      (Addressing himself to the CADETS*)*
                                I can despise
                      Your taunts. 'Tis well known how   15
                      I bear me in the war; yesterday, they saw the rage
                      With which I beat back the Count of Bucquoi;
                      Assembling my own men, I fell on his,
                      And charged three separate times!

CYRANO   *(Without lifting his eyes from his book)*
                      And your white scarf?   20

DE GUICHE   *(Surprised and gratified)*
                      You know that detail? Troth! It happened thus.
                      While recalling the troops
                      For the third charge, a band of fugitives
                      Bore me with them, close by the hostile ranks.

I was in peril—capture, sudden death!—   25
When I thought of the good expedient
To loosen and let fall the scarf which told
My military rank; thus I contrived—
Without attention waked—to leave the foes,
And suddenly returned, reinforced   30
With my own men, to scatter them!
(The CADETS *pretend not to be listening. They wait.)*
                          And now,
What say you, sir?

CYRANO   I say, that Henry IV*

       Henry IV: the king of France
                   (1589–1610)

Had not, by any dangerous odds, been forced
To strip himself of his white helmet plume.
(Silent delight)

DE GUICHE   The ruse succeeded, though!
(Same suspension of play, etc.)

CYRANO   Oh, may be! But   35
One does not lightly abdicate the honor
To serve as target to the enemy.
(Increasing satisfaction among the CADETS *as the games
resume)*
Had I been present when your scarf fell low—
Our courage, sir, is of a different sort—
I would have picked it up and put it on.   40

DE GUICHE   Oh, ay! Another Gascon boast!

CYRANO   A boast?
Lend it to me. I pledge myself, tonight,
With it across my breast, to lead th' assault.

DE GUICHE   Another Gascon vaunt!*   **vaunt:** boastful remark
You know the scarf lies with the enemy,   45
Upon the brink of the stream.
The place is riddled now with shot—
No one can fetch it hither!

CYRANO   *(Drawing the scarf from his pocket, and holding it out
to him)*
                 Here it is.

(Silence. The Cadets stifle their laughter in their cards and dice-boxes. De Guiche turns and looks at them; they instantly become grave and set to play. One of them whistles indifferently the air just played by the fifer.)

De Guiche   (Taking the scarf)
I thank you. It will now enable me
To make a signal that I had forborne   50
To make—till now.
(He goes to the rampart, climbs it, and waves the scarf thrice.)

All   What's that?

Sentinel   (From the top of the rampart)
See you the man down there, who runs?

De Guiche   (Descending)
'Tis a false Spanish spy
Who is extremely useful to my ends.
The news he carries to the enemy   55
Are those I prompt him with—so, in a word,
We have an influence on their decisions!

Cyrano   Scoundrel!

De Guiche   (Carelessly knotting on his scarf)
'Tis opportune. What were we saying?
Ah! I have news for you. Last evening
To victual us, the marshal did attempt   60
A final effort—secretly he went
To Dourlens, where the king's provisions be.
But—to return to camp more easily—
He took with him a goodly force of troops.
Those who attacked us now would have fine sport!   65
Half of the army's absent from the camp!

Carbon   Ay, if the Spaniards knew,
'Twere ill for us—but they know nothing of it?

De Guiche   Oh! they know.
They will attack us.

Carbon   Ah!

DE GUICHE	For my false spy 70 Came to warn me of their attack. He said, "I can decide the point for their assault; Where would you have it? I will tell them 'tis The least defended—they'll attempt you there." I answered, "Good. Go out of camp, but watch 75 My signal. Choose the point from whence it comes."
CARBON	*(To the* CADETS*)* Make ready! *(All rise; sounds of swords and belts being buckled.)*
DE GUICHE	'Twill be in an hour.
FIRST CADET	Good! *(They all sit down again and take up their games.)*
DE GUICHE	*(To* CARBON*)* Time must be gained. The marshal will return.
CARBON	How gain it?
DE GUICHE	You will all be good enough To let yourselves to be killed.
CYRANO	Vengeance! oho! 80
DE GUICHE	I do not say that, if I loved you well, I had chosen you and yours. But, as things stand— Your courage yielding to no corps the palm— I serve my king, and serve my grudge as well.
CYRANO	Permit that I express my gratitude— 85
DE GUICHE	I know you love to fight against five score; You will not now complain of paltry odds. *(He goes upstage with* CARBON*.)*
CYRANO	*(To the* CADETS*)* We shall add to the Gascon coat of arms, With its six bars of blue and gold, one more— The blood-red bar that was a-missing there! 90

(DE GUICHE *speaks in a low voice with* CARBON *at the back. Orders are given. Preparations go forward.* CYRANO *goes up to* CHRISTIAN, *who stands with crossed arms.*)
Christian!
(Putting his hand on CHRISTIAN's *shoulder)*

CHRISTIAN
(Shaking his head)
                    Roxane . . .

CYRANO
                              Alas!

CHRISTIAN
At least, I'd send my heart's farewell to her
In a fair letter!

CYRANO
                    I had suspicion it would be today,
(Drawing a letter out of his doublet)
And had already writ . . .

CHRISTIAN
                              Show!

CYRANO
                              Will you . . . ?

CHRISTIAN
(Taking the letter)
Ay!
(He opens and reads it.)
    Hold!

CYRANO
          What?

CHRISTIAN
                    Here,   95
This little spot!

CYRANO
(Taking the letter, with an innocent look)
                    A spot?

CHRISTIAN
                              A tear!

CYRANO
Poets, at last—by dint of counterfeiting—
Take counterfeit for true—that is the charm!
This farewell letter—it was passing sad,
I wept myself in writing it!

CHRISTIAN
                              Wept? why?   100

CYRANO
Oh! death itself is hardly terrible,
But, ne'er to see her more! That is death's sting!

For I shall never . . .
(CHRISTIAN *looks at him.*)
                                    We shall . . .
(*Quickly*)
                                              I mean, you shall . . .

CHRISTIAN   (*Snatching the letter from him*)
                   Give me that letter!
                   (*A rumor, far off in the camp*)

VOICE OF SENTINEL   Who goes there? Halloo!
                   (*Shots—voices—carriage-bells*)

CARBON   What is it?

SENTINEL   (*On the rampart*)
                            'Tis a carriage!
                   (*All rush to see.*)

CRIES   In the camp?   105
                   It enters! It comes from the enemy!
                   Fire! No! The coachman cries! What does he say?
                   "On the king's service!"
                   (*Everyone is on the rampart, staring. The bells come
                   nearer.*)

DE GUICHE   The king's service? How?
                   (*All descend and draw up in line.*)

CARBON   Hats off, all!

DE GUICHE   The king's! Draw up in line!
                   Let him describe his curve as it befits!
                   (*The carriage enters at full speed, covered with dust and
                   mud. The curtains are drawn close. Two* LACKEYS *behind.
                   It is pulled up suddenly.*)

CARBON   Beat a salute! 110
                   (*A roll of drums. The* CADETS *uncover.*)

DE GUICHE   Lower the carriage steps!
                   (*Two* CADETS *rush forward. The door opens.*)

ROXANE   (*Jumping down from the carriage*)
                            Good day!

(All are bowing to the ground, but at the sound of a woman's voice every head is instantly raised.)

DE GUICHE   On the king's service! You?

ROXANE   Ay,—King Love's!
            What other king?

CYRANO   *(Aside)*
                              God is good!

CHRISTIAN   *(Rushing forward)*
                                        Why have you come?

ROXANE   This siege—'tis too long!

CHRISTIAN   But why?

ROXANE   I will tell you all!

CYRANO   *(Aside)*
            Do I dare look at her?

DE GUICHE	You cannot remain here!

ROXANE	But I say yes! 5
	Who will push a drum hither for me?
	(She seats herself on the drum they roll forward.)
	    So! I thank you.
	(She laughs.)
	My carriage was fired at! Look!
	Would you not think 'twas made of a pumpkin, like
	Cinderella's chariot in the tale,
	And the footmen out of rats?
	(Sending a kiss with her lips to CHRISTIAN*)*
	    Good morrow! 10
	(Examining them all)
	You look not merry, any of you!
	Ah! know you that 'tis a long road to get to Arras?
	(Seeing CYRANO*)*
	Cousin, delighted!

CYRANO	*(Coming up to her)* But how . . . ?
ROXANE	How found I the way to the army? Simply enough, I followed the country laid waste. 15 Ah, what horrors there! Had I not seen, Then I could never have believed it! Well, gentlemen, if such be the service of your king, I would fainer serve mine!
CYRANO	But where Did you get through?
ROXANE	Why, through the Spanish lines. 20
FIRST CADET	For subtle craft, give me a woman!
DE GUICHE	But how did you Pass through their lines?
LE BRET	Faith! that must have been A hard matter!
ROXANE	No—I but drove quietly forward, And when some hidalgo* of haughty mien Would have stayed me, lo! 25

hidalgo: low-ranking Spanish nobleman

I showed at the window my sweetest smile, and these
Señors being (with no disrespect to you) the most
Gallant gentlemen in the world—I passed on!

CARBON   True, that smile is a passport!

DE GUICHE   You must leave this place!

ROXANE   I?   30

LE BRET   No time to lose.

ROXANE   But wherefore must I?

CHRISTIAN   *(Embarrassed)*
                                      'Tis that . . .

CYRANO   *(The same)*
              In three quarters of an hour . . .

DE GUICHE   *(The same)*
                                      Or for . . .

CARBON   *(The same)*
                                      It were best . . .

LE BRET   *(The same)*
              You might . . .

ROXANE   You are going to fight? I stay here.

ALL   No, no!

ROXANE   He is my husband!
              (She throws herself into CHRISTIAN's *arms.)*
              They shall kill us both together!   35

CHRISTIAN   Why do you look at me thus?

ROXANE   I will tell you why!

DE GUICHE   *(In despair)*
              'Tis a post of mortal danger!

ROXANE	*(Turning round)* <div align="center">Mortal danger!</div>
CYRANO	Proof enough, that he has put us here!
ROXANE	*(To DE GUICHE)* So, sir, you would have made a widow of me?
DE GUICHE	Nay, on my oath . . .
ROXANE	<div align="right">I will not go! I am reckless now, 40</div>And I shall not stir from here! Besides, 'tis amusing!
CYRANO	Oh-ho! So she is a heroine!
ROXANE	Monsieur de Bergerac, I am your cousin.
CADET	We will defend you well!
ROXANE	*(More and more excited)* I have no fear of that, my friends! 45 But— *(Looks at DE GUICHE)* Were it not wisest that the count retire? They may begin the attack.
DE GUICHE	<div align="right">That is not to be brooked!</div>I go to inspect the cannon and shall return. You have still time—think better of it!
ROXANE	Never! *(DE GUICHE goes out.)*
CHRISTIAN	*(Entreatingly)* Roxane!
ROXANE	<div align="center">No!</div>
FIRST CADET	<div align="center">She stays!</div>
CARBON	*(To ROXANE)* Pray, open the hand that holds your kerchief.
ROXANE	*(Opens her hand, and the handkerchief falls)* <div align="right">Why?</div>*(The whole company starts forward to pick it up.)*

SCENE vi

CARBON	*(Quickly raising it)* My company had no flag. But now, by my faith, They will have the fairest in all the camp!
ROXANE	*(Smiling)* 'Tis somewhat small.
CARBON	*(Tying the handkerchief onto the staff of his lance)* But—'tis of lace! 5
CADET	*(To the rest)* I could die happy, having seen so sweet a face, If I had something in my stomach—were it but a nut!
CARBON	*(Who has overheard, indignantly)* Shame on you! What, talk of eating when a lovely woman—
ROXANE	But your camp air is keen; I myself am famished. Pasties, cold fricassee, old wines— 10 There is my bill of fare. Pray bring it all here.
CADET	*(Aside)* All that?
ANOTHER	But where on earth find it?
ROXANE	*(Overhears; sweetly)* In my carriage.
ALL	How?
ROXANE	Now serve up—carve! Look a little closer At my coachman, gentlemen, and You will recognize a man most welcome. 15 All the sauces can be sent to table hot, if we will!
CADETS	*(Rushing to the carriage)* Ragueneau!
ROXANE	*(Looking after them)* Poor fellows!
CADETS	*(Acclamations)* Ah! Ah!

CYRANO	*(Kissing her hand)* Kind fairy!
RAGUENEAU	*(Standing on the box like a quack doctor at a fair)* Gentlemen! *(General delight)*
CADETS	Bravo! Bravo!
RAGUENEAU	The Spaniards, gazing on a lady so dainty fair, Overlooked the fare so dainty! *(Applause)*
CYRANO	*(In a whisper to* CHRISTIAN*)* Hark, Christian! 20
RAGUENEAU	And, occupied with gallantry, Perceived not— *(His draws a plate from under the seat and holds it up)* The galantine!* *(Applause. The galantine passes from hand to hand.)*
CYRANO	*(Still whispering to* CHRISTIAN*)* Prithee, one word!
ROXANE	*(As the* CADETS *return with their arms full of provisions, calls)* Christian, come, make yourself of use! *(*CHRISTIAN *turns to her at the moment when* CYRANO *was leading him aside. She arranges the food with his aid and that of the two imperturbable footmen.)*
FIRST CADET	We shall not die without having had a gullet-full— *(Quickly correcting himself on seeing* ROXANE*)* Pardon! A Balthazar feast! *(Tumult; laughter)*
ROXANE	*(Throwing a folded tablecloth at* CYRANO'S *head)* Unfold me that napkin— 25 Come, come! Be nimble!
RAGUENEAU	*(Waving a lantern)* Each of the carriage lamps is a little larder!

> galantine: a dish of boned and stuffed meat or fish, poached and served cold

CYRANO	*(In a low voice to* CHRISTIAN, *as they arrange the cloth together)* I must speak with you before you speak to her.
RAGUENEAU	My whip handle is an Arles sausage!
ROXANE	*(Pouring out wine, helping)* Since we are to die, let the rest of the army 30 Shift for itself. All for the Gascons! And mark! If de Guiche comes, let no one invite him! *(Going up to* CHRISTIAN*)* What will you?
CHRISTIAN	Nothing.
ROXANE	Nay, nay, take this biscuit, Steeped in muscat; come! but two drops!
CHRISTIAN	*(Trying to detain her)* Oh! tell me why you came?
ROXANE	Hush! In a few minutes—35 My first duty is to these poor fellows.
LE BRET	*(Who had gone up to pass a loaf on the end of a lance to the sentry on the rampart)* De Guiche!
CYRANO	Quick! Hide flasks, Plates, pie-dishes, game-baskets! Hurry! Let us all Look hungry! *(To* RAGUENEAU*)* Up on your seat! Is everything covered up? 40 *(In an instant all has been pushed into the tents or hidden under doublets, cloaks, and hats.* DE GUICHE *enters hurriedly—stops suddenly, sniffing the air. Silence.)*
DE GUICHE	It smells good here.
A CADET	*(Humming)* Lo! Lo-lo!
DE GUICHE	*(Looking at him)* What is the matter? You are very red.

SCENE vii

THE CADET	Nothing! 'Tis my blood Boiling at the thought of the coming battle!
ANOTHER	Poum, poum—poum . . .
DE GUICHE	*(Turning round)* What's that?
THE CADET	Nothing! 'Tis a song!—a little— 5
DE GUICHE	You are merry, my friend!
THE CADET	The approach of danger Is intoxicating!
DE GUICHE	*(Calling* CARBON DE CASTEL-JALOUX, *to give him an order)* Captain! I— *(He stops short on seeing him.)* Plague take me! But you look bravely, too!
CARBON	*(Crimson in the face, hiding a bottle behind his back with an evasive movement)* Oh!
DE GUICHE	I have one cannon left, And have had it carried there— *(He points behind the scenes.)* In that corner. Your men can use it in case of need. 10
ANOTHER	*(With an ingratiating smile)* Kind solicitude!
DE GUICHE	*(Shrugging his shoulders, then going quickly to* ROXANE*)* Madame, what decision do you deign to take?
ROXANE	I stay here.
DE GUICHE	You must fly!
ROXANE	No! I will stay.
DE GUICHE	Since things are thus, Give me a musket, one of you!

CARBON	Wherefore?
DE GUICHE	Because I too 15
	Mean to remain.
CYRANO	At last! This is true valor, sir!
FIRST CADET	Then you are Gascon after all,
	Spite of your lace collar?
ROXANE	What is all this?
DE GUICHE	I leave no woman in peril.
SECOND CADET	*(To the first)*
	Hark you!
	Think you not we might give him something to eat? 20
	(All the food reappears as if by magic.)
DE GUICHE	*(Whose eyes sparkle)*
	Victuals!
THIRD CADET	Yes, you'll see them coming from under every coat!
DE GUICHE	*(Controlling himself, haughtily)*
	Do you think I will eat your leavings?
CYRANO	*(Saluting him)*
	You make progress.
DE GUICHE	I will fight without br-r-eaking my fast! 25
FIRST CADET	*(With wild delight)*
	He has got the accent!
DE GUICHE	*(Laughing)*
	Have I?
FIRST CADET	'Tis a Gascon!
	(All begin to dance.)
CARBON	*(Who had disappeared behind the rampart, reappearing on the ridge)*
	I have drawn my pikemen up in line.
	They are a resolute troop.

(He points to a row of pikes, the tops of which are seen over the ridge.)

DE GUICHE (Bowing to ROXANE)
Will you accept my hand, and accompany me
While I review them?   30
(She takes it, and they go up toward the rampart. All uncover and follow them.)

CHRISTIAN (Going to CYRANO, eagerly)
Tell me quickly!
(As ROXANE appears on the ridge, the tops of the lances disappear, lowered for the salute, and a shout is raised. She bows.)

PIKEMEN (Outside)
Vivat!

CHRISTIAN   What is this secret?

CYRANO   If Roxane should . . .

CHRISTIAN Should?

CYRANO   Speak of the letters . . .

CHRISTIAN   Yes, I know!

CYRANO Do not spoil all by seeming surprised . . .

CHRISTIAN   At what?

CYRANO I must explain to you! Oh! 'tis no great matter—I but   5
Thought of it today on seeing her. You have . . .

CHRISTIAN   Tell quickly!

CYRANO You have written to her oftener than you think . . .

CHRISTIAN   How so?

CYRANO Thus, 'faith! I had taken it in hand
To express your flame for you!
At times I wrote without saying, "I am writing!"

CHRISTIAN	Ah! 10
CYRANO	'Tis simple enough!
CHRISTIAN	But how did you contrive, Since we have been cut off, thus, to . . .
CYRANO	Oh! Before dawn I was able to get through.
CHRISTIAN	*(Folding his arms)* That was simple, too? And how oft, pray you, have I written? Twice in the week? Three times? Four? 15
CYRANO	More often still.
CHRISTIAN	What! Every day?
CYRANO	Yes, every day— Twice.
CHRISTIAN	*(Violently)* And that became so mad A joy for you, that you braved death . . .
CYRANO	*(Seeing* ROXANE *returning)* Hush! Not before her! *(He goes hurriedly into his tent.)*
ROXANE	*(Running up to* CHRISTIAN*)* Ah, Christian, at last!
CHRISTIAN	*(Taking her hands)* Now tell me why— 20 Why, by these fearful paths so perilous— Across these ranks of ribald* soldiery, You have come?
ROXANE	Love, your letters brought me here!
CHRISTIAN	What say you?

ribald: vulgar or lewd, especially referring to humor

ROXANE	'Tis your fault if I ran risks! Your letters turned my head! Ah! All this month, How many! and the last one ever bettered The one that went before!

25

CHRISTIAN	What! for a few Inconsequent love letters!

ROXANE	Hold your peace! Ah! You cannot conceive it! Ever since That night, when, in a voice all new to me, Under my window you revealed your soul— Ah! Ever since I have adored you! Now Your letters all this whole month long! meseemed As if I heard that voice so tender, true, Sheltering, close! Thy fault, I say! It drew me, The voice o' th' night! Oh! Wise Penelope Would ne'er have stayed to broider on her hearthstone, If her Ulysses could have writ such letters! But would have cast away her silken bobbins, And fled to join him, mad for love as Helen!*

30

35

40 **Helen:** mythological beauty over whom the Trojan War was fought

CHRISTIAN	But . . .

ROXANE	I read, read again— Grew faint for love; I was thine utterly. Each separate page was like a petal, loosed From your own soul, and wafted thus to mine. Imprinted in each burning word was love Sincere, all-powerful—

45

CHRISTIAN	A love sincere! Can that be felt, Roxane!

ROXANE	Ay, that it can!

CHRISTIAN	You come . . . ?

ROXANE	O, Christian, my true lord, I come— I come to crave your pardon. (Ay, 'tis time To sue for pardon, now that death may come!) For the insult done to you when, frivolous, At first I loved you only for your face!

50

CHRISTIAN	*(Horror-stricken)*
	Roxane!

ROXANE	And later, love—less frivolous—
	Like a bird that spreads its wings, but cannot fly—
	Arrested by your beauty, by your soul 55
	Drawn close—I loved for both at once!

CHRISTIAN	And now?

ROXANE	Ah! You yourself have triumphed,
	And now, I love you only for your soul!

CHRISTIAN	*(Stepping backward)*
	Roxane!

ROXANE	Be happy. To be loved for beauty—
	A poor disguise that time so soon wears threadbare— 60
	Must be to noble souls, to souls aspiring,
	A torture. Your dear thoughts have now effaced
	That beauty that so won me at the outset.
	Now I see clearer—and I no more see it!

CHRISTIAN	Oh!

ROXANE	You are doubtful of such victory? 65

CHRISTIAN	*(Pained)*
	Roxane!

ROXANE	I see you cannot yet believe it.
	Such love . . . ?

CHRISTIAN	I do not ask such love as that!
	I would be loved more simply; for . . .

ROXANE	For that
	Which they have all in turns loved in thee?
	Shame! Oh, be loved henceforth in a better way! 70

CHRISTIAN	No! The first love was best!

ROXANE	Ah! How you err!
	'Tis now that I love best—love well! 'Tis that
	Which is thy true self, see! that I adore!
	Were your brilliance dimmed . . .

474 TONE

CHRISTIAN	Hush!
ROXANE	I should love still! Ay, if your beauty should today depart . . .
CHRISTIAN	Say not so! 75
ROXANE	Ay, I say it!
CHRISTIAN	Ugly? How?
ROXANE	Ugly! I swear I'd love you still!
CHRISTIAN	Oh no!
ROXANE	Are you content at last?
CHRISTIAN	*(In a choked voice)* Ay!
ROXANE	What is wrong?
CHRISTIAN	*(Gently pushing her away)* Nothing . . . I have two words to say—one second . . .
ROXANE	But—
CHRISTIAN	*(Pointing to the CADETS)* Those poor fellows, shortly doomed to death— 80 My love deprives them of the sight of you. Go—speak to them—smile on them ere they die!
ROXANE	*(Deeply affected)* Dear Christian! *(She goes up to the CADETS, who respectfully crowd round her.)*
CHRISTIAN	*(Calling toward CYRANO's tent)* Cyrano!
CYRANO	*(Reappearing, fully armed)* What? Why so pale?
CHRISTIAN	She does not love me!

SCENE ix

CYRANO	What?
CHRISTIAN	'Tis you she loves!
CYRANO	No!
CHRISTIAN	For she loves me only for my soul!
CYRANO	Truly?
CHRISTIAN	Yes!
	Therefore, 'tis you she loves! And you—love her! 5
CYRANO	I?
CHRISTIAN	Oh, I know it!
CYRANO	Ay, 'tis true!
CHRISTIAN	You love to madness!
CYRANO	Ay! And worse!
CHRISTIAN	Then tell her so!
CYRANO	No!
CHRISTIAN	And why not?
CYRANO	Look at my face! Be answered!
CHRISTIAN	She'd love me were I ugly.
CYRANO	Said she so? 10
CHRISTIAN	Ay! In those words!
CYRANO	I'm glad she told you that! But, pooh! Believe it not! I am well pleased She thought to tell you. Take it not for truth. Never grow ugly—she'd reproach me then! 15
CHRISTIAN	That I intend discovering!
CYRANO	No! I beg!

CHRISTIAN	Ay! She shall choose between us! Tell her all!
CYRANO	No! No! Spare me this!
CHRISTIAN	Because my face is haply fair, Shall I destroy your happiness? 20 'Twere too unjust!
CYRANO	And I, because by nature's freak I have The gift to say all that perchance you feel— Shall I be fatal to your happiness?
CHRISTIAN	Tell all!
CYRANO	It is ill done To tempt me thus!
CHRISTIAN	Too long I've been 25 A rival to myself—
CYRANO	Christian!
CHRISTIAN	Our union, Without witness—secret— Clandestine—can be easily dissolved.
CYRANO	He still persists!
CHRISTIAN	I will be loved myself—or not at all! 30 I'll go see what they do—there, at the end Of the post speak to her, and then let her choose One of us two!
CYRANO	It will be you.
CHRISTIAN	I pray so! *(He calls.)* Roxane!
CYRANO	No! No!
ROXANE	*(Coming up quickly)* What?

CHRISTIAN	Cyrano Has things important for your ear. *(She hastens to* CYRANO. CHRISTIAN *goes out.)*
ROXANE	Important? How? 35
CYRANO	*(In despair)* He's gone! *(To* ROXANE*)* 'Tis naught! Oh, you know how he sees importance in a trifle!
ROXANE	Did he doubt of what I said? Ah, yes, I saw he doubted!
CYRANO	*(Taking her hand)* But are you sure you told him all the truth?
ROXANE	Yes, I would love him were he . . . 5 *(She hesitates.)*
CYRANO	Does that word embarrass you before my face, Roxane?
ROXANE	I . . .
CYRANO	'Twill not hurt me! Say it! If he were ugly!
ROXANE	Yes, ugly! *(Musket report outside)* Hark! I hear a shot!
CYRANO	Hideous?
ROXANE	Hideous.
CYRANO	Disfigured?
ROXANE	Ay!
CYRANO	Grotesque?
ROXANE	He could not be grotesque to me! 10
CYRANO	You'd love the same?

ROXANE	The same—nay, even more!
CYRANO	*(Losing command over himself—aside)* It's true, perchance, love waits me there! *(To ROXANE)* I . . . Roxane . . . listen . . .
LE BRET	*(Entering hurriedly—to CYRANO)* Cyrano!
CYRANO	*(Turning round)* What?
LE BRET	Hush! *(He whispers something to him.)*
CYRANO	*(Letting go ROXANE's hand and exclaiming)* Ah!
ROXANE	What is it?
CYRANO	*(To himself—stunned)* All is over now. *(More shots)*
ROXANE	What is the matter? Hark! Another shot! *(She goes up to look outside.)*
CYRANO	It is too late, now I can never tell! 15
ROXANE	*(Trying to rush out)* What has chanced?
CYRANO	*(Rushing to stop her)* Nothing! *(Some CADETS enter, trying to hide something they are carrying, and close round it to prevent ROXANE's approaching.)*
ROXANE	And those men? *(CYRANO draws her away.)* What were you just about To say before . . . ?

CYRANO	Nothing now, I swear!
	(Solemnly)
	I swear that Christian's soul, his nature, were—
	(Hastily correcting himself)
	Nay, that they are, the noblest, greatest . . .
ROXANE	*(Catches at the word)*
	Were?
	(With a loud scream)
	Oh!　20
	(She rushes up, pushing everyone aside.)
CYRANO	All is over now!
ROXANE	*(Seeing* CHRISTIAN *lying on the ground, wrapped in his cloak)*
	O Christian!
LE BRET	*(To* CYRANO*)*
	Struck by first shot of the enemy!
	*(*ROXANE *flings herself down by* CHRISTIAN*. Fresh reports of cannon—clash of arms—clamor—beating of drums.)*

CARBON	*(With sword in the air)* O come! Your muskets. *(Followed by the* CADETS, *he passes to the other side of the ramparts.)*
ROXANE	Christian!
CARBON	*(From the other side)* Ho! Make haste!
ROXANE	Christian!
CARBON	Form line!
ROXANE	Christian!
CARBON	Handle your match! *(*RAGUENEAU *rushes up, bringing water in a helmet.)*
CHRISTIAN	*(In a dying voice)* Roxane!
CYRANO	*(Quickly, whispering into* CHRISTIAN's *ear, while* ROXANE *distractedly tears a piece of linen from his breast, which she dips into the water)* I told her all. She loves you still. *(*CHRISTIAN *closes his eyes.)*
ROXANE	How, My sweet love?
CARBON	Draw ramrods!
ROXANE	*(To* CYRANO*)* He is not dead?
CARBON	Open your charges with your teeth!
ROXANE	His cheek Grows cold against my own!
CARBON	Ready! Present!
ROXANE	A letter! 'Tis for me! *(She opens it.)*

25

CYRANO	*(Aside)* My letter!
CARBON	Fire! *(Musket reports—shouts—noise of battle)*
CYRANO	*(Trying to disengage his hand, which* ROXANE *on her knees is holding)* But, Roxane, hark, they fight!
ROXANE	Stay yet awhile. 30 For he is dead. You knew him, you alone. *(Weeping quietly)* Ah, was not his a beauteous soul, a soul Wondrous!
CYRANO	*(Standing up—bareheaded)* Ay, Roxane.
ROXANE	An inspired poet?
CYRANO	Ay, Roxane.
ROXANE	And a mind sublime?
CYRANO	Oh, yes!
ROXANE	A heart too deep 35 For common minds to plumb, A spirit subtle, charming?
CYRANO	*(Firmly)* Ay, Roxane.
ROXANE	*(Flinging herself on the dead body)* Dead, my love!
CYRANO	*(Aside—drawing his sword)* Ay, and let me die today, Since, all unconscious, she mourns me—in him! *(Sounds of trumpets in the distance.)*
DE GUICHE	*(Appearing on the ramparts, bareheaded, with a wound on his forehead—in a voice of thunder)*

It is the signal! Trumpet flourishes!   40
The French bring the provisions into camp!
Hold but the place awhile!

ROXANE   See, there is blood
Upon the letter—tears!

A VOICE   *(Outside—shouting)*
Surrender!

CADETS   No!

RAGUENEAU   The danger's ever greater!

CYRANO   *(To* DE GUICHE*)*
I will charge! Take her away!   45

ROXANE   *(Kissing the letter—in a half-extinguished voice)*
O God! His tears! His blood! . . .

RAGUENEAU   *(Jumping down from the carriage and rushing toward her)*
She's swooned away!

DE GUICHE   *(On the rampart—to the* CADETS*—with fury)*
                              Stand fast!

VOICE   *(Outside)*
Lay down your arms!

CADETS   No!

CYRANO   *(To* DE GUICHE*)*
Now that you have proved your valor, sir, save her!

DE GUICHE   *(Rushing to* ROXANE, *and carrying her away in his arms)*
So be it! Gain but time, the victory's ours!

CYRANO   Good.   50
(Calling out to ROXANE, *whom* DE GUICHE, *aided by*
RAGUENEAU, *is bearing away in a fainting condition)*
Farewell, Roxane!
(Tumult. Shouts. CADETS *reappear, wounded, falling on
the scene.* CYRANO, *rushing to the battle, is stopped by*
CARBON DE CASTEL-JALOUX, *who is streaming with blood.)*

CARBON	We are breaking! I am wounded—wounded twice!
CYRANO	*(Shouting to the Gascons)* Ho, Gascons! Never turn your backs! *(To* CARBON, *whom he is supporting)* Have no fear! I have two deaths to avenge— My friend who's slain— 55 And my own dead happiness! *(They come down,* CYRANO *brandishing the lance to which is attached* ROXANE'S *handkerchief.)*

Curtain

About the Drama

1. Judging by her actions in Act IV, how is it possible to consider Roxane a dynamic character?

2. Name one internal and one external conflict that emerge as a result of Roxane's development.

3. Describe Rostand's tone toward Christian in Act IV, citing examples of Christian's words and acts from the text.

4. Why does Cyrano refuse to tell Roxane he loves her after Christian dies?

5. One theme evident throughout the play—and especially in Act IV—is the nobility inherent in self-sacrifice. How does the action of Act IV comment on this theme? Cite and explain how at least three events in Act IV reflect this theme.

Act V

Cyrano's Gazette

Fifteen years later, in 1655, the park of the convent occupied by the Ladies of the Cross, at Paris.

At the curtain rise the nuns are coming and going across the park; several are seated on the bench around MOTHER MARGUERITE. The leaves are falling.

SISTER MARTHA — *(To* MOTHER MARGUERITE*)*
Sister Claire glanced in the mirror,
Once—nay, twice, to see if her coif suited.

SCENE i

MOTHER MARGUERITE — *(To* SISTER CLAIRE*)*
'Tis not well.

SISTER CLAIRE — But I saw Sister Martha take a plum
Out of the tart.

MOTHER MARGUERITE — *(To* SISTER MARTHA*)*
That was ill done,
My sister.

SISTER CLAIRE — A little glance!   5

SISTER MARTHA — And such a little plum!

MOTHER MARGUERITE — I shall tell this to
Monsieur Cyrano.

SISTER CLAIRE — Nay, prithee do not!
He will mock!

SISTER MARTHA — He'll say we nuns
Are vain!

SISTER CLAIRE — And greedy!

MOTHER MARGUERITE — *(Smiling)*
Ay, and kind!

SISTER CLAIRE — Is it not true, pray, Mother Marguerite,   10
That he has come, each week, on Saturday
For ten years, to the convent?

MOTHER MARGUERITE	Ay! And more! Ever since—fourteen years ago—the day His cousin brought here, 'midst our woolen coifs, The worldly mourning of her widow's veil. 15
SISTER MARTHA	He only has the skill to turn her mind From grief—unsoftened yet by time—unhealed!
ALL	He is so droll! It's cheerful when he comes! He teases us! But we all like him well! We make him pasties of angelica!
MOTHER MARGUERITE	He's poor. 20
SISTER MARTHA	Who told you so, dear Mother?
MOTHER MARGUERITE	Monsieur Le Bret.
SISTER MARTHA	None help him?
MOTHER MARGUERITE	He permits not. *(In an alley at the back* ROXANE *appears, dressed in black, with a widow's coif and veil.* DE GUICHE, *imposing-looking and visibly aged, walks by her side. They saunter slowly.* MOTHER MARGUERITE *rises.)* 'Tis time we go in; Madame Madeleine walks in the garden with a visitor.
SISTER MARTHA	*(To* SISTER CLAIRE, *in a low voice)* The Marshal of Grammont? 25
SISTER CLAIRE	*(Looking at him)* 'Tis he, I think.
SISTER MARTHA	'Tis many months now Since he came to see her.
THE SISTERS	He is so busy! The court, the camp!
SISTER CLAIRE	The world!
	(They go out. DE GUICHE *and* ROXANE *come forward in silence and stop close to the embroidery frame.)*

SCENE ii

DE GUICHE	And you stay here still—ever vainly fair, Ever in weeds?

ROXANE	Ever.
DE GUICHE	Still faithful?
ROXANE	Still.
DE GUICHE	*(After a pause)* Am I forgiven?
ROXANE	Ay, since I am here.
DE GUICHE	His was a soul, you say?
ROXANE	Ah! when you knew him!

5

DE GUICHE	Ah, may be! I, perchance, too little knew him! And his last letter, ever next your heart?
ROXANE	Hung from this chain, a gentle reliquary.*

reliquary: relic used in religious ceremony, usually reputed to have belonged to some saint or martyr

DE GUICHE	And, dead, you love him still?
ROXANE	At times, meseems He is but partly dead—our hearts still speak, As if his love, still living, wrapped me round!

10

DE GUICHE	*(After another pause)* Cyrano comes to see you?
ROXANE	Often, ay. Dear, kind old friend! We call him my "Gazette." He never fails to come. Beneath this tree They place his chair, if it be fine; I wait, I broider; the clock strikes; at the last stroke I hear—for now I never turn to look, Too sure to hear his cane tap down the steps. He seats himself; with gentle raillery He mocks my tapestry that's never done; He tells me all the gossip of the week— *(LE BRET appears on the steps.)* Why, here's Le Bret! *(LE BRET descends.)* How goes it with our friend?

15

20

LE BRET	Ill! Very ill.

DE GUICHE	How?

ROXANE

(To DE GUICHE*)*
He exaggerates!

LE BRET

All that I prophesied—desertion, want!   25
His letters now make him fresh enemies!
Attacking the sham nobles, sham devout,
Sham brave, the thieving authors—all the world!

ROXANE

Ah! But his sword still holds them all in check;
None get the better of him.

DE GUICHE

(Shaking his head)
Time will show!   30

LE BRET

Ah, but I fear for him—not man's attack—
Solitude, hunger, cold December days,
That wolf-like steal into his chamber drear—
Lo! The assassins that I fear for him!
Each day he tightens by one hole his belt.   35
That poor nose—tinted like old ivory;
He has retained one shabby suit of serge.*   **serge**: wool

DE GUICHE

Ay, there is one who has no prize of Fortune—
Yet is not to be pitied!

LE BRET

(With a bitter smile)
My lord marshal!

DE GUICHE

Pity him not! He has lived out his vows,   40
Free in his thoughts, as in his actions free!

LE BRET

(In the same tone)
My lord!

DE GUICHE

(Haughtily)
True! I have all,
And he has naught.
Yet I were proud to take his hand!
(Bowing to ROXANE*)*
Adieu!

ROXANE

I go with you.
*(*DE GUICHE *bows to* LE BRET *and goes with* ROXANE *toward the steps.)*

DE GUICHE   (*Pausing, while she goes up*)
                              Ay, true—I envy him.   45
             Look you, when life is brimful of success
             Though the past hold no action foul—one feels
             A thousand self-disgusts, of which the sum
             Is not remorse, but a dim, vague unrest;
             And, as one mounts the steps of worldly fame,   50
             The duke's furred mantles trail within their folds
             A sound of dead illusions, vain regrets,
             A rustle—scarce a whisper—like as when,
             Mounting the terrace steps, your mourning robe
             Sweeps in its train the dying autumn leaves.   55

ROXANE   (*Ironically*)
             You are pensive?

DE GUICHE   True! I am!
             (*As he is going out, suddenly*)
                              Monsieur Le Bret!
             (*To* ROXANE)
             A word, with your permission?
             (*He goes to* LE BRET, *and in a low voice*)
                              True, that none
             Dare to attack your friend—but many hate him.
             Yesterday, at the queen's card-play, 'twas said,
             "That Cyrano may die—by accident!"   60
             Let him stay in, be prudent!

LE BRET   (*Raising his arms to heaven*)
                              Prudent! He!
             He's coming here. I'll warn him—but . . .

ROXANE   (*Who has stayed on the steps, to a* SISTER *who comes toward her*)
             What is it?

THE SISTER   Ragueneau would see you, madame.

ROXANE   Let him come.
             (*To* DE GUICHE *and* LE BRET)
                              He comes to tell his troubles.
             Having been an author (Save the mark!)—   65
             Poor fellow—now by turns he's singer,

LE BRET   Bathing-man,

ROXANE   Beadle,*

beadle: minor church official
employed to usher and keep
order during services

LE BRET   Actor,

ROXANE   Wig-maker,

LE BRET   Teacher of the lute—

ROXANE   What will he be today, by chance?

RAGUENEAU   *(Entering hurriedly)*
Ah! Madame!
(He sees LE BRET*)*
                  Ah! You here, sir!

SCENE iii

ROXANE   *(Smiling)*
Tell all your miseries
To him; I will return anon.

RAGUENEAU   But, madame—
*(*ROXANE *goes out with* DE GUICHE. RAGUENEAU *goes
toward* LE BRET.*)*
Since you are here, 'tis best she should not know!
I was going to your friend just now—was but   5
A few steps from the house, when I saw him
Go out. I hurried to him. Saw him turn
The corner . . . suddenly, from out a window
Where he was passing—was it chance? may be!
A lackey let fall a large piece of wood.   10

LE BRET   Cowards! O Cyrano!

RAGUENEAU   I ran—I saw . . .

LE BRET   'Tis hideous!

RAGUENEAU   Saw our friend, sir—
Struck to the ground—a large wound in his head!

LE BRET   He's dead?

RAGUENEAU   No—but—I bore him to his room . . .
Ah! His room! What a thing to see! That garret!   15

LE BRET   He suffers?

RAGUENEAU	No, his consciousness has flown.
LE BRET	Saw you a doctor?
RAGUENEAU	One was kind—he came.
LE BRET	My poor Cyrano! We must not tell this To Roxane suddenly. What said the doctor?
RAGUENEAU	Said? what, I know not—fever, meningitis! 20 Ah! If you could see him—his head all bound up! But let us haste! There's no one by his bed! And if he tries to rise, sir, he might die!
LE BRET	*(Dragging him toward the right)* Come! Through the chapel! 'Tis the quickest way!
ROXANE	*(Appearing on the steps, and seeing* LE BRET *go away by the colonnade leading to the chapel door)* Monsieur Le Bret! *(*LE BRET *and* RAGUENEAU *disappear without answering)* Le Bret goes—when I call! 25 'Tis some new trouble of good Ragueneau's. *(She descends the steps.)*
ROXANE	Ah! What a beauty in September's close! My sorrow's eased. April's joy dazzled it, But autumn wins it with her dying calm. *(She seats herself at the embroidery frame. Two* SISTERS *come out of the house and bring a large armchair under the tree.)* There comes the famous armchair Where he sits, dear faithful friend! 5
SISTER MARTHA	It is the parlor's best!
ROXANE	Thanks, sister. *(The* SISTERS *go.)* He'll be here now. *(She seats herself. A clock strikes.)* The hour is striking. My silks? Why, now, the hour's struck! How strange To be behind his time, at last, today! Nothing could hinder him . . . 10

SCENE iv

A SISTER	*(Coming to the steps)*
	Monsieur de Bergerac.

ROXANE	*(Without turning round)* What was I saying? *(She embroiders. CYRANO, very pale, his hat pulled down over his eyes, appears. The SISTER who had announced him retires. He descends the steps slowly, with visible difficulty in holding himself upright, bearing heavily on his cane. ROXANE still works at her tapestry.)* Time has dimmed the tints . . . How harmonize them now? *(To CYRANO, with playful reproach)* Late! For the first time, All these fourteen years! 5
CYRANO	*(Who has succeeded in reaching the chair and has seated himself—in a lively voice, which is in great contrast with his pale face)* Ay! It is villainous! I raged—was stayed . . .
ROXANE	By?
CYRANO	By a bold, unwelcome visitor.
ROXANE	*(Absently, working)* Some creditor?
CYRANO	Ay, cousin, the last creditor Who has a debt to claim from me. 10
ROXANE	And you have paid it?
CYRANO	No, not yet! I put it off; Said, "Cry you mercy; this is Saturday, When I have got a standing rendezvous That naught defers. Call in an hour's time!" 15
ROXANE	*(Carelessly)* Oh, well, a creditor can always wait! I shall not let you go ere twilight falls.
CYRANO	Haply, perforce, I quit you ere it falls! *(He shuts his eyes and is silent for a moment. A light breeze causes the leaves to fall.)* Autumn leaves!

ROXANE   (*Lifting her head, and looking down the distant alley*)
            Soft, golden brown, like a Venetian's hair.   20
            See how they fall!

CYRANO   Ay, see how brave they fall,
            In their last journey downward from the bough,
            To rot within the clay; yet, lovely still,
            Hiding the horror of the last decay,
            With all the wayward grace of careless flight!   25

ROXANE   What, melancholy? You?

CYRANO   (*Collecting himself*)
                              Nay, nay, Roxane!

ROXANE   Then let the dead leaves fall the way they will,
            And chat. What, have you nothing new to tell,
            My Court Gazette?

CYRANO   Listen.

ROXANE   Ah!

CYRANO	*(Growing whiter and whiter)*
	Saturday the nineteenth, having eaten to excess 30
	Of pear-conserve, the king felt feverish;
	The lancet quelled this treasonable revolt,
	And the august pulse beats at normal pace.
	At the queen's ball on Sunday, thirty score
	Of best white waxen tapers were consumed. 35
	Our troops, they say, have chased the Austrians.
	Four sorcerers were hanged. The little dog
	Of Madame d'Athis took a dose . . .

ROXANE	I bid
	You hold your tongue, Monsieur de Bergerac!

CYRANO	Monday, not much—Claire changed protector.

ROXANE	Oh! 40

CYRANO	*(Whose face changes more and more)*
	Tuesday, the court repaired to Fontainebleau.
	Wednesday, the Montglat said to Comte de Fiesque . . .
	No! Thursday—Mancini, Queen of France! (almost!)
	Friday, the Monglat to Count Fiesque said—"Yes!"
	And Saturday the twenty-sixth . . .
	(He closes his eyes. His head falls forward. Silence)

ROXANE	*(Surprised at his voice ceasing, turns round, looks at him, and rising, terrified)*
	He swoons! 45
	(She runs toward him crying)
	Cyrano!

CYRANO	*(Opening his eyes, in an unconcerned voice)*
	What is this?
	(He sees ROXANE *bending over him, and, hastily pressing his hat on his head, and shrinking back in his chair)*
	Nay, on my word
	'Tis nothing! Let me be!

ROXANE	But—

CYRANO	That old wound
	Of Arras, sometimes—as you know . . .

ROXANE	Dear friend!

CYRANO	'Tis nothing, 'twill pass soon;
	(He smiles with an effort.)
	See—it has passed!

ROXANE	Each of us has his wound; 50
	Ay, I have mine—never healed up—
	Not healed yet, my old wound!
	(She puts her hand on her breast.)
	'Tis here,
	Beneath this letter brown with age,
	All stained with teardrops, and still stained with blood.
	(Twilight begins to fall.)

| CYRANO | His letter! Ah! You promised me one day 55 |
| | That I should read it. |

| ROXANE | What would you? |
| | His letter? |

| CYRANO | Yes, I would fain, today . . . |

| ROXANE | *(Giving the bag hung at her neck)* |
| | See! Here it is! |

| CYRANO | *(Taking it)* |
| | Have I your leave to open? |

| ROXANE | Open—read! |
| | *(She comes back to her tapestry frame, folds it up, sorts her wools.)* |

CYRANO	*(Reading)*
	"Roxane, adieu! I soon must die!
	This very night, beloved; and I 60
	Feel my soul heavy with love untold.
	I die! No more, as in days of old,
	My loving, longing eyes will feast
	On your least gesture—ay, the least!
	I mind me the way you touch your cheek 65
	With your finger, softly, as you speak!
	Ah me! I know that gesture well!
	My heart cries out! I cry, 'Farewell!' "

| ROXANE | But how you read that letter! One would think . . . |

CYRANO   *(Continuing to read)*
                 "My life, my love, my jewel, my sweet,   70
                 My heart has been yours in every beat!"
                 (The shades of evening fall imperceptibly.)

ROXANE   You read in such a voice—so strange—and yet—
                 It is not the first time I have heard that voice!
                 (She comes nearer very softly, without his perceiving it,
                 passes behind his chair, and, noiselessly leaning over him,
                 looks at the letter. The darkness deepens.)

CYRANO   "Here, dying, and there, in the land on high,
                 I am he who loved, who loves you—I . . ."   75

ROXANE   *(Putting her hand on his shoulder)*
                 How can you read? It is too dark to see!
                 (He starts, turns, and sees her close to him. Suddenly
                 alarmed, he holds his head down. Then in the dusk, which
                 has now completely enfolded them, she says, very slowly,
                 with clasped hands)
                 And, fourteen years long,
                 He has played this part of the kind old friend
                 Who comes to laugh and chat.

CYRANO   Roxane!

ROXANE   'Twas you!

CYRANO   No, never; Roxane, no!

ROXANE   I should have guessed,   80
                 Each time he said my name!

CYRANO   No, it was not I!

ROXANE   It was you!

CYRANO   I swear!

ROXANE   I see through all the generous counterfeit—
                 The letters—you!

CYRANO   No.

ROXANE   The sweet, mad love-words! You!

| CYRANO | No! | 85 |

ROXANE   The voice that thrilled the night—You, you!

CYRANO   I swear you err.

ROXANE   The soul—it was your soul!

CYRANO   I loved you not.

ROXANE   You loved me not?

CYRANO   'Twas he!

ROXANE   You loved me!

CYRANO   No!

ROXANE   See! How you falter now!

CYRANO   No, my sweet love, I never loved you!   90

ROXANE   Ah—things dead, long dead. See! How they rise again!
Why, why keep silence all these fourteen years,
When, on this letter, which he never wrote,
The tears were your tears?

CYRANO   *(Holding out the letter to her)*
                              The blood was his.

ROXANE   Why, then, that noble silence—kept so long—   95
Broken today for the first time—why?

CYRANO   Why?
(LE BRET and RAGUENEAU enter running.)

LE BRET   What madness! Here? I knew it well!

CYRANO   *(Smiling and sitting up)*
What now?

LE BRET   He has brought his death by coming, madame.

ROXANE   Ah, then! That faintness of a moment since . . . ?   100

CYRANO	Why, true! It interrupted the Gazette—
	Saturday, twenty-sixth, at dinner time,
	Assassination of de Bergerac.
	(He takes off his hat; they see his head bandaged.)
ROXANE	What says he?
	Cyrano! His head all bound! Ah, what has chanced?
	How? Who?
CYRANO	To be struck down, 105
	Pierced by sword i' the heart, from a hero's hand!
	That I had dreamed. O mockery of Fate!
	Killed, I! Of all men—in an ambuscade!
	Struck from behind, and by a lackey's hand!
	'Tis very well. I am foiled, foiled in all, 110
	Even in my death.
RAGUENEAU	Ah, monsieur!
CYRANO	*(Holding out his hand to him)*
	Ragueneau, weep not so bitterly!
	What do you now, old comrade?
RAGUENEAU	*(Amid his tears)*
	Trim the lights for Moliere's stage.
CYRANO	Moliere!
RAGUENEAU	Yes; but I shall leave to-morrow. 115
	I cannot bear it! Yesterday, they played
	"Scapin"—I saw he'd thieved a scene from you!
LE BRET	What! A whole scene?
RAGUENEAU	Oh, yes, indeed, monsieur,
	The famous one, "What in the world is he doing?"
LE BRET	Moliere has stolen that?
CYRANO	Tut! He did well! 120
	(To RAGUENEAU*)*
	How went the scene? It told—I think it told?
RAGUENEAU	*(Sobbing)*
	Ah! How they laughed!

CYRANO	Look you, it was my life
	To be the prompter everyone forgets!
	(To ROXANE*)*
	That night when 'neath your window Christian spoke
	Under your balcony, you remember? Well! 125
	There was the allegory of my whole life.
	I, in the shadow, at the ladder's foot,
	While others lightly mount to Love and Fame!
	Just! Very just! Here on the threshold drear
	Of death, I pay my tribute with the rest, 130
	To Moliere's genius—Christian's fair face!
	(The chapel-bell chimes. The nuns are seen passing down
	the alley at the back to say their office.)
	Let them go pray, go pray, when the bell rings!

| ROXANE | *(Rising and calling)* |
| | Sister! Sister! |

CYRANO	*(Holding her fast)*
	Call no one. Leave me not;
	When you come back, I should be gone for aye.
	(The nuns have all entered the chapel. The organ
	sounds.)
	I was somewhat fain for music—hark! 'tis come. 135

| ROXANE | Live, for I love you! |

CYRANO	No, in fairy tales
	When to the ill-starred prince the lady says
	"I love you!" all his ugliness fades fast—
	But I remain the same, up to the last!

| ROXANE | I have marred your life—I, I! |

CYRANO	You blessed my life! 140
	Never on me had rested woman's love.
	My mother even could not find me fair.
	I had no sister; and, when grown a man,
	I feared the mistress who would mock at me.
	But I have had your friendship—grace to you— 145
	A woman's charm has passed across my path.

| LE BRET | *(Pointing to the moon, which is seen between the trees)* |
| | Your other lady-love is come. |

CYRANO	*(Smiling)*
	I see.

ROXANE	I loved but once, yet twice I lose my love!

CYRANO	Hark you, Le Bret! I soon shall reach the moon.
	Tonight, alone, with no projectile's aid! 150

LE BRET	What are you saying?

CYRANO	I tell you, it is there,
	There, that they send me for my paradise,
	There I shall find at last the souls I love,
	In exile—Galileo—Socrates!

LE BRET	*(Rebelliously)*
	No, no! It is too clumsy, too unjust! 155
	So great a heart! So great a poet! Die
	Like this? What, die . . . ?

CYRANO	Hark to Le Bret,
	Who scolds!

LE BRET	*(Weeping)*
	Dear friend . . .

CYRANO	*(Starting up, his eyes wild)*
	What ho! Cadets of Gascony!
	The elemental mass—ah yes! The hic . . .

LE BRET	His science still—he raves! 160

CYRANO	Copernicus said . . .

ROXANE	Oh!

CYRANO	"But what in the world is he doing?
	But what in the world is he doing in the galleys?"
	(He declaims.)
	Philosopher, metaphysician,
	Rhymer, brawler, and musician, 165
	Famed for his lunar expedition,
	And the unnumbered duels he fought,
	And lover also—by interposition!
	Here lies Hercule Savinien

De Cyrano de Bergerac,   170
Who was everything, yet was naught.
I cry you pardon, but I may not stay;
See the moon-ray that comes to call me hence!
(He has fallen back in his chair; the sobs of ROXANE
recall him to reality; he looks long at her, and, touching
her veil)
I would not bid you mourn less faithfully
That good brave Christian; I would only ask   175
That when my body shall be cold in clay
You wear those sable mourning weeds for two,
And mourn awhile for me, in mourning him.

ROXANE   I swear it you!

CYRANO   *(Shivering violently, then suddenly rising)*
                Not there! What, seated? No!
                (They spring toward him.)
                Let no one hold me up—   180
                (He props himself against the tree.)
                Only the tree! It comes. E'en now
                My feet have turned to stone,
                My hands are gloved with lead!
                (He stands erect.)
                But since Death comes,
                I meet him still afoot, and sword in hand!   185
                (He draws his sword.)

LE BRET   Cyrano!

ROXANE   *(Half fainting)*
                    Cyrano!

CYRANO   Why, I well believe
                He dares to mock my nose? Ho! Insolent!
                What say you? It is useless? Ay, I know—
                But who fights ever hoping for success?
                I fought for lost cause, and for fruitless quest!   190
                You there, who are you! You are thousands!
                Ah! I know you now, old enemies of mine!
                (Strikes in air with his sword)
                Falsehood! Have at you! Ha! and Compromise!
                Prejudice, Treachery!
                (Strikes)
                            Surrender, I?

Parley? No, never! You too, Folly—you?   195
I know that you will lay me low at last;
Let be! Yet I fall fighting, fighting still!
(Makes passes in the air and stops, breathless)
You strip from me the laurel* and the rose!
Take all! Despite you there is yet one thing
I hold against you all, and when, tonight,   200
I enter Christ's fair courts, and, lowly bowed,
Sweep with doffed casque* the heavens' threshold blue,
One thing is left, that, void of stain or smutch,
I bear away despite you.
(Springs forward, his sword raised. The sword falls from his hand; he staggers, falls back into the arms of LE BRET *and* RAGUENEAU.)*

laurel: a type of evergreen tree; wreaths of laurel were given in ancient times as a mark of honor.

casque: a helmet

ROXANE   *(Bending and kissing his forehead)*
                            'Tis?

CYRANO   *(Opening his eyes, recognizing her, and smiling)*
                            My honor.

                    Curtain

About the Drama

1. Why is it symbolically appropriate that the action of Act V takes place in the autumn?

2. Read Le Bret's speech on page 488, lines 31–37. What does Le Bret fear for Cyrano? Why?

3. What is Rostand's tone toward de Guiche in Act V?

4. Explain what Roxane means when she says, "I loved but once, yet twice I lose my love!"

5. By the end of the play, has Cyrano changed in his devotion to his ideals? How can you tell?

About the Author

Edmond Rostand (1868–1918) wrote French verse drama in the Romantic style for an audience that craved plays full of heroism, wit, and poetic language. *Cyrano de Bergerac,* Rostand's best-known work and the one that established his reputation, more than satisfied the desires of his audience.

The son of a poet, Rostand studied the liberal arts in Paris and enjoyed composing plays for a form of puppet theater called marionette theater. He wrote his first play at age twenty; more and better plays as well as poems and essays followed.

Cyrano de Bergerac was written in 1897 when Rostand was twenty-nine. Another play followed in 1900, and by 1901 Rostand's reputation as a French playwright was secure. After his election in 1901 to the prestigious French Academy, a sickly Rostand retired and went to live in the country. In 1910 he wrote another play in the form of a fable. Featuring the well-known French character Chanticleer the Rooster, this play was not a success. Rostand, however, continued to write poetry and drama well into the years of World War I. At his death in 1918, Rostand was considered the unofficial poet laureate of France.

The work that you have just read, *Cyrano de Bergerac*, stands as one of the greatest examples of drama in world literature. Strictly defined, **drama** is literature written to be acted. Dramas are also commonly referred to as **plays**, and the authors of these works are referred to as **dramatists** or **playwrights**. Though drama relies heavily on dialogue as a means to advance the action of the story, many dramatists also employ **stage directions** that assist the reader in visualizing the action and help the director in setting the scene for the audience. Sometimes details of exposition, such as lapses in time, are contained in the stage directions.

Dramas are often separated into major units called **acts**, which are then further subdivided into scenes. A **scene** is one unit of dialogue or a single situation within an act. A scene usually has no gaps in time or changes in setting as there might be between scenes or acts, and it is usually marked by the entrance or exit of an actor or actors. From ancient Rome until the late nineteenth century, plays generally comprised five acts. In the late nineteenth century, however, dramatists began experimenting with patterns of three or four acts. Indeed, many modern playwrights specialize in one-act plays, which have their origin with Euripides and his fourth-century play, *The Cyclops*.

Much of world drama can be classified into two categories: **tragedy** and **comedy**. Though these terms may also be used to refer to prose works, both originated with drama and are most commonly used when discussing dramatic works. As discussed in Unit 2, tragedies generally depict serious issues and usually end with a catastrophe (most often death) for the protagonist. Comedies, however, usually concern light-hearted matters (often related to courtship and love) but may also be satirical. Usually, the characters in a comedy meet a happy end. (In Shakespeare, the central male and female characters often marry.) Critics have been divided over how to strictly classify *Cyrano de Bergerac*, given its ending. Think about how you would classify the play.

1. What are the differences between a **scene** and an **act**?

2. How do the endings of **comedy** and **tragedy** differ?

3. What important functions do **stage directions** accomplish? Consider the stage directions in Act V of *Cyrano de Bergerac*. What element of symbolism can be found in them?

4. Critics disagree about how to classify *Cyrano de Bergerac*. Given what you have learned about comedy and tragedy, which term would you use to classify this **drama**? Explain.

5. What is the moral tone of *Cyrano de Bergerac*? How does this reflect Rostand's worldview?

6. How do you respond to Rostand's worldview?

UNIT VI REVIEW

REMEMBER THE TERMS

Review the following terms from the opening essay, "Tone," and the Thinking Zone pages. Be prepared to discuss their meanings and uses.

tone	drama
overstatement	play
hyperbole	dramatist/playwright
understatement	stage directions
satire	act
moral tone	scene
analogy	tragedy
allusion	comedy

APPLY THE CONCEPTS

Answer the following questions about how the literary concepts you have studied are used in this unit.

1. Who or what does Max Beerbohm satirize in "The Crime"?

2. Identify one clue in "The Crime" that indicates that Beerbohm's tone is humorous.

3. Beerbohm's characterization of the book burning as a "crime" may be considered what figure of speech?

4. How does Beerbohm's use of hyperbole and understatement affect the tone of "The Crime"?

5. From what point of view is "The Crime" written? Why does this point of view work well for the essay?

6. According to what you have read, simile and metaphor may be classified as what type of figure of speech?

7. Identify the tone of Gwendolyn Brooks toward the actions of the pool players in "We Real Cool."

8. How can we say that "We Real Cool" demonstrates a positive moral tone?

9. Explain Rostand's tone toward the theatergoers in Act I of *Cyrano de Bergerac*.

10. Explain why it is appropriate that Cyrano often uses hyperbole in his witticisms.

11. Name one allusion to classical mythology in Act I of *Cyrano de Bergerac*.

12. Explain the difference between tone and atmosphere (or mood).

13. What is Rostand's tone toward the main character in *Cyrano de Bergerac*?

14. In Act III, Cyrano's speaking on behalf of Christian to Roxane and Roxane's purposeful misreading of de Guiche's letter illustrate which of the play's themes?

15. Name one occurrence in Act IV (the battle scene) that points to the theme of the nobility of self-sacrifice.

16. Besides the two identified above (questions 14 and 15), name another of the play's themes.

17. Name an internal conflict that results from Roxane's revelation in Act IV that she now loves Christian only for his soul as revealed in his letters.

EVALUATE THE IDEAS

Identify each of the following statements as true or false. If false, rewrite the underlined portion of the sentence to make it true.

18. At the end of "The Crime," Beerbohm alludes to the biblical book of Proverbs.

19. Cyrano's description of his nose as a "peninsula" is an example of hyperbole.

20. When, during the course of Act I of *Cyrano de Bergerac*, Cyrano asks for a jawbone with which to "slaughter every man of you," Rostand is employing stage directions.

21. Cyrano's statement to Roxane that she was "not ill to see" is an example of understatement.

22. Max Beerbohm alludes to Shakespeare's *Hamlet* at the beginning of "The Crime."

23. Allusion may be considered an implied type of hyperbole.

24. The action of Act V of *Cyrano de Bergerac* takes place during the autumn.

25. Judging by her actions and words throughout *Cyrano de Bergerac*, Roxane is best considered a static character.

26. A drama usually has several <u>scenes</u> within a single <u>act</u>.

27. One function of <u>stage directions</u> is that they help to set the scene for a drama.

28. In her poem "We Real Cool," Brooks uses <u>end rhyme</u>.

WRITE A RESPONSE

Completely answer the following questions.

29. How is it possible for an author to adopt a critical tone toward a character while remaining sympathetic to him or her?

30. How does an author's moral tone in a story reveal his worldview?

31. Explain how Rostand's portrayal of Cyrano's dealings with Roxane and Christian illustrate both a positive and a negative moral tone.

32. Respond to one of the pieces of literature in this unit from a Christian worldview. Use Scripture to defend your response.

GLOSSARY OF LITERARY TERMS

abstract concept. A concept that cannot be perceived by the five senses but must instead be discussed in general terms by describing the image's attributes or its effects upon a concrete subject.

act. A major division in the action of a **play**.

action. What a **character** does.

adaptation. A rewritten version of an author's work that has been changed for reasons such as length or readability.

allegory. A type of **extended metaphor** that forms a story with two levels of meaning.

alliteration. The repetition of initial consonant sounds.

allusion. A reference within a work to something else, usually another artistic work.

analogy. A detailed comparison of one thing to another dissimilar thing.

anapestic foot. **Poetic foot** that contains two unstressed and then one stressed syllable.

anaphora. The repetition of words or phrases at the beginnings of lines of poetry or grammatical units.

anecdote. A short narrative of a single interesting or amusing incident.

antagonist. A force or **character** who struggles against the **protagonist**.

apostrophe. A speech, poem, or other work addressing an absent person, abstraction, or inanimate object.

assonance. The repetition of similar vowel sounds in a series of words.

atmosphere. The mood or emotion that the reader is supposed to share with the **characters**.

authorial intent. The reason that an author composed his or her work.

autobiographical essay. A short selection written by the author about his experience(s) and focused on a particular event or happening.

ballad. A narrative poem often derived from folklore and originally intended to be sung or recited.

biographical sketch. A brief descriptive **biographical** essay. See also **sketch**.

biography. A **nonfiction** account in which the author tells the true events that make up the life of a real individual other than himself.

blank verse. Unrhymed **iambic pentameter**.

caesura. A pause in the middle of a line of poetry, usually indicated by a mark of punctuation.

character. A person or being who performs the action of the story.

character flaw. An incidental weakness or serious moral fault that a character reveals through the story.

character motivation. See **motivation**.

character trait. How a character thinks or acts.

chiasmus. An alternate form of **parallelism** that inverts the parallel structure, keeping the elements of the original phrase, clause, or sentence but reversing them in the following unit.

chronological order. The order in which events actually occur in a story.

cinquain. A poem in which the following are true: The first line contains one stressed syllable; the second, two; the third, three; and the fourth, four. The fifth line, like the first, has only one stressed syllable.

cliché. A phrase, **idiom**, or expression that has become so overused that it often detracts from rather than contributes to a story.

cliffhanger. **Suspenseful** situations strategically placed throughout different parts or chapters of a longer work.

climax. The point at which the **plot** reaches the moment of highest emotional intensity.

comedy. **Drama** that focuses on light-hearted matters such as courtship and love and that may also be satirical.

concrete language. Words that appeal to one or more of the five senses.

conflict. The opposition of two or more **characters** or forces; the three main conflicts are **man against a greater force, man against man, and man against himself.**

conflict resolution. The opposing forces in a particular **conflict** come to grips with the issues at hand.

connotative meaning. The meaning of a word plus all of its implications and emotional associations.

consonance. The repetition of terminal consonant sounds (as in "bit . . . fight . . . let") and, more rarely, of internal consonants that creates extra emphasis on the words involved.

context. The influence of factors surrounding a work of literature that may provide additional insight into its meaning.

couplet. A pair of rhymed lines.

crisis. The major turning point for the main **character**; the point at which something happens that affects the outcome of the story and determines the future of the main **character**.

criticism. The analysis of a literary work.

dactylic dimeter. See **dactylic foot** and **dimeter.**

dactylic foot. **Poetic foot** that contains one stressed and then two unstressed syllables.

denotative meaning. The exact definition of a word as found in a dictionary.

dénouement. See **resolution.**

description. Writing that seeks to aid the reader in seeing or feeling whatever the author is trying to convey.

detective fiction. **Fiction** in which a recurring character (a detective) investigates and solves crimes.

developing character. A **character** who changes as the story progresses.

dialect. **Dialogue** written to reflect qualities of a character's speech.

dialogue. A conversation between **characters.**

diary. See **journal.**

dimeter. A line of verse consisting of two metrical feet.

direct characterization. Type of character description in which straightforward details tell the reader about the character.

drama. Literature written to be acted.

dramatic irony. A type of **irony** in which the reader is aware of a **plot** development of which the **characters** of the story are unaware.

dramatic monologue. A literary form, usually **poetry**, in which a single **character** speaks either to himself or to another character.

dramatist. See **playwright.**

dynamic character. A changing or **developing character.**

end rhyme. **Rhyme** that occurs at the ends of corresponding lines of **poetry.**

end-stopped lines. Lines of **poetry** that end with a natural pause indicated by punctuation.

English sonnet. **Poetry** whose thought is usually distributed over three **quatrains** with a concluding **couplet**, the whole rhyming *abab cdcd efef gg.*

enjambment. A poetic device in which lines flow past the end of one verse line and into the next with no punctuation at the end of the first verse line.

epic. A long **narrative poem** about a great hero expressed in a formal, dignified **style.**

epilogue. An addition to a story's ending that expounds on the fortunes of the main **character** or on the significance of the story's conclusion.

essay. A work that seeks to state a **point of view**, discuss a subject, or persuade a reader to accept an argument.

euphemism. A mild, indirect, or vague term that substitutes for a harsh, blunt, or offensive one.

explicit theme. A **theme** stated outright within a work of literature.

exposition. The part of a story's **plot** that introduces the reader to the **setting**, the **characters**, and the situation.

extended metaphor. A **metaphor** that is developed beyond a single sentence or comparison.

external conflict. Conflict that occurs between a **character** and an outside force (such as society or nature).

eye rhyme. Word pairs that are spelled alike but pronounced differently.

fable. A brief fanciful story that seeks to expand on a **moral.**

falling action. The events that unfold the results of the **crisis** and lead to the conclusion.

fiction. A work that contains events and **characters** invented by the author.

figurative language. An artful deviation from literal speech.

first-person point of view. The **point of view** in which the author, as one of the **characters,** refers to himself as *I* throughout the piece.

flashback. A reference to events that occurred before the action of the main story or to action that occurred before the time that the **narrator** is speaking.

flat character. A **character** with little individuality whose mindset the reader knows little about.

foil character. A **character** used to emphasize another character's opposing traits within a work.

folklore. The collective term for the tales and **myths** passed along primarily by word of mouth within a society or culture.

folktale. A short tale passed along by word of mouth throughout a given culture.

foot. See **poetic foot.**

foreshadowing. Hinting at events that will occur later in a story.

frame story. A story that contains another story or an introductory story from which another story springs.

free verse. Poetry with no distinguishable **rhyme, meter,** or line length.

genre. A type or category of literature.

haiku. A seventeen-syllable poem about nature, composed of three lines of five, seven, and five syllables. Example: "Daffodils in spring / Lift their golden trumpets and / Breathe a melody."

hero/heroine. A male or female **protagonist** who behaves virtuously in a story.

historical fiction. A fictional story that employs authentic historical **characters** or **settings.**

humor. A **genre** that seeks to amuse the reader through **wordplay, irony,** or other means.

hyperbole. A type of obvious **overstatement** used by writers to make a point.

iamb. A type of **poetic foot** that contains one unstressed syllable followed by one **stressed syllable** (also known as an **iambic foot**).

iambic foot. Poetic foot that contains one unstressed and then one **stressed syllable.**

iambic pentameter. Meter with five **iambs** in each line of a poem.

idiom. An expression that is unique to itself and cannot be defined from the meanings of the individual words (e.g., *pass the buck*).

imagery. Descriptive words or phrases used to create an impression.

implicit theme. A **theme** that is not stated outright but must be discerned from the details that the author includes in the work.

inciting incident. The incident that sets the events of the **conflict** in motion.

indirect characterization. Type of characterization in which the reader must infer **character traits** from information shown by the author.

informal essay. A type of **essay** in which the writer adopts a friendly or conversational tone with the reader (also known as a *personal essay*).

in media res. Latin literary term meaning "in the middle of events."

internal conflict. Conflict that occurs between a **character** and his own thoughts, emotions, or beliefs.

internal rhyme. Rhyme that occurs between words within a single line of poetry.

irony. The use of language to convey meaning other than what is stated or a contradiction in what is expected to happen and what actually happens.

Italian sonnet. Poetry whose first eight lines (an octave, rhyming *abbaabba*) form a distinct unit of thought and whose last six lines (a sestet, rhyming variously with two or three new rhymes) form another.

journal. An informal (often daily) record of a person's life.

limited-omniscient point of view. Viewpoint of a narrative in which the author tells the story in third person and "gets inside" only one of the **characters,** usually the central **character.**

limited point of view. The **point of view** that limits the reader's scope of knowledge about the thoughts and feelings of the story's **characters.**

literal meaning. A standard definition of a word or expression.

litotes. A form of **understatement** that expresses a positive statement by denying its opposite (e.g., *That girl is no slacker*).

local color. Re-creates the dress, **dialect,** geography, social practices, and general **worldview** of a specific region.

memoir. A type of **nonfiction** that recounts a personal recollection of the author.

metaphor. An expression of one thing in terms of another.

meter. The regular arrangement of **stressed** and unstressed **syllables** in a poem.

monologue. An extended speech or piece of writing in which a single **character** reveals his thoughts.

moral. A simple statement that sums up a truth about life.

moral tone. Application of a person's philosophy through the ethics that the individual embraces.

motivation. The reason that a **character** behaves as he or she does.

myth. A fictional story that was at one time held to be true within a certain cultural group.

narrative poem. A poem that tells a story.

narrator. The individual telling the story to the reader.

nonfiction. Prose that tells of real people and events.

normative character. The **character** sometimes called simply "the norm," who models and articulates the author's ethics throughout the story.

novel. An extended work of fictional **prose.**

novella. A **prose** work of medium length, longer than a **short story** yet shorter than a novel.

omniscient viewpoint. The viewpoint taken by an author who tells his story in third person and who, as the storyteller, "knows all."

onomatopoeia. The use of words that sound like what they mean (e.g., *hiss, buzz*).

oral tradition. The audible means by which much **folklore** and mythology were transferred from person to person before the prevalent use of written language.

overstatement. The exaggeration of details surrounding the events of a story.

parable. A brief story told to illustrate or clarify a truth, often biblical in nature.

paradox. A statement that seems to be self-contradictory yet actually makes sense when applied at the right moment.

parallelism. Similarity in the structure of two or more phrases, clauses, or sentences.

perfect rhyme. See **rhyme.**

persona. The person created by the author to tell the story, affecting the way the story is told.

personification. Giving human characteristics to something that is not human.

perspective. The author's mental view or outlook that influences his account of a story.

persuasion. Argument that motivates the listener to change not only his ideas but also his actions.

play. See **drama**.

playwright. The author of a **drama** or **play**.

plot. A series of events arranged to produce a definite sense of movement toward a specific goal.

plot twist. A **plot** development that violates the reader's expectations.

poetic foot. The specific combination of two or three **stressed** and/or unstressed **syllables** that predominantly repeats throughout the poem's lines.

poetic justice. The term given to the reward or punishment that a **character** receives for his virtue or vice within a story.

poetry. Artfully compressed thought in the form of elevated expression.

point of view. The perspective or angle from which a story is told.

prologue. An introduction to a literary work.

propaganda. Literature plainly written to persuade the reader to espouse the author's position on a significant issue of his time.

prose. Writing that resembles speech and differs from **poetry**, such as a **short story** or an **essay**.

prose poem. Writing that unites the two most basic literary forms, drawing on both the meterless structure of prose and the sensory images, sound devices, and compressed speech of poetry.

protagonist. The main **character** of a story.

proverb. A brief but wise saying.

pun. A type of **wordplay** in which the author combines two word meanings within a sentence.

pyrrhic foot. **Poetic foot** that has two unstressed syllables.

quatrain. A **stanza** or poem of four lines.

refrain. A line or group of lines repeated throughout a poem.

repetition. In **poetry**, the act of creating patterns by repeating not only sounds but also words, lines, **meter**, or syntax.

resolution. The final outcome of a story and the last element of the **plot** (also known as the dénouement) in which the major complications are explained or settled.

rhyme. Identical sounds in the last stressed vowel and all of the sounds following that vowel in two or more words.

rhymed verse. **Verse** having **end rhyme** and regular **meter**.

rhyme scheme. The pattern of **rhyme** sounds in a poem or in a **stanza** of **poetry**.

rhythm. A regular pace or beat.

rising action. The events that follow the **inciting incident** and lead up to the **crisis** in a story.

round character. A **character** who is complex and often undergoes changes in his actions and thoughts.

sarcasm. A type of **irony** that takes the form of mock praise.

satire. Corrective ridicule of some object of scorn usually outside of the literature itself.

scansion. The process of identifying the two major features of **meter** in a particular poem.

scene. In a **drama**, a subdivision of an **act** that does not contain a change of time or place.

setting. The time, place, and way of life in which the action of the story occurs.

shaped poem. A poem that rarely follows any specific **stanza** or **verse form** but is shaped in an image that supports the subject of the poem.

short story. A brief work of **prose fiction**.

simile. A comparison of two unlike objects using *like* or *as*.

situational irony. A type of **irony** in which a story's events violate normal expectations.

sketch. A brief descriptive **essay**.

slant rhyme. **Rhyme** between two words with similar but slightly mismatched sounds (e.g., star and door).

soliloquy. A form of speech in which a **character** who believes himself to be alone discloses his innermost thoughts.

sonnet. A lyric poem of fourteen lines. The two most common types of sonnet are the **Italian** (or Petrarchan) and the **English** (or Shakespearean).

spondaic foot. **Poetic foot** that repeats two **stressed syllables**.

stage directions. Instructions for lighting, movement, and action included within a **drama** script.

stanza. Divisions of a poem based on thought, **meter,** or **rhyme** and usually recognized by the number of lines they contain.

static character. A **character** who remains essentially the same throughout the story.

stream of consciousness. A type of writing in which the author attempts to reproduce the flow of thoughts in a character's mind with little attention to grammar or logic.

stressed syllable. A syllable that receives greater emphasis when pronounced.

structure. Chronological framework that emphasizes the narrative qualities of a piece.

style. An author's manner of expression in **prose** or **verse,** in written or oral discourse.

subplot. A secondary **plot** within a piece of literature that accompanies the main **plot** yet is lesser in importance or significance.

surprise ending. A **plot twist** at the end of a story.

suspense. Reader anxiety resulting from the author's withholding of **plot** details.

symbol. A person, place, thing, or idea that means something in addition to itself.

symbolism. The use of **symbols.**

sympathetic character. A **character** with whom the reader identifies or for whom the reader has favorable feelings.

synesthesia. Describing one sense experience in terms of another.

theme. A recurring or emerging idea in a work of literature.

third-person point of view. The **point of view** in which the author refers to the **characters** as *he, she,* or *it.*

tone. The attitude of an author toward his or her subject.

traditional forms. **Poetry** that uses a broad spectrum of techniques and patterns to organize poetic lines.

tragedy. Literature whose **protagonist**'s flaws cause him tremendous suffering that eventually results in a catastrophe, or disastrous conclusion.

tragic flaw. The **protagonist**'s most significant flaw that triggers the **tragic hero**'s downfall.

tragic hero. The **protagonist** in a tragedy.

trochaic foot. **Poetic foot** that contains a **stressed** and then an unstressed **syllable.**

understatement. The representation of something as less important than it truly is.

universal theme. An idea about life that is found throughout world literature because it can be understood by people of all times and places.

unsympathetic character. A **character** with whom the reader cannot identify or for whom the reader has strong feelings of dislike.

verbal irony. **Irony** occurring when an author's or **character**'s meaning differs from what he or she expresses in words.

verse. A composition written in **meter.**

verse forms. Specific combinations of **rhyme** and **meter.**

villain. An evil or cruel **antagonist.**

wordplay. Witty or clever verbal exchange.

worldview. The viewpoint from which a person examines the world and draws conclusions.

INDEX

Entries in SMALL CAPITALS refer to artists and authors. Entries in *italics* refer to titles of paintings and literary selections. Entries in **bold** refer to literary terms.

Illustrators

Miss Hinch Stephanie True, Sarah Ensminger

Top Man Tom Halverson, Sarah Ensminger

Through the Tunnel Stephanie True, Sarah Ensminger

The Duel Preston Gravely

Under the Lion's Paw Stephanie True, Kathy Pflug

from *Treasure Island* Stephanie True, Del Thompson

Phaëthon Del Thompson, Heather Stanley

The Revolt of Mother Stephanie True, Heather Stanley

Neighbour Rosicky Stephanie True, Heather Stanley

from *Don Quixote* Sandy Mehus, Jennifer Lowry

The Silver Mine Sandy Mehus

Beauty and the Beast Stephanie True

Quality Cheryl Weikel, Preston Gravely

Dr. Heidegger's Experiment Courtney Godbey

The Forty Thieves Angela Merzib

The Open Window Del Thompson

After the Battle John Roberts

The Age of Miracles Dave Schuppert

John 9 John Roberts

The Necklace Mary Ann Lumm, Paula Cheadle

The Possibility of Evil Amber Cheadle

In the Ring with Jack Dempsey Steve Christopher

The Adventure of the Beryl Coronet Stephanie True, Preston Gravely

Allen-a-Dale Preston Gravely

The Altar Preston Gravely

The Crime Dana Thompson

PHOTOGRAPH CREDITS

The following agencies and individuals have furnished materials to meet the photographic needs of this textbook. We wish to express our gratitude to them for their important contribution.

Amistad Research Center
The Art Institute of Chicago
Art Resource
BJU Press Files
The Bridgeman Art Library
Fotolia.com
Getty Images
The Granger Collection

iStockphoto.com
JupiterImages Corporation
Library of Congress
The M.C. Escher Company-The Netherlands
PhotoDisc
Shutterstock Images
Unusual Films

COVER
The Starry Night, June 1889 (oil on canvas) by Vincent van Gogh (1853–90), ©Museum of Modern Art, New York, USA/ The Bridgeman Art Library Nationality / copyright status: Dutch / out of copyright (painting inside frame); Shutterstock Images LLC/Mike Irwin (frame); BJU Press Files (back of man)

FRONT MATTER
The Starry Night, June 1889 (oil on canvas) by Vincent van Gogh (1853–90), ©Museum of Modern Art, New York, USA/ The Bridgeman Art Library Nationality / copyright status: Dutch / out of copyright i, xiii (painting inside frame); Shutterstock Images LLC /Mike Irwin i, xiii (frame); BJU Press Files i (back of man); © iStockphoto.com/leezsnow vii (frame); *A Literary Joust*, 2006 (w/c on paper) by Jonathan Wolstenholme (b. 1950) (Contemporary Artist) © Private Collection/ ©Portal Gallery Ltd/ The Bridgeman Art Library Nationality / copyright status: English / in copyright vii (painting inside frame); Grant Wood, American, 1891–1942, *American Gothic*, 1930, Oil on beaver board, 30 11/16 × 25 11/16 in. (78 × 65.3 cm) unframed, Friends of American Art Collection, 1930.934, The Art Institute of Chicago. Photography©The Art Institute of Chicago. viii; Shutterstock Images LLC/fritzkocher ix (frame); *Funeral Procession* by Ellis Wilson used by permission of Amistad

Research Center ix (painting inside frame); © iStockphoto.com/gbrundin x (frame); *Boaters on the Yerres* (oil on canvas) by Gustave Caillebotte (1848–94) ©Private Collection/ The Bridgeman Art Library Nationality / copyright status: French /out of copyright x (painting inside frame); ©iStockphoto.com/evirgen xi (frame); M.C. Escher's "Relativity" © 2017 The M.C. Escher Company-The Netherlands. All rights reserved. xi (drawing inside the frame); ©iStockphoto.com/anirav xvii

UNIT 1
©iStockphoto.com/leezsnow xx (frame); *A Literary Joust*, 2006 (w/c on paper) by Jonathan Wolstenholme (b. 1950) (Contemporary Artist) ©Private Collection / ©Portal Gallery Ltd/ The Bridgeman Art Library Nationality / copyright status: English / in copyright xx (painting inside frame); ©iStockphoto.com/poco_bw 47; Library of Congress 49

UNIT 2
Photography © The Art Institute of Chicago. 68; ©iStockphoto.com/LPETTET 99; "La Belle Ferronnière" by Leonardo da Vinci/Wikimedia Commons/Public Domain 153